Treat this book with care and respect.

It should become part of your personal and professional library. It will serve you well at any number of points during your professional career.

Macroeconomics
A Model Building Approach

Laurence H. Meyer
Associate Professor of Economics
Washington University

Published by
H80 SOUTH-WESTERN PUBLISHING CO.

CINCINNATI   WEST CHICAGO, ILL.   DALLAS   PELHAM MANOR, N.Y.   PALO ALTO, CALIF.

Copyright © 1980
by South-Western Publishing Co.
Cincinnati, Ohio

ALL RIGHTS RESERVED

The text of this publication, or any part thereof, may not be reproduced or transmitted in any form or by any means, electronic or mechanical, including photocopying, recording, storage in an information retrieval system, or otherwise, without the prior written permission of the publisher.

Library of Congress Catalog
Card Number: 79–63754

ISBN: 0–538–08800–1

12345678Ki76543210
Printed in the United States of America

PREFACE

The title of this book highlights its distinctive feature: an emphasis on the construction and use of macroeconomic models. Most macro texts build simple models of the sort I develop, but few exploit the models and none, to my knowledge, consider the properties of the models as fully or treat as many refinements and applications. My motivation for emphasizing model building and manipulation is twofold. First, I believe that a major benefit derived from studying economics should be the development of the ability to solve problems. Students should not take on a passive role, acting merely as recipients of the information fed them by their instructors. Rather, they should be encouraged to be active, to learn to derive the results for themselves. In the process of building and manipulating models, the students develop a deep understanding of the functioning of the economy. Second, the use of a basic model unifies the material. Instead of a series of seemingly unrelated topics, the model building approach results in a more thoroughly integrated and cohesive treatment. Thus, the model building approach provides the vehicle for a *cohesive* and *cumulative* treatment of the material and for an approach that emphasizes *problem solving*. The various theories of consumption, investment, and demand for money are not treated as unrelated elements but as part of a system used to determine output, prices, and interest rates.

We begin in Chapter 1 by developing concepts relevant to the development of macroeconomic models, and by the end of Chapter 4 we have developed simple working hypotheses about the supply and demand functions in the various sectors and markets. We proceed to the development of model solution and manipulation skills, first in terms of the simple Keynesian cross (Chapter 6) and then in terms of two complementary versions of the *IS-LM* model (a fixed price-variable output or "Keynesian" version and a fixed output-variable price or classical version, Chapters 7–10). Chapter 11 introduces some simple extensions that allow for variable prices and output. All solutions of the models are achieved by using both graphs and, where possible, algebra. In all cases there are careful verbal explanations of the meaning of the results.

The first 11 chapters are the core of the book. Much can be learned from the simple models developed in these chapters, and the complications introduced later can be quite easily grasped and integrated once these models are thoroughly mastered. But the simple models are only the beginning of the model building process. In Parts III through V we introduce refinements and discuss their implications for the way the economy responds to disturbances and policy changes. Chapters typically come in pairs, where the first introduces a respecification of the basic supply and demand functions that were introduced in Chapter 4 and the second integrates the respecified function into the basic model and develops its implications for income, price, and interest rate determination.

Part III refines the aggregate demand sector, introducing the life cycle model of consumption and exploring the implications of respecifying the consumption function to include expected income and wealth as arguments. Also introduced are income-induced investment, the accelerator, and lags in the response to changes in the demand for capital. We discuss the implications of income-induced investment for stability, the implications of the accelerator for the explanation of business cycles, and the implications of lags for the short-run response to monetary and fiscal policies.

Part IV then refines the aggregate supply side of the model. Here the critical refinement is the introduction of the Phillips curve and the development of the implications of its alternative specifications in Chapter 18 (the traditional specification based on asymmetrical response of wages to excess supply and demand, the expectations-augmented natural rate version, and assorted eclectic specifications). In this part we also discuss alternative approaches to explaining the response of employment to changes in aggregate demand (both the nonmarket clearing and short-run money illusion approaches).

The financial sector is refined in Part V. We develop alternative specifications of the demand for money in Chapter 19 (transactions and portfolio approaches) and the relation between the demands for money and bonds, the role of government and private sector financing constraints for the supply of bonds, and the term structure of interest rates in Chapter 20. The next three chapters consider the implications of these modifications with an emphasis on the implications of a wealth effect in the demand for money and of government and private financing constraints for the crowding-out of private expenditures by government expenditures.

The treatment is *comprehensive* yet *flexible*. It covers a full range of topics that are typically emphasized in intermediate macro and first semester graduate macro courses. It does not include material on formal difference and differential equation models of business cycles (although we discuss the role of the accelerator and provide a simulation of a multiplier-accelerator model to show its potential for generating cycles) or neoclassical growth models (although we discuss the sources of growth). It is flexible in that the instructor is free to rearrange the order of Parts III, IV, V, and VII and to pick and choose among the various topics covered. In general we integrate the refinements in each part into the simple model developed in Parts I and II. This permits an instructor to rearrange material and to exclude some chapters without seriously damaging either the integrating role of the model or the cumulative element in the development of extensions of the model. Part VI, Policy, on the other hand, draws on all the material in Parts I through V, pulling together their implications for the nature and effectiveness of stabilization policy.

Our policy chapters in Part VI (three separate chapters on monetary, fiscal, and income policies) have four basic elements: (1) they draw together the implications of all the material in Parts I through V for the response to policy changes, (2) they discuss important institutional features of the policy process (e.g., the budget process, the Federal Reserve System), (3) they present empirical evidence on the response of output to policy changes from both structural models and reduced forms, and (4) they discuss the difficulties in implementing stabilizing discretionary policy (the role of lags, stochastic disturbances, multiplier uncertainty, instrument instability, and conflicting objectives).

Preface

Part VII extends the model to the case of an open economy. In Chapter 27, foreign trade and international capital flows are introduced into the basic model. Chapter 28 discusses the nature and limitations of stabilization policies in an open economy.

In conclusion, let me review the distinctive features of my book. I make use of relatively simple macro models throughout the book. I integrate into the basic *IS-LM* framework an impressive amount of conventional wisdom in macroeconomics and perhaps even some wisdom that is not yet as conventional as it should be. The model building approach permits a unified, cohesive treatment which is cumulative and comprehensive, yet flexible. Some of the topics included that receive less attention in most other intermediate macro texts are:

- the impact of monetary change on real and nominal interest rates
- stability analysis and the correspondence principle
- the role of Walras' Law and the balance sheet identity in stock-flow models
- the role of both government and private sector financing constraints
- the role of the bond markets in the crowding-out effect
- the long-run analysis of fiscal policy
- the role of the equity market in consumption and investment decisions
- the distinction between notional and effective demand curves in the labor and commodity markets
- the implications of the life cycle hypothesis (via the role of expected income and wealth effects) for the effectiveness of monetary and fiscal policies
- the theory underlying the use of intermediate targets in the conduct of monetary policy
- alternative models of expectations formation (adaptive vs. rational)
- Okun's Law
- the term structure of interest rates
- empirical evidence on policy multipliers based on both structural models and reduced-form equations
- the endogenous process of wealth accumulation
- rules vs. discretion
- the theory underlying the benefits and costs associated with the use of mandatory wage and price controls
- the impact of exogenous supply shocks
- the long-run vs. the short-run Phillips curves and the implications of a vertical long-run Phillips curve and of asymmetry in the response of wage change to excess supply and demand
- the specification of asset equilibrium in discrete or period models
- the implications of lags for instrument instability
- the implications of uncertainty for the conduct of policy
- the monetarist critique of income-expenditure structural models and the income-expenditure counterattack on monetarist reduced forms
- the monetary approach to the balance of payments

Acknowledgments

During the preparation of this book I benefited from comments and suggestions from a number of colleagues and many students. Edward Greenberg, Edward Kalachek, and Fredric Raines, colleagues at Washington University, Basil Moore, Wesleyan University, Geoffrey Wood, City College, London, and Wolfgang Mayer, University of Cincinnati, each made helpful comments on several chapters. Two of my former students, William Hart, Miami University, and Joel Prakken, IBM, read and made helpful comments on several drafts of most of the chapters. And a special thanks is due to Lloyd Valentine, University of Cincinnati, who read and made detailed comments on the entire manuscript, helping me both to avoid at least some errors I otherwise would have made and to improve the clarity of my exposition. Many shared the burden of typing the numerous drafts of the manuscript, but a special thanks is due to Mary Kastens and Linda Beck, who did the major portion of the typing. Above all, I am grateful to my many former students, on whom I unrelentingly experimented to develop the approach presented in this book. Their comments and encouragement along the way were invaluable.

Laurence H. Meyer

CONTENTS

- Preface iii

PART I CONCEPTS, MEASUREMENT, AND DEVELOPMENT OF THE BASIC MODEL

- **Chapter 1. Basic Concepts in Macroeconomics** 2
  - Microeconomics vs. Macroeconomics 3
  - Macroeconomic Problems 3
  - Flows and Stocks 5
  - Continuous and Period Analysis 6
  - Economic Models 7
  - Relationships Among Variables in Economic Models 8
  - Two Illustrative Models and the Distinction Between Endogenous and Exogenous Variables 14
  - Structural Equations and Reduced Forms 17
  - Appendix   Theoretical vs. Statistical Specifications of Hypotheses ... 18
  - Review Questions 21
  - Problems 21
  - Exercise 23

- **Chapter 2. The Measurement of Macroeconomic Variables** 24
  - National Income Accounts 24
  - Price Indices 33
  - Balance Sheets 38
  - Review Questions 47
  - Problems 47
  - Exercises 49

- **Chapter 3. Potential Output and the Cyclical and Secular Performance of the U.S. Economy** 50
  - The Measurement of Employment and Unemployment 50
  - The Meaning of Full Employment 52
  - Business Cycles 54
  - Potential Output: Growth and Cycles 56
  - The Price Level and Inflation 59
  - Review Questions 60
  - Problem 61
  - Exercises 61

Contents

○ **Chapter 4. The Development of the Basic Model**   62

    Sectors and Markets 62
    Economic Decisions of the Three Sectors 63
    The Simplified Balance Sheets of the Three Sectors....................... 64
    The Behavior of Households, Businesses, and Government........... 65
    Supply, Demand, and Equilibrium in the Four Markets................. 80
    Review Questions 82
    Problems.. 83

○ **Chapter 5. Classical and Keynesian Versions of the Basic Model**   84

    Classical and Keynesian Assumptions and the Treatment of the
        Labor Market... 84
    The Conditions Under Which Models Yield Unique Solutions....... 89
    Redundant Market Analysis... 91
    Classical and Keynesian Versions... 96
    Review Questions 97
    Problems.. 98

PART II COMPARATIVE STATIC ANALYSIS WITH THE BASIC MODEL

○ **Chapter 6. The Keynesian Cross: A Simple but Incomplete Model**   100

    The Simple Consumption Multiplier Model 100
    Adding the Government Sector 113
    Review Questions... 118
    Problems 118

○ **Chapter 7. Derivation and Interpretation of the Slopes of the *IS* and *LM* Curves in the Keynesian and Classical Models**   122

    Keynesian Model.. 122
    Classical Model 126
    Appendix   The Slope of the Classical *IS* Curve When There Is a
        Wealth Effect.. 131
    Review Questions... 132
    Problems 132

○ **Chapter 8. Sources of Disturbances and Shifts in the *IS* and *LM* Curves**   134

    Policy Instruments and Nonpolicy Disturbances............................. 134
    Shifts in the *IS* Curve 137
    Shifts in the *LM* Curve 140
    Money-Financed Fiscal Policy—Shifts in Both the *IS* and *LM* Curves........... 142
    Review Questions... 143
    Problems 144

Chapter 9. A Comparative Static Analysis of the Classical Model — 146

The Adjustment Mechanism in the Classical Model	147
Conditions Under Which the Classical Adjustment Mechanism Breaks Down	150
Real vs. Nominal Rates	154
Response of the Classical System to Various Disturbances	155
Important Propositions Based on the Classical Model	158
Appendix Mathematical Derivation of the Multipliers for the Classical Model	167
Review Questions	169
Problems	169

Chapter 10. A Comparative Static Analysis of the Keynesian Model — 171

Disequilibrium Assumptions for the Keynesian Model	172
Deriving the Reduced Forms for the Keynesian Model	173
Interpreting Multipliers—Direct Impacts and Feedback Responses	174
Comparative Static Results	175
Important Properties of the Keynesian Model	179
The Relative Effectiveness of Monetary and Fiscal Policies	185
Appendix A Numerical Example of Income Determination in the Keynesian Model	189
Review Questions	190
Problems	190

Chapter 11. Aggregate Supply and Demand Analysis — 192

The Aggregate Supply Curve	192
The Aggregate Demand Curve	198
The Aggregate Supply Curve and the Response of Output to Demand Disturbances	200
The Response of the Price Level to Demand and Supply Disturbances	202
Review Questions	208
Problems	208

PART III REFINEMENTS OF THE REAL SECTOR: AGGREGATE DEMAND

Chapter 12. Consumption — 210

Income and Consumption	210
The Absolute Income Hypothesis (AIH)	212
Empirical Evidence	213
Life Cycle Hypothesis (LCH)	216
Appendix A The Definition of Consumption	224
Appendix B The Relative Income Hypothesis	225
Appendix C The Permanent Income Theory	227
Review Questions	229
Problems	229

Contents

Chapter 13. The Implications of the Life Cycle Hypothesis — 231

Consumption as a Function of Current and Lagged Values of Income — 231
Wealth Effects — 236
Review Questions — 245
Problems — 246

Chapter 14. Investment — 247

The Microfoundations of the Demand for Capital — 248
Time, Uncertainty, Disequilibrium, and the Demand for Capital — 250
The Internal Rate of Return and Present Value Rules:
 Toward a Theory of Net Investment — 254
Alternative Models of Investment — 256
The Production Function, the Demand for Capital, and Investment — 263
Appendix A A Comparison of the i and PV Rules — 266
Appendix B A Simplified Derivation of Jorgenson's Model of Optimal Capital
 Accumulation — 268
Appendix C Applications to Other Components of Aggregate Demand — 269
Review Questions — 274
Problem — 274

Chapter 15. The Implications of Alternative Specifications of the Investment Function — 275

Induced Investment — 275
The Accelerator — 283
Lagged Adjustment of Investment to a Change in the Interest Rate — 292
Review Questions — 294
Problems — 294

PART IV REFINEMENTS OF THE REAL SECTOR: AGGREGATE SUPPLY

Chapter 16. The Demand for and Supply of Labor — 296

The Demand for Labor — 296
The Supply of Labor — 302
Equilibrium in the Labor Market and Unemployment — 310
The Meaning of Full Employment — 314
Review Questions — 317
Problems — 318

Chapter 17. The Response of Output and Employment to Aggregate Demand — 319

Unemployment and Labor Market Disequilibrium — 319
Money Illusion and Cyclical Variation in Employment and Output — 327
Appendix A The Sources of Economic Growth — 332

Appendix B Cyclical Movements in Employment and Output: Okun's Law.	334
Review Questions	336
Problem	336

Chapter 18. The Phillips Curve — 337

The Classical Adjustment Mechanism	338
The Traditional Specification of the Phillips Curve	339
Inflation Expectations and the Phillips Curve—The Natural Rate View	351
Appendix A Eclectic Specifications of the Phillips Curve	359
Appendix B Models of Expectations Formation	362
Review Questions	365
Problems	366

PART V   REFINEMENTS OF THE FINANCIAL SECTOR

Chapter 19. The Demand for Money — 368

The Functions of Money and the Central Issue in the Theory of the Demand for Money	368
The Transactions Demand for Money	371
The Asset Demand for Money	375
Empirical Evidence	385
Appendix A The Definition of Money	388
Appendix B The Implications of the Integer Constraint in the Transactions Model of the Demand for Money	389
Review Questions	390
Problems	391

Chapter 20. The Supply and Demand for Bonds and the Term Structure of Interest Rates — 392

The Balance Sheet Identity and the Demand for Bonds	392
Financing Constraints and the Supply of Bonds	394
The Term Structure of Interest Rates	397
Appendix A The Equivalence of the Adding-Up Restrictions in the Continuous and Period Specifications	404
Appendix B A Three-Asset Model	406
Review Questions	408
Problems	408

Chapter 21. The Implications of Alternative Specifications of the Demand for Money — 409

The Implications of Extreme Values of the Interest Responsiveness of the Demand for Money	409
The Implications of Wealth in the Money Demand Function	420
Review Questions	425
Problems	426

Chapter 22. The Bond Market and Crowding-Out — 427

The Bond Market and Crowding-Out 427
Implications of the Term Structure Equation for Fiscal and Monetary Policy Multipliers 429
The Government Budget Constraint and the Long-Run Effect of Fiscal Policy — 431
Appendix A   Implications of a Three-Asset Model 435
Appendix B   The Effect of Bond Financing after the Initial Period 436
Review Questions 437
Problems 437

Chapter 23. A Model of the Money Supply Process and the Implications of an Endogenous Money Supply — 439

The Federal Reserve System, Commercial Banks, and the Money Supply Process — 439
Models of the Money Supply Process 443
The Implications of an Endogenous Money Supply 449
Review Questions 452
Problems 452

PART VI   POLICY

Chapter 24. Monetary Policy — 456

The Institutions of Monetary Policy 456
The Instruments of Monetary Policy 458
The Channels of Monetary Policy 460
Empirical Evidence on Monetary Policy Multipliers 464
Problems in the Execution of Monetary Policy 466
Rules vs. Discretion 471
Appendix A   The Problem of Instrument Instability 475
Appendix B   The Implications of Uncertainty and Incomplete Information 476
Review Questions 484
Problems 484
Exercise 485

Chapter 25. Fiscal Policy — 486

Fiscal Institutions 486
The Economic Stimulus of the Budget and Measuring Discretionary Policy Changes 490
Built-In Stability 492
The Response of Income to Discretionary Fiscal Actions 496
Evidence on the Response to Fiscal Actions 499
The Monetarist Critique and Income-Expenditure Counterattack 501
Review Questions 505
Problems 506
Exercise 507

Chapter 26. Incomes and Other Supply-Oriented Policies — 508

The Motivation for Supply Policies 508
Wage-Price Guideposts 512
Mandatory Wage and Price Controls 518
Indexation 525
Other Supply-Oriented Policies 527
Review Questions 529
Problems 530

PART VII EXTENSION TO AN OPEN ECONOMY

Chapter 27. Trade and International Capital Flows in Macroeconomic Analysis — 532

The Balance of Payments 532
The Exchange Rate, Relative Prices, Absolute Prices, and Real Income 535
The Foreign Exchange Market 538
Integrating Trade and International Capital Flows into the $IS\text{-}LM$ Model 544
Methods and Systems of Balance of Payments Adjustment 554
Review Questions 561
Problems 562

Chapter 28. Macroeconomic Policy in an Open Economy — 563

The Keynesian Open Economy Model Under Fixed Exchange Rates 563
The Classical Open Economy Model Under Fixed Exchange Rates 570
The Keynesian Open Economy Model Under Flexible Exchange Rates 574
The Classical Open Economy Model Under Flexible Exchange Rates 579
Appendix A   A Monetarist Model of the Balance of Payments and World Inflation 581
Review Questions 582
Problems 583

Index — 585

Part I

Concepts, Measurement, and Development of the Basic Model

Chapter 1. Basic Concepts in Macroeconomics
2. The Measurement of Macroeconomic Variables
3. Potential Output and the Cyclical and Secular Performance of the U.S. Economy
4. The Development of the Basic Model
5. Classical and Keynesian Versions of the Basic Model

Chapter 1

Basic Concepts in Macroeconomics

The total value of current production in the U.S. economy during 1977 was $1.89 trillion. On the other hand, the productive capacity of the economy, the value of output the economy was capable of producing if all its factors of production (e.g., its labor force and stock of equipment) were fully employed, was about $2.0 trillion. This means that there was a gap of about $100 billion between actual and potential output.[1] What determines the actual and potential rates of output and how can economic policy be used to close this gap? These questions are two of the most important encountered in the study of macroeconomics.

One reason for caution in the conduct of economic policy in 1977 was the concern that policies which stimulated production would also result in an acceleration in the rate of inflation, the rate at which the prices of currently produced goods and services in the economy are increasing. That rate was 6.5 percent in 1977 despite the sizable gap between actual and potential output and a 7.0 percent rate of unemployment, well above the rate associated with a fully employed labor force. Why was the inflation rate so high in 1977 despite the gap between actual and potential output and the high rate of unemployment and what is the relation between changes in the inflation rate and changes in the level of unemployment? Is it possible to design policies to moderate inflation without simultaneously reducing output and increasing unemployment? This set of questions along with the set at the end of the first paragraph constitute the central issues in macroeconomics. They are issues of overriding national concern, the issues on which Presidential campaigns are won and lost, and some of the issues which motivate the content of this book.

The distinctive feature of our approach to these issues is the emphasis on model building. We develop models which explain how the behavior of households, businesses, and government interact to determine the broad economic aggregates in the economy.

---

[1] The data on potential output are based on the series presented by the Council of Economic Advisors, *The Economic Report of the President,* January, 1978 (Washington: U.S. Government Printing Office, 1978), p. 84.

In the remainder of the chapter we introduce the basic concepts that we will employ in the development of macroeconomic models and we discuss the usefulness of models in explaining observed regularities among the broad economic aggregates and in making predictions about the response of those aggregates to various disturbances and policy actions. Before we turn to the development of the basic concepts, we will clarify the scope of macroeconomics, first by differentiating it from microeconomics and then by identifying in more detail the problems with which macroeconomics is concerned.

MICROECONOMICS VS. MACROECONOMICS

Microeconomics is the study of decision making by individual economic agents, and *macroeconomics* is the study of the relation among broad economic aggregates. Thus, macroeconomics studies the outcome of individual decision making by economic agents for the behavior of broad sectors of the economy (e.g., households, businesses) and for the determination of aggregate variables (e.g., total output, the overall price level). The aggregation which distinguishes macro from micro takes place over both transactors (e.g., businesses, households) and items being transacted (e.g., consumer goods, capital goods, labor services).

For example, microeconomics studies the supply of individual commodities by individual firms, while macroeconomics studies the supply of total output by the entire economy. Microeconomics studies the demand for individual commodities by individual households, while macroeconomics studies the demand for consumer goods by the household sector. And microeconomics is concerned with relative prices, while macroeconomics is concerned with the overall or absolute price level. However, even the study of microeconomics involves some aggregation and the study of macroeconomics involves some disaggregation. The study of the market supply and demand for a particular commodity, for example, is part of microeconomics. Thus, aggregation across a sector remains microeconomics as long as consumption or production of a single commodity rather than aggregate consumption or production is being studied. The study of the composition of output among consumption, investment, and government services, on the other hand, is still part of macroeconomics.

Microeconomics remains the foundation of the theories used to explain the behavior of the household and business sectors. After all, the aggregate behavior of each sector and of the whole economy results from the decisions of individual economic agents. In the course of our analysis, for example, we will discuss the relation of the micro theory of the labor-leisure choice to the macro specification of the supply of labor and the relation of the micro theory of factor employment to the macro theories of labor demand and investment.

MACROECONOMIC PROBLEMS

The Employment Act of 1946 made explicit the federal government's commitment to design and execute policies to achieve and maintain a high level of employment. Other macroeconomic goals simultaneously sought include a stable price level and a high rate of economic growth. These goals identify the three major macroeconomic problems: unemployment, inflation, and economic growth.

Growth in per-capita output is desirable because it permits improvement in living standards. We have recently become painfully aware that economic growth brings burdens as well as benefits—increased pollution and congestion as well as rising per-capita consumption of goods. Nevertheless, growth of productive capacity remains a widely accepted economic objective. Indeed, there is growing concern that capital accumulation is proceeding too slowly to permit continued economic growth at rates we have achieved in the recent past.

Actual output does not always expand at precisely the rate of growth of the economy's productive capacity. A second problem is the instability in the growth of actual output relative to the economy's productive capacity and the resulting variation in the rate of unemployment. A major part of this book is devoted to modeling the determination of the level of output and employment, analyzing the sources of unemployment and causes of the cyclical variation in the unemployment rate, and exploring the use of macroeconomic policy to maintain full employment.

The cost of unemployment is both the output lost by failure to utilize all the economy's resources and the financial and psychological burden on the unemployed. In Chapter 3 we will discuss Okun's Law, which relates increases in unemployment to output losses associated with departures of actual output from its potential level. According to Okun's Law, each one percentage-point increase in the unemployment rate costs the economy 3 percent in lost output. With output in 1976 of $1.7 trillion, each 1 percent increase in unemployment costs the economy $51 billion in output. Recessions typically involve increases in the unemployment rate of at least a couple of percentage points. The costs of such temporary departures from full employment are therefore quite large and, along with the financial and psychological burdens on the unemployed, justify the concern with maintaining full employment.

The cost of *inflation* (a situation in which there are continuing and appreciable increases in the price level) is more difficult to assess. It is important to distinguish perfectly anticipated and imperfectly anticipated inflation. In a fully anticipated inflation, all contracts and economic decisions will reflect full knowledge of the rate of inflation. As we will show more fully in subsequent chapters, nominal interest rates will rise by the amount of the inflation so that real interest rates will be unaffected. In addition, wages, taxes, social security payments, etc., will all be adjusted to the rate of inflation. Relative prices and therefore resource allocation should be unaffected.

However, there is a cost associated even with a fully anticipated inflation. This cost results from the fact that the explicit interest rate on money, generally fixed at zero, cannot respond to fully anticipated inflation. Relative rates of return will therefore be affected and resource allocation will be distorted.

Interest is not generally paid on money, the sum of demand deposits and currency. It would, however, be simple to pay interest on demand deposits and, in fact, banks in New England are allowed to pay interest on checking deposits. In a fully anticipated inflation we assume all banks would be permitted to pay interest on demand deposits. Paying interest on currency, on the other hand, would be quite difficult. As nominal interest rates rose in response to a fully anticipated inflation, the opportunity cost of holding currency relative to bonds would increase and there would be an incentive to economize on currency holdings. Spending units would hold less currency relative to transactions and, as a consequence, make more trips to the bank. These added trips to the bank represent the most important cost associated with fully anticipated inflation; this cost is sometimes referred to as the "shoe-leather" cost of fully anticipated inflation.

This cost may seem trivial and an unlikely source of the public antipathy toward inflation. But the fact is that inflation is typically episodic rather than steady and therefore only imperfectly anticipated. The costs of unanticipated inflation are the arbitrary redistribution of income and wealth and the changes in relative prices and distortions in resource allocation that result. The classic example of inflation-induced redistribution is from creditors to debtors; i.e., when inflation is unanticipated, the real value of the loan repayment (principal and interest) will be smaller than had been expected at the time the loan was made so that the lender is worse off and the borrower better off. Many other types of arbitrary redistributions occur in such a situation—from those who adjust slowly to inflation to those who adjust more rapidly. Sellers (including sellers of labor services) who are quick to raise prices gain at the expense of those who are slow. Individuals whose incomes are fixed in nominal terms (such as elderly people on pensions) suffer greatly.

All of this suggests that the avoidance of inflation is a desirable goal of macroeconomic policy. However, it is sometimes suggested that unemployment can be reduced if we accept a constant rate of inflation. In this case there may be a conflict between maintaining high employment and price stability. We will discuss the nature and source of inflation and the relation between inflation and unemployment in considerable detail—first in Chapter 9 and then more fully in Chapters 17 and 18. We will discuss policies designed to combat inflation in those chapters and also in Chapters 24 and 26.

FLOWS AND STOCKS

The level of output, the price level, the level of employment, the capital stock, the money supply, and the interest rate are some of the variables studied in macroeconomics. It is important to understand that these variables are not all dimensioned identically in relation to time. There are two basic types of variables: flows and stocks. Still other variables are ratios involving stocks and/or flows. A *flow* is a variable that can only be measured *per unit of time*. For example, output is measured as a rate per unit of time—X number of units per year or Y dollars per year. Similarly, consumption, investment, and government expenditures are flow variables. A *stock* is a variable that must be measured at a specific moment in time. The money supply is measured as X dollars on June 1, 1971. The capital stock, the level of employment, and the supply of government and private bonds are all stocks.

Some macroeconomic variables are neither flows nor stocks. These can be interpreted as one of the following types of *ratios*: (1) *ratio of stocks*—The unemployment rate is the ratio of the stock of unemployed persons to the total labor force. (2) *ratio of flows*—The price level can be interpreted as the ratio of the flow of cash to the flow of goods. (3) *ratio of flows to stocks*—Income velocity is the ratio of income (a flow) to the money supply (a stock). The interest rate is the ratio of the per-period return on a bond (a flow) and the principal (a stock).

CONTINUOUS AND PERIOD ANALYSIS

Economic models involve both flow and stock variables. For example, the *IS-LM* analysis in Part II studies the simultaneous equilibrium in the markets for output (a flow) and money (a stock). Since flows and stocks are dimensioned differently with respect to time, the concept of simultaneous equilibrium in stock and flow markets turns out to be a rather subtle concept.[2]

In Figure 1.1 we depict the relation between stock (S) and flow (F) variables over a period from t to $t + \Delta t$. The flow variable is defined as expenditures or production over the unit interval (say, one year) of the analysis (Δt). Stocks can be measured at the beginning of the period (*BOP*), at the end of the period (*EOP*), or at any other moment during the interval. We could define equilibrium in stock markets in terms of either beginning- or end-of-period supplies of and demands for stocks, or we could define equilibrium in terms of average values of supplies and demands over the interval. But there seems to be an element of arbitrariness in combining any of these specifications of stock equilibrium with the concept of flow equilibrium *over the period*.

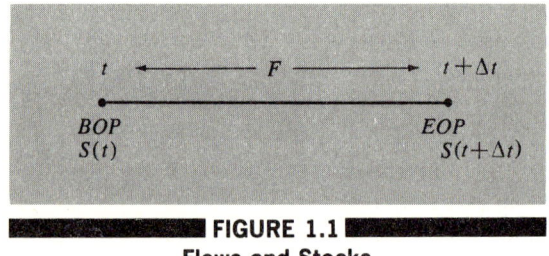

FIGURE 1.1
Flows and Stocks

To get a precise solution to this problem, we could collapse the period (Δt) to a single instant. Then the beginning and end of the period converge and the meaning of simultaneous equilibrium in stock and flow markets becomes clearcut. This specification of stocks and flows is called *continuous analysis*. The flows are instantaneous rates of change at the moment t, and the stocks are defined at the same point in time. This may not seem like a useful type of analysis, given that our observations of broad economic aggregate flows, such as income and production, are generally available only in quarterly or at best monthly data. But the fact that our data may only be available as averages over discrete periods does not imply that theoretical

---

[2] Our treatment of stocks and flows is strongly influenced by the excellent discussion of these issues by Duncan Foley in "On Two Specifications of Asset Equilibrium in Macroeconomic Models," *Journal of Political Economy*, Vol. 83 (April, 1975), pp. 303–324.

models of the economy cannot be meaningfully formulated in continuous terms. Nevertheless, discrete or period analysis is easier to understand and we will concentrate on that approach in the text.

In *discrete* or *period analysis*, flows are measured over some discrete period; e.g., a month, a quarter, or a year.[3] Thus, we measure *GNP*, the comprehensive measure of the flow of current production, as production per quarter or per year.[4] We will interpret simultaneous equilibrium of stock and flow markets in our period-type models as corresponding to equilibrium in flow markets over the period (Δt) and equilibrium in stock markets at the end of the period ($t + \Delta t$). This end-of-period specification of stock equilibrium is convenient because it permits us to develop clearly the interaction of stocks and flows over the unit interval of our analysis. In our early model manipulation in Part II we will use simple forms of our model which insure that the distinction between beginning- and end-of-period specifications of stocks will not influence the results of the analysis. In Part III and particularly in Part V we will explicitly develop the end-of-period specification of asset market equilibrium.

ECONOMIC MODELS

The basic approach used in this text is to develop models which specify the behavior of households (consumption, demand for money and bonds, supply of labor), businesses (investment, demand for labor, supply of private bonds), and government (government expenditures, taxes, supplies of money and government bonds) and to use these models to understand how the interaction among these sectors determines the key macro variables such as output, prices, and interest rates. But what is a model and what is the purpose of developing models?

A *model* is a rigorous representation of a theory, usually in mathematical form. A *theory* is a plausible principle or set of principles offered to explain phenomena (e.g., the determination of price and quantity in a particular market or the determination of aggregate output and the price level in the entire economy). A theory includes definitions, a set of assumptions, and one or more hypotheses. The *definitions* identify the variables to which the hypotheses apply. The *assumptions* specify the conditions

---

[3] For those with some background in calculus, the relationship between the instantaneous rate of flow, f, and the period analysis concept of a flow, F, is given by

$$F = \int_{t=0}^{n} f \, dt$$

where t, the index of instants of time, runs from the beginning of the period ($t = 0$) to the end of the period ($t = n$). Thus, F is simply the cumulative effect of the instantaneous rates of change over the period of analysis. If f is constant over the interval, Δt, the period specification of the flow over that interval is $F = f \Delta t$.

[4] Often when we measure *GNP* and other flows over a quarter, we dimension them at annual rates. For example, an increase in *GNP* by $20 billion in a given quarter corresponds to an annual rate of increase of $80 billion. Similarly, a 1 percent increase in *GNP* over a quarter corresponds to an annual rate of increase of 4 percent per year; i.e., if the economy continued to expand for a full year at the rate achieved in the quarter, it would expand by 4 percent over the year.

under which the theory applies. And the *hypotheses* are testable propositions about the relation between two or more variables. The purpose of models is both to *explain observed regularities* (e.g., the cyclical variation in the unemployment rate and the relation between inflation and unemployment) and to *permit prediction* of the future course of variables (e.g., the response of income to a cut in tax rates or the effect of an increase in government spending on interest rates and capital spending).

The explicit models used in economics are sometimes criticized for the enormous simplification of reality they involve. But this is precisely the purpose of theory—to isolate from the complex interrelations of reality those simpler relations which permit us to explain a large part of the observed regularities we encounter. The ultimate test of a theory is not how well it mirrors the details of the process determining the phenomenon being explained, but the conformity with experience of the predictions based on that theory.[5] Of course, the richer the detail of the model, the greater the number of specific predictions we will be able to make.

RELATIONSHIPS AMONG VARIABLES IN ECONOMIC MODELS

Models, we noted above, are mathematical representations of theories which, in turn, involve relations among variables. There are three basic types of relationships among variables that we will use in developing our models: (1) identities, (2) functional relationships, and (3) equilibrium conditions.

This is our first opportunity to introduce explicit mathematical notation. Our use of mathematics is primarily confined to the use of functional notation and algebra. Calculus is occasionally used in footnotes and appendices and only rarely in the main body of the text. The use of mathematical notation and of explicit solutions of the simple models permits us to make precise the relationships among macroeconomic variables that are the heart of macroeconomic analysis.

We recognize, however, that some students view any use of mathematics with anxiety. To these individuals, the use of such mathematical notation signals that the material must be difficult, obscure, or beyond their grasp. It is sometimes difficult to overcome such fears. By gradually introducing the notation and by beginning with quite simple models, we hope that we can persuade even those students who cringe at the sight of an equation (much less the solution of a set of equations) to continue, and that we can convince students that the mathematical techniques employed in the text are both quite simple and very useful in developing a thorough understanding of macroeconomics. Now we turn to the three types of relations we employ in our models.

Identities

An *identity* is a relationship between variables that is true by definition. For example, the relationship between total output (X) and its components [consumption

---

[5] For an excellent discussion of the nature of models, see Milton Friedman, "The Methodology of Positive Economics," in *Essays in Positive Economics* (Chicago: The University of Chicago Press, 1953), pp. 3–43.

Chapter 1 • Basic Concepts in Macroeconomics

(C), investment (I), and government spending (G)] is an identity.[6]

$$X \equiv C + I + G \tag{1.1a}$$

Another identity defines disposable income of households (Y) as total income or GNP (X) minus taxes net of transfers (T).

$$Y \equiv X - T \tag{1.1b}$$

Given that identities are true by definition, they are not subject to testing by collecting data and verifying the relation. The issue is usefulness, not correctness. An identity isolates components of a variable that permit more precise modeling of a sector's behavior [in the case of identity (1.1b)] or more accurate analysis of the aggregate economy's behavior [in the case of identity (1.1a)]. Thus, the GNP identity separates the total output into three categories, each of which is determined by a different sector of the economy and is influenced by different sets of variables. This decomposition is very useful in constructing models to explain the determination of aggregate income. The second identity, identity (1.1b), isolates another component of GNP, disposable income, that is useful in explaining household consumption spending (C). As we proceed, we will encounter numerous other useful identities, including the household balance sheet identity and the business and government sector's financing constraints, that will prove similarly useful in our development of macroeconomic models.

○ Functional Relationships

A *functional relationship* describes the systematic dependence of one variable (the *dependent variable*) on one or more other variables (the *independent variables*); i.e., a functional relationship is a *testable hypothesis* about the determinants of some variable.

Functional Notation. Assume there are three variables X, Y, and Z that are interrelated according to some hypothesis; e.g., X depends on, is a function of, Y and Z. This means that movement in Y and/or Z induces movement in X. We can write this hypothesis in mathematical notation as

$$X = F(Y, Z). \tag{1.2}$$

where Y, Z are independent variables, X is the dependent variable, and F is the symbol indicating existence of a functional relation.

This is simply a shorthand way of writing that X depends on Y and Z. X is said to

---

[6] To simplify the discussion, we have ignored the existence of imports and exports. We confine most of our analysis to a closed economy (i.e., one without foreign trade) until Chapters 27 and 28.

be the dependent variable and Y and Z are the independent variables. The symbol F simply indicates the existence of a functional relation or systematic dependence of X on Y and Z.

Functional Form. When we work with functional relations, it will generally be useful to specify precisely the functional form, the explicit nature of the relation among X, Y, and Z. We will use only two explicit functional forms: the *additive* or *linear* form and the *multiplicative* or *log-linear* form.

1. *The Linear Specification.* The linear specification of equation (1.2) is

$$X = a + bY + cZ \qquad (1.2a)$$

where a is a constant term (constant term) and b and c are constant parameters which indicate the relation between changes in Y and Z and changes in X. The linear specification is the simplest to work with, and most of the equations we work with will be linear.

The parameters in the linear specification indicate the ratio of the change in the dependent variable to a unit change in an independent variable, holding constant all other independent variables; i.e., $b = \Delta X / \Delta Y$ and $c = \Delta X / \Delta Z$.

2. *The Multiplicative Form.* The second common type of functional specification (used often in the specification of production, investment, and money demand functions) is the multiplicative form. If the function given by equation (1.2) is presumed to be multiplicative in the independent variables, it can be rewritten as

$$X = A Y^\alpha Z^\beta \qquad (1.2b)$$

where A is some constant and α and β are constant elasticities of X with respect to Y and Z, respectively. The *elasticity* of the dependent variable with respect to an independent variable is the ratio of the percentage change in the dependent variable to the percentage change in the independent variable, holding all other independent variables constant. Thus, the elasticity of X with respect to Y is

$$\epsilon_{XY} = \frac{\% \Delta X}{\% \Delta Y} = \alpha.$$

To derive the elasticity interpretation of parameters in the multiplicative specification, take logs of equation (1.2b).

$$\ln X = \ln A + \alpha \ln Y + \beta \ln Z \qquad (1.2b')$$

where $\ln$ is the symbol for the natural logarithm or logarithm to the base e. Taking first differences

$$\Delta \ln X = \alpha \Delta \ln Y + \beta \Delta \ln Z$$

where Δ is the symbol for "change in" or "first difference of." The change in the natural log of a variable is approximately the percentage change; i.e., $\Delta \ln X \simeq \%\Delta X$, etc. Therefore,

$$\alpha = \frac{\Delta \ln X}{\Delta \ln Y} \simeq \frac{\%\Delta X}{\%\Delta Y} = \epsilon_{XY}.$$

Parameters. The parameters of a functional relationship describe the effect of a change in the independent variables on the dependent variable. In the general functional form, the partial derivatives F_Y and F_Z provide this information. In the linear specification the parameters are the constant coefficients of Y and Z, a and b, equal to $\Delta X/\Delta Y$ and $\Delta X/\Delta Z$, respectively. The parameters of the multiplicative specification are the constant elasticities, α and β. The essential feature of the interpretation of functional parameters is the *ceteris paribus* ("all other things being constant") restriction: the functional parameters indicate the effect of a change in one independent variable on the dependent variable, holding all other influences on the dependent variable constant.

Types of Functional Relations in Economic Models. We will encounter two types of functional relations in economic models: behavioral equations and technical equations.

1. *Behavioral Equation.* A behavioral equation expresses a hypothesis about the behavior of some economic agent or about the collective behavior of some group of economic agents. For example, the consumption function presents a hypothesis about the spending decision by households. One such hypothesis is that consumption expenditures (C) depend on disposable income (Y) and wealth (a). We can express the hypothesized dependence of C on Y and a as follows:

$$C = C(Y, a) \tag{1.3}$$

C: dependent variable
Y, a: independent variables.

Equation (1.3) indicates that C is a function of (depends upon) Y and a. Generally we employ the same symbol used to identify the dependent variable to identify the functional relationship (in this case, C).

The consumption function we employ in our models is the linear specification of equation (1.3); i.e.,

$$C = \bar{C} + C_y Y + C_a a \tag{1.3'}$$

where C_y and C_a are the constant parameters and $\bar{C}$ is the constant term. The values of C_y and C_a are based on empirical studies of the relation between consumption, income, and wealth. We discuss the nature of the process used to estimate these parameters in the appendix to this chapter, and we discuss the evidence concerning C_y and C_a in more detail in Chapter 12. But the important point to grasp here is that we can express a hypothesis about the behavior of economic agents in the form of quite simple equations. The empirical evidence discussed in Chapter 12 indicates that C_y is about 0.7 and C_a is about 0.05. This means that households increase consumption by about 70 cents for each increase of one dollar in income, and households increase consumption by 5 cents for each one-dollar increase in net wealth.

2. *Technical Equation*. A technical equation describes a functional relationship arising from technical rather than behavioral considerations. An example is the aggregate production function which describes the relationship between output (X) and the factors of production; e.g.,

$$X = F(K, N) \tag{1.4}$$

where K is the capital stock and N is the input of labor services. In this case we have used the symbol F to denote the functional relation between the dependent and independent variables. Equation (1.4) indicates how the factor inputs are transformed into output. It does not describe the behavior of firms or households; rather, it describes the engineering relationship between inputs and outputs.

Using the multiplicative specification of the production function, we can rewrite equation (1.4) as

$$X = A K^\alpha N^\beta \tag{1.4'}$$

where A is a constant and α and β are the elasticities of X with respect to K and N, respectively. Given estimates of A, α and β, we can predict the value of X associated with any set of K and N.

Some of the identities we use in subsequent chapters are multiplicative. For example, output (X) can be expressed as the product of labor input (N) and output per unit of labor input (X/N). The latter variable is referred to as labor productivity ($\rho = X/N$).

$$X \equiv N(X/N) = N\rho \tag{1.5}$$

By taking logs and then first differences, we can relate the growth rate in output to growth rates in labor input and productivity. First, taking logs and first differences, we obtain

$$\Delta \ln X \equiv \Delta \ln N + \Delta \ln \rho. \tag{1.5'}$$

The first differences are changes in the respective variables *over time*; e.g., $\Delta \ln X$ is the change in $\ln X$ between this period and the previous one. The change in the log of a variable is approximately a *percentage* change. Therefore, $\Delta \ln X$ is approximately the proportional or percentage change in output over the period (e.g., the percentage change from one year to the next). We will use dots over variables to express *change over time*; e.g., $\dot{X}$ means change in X per unit of time. Equation (1.5') can be rewritten as

$$\frac{\dot{X}}{X} = \frac{\dot{N}}{N} + \frac{\dot{\rho}}{\rho}. \tag{1.5''}$$

This equation states that the percentage rate of growth of output is the sum of the percentage rates of growth of labor input and productivity.

○ Equilibrium Condition

Equilibrium refers to a state of balance between opposing forces. In economics, equilibrium generally refers to a situation in which supply and demand are in balance in a market. For example, in a flow market, such as the market for currently produced goods and services, equilibrium exists when the quantity that firms want to sell over a given period equals the quantity that buyers want to purchase over the same period. In a stock market, such as the bond market, equilibrium exists when the quantity of bonds that firms wish to have outstanding at a given point in time is just equal to the quantity of bonds that wealth owners want to hold in their portfolios at that moment.

We can further clarify the meaning of equilibrium in terms of a simple supply and demand model.

$$D = D(P) \tag{1.6}$$

$$S = S(P) \tag{1.7}$$

$$S = D \tag{1.8}$$

Equations (1.6) and (1.7) are behavioral equations describing the decision making by buyers and sellers, respectively. Equation (1.6) indicates that the quantity demanded (D) depends on the price level (P); it is a hypothesis about the behavior of buyers. According to equation (1.7), the quantity supplied (S) depends on the price level also; this is a hypothesis about the behavior of sellers. Equation (1.8) is an equilibrium condition; equilibrium requires that supply and demand are in balance. Note that equation (1.8) is *not* an identity because supply and demand are not definitionally equal despite the fact that the quantities bought and sold must always be identical. Supply and demand are *desired* quantities; they represent the amount demanders desire to purchase and suppliers desire to sell at various prices—not the actual quantities that get exchanged. The dependent variable in a behavioral equation always indicates a desired or *ex ante* quantity—not an actual or *ex post* quantity. Only in equilibrium must the *ex post* and *ex ante* values of the variables be equal.

The supply (SS) and demand (DD) curves are depicted in Figure 1.2. The supply curve is upward sloping and the demand curve is downward sloping. The downward-sloping demand curve reflects the hypothesis that a decline in price will induce an increase in the quantity of the commodity demanded. And the upward-sloping supply curve reflects the hypothesis that an increase in the price level is required to induce an increase in the quantity of the commodity supplied. Point E represents the equilibrium position in the market. Any point on DD represents a desired position for buyers and any point on SS represents a desired position for sellers. Only at E are both buyers and sellers content. At the equilibrium price, P_0, (desired) quantity supplied and (desired) quantity demanded are equal. If the price level is higher than the equilibrium price, as at P_1 in Figure 1.2, the quantity supplied (S_1) will exceed the quantity demanded (D_1); $S_1 - D_1$ is a measure of the magnitude of the (excess supply) disequilibrium.

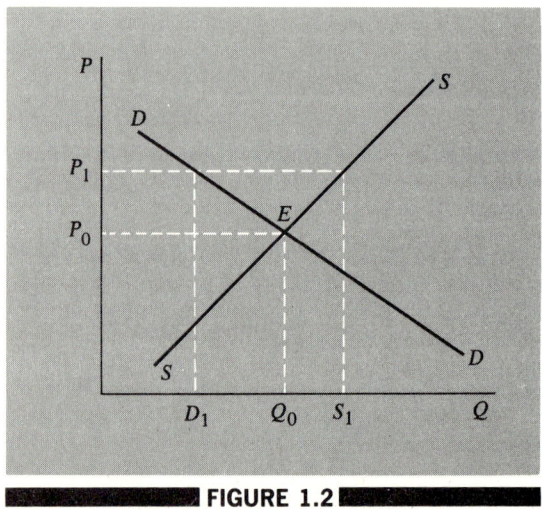

FIGURE 1.2
Equilibrium and Disequilibrium

Note that under voluntary exchange, the "short end" of the market dominates. Let Q denote the actual amount bought and sold. Q is always the lesser of the amount buyers wish to purchase (D) and the amount sellers wish to sell (S); i.e.,

$$Q = \min(D,S). \tag{1.9}$$

In equilibrium $Q_0 = S_0 = D_0$. Both buyers and sellers are satisfied; i.e., at P_0 sellers are able to sell just the amount they would like to sell and buyers are able to purchase just the amount they would like to purchase. Note that in equilibrium, buyers are at a point on their demand curve and sellers are at a point on their supply curve.

TWO ILLUSTRATIVE MODELS AND THE DISTINCTION BETWEEN ENDOGENOUS AND EXOGENOUS VARIABLES

In this section we consider two examples of economic models: a supply and demand model and a multiplier model of income determination. We use these models to clarify the distinction between endogenous and exogenous variables.

The Supply and Demand Model

Let us expand the supply and demand model we introduced in the previous section. Let the supply of a particular agricultural commodity, S_a, depend on its price, P_a, the price of other competing commodities that the firm could produce, P_0, weather conditions, W, and government subsidies, GS.

$$S_a = S(P_a, P_0, W, GS) \tag{1.10}$$

Let the demand depend on P_a, P_0, and the level of income, Y.

$$D_a = D(P_a, P_0, Y) \tag{1.11}$$

In each case we have not included all possible influences on supply and demand. We have isolated those variables which are believed to be the most important in determining movements in the quantity and price of the commodity. This is, as we noted above, the purpose of theory. The equilibrium condition is

$$S_a = D_a. \tag{1.12}$$

○ The Multiplier Model

The *multiplier model* consists of the *GNP* identity, the disposable income identity, and the consumption function.

$$X \equiv C + I + G \tag{1.13}$$

$$Y \equiv X - T \tag{1.14}$$

$$C = C(Y) \tag{1.15}$$

Total expenditures are the sum of consumption, C, investment, I, and government expenditures, G. Disposable income equals *GNP* minus taxes net of transfers, T. Consumption is assumed to be positively related to income. Assuming a linear form for the consumption function,

$$C = \bar{C} + C_y Y \tag{1.15'}$$

where $1 > C_y > 0$.

○ Endogenous vs. Exogenous Variables

Each variable in a model can be classified as being endogenous or exogenous to the model. An *endogenous variable* is one whose value is determined by the model; it is an "unknown" which must be solved for by using the model. An *exogenous variable* is one whose value is determined outside the model; it is datum to be used to determine the values of the unknowns.

We classify exogenous variables as either policy or nonpolicy variables. A *policy variable* (or *instrument*) is purposefully controlled by policy authorities (e.g., the government or the central bank); government subsidies in the supply and demand model and government expenditures in the multiplier model are policy instruments. *Nonpolicy exogenous variables* are other variables whose value we do not explain within the model; changes in these variables are disturbances which affect the values of the endogenous variables. Weather, prices of other commodities, and income are nonpolicy exogenous variables in the supply and demand model; investment is a nonpolicy exogenous variable in the multiplier model. Other exogenous variables that influence supply and/or demand or consumption have been excluded from the theory. These are assumed to influence the variables in the model by affecting the constant term in the various structural equations. For example, an increase in desired saving due to increased consumer pessimism associated with political events would involve a decrease in $\bar{C}$ in equation (1.15′).

We classify endogenous variables as "target" or "goal" variables and "other" endogenous variables. A *goal variable* is an endogenous variable whose value is of ultimate concern to policymakers. We can consider policymakers as having a utility function, the arguments of which are the goal variables. The level of output, the rate of change of prices, and the level of unemployment are obvious candidates for goal variables. When there are multiple targets, it may be impossible for policymakers to simultaneously achieve the most desirable values for each of the goal variables. For example, policymakers desire a low rate of unemployment. But low unemployment rates may be associated with high rates of inflation; i.e., low unemployment and price stability may be incompatible. In this case policymakers must impose their subjective preferences about their distaste for unemployment and inflation to decide which of the possible combinations of unemployment and inflation they should opt for.

There are two ways in which we classify variables as being endogenous or exogenous. The first approach is to classify the variables in relation to the specific model under consideration. For example, while W would be exogenous in any economic model, it would be endogenous in a meteorological model; and although P_0 and Y are exogenous in the supply and demand model, they would be endogenous in a model of the entire economy. On the other hand, we sometimes criticize a model for treating as exogenous a variable that is "in reality" endogenous. Thus, there is also a meaningful distinction between what *is* being treated as exogenous and what *ought to be* treated as exogenous. For example, if we believe we can explain variation in the level of investment in terms of movements in the interest rate, we would question the accuracy of the results given by the Keynesian multiplier model presented above because the model fails to allow for the interaction of investment and other variables in the model.

○ Autonomous vs. Induced Changes in Endogenous Variables

Our equation for consumption, equation (1.15′), includes both a constant term $\bar{C}$ and a term related to income. The constant term is sometimes referred to as the *autonomous* component of consumption, the part of consumption independent of other variables in the model. Thus, there may be an element of exogeneity even in the endogenous variables. The second term in equation (1.15′) is the *induced* component of consumption. There is some ambiguity about the appropriate way to classify the autonomous component of endogenous variables. $\overline{C}$ could be viewed as a parameter in the consumption function. However, we will find that it functions in the model more like an exogenous variable than like parameters such as C_y and C_a. Therefore, we will generally group the autonomous component of the endogenous variables with the exogenous variables.

STRUCTURAL EQUATIONS AND REDUCED FORMS

The identities, functional relationships, and equilibrium conditions that describe the structure of the economy are called *structural equations*; the parameters of behavioral and technical equations are called *structural parameters*. The purpose of constructing models is to use our understanding of the economy to explain the past and predict the future behavior of the unknowns or endogenous variables. To find the value of the unknowns implied by the model, we must *solve* the model. For simple linear models of the type on which we concentrate in this text, it is possible to solve the models for the value of each unknown as a linear function of the exogenous variables; e.g., we could solve the model given by equations (1.13), (1.14), and (1.15) for

$$X = m_1 \overline{C} + m_2 \overline{I} + m_3 \overline{T} + m_4 \overline{G}. \tag{1.16}$$

This type of equation is called a *reduced form*: it reduces the model's structure to a single equation describing the way in which the exogenous variables determine the values of the endogenous variable.

The parameters of the reduced form [m_1, m_2, m_3, and m_4 in equation (1.16)] are called *multipliers*. A multiplier describes the response of an endogenous variable to a change in some exogenous variable, holding constant all other exogenous variables but permitting all other endogenous variables to change at the same time. For example, the coefficient of G, $m_4 = \dfrac{\Delta X}{\Delta G}$, is the change in output associated with a unit change in government expenditures. The multipliers in reduced-form equations are, in turn, combinations of the structural parameters in the model. We will not explicitly solve for the values of the multipliers at this point, although you may find it useful to try to do so yourself. After we have had an opportunity to look at the simple model more carefully, we will solve explicitly for the reduced form. Indeed, one of the distinctive features of our approach is the focus on solving for and interpreting reduced forms.

APPENDIX

Theoretical vs. Statistical Specifications of Hypotheses

One objection often raised about the use of mathematical specifications of relations among economic variables is that they suggest a precision that is inconsistent with both the current state of knowledge and the often imprecise nature of predictions based on such specifications. For example, the consumption function given by equation (1.15') in Chapter 1 might suggest that, given values for $\bar{C}$ and C_y, it is possible to predict with precision the value of consumption associated with any given value of income. But economic theory in general indicates only the independent variables that influence the dependent variable and the *signs* of the relation between movements in independent and dependent variables. It does not generally yield information about the precise magnitude of the parameters. For example, theory suggests that real disposable income is an important determinant of real consumption expenditures and that the propensity to consume is between zero and one. The precise value of C_y cannot be derived explicitly from the theory. To determine the magnitudes of the parameters, it is necessary to use data on observed values of the dependent and independent variables to *estimate* the values of the parameters. Thus, using data on observed values of C and Y, we can estimate the values of $\bar{C}$ and C_y. The predictions based on such an estimated equation will not be precisely correct, and the precision of the predictions provides a measure of the consistency of the hypothesis with observed movements in the dependent and independent variables.

The Theoretical Specification

We begin with a theoretical relation between consumption and income. This relationship will generally be derived from assumptions about the behavior of households; e.g., households maximize utility subject to a resource constraint. Our starting point is therefore a functional relation between consumption and income,

$$C = C(Y). \tag{1A.1}$$

Let us also assume that the relationship is linear so that we can express equation (1A.1) as

$$C = \bar{C} + C_y Y. \tag{1A.1'}$$

This is the theoretical specification of our hypothesis.

The Stochastic Specification

There are many factors other than income that can influence consumption. We noted in this chapter that theory represents an enormous simplification of reality, isolating the essential determinants of a particular variable. Much is left out. The effect of all the left-out factors can be incorporated by adding an error or disturbance term, ϵ, to equation (1A.1').

$$C = \bar{C} + C_y Y + \epsilon \tag{1A.2}$$

We assume that the error term in any period is a *random variable*, a variable whose value is governed by the laws of probability or chance. A random variable may be described by its *probability distribution*; a probability distribution associates each possible outcome of a variable with the probability that it will occur. Two important properties of a probability distribution are its mean and variance. The *mean* or expected value of a probability distribution is a measure of the central tendency or average value of the distribution; more precisely, the mean is defined as a weighted average of all possible outcomes where the weights are the probability that the particular outcome will occur. We generally use the symbol $E(\cdot)$ to denote the expected value of the function of the random variable that is placed in the parentheses. If x itself is placed in the parentheses, we use a special symbol: $E(x) = \bar{x}$. The *variance* is a measure of spread or dispersion of a variable around its mean. We can express the variance of a variable x as the expected value of the function $(x - \bar{x})^2$; i.e.,

$$\text{Var}(x) = E[(x - \bar{x})^2]. \tag{1A.3}$$

We usually assume that the probability distribution associated with the error term is normally distributed with a zero mean. This type of distribution is depicted in Figure 1A.1. The possible outcomes for the variable in question, in this case the error term (ϵ), are measured along the horizontal axis. The probability that the error term will take on a value over a given interval on the horizontal axis is measured by the area under the curve over this interval. The area under the entire curve must therefore equal one. The normal distribution is symmetric around the mean, zero in this case. The expected value of C (the mean value of the probability distribution governing C) is simply the value of the theoretical prediction given by

$$\tilde{C} = \bar{C} + C_y Y \tag{1A.2'}$$

where $\tilde{C}$ designates the predicted value of C associated with a given value of Y. This equation indicates the best guess about the value of C corresponding to any given value of Y. The actual C will diverge from this prediction by some random amount, drawn from the probability

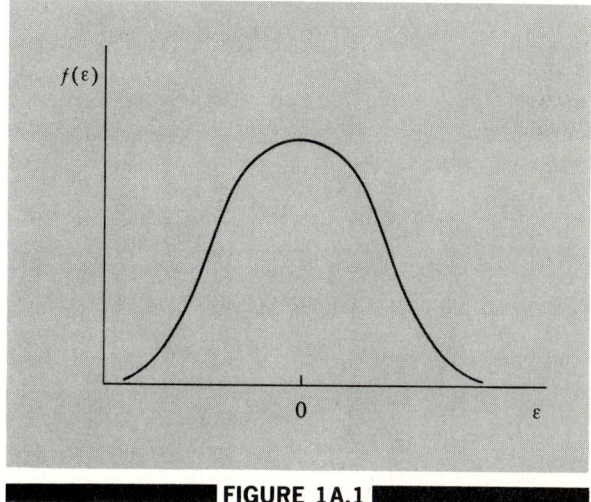

FIGURE 1A.1
The Normal Distribution with Zero Mean

distribution governing ϵ. Thus, even if our theory had correctly identified the key determinant of consumption and even if we knew the true values of $\bar{C}$ and C_y, we could not expect to predict the value of C corresponding to a given value of Y without error. The degree of precision with which we could predict would be governed by the probability that the error term might take on values substantially different from zero; such values are said to be in the tails of the distribution. The next step is to use observed values of C and Y to estimate the values of $\bar{C}$ and C_y.

Testing the Theory[1]

Time series for consumption and income consist of values of C and Y over some period of time; e.g., annual observations from 1954 to 1977. We denote the value of C and Y in period t as C_t and Y_t, where t is the time period index.

To test the theory, we must first estimate the values of $\bar{C}$ and C_y so that we can obtain predictions of C for various levels of Y. We designate the estimated values of $\bar{C}$ and C_y as $\hat{\bar{C}}$ and $\hat{C}_y$. The predicted value of C_t will be

$$\hat{C}_t = \hat{\bar{C}} + \hat{C}_y Y_t, \tag{1A.4}$$

and the prediction error or residual, e_t, will be

$$e_t = C_t - \hat{C}_t. \tag{1A.5}$$

The values of e_t will indicate the degree of fit between the theory and the data.

The first step is to determine the "best" estimates of the parameters. The obvious criterion for "best" is the value of the parameters which minimizes the size of the prediction errors. The specific criterion usually applied in econometric analysis is to select the values of $\bar{C}$ and C_y which *minimize the sum of the squares of the error terms,* $\sum_{t=1}^{n}(e_t)^2$, where n is the number of periods in the time series of C and Y. This procedure is referred to as the *least squares method*. The statistical form of a structural equation is referred to as a *regression* and the estimated parameters are called *regression coefficients*.

A theory is useful to the extent that it permits us to explain a substantial portion of the variation in the variables that the theory is designed to explain; i.e., a theory is useful if the prediction errors are small in relation to the systematic explanatory power of the regression. We therefore need a measure of the degree to which the model explains the movements in the dependent variable. We noted above that the variance of a variable is a measure of its dispersion about its mean; the variance of consumption over its sample period, for example, is given by

$$\text{Var}(C) = \sum_{t=1}^{n}(C_t - \tilde{C})^2/n \tag{1A.6}$$

---

[1] For a more thorough introduction to the estimation of economic relationships, see A. A. Walters, *Introduction to Econometrics* (New York: W. W. Norton & Company, 1970); or Chapter 2 in Richard Schmalensee, *Applied Microeconomics: Problems in Estimation, Forecasting, and Decision-Making* (San Francisco: Holden-Day, 1973).

where $\tilde{C}$ is the mean of consumption over the sample period defined by

$$\tilde{C} = \sum_{t=1}^{n} C_t/n. \tag{1A.7}$$

The explanatory power of the consumption function can be judged by the R^2 statistic, a measure of the percentage of the variance of the dependent variable explained by the regression

$$R^2 = \frac{\text{Var}(C) - \text{Var}(e)}{\text{Var}(C)} = 1 - \frac{\text{Var}(e)}{\text{Var}(C)}. \tag{1A.8}$$

The closer R^2 is to unity, the better the "fit"; i.e., the higher the explanatory power of the regression.

Throughout the text we will discuss the quantitative values of the parameters of our theoretical specifications suggested by the accumulated empirical evidence from econometric analysis. We will not in most cases discuss the full details of the evidence. We will, however, include references to specific econometric studies to allow the interested reader to learn more about the predictive accuracy of the equations and models we discuss.

● REVIEW QUESTIONS

1. Distinguish between microeconomics and macroeconomics. In what way must macroeconomics build on microeconomics?

2. Why is price level stability considered a goal of macroeconomic policy?

3. Why does it matter whether inflation is anticipated or unanticipated?

4. What is the difference between stock and flow variables?

5. Contrast the unique specification of stocks in a continuous model with the choices for the specification of stocks in period models.

6. What is a model and what is the purpose of constructing models?

7. What is the difference between a functional relationship and an identity?

8. What is the distinction between structural and reduced-form equations?

● PROBLEMS

1. "How can supply exceed demand? When someone buys a good, someone else must sell it. The amount bought and the amount sold are always identical. Therefore, supply and demand must always be equal." Comment.

Part I • Concepts, Measurement, and Development of the Basic Model

2. Write down equations corresponding to each of the relations among variables given below. Indicate whether they are identities, functional relationships, or equilibrium conditions. Identify the stock and flow variables.

   (a) The unemployment rate (u) is the ratio of the number of people who are unemployed (U) to the total labor force (L).

   (b) Net wealth of households (a) is the sum of their holdings of money (m), bonds (b), and consumer durables (cd).

   (c) The demand for money (m^d) depends on both the interest rate (r) and the level of income (X).

   (d) The real wage (w) rate is the nominal wage (W) rate divided by the price level (P).

   (e) The supply of labor (N^s) depends on the real wage rate.

   (f) The demand for labor (N^d) depends on the real wage rate.

   (g) Equilibrium exists in the labor market when the supply and demand for labor are equal.

   (h) Consumption (C) depends on disposable income (Y).

   (i) The net wealth of the household at the end of the year (a) equals the net wealth at the beginning of the year ($\bar{a}$) plus the saving of the household over the year (S).

3. Write the money demand and consumption functions described in problem 2 assuming they are both linear relations. Identify the behavioral parameters and discuss their interpretation.

4. The table below provides information on the value of consumption expenditures (C) associated with various levels of disposable income (Y).

Y	C
500	600
750	800
1000	1000
1250	1200

   (a) Plot these pairs of consumption and disposable income. Measure disposable income along the horizontal axis and consumption along the vertical axis.

   (b) Connect the points. What kind of relationship do you observe between consumption and income? What is the sign of the slope and what is the interpretation of the slope?

   (c) Assume that the relationship among the points in your graph holds for all other combinations of Y and C. Find the value of the slope and the vertical axis intercept of the curve relating C and Y.

(d) Write an equation that precisely describes the relationship between consumption and income.

(e) If income is expected to equal $1,500 billion next year, what level do you expect for consumption?

5. Consumption expenditures are a linear function of disposable income. Disposable income is total income or *GNP* minus tax revenues. Tax revenues are proportional to total income. *GNP* is the sum of consumption, investment, and government expenditures. Write out the model that includes all the relations among the variables discussed above. Identify exogenous and endogenous variables, functional relationships and identities, and behavioral parameters.

6. Solve for the reduced form of the model given by equations (1.13) − (1.15).

● EXERCISE

Using the *Wall Street Journal* or the business section of a newspaper, cut out an article dealing with relations among macroeconomic variables. Identify whether the variables are stocks, flows, or ratios. Then write out an equation that corresponds to the one discussed in the article. Is it a functional relation? Is it a reduced-form or a behavioral equation? How could this relation be verified?

Chapter 2

The Measurement of Macroeconomic Variables

The purpose of this chapter is to explain the measurement of the key variables that enter into our models. A word of caution is in order. Like the first chapter, this one involves a large dose of information which will become increasingly meaningful only as the variables discussed are used in succeeding chapters. You may therefore find it useful to refer back to this chapter as the variables are introduced into the models in later chapters.

Theory and facts interact. Facts motivate theory. Theory indicates what data are important to collect and analyze. And theory is useful only if it explains the facts. Your understanding of macroeconomics will be greatly enhanced if you follow the course of macroeconomic variables such as *GNP*, various measures of the price level, interest rates, monetary growth, unemployment rate, and other variables discussed in this chapter. You will appreciate the usefulness of models better when you understand the measurement of the variables involved and you will sharpen your understanding of the interrelation among macro variables through the use of the models.

We begin with a discussion of the accounting framework for income and expenditure flows, called the national income accounts (*NIA*). Next, we discuss the measurement of the overall or absolute price level and the use of price indices to separate movements in real economic activity from movements in the price level. In the final section we develop the accounting framework for stocks and the balance sheets of the economy and of the household, business, and government sectors. Here we also discuss the nature of bonds and equities, the relation between the interest rate and the market price of a bond, and the distinction between real and nominal interest rates.

NATIONAL INCOME ACCOUNTS

The natural starting point is the measurement of the overall level of income and production in the economy. The accounting framework for the income and production statistics for the economy is called the *national income accounts* (*NIA*) and the most widely used measure of macroeconomic activity is the *gross national product* (*GNP*). Our discussion of income and production statistics will therefore focus on the way in which *GNP* is measured and consider the way in which *GNP* can be decomposed into component flows which, in turn, will be important variables in the models we develop below to explain the determination of income.

Theory and Measurement

The *NIA* is concerned with definitions or identities, not with theoretical or functional relationships. Yet theory plays an important role in designing the accounting framework. The problem of *NIA* is not simply statistical information collection; it is not how to obtain numerical estimates of preconceived variables, but rather how to develop good operational definitions of the variables theory suggests are important. In evaluating a particular design for the *NIA*, the critical question is not whether a particular set of definitions is "correct," but rather whether the particular set of definitions is "useful" for testing some theory.

For example, is the disaggregation of total expenditures (X) into consumption (C), investment (I), and government expenditures (G),

$$X \equiv C + I + G, \tag{2.1}$$

useful? Assume the preconceived theory is the Keynesian cross framework. According to the Keynesian cross model we will study in Chapter 6, C depends only on X, I is an exogenous disturbance, and G is a policy-controlled instrument. This definition isolates the three different types of variables that comprise total expenditures and thus organizes the data to test the theory.

Gross National Product

The most widely used measure of macroeconomic activity is the gross national product (*GNP*), the value of all final goods and services produced by a nation over a specified period of time. In the *NIA*, *GNP* is measured from two different perspectives: the value of currently produced goods and services (the product side) and the value of factor incomes that are earned in the process of producing the goods (the income side). In this section we discuss the measurement of currently produced goods and services from each of these perspectives.

The Product to be Included. The basic procedure for measuring the value of currently produced goods and services is to sum the value of expenditures on currently produced goods and services. Therefore, only products that are sold on markets are generally included. In addition, to avoid double-counting, we include expenditures on "final" output only. In this section we discuss the rationale for excluding nonmarket production, the exceptions, the kinds of market transactions which are excluded, and the definition of "final" output.

1. *Nonmarket Production.* In general, we do not include in our measure of *GNP* the value of nonmarket production, such as the value of personally rendered services.

For example, the value of labor services involved in building an extension to one's home is included if the owner hires someone to do the work, but is excluded if the owner does the work. The justification for the exclusion of nonmarket goods is primarily practical rather than theoretical—the difficulty in valuing nonmarket goods. This asymmetrical treatment of market and nonmarket goods, however, makes intertemporal and intercountry comparisons of *GNP* hazardous.

There are two exceptions to the exclusion of nonmarket goods. Current housing services are valued in the market only for rented apartments or houses. To capture the value of all housing services, rent is "imputed" for owner-occupied houses; i.e., an estimate is made of what the rental payment would be if the house were rented rather than owned. In addition, the value of payment in kind is imputed by estimating how much the goods would cost in the market.

2. *Excluded Market Transactions.* Not all market transactions are included in *GNP.* Only market activity that adds to the flow of current goods and services is included. Excluded market transactions include asset exchanges and transfer payments. The payment for a tangible good produced and sold in a previous period but resold in the current period is not included; e.g., the sale of an "old" house or painting. In addition, we do not include the value of capital gains (losses) on existing assets. A capital gain (loss) is the appreciation (depreciation) in the value of an existing asset. Changes in the value of existing assets are excluded from national income because they do not reflect a payment for current services or production. The increase in the value of a house due to inflation, the change in the value of a piece of art over time, and the change in the value of outstanding bonds and equity are examples of capital gains. A *transfer payment* is a payment from one unit to another without any current *quid pro quo* (no current service, production, or exchange) required by the unit receiving the payment. Government transfers include social security and welfare payments. Personal transfers include gifts, inheritance, and charity. Also, interest payments on consumer and government debt are treated as transfer payments, under the assumption that only business loans are "productive," and therefore only the interest on business loans reflects current productive services by the lending unit. Most government debt was accumulated in wartime and the assets financed by the sale of the debt have long since been destroyed. Business transfer payments include the payment of contest prizes. Business transfer payments are not included in national income, the sum of income payments to all the factors of production, for the same reason that government and personal transfers are excluded—they are not a payment for current productive services. But, in contrast to other transfer payments, business transfers are included in *GNP.* We will explain why when we turn to the income side of the *NIA* later in this section.

3. *Final vs. Intermediate Goods.* In valuing the nation's output, we must be careful to avoid double-counting. One way of insuring this is to include only the value of currently produced *final* goods and services. An *intermediate good* is one produced and purchased for resale (with or without further processing) within the accounting period. A *final good* is one produced and either purchased for final use, purchased for ultimate processing and resale in a subsequent period, or not purchased during the period. *Final use* is identified primarily with directly contributing to consumers' well-being. Fuel purchased by a business firm (and used in the current period to produce final output) is an intermediate product whereas fuel purchased by a household is a final good. If we counted both the value of the fuel purchased by the firm and the value of the output produced by the firm, we would be double-counting the value of the fuel, because the price of the firm's output must cover the cost of its inputs; i.e., its price must include the value of its fuel consumption.

Two types of goods which might seem more appropriately classified as intermediate goods, inventory investment and fixed business investment, are nevertheless treated as final goods under the above definitions. Inventory investment and business fixed investment must be included in *GNP* to insure that *GNP* includes all the *production* of goods and services over the accounting period.

a. *Inventory Investment.* If a firm purchases goods for further processing but does not process and sell them in the same period, or if the firm produces output which it does not sell in the same period, the inventory of unfinished and finished goods increases. If we only included the value of output sold to households in *GNP*, we would not be measuring total production. To capture the value of total production, we include the value of the inventory accumulation in our measure of *GNP*.

b. *Fixed Business Investment.* A piece of capital equipment purchased by a firm is an intermediate product in the sense that it will be exhausted in the production of output and its value will ultimately be reflected in the price of the firm's output. If we excluded the value of newly produced capital goods and included only the reduction in the value of the existing capital goods due to their use in producing current output (called *depreciation*), we would fully take into account over time the value of the equipment and avoid double-counting. However, this approach would not provide a measure of the value of *current* production. On the other hand, including the value of newly produced capital goods along with the market value of truly final goods, as is done in the computation of *GNP*, does involve double-counting of capital goods. To avoid double-counting, it is necessary to subtract from *GNP* the depreciation of existing capital goods; the resulting measure of current output is referred to as *net national product* (*NNP*).

NNP avoids double-counting the value of capital goods and is therefore conceptually superior to *GNP*. Nevertheless, *GNP* remains the most widely used measure of total production. The explanation for this apparent inconsistency between theory and practice is the difficulty in measuring the depreciation of existing capital goods. Therefore, despite its conceptual deficiency, *GNP* rather than *NNP* remains the most widely used measure of the economy's current production.

Valuation of the Product. There is an enormous variety of economic goods produced in the economy. Some way must be devised to combine the diverse array of economic goods into a meaningful composite figure—total production. The conventional procedure is to value each economic good at its *market price* and then sum the value of the individual economic goods to get the value of total production. Market price is thus a common denominator into which each good can be converted to allow meaningful comparison.

However, as we noted above, not all goods included in national income pass through the market. For example, payments-in-kind and rental value of owner-occupied homes are included in national income although no explicit market transaction occurs. In such cases, values must be "imputed"; values that approximate the market price of identical goods that do pass through the market are assigned. In the case of payments-in-kind, imputed value of the payments appears as wages on the income side and as personal consumption expenditures on the product side. In the case of rental value of owner-occupied homes, the imputed value appears under rental payments on the income side and under personal consumption expenditures on the product side. The homeowner is treated as a business, renting the house to itself.

The Product Side of the NIA. The 1977 *NIA* is presented in Table 2.1. The components of *GNP* on the product side are consumption, investment, and government expenditures. Consumption expenditures generally account for 60–65 percent of *GNP* (61.1 percent in 1977). This explains the importance of being able to explain consumption in building macroeconomic models. On the other hand, as we will see in later chapters, the most important determinant of consumption is income itself. So, movements in income are for the most part initiated by movements in the other components of *GNP*. This explains the interest in the simplest of the models we consider, the Keynesian cross model, in which movements in investment and government expenditures, both viewed as exogenous, induce movements in both consumption and *GNP*.

More sophisticated macroeconomic models do not generally treat investment as exogenous. We will discuss the theory of investment casually in Chapter 4 and in more detail in Chapter 14. In 1977 investment accounted for 15.5 percent of *GNP*. Over the last 20 years it has generally been about 15–16 percent of *GNP* although it was less than this in both 1975 and 1976, raising some concern about a slowing in the future rate of economic growth. Gross private domestic investment includes business fixed investment, residential construction, and inventory investment. *Fixed business investment* includes expenditures on plant and equipment. These totaled $185.6 billion in 1977, 9.8 percent of *GNP*. Over the past 20 years, plant and equipment spending has generally been in the 9.0–10.5 percent range. *Residential construction* totaled $90.9 billion in 1977, 4.8 percent of *GNP*. This is quite a volatile series, generally falling in the range of 3–5 percent of *GNP*. *Inventory investment* is the value of inventories accumulated during the current period and can be positive or negative (inventory accumulation or decumulation). It has ranged from $16.7 billion in 1966 to −$12 billion in 1975. Although it is only a small fraction of *GNP* in any given year, its movements from year to year often account for a sizeable fraction of the changes in *GNP*.

Government spending at all levels totaled $395.0 billion in 1977, 20.9 percent of *GNP*; of this $145.4 billion was federal spending, and this accounted for 7.7 percent of *GNP*. The government component of *GNP* is confined to spending on currently produced goods and services and thus, as we noted above, excludes all transfer payments. For example, the $198.9 billion of federal government transfer payments in 1977, including social security, unemployment compensation, interest on the outstanding debt, and welfare payments are not included in *GNP*.

Income		Product	
Wages, Salaries, and Supplements	1210.1	Personal Consumption Expenditures	1155.8
Proprietors' Income	97.9	Gross Private Domestic Investment	294.3
Rental Income	25.3	business fixed investment	185.6
Net Interest	100.9	inventory investment	17.8
		residential construction	90.9
Corporate Profits*	140.3		
profits tax	69.2	Government Expenditures	395.0
dividends	41.2	federal	145.4
undistributed profits	61.7	state-local	249.5
IVA	−14.5		
CCAdj	−17.0	Net Exports	−9.0
National Income	1520.3	Gross National Product	1890.4
Indirect Business Taxes	165.2		
Business Transfers	9.0		
Government Subsidies— Surplus of Government Enterprises	2.1		
Statistical Discrepancy	1.0		
Net National Income	1693.4		
Capital Consumption Allowances	197.0		
Gross National Income	1890.4		

* including inventory valuation adjustment and capital consumption adjustment

TABLE 2.1
National Income and Product Account, 1977
(billions of dollars)

The final component is net exports which may be positive or negative. *Exports*, the sale of currently produced domestic goods to other countries, are part of domestic production and must therefore be included in *GNP*. Part of consumption, investment, and government expenditures are for imported goods and do not therefore represent current domestic production. Consequently, we subtract imports to get total domestic production.

The Income Side of the NIA. On the income side, the various forms of income that are generated in the process of producing the output are enumerated. The sum of the income components is called *national income*. The income side of *NIA* includes two other components in addition to national income: "other charges against *GNP*" and depreciation (or capital consumption allowances). These two components must be included to make the two sides balance because the total value of the product is not exhausted in income payments to the owners of the factors of production.

1. *National Income.* There are five components of national income: compensation of employees, proprietors' income, rental income, net interest, and corporate profits. *Compensation of employees* includes wages and salaries, imputed value of income-in-kind, and supplements to wages and salaries such as employer contributions to social security and private pension plans. Compensation of employees has accounted for about 75–80 percent of national income in the 1970s, compared to 70–74 percent in the 1960s. In 1977 it was 79.6 percent of national income. *Proprietors' income* ($97.9 billion or 6.4 percent of *NI* in 1977) includes all monetary income (salaries, interest, and profit) and imputed income-in-kind accruing to sole proprietorships and partnerships. *Rental income* ($25.3 billion or 1.7 percent of *NI* in 1977) includes rental incomes of persons not primarily engaged in the real estate business and imputed rent from owner-occupied homes. Income generated by firms in the real estate business is treated like income from any other business. *Net interest* ($100.9 billion or 6.6 percent of *NI* in 1977) is interest payments to persons from business units. As we noted above, interest payments by households and government are not included in the measurement of national income.

Corporate profits were $140.3 billion, or 9.2 percent of national income in 1977. During the 1970s it has generally been between 7.5 and 9.6 of *NI*, well below the 10.5–13.5 range in the 1960s. This is the most volatile component of national income. In 1972, for example, it was $92.1 billion, or 9.7 percent of *NI*; by 1973 it had plunged to $77.2 billion, only 7.5 percent of *NI*.

The corporate profit component of national income includes two adjustments, one to eliminate capital gains on inventories (*inventory valuation adjustment, IVA*) and the other to reflect the understatement of economic depreciation associated with the use of historic rather than replacement cost of capital goods in calculating depreciation (the *capital consumption adjustment, CCAdj*). When prices are rising, firms realize capital gains on their stocks of inventories. Profits arising from the increase in the value of inventories are viewed as capital gains rather than a reward for current productive services, and are therefore excluded from *NI*. When prices are rising, corporate profits therefore tend to overstate true, economic profit; the negative *IVA* adjustment corrects for this. The inventory valuation adjustment is also included on the product side in the computation of inventory investment. Ignoring the *IVA*, inventory investment would equal the value of end-of-period inventories minus the value of beginning-of-period inventories. But this includes capital gains along with increases in the physical volume of inventories. To calculate the inventory investment component of the *NIA*, therefore, the *IVA* is used to remove the capital gain (or capital loss) component of the change in the value of inventories over the period. If prices rose over the period, for example, the negative *IVA* is used to reduce the value of the change in inventories to obtain the inventory investment component on the product side of the *NIA* and to reduce the corporate profit entry on the income side of the *NIA*. In 1977 the *IVA* was −$14.5 billion, removing a capital gain of that amount from both profits and inventory investment. Also, during periods of rising prices, capital consumption allowances based on historic cost of capital goods understate the economically more meaningful concept of economic depreciation based on replacement cost. *CCA* is therefore understated and corporate profits are overstated. The negative *CCAdj* is used to correct corporate profits and, of course, is also used to raise the value of *CCA*, discussed below.

The *corporate profit tax liability* is based on unadjusted corporate profits (i.e., corporate profits before *IVA* and *CCAdj*). Corporate profits tax liability was 40.3 percent of unadjusted corporate profits in 1977. This proportion varies, of course, with the level and structure of corporate income taxes, as well as with tax treatment of depreciation and other tax incentives. *Dividends*, the portion of after-tax corporate profits paid to the owners of the corporations (the holders of corporate shares or equities), are relatively stable cyclically, compared to profits; the ratio of dividends to profits therefore rises during recessions and falls during expansions. In 1977 the payout ratio (dividends divided by unadjusted after-tax profits) was 40.2 percent. It generally falls in the 40–50 percent range. *Undistributed profits*, also called *retained earnings*, is the most volatile of the components of profit. It fell from $24.2 billion in 1968 to $14.1 billion in 1970 during the 1969–1970 recession, then climbed to $44.4 billion in 1974 before falling about 25 percent to $33.2 billion in 1975 during the 1974–1975 recession.

Altogether the income payments (*NI*) accounted for 80.4 percent of *GNP* in 1977. Other charges against income accounted for 9.4 percent of *GNP* and capital consumption allowances for the remaining 10.4 percent.

2. *Other Charges Against Income.* The market value of final output of goods and services (the right-hand side of the *NIA*) exceeds the value of income payments to factors (the value of national income on the left-hand side of the *NIA*). This reflects the fact that there are some cost elements which affect the price of output that do not simultaneously reflect income payments to factors. These "nonincome" charges include indirect business taxes, business transfers, (minus) government subsidies, and current surplus of government enterprises. We also include among these components statistical discrepancy to offset measurement errors which otherwise would result in the two sides of *NIA* failing to balance.

Indirect business taxes (e.g., sales taxes, excise taxes, and real property taxes paid by business) are treated as a cost of doing business by firms and are passed forward to consumers by raising the price of output. The cost of *business transfers* (e.g., corporate gifts or prizes) must also be reflected in the price of output. Again, there is no corresponding factor service. *Subsidies* by government to businesses result in a price of output less than the factor payments. The receipts to the business firm (including the subsidy) will exceed their expenditures on inputs by the amount of the subsidy. Subsidies are therefore subtracted from the income side so that the two sides balance. *Current surplus of government enterprises* refers to the excess of total revenue over factor payments for government enterprises (e.g., Post Office, TVA). The price of the product was high enough to generate this surplus, but the government is not considered to be a factor of production. Therefore, the surplus is added to the income side to make the two sides balance.

3. *Capital Consumption Allowances* (*CCA*). The value of the product (right-hand side of Table 2.1) must also cover the cost of capital goods as well as the cost of labor services (wages and salaries and proprietors' income), land (rental income), loans (interest), and the opportunity cost of owner's funds (profits). Unlike the other items, however, the price of a newly purchased capital good is not charged as a cost at the time the purchase is made. Instead, the cost is distributed over the lifetime of the piece of capital. The measure of the portion of the cost charged off in the current period is depreciation or capital consumption allowances.

When firms compute the value of their corporate profits, therefore, they deduct allowances for depreciation of the capital goods over the period, not the value of new capital goods purchased that period. For tax purposes, the depreciation or capital consumption allowances must be calculated on the basis of historic costs; i.e., if the capital good depreciated by 10 percent over the period, the firm can deduct 10 percent of the price actually paid for the capital good. The true cost to the firm of the depreciation of the machine, however, is based on its replacement costs (the price of the machine if purchased in the current period), not on what the firm happened to pay for the machine in some earlier period. Therefore, in the *NIA*, the level of the *CCA* is adjusted upward and the value of corporate profits downward from levels used for tax purposes by applying the capital consumption adjustment. Note, however, that the value of all newly produced capital goods does appear on the product side of the *NIA* and the wages and salaries and other factor income generated in the process appear on the income side. If we also include the depreciation each period, we will be double-counting the services of capital goods. To avoid double-counting, we must subtract depreciation from *GNP*; this gives us the net national product (*NNP*) figure shown in Table 2.1. As we noted above, however, *GNP* remains the more widely used measure of economic activity because of lack of confidence in our ability to accurately measure depreciation.

The ratio of *CCA* to fixed gross business investment provides a measure of the percentage of gross investment spending on plant and equipment that was used to replace existing capital stock worn out over the year. Replacement investment has ranged from 53.5 percent to 87.9 percent of gross business fixed investment in the 1970s. During expansions this ratio is generally around 55 percent; during recessions it generally rises above 60 percent. In the steepest postwar recession during 1975, it reached 87.9 percent, reflecting the unusually sharp decline in net investment during this recession.

Personal and Disposable Personal Income. In Table 2.2, we indicate the way in which two other income concepts, personal income (*PI*) and disposable personal income (*DI*), are derived from national income. *Personal income* subtracts from national income the parts of factor payments not paid directly to households and adds on receipts which do not reflect payment for current services. *Disposable personal income* is what remains of personal income after personal income taxes have been deducted.

Personal income differs from national income because part of factor payments does not go to households and because households receive transfer payments as well as factor payments. Part of corporate profits is paid to government (corporate profits tax liability in Table 2.1). The only part of corporate profits which is actually directly paid to households is dividends. Therefore, in deriving *PI*, we subtract corporate profits from *NI*, then add back dividends; alternatively, we could have subtracted corporate profit tax liability and retained earnings from *NI*. Contributions for social insurance also are subtracted from *NI*. *PI* includes all personal interest income, whereas *NI* includes only interest paid to households by business firms. Therefore, we subtract net interest (the interest component of *NI*) and add personal interest income; alternatively, we could have added the other interest components of personal interest income which were excluded from *NI* (government interest payments and interest from other persons). Finally, we include transfer payments, both government and business.

In 1977 personal income was 117.4 percent of *NI*, as the additions were larger than the subtractions. Personal tax payments were 14.8 percent of disposable income.

	National Income	1520.3
−	Corporate Profits	140.3
−	Net Interest	100.9
−	Contributions for Social Insurance	139.0
+	Government Transfer Payments	197.8
+	Personal Interest Income	147.9
+	Dividends	41.2
+	Business Transfer Payments	9.0
=	Personal Income	1536.1
−	Personal Tax Payments	227.5
=	Disposable Personal Income	1308.6

TABLE 2.2

National Income, Personal Income, and Disposable Income, 1977
(billions of dollars)

PRICE INDICES

In our discussion of national income accounting in the previous section, we used money prices as a common denominator to permit us to add the value of all goods and services produced. The change in *GNP* valued at money prices (called *nominal GNP*) over time, therefore, includes changes in both the *physical volume* of goods and services and in the *money prices* of goods and services. But nominal *GNP* itself is not a particularly interesting statistic. We want to know what happens to the physical volume of production and what happens to the overall price level. We therefore need to find a way of separating the change in nominal *GNP* into changes in output and prices.

In this section we consider the procedure for adjusting or "deflating" nominal *GNP* to get a measure of the physical volume of output, called *real GNP*. The procedure is to construct a *price index* and then use the price index to "deflate" nominal *GNP*. Thus, price indices permit us both to measure price change (or inflation) and to deflate other economic series.

Constructing a Price Index

To simplify, assume that *GNP* consists of only four different commodities: food, clothing, haircuts, and capital equipment. Table 2.3 presents data on the price and quantity produced of each item in two years—the base year and the given year.

	Base Year		Given Year	
	Price	Quantity Consumed	Price	Quantity Consumed
Food	$ 2.00	100	$ 3.25	150
Clothing	4.00	50	5.00	60
Capital Goods	10.00	50	12.00	55
Haircuts	1.00	5	3.00	5

TABLE 2.3
Hypothetical Data for Constructing a Price Index

Total output in current dollars (nominal value of output) increased from $905 in the base year to $1,462.50 in the given year. A portion of this increase is attributable to price increases. We would like to determine how much real output increased over this period. The approach we use is to first determine how much prices have risen between the two years and then to adjust the change in nominal output to remove the influence of the price change.

Unweighted (or Equally Weighted) Index. One approach is to find the average price increase of the four commodities. Divide the given-year price by the base-year price for each of the four commodities. Add the four ratios and divide by four.

$$P_u = \left(\frac{3.25}{2.00} + \frac{5.00}{4.00} + \frac{12.00}{10.00} + \frac{3.00}{1.00}\right) / 4 = 1.76$$

This indicates that, on the average, the price of a commodity was 76 percent higher in the given year than the base year.

The general formula for the unweighted index is

$$P_u = \sum_{i=1}^{n} \frac{Pg_i}{Pb_i} / n \qquad (2.2)$$

where Pg_i is the given-year price of the ith commodity and Pb_i is the base-year price of the ith commodity.

The deficiency of the unweighted index is that it gives equal weight to each commodity. Although the price of haircuts increased threefold, we can see from Table 2.3 that haircuts are a very minor component of total output. To remedy this, we construct *weighted price indices* where the weights are the quantities of the commodity purchased. However, we must decide which quantity weights to employ:

Chapter 2 • Measurement of Macroeconomic Variables

the quantities consumed in the base year (base-year weights), the quantities consumed in the current or given year (given-year weights), or those consumed in some other year (other-year weights). The use of such fixed quantity weights implies that price indices measure changes in the cost of some *fixed market basket* of goods. Because the quantities of commodities are held constant, the changes in the costs between any two years provide a measure of the overall increase in prices.

Base-Year Weights. The general formula for the price index with base-year weights is

$$P_b = \frac{\Sigma(Pg_i Qb_i)}{\Sigma(Pb_i Qb_i)} \tag{2.3}$$

where Qb_i is the quantity of the ith good produced in the base year. Using Table 2.3,

$$P_b = \frac{(3.25)(100) + (5.00)(50) + (12.00)(50) + (3.00)(5)}{(2.00)(100) + (4.00)(50) + (10.00)(50) + (1.00)(5)} \tag{2.3'}$$
$$= 1.31.$$

The base-year index has a very precise interpretation: It would have cost 31 percent more in the given year to purchase the goods that were actually purchased in the base year.

Given-Year Weights. Alternatively, we could use given-year quantities as weights.

$$Pg = \frac{\Sigma(Pg_i Qg_i)}{\Sigma(Pb_i Qg_i)} \tag{2.4}$$

From Table 2.3,

$$Pg = \frac{3.25(150) + 5.00(60) + 12.00(55) + 3.00(5)}{2.00(150) + 4.00(60) + 10.00(55) + 1.00(5)}$$
$$= 1.34.$$

The results indicate that it cost 34 percent more to purchase the quantities in the given year than it would have cost them to buy the same quantities in the base year.

Other-Year Weights. A weighted price index can also be computed using weights from a third year. Indices of this type are actually the ones most widely encountered in practice. For example, the *CPI* and *WPI* indices discussed below are of this type.

○ Particular Price Indices

There are a variety of different price indices that are useful to observe. The three most widely quoted price indices are the consumer price index (*CPI*), the wholesale price index (*WPI*), and the implicit *GNP* price deflator (*PGNP*).

The Consumer Price Index. The *consumer price index* is probably the most widely quoted measure of the rate of inflation in the economy. In addition to its use as a deflator for other series and as a measure of inflation, it is the price index employed in *escalator clauses* in labor contracts which provide for automatic increases in nominal wages in response to increases in "the price level." More than 8.5 million workers are covered by collective bargaining agreements which provide for such wage increases in response to movements in the *CPI*.

The base year for the *CPI* is 1967 and the weights are for 1972–1973. The *CPI* measures the price of goods and services bought by urban wage earners. The sample of goods and the weights are based on the *Consumer Expenditure Survey* taken in 1972–1973, and prices are collected from stores in 85 areas. The 85 areas are weighted in proportion to their working populations. In 1977 the *CPI* averaged 181.5, indicating that the cost of the market basket of goods used to form the index had increased 81.5 percent from 1967.

The Wholesale Price Index. The *WPI* measures the price of commodities at their wholesale or primary market level. The *WPI* includes 2200 commodities. The price data are collected partly from questionnaires sent to producers and partly from published price data. The weights are taken from the value of shipments. The base year is 1967 and the weights are from 1963. In 1977 the *WPI* equalled 194.2, indicating that the cost of the sample basket of commodities increased 94.2 percent from 1967 (the base year) to 1977.

The Implicit GNP Price Deflator. To compute a price index for *GNP*, *GNP* is divided into components and each component is deflated by an appropriate price index.

$$GNP\$ = \Sigma E\$_i \qquad (2.5)$$

where $GNP\$$ is nominal *GNP* and the $E\$_i$ are the various components of $GNP\$$. A price index is computed and used to deflate each component. The real value of each component (E_i) is therefore

$$E_i = \frac{E\$_i}{P_i} \qquad (2.6)$$

where P_i is the price index for the ith component. The real value of *GNP* is the sum of the real values of its components,

$$GNP = \Sigma E_i, \qquad (2.7)$$

and the implicit *GNP* price deflator is

$$PGNP = \frac{GNP\$}{GNP}. \qquad (2.8)$$

It is called an implicit index because it is not calculated directly, but rather is implicit in the values of *GNP* and $GNP\$$. This index is only available on a quarterly basis.

In 1977 the value of nominal *GNP* was $1,890.4 billion and of real *GNP*, $1,337.6 billion. The implicit *GNP* deflator was therefore $1890.4/1337.6 = 141.3$, compared to 100.0 in the base year, 1972.

Problems in the Construction of Price Indices

The major deficiencies of the price indices we have discussed are their inability to take into account changes in quality, introduction of new products, and substitution effects.

Quality Improvement. One of the most difficult problems of constructing a price index is the treatment of quality changes. Price indices attempt to measure changes in the price of a constant market basket of goods and services and this means a market basket of constant quality. Price increases that reflect changes in quality should therefore be excluded from the measurement of price indices. If quality of goods progressively improves over time, price indices which failed to remove the effect of quality improvement on the price level would tend to overstate the true rate of inflation.

Recently there have been attempts to quantify the price impact of improved quality. One procedure is to identify the relationship between the price of a good and its quantifiable characteristics. For example, quantifiable characteristics of automobiles include weight (W), length (L), and horsepower (H). An equation relating these characteristics to the price of autos (P) in an initial period can be estimated,

$$P_1 = aW_1 + bL_1 + cH_1 \tag{2.9}$$

where the subscripts refer to the initial period and the coefficients represent the amount consumers are willing to pay for the various characteristics. Assume that both the price and the characteristics of autos change in a later period. The unadjusted price change is

$$\Delta P = P_2 - P_1. \tag{2.10}$$

To adjust the price change for the influence of the quality change, an implicit or *hedonic price index* (P^*) can be computed by making use of the estimated coefficients from equation (2.9).

$$P^* = aW_2 + bL_2 + cH_2 \tag{2.11}$$

Equation (2.11) indicates how much consumers would have been willing to pay for an auto of quality of period 2 in period 1. The quality adjusted price change,

$$\Delta P^* = P_2 - P^*, \tag{2.12}$$

measures the increase in price for an auto of unchanged quality.[1]

---

[1] For a survey of approaches to purging the influence of quality change from the measurement of price changes, see Jack E. Triplett, "The Measurement of Inflation: A Survey of Research on the Accuracy of Price Indexes," in Paul H. Earl (ed.), *Analysis of Inflation* (Cambridge, Mass.: Lexington Books, 1975), pp. 19–82.

The procedure for calculating the *CPI* makes an allowance for quality change, although not via hedonic price indices. Instead, an attempt is made to assess the cost of the quality improvement and adjust the price of the product down by the cost of the quality improvement. The techniques used to correct for quality improvement may undercorrect or overcorrect so that price index changes may be biased upward or downward because of failure to adjust the data accurately for the effect of quality change. Most (but not all) studies find that inflation estimates tend to be upward biased, but it is important to recognize that it is possible for these indices to be downward biased because of overcorrection for quality change.[2]

New Products. The market basket used in price indices is generally revised only infrequently. Therefore, the price indices do not respond rapidly to reflect changes in consumer expenditure patterns. Often new products with increasing market share are not introduced quickly into the indices, while old products with declining market shares are retained too long.

Substitution Effects. Consumers can be expected to substitute in favor of goods whose prices rise less or fall more than general. Therefore, fixed-weight indices involve biases because they ignore such substitutions. An index with base-year weights will tend to overestimate the rise in the cost of living associated with price rises. An index with current-year weights will tend to underestimate the rise in the cost of living associated with price increases. Empirical evidence on the extent of this bias, however, suggests that it has been quite small.[3]

BALANCE SHEETS

In this section, we discuss the measurement and accounting procedures for assets. We begin by defining national wealth and then discuss sectoral balance sheets. Then we consider the properties of the various assets that are held in portfolios and the measurement of holding period yields and real rates of interest.

National Wealth

National wealth consists of the nation's tangible assets (land, structures, consumer durables, business equipment, and inventories) plus its net claims against the rest of the world. The balance sheets of individual units (e.g., households, businesses) and the consolidated balance sheets of the various sectors (e.g., all households, all businesses), on the other hand, include a variety of paper claims (or financial assets) in addition to the real or tangible assets that show up on the national balance sheet.

Sectoral Net Wealth

The *net wealth of a sector* is defined as the total value of its assets (gross assets or gross sectoral wealth) minus the total value of its liabilities. In this section we

---
[2] *Ibid.*, pp. 30–61.
[3] *Ibid.*, pp. 25–30.

will discuss the variety of assets that appear on sectoral balance sheets and explain why the paper claims or financial assets (with the exception of claims against the rest of the world) fail to appear in national wealth. We begin by distinguishing real and financial assets and inside and outside financial assets.

Real vs. Financial Assets. A *real asset* appears only in the balance sheet of its owner. A *financial asset,* in contrast, appears on two balance sheets: as an asset on the balance sheet of its holder and on the liability side of the balance sheet of the issuing unit. It is useful to distinguish two different types of financial assets held by a given sector: inside (financial) assets and outside (financial) assets.

Inside vs. Outside Financial Assets. An *inside asset* is an asset to some unit in the sector *and* a liability to another unit *inside* the same sector. An inside asset is not part of the net wealth of a sector; when the individual accounts of the sector are consolidated into a sectoral account, the asset to the one unit cancels against the liability to the other unit. An *outside asset* is an asset to some unit in the sector, but it is a liability to someone *outside* that sector. *Sectoral net wealth* is therefore the sum of the sector's holdings of real assets and net outside financial assets (outside financial assets minus outside financial liabilities).

○ Sectoral Balance Sheets

Table 2.4 presents the balance sheets of the household, business, and U.S. government sectors as of December 31, 1973. The data are from the flow of funds accounts,[4] and include only financial assets. Therefore, no amount is shown for the tangible assets in each sector's balance sheet.

Note that the gross assets of the household sector include a variety of paper claims against other sectors in addition to the tangible assets owned by the household sector and that households have liabilities to other sectors. The only entry in the household balance sheet which appears in national wealth is the tangible assets held by households. Among household holdings of financial assets, corporate bonds, corporate shares or equities, government securities, currency and demand deposits, and savings and time deposits are all outside assets of the household sector, but are inside assets for the economy as a whole. *Corporate bonds* are liabilities of the business sector. *Equities* are also claims against the business sector, although the conventional accounting procedure of the flow of funds accounts does not include them on the business sector balance sheet. (We will explain the treatment of equities when we turn to the balance sheet of the business sector.) *Government bonds* are a liability of the government sector, *currency* is a liability of the monetary authority (the Federal Reserve System), *demand deposits* are liabilities of the commercial banking system, and *savings and time deposits* are liabilities of the commercial banking and nonbank

---

[4] For an excellent introduction to flow of funds accounts, see *Introduction to Flow of Funds* (Washington: Board of Governors of the Federal Reserve System, February, 1975); and Lawrence S. Ritter, "The Flow of Funds Accounts: A Framework for Financial Analysis," New York University, Graduate School of Business Administration, Institute of Finance, *The Bulletin,* Vol. 52 (August, 1968), pp. 4–31.

(a) Households			
Assets		Liabilities	
Demand Deposits and Currency	170.2	Home Mortgages	379.0
Time and Savings Assets	635.6	Consumer Credit	180.5
commercial banks	287.8	Other	94.8
thrift institutions	347.8		
Life Insurance Reserves	150.3		
Pension Fund Reserves	307.8		
Corporate Shares	744.4		
U.S. Govt. Securities	105.3		
State and Local Govt. Securities	50.5		
Corporate, Foreign Bonds	56.8		
Other	81.4		
	2302.3		661.1
Tangible Assets			
consumer durables			
homes			

continued, p. 41

TABLE 2.4
Sectoral Balance Sheets, December 31, 1973
(billions of dollars)

financial institution sectors.[5] Note that households also emit liabilities (primarily mortgages and consumer credit). These liabilities primarily represent borrowing from financial intermediaries to finance households' acquisition of tangible assets (houses and consumer durables).

The dominant assets of the business sector are its holdings of tangible assets, primarily plant and equipment. However, businesses also hold some financial assets, the largest component of which is loans to other firms (an inside asset of the business

---

[5] Questions have been raised about the treatment of government bonds, currency, and demand deposits in conventional balance sheet accounting. If the private sector discounts the value of the payments required to service the outstanding debt, the present value of the tax payments should just offset the present value of the coupon payments on the government debt so that government bonds should not appear as an asset in private sector portfolios. However, the asset value of government bonds may exceed the present value of tax liabilities for a number of reasons, and the conventional practice is to include the full value of government bonds in private sector net worth. Currency is issued by the Federal Reserve System (FRS) and is generally treated as a liability of the FRS. However, the FRS promises neither interest payments nor repayment of principal; therefore, there is some question about the meaningfulness of treating currency as a liability of the FRS. Demand deposits are traditionally viewed as a liability of the commercial banking sector. This has been questioned on the grounds that commercial banks do not pay interest on such accounts and therefore, like currency, they should not be viewed as liabilities of the issuing unit. However, in this case, banks do retain the obligation to repay the principal on demand in the form of currency. Therefore, demand deposits continue to be included as a liability of the commercial banking sector.

(b) Business

Assets		Liabilities	
Demand Deposits and Currency	55.4	Corp. Bonds	207.5
Time and Savings Assets	21.5	Mortgages	223.4
Trade Credit	240.9	Bank Loans	180.5
Consumer Credit	31.9	Trade Credit	212.6
U.S. Govt., State and Local Govt. Bonds	9.4	Other	101.1
Other	168.9		
	528.0		925.1

Tangible Assets
  plant
  equipment
  inventories

(c) U.S. Government

Assets		Liabilities	
Demand Deposits and Currency	12.6	U.S. Govt. Securities	353.1
Other	90.3	Other	55.5
	102.9		408.6

TABLE 2.4
(continued)

sector). The firms finance the acquisition of capital in part by borrowing from households and financial intermediaries (by the sale of corporate bonds as well as through mortgages and bank loans). Another way in which the business sector finances the acquisition of tangible assets is by the sale of equities or corporate shares to households and financial intermediaries. However, equities, unlike bonds, mortgages, and bank loans, are generally not included on the liability side of the business sector balance sheet because they represent ownership rights in rather than debt claims against firms. Nevertheless, the holders of corporate shares do have claim on the business sectors; they have a claim to the residual income of the firm, the income remaining after all factors of production, including bondholders, have been paid. The present value of the residual income of the business sector can be viewed as the net worth of the corporate sector. But corporations are artificial entities. Their net worth belongs to their owners. Indeed, the household sector is the ultimate owner of all the wealth in the private sector so that the net wealth of the private sector must equal the net worth of the household sector. We find it preferable, therefore, to treat equities, like bonds, as claims against the business sector, so that firms have zero net worth and so that the value of equities in household portfolios can cancel against their value as claims against firms, netting out in the consolidated national balance sheet.

Varieties of Paper Claims

As we have already seen, the financial claims in sectoral portfolios vary considerably in form. In this section, we provide a more formal treatment of the nature of bonds and equities. This will provide the opportunity to introduce the concept of the present value of a stream of returns and permit us to relate changes in the prices of financial assets (capital gains) to changes in interest rates.

A Debt Claim (or Loan or Bond). A *debt claim* or a *bond* represents the transfer of a sum of money (the principal of the loan) from one unit (the creditor or the bondholder) to another unit (the debtor or issuer of the bond) in exchange for the promise to pay a stated amount of interest and to repay the principal at a specified later date. Let P_0 = money lent out in period 0, P_t = money received in period t, and r = rate of interest. We will distinguish several varieties of debt claims: a one-period loan, a multiperiod loan, and a bond.

1. A One-Period Loan. If a unit lends another unit P_0 dollars for one period at the interest rate r, the lending unit will receive

$$P_1 = P_0(1 + r) \qquad (2.13)$$

dollars at the end of the period. For example, if A lends B \$1,000 for one period at a 5 percent rate of interest, B agrees to pay A $P_1 = \$1{,}000(1 + .05) = \$1{,}050$ at the end of the period. The loan agreement stipulates that B is committed to pay A \$1,050 in period $t = 1$. How much is that commitment worth in period $t = 0$? For example, if A needs the money loaned to B immediately after the loan agreement has been made, and A wants to sell the contract committing B to pay \$1,050 in period $t = 1$ to another unit, how much should the other unit offer?

A sum to be paid in the future is not worth the same as a sum to be paid immediately. There are two explanations for this. First, it is usually assumed that people have *positive time preference*; i.e., they prefer to have command over goods and services immediately rather than later. After all, if I have the money now I can use it now or later; therefore, I gain flexibility by having the funds now rather than later. Secondly, if there are interest-earning assets, the funds received now can be invested and will be worth more in the future. Assume unit C has the opportunity to invest in an asset paying 5 percent for one period. How much would C be willing to pay A for the right to the \$1,050 due from B in period $t = 1$? C will be willing to pay \$1,000.

In general, we find the *present value* (P_0) of a sum due in one period (P_1) by the formula

$$P_0 = \frac{P_1}{1 + r}. \qquad (2.13')$$

P_1 is *discounted* to the present using the discount rate, r; r is the opportunity cost of foregoing the next best investment opportunity available to the unit.

Chapter 2 • Measurement of Macroeconomic Variables

2. A Multiperiod Loan. A *multiperiod loan* is a commitment due at a specified future date, t periods away. If A lends B P_0 dollars for t periods at the per-period rate of interest r, B will pay A

$$P_t = P_0(1+r)^t \tag{2.14}$$

dollars in period t. If the interest rate is r per period, B will owe

$$P_1 = P_0(1+r)$$

at the end of one period. This is the amount of the loan outstanding in period 1. The amount due after two periods is

$$P_2 = P_1(1+r) = P_0(1+r)^2.$$

The amount due after t periods is given by equation (2.14).

What is the present value of a sum due t periods in the future? Assuming a discount rate equal to r,

$$P_0 = \frac{P_t}{(1+r)^t}. \tag{2.14'}$$

3. A Bond. A *bond* is a debt claim or loan in which the unit issuing the bond makes a commitment to make a series of payments at specified times in the future to the unit holding the bond. There are two types of bonds: (a) a *fixed coupon-variable price bond* and (b) a *fixed price-variable coupon bond*. Let MV = price or market value of the bond, R = per-period coupon, PV = principal or par value of the bond, and r = per-period rate of interest.

a. *Fixed Coupon-Variable Price Bond.* In this case, the issuing unit promises to pay a certain constant sum, called a *coupon*, each period for a specified number of periods; the issuing unit generally also promises to repay the principal of the loan, PV, at a specified date in the future. How much will this commitment be worth? The present value of the set of commitments (the market value of the bond) is given by

$$MV = \frac{R}{1+r} + \frac{R}{(1+r)^2} + \frac{R}{(1+r)^3} + \cdots + \frac{R}{(1+r)^t} + \frac{PV}{(1+r)^t} \tag{2.15}$$

for a bond committing the issuing agent to pay the coupon R for t periods and to repay the principal in period t. When the bond is issued, it generally sells at *par*; i.e., the present value or market value is equal to the principal of the loan. Thus, the price of the bond reflects the market's judgement about the present value of the stream of returns the bondholder expects to receive.

Part I • Concepts, Measurement, and Development of the Basic Model

To develop the properties of this type of bond for the simplest case, assume that the issuing agent promises to pay a certain periodic coupon forever. This type of bond is called a *perpetuity* or *consol*. The formula for the price of a perpetuity is derived by letting $t \to \infty$ in equation (2.15) which reduces to

$$MV = \frac{R}{r}. \qquad (2.16)$$

When the bond is issued, $MV = PV$ and the interest rate at date of issue is $r = R/PV$.

The market rate r can always be computed by

$$r = \frac{R}{MV}. \qquad (2.16')$$

Since the coupon is fixed at the time the bond is issued, the only way the market interest rate can vary is for the price of the bond to change.

Assume a perpetuity is issued at $P = 1000$ and $R = 50$. The initial interest rate is 5 percent. If a perpetuity is offered in a subsequent period at $PV = 1000$ and $R = 100$ (an initial interest rate of 10 percent), holders of the first bond will prefer the second; they will attempt to sell the first bond to buy the second bond. As they attempt to sell the first bond, the price of that bond will fall until it pays the same market interest rate as the second bond; the price of the first bond will fall to 500 so that $r_1 = 50/500 = 10\%$. This example illustrates the *inverse relationship between the price and market interest rate for a fixed coupon-variable price bond*. This relationship holds for the general case as well as for the perpetuity.

The holder of a fixed coupon-variable price bond is not interested exclusively in the prevailing market interest rate. Rather, the holder wants to know the percentage gain in wealth that can be expected from holding this asset over some relevant horizon (the holding period); i.e., the holder wants to know the expected *holding period yield*, not the market interest rate. Assume the bond is bought at a price MV_0 and held for one period; at the end of the period its market value is MV_1. The holding period yield, y, is

$$y = \frac{R}{MV_0} + \frac{MV_1 - MV_0}{MV_0}. \qquad (2.17)$$

The first term is the percentage return on the bond on account of the coupon payment. The second term is the capital gain (if positive) or capital loss (if negative) due to the change in the price of the bond over the holding period. For example, if the bond is purchased at $MV_0 = 1000$ and pays a coupon $R = 50$ and appreciates to $MV_1 = 1050$ in the next period, the holding period yield is 10 percent.

$$y = \frac{50}{1000} + \frac{1050 - 1000}{1000} = \frac{100}{1000} = .10$$

b. *Fixed Price-Variable Coupon Bond.* In this case, the coupon promised by the issuing unit varies but the principal of the loan remains unchanged. An example is a savings account. A depositor places a certain sum in an account. The bank promises to pay a periodic interest rate on the deposit, subject to change by the bank. Assume a depositor places $1,000 in an account when the interest rate posted by the bank is 5 percent. If the bank immediately alters its interest rate to 6 percent, the depositor can still withdraw the full amount of the deposit. However, if the deposit is kept in the bank, it will yield $60 at the end of the year rather than $50. Thus, the market value of the deposit does not vary with the interest rate.

Equity (Common Stock). When someone purchases a unit of equity rather than a bond from a business firm, that person is purchasing ownership rights rather than lending to the business. The market value of a unit of equity represents the present value of the firm's residual income (profits). *Profits* (Π) equal revenue (R) minus costs (C),

$$\Pi = R - C. \tag{2.18}$$

For the purpose of illustrating the present value calculation implicit in the valuation of equities, we treat capital as a perpetuity, paying an uncertain profit, Π, each period. The expected profit level may depend on the current level of economic activity, X.

$$\dot{\Pi} = \Pi(X) \tag{2.19}$$

where $\dot{\Pi}(X) > 0$. The market value of equity (MVE) is derived by finding the present value of the stream of profits; i.e.,

$$MVE = \frac{\Pi(X)}{r}. \tag{2.20}$$

An increase in expected profit income increases the market value of equity; an increase in the interest rate reduces it.

○ Real vs. Nominal Rates of Return

We assume that lenders and borrowers make decisions on the basis of (expected) real rates of return; i.e., the lender is concerned with the percentage increase in purchasing power of the sum loaned, not with the percentage increase in the number of dollars received upon repayment of the loan. For example, assume the one-year market interest rate is 10 percent. A sum of $100 loaned for one year will yield $110 at the end of the year; i.e., $100 \cdot (1 + .10) = \$110$. But the increase in purchasing power did not increase by 10 percent if the price level of goods increased also. If prices increased by 5 percent over the year, for example, the real value of the $100 principal repaid at the end of the year can be found by deflating the principal by the price index which gives the relation between the price level of goods at the beginning and end of the year. If prices increased by 5 percent and the first year is the base year, the price index at the end of the year will be 1.05 and the real or deflated value of the principal will be $100/1.05 = 95.2$. The interest payment also must be deflated. The $10 received at the end of the year is only worth $10/1.05 in real terms (i.e., in terms of base-year prices). Therefore, the real rate of return, the increase in purchasing power over the year, is

$$\left[\frac{(100+10)}{1.05} - 100\right]/100 = 4.76.$$

In general, to find the real rate of interest, we must deflate the value of the principal and accumulated nominal interest income at the end of the period $(1 + r)$ by an appropriate price index $1 + \dot{P}/P$;

$$1 + i = \frac{1+r}{1+\dot{P}/P} \tag{2.21}$$

where $\dot{P}/P$ is the rate of inflation over the period used to define the per-period nominal rate of interest (r). Thus, $1 + i$ is the purchasing power in terms of real goods of the nominal sum, $1 + r$, available at the end of the period. Equation (2.21) can also be rewritten as

$$1 + r = (1 + i)(1 + \dot{P}/P) \tag{2.21'}$$

by multiplying the real sum available at the end of the period by the price index to obtain the nominal sum available at the end of the period.

Equation (2.21') can be rewritten, in turn, as

$$r = i + i(\dot{P}/P) + \dot{P}/P. \tag{2.21''}$$

To maintain an unchanged real rate, i, the nominal rate r would have to rise in response to inflation by an amount to compensate both for the decline in the real value of the interest payment and for the decline in the real value of the principal. The $i(\dot{P}/P)$ term captures the increase in the nominal rate to compensate for the decline in the real value of the nominal interest payment. The $\dot{P}/P$ term captures the increase in r required to compensate for the decline in the real value of the principal. Note that the real interest rate i is also the nominal rate in the absence of inflation. The $i(\dot{P}/P)$ term will generally be quite small and is usually ignored, leaving

$$r = i + \dot{P}/P. \tag{2.22}$$

The nominal rate, r, is the sum of the real rate, i, and the inflation rate, $\dot{P}/P$. Alternatively, the real rate is

$$i = r - \dot{P}/P, \tag{2.22'}$$

the nominal rate minus the inflation rate. However, if either i or $\dot{P}/P$ is larger than .03, the complete formula should be employed in the calculation.

Note that equation (2.21″) is an identity. [Equation (2.22) is only an approximation to the identity.] We cannot use it to determine the impact on nominal rates of an increase in the expected rate of inflation, unless we already know the impact of this change on the real rate. We will discuss the effect of changes in the expected inflation rate on nominal and real rates of interest in Chapter 9.

● REVIEW QUESTIONS

1. How do we avoid double-counting in the computation of *GNP*?

2. If *GNP* is the value of final output, why do we include inventory investment and fixed business investment?

3. Why are government transfer payments excluded from *GNP*?

4. In light of your answer to question 3, why are business transfer payments included?

5. Why are capital consumption allowances included as a component of *GNP* on the income side of the national income accounts?

6. What are the uses of price indices?

7. Why are unweighted price indices unsatisfactory?

8. What is the distinction between real and financial assets and between inside and outside assets?

9. What is the distinction between bonds and equities?

10. What is the difference between the market interest rate and the holding period yield?

11. Define the real interest rate.

● PROBLEMS

1. Use the following data to compute national income, net national product, gross national product (using both income and product sides of *NIA*), personal income, and disposable personal income.

Wages, Salaries, and Supplements	1000
Proprietors' Income	100
Net Interest Paid by Business Sector	75
Rental Income	20
Corporate Profits Tax	65
Dividends	30
Undistributed Corporate Profits	30

Interest Payments on Government Debt	75
Government Transfer Payments	200
Personal Tax Payments	200
Consumption	1050
Investment	300
Government Spending on Goods and Services	300
Capital Consumption Allowances	175
Business Transfer Payments	5
Indirect Business Taxes	150

2. (a) Given the following information on nominal and real *GNP*,

	GNP $	Real GNP
1974	1306.6	1214.0
1975	1413.2	1191.7

compute the implicit *GNP* deflator and the rate of inflation from 1974 to 1975.

(b) The economy consists of two goods—consumptions goods (*C*) and investment goods (*I*). Prices and quantities produced in two years are presented below:

	P_1	Q_1	P_2	Q_2
C	25	1000	30	1200
I	75	200	85	300

Find nominal income in years 1 and 2 and the rate of increase between years 1 and 2.

Compute a base-year price index.

Find real incomes in years 1 and 2 and the percentage change between years 1 and 2.

Find the rate of inflation between years 1 and 2.

3. The following items are sufficient to complete balance sheets for the household and business sectors, for the consolidated private sector, and for the entire economy.

Capital held by businesses (K^b) = 200
Consumer durables held by households (K^h) = 50
Housing stock (K_H) = 75
Household holdings of government securities (B_g^h) = 50
Household holdings of business bonds (B_p^h) = 100
Household holdings of money (M^h) = 100
Household holdings of equities (E^h) = 100
Money issued by the government (M) = 100

(a) Complete the balance sheets of the household and business sectors, of the consolidated private sector, and of the entire economy.

(b) What is the relationship between household net worth and net private wealth? Why?

(c) Households do not hold any of the business capital stock (K^b), yet they are the ultimate owners of the businesses. How does the value of K^b show up in household net worth?

(d) What financial assets are inside and outside for (a) the household sector and (b) the consolidated private sector?

4. (a) A perpetuity that promises to pay $50 per year sells at $1,000. What is the market rate of interest?

(b) If the market interest rate increases to 8 percent, what happens to the price of the bond?

(c) Assume that the rate is expected to fall from 5 percent to 4 percent over the next year. What is the expected holding period yield?

(d) Use the price index computed above in problem 2(b) to find the real holding period yield.

● EXERCISES

1. Using the most recent issue of the *Economic Report of the President, Survey of Current Business*, or other source, update the *NIA* table for the latest year available. Calculate the ratios of consumption, investment, and government expenditures to *GNP* and compare with figures presented in this chapter.

2. Using the same statistical source as above, find the value of the *CPI, WPI*, and implicit price deflator for *GNP* for the latest year available and compute inflation rates for the three price indices from the previous year to the latest available year.

Chapter 3

Potential Output and the Cyclical and Secular Performance of the U.S. Economy

In this chapter we introduce the concept of potential output and use the potential output series to separate movements in output into a long-term or secular trend component and a short-run or cyclical component. We begin by discussing the measurement of employment and unemployment, the sources of unemployment, and the meaning of full employment. The unemployment rate is a measure of the degree of utilization of the economy's labor resources. Potential output, introduced in the second section, is the amount of output that could be produced if the economy's resources were "fully" utilized and full utilization of resources is generally defined in relation to the unemployment rate. After defining potential output, we discuss the sources of growth in potential output, the cyclical experience of actual relative to potential output, and Okun's Law which relates cyclical movements in output and unemployment.

The comparison of actual and potential series provides a picture of the economy's cyclical experience. In the third section we discuss the nature of business cycles, the meaning of a recession, and the duration and amplitude of postwar cycles. In the final section we consider the relation between inflation and the cyclical pattern of the economy.

○ THE MEASUREMENT OF EMPLOYMENT AND UNEMPLOYMENT

In this section we will discuss the way in which employment and unemployment are defined and measured, provide a brief sketch of the sources of unemployment, and discuss the meaning of "full employment."

○ Defining Employment and Unemployment

The Bureau of the Census takes a monthly sample survey of the labor force (16 years of age or older) for one week of each month. The monthly estimate of employment is then computed by "blowing up" the sample findings. A person is considered *employed* if at any time during the survey week he or she (1) was at work for a private or government employer; (2) was self-employed; (3) was an unpaid family worker for 15 hours or more; or (4) had a job but was not at work because of vacation, illness, labor dispute, or bad weather. A person is considered *unemployed* if she or he was 16 years of age or older and did not work at all during the survey week but was available for work and (1) was engaged in some specific job-seeking activity (e.g., visited an employment service, made application for a job) during the past four weeks, (2) was waiting to be recalled to a job from which he or she had been laid off, (3) was waiting to report to a new job within 30 days, or (4) would have been looking for a job but was temporarily ill.[1]

The *civilian labor force* (LF) is the sum of employed and unemployed persons (E and U, respectively).

$$LF = E + U \tag{3.1}$$

The *unemployment rate* is the percentage of unemployed in the total labor force

$$u = \frac{U}{LF} 100. \tag{3.2}$$

○ Types of Unemployment

There are three major classifications of unemployment: frictional, structural, and demand deficiency.

Frictional Unemployment. Frictional unemployment is unemployment attributed to "frictions" (or immobilities) in the labor market which prevent or impede instantaneous adjustment of labor supply to changes in the location of the demand for labor and prevent many voluntary movements from one job to another from being accomplished without any intervening periods of unemployment. Some amount of frictional unemployment is inevitable in a dynamic economy with a growing labor force and constant changes in the composition of demand, the technology for producing output, and the life cycle status and aspirations of workers. Frictional unemployment is of short duration, no longer than from one to four months. Sometimes the concept is limited to unemployment which does not exceed unfilled vacancies; i.e., the problem is not lack of jobs but matching the job with the appropriate worker. Therefore, no change in aggregate economic activity is required to permit reemployment; all that is required is time for workers to search and match up with the available job opening. The magnitude of frictional unemployment is the subject of considerable uncertainty though it is often estimated at about 2 percent of the labor force.

Structural Unemployment. Structural unemployment is a long-run or chronic version of frictional unemployment. Again, it arises because of the inability of labor supply

---

[1] For a more detailed discussion of the measurement of unemployment, see U.S. Department of Labor, Bureau of Labor Statistics, *How the Government Measures Unemployment* (Washington: U.S. Government Printing Office, 1977).

Part I • Concepts, Measurement, and Development of the Basic Model

to adjust to shifts in the occupational or geographic pattern of demand. The major difference between frictional and structural unemployment is the ease with which matching up between jobs and persons can be expected to occur. In the case of structural unemployment, the vacant job is likely to demand different skills than the unemployed person possesses or plans to acquire or the vacant job is likely to be far removed geographically from the unemployed person. It would generally be considered unreasonable or impossible to expect a matching up to occur without government assistance. Retraining and/or relocation are necessary to effect the matching up. These may require a considerable sum of money, a sum beyond the means of the individuals concerned. In addition, there may be great uncertainty about the success of any individually initiated retraining or relocation, and it is quite unlikely that individuals who require it could borrow funds in the private market to finance the retraining and/or relocation. Structural unemployment has generally been estimated to be less than 1 percent of the labor force, with many estimates placing it below 0.5 percent of the labor force.

Demand Deficiency Unemployment. The cure for frictional unemployment is time and search. The cure for structural unemployment is retraining and/or relocation. In each case there are jobs available for the unemployed, but they are in different firms, occupations, geographic areas, or skill categories. *Demand deficiency unemployment* arises because there is an insufficient number of jobs; total aggregate demand is insufficient to generate jobs for all those who want to work at prevailing wage rates. Thus, demand deficiency unemployment exists when there is disequilibrium in the labor market; i.e., when supply exceeds demand. To persist, the labor market must remain in disequilibrium. Therefore, demand deficiency unemployment is typically associated with the failure of wages and prices to move rapidly enough to maintain labor market equilibrium. However, the ultimate source of demand-deficient unemployment is the deficiency of demand for output. Consequently, adaptive behavior by the unemployed alone will not be sufficient to eliminate such unemployment. Only in so far as the adaptive behavior of the unemployed results in an increase in the demand for output will it be successful in eliminating such unemployment. The concept of demand deficiency unemployment will be considered further in Chapter 17.

THE MEANING OF FULL EMPLOYMENT

One of the key concepts we use throughout the text is "full employment." We noted in Chapter 1 that the maintenance of full employment is one of the most important objectives of macroeconomic policy. Yet defining full employment is one of the more difficult tasks in macroeconomic analysis. We will discuss the alternative approaches to the definition of full employment in Chapter 16. For now, we want to clarify what full employment is not and introduce a simple definition that we will be able to use until we refine the analysis of the labor market in Part IV.

Full employment is *not* zero unemployment. We noted above that there are always workers moving between jobs or entering the labor force. Often some period of unemployment occurs in such cases. In addition, there are always some unfilled jobs or vacancies. The existence of unemployment and vacancies is not incompatible with full employment. We will view *full employment* as a situation of *equilibrium* in the labor market in which demand and supply of labor are equal and there is no demand deficiency unemployment. Unemployment and vacancies exist, but because of the balance between unemployment and vacancies, the unemployment at full employment is viewed as frictional, not demand deficient.

The unemployment rate in the postwar period is depicted in Figure 3.1. The unemployment rate has been as low as 2.5 percent (in 1953) and as high as 9.1 percent (in 1975) during the postwar period. The level of the unemployment rate at full employment was generally viewed as 4 percent during the 1960s. The Council of Economic Advisors in 1962 specified this rate as an appropriate measure of full employment and as the target for macroeconomic policy. Recent studies of the labor

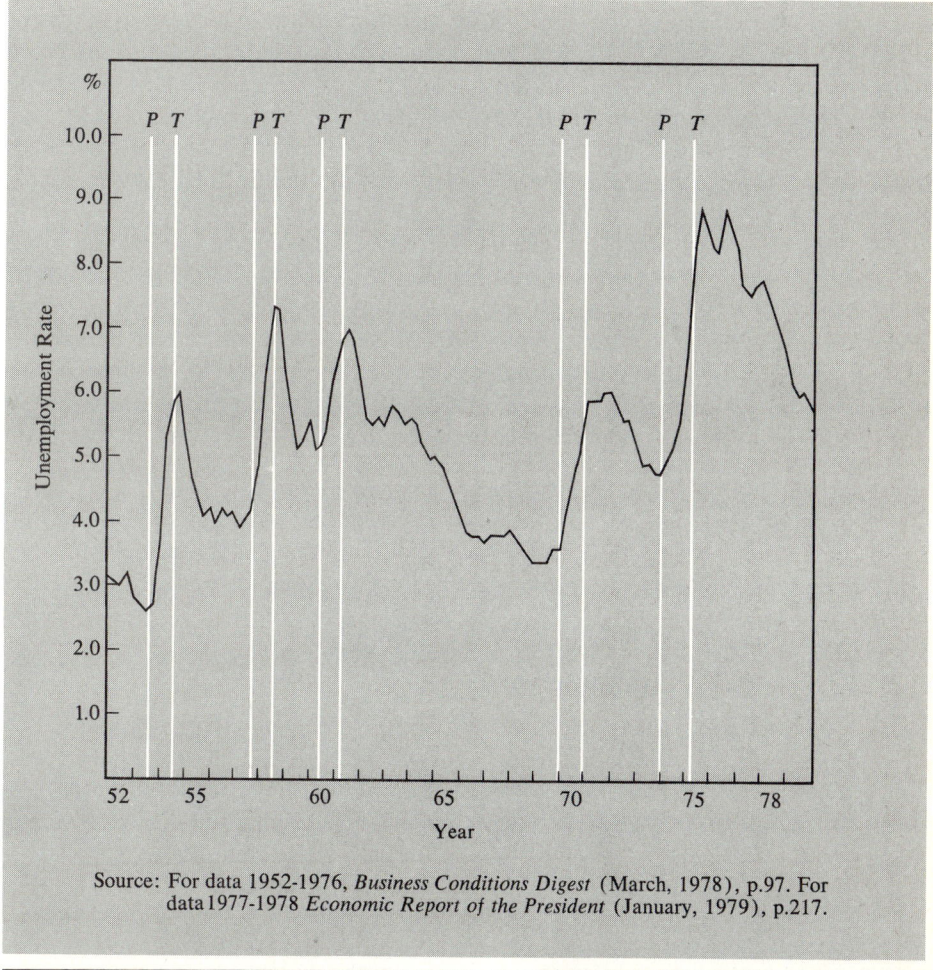

Source: For data 1952-1976, *Business Conditions Digest* (March, 1978), p.97. For data 1977-1978 *Economic Report of the President* (January, 1979), p.217.

FIGURE 3.1
Total Unemployment Rate
(percent scale)

market have suggested that the unemployment rate associated with full employment has increased over the 1970s and the Council of Economic Advisors raised the rate it associated with full employment to 4.9 percent in 1976. For now, we will view the unemployment rate at full employment as lying in the 4–5 percent range. But we will return to this problem in Part IV.

BUSINESS CYCLES

The economy is not always at full employment. Instead, output and employment are subject to cycles. *Business cycles* refer to the recurrent episodes of expansion and contraction in aggregate economic activity. The National Bureau of Economic Research (NBER) has developed a generally accepted procedure for dating the peaks and troughs of business cycles. The NBER procedure takes into account the movements of a large number of aggregate time series and identifies cyclical turning points on the basis of the amplitude, duration, and degree of diffusion of the movements in the various time series. A simple rule that generally yields similar conclusions is that a *recession* occurs if real *GNP* declines for two or more consecutive quarters. Thus, recessions or contractions are identified with declines in the absolute level of output.

Table 3.1 gives the *reference dates* (peaks and troughs) of postwar business cycles and the duration of expansions and contractions. The reference dates are those identified by the NBER. *Contractions* are measured from a trough to the previous peak. *Expansions* are measured from a trough to the subsequent peak. The *duration* of the full cycle can be measured either from a trough to the previous trough or from a peak to the previous peak. Note that the average contraction lasts almost one year while the average expansion lasts four years. A full cycle averages five years.

Business Cycle Reference Date		Contraction (T from previous P)	Expansion (T to P)	Cycle (T from previous T)	Cycle (P from previous P)
Trough (T)	Peak (P)				
Oct., 1945	Nov., 1948	—	37	—	45
Oct., 1949	July, 1953	11	45	48	56
May, 1954	Aug., 1957	10	39	55	49
Ap., 1958	Ap., 1960	8	24	47	32
Feb., 1961	Dec., 1969	10	106	34	116
Nov., 1970	Nov., 1973	11	36	117	47
Mar., 1975		16		52	
Average all cycles 6 cycles: 1945–1975		11	48	59	58

TABLE 3.1
Postwar Business Cycles

This average duration of expansion is, however, somewhat misleading. The average duration exceeds the duration of five of the six postwar expansions, reflecting the unusually long expansion from 1961–1969 (106 months). Eliminating the 1961–1969 expansion, the other five postwar expansions averaged 36 months, and full cycles (measured peak to peak) averaged 46 months.

The corresponding averages for 26 business cycles from 1854–1961 are: contractions, 19 months; expansions, 30 months; and full cycles, 49 months. Over this longer period, contractions are almost twice as long as in the postwar period and contractions are two-thirds as long as expansions. Eliminating the 1961–1969 expansion, postwar cycles have been only slightly shorter than the longer period experience but the distribution between contraction and expansion has shifted in favor of shorter contractions (11 months versus 19 months) and longer expansions (36 months versus 30 months).

There have been six recessions in the postwar period. We have already noted that the average duration of postwar recessions has been just under one year. We define the *amplitude of a recession* as the percentage decline in real *GNP* from the peak quarter to the trough quarter. We must use quarterly figures because there are no monthly *GNP* statistics. The durations and amplitudes of the six postwar recessions are given in Table 3.2. The average decline has been just over 2.5 percent.

Recession	Duration	Amplitude
Nov., 1948 to Oct., 1949	11	1.4
July, 1953 to May, 1954	10	3.3
Aug., 1957 to April, 1958	8	3.2
April, 1960 to Feb., 1961	10	1.2
Dec., 1969 to Nov., 1970	11	1.1
Nov., 1973 to March, 1975	16	5.7
Average all cycles 6 cycles: 1948–1975	11	2.7

TABLE 3.2
Amplitude of Postwar Recessions

Note that the 1974–1975 recession is the sharpest of the postwar period, four times as deep as the two previous recessions and over 70 percent deeper than the next sharpest decline. The amplitude of postwar cycles has been mild compared with the declines of the 1920s and 1930s in which output dropped by more than one-third. Although postwar recessions are both shorter and milder than prewar contractions, the business cycle is by no means obsolete. The distinctive feature of the postwar cyclical experience is the absence of any serious depression such as occurred in the 1870s, the 1890s, and the 1930s. The postwar recessions, on the other hand, resemble the minor cycles of prewar experience.

The milder pattern of cyclical experience, particularly through the mid-1960s, led to increased optimism about our ability to control or at least moderate the business cycle. Credit was jointly given to the increased importance of built-in stabilizers, banking and financial reforms, the acceptance of full employment as a goal for macroeconomic policy, and the willingness to use discretionary monetary and fiscal policies to achieve and maintain full employment.

In the decade following the mid-1960s, however, this confidence in our ability to moderate the course of the business cycle has been eroded by a series of sharp financial disturbances, increased instability in both prices and output, and the sharpest recession in the postwar period. The instability in prices and output in the last decade seemed to be closely related in that the recessions and financial disturbances appeared to be initiated or at least aggravated by the attempt of policymakers to bring inflation under control.

POTENTIAL OUTPUT: GROWTH AND CYCLES

The path of output over time can be decomposed into a trend rate of growth and a cyclical pattern of actual output relative to the trend. The *trend rate of growth* reflects growth in the quantities of productive inputs (labor and capital) as well as improvements in knowledge and skill that permit larger output from a given set of resources. The latter source of output growth is generally referred to as *technological change*. The cyclical pattern of actual output relative to the trend reflects changes in the degree to which existing resources are utilized.

The concept of potential output introduced in Chapter 1 is a measure of the level of output associated with a constant, high degree of labor force utilization, the utilization rate at "full employment." The rate of growth of potential output measures the economy's rate of trend growth. The deviation of actual from potential reflects cyclical experience.

Defining Potential Output

We can clarify the meaning of potential output by considering the economy's aggregate production function:

$$X = F(N, K). \tag{3.3}$$

According to equation (3.3), the rate of production (X) is related to the size of the capital stock (K) and the input of labor services (N). Over time the available supply of labor services grows, primarily due to increases in population, and the capital stock grows due to net investment. To simplify, we ignore the existence of technological change. Over any period, on the other hand, the economy may fail to utilize all the available inputs. Machines may be idle and people who would like to work may be unemployed. To simplify, we will view the capital stock as always being "employed" and relate cyclical movements in output to changes in the degree to which available labor is utilized. *Potential output* can then be defined as the level of output associated with the fixed capital stock ($\bar{K}$) and a full employment level of labor input (N_f).

$$X_p = F(N_f, \bar{K}) \tag{3.3'}$$

The *GNP* Gap and Okun's Law

The *GNP gap* is the difference between potential output and the prevailing level of output. Actual output varies relative to full employment as employment varies relative to its full employment level and, therefore, as unemployment varies relative to its full employment level. The relation between movements in the *GNP* gap and unemployment has been studied by Arthur Okun.[2] He estimated that each 1.0 percentage-point reduction in the unemployment rate is associated with a 3.2 percentage-point reduction in the the *GNP* gap. This relation has become known as *Okun's Law*. It can be summarized by the following equation,

$$\frac{X_p - X}{X} = 0.032(u - u_f) \tag{3.4}$$

where u, the unemployment rate, is measured in percentage points (e.g., 4.0 is 4 percent).

There is some controversy about the rate at which potential output is growing. We will discuss the growth in potential output in more detail in an appendix to Chapter 17. For the moment, we will use 4 percent as the economy's trend rate of growth, although some estimates place the growth in potential output at or below 3.5 percent per year. From equation (3.4) we can see that a 4 percent rate of growth in potential output means that actual output must grow at about 4 percent per year just to maintain the unemployment rate constant. In order to reduce the unemployment rate by 1.0 percentage point over a year, therefore, output must increase by 7.2 percent: 4 percent to offset the growth in potential output and another 3.2 percent to permit a 1.0 percentage-point reduction in the unemployment rate.

Cyclical Behavior of Actual Relative to Potential Output

The cyclical behavior of the economy can be depicted by comparing the actual level of output with the level of potential output. During recessions, output declines while potential output continues to grow. This gives rise to the "*GNP* gap," the difference between potential and actual output, discussed in the previous section. The *GNP* gap is thus a measure of the output loss associated with recessions.

Figure 3.2 presents actual and potential real *GNP* since 1952. The NBER cyclical reference dates are included on the chart. The chart makes clear the decline in actual output that characterizes each recession and the tendency of output to return to its potential level during the expansions. However, some recoveries have been incomplete; i.e., output declines again before it has returned to potential output. This is particularly clear in the case of the recovery from the 1957–1958 recession which was interrupted by the 1960–1961 recession well before potential output had been achieved. On the other hand, the long expansion following the 1960–1961 recession returned output

---

[2] Arthur Okun, "Potential *GNP*: Its Measurement and Significance," *Proceedings* of the Business and Economic Statistics section of the American Statistical Association, 1962.

58 Part I • Concepts, Measurement, and Development of the Basic Model

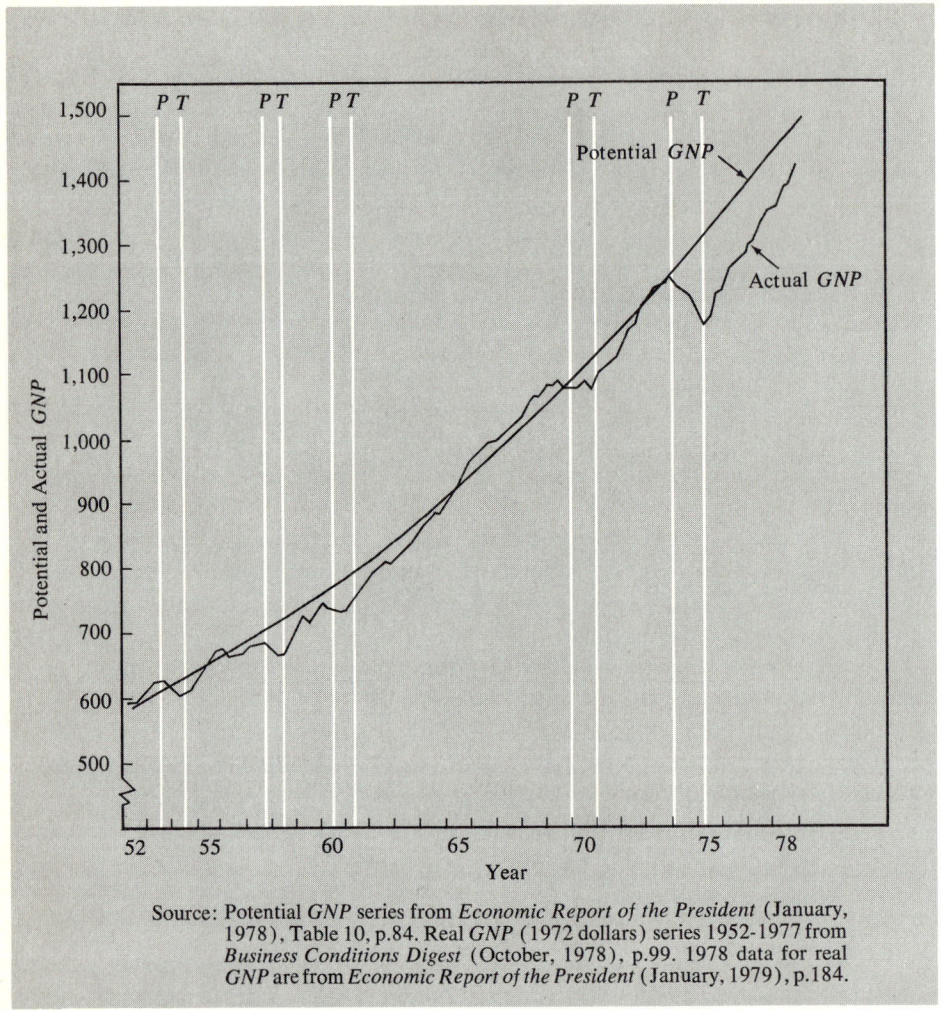

Source: Potential GNP series from *Economic Report of the President* (January, 1978), Table 10, p.84. Real GNP (1972 dollars) series 1952-1977 from *Business Conditions Digest* (October, 1978), p.99. 1978 data for real GNP are from *Economic Report of the President* (January, 1979), p.184.

FIGURE 3.2
Actual and Potential Real Gross National Product

to the potential output level by 1966, and the economy remained at full capacity until the 1969–1970 recession. In fact, Figure 3.2 indicates that actual output exceeded potential output during the 1966–1969 period. This reflects the fact that potential output is defined as the level of output associated with the target 4 percent unemployment rate, and during this period unemployment remained slightly below 4 percent.

From Okun's Law, it is evident that the *GNP* gap and the unemployment rate are intimately related. Note from Figure 3.1 that the unemployment rate rises sharply during recessions and then declines during expansions. However, the unemployment rate occasionally rises during an expansion. This reflects the fact that to keep the unemployment rate unchanged, output must rise by about 4 percent a year (the rate of growth of potential output); i.e., a 4 percent rate of growth of output is just sufficient to absorb new entrants to the labor force and offset the effects of increased productivity of the labor force. To reduce the unemployment rate, output must advance at a rate in excess of 4 percent per year. During expansions, unemployment will rise if the rate of increase in output falls below 4 percent per year. Such episodes are sometimes referred to as "growth recessions."

Rates of Expansion of Output: Long-Run Growth vs. Cyclical Experience

The long-term or secular rate of growth of the economy can be measured by the rate of growth of potential output. Over the postwar period, potential output has grown at a 3.5–4 percent rate. This secular increase in real *GNP* reflects the growth of population and hence of the labor force and the secular increase in labor productivity (output per worker-hour). The secular increase in labor productivity, in turn, reflects the effects of growth in the capital stock relative to labor, technological advance, education, and on-the-job training.

This secular growth rate in potential output sets a limit on the rate at which output can expand once full employment is achieved. During recoveries from recessions, on the other hand, the economy begins from an output level well below potential output and can therefore expand at a rate in excess of 4 percent per year until full employment is approached. For example, the rate of advance in real *GNP* during a quarter often reaches as high as 8.5 percent at an annual rate during recoveries and has reached as high as 12 percent. The highest growth rates over a full year during the postwar period were the 8.7 and 8.1 percent rates recorded in 1950 and 1951, respectively.

Real *GNP* has rarely declined in excess of a 4 percent annual rate during a quarter. However, during the most recent and sharpest of the postwar recessions, real *GNP* declined at a 7.5 percent rate in the last quarter of 1974 and at a 9.2 percent rate during the first quarter of 1975. The largest full-year decline in real *GNP* in the postwar period was the 2 percent decline in 1975.

THE PRICE LEVEL AND INFLATION

One of the important features of our economy is the failure of prices to decline during recessions. In fact, the *GNP* price deflator has declined in only three quarters during the entire period, and the last time was in 1954! During the two most recent recessions, prices continued to rise. This coexistence of inflation and recessions is a topic we will consider in great depth in Part IV. The relation between inflation and unemployment is one of the most important and least understood macroeconomic relationships. The relationship between the inflation and unemployment rates from 1954 to 1977 is depicted in Figure 3.3. During the 1950s and 1960s, there was an evident tendency for high inflation rates to be associated with low unemployment rates, and it appeared that lower inflation rates could be achieved at higher unemployment rates. However, this simple relation broke down in the 1970s. The relation between inflation and unemployment will be studied in detail in Part IV.

Part I • Concepts, Measurement, and Development of the Basic Model

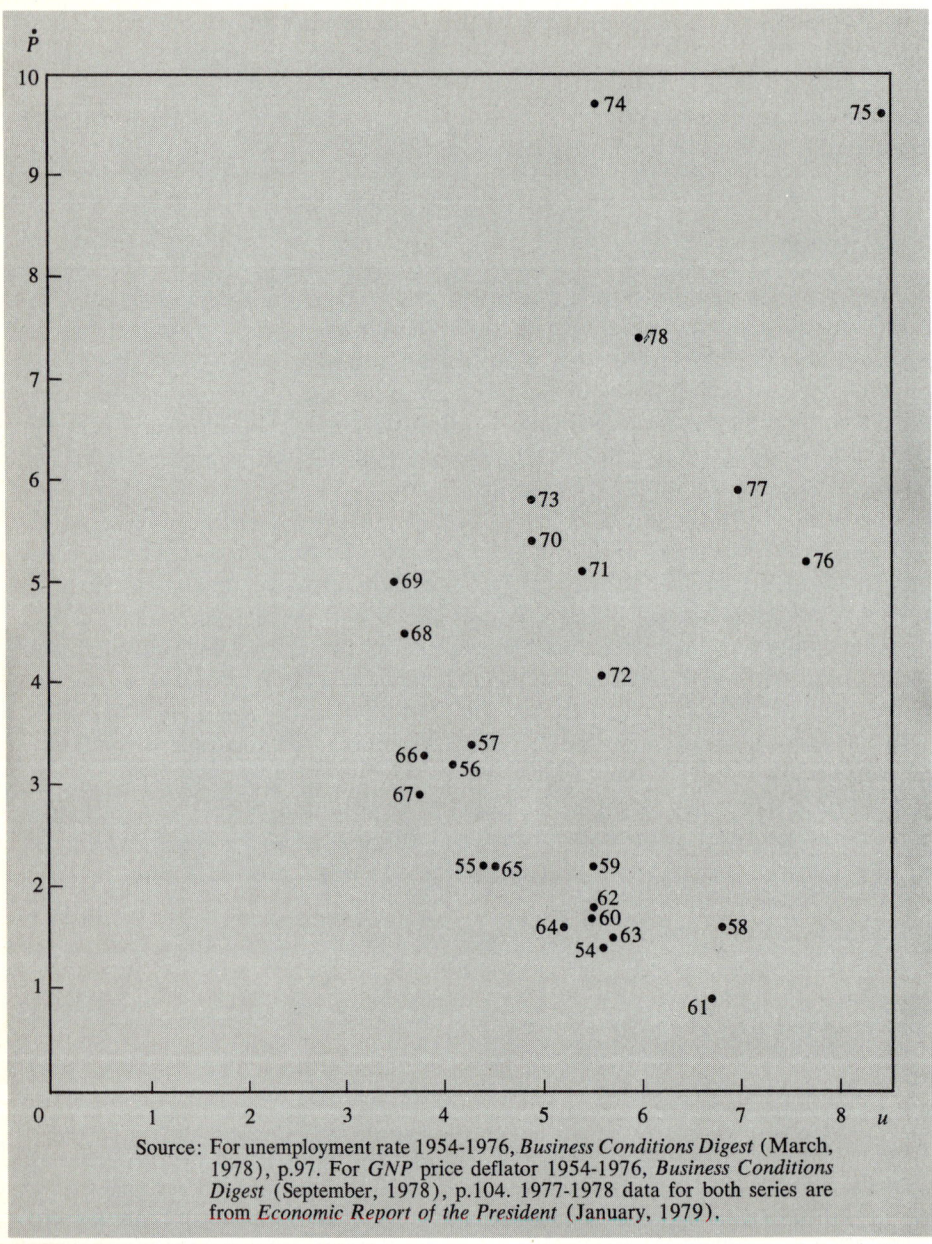

FIGURE 3.3
Inflation and Unemployment

● REVIEW QUESTIONS

1. What is the distinction between being unemployed and not being in the labor force?
2. Is a worker who has been temporarily laid off from a job but expects to be recalled to that job employed or unemployed?

Chapter 3 • Performance of the U.S. Economy

3. Distinguish between frictional and demand deficiency sources of unemployment.

4. What do we mean by full employment?

5. What is a recession?

6. Define potential output and discuss the usefulness of the potential output concept.

● PROBLEM

Assume the unemployment rate is 6.5 percent. How much would *GNP* have to increase, based on Okun's Law, to reduce the unemployment rate to 5 percent within a year?

● EXERCISES

1. Update Tables 3.1 and 3.2.

2. Calculate the level of potential output and *GNP* gaps for the most recent data using Okun's Law.

3. Find the unemployment rate for the latest year available. Did the movement in the inflation rates relative to the change in the unemployment rate conform to the simple trade-off model?

Chapter 4

The Development of the Basic Model

In this chapter we develop our basic model. No attempt is made at this point to rigorously derive the specifications of our behavioral macroeconomic relations. Rather, we will begin with simple working hypotheses about the determination of consumption, investment, labor supply and demand, and money and bond demands. This simple model will be used to develop an understanding of the determination of output, prices, and interest rates in Part II. After the basic model has been fully explained and exploited, we will take a more careful look in Parts III, IV, and V at each component of the model, deriving the behavioral macro relations from micro theory. As we do so, more sophisticated theories of consumption, investment, etc., will be introduced and we will consider how these modifications of our behavioral macro relations affect the determination of output, prices, interest rates, and other important macroeconomic variables.

In the first section, the sectors and markets are identified and the economic decisions of each sector are outlined. In the second section, we present the simplified balance sheets of the three sectors. The third section presents working hypotheses concerning each of the economic decisions. And in the final section, we combine the hypotheses about sectoral behavior to derive supply and demand equations in each of the markets.

◯ SECTORS AND MARKETS

There are three sectors in our model: household, business, and government. Thus, with the exception of our discussion of the commercial banking sector in Chapter 23, we do not explicitly include financial intermediaries; instead, we assume business and government borrow directly from households. Also, we consolidate the government sector and the monetary authority into a single policymaking authority. Our model includes four markets: goods, labor, money, and bonds. As is conventional in simple macro models, our model is a "one good" model; i.e., it does not explicitly allow for different types of output with different price levels. The price level of this single output is the economy's aggregate price level, corresponding to the implicit

GNP price deflator discussed in Chapter 2. The financial sector includes only two assets: money and a single type of bond, issued by both firms and government. Only in Chapters 20 and 22 do we allow explicitly for different types of bonds or distinguish explicitly between bonds and equities.

ECONOMIC DECISIONS OF THE THREE SECTORS

Table 4.1 summarizes the decisions made by each of the sectors and Table 4.2 summarizes the interaction of the three sectors in the four markets.

Household Sector

Households supply labor services to the business sector; N^s is the desired supply of labor and N is the actual level of employment. Consumption expenditures (C) is the household sector's demand for currently produced goods and services. Households are assumed to hold all the financial assets in the economy. Bonds issued by the government and business sectors are assumed to be perfect substitutes to households; thus, the total value of household bonds (B) is the sum of the value of bonds issued by business and government sectors (B_p and B_g, respectively).

Sector	Decisions	
	Supply	Demand
Household	Labor (N^s)	Consumption (C) Money (M^d) Bonds (B_g^d, B_p^d)
Business	Output (X) Bonds (B_p)	Labor (N^d) Investment (I)
Government	Money (M) Bonds (B_g)	Government Expenditures (G)

TABLE 4.1
Decisions of the Three Sectors

Business Sector

We assume that the business sector supplies all of the output (X) in the economy. Businesses also demand a portion of currently produced output, investment (I). We do not explicitly distinguish between the components of investment in the model. The business sector also demands labor services (N^d).[1] The business sector is assumed to finance its acquisition of capital exclusively by selling financial claims (business sector "bonds," B_p) to households. Portfolio behavior of the business sector is confined to matching liability issue (B_p) with asset acquisition (capital, K).

---

[1] We assume that the business sector alone demands labor services, although in reality, government and household sectors also demand a portion of labor services.

We treat these financial claims issued by business firms as perfect substitutes for government bonds in household portfolios to allow us to retain a simple two-asset framework in the models we will use throughout most of the text. In reality, these financial claims should differ from government bonds in at least two respects. First, if viewed as bonds, there should be some risk of default on bonds issued by the business sector; government liabilities, on the other hand, are considered free of default risk because the government can meet its interest payments out of its tax collections. The single type of financial claims issued by the business sector, on the other hand, might be viewed more appropriately as an equity rather than a bond. In this case, the instrument should have a variable coupon (depending on the size of residual income of firms) rather than a fixed coupon as in the case of a government bond. However, we ignore these differences, as we noted above, in order to retain the two-asset framework.

Markets	Participants	
	Supply	Demand
Labor	Households (N^s)	Business (N^d)
Output	Business (X)	Households (C) Business (I) Government (G)
Money	Government (M)	Households (M^d)
Bond	Government (B_g) Business (B_p)	Households (B_g^d, B_p^d)

TABLE 4.2
Interaction of the Three Sectors in the Four Markets

○ Government Sector

Government supplies money (M) and government bonds (B_g). Government demands a portion of output (G), imposes taxes (T_x), and makes transfer payments (T_r).

○ THE SIMPLIFIED BALANCE SHEETS OF THE THREE SECTORS

We have simplified the balance sheets of the three sectors relative to those which appeared in Chapter 2. The simplified balance sheets are presented in Table 4.3. In particular we have assumed that households hold all money and bonds, that businesses hold all the physical capital, that businesses issue only a single form of financial claim, and that there is no banking system or nonbank financial intermediaries (and therefore no demand deposits, savings deposits, business loans, mortgages, or installment credit). Some of these restrictions will be relaxed in subsequent chapters. Note that capital is offset on the liability side of the business sector balance sheet by "bonds"

	Household Sector	
Assets		Liabilities
Money M Bonds B_g, B_p		

	Business Sector	
Assets		Liabilities
Capital K		Bonds B_p

	Government Sector	
Assets		Liabilities
		Money M Bonds B_g

TABLE 4.3
Sectoral Balance Sheets

issued by businesses; this reflects the assumption that firms must finance the acquisition of capital by selling financial claims to households.

$$K \equiv \frac{B_p}{P} \tag{4.1}$$

The value of the capital stock shows up in the household portfolios via household holdings of private "bonds"; i.e., households, the ultimate wealth-owning units, indirectly hold the economy's capital stock via their holdings of private bonds. We can therefore write real net wealth of households as

$$a \equiv m + b_g + b_p \tag{4.2a}$$

where m is their holdings of money and b_g and b_p are the holdings of government and private bonds, respectively (all in real terms), or as

$$a \equiv m + b_g + K, \tag{4.2b}$$

given that $K \equiv b_p$.

THE BEHAVIOR OF HOUSEHOLDS, BUSINESSES, AND GOVERNMENT

In the previous section we discussed the various decisions made by our three decision-making units: households, businesses, and government. In this section we will present working hypotheses about each of these decisions.

○ Households

Households demand a portion of currently produced output (*consumption*), supply labor to businesses, and hold all the money and bonds issued by government and businesses.

The Consumption Function. Households demand current output from business firms for consumption. Our working hypothesis is that real consumption expenditures (C) are positively related to real disposable income (Y) and the real value of household net worth (a). We can write down this working hypothesis in general functional form as

$$C = C(Y, a) \tag{4.3}$$

or in linear form as

$$C = \bar{C} + C_y Y + C_a a. \tag{4.3'}$$

We assume there is some positive autonomous component of consumption ($\bar{C}$), that the marginal propensity to consume out of disposable income is between zero and one ($1 > C_y > 0$), and that the marginal propensity to consume out of net wealth is between zero and one ($1 > C_a > 0$).

The rationale for this hypothesis is that household demand for current output should be directly related to resources at the disposal of households. These resources include both disposable income and net wealth. *Disposable income* is the *flow* of spendable income over some period (e.g., over a year) and *net wealth* is the stock of resources at the beginning of the period. Thus, income and net wealth are the resources available for spending over the period. The larger the economic resources of households, the larger will be their demand for current output. Further, the propensity to spend out of a *recurring flow* (disposable income) should be larger than the propensity to spend out of an *exhaustible stock* (net wealth); therefore, $C_y > C_a$.

When we use numerical values for our parameters, we will set $C_y = .7$ and $C_a = .05$. These values reflect the evidence based on econometric studies of consumption which we will discuss further in Chapter 12. $C_y = \Delta C / \Delta Y = .7$ means that each $1 billion increase in disposable income induces a $0.7 billion increase in consumption expenditures; and $C_a = \Delta C / \Delta a = .05$ means that each $1 billion increase in wealth induces a $50 million increase in consumption. Given the values of $\bar{C}$, C_y, and C_a, we can use equation (4.3') to predict the value of consumption for any given set of income and wealth.

There are two identities that relate to household decisions in the output market.

The Definition of Disposable Income. Disposable income is defined as *GNP* (X in our notation) minus personal taxes net of transfer payments (T); all variables are in real terms.

$$Y \equiv X - T \tag{4.4}$$

A more complex definition was introduced in Chapter 2, but for the simple structure of our model here, this one suffices.

Chapter 4 • The Development of the Basic Model

The Household Budget Constraint. Households can either spend or save their disposable income. Therefore, we can relate actual values of disposable income, consumption, and saving via the following identity, called the *household budget identity:*

$$Y \equiv C + S. \tag{4.5}$$

A related identity, referred to as the *household budget constraint* (*HBC*), requires that *desired* consumption and *desired* saving sum to disposable income; i.e.,

$$Y \equiv C(\ ) + S(\ ) \tag{4.6}$$

where $C(\ )$ and $S(\ )$ are desired consumption and saving, respectively. Given that all disposable income that is not consumed must, by definition, be saved, the *HBC* requires that households must desire to save the portion of income they do not want to consume. This simply insures that household decisions involving income, consumption, and saving are internally consistent.

We now specify an explicit saving function,

$$S = S(Y, a) \tag{4.7}$$

or

$$S = \bar{S} + S_y Y + S_a a, \tag{4.7'}$$

and consider the relation among the parameters in the consumption and saving functions required by the household budget constraint. These restrictions on the parameters in the consumption and saving functions, usually referred to as *adding-up restrictions*, impose the internal consistency in household decisions involving income, consumption, and saving. To derive them, substitute the linear specifications of consumption and saving functions [equations (4.3') and (4.7'), respectively] into the *HBC* [equation (4.6)] and take first differences. First, assuming $\Delta a = 0$, we obtain

$$C_y + S_y \equiv 1. \tag{4.8a}$$

Then, assuming $\Delta Y = 0$, we get

$$C_a + S_a \equiv 0.[2] \tag{4.8b}$$

The first condition requires that the increment in desired consumption and saving induced by an increase in income must just exhaust the increase in income. This, in turn, requires that $S_y \equiv 1 - C_y$. For example, if disposable income increases by $1,000 and the household increases desired consumption by $800, desired saving

---

[2] These can be derived using the general functional forms for desired saving and consumption by simply taking partial derivatives of equation (4.6) with respect to Y and a, respectively. Note that the *wealth variable* is defined as beginning-of-period wealth so that increases in income do not affect wealth in the same period.

must increase by $200. The second condition requires that any increase in desired consumption induced by an increase in wealth be matched by an equivalent decline in desired saving. Given income, an increase in consumption can only occur with an equivalent decline in saving; therefore, $S_a \equiv -C_a$. The adding-up restrictions imply that the saving function can be written as

$$S = (1 - C_y) Y - C_a a - \bar{C}. \tag{4.7''}$$

This analysis demonstrates that it is not necessary to specify separate equations for desired consumption and saving. Once we have specified the consumption function, the specification of the saving function is also determined.

The Supply of Labor. Households supply labor to business firms. We assume that the supply of labor services (N^s) is positively related to the real wage rate (W/P); i.e., an increase in the real wage rate is required to induce an increase in the supply of labor services.

$$N^s = N^s(W/P) \tag{4.9}$$

The *real wage rate* is the opportunity cost associated with another hour of leisure. An increase in the real wage increases the cost of leisure and thereby induces substitution of work for leisure; this is the *substitution effect*. But an increase in the real wage also increases the amount of income the household can earn. The household may prefer to purchase more leisure along with more of other goods with this higher income; this is the *income effect*. If leisure is a *normal good* (one for which demand increases with income), an increase in the real wage will induce an increase in leisure via the income effect. The net effect is ambiguous. Our assumption that labor supply and the real wage rate are positively related reflects the presumption that the substitution effect dominates. This is the basis for the positively sloped labor supply curve in Figure 4.1. A more formal treatment of the labor supply decision will be presented in Chapter 16.

The Demand for Money. We assume that households hold all the financial assets in the economy (and no real assets). There are only two types of financial assets: money and bonds. Money pays no explicit rate of interest. Money is the medium of exchange, and all purchases of output and all sales of labor are transacted with money. Households therefore want to hold some part of their wealth in the form of money to facilitate transactions.

It is useful to depict the portfolio as consisting of two components: the *transactions* component and the *investment* component. At the beginning of each period, the unit receives an income payment, a portion of which will be spent over the period. The portion that the unit intends to spend is the transactions portion of its portfolio. This component is gradually exhausted over the period, then renewed again at the beginning of the next period. The investment portion of the portfolio increases with the saving out of each period's income.

First, consider the composition of the transactions portion of the portfolio. Assume the interest paid on bonds represents a certain return. Why would wealth owners hold money and forego this return? The fact that the wealth must ultimately be converted to money to make transactions is not sufficient to rule out holding all wealth in bonds and selling bonds only at the instant of a transaction. What precludes such a strategy is the existence of exchange costs for moving between money and bonds. *Exchange costs* are sometimes *implicit*—the imputed cost associated with the time required to go to the savings bank (not included in the current model) and acquire cash—and sometimes *explicit*—the brokerage fee charged to buy or sell bonds in the open market. Given exchange costs, the strategy of holding all wealth in bonds and selling bonds at the instant of each transaction becomes costly. However, if the interest rate is high enough and the period between receipt of income and expenditures is long enough, the interest gain from holding bonds for a while may more than compensate for the exchange cost of buying, then selling the bonds. The higher the interest rate, the greater the cost of holding money relative to bonds in the transactions portfolio, and the smaller the demand for money. The larger the value of total transactions, the greater the need for the medium of exchange, and the greater the demand for money.

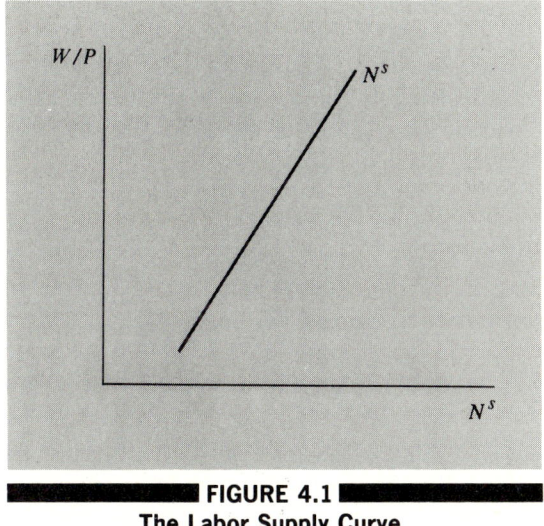

FIGURE 4.1
The Labor Supply Curve

Now consider the composition of the investment component of portfolios. Households may want to hold a portion of their investment portfolio in money; i.e., they may wish to *diversify* their portfolios rather than holding all wealth not required for transaction purposes in bonds. One explanation for such portfolio diversification is that the return on bonds may be uncertain; by increasing the proportion of money in portfolios, households can sacrifice some potential earnings for increased certainty about the value of their assets.

These assumptions can be embodied in a money demand function of the following form:

$$\frac{M^d}{P} = L(r, X, a) \tag{4.10}$$

or in its linear specification

$$\frac{M^d}{P} = \bar{L} + L_r r + L_x X + L_a a. \tag{4.10'}$$

We assume that $L_x > 0$ (reflecting the transactions motive for holding money), $L_r < 0$ (reflecting the fact that the interest rate is the opportunity cost of holding money), and $1 > L_a \geq 0$ (reflecting the portfolio diversification motive). L is the traditional symbol for the demand for money, reflecting Keynes's reference to the demand for money as liquidity preference.

$L_r = \Delta L/\Delta r$ is the change in the demand for money associated with a change in the rate of interest. If $L_r = -20$, a one percentage-point decline in the interest rate increases the demand for money by $20 billion. $L_x = \Delta L/\Delta X$ is the change in the demand for money induced by an increase in the level of real income (transactions). If $L_x = .2$, then a $1 billion increase in real income increases the demand for money by $200 million. $L_a = \Delta L/\Delta a$ is the change in the demand for money induced by an increase in wealth. If $L_a = .1$, a $1 billion increase in wealth increases the demand for money by $100 million.

The Household Demand for Bonds. Households hold bonds issued by government and by business firms. To simplify the model, we will assume that government and business bonds are perfect substitutes to households. Therefore, we need only talk about household demand for bonds (B) where

$$B = B_g + B_p. \tag{4.11}$$

Again, to simplify our model, we assume initially that both bonds are of the fixed price-variable coupon type. The demand for bonds is given by

$$\frac{B^d}{P} = B(r, X, a) \tag{4.12}$$

in its general form, and

$$\frac{B^d}{P} = \bar{B} + B_r r + B_x X + B_a a \tag{4.12'}$$

in its linear form. We postpone discussion of the signs of the parameters of the bond demand equation until we have introduced the balance sheet constraint.

The Household Balance Sheet Constraint. Household portfolios include money and bonds. The household *balance sheet identity* (*BSI*) defines net wealth of households as the sum of their holdings of money and bonds.

$$A \equiv M + B \tag{4.13}$$

where A, M, and B are nominal values of net wealth, money, and bond holdings.

Real net wealth is defined as

$$a = \frac{A}{P} \tag{4.14}$$

where P is the price level and the *BSI* in real terms is

$$a \equiv m + b \tag{4.13'}$$

where m and b are real money and bond holdings, respectively. In the *BSI*, the values of money and bonds are *actual* values. A related identity, referred to as the *balance sheet constraint* (*BSC*), relates the sum of *desired* values of money and bond holdings (the demands for money and bonds) and the value of net wealth.

$$a \equiv L(r,X,a) + B(r,X,a) \tag{4.15}$$

The *BSC* requires that desired money and bond holdings sum to total wealth.[3] Given that money and bonds are the only assets available to households, and that household wealth must therefore be held in some combination of these assets, the sum of household demands for money and bonds must just exhaust wealth. Note that asset demand equations specify how households want to hold their wealth, *not* how much wealth they want to hold; i.e., the money and bond demand equations indicate desired *portfolio composition*, not the desired size of the portfolio.[4] Thus, the money demand equation indicates how much wealth households want to hold in money; given that the only other form of holding wealth is bonds, consistency requires that the demand for bonds must be identical to wealth minus the demand for money. Thus, the bond demand equation is implicit in the money demand equation, given the *BSC*.

$$B(r,X,a) \equiv a - L(r,X,a) \tag{4.15'}$$

Using the *BSC*, we can derive *adding-up conditions*, restrictions on the parameters of the asset demand equations required for internal consistency in wealth owners' portfolio transactions. To do so we substitute linear specifications for money and bond demands, take first differences, and assume Δr and Δa are zero—then ΔX and Δa are zero, etc.; alternatively, we take partial derivatives of the *BSC* with respect to X, r, and a, respectively. This yields

$$0 \equiv L_x + B_x \tag{4.16a}$$

$$0 \equiv L_r + B_r \tag{4.16b}$$

$$1 \equiv L_a + B_a. \tag{4.16c}$$

---

[3] Note the similarity to the household budget constraint. The *HBC* enforces consistency in household *flow* decisions involving consumption, saving, and income; the *BSC* enforces consistency in household *stock* transactions.

[4] The consumption (saving) function indicates the incremental demand for wealth; i.e., it specifies the amount that units desire to add to their wealth.

A change in income or interest rates, *holding wealth constant*, induces a shift in desired portfolio *composition*: any increase in desired money balances must be matched by an equivalent decline in desired bond holdings. These restrictions are given by conditions (4.16a) and (4.16b) and imply that $B_x \equiv -L_x$ and $B_r \equiv -L_r$. According to condition (4.16c), any increase in wealth must induce increases in desired money and bond holdings which just exhaust the increase in wealth; therefore, $B_a \equiv 1 - L_a$. Thus, the signs of the parameters of the bond demand equation are $B_r > 0$ (r is the interest rate on bonds), $B_x < 0$ (reflecting transactions demand for money at the expense of bonds), and $1 \geq B_a > 0$ (implying portfolio diversification). The use and interpretation of these restrictions is sufficiently subtle so that we will refrain from making much use of them until we first discuss their derivation and interpretation in continuous and period models in Chapter 20. It is easier to understand the adding-up conditions when wealth and the demands for money and bonds are specified as beginning-of-period values. In Chapter 20 we will show that the adding-up restrictions are the same in both beginning- and end-of-period specifications.

The Perpetual Inventory Definition of Wealth. The *BSI* defines *household wealth* as the "sum of the assets" held by households.[5] This is a convenient definition in the beginning-of-period specification of our model in which the supplies of all assets (and, therefore, household wealth) are assumed to be fixed over the period. In our end-of-period specification, however, wealth is endogenous; end-of-period wealth of households (a) depends on beginning-of-period (end of the last period) wealth ($\bar{a}$) and wealth accumulation over the period. Households accumulate wealth by saving (not consuming) a portion of their income.[6] Therefore, we can define end-of-period wealth as

$$a \equiv \bar{a} + S. \tag{4.17}$$

This is generally referred to as the *perpetual inventory definition of wealth*. When we model end-of-period demands for assets, it will be planned end-of-period wealth, where S is desired saving in equation (4.17), that enters as the constraint on end-of-period household asset demands.

○ Businesses

Business firms supply all output, demand a portion of current output (investment), demand labor services, and supply bonds.

The Production Function. Firms transform inputs into output. We assume there are two homogeneous inputs: labor and capital. The aggregate *production function* indicates the maximum output that can be produced from any combination of the two inputs:

$$X = F(N, K). \tag{4.18}$$

---

[5] Note that there are no liabilities in the present model. If there were, the relevant wealth concept would be net wealth, assets minus liabilities.

[6] Wealth can also change via revaluations of the price of existing assets (capital gains and losses). We ignore capital gains and losses at this point. We discuss their role in Chapter 13.

The production function is not a behavioral relation; rather, it is a technical relation describing the nature of engineering knowledge.

In the models we employ, we generally assume that the capital stock is fixed; more precisely, we ignore the impact of any changes in the capital stock on the productive capacity of the economy. This is considered appropriate for demand-oriented, short-run models of income determination. The changes in K over the period under consideration are negligible in relation to the initial capital stock.

The relation between output (X) and labor input (N) is depicted in Figure 4.2. The shape of this curve reflects an important regularity that we will make use of at various points in the text: the *law of diminishing returns*. As labor input increases, output increases; therefore, the production function is positively sloped. But as labor input is increased, the increment in output (ΔX) associated with equal successive increments in labor input (ΔN) ultimately declines. Another way of stating this is that the *marginal physical product* of labor ($F_N = \Delta X/\Delta N$), the increment in output associated with an increment in labor input, ultimately declines. The law of diminishing returns applies over the entire range of the production function depicted in Figure 4.2. The slope of the production function, $\Delta X/\Delta N$, is the marginal product of labor; the slope is positive but declines as N increases.

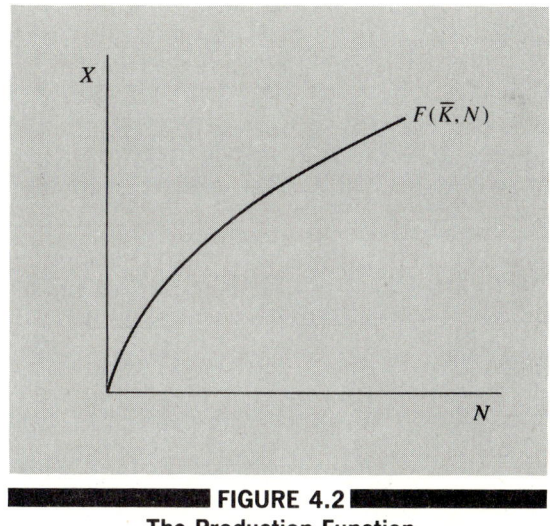

FIGURE 4.2
The Production Function

The Demand for Labor. Given that the capital stock and the state of the arts or technology are fixed, firms can vary their output only by altering their demand for labor. The profit-maximizing level of labor input occurs where the marginal revenue product of labor ($MRP_N = P \cdot F_N$) equals the wage rate (W),

$$PF_N = W, \tag{4.19a}$$

or equivalently, where the marginal physical product of labor equals the real wage,

$$F_N = \frac{W}{P}. \tag{4.19b}$$

The condition that $PF_N = W$ is simply the marginal revenue (associated with hiring another unit of input) equal to the marginal cost (associated with hiring another unit of input) condition for profit maximization. The *marginal revenue* associated with hiring another unit of labor is the product of the amount of output that the additional labor will yield (equal to $F_N = \Delta X/\Delta N$, the marginal product of labor) and the increment in revenue associated with another unit of output (marginal revenue or price, P, assuming the firm is a perfect competitor or price taker in its product market). The *marginal cost* of hiring another unit of labor is simply the wage rate (assuming the firm is a perfect competitor or price taker in the labor market). If $PF_N > W$, firms increase revenue more than cost and thereby increase profit by hiring an additional unit of labor. As the firm hires additional labor, the marginal physical product of labor (F_N) declines due to the law of diminishing returns. Therefore, as the firm hires additional labor, the equality between PF_N and W is obtained. From condition (4.19b), it is clear that the demand for labor depends on the real wage rate,

$$N^d = N^d(W/P), \tag{4.20}$$

where N^d and W/P are inversely related. The labor demand curve is depicted in Figure 4.3. At point a, N_0 is the profit-maximizing level of labor input associated with a real wage of $(W/P)_0$. An increase in P or a decline in W (in either case a decline in the real wage) results in $PF_N > W$ and an incentive to expand employment. A decline in the real wage rate to $(W/P)_1$, for example, increases the demand for labor to N_1 in Figure 4.3.

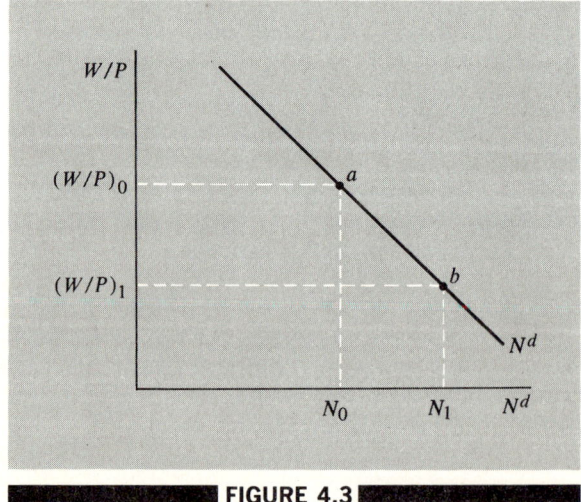

FIGURE 4.3
The Labor Demand Curve

There is an important assumption implicit in this formulation: firms are assumed to be able to sell all the output they produce at the prevailing price level for output. If, however, firms find that they cannot sell all they want to at the prevailing price, equation (4.20) no longer describes their demand for labor. Given their capital stock, their demand for labor is constrained by the demand for output. The output-constrained demand for labor can be derived directly from the production function; it is the amount of labor input required to accommodate the demand for output.

$$N^d = F^*(K, X) \qquad (4.20')$$

The notation employed for the effective demand function, F^*, is to remind us that the effective demand equation is derived by solving the production function for N in terms of K and X. Given the capital stock, the production function indicates the amount of labor services required to produce the output being demanded.

Equation (4.20) is usually referred to as the "notional" demand for labor and equation (4.20') as the "effective" demand or output-constrained demand for labor. *Notional* means "imaginary, not actual." When the effective demand curve is relevant, the notional curve describes how much labor would be demanded under the "imaginary" condition that firms could sell all the output they wished at the prevailing price level. On the other hand, there are conditions under which firms can indeed sell all they wish at the prevailing price level, and in such circumstances the notional curve gives the *actual* demand for labor!

The notional and effective demand functions for labor are depicted in Figure 4.4b. The *notional demand curve* is simply the inverse relation between the real wage and the demand for labor, depicted in Figure 4.3. The *effective demand curve*, derived from the production function in Figure 4.4a, simply indicates the labor input required to satisfy the prevailing level of demand for output. In Figure 4.4a, we assume that the notional demand curve is applicable when the demand for output is equal to X_0. At $(W/P)_0$, firms demand N_0 in labor services and can sell the resulting output at the prevailing price. If the demand for output declines to X_1, firms will cut back their demand for labor even if the real wage rate remains at $(W/P)_0$. The demand for labor when aggregate demand is X_1 is N_1, and the effective demand curve for labor is a vertical line at N_1 in Figure 4.4b. Note that the effective demand curve only applies up to point A, above which the notional demand curves become relevant again; i.e., at a high enough real wage rate, the demand for labor will contract to the point where firms are able to sell all the output they would produce by operating on their notional demand curve.

The Investment Function. The investment function is difficult to incorporate into an equilibrium framework. Net investment, after all, occurs when firms find that their capital stock is different from their optimal or profit-maximizing capital stock. Thus, *net investment* is a *disequilibrium* phenomenon. Once firms have achieved their optimal capital stock, the only investment that occurs is replacement investment.

The first step is to determine the factors affecting the profit-maximizing stock of capital. Given the level of employment, firms maximize profits by demanding capital to the point where the marginal revenue product of capital equals the price

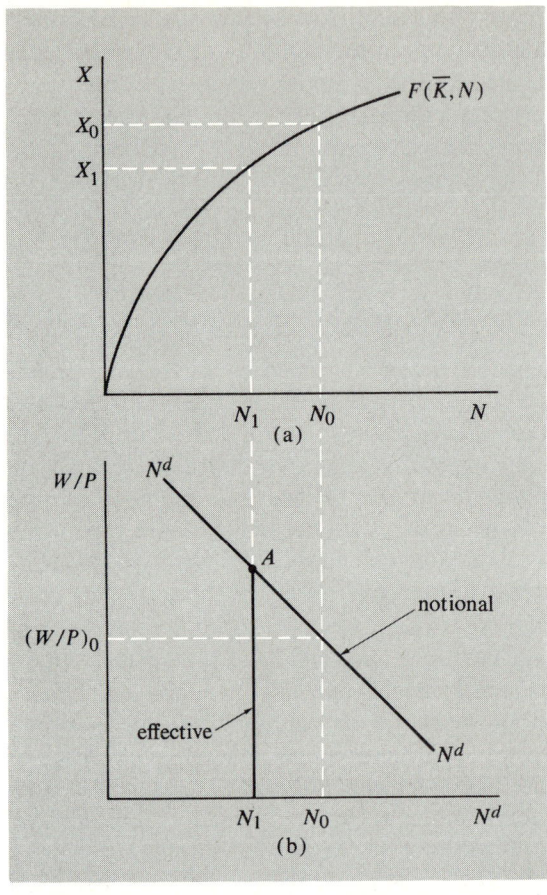

FIGURE 4.4
The Notional and Effective Demand Curves
for Labor

of capital services. The price of labor services is simply the nominal wage rate. But what is the price of capital services? When a firm buys a piece of capital, it does not charge the full price as a cost in the period in which the capital is purchased. The piece of capital will last several periods and the firm, therefore, spreads the cost of the capital good over its life; this is called *amortizing* the cost of the capital good. Assuming the capital good depreciates in value by δ each period ($1 > \delta > 0$), the firm charges itself δP each period as a cost of capital; P is the price of the capital good at the time of purchase, equal to the price level of all current output under the assumptions of our model. δ is about .10 for fixed business investment; i.e., capital goods on the average depreciate about 10 percent per year.

This, however, is only part of the cost of capital goods. There is also a cost associated with the funds tied up in the capital good. If these funds were borrowed, the additional cost is an explicit borrowing cost. If the funds are not borrowed, there is still an *opportunity cost* associated with their use: the rate the firm could have earned by using these funds in the next best use. Letting r represent the explicit borrowing or imputed opportunity cost, the full cost of capital (c) can be expressed as

$$c = (r + \delta) P. \tag{4.21}$$

The profit-maximizing condition can be expressed as

$$PF_K = (r + \delta) P \tag{4.22}$$

or

$$F_K = r + \delta \tag{4.22'}$$

where $P \cdot F_K$ is the marginal revenue product of capital (the marginal physical product of capital, F_K, times the price of output). Note that the P's cancel out in equation (4.22) because of the assumption that the price of newly produced capital goods equals the price of output in general. If $PF_K > c$, then the additional revenue (per period) the firm can obtain by adding an additional unit of capital (the price of output times the additional output associated with one more unit of capital) exceeds the cost of acquiring the capital (the per-period cost of capital services, c, not the purchase price of a unit of capital), and the firm can therefore increase profits by acquiring an additional unit of capital. As K increases, F_K declines via the law of diminishing returns and the equality $PF_K = c$ is ultimately obtained.

From the profit-maximizing condition, equation (4.22'), it is clear that the demand for capital depends on the cost of capital services, c. If $F_K = c/P$ initially, a decline in c (e.g., via a decline in the interest rate) would result in $F_K > c/P$ and an incentive to expand the capital stock. The demand for capital is therefore an inverse function of c. We treat δ as a technologically fixed rate of depreciation and therefore relate the demand for capital directly to the variable component of c, the interest rate:

$$K = K(r) \tag{4.23}$$

where $K_r < 0$.

Investment occurs to replace worn-out capital and to bring the actual capital stock into line with the desired capital stock. We can write gross investment (I) as the sum of net investment (I_N) and replacement investment ($I_R = \delta K$).

$$I \equiv I_N + \delta K \tag{4.24}$$

where replacement investment is the depreciation rate times the existing capital stock. Net investment occurs at a rate proportional to the gap between desired (K^*) and actual (K) capital stock.

$$I_N = \beta(K^* - K) \tag{4.25}$$

β is called the *speed-of-adjustment coefficient* and is expected to be between zero and one. $\beta = 1$ means that firms completely adjust their capital stocks to changes in the demand for capital within the unit period of the analysis. In this case,

$$I = K(r) - (1 - \delta)K. \tag{4.26}$$

Since we will treat both δ and K as constants, we can rewrite this equation as

$$I = I(r) \tag{4.26'}$$

or

$$I = \bar{I} + I_r r \tag{4.26''}$$

where $I_r = \Delta I/\Delta r$ is the change in the rate of investment induced by an increase in the rate of interest. If $I_r = -20$, a one percentage-point increase in the interest rate induces a $20 billion decline in investment.

The interpretation of this equation remains tricky even after all the simplifying assumptions we have made. This equation permits us to determine the level of investment expenditures over a year in response to a change in the interest rate. Once the investment has adjusted the actual capital stock to its desired level, only replacement investment occurs. But for short-run models of income determination, equation (4.26′) provides the required relationship to determine current *GNP*: the amount investment will change this year in response to a change in the interest rate.

The Supply of Bonds. The business sector raises funds to purchase capital by selling bonds to the household sector. We assume firms pay out all their income to households so that all capital must be externally financed. We can relate the supply of bonds to the value of the capital stock

$$B^S = PK. \tag{4.27}$$

This relation holds true in the long run for bonds. If prices rise, firms must eventually issue a larger nominal stock of bonds to replace worn-out capital at the new higher price. If we think of the financial claims issued by firms as equities, on the other hand, an increase in the price level, *ceteris paribus*, should be reflected immediately in a higher nominal value of capital and hence equities. For our end-of-period models, we must relate the end-of-period supply of bonds by firms to the investment decision. The change in the supply of bonds over the period of analysis must be equal to the value of net investment over the period. For our short-run model, we will assume all investment is net investment. We refer to the relationship between investment and bond supply as the *investment financing constraint.*

$$\frac{\Delta B^S}{P} \equiv I. \tag{4.28}$$

○ The Government Sector[7]

Government demands a portion of current output (government expenditures on goods and services, G), issues money (M) and bonds (B_g), taxes (T_x), and makes transfer payments to households (T_r).

Government Expenditures. There are two types of government outlays: expenditures on goods and services (G) and transfer payments (T_r). We assume that real government expenditures on goods and services are exogenous.

Tax Revenues. In our initial use of the model we will assume that real tax revenues (T_x) are exogenous. Because transfer payments and taxes enter the model symmetrically (although with opposite signs, of course), we combine the two variables into real tax revenues net of transfer payments ($T \equiv T_x - T_r$). Eventually we will endogenize tax revenues by assuming that tax rates are fixed and that tax revenues vary proportionately with income.

The Government Financing Constraint and the Supply of Government Bonds. Like the business sector, the government sector must finance its current expenditures. As we noted above, there are two types of expenditures: expenditures on goods and services (G) and transfer (T_r) payments. There are three sources of finance: current inflows in the form of tax revenue (T_x), changes in the supply of government bonds (ΔB_g), and changes in the supply of money (ΔM). The government financing constraint (*GFC*) requires that the total expenditures must be financed by some combination of the three sources of finance:

$$G + T_r \equiv T_x + \frac{\Delta B_g}{P} + \frac{\Delta M}{P}. \tag{4.29}$$

Combining the T_x and T_r variables into net tax receipts (T), we rewrite the *GFC* as

$$G \equiv T + \frac{\Delta B_g}{P} + \frac{\Delta M}{P}. \tag{4.29'}$$

Note that since G and T are both in real terms, the amount of the change in nominal money and bonds required to finance the real government deficit, $G - T$, depends on the price level.

The government financing constraint has two important implications for our model. First, it implies that the fiscal instruments are *interdependent*. Given the values of G, T, and $\Delta M/P$, there is only one possible value of $\Delta B_g/P$—the value consistent with the *GFC*. Therefore, we can only make independent decisions about three of the four government instruments; the fourth becomes an endogenous variable, determined by the other three, given the *GFC*. Which of the four instruments to select as the

---

[7] In modeling the government sector, we confine ourselves to federal government spending and taxing. An additional sector could be added for state and local government spending and taxing.

residual is a matter of convenience. Usually we will select $\Delta B_g/P$ as endogenous, the residual which takes on the value necessary to satisfy the *GFC*. Note, however, that the *GFC* only enters into our model in the end-of-period (*EOP*) specification. We use it in the *EOP* model to determine the end-of-period supply of government bonds required by the decisions about G, T, and $\Delta M/P$. Secondly, the government budget constraint also implies that, if the financing of a deficit affects the economy, the economy cannot be in full equilibrium unless the budget is balanced. If G is increased and maintained at its new level indefinitely, the resulting deficit must be financed not only in the initial period when G is increased, but in each subsequent period as well. The models we develop generally yield only short-run effects of fiscal policy; in Chapter 22, however, we discuss the long-run response to fiscal policy and trace out the full implications of deficit financing for the equilibrium response of income to changes in fiscal instruments. In addition, by using the end-of-period specification of our model in Chapter 22, even our short-run analysis of fiscal policy takes into account the effect of changes in the outstanding supply of government bonds associated with financing a deficit.

The Nominal Money Supply Is Exogenous. The government issues all the money in our model. In Chapter 23 we introduce a banking sector, permitting the private sector as well as the government to issue money. The government issues money to finance the current budget deficit or to purchase existing government debt. The latter policy is called an *open market operation*; the government purchases its own securities in the open market. Open market operations are traditionally carried out by the central bank; in the U.S. case, by the Federal Reserve System (or Fed). The Treasury makes decisions (within constraints imposed by Congress) concerning G, T, and the value of B_g outstanding, some of which is held by the private sector and the rest by the Fed. The Fed makes decisions about the size of the money supply, increasing or decreasing the money supply by buying or selling government securities. Therefore, the stock of outstanding government bonds (government bonds held outside the Fed) is jointly determined by the Treasury and the Fed while G and T are uniquely determined by the Treasury, and M is uniquely determined by the Fed. To simplify our model, we consolidate the Treasury and the Fed into a single policy bureau, subject to the *GFC*.

SUPPLY, DEMAND, AND EQUILIBRIUM IN THE FOUR MARKETS

In the previous section we presented working hypotheses about the decisions made by each of the sectors. In this section we consider how these decisions determine the supply and demand in each market and introduce the equilibrium conditions in each of the markets.

The Output Market

$$X^d = C(Y,a) + I(r) + \bar{G} \qquad (4.30)$$

$$X^s = F(\bar{K}, N^d) \qquad (4.31)$$

$$X^s = X^d \qquad (4.32a)$$

$$X = X^d \qquad (4.32b)$$

The aggregate *demand* for output (X^d), equation (4.30), is the sum of the demands of each of the three sectors: desired consumption by households [from equation (4.3) above], desired investment by business firms [from equation (4.26') above], and government expenditures on goods and services (an exogenously determined policy variable). The desired *supply* of output (X^s) is determined by the production function, the fixed capital stock, and the desired labor input [equation (4.31)]. If firms can sell all the output they would like to at the prevailing price level for output, the supply of output is determined by the notional demand for labor [equation (4.20) above] and the production function [equation (4.18) above]. However, if firms cannot sell all the output they would like to at the prevailing price level, the amount of output they will choose to produce will be limited to the amount demanded. In this case, the demand for output determines the supply of output. The equilibrium condition in the output market, equation (4.32a), requires equality between supply and demand for output. In the output-constrained case, this reduces to the equality of actual output and demand for output, as in equation (4.32b).

⃝ The Labor Market

$$N^d = N^d(W/P) \qquad (4.20)$$

$$N^d = F^*(K, X) \qquad (4.20')$$

$$N^s = N^s(W/P) \qquad (4.9)$$

$$N^s = N^d \qquad (4.33)$$

The *demand* for labor is a function of the real wage rate if firms can sell all the output they would like to at the prevailing price level [equation (4.20)]; otherwise, it is determined by the demand for output via the production function [equation (4.20')]. The *supply* of labor depends on the real wage rate [equation (4.9)]. *Equilibrium* exists when the supply and demand for labor are equal [equation (4.33)].

⃝ The Money Market

$$\frac{M^d}{P} = L(r, X, a) \qquad (4.10)$$

$$M^s = \bar{M} \tag{4.34}$$

$$M^s = M^d \tag{4.35}$$

The *demand* for real money balances is a function of income, wealth, and the interest rate [equation (4.10)]. The *supply* of nominal money balances is exogenous. Its value is determined by open market operations (monetary policy) and, in the end-of-period specification, by any money issue associated with financing a government deficit.[8] *Equilibrium* exists when the supply of and demand for money are equal.

The Bond Market

$$\frac{B^d}{P} = B(r, X, a) \tag{4.12}$$

$$\frac{B^s}{P} = \frac{\bar{B}}{P} + \left(G - T - \frac{\Delta M}{P}\right) + I(r) \tag{4.36}$$

$$B^s = B^d \tag{4.37}$$

The *demand* for bonds depends on income, wealth, and the rate of interest. The nominal supply of bonds can be altered only by open market operations in the beginning-of-period specification of the model. In the end-of-period specification, the (end-of-period) supply of bonds depends on the beginning-of-period supply of bonds ($\bar{B}$) and increases in the supply of bonds to finance both the portion of the government deficit not financed by money issue and the net investment over the period. Equilibrium exists when the supply of and demand for bonds are equal.

REVIEW QUESTIONS

1. The three behavioral hypotheses which are most important in the models in subsequent chapters are the consumption, money demand, and investment functions. Write the linear specifications of each function, rationalize the choice of independent variables, and explain the signs of the behavioral parameters.

---

[8] This sharp distinction between the implications of beginning- and end-of-period specifications of asset market equilibrium applies only to the one-period multiplier analysis we focus on initially. In longer run analysis, money and bond issues associated with financing a deficit in period t will increase money and bond supplies at the beginning of period $t + 1$ in the beginning-of-period specification.

2. Explain the household budget and balance sheet constraints. Why are these relations necessary to insure consistency in sectoral decisions involving flows and stocks, respectively?

3. Explain the role of business and government sector financing constraints in specifying the determinants of the supply of bonds.

4. Why is the investment function inherently more difficult to integrate into our comparative static analysis than consumption and money demand functions?

5. What relation do you expect between (a) C_y and C_a, (b) C_y and S_y, and (c) L_r and B_r? Explain each relation.

6. What is the distinction between the notional and effective demand curves for labor?

7. Explain why the demand for labor is inversely related to the real wage rate in the notional labor demand function.

● PROBLEMS

1. "It is obvious that the interest rate would affect the demand for bonds. It is not so obvious that the interest rate should affect the demand for money." Comment.

2. "There is no long-run relation between net investment and the rate of interest." Comment.

3. "A *once-and-for-all* increase in government expenditures requires *continuing* increases in the supply of money or bonds." Comment.

Chapter 5

Classical and Keynesian Versions of the Basic Model

The model developed in Chapter 4 consists of supply, demand, and equilibrium conditions in the four markets. In this chapter we will reduce the model to two alternative versions, each of which consists of two unknowns and equilibrium conditions in two markets. First, we discuss how assumptions about price-wage flexibility permit us to drop the labor market from explicit analysis and allow us to work with two simple versions of our basic model: a fixed output-variable price level version which we refer to as the *classical version* and a fixed price level-variable output version which we refer to as the *Keynesian version*. These two versions are not viewed as competing models of the economy but as complementary models, each of which has relevance to a particular set of circumstances.

In the second section we discuss an important aspect of model building: under what conditions will the model yield a unique solution for the values of the unknowns. The models that we are working with as we begin this section involve three equations (equilibrium conditions in the commodity, money, and bond markets) but only two unknowns (interest rate and price level in the classical case and interest rate and output in the Keynesian version). On the other hand, we find that we need an equal number of independent equations and unknowns to have a unique solution to a model. The task therefore is to demonstrate that only two of the equations are independent. We demonstrate this in the final section of the chapter.

CLASSICAL AND KEYNESIAN ASSUMPTIONS AND THE TREATMENT OF THE LABOR MARKET

Assumptions about price and wage flexibility permit us to drop the labor market from an explicit role in the use of our models in the next several chapters. If prices and wages are flexible, there is a unique equilibrium in the labor market and therefore a unique equilibrium level of employment. The only role of the labor market is to identify the benchmark of full employment to which the rest of the model must adjust. An alternative assumption, that wages and prices are fixed, results in a completely different role for the labor market. Employment now passively adjusts to the demand for output determined in the other three markets. There is no feedback from the labor market to the rest of the model. Therefore, the labor market can be dropped from our analysis of the determination of output and the interest rate. The dropping of the labor market from explicit treatment is solely for the purpose of initially simplifying the analysis. It permits us to develop some essential properties of our macro model which carry over into more sophisticated specifications in subsequent chapters. In particular, the labor market is reintroduced in a limited way in Chapter 11 and in more detail in Part IV where we refine our analysis of employment and inflation theory. We will find there that the analysis of the labor market has a most important place in modern macroeconomic analysis. While we work with the two simple versions, it should be understood that they are complements, not substitutes; i.e., they are not two alternative models of the way the economy works, but rather two parts of an overall explanation of aggregate behavior. The relevance of each version will be shown to depend on both the nature of the *initial conditions* (proximity to full employment) and the *time horizon* over which we view the response to some disturbance.

○ The Classical Assumptions: Price and Wage Flexibility

The approach we employ to investigate the properties of our models relies on a comparison of alternative equilibrium positions (i.e., comparing equilibrium values of our unknowns before and after some disturbance). This method is called *comparative statics*. If prices and wages are perfectly flexible, there will be a unique equilibrium level of employment; i.e., the equilibrium value of employment will always be the same, whatever the level of government expenditures, taxes, money supply, etc., and we can therefore treat employment as predetermined at this unique equilibrium value,

$$N = \bar{N}_f, \tag{5.1}$$

and drop the labor market from further consideration. From the production function, if $N = N_f$, X must be $X_f = F(\bar{K}, N_f)$ so that the equilibrium level of output is also invariant with respect to disturbances and policy changes and output can also be treated as a predetermined variable in the rest of the model.

$$X = \bar{X}_f \tag{5.2}$$

The determination of employment and the associated level of output is depicted in Figure 5.1. In Figure 5.1a we illustrate how this full employment level of employment determines the unique full employment level of output via the production function. In Figure 5.1b we depict the unique equilibrium level of employment determined by the supply and demand for labor.

The classical version of our model is therefore a supply-oriented full employment model. Although this model differs in many ways from the models that are generally associated with classical economists,[1] it does capture, in our view, the essential properties of these models: a long-run equilibrium perspective and confidence in the efficacy of price-wage adjustments in moving the economy back to full employment after being displaced by exogenous shocks. This version of our model is useful for analyzing the response of interest rates and prices to disturbances that are maintained over long periods. For example, in Chapter 9 we will use this version to investigate the response of inflation to a continuing monetary expansion and the response of real and nominal interest rates to a sustained inflation.

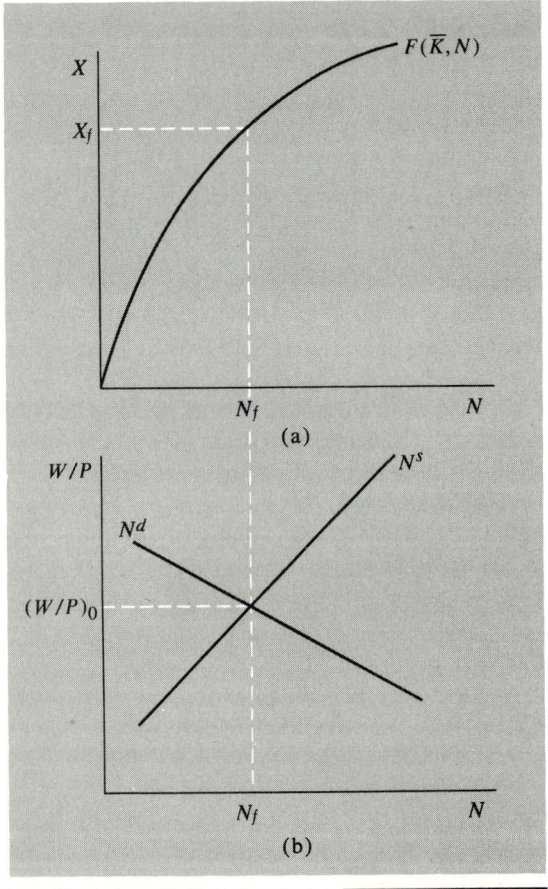

FIGURE 5.1
The Classical Model: Unique Equilibrium Levels of Employment and Output

---

[1] The term "classical economists" is generally used to identify all the followers of Adam Smith (1723–1790) through Ricardo (1772–1823) and J. S. Mill (1806–1878). See Mark Blaug, *Economic Theory in Retrospect* (Homewood, Illinois: Richard D. Irwin, Inc., 1968). Keynes also includes among the classical economists those who "adopted and perfected" the theory of this earlier group, including Marshall (1842–1924) and Pigou (1877–1959). See John Maynard Keynes, *The General Theory of Employment, Interest and Money* (New York: Harcourt, Brace and World, Inc., 1936), p. 3.

Keynesian Assumptions: Rigid Prices and Wages

An alternative assumption is that both the nominal wage rate (W) and the price level (P) are exogenous:

$$W = \overline{W} \tag{5.3}$$

and

$$P = \overline{P}. \tag{5.4}$$

This makes the real money supply, $m = M/P$, and the real wage rate, $w = W/P$, exogenous variables.

The Keynesian assumptions apply when there is deficient aggregate demand and, as a consequence, employment is below the full employment level.[2] It is not necessary that prices and wages be perfectly rigid to make the Keynesian version an interesting one. As long as price adjustments are slow, output may bear most of the initial burden of adjusting to disturbances. Given that we are not undertaking a full dynamic analysis and are concentrating on the short-run response to disturbances, we will get a better approximation to the impact of disturbances by assuming prices and wages rigid and deriving the implied response of output than by assuming that price and wage adjustments quickly offset the effect of any disturbances on output. Later in the analysis we will allow for variation in both prices and output. We do so first by introducing the aggregate supply curve in Chapter 11; this allows for prices to vary even if the nominal wage rate remains fixed. More detailed analysis of the short-run response of the economy to disturbances with variable wages, prices, and output requires the introduction of the Phillips curve, which describes the response of nominal wages to labor market disequilibrium and expected inflation. We devote most of Part IV to the refinement of short-run analysis with variable wages, prices, and output. Nevertheless, we believe that by beginning with simpler models, we will promote clearer understanding of the more complicated models to come. And the fixed price model we use in Part II is extremely useful in clarifying many important aspects of the economy's short-run response to disturbances that will carry over in the more complicated models introduced later.

The demand for labor in the Keynesian case is determined by the prevailing level of output via the production function. Figure 5.2 depicts the production function; given the level of output $X_0 < X_f$, the level of employment required to produce X_0 can be read off the production function. The labor demand curve is a vertical line at the level of employment corresponding to X_0 on the production function.

To further clarify the role of the labor market in the Keynesian version, it is useful to note a special property of this model. It is said to be *recursive*. This means it can be split into two subsectors and solved sequentially. One subsector consists of the equilibrium conditions in the commodity, money, and bond markets. These

---

[2] The price level is always assumed to be flexible upward when the economy begins from a position of full employment. The classical model remains the appropriate framework for analyzing the economy's response to disturbances which increase aggregate demand in this case.

conditions can be solved to determine the equilibrium level of all variables other than employment (i.e., the interest rate and the level of output). Given the equilibrium level of output, the labor market equations (actually the production function) determine the level of employment. Because the labor market equations are not needed to determine the equilibrium values of r or X, we can drop the labor market equations from explicit analysis in the Keynesian version.

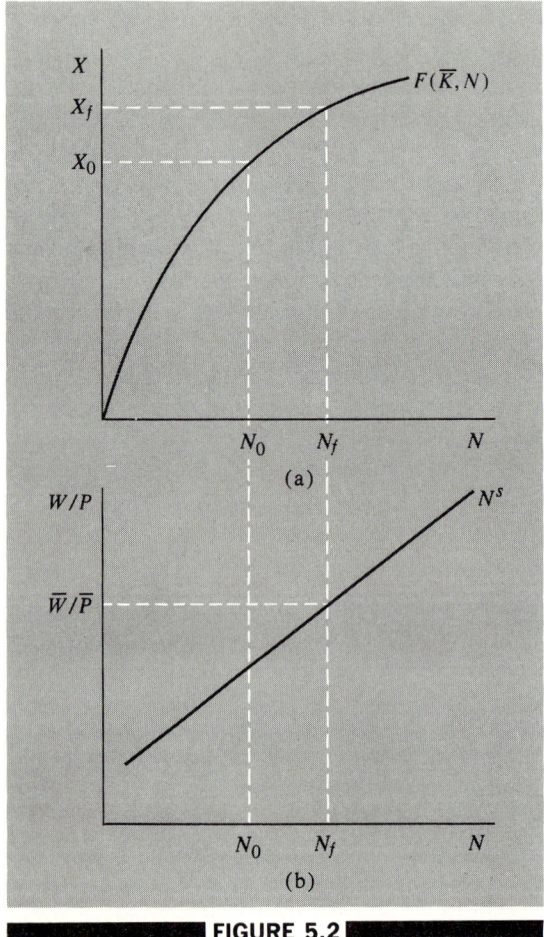

FIGURE 5.2
The Keynesian Model: The Effective Demand for Labor

The Keynesian version of the basic model captures the key insight of Keynes and Keynesian economics—the importance of *effective demand* in the determination of the *actual* level of employment and output. Instead of aggregate demand adjusting to a unique equilibrium level of aggregate supply, as in the classical version, aggregate supply adjusts to accommodate aggregate demand. Our choice of the label "Keynesian" for this model is justified by this focus on aggregate demand as the key determinant of the prevailing level of output. It is not intended to represent "the" model Keynes had in mind in the *General Theory*.³

THE CONDITIONS UNDER WHICH MODELS YIELD UNIQUE SOLUTIONS⁴

We now have eliminated the labor market from the model and have two versions, each of which has three equations and two unknowns. The three equations are the equilibrium conditions in the commodity, money, and bond markets in each version. The two unknowns are the interest rate and price level in the classical version and the interest rate and output in the Keynesian version. As we noted in Chapter 1, we build models to explain and predict the values of the unknowns. We do so by *solving* the model for the unknowns. The issue we take up here is under what conditions models will yield unique solutions for the unknowns. We find that equality of unknowns and independent equations is a general condition for a unique solution. This means that we must demonstrate that only two of the three equilibrium conditions are independent to insure a unique solution to our model. We show in the final section that this is in fact the case.

The Counting Rule

The *counting rule* states that *equality between the number of equations and unknowns* is required for and assures a unique solution to a system of equations. The counting rule, however, is neither a necessary nor sufficient condition for a unique solution to a system of equations. It applies only when the equations are linear, consistent, and independent. In this section we will illustrate these concepts using *IS* and *LM* curves for the Keynesian version of our model.

We will discuss *IS* and *LM* curves in great detail in the next four chapters. At this point, all you need to know is that the *IS* and *LM* curves are *equilibrium conditions* in the commodity and money markets, respectively. We noted that in the Keynesian model we have two unknowns: interest rate (r) and output (X). The *LM* curve in Figure 5.3 is the locus of combinations of r and X for which supply and demand for money are equal. The *IS* curve is the locus of combinations of r and X for which the supply and demand for output are equal. Do not worry at this point about why the *LM* curve is upward sloping and the *IS* curve is downward sloping. All we are interested in now is whether there will be a *unique solution* for r and X; i.e., in terms of Figure 5.3, whether there is a *single intersection* of the *IS* and *LM*

---

³ There has been considerable controversy about the nature of the model implicit in Keynes's *The General Theory of Employment, Interest and Money.* Our interest in this text lies in presenting macroeconomic models which reflect current understanding of the behavior of households and firms and of the macro economy, not in discussing the history of the doctrine. We therefore avoid the traditional "Keynes vs. the classics" discussion. For a particularly insightful discussion of the continued relevance of Keynes's view of macroeconomics, see James Tobin, "How Dead Is Keynes?", *Economic Inquiry*, Vol. XV, No. 4 (October, 1977).

⁴ For excellent discussions of the mathematical properties of models, see Laurence Mauer, "The Patinkin Controversy: A Critique," *Kyklos,* Vol. 19 (1966), pp. 299–314; and Harry Johnson, *Macroeconomics and Monetary Theory* (Chicago: Aldine-Atherton, Inc., 1972), pp. 105–107.

curves. When a unique intersection exists, then there is a unique solution—a single set of values for r and X for which both markets are in equilibrium. Although there are many combinations of r and X consistent with equilibrium in the commodity market (all combinations along the *IS* curve) and many combinations consistent with equilibrium in the money market (all combinations along the *LM* curve), there is only one combination of r and X that is consistent with *simultaneous* equilibrium in the commodity and money markets (the combination that is on both *IS* and *LM* curves, r^* and X^*).

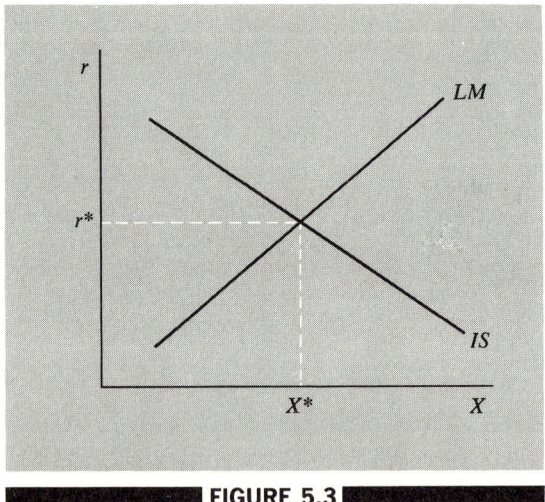

FIGURE 5.3

IS and *LM* Curves: A Unique Solution

○ Consistency and Independence

According to the counting rule, the *IS* and *LM* curve analysis should yield a unique solution because it involves two equations and two unknowns. But we noted that this rule is only valid if the equations are linear, consistent, and independent. The *IS* and *LM* curves in Figure 5.3 are linear (i.e., straight lines). A system of equations is *consistent* if there exists *at least one* set of values for the unknowns which satisfies all equations; i.e., if there is at least one intersection of the *IS* and *LM* curves. The *IS* and *LM* curves depicted in Figure 5.3 are consistent, but those depicted in Figures 5.4a and 5.4b are not. In Figure 5.4a the *IS* and *LM* curves are parallel and have no intersection point.

The curves in Figure 5.4b are mathematically consistent in that a unique solution exists at point *A*. However, point *A* is not an *economically meaningful* solution. Some variables can be positive or negative; e.g., net fixed investment and inventory investment. However, others can only be zero or positive; e.g., output and the price level. Other restrictions on economically meaningful solutions are more complicated. For example, the rate of interest cannot be more negative than the cost of storing money; otherwise, individuals would demand an infinitely large amount of loans, driving the interest rate above this threshhold. Therefore, a solution as in Figure 5.4b that required a substantially negative interest rate would not be economically meaningful. Thus, the *IS* and *LM* curves in Figure 5.4b are also inconsistent.

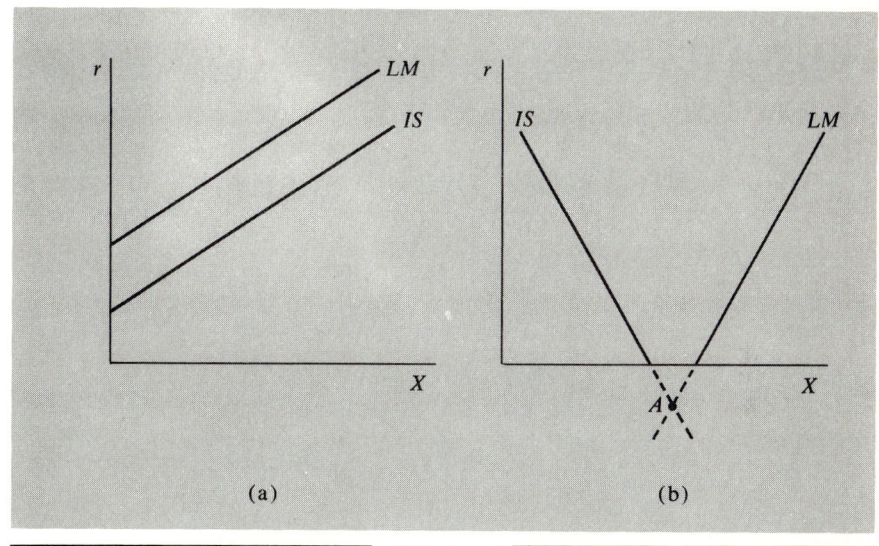

FIGURE 5.4
Inconsistent *IS* and *LM* Curves

The equations of a model are *independent* if no one of the equations is necessarily satisfied by the values of the unknowns which satisfy all the other equations. This is the property of equations that we will use in the final section to demonstrate why we can drop the bond market from our analysis. The *IS* and *LM* curves depicted in Figure 5.5 lie one on top of the other; *any* combination of r and X which is consistent with commodity market equilibrium (i.e., on the *IS* curve) is also consistent with equilibrium in the money market (i.e., is also on the *LM* curve). The *IS* and *LM* curves are dependent in this case and there will be an infinite number of solutions for r and X which are consistent with simultaneous equilibrium in the commodity and money markets (all points along the common *IS-LM* curve).

We conclude that if the equations are linear, equality of unknowns and equations guarantees a unique solution if the equations are also consistent and independent. If the equations are linear and consistent but dependent (as in Figure 5.5), there will be an infinite number of solutions. If the equations are inconsistent (as in Figures 5.4a and 5.4b), there will be no solution.

REDUNDANT MARKET ANALYSIS

We have now demonstrated the conditions under which our linear *IS* and *LM* curves will yield a unique solution. But we entered this section with two versions of our basic model, each with *three* equilibrium conditions (in the commodity, money, and bond markets) and only *two* unknowns (r and P or r and X). If we can find a reason for eliminating the bond market (or any of the other two equilibrium conditions), we are home free: two equations in two unknowns. The solution is evident. If one of the three equilibrium conditions is not independent, we really only have two independent equations. The problem is, therefore, to demonstrate *why* one equilibrium condition is *redundant*. The precise explanation for the fact that one market is redundant depends on the way we relate flows and stocks in our model.

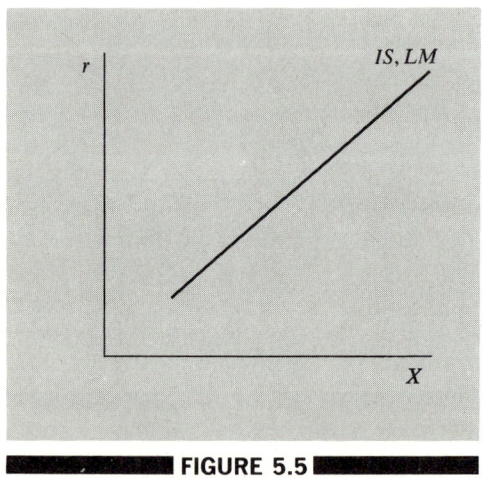

FIGURE 5.5
**Dependent *IS* and *LM* Curves:
An Infinite Number of Solutions**

○ Flows and Stocks in Continuous and Period Models[5]

In continuous models, flow variables are dimensioned as instantaneous rates of change. If we confine our analysis to instantaneous effects of disturbances, *flows do not affect stocks*; e.g., the rate of saving at time t does not affect wealth at time t, and neither government deficits nor investment at time t affects the supply of bonds outstanding at time t. Of course, over a discrete interval of time, flows will generate changes in stocks. The analysis of this relation between flows and stocks over discrete periods is more easily handled in period-type models.

To clarify the difference between the continuous and period specifications, consider the relation between the measurement of flow variables in the two approaches. If s is the instantaneous rate of saving, the way saving is dimensioned in a continuous model, the period counterpart, S, is defined as

$$S = s\Delta t \tag{5.5}$$

---

[5] The analysis in this section builds on the analysis of Josef May, "Period Analysis and Continuous Analysis in Patinkin's Macroeconomic Model," *Journal of Economic Theory*, Vol. 2 (1970), pp. 1–9; and Duncan Foley, "On Two Specifications of Asset Equilibrium in Macroeconomic Models," *Journal of Political Economy*, Vol. 83 (April, 1975), pp. 303–324.

where Δt is the interval of the period being studied. S is measured in dollars over the period. Wealth at the end of the interval in the period model is given by

$$a = \bar{a} + s\Delta t \tag{5.6}$$

where $\bar{a}$ is wealth at the beginning of the period. Continuous analysis is a limiting case of period analysis where the interval Δt goes to zero; therefore, in continuous analysis $a = \bar{a}$ because $s\Delta t \to 0$ as $\Delta t \to 0$. Thus, wealth is exogenous at the moment t in continuous analysis, but endogenous over the unit interval of our period approach.

We will now consider the rationale for dropping one of our three remaining markets in continuous and period models.

○ The Balance Sheet Constraint in Continuous Models

At a given moment, there is a certain amount of money and bonds outstanding and the sum of these outstanding financial assets equals the net wealth of households. The definition of wealth is given by the balance sheet identity (BSI) introduced in Chapter 4.

$$\bar{a} \equiv \bar{m} + \bar{b} \tag{5.7}$$

A related identity also introduced in Chapter 4, the balance sheet constraint (BSC), given by equation (5.8), is a logical proposition about asset demands; it requires that household demands for money and bonds just sum to the existing value of household wealth:

$$\bar{a} \equiv L(\ ) + B(\ ). \tag{5.8}$$

Households must hold wealth in either money or bonds; the amount they do not want to hold in money, they must want to hold in bonds. Using equation (5.7) to define $\bar{a}$, we can rewrite equation (5.8) as

$$0 \equiv [L(\ ) - \bar{m}] + [B(\ ) - \bar{b}]. \tag{5.8'}$$

According to equation (5.8'), the sum of the excess demands across the two asset markets must sum to zero. This result provides the rationale for treating *either the money or the bond markets as the redundant market*; if the money market is in equilibrium for any combination of r, X, and $\bar{a}$, the bond market must also be in equilibrium at those same values. The bond market is then a mirror image of the money market (the excess supply of bonds is identically equal to the excess demand for money) and adds no additional restrictions on the values of the unknowns.

We can relate this situation to our analysis in the previous section. The equilibrium conditions in the money and bond markets are *dependent*. Any combination of r and X which is consistent with equilibrium in the money market (on the LM curve) *must* also be consistent with equilibrium in the bond market (on the curve depicting all combinations of r and X consistent with bond market equilibrium, the BB curve).

Thus, the *LM* and *BB* curves lie one on top of the other in this case, as in Figure 5.6. We can use either the *LM* or *BB* curve along with the *IS* curve to solve for unique values of r and X.

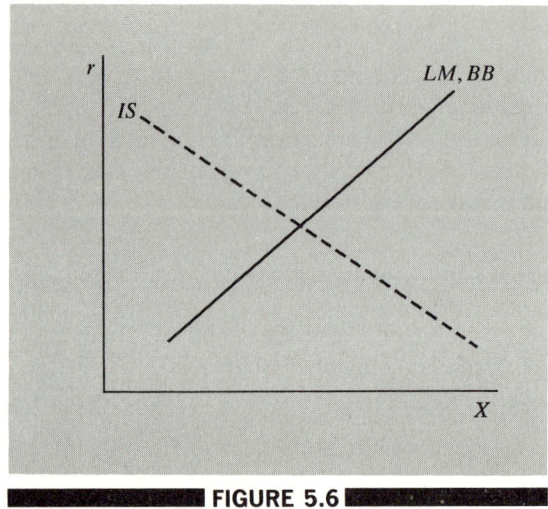

FIGURE 5.6
Dependent *LM* and *BB* Curves

○ Walras' Law and Period Models

In the end-of-period (*EOP*) specification of period models, we focus on the values of asset supplies and demands *at the end of a discrete interval*.[6] The balance sheet constraint is written in this case as

$$\bar{a} + S(\ ) \equiv L(\ ) + B(\ ) \tag{5.9}$$

where $\bar{a}$ is now defined as the beginning-of-period value of real wealth, $S(\ )$ is desired saving over the period, and $L(\ )$ and $B(\ )$ are desired holding of money and bonds at the end of the interval. $\bar{a} + S(\ )$ is the desired wealth position at the end of the interval, and the *BSC* requires that the sum of asset demands at the end of the interval just equals the desired wealth. We can rewrite this as

$$S(\ ) = [L(\ ) - \bar{m}] + [B(\ ) - \bar{b}], \tag{5.9'}$$

indicating that desired saving must just be matched by desired accumulation in money and bonds over the period. The *BSC* still imposes restrictions on parameter values in the asset demand equations, but it no longer provides a basis for dropping one of the markets.

---

[6] It is also possible to define asset market equilibrium in period models in terms of wealth and asset supplies and demands *at the beginning of the interval*. The analysis in this case resembles the continuous analysis. When we refer to period analysis in this discussion, we will always specify asset market equilibrium in terms of *end-of-period* supplies and demands.

Chapter 5 • Classical and Keynesian Versions of the Basic Model

To develop a rationale for dropping one market, we must convert the *BSC* into a statement about excess demands in the three markets. $S(\ )$ is of course just equal to $X - C(\ )$. Let us subtract $I(\ )$, desired investment, from both sides of equation (5.9). For the moment we ignore the government sector.

$$\underbrace{X - C(\ ) - I(\ )}_{\text{excess supply of commodities}} \equiv \underbrace{[L(\ ) - \bar{m}]}_{\text{excess demand for money}} + \underbrace{\{B(\ ) - [\bar{b} + I(\ )]\}}_{\text{excess demand for bonds}} \qquad (5.10)$$

The left-hand side of equation (5.10) is the excess supply in the goods market— the supply of output, X, minus the demand for output, $C(\ ) + I(\ )$. The terms on the right-hand side of equation (5.10) are the excess demands in the money and bond markets, respectively (in each case, the end-of-period demands minus the end-of-period supplies). Note that the end-of-period desired supply of bonds equals the beginning-of-period bonds plus planned issues of bonds to finance investment over the period. Thus, equation (5.10) requires that the sum of the excess demands across the goods and assets markets must sum to zero in this specification of the model. This relation is referred to as *Walras' Law*.

To add the government sector, note that desired saving equals $X - C(\ ) - \bar{T}$. Subtracting G from both sides and adding T to both sides yields

$$X - C(\ ) - I(\ ) - \bar{G} \equiv [L(\ ) - \bar{m}] + \{B(\ ) - [\bar{b} + I(\ ) + \bar{G} - \bar{T}]\}. \qquad (5.10')$$

Once again the left-hand side is the excess supply of commodities and the terms on the right are the excess demands for money and bonds, respectively. The end-of-period supply of bonds now depends on both planned investment and the government deficit.

If we find the values of r and X which are consistent with equilibrium in any two of the three markets, these values must also be consistent with equilibrium in the third market, according to Walras' Law. Therefore, we can use any two of the three markets to solve for the equilibrium values of r and X. The third market is simply dropped from the formal solution to the model. Walras' Law permits us to treat any of the three markets as redundant, even the commodity market. To preserve similarity to conventional *IS-LM* analysis, we will continue to drop the bond market.

The picture of the *IS*, *LM*, and *BB* curves looks like Figure 5.7. We know from equation (5.10) that any set of r and X that is consistent with equilibrium in two markets must also be consistent with equilibrium in the third. If r^* and X^* are consistent with equilibrium in the money and commodity markets, the *IS* and *LM* curves intersect at r^* and X^*; then, by equation (5.10), the *BB* curve must also go through this point. Therefore, the *BB* curve adds no new information and imposes no restrictions on the solution not already embedded in the *IS* and *LM* curves. It is redundant.

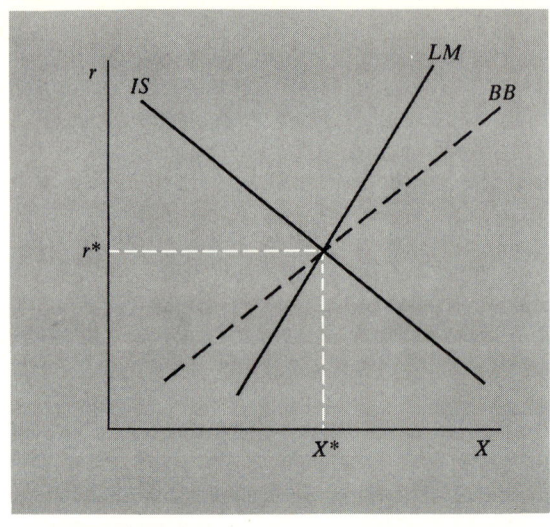

FIGURE 5.7
The Implications of Walras' Law:
One Equilibrium Condition Is Redundant

CLASSICAL AND KEYNESIAN VERSIONS

We can now summarize the two versions of our basic model. To simplify the analysis in Part II, we assume that neither the consumption nor money demand function includes wealth as an argument. We treat our flow and stock variables as defined in the discrete or period case. *Expenditures* are flows over a unit interval, and we view the *unit interval* as a period of one year. We will generally define our *stock variables* as values at the end of the interval, although the importance of the distinctions between continuous, beginning- and end-of-period specifications is virtually eliminated by the simplifying assumptions that $C_a = 0$ and $L_a = 0$. In Part III we will relax the assumption that $C_a = 0$ and in Part IV we will relax the assumption that $L_a = 0$. Our two equilibrium conditions can be written as

$$X = C(Y) + I(r) + \bar{G} \tag{5.11}$$

$$\frac{M}{P} = L(r, X) \tag{5.12}$$

where

$$Y = X - \bar{T}. \tag{5.13}$$

Substituting equation (5.13) into equation (5.11) permits us to represent our model as a system of two equations in three unknowns (r, P, and X). Such a system cannot in general be solved. Imposing the classical and Keynesian assumptions about price and wage flexibility yields two alternative systems of two equations in two unknowns.

○ The Classical Version

In the classical version $X = \bar{X}_f$ and the two equilibrium conditions become

$$\bar{X}_f = C(\bar{X}_f - \bar{T}) + I(r) + \bar{G} \tag{5.14}$$

$$\frac{\bar{M}}{P} = L(r, \bar{X}_f). \tag{5.15}$$

The exogenous variables are $\bar{G}$, $\bar{T}$, and $\bar{M}$, and the endogenous variables are P and r.

○ The Keynesian Version

In the Keynesian version we assume $P = \bar{P}$ so that $\bar{m} = \bar{M}/\bar{P}$ and

$$X = C(X - \bar{T}) + I(r) + \bar{G} \tag{5.16}$$

$$\bar{m} = L(r, X). \tag{5.17}$$

The exogenous variables are $\bar{G}$, $\bar{T}$, and $\bar{m}$, and the endogenous variables are r and X.

We will use these two versions of *IS-LM* analysis to develop the essential properties of income, price, and interest rate determination in Chapters 9 and 10. Before we do so, we will introduce a simpler model in Chapter 6 and then develop the graphical approach to solving the two versions of the *IS-LM* model in Chapters 7 and 8.

● REVIEW QUESTIONS

1. Why is it permissible in the classical model to treat employment and output as predetermined variables?

2. Prices and wages are obviously variable. What can be learned from models which assume rigid prices and wages?

3. In what sense are the classical and Keynesian versions complements?

4. State the counting rule and discuss why it is not a sufficient condition for a unique solution to a model.

5. Describe the relation between flow variables in continuous and period analysis and the relation between flows and stocks in the two approaches. Use as an example the relation between investment and the capital stock.

6. Why is Walras' Law not a constraint on instantaneous flow demands and stock demands at the instant the flows are defined in continuous analysis?

7. Show how the equation for Walras' Law collapses to the balance sheet constraint when the period is reduced toward zero.

8. How is redundant market analysis related to the concept of dependence?

PROBLEMS

1. Plot the following linear equations and determine whether the system has a unique solution. If not, identify which condition required for the validity of the counting rule is violated.

   (a) $y = 5 + x$

   $y = 10 + x$

   (b) $y = 5 + x$

   $2y = 10 + 2x$

   (c) $y = 5 + x$

   $y = 10 + 2x$

2. Consider the following *nonlinear* systems. In which case(s) does a unique solution exist?

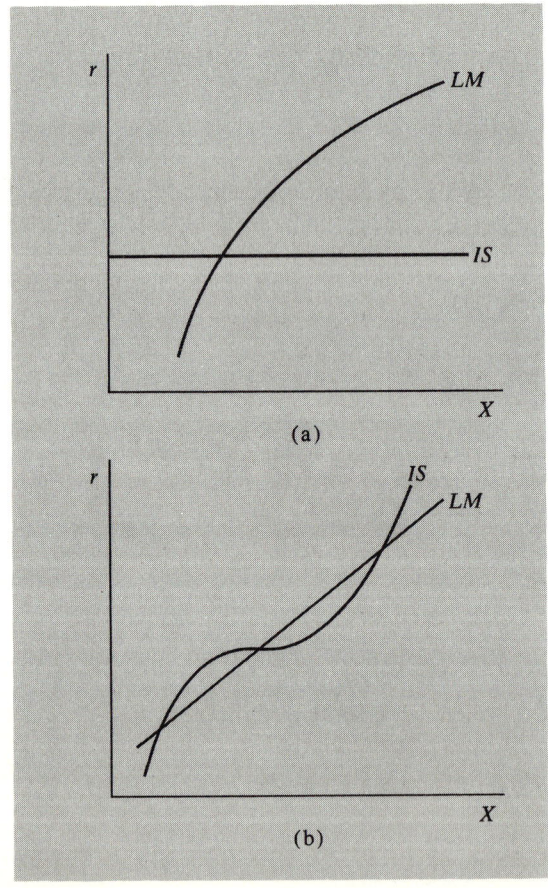

Part II

Comparative Static Analysis with the Basic Model

    Chapter 6. The Keynesian Cross: A Simple but Incomplete Model
                   7. Derivation and Interpretation of the Slopes of the *IS* and *LM* Curves in the Keynesian and Classical Models
                   8. Sources of Disturbances and Shifts in the *IS* and *LM* Curves
                   9. A Comparative Static Analysis of the Classical Model
                 10. A Comparative Static Analysis of the Keynesian Model
                 11. Aggregate Supply and Demand Analysis

Chapter 6

The Keynesian Cross: A Simple but Incomplete Model

Before we proceed to analyze the classical and Keynesian versions of the *IS-LM* framework that we discussed in the previous chapter, we introduce a much simpler model. The equilibrium level of output is determined exclusively by the supply and demand for commodities. This simple model, when presented graphically, is often referred to as the Keynesian cross (*KC*) model. The rationale for beginning with this model is its usefulness for reinforcing some of the basic concepts introduced in Chapter 1 (e.g., identities, equilibrium conditions, reduced-form equations, and multipliers), for providing some exercise in solving simple macroeconomic models, and for introducing several important new concepts, such as comparative statics, dynamics, and the stability of equilibrium. After we have solved the simple *KC* model graphically and mathematically, we expect that the manipulations involved in solving the more complicated *IS-LM* model will seem less difficult than if we had proceeded directly to that model.

THE SIMPLE CONSUMPTION MULTIPLIER MODEL

The single equilibrium condition in the Keynesian cross model is the equality between the supply of and the demand for output. The supply of output responds to accommodate the demand for output. Therefore, we can write the equilibrium condition in terms of the equality between actual output (X) and the demand for output (X^d) as

$$X = X^d. \tag{6.1}$$

We begin by ignoring the government sector. Output (X) is therefore defined as the sum of consumption (C) and investment expenditures (I)

$$X \equiv C + I \tag{6.2}$$

and the demand for output (X^d) as the sum of desired consumption and investment. Desired consumption is assumed to depend on income only:

$$C = C(X), \tag{6.3}$$

or, assuming a linear function,

$$C = \bar{C} + C_x X \tag{6.3'}$$

where $\bar{C}$ is a constant (autonomous component of desired consumption) and C_x is the marginal propensity to consume out of income.

○ Two Versions of the Equilibrium Condition

There are two equivalent ways of expressing the equilibrium condition in the output market. The first, equation (6.1), requires equality of the supply and demand for output. Substituting *desired* consumption and investment for actual values in the *GNP* identity we get

$$X = \overbrace{\bar{C} + C_x X + \bar{I}}^{X^d} \tag{6.4a}$$

where $\bar{I}$ is the exogenous level of desired investment.

To derive the second form of the equilibrium condition, we make use of the relation between income, saving, and consumption. Recall from Chapter 4 that the household budget identity defines the uses of income by households; in the present model income must be consumed or saved. Therefore, $X \equiv C + S$ where S is household saving. Consistency in household decisions involving flows requires that desired consumption and desired saving just exhaust household income; we called this the household budget constraint in Chapter 4: $X \equiv C(X) + S(X)$ where $S(X)$ is desired saving. Given this relation between income, desired consumption, and desired saving, once we have specified explicitly the relationship between income and desired consumption, we have implicitly specified the relation between income and desired saving.

$$S(X) \equiv X - C(X) \tag{6.5}$$

The equilibrium condition, equation (6.4a), can be rewritten as $X - C(X) = I$ or, using equation (6.5), as

$$S(X) = \bar{I}. \tag{6.4b}$$

Thus, the equality of the supply and demand for output is equivalent to the equality of desired saving and desired investment. Note that there is also an *identity* relating saving and investment. From the *GNP* identity, $I \equiv X - C$; from the household budget identity, $S \equiv X - C$. Therefore, we can write

$$S \equiv I. \tag{6.6}$$

The portion of output not purchased by households (S) is identically equal to the purchase of currently produced goods by firms (I). How can this *identity* be reconciled with the preceding *equilibrium condition?* The explanation is the distinction between *desired* and *actual* values of the variables. According to equation (6.4b), equilibrium requires the equality of *desired* saving, $S(X)$, and *desired* investment, $\bar{I}$; i.e., equilibrium requires that the portion of income that households do not *desire* to spend on output must be just offset by the *demand* for output by business firms. The identity states that, irrespective of whether or not the output market is in equilibrium, *actual* saving and *actual* investment are always equal.

To clarify further how $S(X) > \bar{I}$ is compatible with $S \equiv I$, let us assume that households always realize their consumption (saving) plans but firms are sometimes unable to realize their investment plans. This means that actual saving will always be equal to desired saving but actual investment may deviate from desired investment. We define *actual investment* as the sum of desired or planned investment, $\bar{I}$, and unintended investment, I^u.

$$I \equiv \bar{I} + I^u \tag{6.7}$$

Unintended investment takes the form of unplanned accumulation of inventories, unintended inventory investment. If firms produce more than consumers and firms want to purchase, they end up being unable to sell a portion of the output, and this portion is retained as inventories by the firms. Of course, the firms did not want to accumulate these inventories, so the level of production cannot be an equilibrium one. It is the I^u term, undesired investment, which always makes up the difference between actual output and the demand for output so that $X \equiv C + I$ whether or not $X = C(X) + \bar{I}$. When unintended inventory accumulation is zero ($I^u = 0$), then actual investment equals planned investment and both the equilibrium condition and the identity are satisfied.

○ Graphical Solution of the Model

The *KC* model consists of one equation [either (6.4a) or (6.4b)] in one unknown (X). The model can be solved mathematically or graphically (using the "Keynesian cross"). We will develop the graphical solution first. The linear version of the consumption function is plotted in Figure 6.1 where we have set $\bar{C} = 15$ and $C_x = .8$. The equation for the consumption function is therefore

$C = 15 + .8X.$

The constant term is the vertical axis intercept (the value of C when $X = 0$) and the coefficient of X is the slope ($\Delta C / \Delta X$). The saving function is plotted on the same graph; using the fact that $S(\ ) \equiv X - C(\ )$,

$S = -15 + .2X.$

To derive the saving function graphically from the consumption function, we include a 45° line along which output (measured along the horizontal axis) is equal to the sum of desired consumption and saving (measured along the vertical axis). Desired saving at any level of X is simply that level of X minus desired consumption at that level of income. We can therefore measure desired saving in Figure 6.1 as $b - a$, $X - C(X)$, or $b' - a'$, $S(X)$.

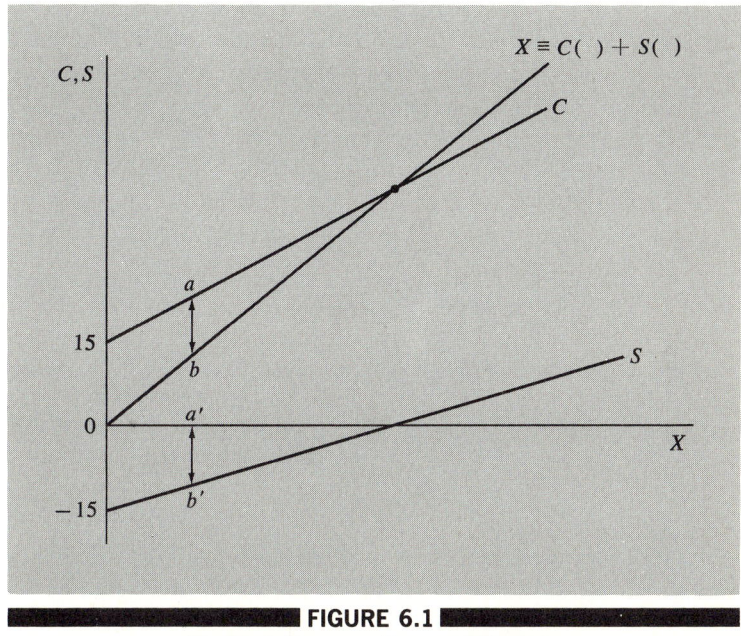

FIGURE 6.1
Desired Consumption and Saving

In Figure 6.2a we measure X^d along the vertical axis and actual output, X, along the horizontal axis. The equilibrium value of X is the one for which $X = X^d$; therefore, the equilibrium must lie along the straight line from the origin with a slope of one (again, a 45° line). We can also plot on Figure 6.2a the relationship between X^d and X. To plot the X^d curve we simply add the exogenous level of I to the value of C we found at each level of X in Figure 6.1. Assuming $\bar{I} = 25$, $X^d = 15 + .8X + 25$, or

$$X^d = 40 + .8X.$$

Thus, the X^d and C curves have identical slopes; the constant vertical difference between the two curves is the constant level of $\bar{I}$. The X^d curve gives the value of X^d at alternative values of X. The intersection of the X^d and $X \equiv X^d$ curves is the equilibrium value of X. In Figure 6.2a, this occurs at $X = 200$.

An alternative but equivalent graphical approach is depicted in Figure 6.2b. It makes use of the alternate version of the equilibrium condition given by the equation: $S(X) = \bar{I}$. The saving curve was already derived in Figure 6.1. The investment curve is simply a horizontal line at $\bar{I} = 25$. The equilibrium value of X is the value of X for which desired saving and investment are equal; i.e., the value of X at which the

S and I lines intersect. This, of course, must be at $200. Thus, the equilibrium value of X (designated by $\tilde{X}$) is the only value of X for which $\tilde{X} = C(\tilde{X}) + \bar{I}$ or $S(\tilde{X}) = \bar{I}$.

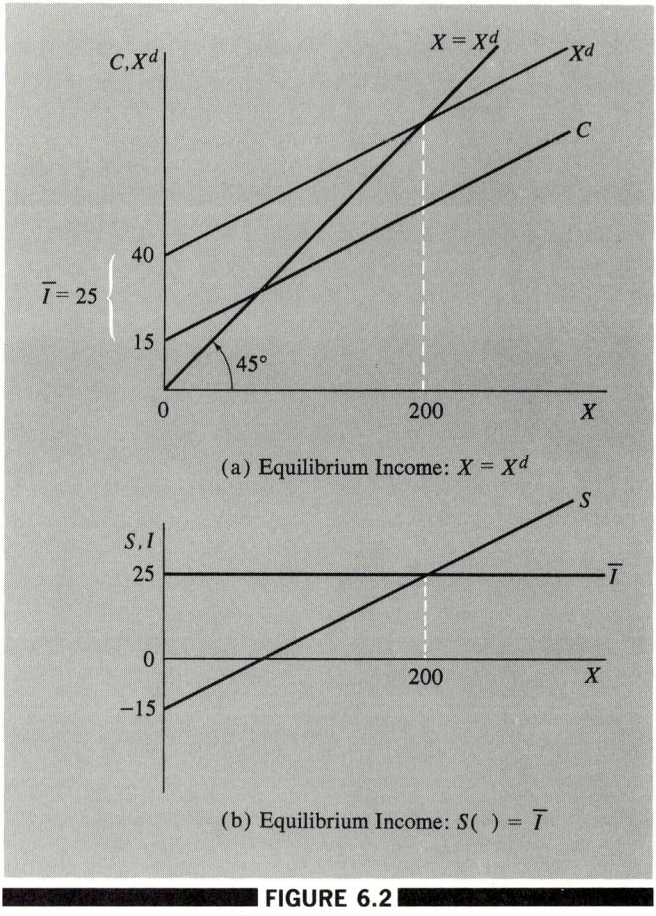

FIGURE 6.2
Determining Equilibrium Income

○ Reduced Forms and the Explicit Solution to Models

We can solve this model mathematically as well. To find the equilibrium value of X, we solve for X in terms of exogenous variables and structural parameters, the values of which we know. The model consists of two equations: the *GNP* identity [equation (6.2)] and the consumption function [equation (6.3′)]. To solve for X, we begin by substituting the desired values of consumption and investment for actual values in the *GNP* identity, converting it to an equilibrium condition in the commodity market (supply of output equal to demand for output); this gives us equation (6.4a) discussed above. Equation (6.4a) has only one unknown (X) and can generally be solved for the unique value of X which is consistent with equilibrium in the commodity market. We show the step-by-step solution below:

$$X = \bar{C} + C_x X + \bar{I}$$
$$X - C_x X = \bar{C} + \bar{I}$$
$$(1 - C_x) X = \bar{C} + \bar{I}$$
$$X = \frac{1}{1 - C_x} \bar{C} + \frac{1}{1 - C_x} \bar{I}. \tag{6.8}$$

This is referred to as a *reduced-form* equation. In fact, this is the explicit solution of the reduced form we discussed in Chapter 1. It expresses a single endogenous variable in terms of the exogenous variables and the model parameters. The coefficients of the exogenous variables are called *multipliers*. A multiplier describes the response of an endogenous variable to a change in an exogenous variable, holding constant all other exogenous variables. For example, the response of output to a change in investment is $\Delta X/\Delta I = 1/(1 - C_x)$. Using the reduced-form equation along with assumed values for C_x, $\bar{C}$, and $\bar{I}$, we can find the precise value of equilibrium income:

$$X = \frac{1}{1 - .8}(15) + \frac{1}{1 - .8}(25) = \frac{1}{.2}(40) = 200.$$

○ Equilibrium and Disequilibrium

When the economy is in equilibrium, all plans are realized. When the economy is not in equilibrium, however, there is a discrepancy between actual and planned values of consumption (saving) and/or actual and planned values of investment. We assumed above that consumption plans are always realized so that disequilibrium will be associated with the failure of business firms to realize their investment plans; i.e., in disequilibrium there will be unintended investment (or disinvestment). In Figure 6.3 we illustrate the relation between actual output and the demand for output in equilibrium and disequilibrium.

At $\tilde{X}$ in Figure 6.3 the equilibrium level of output is $\tilde{X} = C(\tilde{X}) + \bar{I}$ so that $I^u = 0$. At X_1, on the other hand, $C(X_1) + \bar{I} > X_1$; this is a situation of excess demand for output. Of course, actual output still equals the sum of actual consumption (assumed to be always the same as desired consumption) and actual investment (the sum of desired and undesired investment). Thus, $X_1 \equiv C(X_1) + \bar{I} + I^u$ and I^u must be negative; i.e., at X_1 demand for output exceeds current production and producers meet demand by drawing down their inventories. The unplanned decline in inventories signals firms that production is insufficient to meet demand, and firms respond by increasing production to a level consistent with aggregate demand. Only when X has been increased to $\tilde{X}$ will $I^u = 0$ and firms' actual and planned investment be equal.

The response of actual output to disequilibrium in the output market is based on a hypothesis about the way in which economic agents respond to commodity market disequilibrium: the rate of change in output ($\dot{X}$) is proportional to the gap between the demand for output and the current level of production.

$$\dot{X} = a(X^d - X) \tag{6.9}$$

where a is a positive constant. This can also be written as

$$\dot{X} = a[\bar{I} - S(X)] = -aI^u. \tag{6.9'}$$

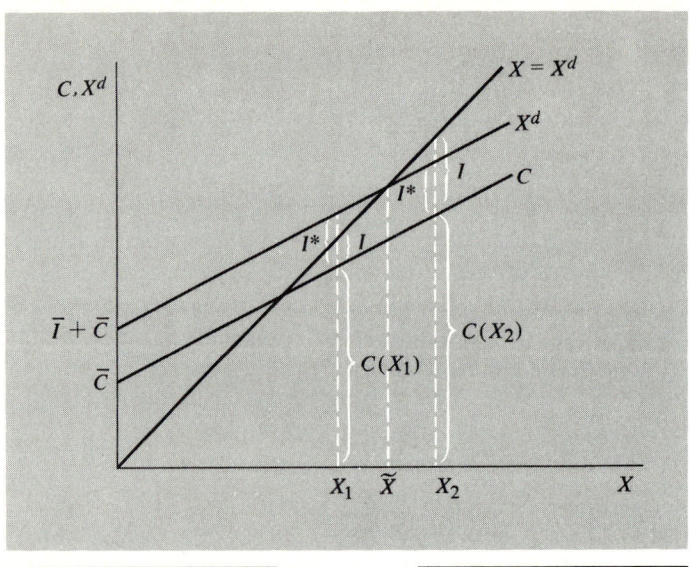

FIGURE 6.3
Equilibrium and Disequilibrium

Equilibrium requires $X = X^d$, $S(X) = \bar{I}$, and $I^u = 0$. If the economy is at X_1, $X^d > X$, $\bar{I} > S(X)$, and $I^u < 0$; in response to this excess demand, firms expand production, increasing X. This continues until $\tilde{X}$ is reached.

Now consider an initial value of X in excess of the equilibrium value; e.g., X_2 in Figure 6.3. At X_2, $X_2 > C(X_2) + \bar{I}$; i.e., demand falls short of the amount necessary to just exhaust firms' production. Therefore, there is unplanned inventory accumulation; i.e., $X_2 - [C(X_2) + \bar{I}] = I^u > 0$. This undesired build-up in inventories signals firms that their production exceeds demand, and firms respond by cutting production to a level compatible with demand; i.e., from X_2 to $\tilde{X}$.

Note that the cutback in production will be *greater* than the initial excess of production over demand; i.e., $X_2 - \tilde{X} > I^u$. This is a reflection of the multiplier mechanism. As firms cut production, income falls; as income falls, demand falls even more. Nevertheless, each decline in X induces a decline in X^d which is smaller in absolute value than the decline in X; therefore, the decline in X does reduce and eventually eliminate excess supply of output. In the present model, each dollar decline in output reduces demand by 80 cents; i.e., each dollar decline in X reduces excess supply by only 20 cents. Therefore, the change in X required to eliminate the given excess supply is five times the initial excess supply. The multiplier in this model is five! For example, assume $X_2 = 300$. Then $X^d = 15 + .8(300) + 25 = 40 + 240 = 280$. Excess supply is $X_2 - X^d = I^u = 20$. The decline in X required to restore equilibrium is $X_2 - \tilde{X} = 300 - 200 = 100 = 5 \cdot (20)$.

○ The Multiplier

To further develop the concept of the multiplier, we will explicitly introduce a dynamic version of the consumption function so that we can observe the multiplier process working itself out gradually over time. We will assume that expenditures induce immediate changes in income and output but that this period's consumption depends on last period's income; i.e., there is a lag of one period between receipt of income and the expenditure decision based on income. The dynamic version of our consumption function can be written as

$$C_t = bX_{t-1} \tag{6.10}$$

where C_t is desired consumption in period t, X_{t-1} is actual income in period $t-1$, and b is the constant marginal propensity to consume out of income. Investment is exogenous, equal to $\bar{I}$ each period, and we have eliminated the autonomous component of consumption to simplify the exposition. Equilibrium therefore requires that

$$X_t = bX_{t-1} + \bar{I} \tag{6.11}$$

and

$$X_t = X_{t-1}. \tag{6.12}$$

If equation (6.11) holds but equation (6.12) does not, the system will not remain at X_t. To find the equilibrium value of X, set $X_t = X_{t-1} = \tilde{X}$ and solve for $\tilde{X}$:

$$\tilde{X} = \frac{1}{1-b} \bar{I}. \tag{6.13}$$

This is the same result as in the static version of the model.

Assume that we begin from a position of full equilibrium in period $t = 0$. This means that

$$X_0 = bX_{-1} + \bar{I}$$

and $X_0 = X_{-1}$. Now consider the response of income to a sustained one-dollar increase in desired investment, beginning in period $t = 1$. The one-dollar increase in desired investment increases aggregate demand and income by one dollar in period 1; i.e.,

$$X_1 = bX_0 + (\bar{I} + 1) = (bX_0 + \bar{I}) + 1 = X_0 + 1.$$

Note that the increase in income in period 1 does not affect consumption in that period because consumption in period 1 depends on income in the previous period; last period's income is, of course, unaffected by any disturbances in the current period. Therefore, the increase in desired investment increases output, income, and aggregate demand dollar-for-dollar in the first period.

In period 2, consumption will increase because income in period 1 exceeds income in period 0.

$$X_2 = b(X_1) + (\bar{I} + 1) = b\overbrace{(X_0 + 1)}^{X_1} + (\bar{I} + 1) = \underbrace{bX_0 + \bar{I}}_{X_0} + 1 + b$$

Subtracting the equation for X_2 from the one for X_1, we find that $X_2 - X_1 = b$. Income in period 2 increases by $\$b$ over income in period 1. Income in period 3 is

$$X_3 = b(X_2) + (\bar{I}+1) = b(\overbrace{X_0 + 1 + b}^{X_2}) + (\bar{I}+1) = \underbrace{bX_0 + \bar{I}}_{X_0} + 1 + b + b^2.$$

Continuing this approach yields

$$X_n = \underbrace{bX_0 + \bar{I}}_{X_0} + 1 + b + b^2 + b^3 + \ldots + b^{n-1}.$$

Multiplying the equation directly above by b gives us

$$bX_n = bX_0 + b + b^2 + b^3 + \ldots + b^{n-1} + b^n.$$

Subtracting this equation from the equation for X_n yields

$$X_n - bX_n = X_0 - bX_0 + 1 - b^n.$$

For large values of n, b^n approaches zero. Therefore,

$$X_n - bX_n = X_0 - bX_0 + 1$$

$$(1-b)X_n = (1-b)X_0 + 1$$

$$X_n = X_0 + \frac{1}{1-b} \tag{6.14}$$

and

$$\Delta X = X_n - X_0 = \frac{1}{1-b} = \text{the } \textit{multiplier}. \tag{6.14'}$$

A dollar increase in $\bar{I}$ is converted into a $\frac{1}{1-b}$ dollars increase in X.

The multiplier mechanism reflects the existence of a *positive feedback* response in the model. Any disturbance generates direct impacts and indirect or feedback responses on income. In the present case, the direct impact of an increase in $\bar{I}$ is the one-dollar increase in X in period 1. *Feedback responses* are changes in demand induced by changes in income. There are no feedback responses in the first period. In the second period, households respond to the increase in income in the previous period. Consumption depends on income; therefore, as income increases, consumption increases also. This positive feedback response of consumption to the initial increase in income *multiplies* the effect of the initial change in $\bar{I}$ on income.

Comparative Statics and Dynamics

The basic approach we employ to develop the properties of our models is called comparative statics. In *static analysis* there is no reference to time and only equilibrium positions are studied. *Comparative statics* involves the comparison of equilibrium positions before and after some once-and-for-all change in an exogenous variable. The ratio between the change in the equilibrium value of the endogenous variable and the change in the exogenous variable is called the *equilibrium multiplier*. For example, in the model presented above, the equilibrium multiplier associated with an autonomous increase in investment is $\Delta X/\Delta I = 1/(1 - C_x)$. Comparative static analysis is not concerned with the time path of the endogenous variables between the old and new equilibrium values, with how long it takes for the system to reach the new equilibrium, or, indeed, with whether the system even moves to the new equilibrium in response to a change in an exogenous variable. These are problems that require *dynamic analysis*.

The model used above to develop the time path of the response of income to a change in investment is an example of a dynamic model. Time enters in a fundamental way because variables in one period (consumption) are related to variables in some other period (income). We will use this model to further develop the nature of dynamic analysis. Our comparative static analysis of that model indicated that equilibrium income would increase by a multiple of the increase in investment. We found that the multiplier depended on the value of the marginal propensity to consume:

$$\frac{\Delta X}{\Delta I} = \frac{1}{1 - C_x}.$$

The dynamic analysis provides additional information: the precise time path of income in response to the change in investment. Assume, for example, that $C_x = .8$. Then we know that a $1 billion increase in investment will generate a $5 billion increase in equilibrium income. But the first period response will be only $1 billion. In the second period, income will increase by another $800 million, and in each succeeding period income will increase by smaller and smaller amounts until the system converges to equilibrium and the sum of the changes just equals $5 billion. The change in income each period and the cumulative change in income over time is presented in Table 6.1. The change in income over time is depicted in Figure 6.4. We can see from both the table and the corresponding diagram that the changes in income become progressively smaller and the level of income ultimately converges to the new equilibrium level in this case.

What if C_x is greater than one? The equilibrium multiplier in this case is negative! This result seems counterintuitive. C_x controls the size of positive feedback in the model; the larger C_x, the greater the income-induced increase in aggregate demand in response to the initial increase in income and the larger the change in X we should anticipate. As long as C_x is between zero and one, this is the result we obtain. In Table 6.2 we present the values of the multiplier for various values of C_x. As C_x increases from .5 to .9, the multiplier increases from 2.0 to 10.0. As C_x approaches 1.0, the multiplier approaches infinity. But once C_x increases beyond 1.0, the multiplier turns negative.

Period	Δ Income	Cumulative Δ
1	1.0	1.0
2	0.8	1.8
3	0.64	2.44
4	0.512	2.952
5	0.4096	3.3616
6	0.32768	3.68928
7	0.262144	3.951424
8	0.2097152	4.1611392
9	0.1677721	4.3289113
10	0.1342176	4.4631289
11	0.107374	4.5705029
12	0.0858992	4.6564021
13	0.0687193	4.7251214
14	0.0549754	4.7800968
15	0.0439803	4.8240771
16	0.0351842	4.8592613
.		
.		
.		
.		
.		
∞	0	5.0

TABLE 6.1
The Time Path of Income in Response to a
$1 Billion Increase in Investment When $C_x = .8$
(in billions of dollars)

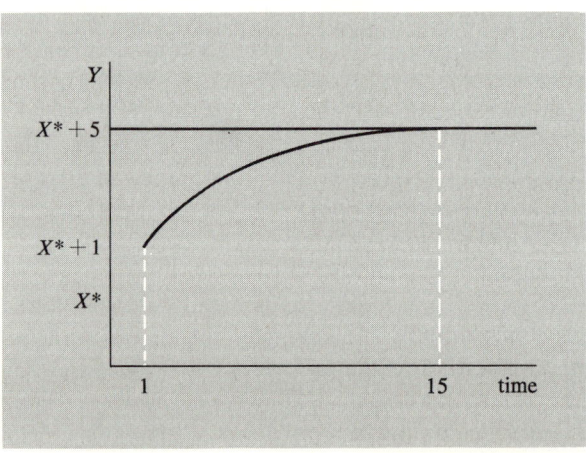

FIGURE 6.4
The Response of Income to a Once-and-for-All
Change in Investment: The Stable Case

Chapter 6 · The Keynesian Cross: A Simple but Incomplete Model

C_x	$1/(1 - C_x)$
.5	2.0
.6	2.5
.7	3.33
.8	5.0
.9	10.0
.95	20.0
.99	100.0
1.0	∞
1.1	−10

TABLE 6.2
The Value of the Multiplier for Alternative Values of C_x

To develop the implications of this counterintuitive reversal in the sign of the multiplier, we will do a dynamic analysis of the case where $C_x > 1$. The result for $C_x = 1.2$ is reported in Table 6.3 and depicted in Figure 6.5. Note that the increments in income become progressively larger rather than progressively smaller in this case. Therefore, the changes in income do not converge to zero and the cumulative change does not converge to some finite value. Instead, income increases in an *unbounded* fashion in the *opposite* direction from the new equilibrium. We refer to systems where endogenous variables do not converge to their equilibrium following some disturbance as *unstable systems*. Conversely, systems in which endogenous variables do converge to their equilibrium values following disturbances are called *stable systems*.

Period	Δ Income	Cumulative Δ
1	1.0	1.0
2	1.2	2.2
3	1.44	3.64
4	1.728	5.368
5	2.0736	7.4416
∞	∞	∞

TABLE 6.3
The Time Path of Income in Response to a
$1 Billion Increase in Investment When $C_x = 1.2$
(in billions of dollars)

In Figure 6.6 we show stable and unstable cases of the Keynesian cross diagram. In the stable case, the disequilibrium response always moves the system in the direction of equilibrium. For example, if income is above the equilibrium ($X_0 > \tilde{X}$), there will be excess supply in the output market ($X > X^d$) and firms will have an incentive to reduce output ($\dot{X} < 0$). In the unstable case, on the other hand, the disequilibrium response moves the system away from the equilibrium. If income is at X_0 in Figure 6.6b, there is excess demand in the commodity market ($X^d > X$) and producers

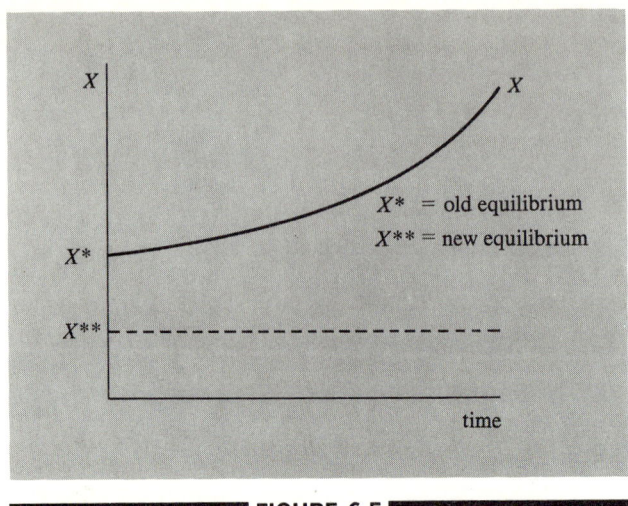

FIGURE 6.5
The Response of Income to a Once-and-for-All
Change in Investment: The Unstable Case

respond by increasing output ($\dot{X} > 0$), moving the system progressively further and further from equilibrium.

The new equilibrium in the unstable case is not very interesting because the system does not even move in the direction of the new equilibrium. Because comparative statics yields information about equilibrium values only and not about the time path in response to disturbances, it is useless in the analysis of the response of income to disturbances in such cases.

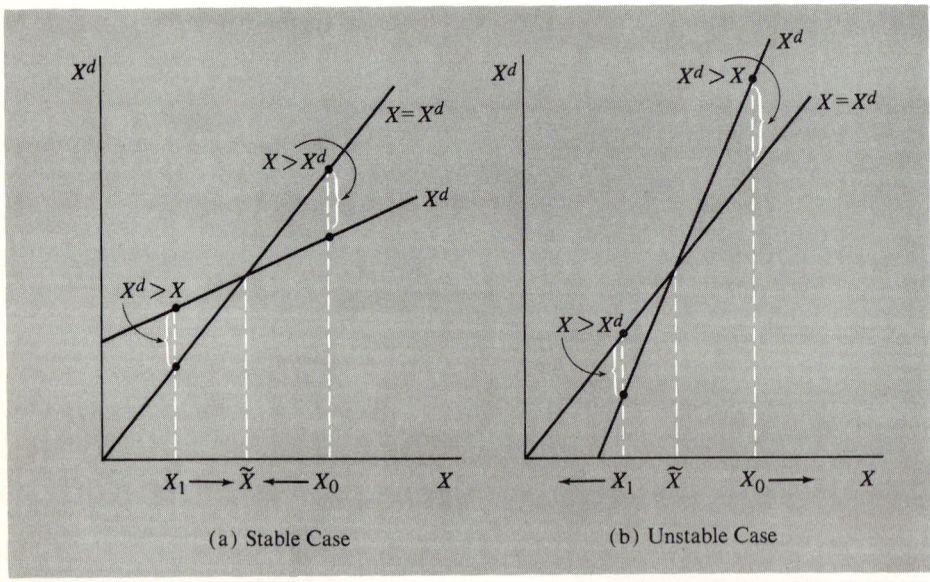

FIGURE 6.6
The Stability of the Keynesian Cross Model

Chapter 6 • The Keynesian Cross: A Simple but Incomplete Model

Comparative statics is only a useful approach to analyzing the response to disturbances in stable systems. Therefore, it is important to analyze the stability of the system before undertaking comparative static analysis. This illustrates the *correspondence principle,* introduced by Paul A. Samuelson: ". . . the problem of stability of equilibrium is intimately tied up with the problem of deriving fruitful theorems in comparative statics. This duality constitutes . . . the *correspondence principle.*"[1]

We can use the dynamic analysis in two alternative ways. First, we can determine the conditions under which the model will be stable and judge whether or not these conditions are likely to be fulfilled. In the present model, the stability condition is $b < 1$. We noted in Chapter 4 that the theory underlying the simple consumption function suggests that $b \equiv C_x$ should be a positive number between zero and one and that empirical evidence confirms this. Therefore, if this model accurately reflects the income determination process, comparative statics will yield fruitful insights about the response of income to disturbances. A second use of dynamics is to impose restrictions on parameters to insure stability when observation of the behavior of the economy suggests that it corresponds to a stable system. In this case, the stability of the model requires $b < 1$ and we could impose this restriction even if the theory underlying the consumption function was ambiguous about whether b was greater or less than one. However, we should be cautious about rejecting all unstable cases as being unreasonable. We will see in Chapter 15 that unstable models provide a possible explanation of business cycle behavior when combined with constraints on the magnitude of upward and downward movements (floors and ceilings).

ADDING THE GOVERNMENT SECTOR

We now expand the model to include government expenditures (G) and tax payments net of transfer payments (T)—both assumed to be exogenous. The *GNP* identity is now

$$X \equiv C + I + G \tag{6.15}$$

and the consumption function is respecified in terms of disposable rather than total income, where disposable income (Y) is defined as

$$Y \equiv X - T. \tag{6.16}$$

The consumption function is

$$C = C(Y) \tag{6.17}$$

or

$$C = \bar{C} + C_y Y. \tag{6.17'}$$

The household budget identity in this case is $Y \equiv C + S$.

---

[1] Paul A. Samuelson, *Foundations of Economic Analysis* (Cambridge, Mass.: Harvard University Press, 1947), p. 258.

○ Two Versions of the Equilibrium Condition

The equilibrium condition can be written either as

$$X = C(Y) + \bar{I} + \bar{G} \tag{6.18a}$$

or as

$$X - C(Y) = \bar{I} + \bar{G}. \tag{6.18b}$$

Equation (6.18a) expresses the equilibrium condition in terms of equality of supply and demand for output. Equation (6.18b) demonstrates that this is equivalent to requiring that the portion of output which households do not demand is just equal to the demand for output by the business and government sectors. Households do not demand all of output because (1) the income available to purchase output (disposable income) is less than the total value of output (i.e., $Y < X$ because $T > 0$) and (2) households desire to save a fraction of their disposable income. The left-hand side of equation (6.18b) can be rewritten as

$$X - C(Y) \equiv \underbrace{(X - Y)}_{(1)} + \underbrace{[Y - C(Y)]}_{(2)}$$

to highlight the two reasons why households do not demand all the output. From the definition of disposable income we know that $X - Y \equiv T$ and from the household budget identity we know $Y - C(Y) \equiv S(Y)$; therefore, equation (6.18b) can be rewritten as

$$S(Y) + \bar{T} = \bar{I} + \bar{G}. \tag{6.18b'}$$

Defining government saving (Sg) as government receipts (Tx) minus expenditures ($Tr + G$),

$$Sg \equiv T - G \tag{6.19}$$

where $T \equiv Tx - Tr$, equation (6.18b) can be rewritten as

$$S(Y) + \overline{Sg} = \bar{I}. \tag{6.18b''}$$

Note that $S(Y) + \overline{Sg} \equiv X - C(Y) - \bar{G}$. Therefore, equation (6.18b'') requires that the portion of output not demanded by households *and* government must be demanded by businesses in equilibrium.

○ Solving the Model

There are three exogenous variables in the model now, $\bar{I}$, $\bar{T}$, and $\bar{G}$, along with the autonomous component of consumption, $\bar{C}$. The reduced-form equation for X

can be derived by substituting for Y in equation (6.18a) [assuming $C(Y)$ is linear in Y] and solving for X.

$$X = \bar{C} + C_y(X - \bar{T}) + \bar{I} + \bar{G}$$

$$X = \frac{1}{1 - C_y} \bar{C} + \frac{1}{1 - C_y} \bar{I} + \frac{1}{1 - C_y} \bar{G} - \frac{C_y}{1 - C_y} \bar{T} \tag{6.20}$$

The multiplier for G is the same as that for the autonomous component of consumption ($\bar{C}$) and exogenous investment ($\bar{I}$). The multiplier for $\bar{T}$ is of the opposite sign and smaller in absolute value than the multipliers for $\bar{I}$, $\bar{C}$, and $\bar{G}$.

Assuming $T = 20$, and $G = 30$, the X^d curve in the Keynesian cross diagram, Figure 6.7, becomes

$$X^d = 70 + .8(X - 20) = 54 + .8X.$$

Equilibrium occurs at $X = 270$. This can be confirmed by substituting in equation (6.20).

$$X = 5[15 + 25 + 30 + -.8(20)] = 270$$

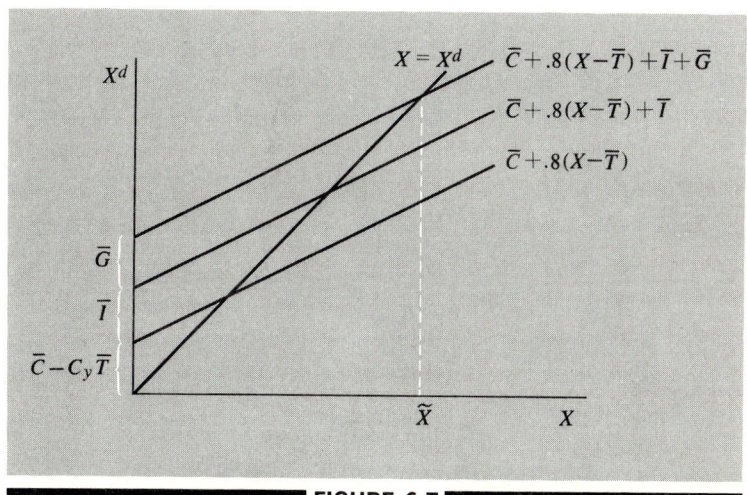

FIGURE 6.7
Income Determination with the Government Sector Included

The direct impact of a dollar change in $\bar{G}$, $\bar{C}$, and $\bar{I}$ on aggregate demand and hence income is one dollar. In terms of the Keynesian cross diagram, a one-dollar change in $\bar{C}$, $\bar{I}$, or $\bar{G}$ shifts the X^d curve up by one dollar at each level of X. The direct impact of a one-dollar change in $\bar{T}$ is on Y and its initial impact on X is via C. A one-dollar decrease in $\bar{T}$ increases Y by one dollar, but a one-dollar increase in Y increases C by only C_y dollars where $1 > C_y > 0$; a decrease in T of one dollar, therefore, shifts the X^d curve upward by only C_y dollars at each value of X.

Part II · Comparative Static Analysis with the Basic Model

The C_y in the numerator of the multiplier for $\bar{T}$ represents the *direct impact* (meaning initial or first-round impact) of a change in $\bar{T}$ on aggregate demand and hence income. The total effect is this first-round impact times the basic multiplier for the model, $\left(\frac{1}{1-C_y}\right)$. This basic multiplier summarizes the income-induced or feedback responses and is independent of how the initial impact on income arises. We always write the multipliers so that the parameters that control the direct impact appear in the numerator and the parameters that control the feedback response appear in the denominator. One over the denominator [e.g., $1/(1 - C_y)$, in this case] is always the basic model multiplier which is applied to all first-round impacts to determine the total effect of each exogenous disturbance.

○ The Balanced-Budget Multiplier

There is a special case of interest—the effect of an increase in government expenditures financed by an equal increase in tax payments. This is called *balanced-budget fiscal policy* (as opposed to deficit-financed fiscal policy). To derive the *balanced-budget multiplier*, we note from equation (6.20) that, assuming $\Delta \bar{C} = \Delta \bar{I} = 0$,

$$\Delta X = \frac{1}{1-C_y}\Delta G - \frac{C_y}{1-C_y}\Delta T.$$

For a balanced-budget fiscal operation, $\Delta G = \Delta T$; therefore,

$$\Delta X = \frac{1-C_y}{1-C_y}\Delta G = \Delta G. \tag{6.21}$$

A tax-financed increase in G increases income by the amount of the increase in G. The balanced-budget multiplier is one!

$$\frac{\Delta X}{\Delta G} = 1$$

Taxes and government expenditures have different first-round impacts; therefore, equal changes in G and T alter the equilibrium level of income. The direct impact of a one-dollar increase in G is one dollar. The direct impact of a one-dollar increase in T is $-C_y$ dollars. The net first-round impact on income of one-dollar increases in G and T is therefore $1 - C_y$. This times the basic multiplier is the total effect of the operation. Consider the definition of disposable income. Equal increases in G and T will leave Y unaffected. The increase in G directly increases X^d and hence initially increases X by an equal amount. The increase in T just offsets the initial increase in X so that Y remains unchanged. If Y remains unchanged, C also remains unchanged. I is exogenous. Therefore, X^d and hence X increase dollar-for-dollar with the increase in G. This result is independent of the value of C_y. The result that equal changes in G and T affect equilibrium income is a general one, applicable to all the models we consider. The result that income increases dollar-for-dollar with the increase in G and T, however, is specific to the present model.

○ Built-In Stability

Tax revenues were treated as an exogenous variable above. A more accurate modeling of tax revenues is to treat tax *rates* as fixed parameters and tax *revenues* as a function of income. A simple approach is to assume a proportional income tax.

$$T = tX \qquad (6.22)$$

where t is the tax rate and $1 > t > 0$. Adding this equation to our model and solving for X yields

$$X = \bar{C} + C_y(X - tX) + \bar{I} + \bar{G}$$
$$X = \bar{C} + (1 - t)C_y X + \bar{I} + \bar{G}$$
$$X = (1 - t)C_y X + \bar{C} + \bar{I} + \bar{G}$$

$$X = \frac{1}{1 - (1 - t)C_y}(\bar{C} + \bar{I} + \bar{G}). \qquad (6.23)$$

Note that T no longer appears among the exogenous variables on the right of the reduced-form equation and that t now enters the multiplier that applies to each of the exogenous components of aggregate demand.

The multiplier with endogenous tax revenues is unambiguously smaller than the multiplier with exogenous tax revenue:

$$\frac{1}{1 - (1 - t)C_y} < \frac{1}{1 - C_y}.$$

This reflects the role of endogenous tax revenues as an automatic or *built-in stabilizer.* Consider the economy's response to an autonomous decline in investment. If tax revenues are exogenous, GNP and disposable income initially fall dollar-for-dollar with investment, and as consumption declines, GNP and disposable income decline further. When tax revenues are proportional to income, GNP initially declines dollar-for-dollar with investment, but the decline in disposable income is moderated by the fall in tax revenues. Disposable income falls by less than GNP, so consumption declines by less. The net result is a smaller income-induced decline in consumption and a smaller displacement of income from its initial position. The multiplier in this model is based entirely on a positive feedback response (a single positive income-induced effect on aggregate demand). The existence of built-in stability reduces the positive feedback and thereby reduces the model multiplier.

Income-Induced Investment

Up to this point we have treated investment as exogenous. One simple model of investment that we could include easily in the Keynesian cross model allows for income-induced investment.

$$I = \bar{I} + I_x X \tag{6.24}$$

where $I_x > 0$. One rationale for income-induced investment is the hypothesis that investment depends on profits and profits depend on the overall level of economic activity. We will discuss income-induced investment further in Chapters 14 and 15. Here we simply explore its implications in this model. It should be clear that adding income-induced investment increases the positive feedback and therefore increases the response of output to disturbances. Note however that it also increases the possibility that the model will be unstable. To see this, solve for the reduced form.

$$X \equiv C + I + G$$
$$X = \bar{C} + C_y(X - \bar{T}) + \bar{I} + I_x X + \bar{G}$$
$$X - C_y X - I_x X = \bar{C} - C_y \bar{T} + \bar{I} + \bar{G}$$

$$X = \frac{1}{1 - C_y - I_x}(\bar{C} - C_y \bar{T} + \bar{I} + \bar{G}) \tag{6.25}$$

The multiplier is larger than if $I_x = 0$ provided that $C_y + I_x < 1$. If $C_y + I_x > 1$, the model is unstable and comparative static multipliers no longer are meaningful.

REVIEW QUESTIONS

1. "Saving equals investment. An increase in saving (decline in consumption) is therefore always matched by an increase in investment so that aggregate demand and aggregate supply are *always* equal." Comment.

2. Explain the meaning of comparative statics and contrast this type of analysis with dynamics.

3. Why is it important to determine that the model is stable before employing comparative static analysis?

PROBLEMS

1. Find the equilibrium levels of income and consumption and the multipliers for changes in government expenditures, taxes, and autonomous investment for the following model.

Chapter 6 • The Keynesian Cross: A Simple but Incomplete Model

$$X \equiv C + I + G$$
$$C = \bar{C} + C_y Y$$
$$Y \equiv X - T$$

Assume $\bar{C} = 100$, $G = 200$, $\bar{T} = 175$, $\bar{I} = 150$, and $C_y = .8$.

2. Now assume that investment varies with the level of income

$$I = \bar{I} + I_x X$$

where $\bar{I}$ is the autonomous component of investment and $I_x > 0$. The consumption function, GNP, and disposable income identities are the same as in problem 1. Solve for the reduced form for income. Assuming $I_x = .1$, compare the basic multiplier to the one derived in problem 1.

3. Assume that $C_y = 1.2$ in the model presented in problem 1. What is the multiplier for an increase in investment? Explain.

4. Now assume that taxes are proportional to income in the model in problem 1; i.e., $T = tX$. Let $t = .4$ and $C_y = 1.2$. Find the income multiplier for a change in investment in this case and explain the difference from the result in problem 3.

5. The following equations were estimated over the 1960–1966 period:

$$C = 2.48 + 0.91 Y$$
$$Y = -2.38 + 0.70 X$$

where C is consumption, X is GNP, and Y is disposable income. What behavioral and/or technical relations does each equation describe? Assuming both government expenditures and investment are exogenous, derive the multiplier for an increase in government expenditures on GNP.

6. Use the following information to construct an economic model. Assume all behavioral relations are linear.

Consumption (C) is positively related to disposable income (Y); there is also an autonomous component ($\bar{C}$). Disposable income is defined as GNP (X) minus corporate profits (π) plus dividends (DIV) minus personal taxes (T). Corporate profits are a function of GNP; the higher the GNP, the higher the level of corporate profits. Corporations pay out a a fixed proportion of profits in dividends and a fixed proportion goes to the government in corporation income tax payments (Tc). Corporate profits remaining after dividends and corporate income tax payments are called undistributed profits (π^u). Investment (I) depends positively on undistributed profits; there is also an autonomous component ($\bar{I}$). Personal taxes are positively related to GNP; there is also an autonomous component ($\bar{T}$). GNP is the sum of consumption, investment, and government expenditures on goods and services (G). Government expenditures on goods and services are exogenous.

(a) Construct an economic model from the above information. Write down an explicit equation for each of the economic relationships described. Indicate which variables are exogenous and which are endogenous. Identify the signs of all the parameters. Specify what type of relationship each equation is (e.g., behavioral, technical, identity, equilibrium, etc.).

(b) Derive the reduced-form equation for *GNP*.

(c) Use the following values of parameters and values of exogenous variables to determine the value of the multipliers in your reduced-form equation for *GNP* and the equilibrium levels of income, consumption, and investment.

—The marginal propensity to consume out of disposable income is .80.
—There is an autonomous component of consumption, set initially at $75 billion.
—The marginal personal tax rate is .25.
—There is an autonomous component of personal taxes = $50 billion.
—Profits are 10 percent of *GNP*.
—Corporations pay out 25 percent of profits in dividends.
—The marginal and average corporate tax rate is 50 percent.
—Each $1 increment in undistributed corporate profits induces $4 of investment.
—There is an autonomous component of investment = $75 billion.
—Government expenditures = $250 billion.

7. According to the paradox of thrift, an attempt to increase saving may result in a decline in saving. Verify whether or not this is possible in the Keynesian cross model; use the *KC* model with autonomous investment and then use the *KC* model with income-induced investment (i.e., $I = \bar{I} + I_x X$). Support your answer with either a mathematical or a graphical solution of the model for the response of equilibrium saving to an autonomous increase in desired saving. (Hint: The saving function is $S = \bar{S} + S_y Y$. The question concerns the response of S to an increase in $\bar{S}$, the autonomous component of saving.)

8. "The balanced-budget multiplier is always unity." Verify this quote with respect to the two versions of the Keynesian cross model identified in problem 7 (with autonomous investment and with income-induced investment).

9. Assume the government decides to use fiscal policy to achieve a target level of income X^T, equal to $2,500. Find the change in

(a) government expenditures (holding tax revenues constant) and

(b) taxes (holding G constant) that would be consistent with achieving X^T.

(c) Is there a unique value of the change in the government budget deficit $(G - T)$ that would be consistent with achieving X^T? Why or why not?

(d) If not, derive the expression for the combinations of changes in G and T just consistent with achieving X^T.

10. (a) Assume that Congress passes a law requiring the Administration to conduct fiscal policy so as to maintain a balanced budget. The government decides to vary the level of government expenditures in order to maintain G equal to tax revenues (which will vary with income). Find the value of the investment multiplier in this case.

(b) Now assume that the government decides to maintain G at a fixed level ($\bar{G} = 200$) and vary tax rates to maintain tax revenues equal to $\bar{G}$. Find the investment multiplier and the government expenditure multiplier. Can you explain the size of the government expenditures multiplier?

(c) Compare the following four cases:

(1) $T = \bar{T}$ (as in problem 1)
(2) $T = tX$ (as in problem 4)
(3) G set to equal tax revenue (as in problem 10a)
(4) t set to raise revenue equal to G (as in problem 10b)

Which case has the greatest built-in stability? Include a precise definition of built-in stability. Which is least stable? Explain your conclusions. Would you recommend that Congress pass such legislation?

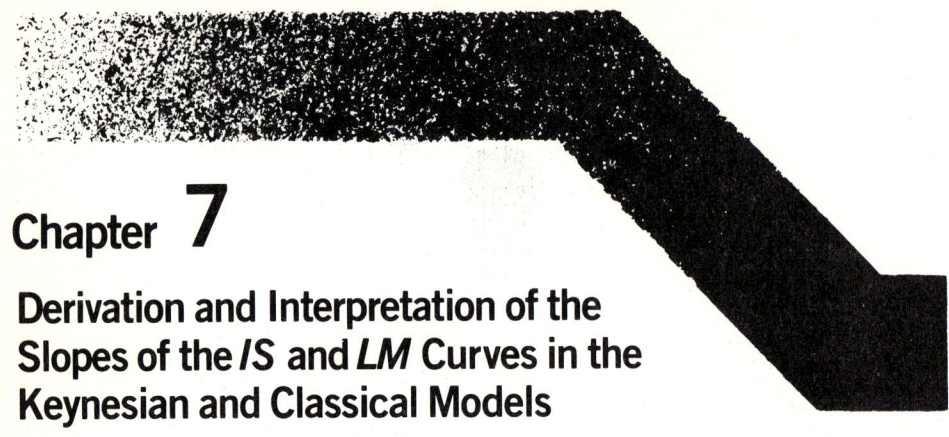

Chapter 7

Derivation and Interpretation of the Slopes of the *IS* and *LM* Curves in the Keynesian and Classical Models

Chapters 7 and 8 develop the graphical approach (*IS* and *LM* curves) to the analysis of the Keynesian and classical versions of our model. Recall from Chapter 5 that our basic model developed in Chapter 4 can be reduced to two alternative models of two equations and two unknowns. The Keynesian version treats the nominal wage and the price level as exogenous variables and is used to solve for the equilibrium values of output and the interest rate. The classical version treats the equilibrium values of employment and output as predetermined variables and is used to solve for equilibrium values of the price level and the interest rate. In each version the two equations used to solve for the two unknowns are the equilibrium condition in the output market (the *IS* curve) and the equilibrium condition in the money market (the *LM* curve).

In this chapter we introduce the *IS* and *LM* equations for both the Keynesian and classical versions and derive the slopes of the curves which graphically depict these equations. In the next chapter we will discuss the exogenous variables which determine the positions of the *IS* and *LM* curves. To simplify the solution of the model in Part II, we initially assume that there are no wealth effects in either the consumption or money demand functions; i.e., $C_a = 0$ and $L_a = 0$. We will relax these assumptions in Part III (for C_a) and Part IV (for L_a). We employ the discrete end-of-period specification of the model, although the continuous, beginning-of-period and end-of-period specifications yield identical multipliers when $C_a = 0$ and $L_a = 0$ for all disturbances and policy changes except money-financed changes in G or T.

○ KEYNESIAN MODEL

The Keynesian model consists of two equations (the equilibrium conditions in the commodity and money markets) and two unknowns (r and X). The *IS* and *LM* curves depict the combinations of the two unknowns that are consistent with commodity and money market equilibrium, respectively.[1] We can see from Figure 7.1 that although there are many combinations of r and X consistent with commodity market equilibrium (all combinations of r and X along the *IS* curve) and many combinations consistent with money market equilibrium (all the points along the *LM* curve), there will only be one combination of r and X consistent with *simultaneous* equilibrium in the commodity and money markets. This combination is the equilibrium values of r and X, r^* and X^*, in Figure 7.1.

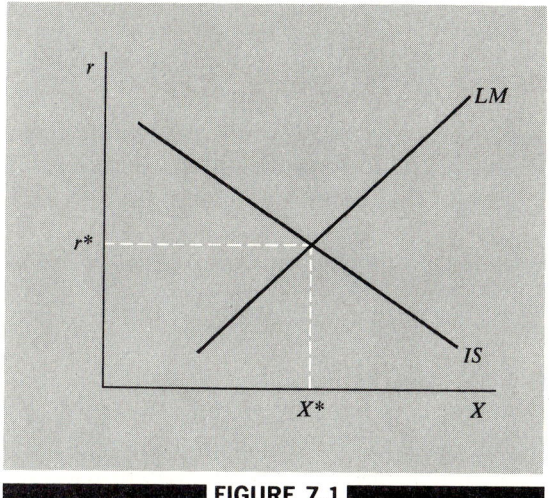

FIGURE 7.1
IS and *LM* Curves for the Keynesian Model

The essential insight to understanding *IS-LM* analysis, then, is that each curve corresponds to equilibrium in one of the markets and that equilibrium of the economy requires *simultaneous* equilibrium in both markets (which will also imply equilibrium in the excluded bond market, as we know from our analysis in Chapter 5). Simultaneous equilibrium, in turn, requires a solution for the unknowns which lies on *both IS* and *LM* curves; e.g., in Figure 7.1, r^* and X^* are the only combination of r and X consistent with simultaneous equilibrium in the money and commodity markets. In Chapter 5 we discussed the conditions under which a system of equations (or curves) would yield a unique solution for the unknowns. We determined that equality of equations and unknowns was a necessary and sufficient condition when the two equations were linear, consistent, and independent, as is the case in our Keynesian *IS-LM* model. This property of *IS-LM* analysis is illustrated by the single intersection of the *IS* and *LM* curves in Figure 7.1.

In this section we will explain the *slope* of the Keynesian *IS* and *LM* curves. Next, we will consider the slopes of the *IS* and *LM* curves in the classical version. In the following chapter we will discuss the way in which the exogenous variables determine the *positions* of the two curves.

---

[1] The curves are named for the key variables in the two equilibrium conditions: *IS* refers to investment (I)-saving (S) equilibrium and *LM* refers to money demand (L)-money supply (M) equilibrium.

Part II · Comparative Static Analysis with the Basic Model

The *IS* Curve

The *IS* curve is the locus of combinations of r and X which correspond to *equilibrium* in the commodity market for *given values of the exogenous variables* which influence the demand for output (government expenditures, G, taxes net of transfers, T, and the autonomous component of private aggregate demand, Z). For given values of G, T, and Z, the *IS* curve represents the combinations of r and X for which aggregate demand equals aggregate supply or, equivalently, it represents the combinations of r and X for which desired saving equals desired investment. The *IS* curve is given by

$$X = C_y(X - \bar{T}) + I_r r + \bar{Z} + \bar{G}. \tag{7.1}$$

Assuming C_y and I_r are constants, equation (7.1) is the equation for a straight line. To find its slope in the r-X plane, we simply solve equation (7.1) in terms of r.

$$r = \underbrace{\frac{1 - C_y}{I_r}}_{\text{slope}} X - \underbrace{\left[\frac{1}{I_r}(\bar{Z} + \bar{G}) - \frac{C_y}{I_r}\bar{T}\right]}_{\text{intercept}} \tag{7.2}$$

The coefficient of X is the slope of the *IS* curve and the second term is the r-axis intercept. Assuming $1 > C_y > 0$ and $I_r < 0$, the slope of the *IS* curve is negative.

The negative slope means that if r falls, X must rise to restore commodity market equilibrium. Figure 7.2 will help to clarify why the *IS* curve must be negatively sloped. Assume that one position of real sector equilibrium is given by point a. If r declines, aggregate demand will increase because $I_r < 0$; i.e., a decline in r will increase investment and hence aggregate demand. Therefore, there will be excess demand in the output market at point b.[2] In order to restore real sector equilibrium at r_1, X must change so as to eliminate the excess demand gap at b. Note that when X changes, aggregate demand changes in the same direction but by a smaller amount, assuming that $1 > C_y > 0$. This means that increasing X increases aggregate supply by more than it increases aggregate demand. An increase in X, therefore, tends to close the excess demand gap. If the gap is one dollar, X will have to rise by a multiple of one dollar to close the gap. A one-dollar increase in X closes the gap by $1 - C_y$; if $C_y = .8$, a one-dollar rise in X only closes the gap by 20 cents and an increase of X of five dollars will be required to close the gap in full. This is simply a reflection of the multiplier principle.[3] We conclude that r and X must be

---

[2] If $C_y(X_0 - \bar{T}) + I_r(r_0) + \bar{Z} + \bar{G} = X_0$, then $C_y(X_0 - \bar{T}) + I_r(r_1) + \bar{Z} + \bar{G} > X_0$, if $I_r < 0$ and $r_1 < r_0$.

[3] How much will X have to increase to restore equilibrium following a given decline in r? To answer that precisely we have to know the magnitude of the parameters C_y and I_r. We can immediately determine the influence of each parameter on the slope of the curve from equation (7.2). An increase in either C_y or I_r reduces the slope of the *IS* curve. An increase in C_y reduces the extent to which an increase in X closes the excess demand gap; i.e., as aggregate demand rises by more in response to the increase in aggregate supply, aggregate supply will have to increase by more to eliminate any given excess demand gap. Therefore, the change in X required to restore equilibrium at a lower r will be greater, the larger is C_y. An increase in I_r increases the magnitude of the disequilibrium at b; i.e., the larger I_r, the larger the increase in aggregate demand for a given decline in r. The larger the excess demand at b, the greater the change in X required to restore equilibrium in the commodity market.

inversely related along the *IS* curve: a decline in r which increases aggregate demand must be offset by a rise in X which increases output relative to aggregate demand.

Just as all points on the *IS* curve correspond to combinations of r and X which are consistent with commodity market equilibrium, all points off the *IS* curve are associated with either excess demand or excess supply in the commodity market. All points below or to the left of the *IS* curve (such as point b in Figure 7.2) are associated with excess demand, and all points above or to the right of the *IS* curve are associated with excess supply of output.

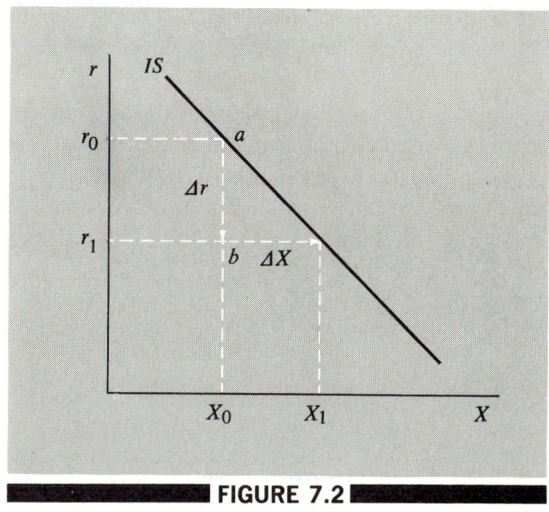

FIGURE 7.2
Keynesian *IS* Curve

○ The *LM* Curve

The *LM* curve is the locus of combinations of r and X consistent with *equilibrium* in the money market, for a constant level of the real money supply, $\bar{m}$, and the autonomous component of the real demand for money, $\bar{L}$; i.e., it represents the combinations of r and X for which the real demand for money equals the exogenously given real money supply. The *LM* curve is given by equation (7.3).

$$\bar{m} = L_r r + L_x X + \bar{L} \tag{7.3}$$

Assuming L_x and L_r are constants, equation (7.3) is a straight line in the r-X plane. Solving in terms of r yields

$$r = -\underbrace{\frac{L_x}{L_r}}_{\text{slope}} X + \underbrace{\frac{1}{L_r}(\bar{m} - \bar{L})}_{\text{intercept}}. \tag{7.3'}$$

The coefficient of X is the slope of the *LM* curve and the second term on the right is the r-axis intercept. Assuming $L_r < 0$ and $L_x > 0$, the *LM* curve is positively sloped.

The positive slope of the *LM* curve implies that if X increases, r must also increase to maintain equilibrium in the money market at a constant level of $\bar{m}$ and $\bar{L}$. Assume that one point of equilibrium in the monetary sector occurs at the combination of r_0 and X_0 (point *a*) in Figure 7.3. If X were to increase to X_1 while r remained at r_0, the money market would no longer be in equilibrium. As $L_x > 0$, an increase in X increases the demand for money relative to the fixed supply. Point *b* corresponding to the combination of r_0 and X_1 is therefore a position of excess demand in the money market.[4] To restore equilibrium at the higher value of X, r must increase because an increase in r will reduce the demand for money ($L_r < 0$).[5] We conclude that r and X must be positively related along the *LM* curve: an increase in X which raises the demand for money must be offset by an increase in r which reduces the demand for money.

Just as all points on the *LM* curve correspond to combinations of r and X which are consistent with money market equilibrium, all points off the *LM* curve are associated with either excess supply or excess demand in the money market. All points below or to the right of the *LM* curve (such as point *b* in Figure 7.3) are positions of excess demand and all points above or to the left of the *LM* curve are positions of excess supply.

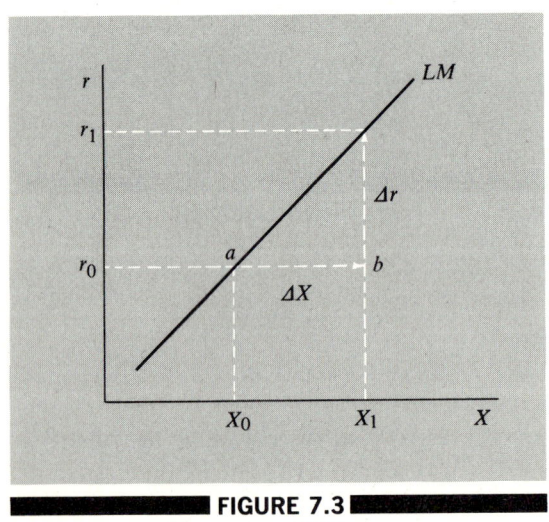

FIGURE 7.3
Keynesian *LM* Curve

CLASSICAL MODEL

The classical model also consists of two equations (the equilibrium conditions in the commodity and money markets) and two unknowns (r and P). Although the

---

[4] Assuming that $L(r_0, X_0) = \bar{m}$ at point *a*, $L(r_0, X_1) > \bar{m}$ at point *b* if $L_x > 0$ and $X_1 > X_0$.

[5] How much must r rise to close the gap between supply and demand? The answer depends on the precise values of L_x and L_r. The larger L_x, the greater disequilibrium associated with the rise in X to X_1 and therefore, given L_r, the greater the rise in r required to restore equilibrium. The smaller L_r, the smaller the change in the demand for money for a given change in r; therefore, the larger the change in r required to bring about any given change in the demand for money.

LM curve is nonlinear in this case, we generally expect a unique solution for the unknowns, or in terms of Figure 7.4, a single intersection between the *IS* and *LM* curves.

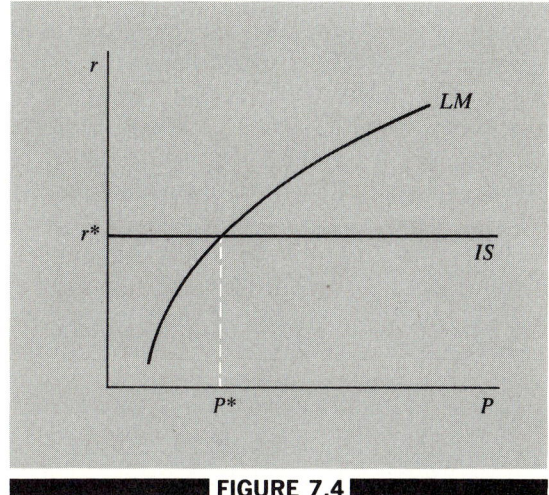

FIGURE 7.4
The *IS* and *LM* Curves in the Classical Model

The *IS* and *LM* curves in the classical model are, as in the Keynesian model, the combinations of the two unknowns consistent with equilibrium in the commodity and money markets, respectively. As we will demonstrate below, there is only one interest rate consistent with commodity market equilibrium, and commodity market equilibrium is completely independent of the price level. Therefore, the *IS* curve is shown as a horizontal line at the unique equilibrium interest rate, r^*. On the other hand, there are numerous combinations of r and P consistent with money market equilibrium (all points along the *LM* curve). And there is only one combination of r and P compatible with *simultaneous equilibrium* in the commodity and money markets; i.e., one pair of r and P that is on both *IS* and *LM* curves: r^* and P^* in Figure 7.4.

In this section we explain the slopes of the classical *IS* and *LM* curves. In the next chapter we discuss the way in which the exogenous variables determine the positions of the two curves.

○ The *IS* Curve

The *IS* curve is now the locus of combinations of r and P consistent with equilibrium in the commodity market, given the level of output, the level of real government expenditures, real taxes, and real autonomous private demand. As output is predetermined at the full employment level in the classical model, the *IS* curve represents the combinations of r and P for which the total demand for output equals the fixed aggregate supply. Alternatively, it represents the combinations of r and P for which desired real saving at the full employment level of output equals desired real investment.

The *IS* curve for the classical model is given by the equation

$$\bar{X}_f = C_y(\bar{X}_f - \bar{T}) + I_r r + \bar{Z} + \bar{G}. \tag{7.4}$$

Note that P does not appear in equation (7.4). There is one equation and one unknown; therefore, equation (7.4) can generally be solved for a unique value of r. If the IS curve is of the form given by equation (7.4), there is a unique equilibrium interest rate determined exclusively by real sector forces in the classical model. The IS curve corresponding to equation (7.4) will be a horizontal line at the equilibrium interest rate (as depicted in Figure 7.5). This indicates that changes in the price level have no effect on the real sector; i.e., given X_f, T, and G, the real sector can be in equilibrium at any price level as long as $r = r_0$. All points below the IS curve are points of excess demand; all points above the IS curve are points of excess supply.

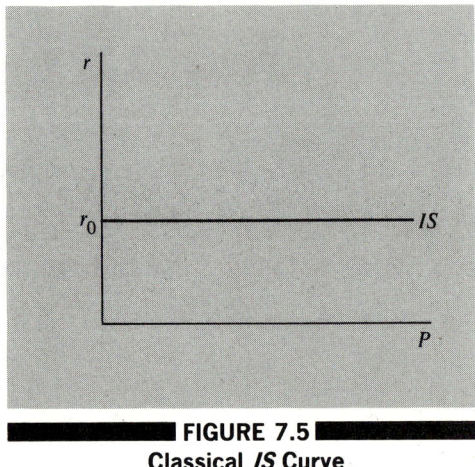

FIGURE 7.5
Classical IS Curve

○ The LM Curve

The LM curve is the locus of combinations of r and P consistent with equilibrium in the money market for given values of the nominal money supply, $\bar{M}$, and the autonomous component of the real demand for money, $\bar{L}$. It represents the combinations of r and P for which the real demand for money equals the real supply or, alternatively, the combinations of r and P for which the nominal demand for money equals the exogenous nominal supply.

The LM curve for the classical model is

$$\frac{\bar{M}}{P} = L_r r + L_x \bar{X}_f + \bar{L}. \tag{7.5}$$

Note that the LM curve is nonlinear in the r-P space in the classical model. To find the slope, we must use calculus. Taking the total derivative of equation (7.5) and solving for dr/dP, assuming $d\bar{X}_f = d\bar{M} = d\bar{L} = 0$, yields

$$\left.\frac{dr}{dP}\right|_{LM} = \frac{-M/P^2}{L_r}. \tag{7.6}$$

Assuming $L_r < 0$, the slope is positive. Note that the slope depends on P (reflecting the nonlinearity of the relation).

The positive slope indicates that if r increases, P must also rise to maintain equilibrium in the money market with a constant nominal money supply. Assume that the combination of r_0 and P_0 (point a) in Figure 7.6 corresponds to an equilibrium position in the money market. If the interest rate increased to r_1 but the price level remained unchanged, the money market would be out of equilibrium at point b. An increase in r reduces the real demand for money relative to the unchanged real supply; alternatively, it reduces the nominal demand relative to the fixed nominal supply.[6] Point b is therefore a position of excess supply of money. To restore equilibrium, P must rise because an increase in P reduces the real supply relative to the real demand for money or, alternatively, the increase in P increases the nominal demand relative to the fixed nominal supply.[7] We conclude that r and P must be

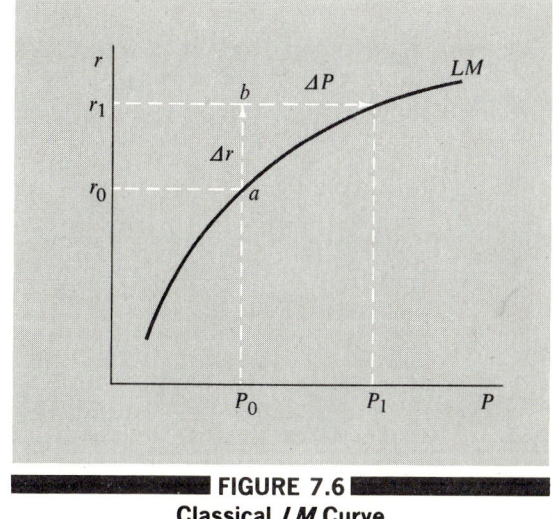

FIGURE 7.6
Classical LM Curve

---

[6] If $\frac{M}{P_0} = L_r r_0 = L_x X_f + \bar{L}$ at point a, then $\frac{M}{P_0} > L_r r_1 + L_x \bar{X}_f + \bar{L}$ at point b, if $r_1 > r_0$ and $L_r < 0$.

[7] How much must P rise? That depends on the change in r, the initial level of P, the initial level of M, and the magnitude of L_r. The smaller L_r, the smaller the excess supply of money due to a given change in the rate of interest; therefore, the smaller the change in P required to reequilibrate the money market.

The smaller the M, the larger the change in P required to restore equilibrium following a given change in r. This reflects the fact that the smaller the M, the smaller the change in the real money supply (M/P) for any given change in P; therefore, the larger the change in P required to achieve a given change in the real money supply.

The smaller the initial P, the smaller the change in P required to restore equilibrium. This reflects the fact that the smaller the P, the greater the change in the real money supply associated with a given change in P; therefore, the smaller the change in P required to produce a given change in the real money supply.

positively related along the classical *LM* curve: an increase in r which reduces the real demand for money must be offset by a rise in P which reduces the real supply of money. All points below or to the right of the *LM* curve are positions of excess demand and all points above or to the left of the *LM* curve are positions of excess supply in the money market.

…
Chapter 7 • Slopes of *IS* and *LM* Curves in Keynesian and Classical Models

APPENDIX

The Slope of the Classical *IS* Curve When There Is a Wealth Effect

The addition of a wealth term including outside financial assets fixed in nominal value to the consumption function alters the slope of the *IS* curve. The *IS* curve in the case is given by

$$\bar{X}_f = C_y(\bar{X}_f - \bar{T}) + C_a a + I_r r + \bar{Z} + \bar{G}. \tag{7A.1}$$

We employ the beginning-of-period specification where nominal wealth of households (A) is exogenous and define real wealth as

$$a = \frac{\bar{A}}{P}. \tag{7A.2}$$

To derive the slope of the *IS* curve corresponding to equation (7A.1), take the total derivative of equation (7A.1) and solve for dr/dP. $d\bar{X}_f = d\bar{A} = d\bar{G} = d\bar{T} = 0$ because X, A, T, and G are exogenous. This yields

$$\left.\frac{dr}{dP}\right|_{IS} = \frac{-C_a \bar{A}/P^2}{I_r}. \tag{7A.3}$$

Assuming $C_a > 0$, $I_r < 0$, and $\bar{A} > 0$, the slope of the *IS* curve is negative, and the *IS* curve will be nonlinear even if C_a and I_r are constants.[1]

To clarify why the *IS* curve is negatively sloped when $\bar{A} > 0$ and $C_a > 0$, assume one combination of r and P consistent with real sector equilibrium, given $\bar{A}$, $\bar{T}$, $\bar{Z}$, and $\bar{G}$, is r_0 and P_0 (point *a*) in Figure 7A.1. If the interest rate were at r_1 rather than r_0, there would be excess demand in the output market since a lower interest rate implies a larger aggregate demand.[2] What must happen to P to restore equilibrium in the output market? The supply of output is fixed. P must change to reduce aggregate demand so that it is again equal to the fixed supply of output. An increase in P will reduce aggregate demand via the wealth effect; as P increases, the real value of net private wealth, a, declines, and as $C_a > 0$, the decline in a generates a decline in aggregate demand.[3]

---

[1] This means that even if we assume that the aggregate demand function is linear in its arguments, as we have written it in equation (7A.1), the *IS* curve will be nonlinear in the *r-P* space. Because of this nonlinearity, we cannot derive the slope of the *IS* curve algebraically.

[2] If $C_y(\bar{X}_f - \bar{T}) + C_a \left(\frac{\bar{A}}{P_0}\right) + I_r r_0 + \bar{Z} + \bar{G} = \bar{X}_f$ at point *a*, then $C_y(\bar{X}_f - \bar{T}) + C_a \left(\frac{\bar{A}}{P_0}\right) + I_r r_1 + \bar{Z} + \bar{G} > \bar{X}_f$ at point *b* if $r_1 < r_0$ and $I_r < 0$.

[3] How much must P decline to restore equilibrium? That depends on the size of A, the value of C_a and I_r, and the initial value of P. The larger is I_r, the greater the disequilibrium at *b*. Given the magnitude of the disequilibrium at *b*, the magnitude of the rise in P required to restore equilibrium will be smaller, the larger the values of A and C_a. The larger the value of A, the greater the change in wealth for a given change in P; the larger is C_a, the larger the effect on aggregate demand of a given change in real wealth. In both cases, a smaller change in P will be required to restore equilibrium.

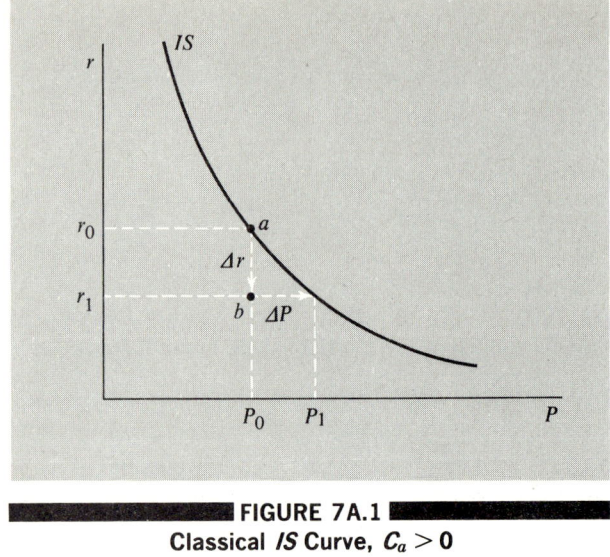

FIGURE 7A.1
Classical *IS* Curve, $C_a > 0$

● REVIEW QUESTIONS

1. What is the difference between the nature of the *IS* and *LM* curves and the supply and demand curves you are familiar with from your introductory micro course?

2. How do you know from Figure 7.1 that the system of equations in the Keynesian model yields a unique solution for the unknowns?

3. What do all points *along* the *IS* curve have in common? What do all points *above* the *IS* curve have in common?

4. Give a clear verbal explanation for the sign of the slope of (a) the *IS* curve and (b) the *LM* curve in the Keynesian model.

5. Why are *r* and *P* rather than *r* and *X* represented on the axes in the classical model *IS-LM* diagram?

6. Give a clear, verbal explanation of the sign of the slopes of (a) the *IS* curve and (b) the *LM* curve in the classical model.

● PROBLEMS

1. Compare the levels of consumption and investment at points *a* and *b* in Figure 1, page 133 (based on the form of the *IS* curve developed in this chapter). Explain.

Chapter 7 · Slopes of *IS* and *LM* Curves in Keynesian and Classical Models

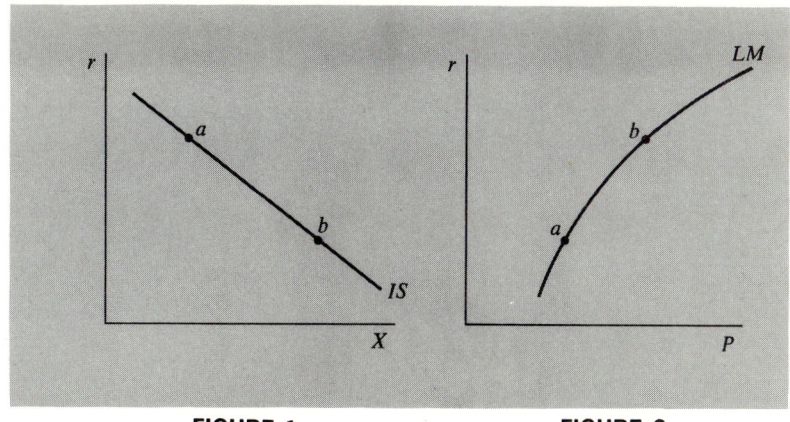

FIGURE 1 **FIGURE 2**

2. What is the relation between the real money supply at points *a* and *b* in Figure 2? Explain.

3. Show the shape of the Keynesian *IS* curve when (a) $I_r = 0$ and (b) $I_r = -\infty$.

4. Show the shape of the Keynesian and classical *LM* curves when (a) $L_r = 0$ and (b) $L_r = -\infty$.

5. Find the slopes of the following *IS* and *LM* curves for the Keynesian version:

    $X = .8Y - 25r + \bar{G} + \bar{Z}$

    $m = .2X - 25r + \bar{L}$

    Find the slope of the following classical *IS* curve:

    $\bar{X} = .8Y - 25r + \bar{G} + \bar{Z}$

6. As income rises, we generally find that interest rates also increase. We can use the slope of the *LM* curve in the Keynesian version to illustrate how our model captures this regularity. Assume that some disturbance unassociated with the supply or demand for money increases income. If income rises by $10 billion, use the slope of the *LM* curve to calculate how much the interest rate must rise to maintain equilibrium in the money market. Use the parameter values employed in problem 5.

7. The monetary authority uses monetary policy (open market operations) to affect aggregate demand by initially influencing the rate of interest. The *IS* curve indicates the relationship between the interest rate and equilibrium income, given exogenous levels of *G*, *T*, and private demand. Use the slope of the *IS* curve derived above to calculate the size of the decline in interest rates required to increase income by $10 billion.

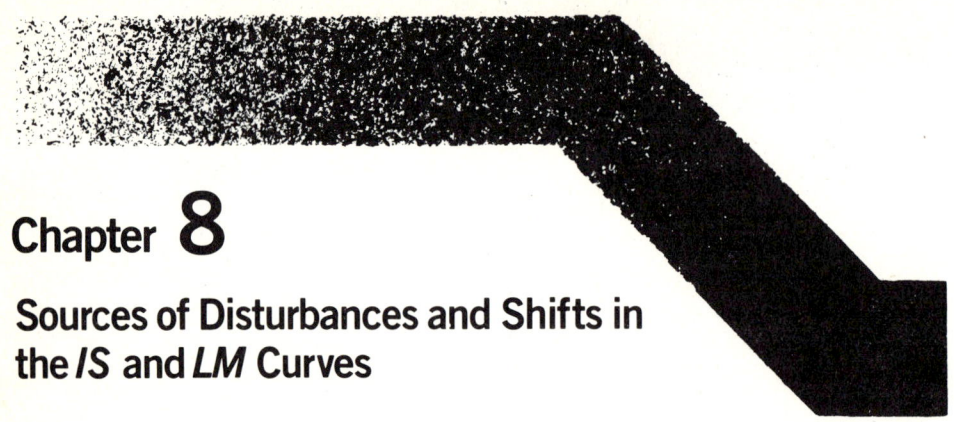

Chapter 8

Sources of Disturbances and Shifts in the *IS* and *LM* Curves

While the parameters of the model determine the *slopes* of the *IS* and *LM* curves, the exogenous variables determine the *positions* of the two curves. Changes in the exogenous variables result in *shifts* in one or both curves. In this chapter we will review the exogenous variables in our models and indicate how each affects the *IS* and *LM* curves.

This chapter develops the graphical technique which we will employ in the next two chapters to uncover the implications of the classical and Keynesian models for the response of the price level, output, and the interest rate to policy changes and nonpolicy disturbances. The methodology used in those chapters is *comparative statics*, discussed previously in Chapter 6. Comparative statics involves a comparison of equilibrium positions before and after a shift in one or more exogenous variables. For example, we might compare equilibriums before and after a change in the money supply. To explore the effects of this change in the *IS-LM* framework, we must first determine how an increase in the money supply shifts the *IS* and/or *LM* curves. In the current specification of our model, an increase in the money supply will shift only the *LM* curve.

The shift in the *LM* curve and the new and old equilibriums in the classical and Keynesian models are depicted in Figures 8.1a and 8.1b. From these figures we can determine that an increase in the money supply leaves the interest rate unchanged and increases the price level in the classical model and increases output and lowers the interest rate in the Keynesian model. We will explain and reconcile these results in Chapters 9 and 10. In this chapter, we devote ourselves to the narrower task of first identifying the exogenous variables whose movements will shift the *IS* and *LM* curves and then explaining how shifts in each exogenous variable affect the positions of the *IS* and *LM* curves.

POLICY INSTRUMENTS AND NONPOLICY DISTURBANCES

Our models include two types of exogenous variables: *policy instruments* and *nonpolicy disturbances*.

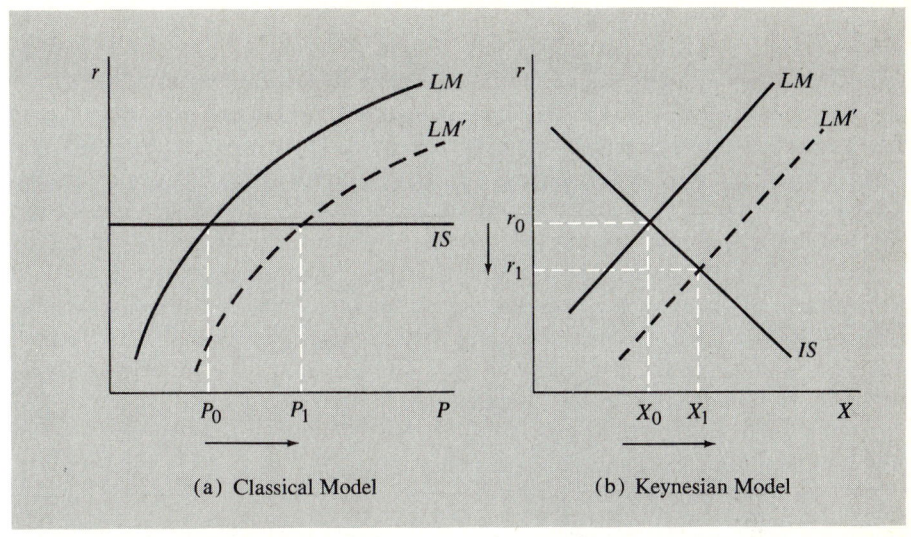

FIGURE 8.1
Comparative Statics with *IS-LM* Analysis:
The Effect of an Increase in the Money Supply

○ Policy Instruments

Policy instruments are variables directly controlled by the government. In our model the policy instruments are real government expenditures on goods and services (G), real tax receipts net of transfer payments (T), and the money supply [the real money supply in the Keynesian model (m) and the nominal money supply in the classical model (M)].

In reality, neither tax revenues nor the money supply is directly controlled by policy authorities. The government sets tax *rates* and tax revenues vary with income. And the money supply is jointly determined by action of the Federal Reserve System and the behavior of banks and the nonbank public. At this stage, however, we simplify the analysis by assuming that both tax revenues and the money supply are directly controlled by the policy authorities. We will relax these assumptions in subsequent chapters. For our purposes, we can view all policy decisions as being made by a unified policy agency. We need not, at this stage of analysis, distinguish the Treasury and the Federal Reserve System. In our policy chapters in Part VI we will discuss the specific institutions that initiate and implement these policies.

The policy instruments are interrelated via the *government financing constraint* (*GFC*). For the Keynesian version, the *GFC* can be written as

$$G \equiv T + \Delta m + \Delta b_g \tag{8.1}$$

where Δm and Δb_g are the changes in the supplies of money and government bonds over the period used to define the flow variables G and T. The *GFC* requires that government expenditures be financed by some combination of net taxes, issue of money, and/or bonds. We can rewrite the *GFC* as

Part II · Comparative Static Analysis with the Basic Model

$$\bar{D} + \Delta G \equiv \Delta T + \Delta m + \Delta b_g \tag{8.1'}$$

where $\bar{D}$ is the government budget deficit inherited from the previous period; i.e., if there was a deficit of $\bar{D}$ in the previous period, the deficit will also be $\bar{D}$ in the current period if G and T remain unchanged.

In this and the next two chapters, we assume all inherited deficits are financed by the sale of bonds to private sector units. Note that in the current specification of our model, changes in the supply of bonds do not have any direct impact on either the IS or LM curve. Therefore, the financing of an inherited deficit via bond sales will not affect the prevailing equilibrium values of the endogenous variables. Unless otherwise stated, we will also assume that changes in G and T are financed by changes in the supply of bonds and that all changes in the money supply are introduced via purchase or sale of bonds (open market operations). In Part V, we refine the specification of the model to allow bond financing to affect the response of the economy to deficit-financed fiscal policy.

We can now summarize the policy changes we will study in this and subsequent chapters. There are two basic classes of fiscal policy: debt-financed and balanced-budget fiscal policies. *Debt-financed fiscal policies* are changes in government expenditures (G) or taxes net of transfers (T) financed by the sale of bonds to households (or by the retirement of outstanding bonds in the case of increases in T or declines in G). *Balanced-budget fiscal policy* refers to equal increases (or decreases) in government expenditures and tax revenues. *Monetary policy* is confined to open market operations (*OMO*) throughout most of the text. An *open market purchase* (*OMP*) is a purchase of bonds from the public with newly issued money; this is the way in which the policy authority increases the money supply. An *open market sale* (*OMS*) is the sale of government bonds by the policy authority to the public; this is the way the policy authority reduces the stock of money outstanding.

○ Nonpolicy Disturbances

The *nonpolicy disturbances* are the constant terms or shift parameters $\bar{Z}$ and $\bar{L}$ in the IS and LM curves, respectively. $\bar{Z}$ is the autonomous component of private aggregate demand (the sum of the autonomous components of consumption and investment). Autonomous decreases in saving (or, equivalently, autonomous increases in consumption) and autonomous increases in investment are introduced into our model via increases in $\bar{Z}$. Exogenous changes in $\bar{Z}$ in our model reflect the fact that our theories of consumption and investment behavior do not permit us to predict precisely the value of C and I corresponding to given values of Y and r; i.e., sometimes there are shifts in the C and/or I functions for reasons we either cannot explain or for reasons we have not been able to capture in our model. Keynes, for example, emphasized the volatile nature of the investment function. Investment demand depends on expectations about the future and such expectations can change dramatically for reasons we simply are unable to model. Such shifts in the I function will be reflected by a volatile $\bar{Z}$ in our models.

$\bar{L}$ is the autonomous component of the real demand for money. Exogenous changes in $\bar{L}$ reflect our inability to predict precisely the demand for money associated with given values of X and r. Thus, the money demand function sometimes shifts for reasons we have not been able to capture in our model.

The *IS* and *LM* curves are given by equations (8.2) and (8.3) below (where $X = \bar{X}_f$ in the classical model and $P = \bar{P}$ in the Keynesian model). Table 8.1 summarizes the exogenous variables which shift the *LM* and *IS* curves in the classical and Keynesian models.

$$\frac{\bar{M}}{P} = L_r r + L_x X + \bar{L} \tag{8.2}$$

$$X = C_y(X - \bar{T}) + I_r r + \bar{Z} + \bar{G} \tag{8.3}$$

Version	LM	IS
Classical	$\bar{M}, \bar{L}$	$\bar{T}, \bar{Z}, \bar{G}$
Keynesian	$\bar{m}, \bar{L}$	$\bar{T}, \bar{Z}, \bar{G}$

TABLE 8.1
Shifts in *IS* and *LM* Curves

In the next two sections we will explain precisely how shifts in each exogenous variable affect the *IS* and *LM* curves. The basic procedure is as follows: hold one of the unknowns constant (e.g., r or X in the Keynesian version) and determine how the other unknown must vary to restore commodity or money market equilibrium at the new value of the exogenous variable. This identifies a point on the new *IS* or *LM* curve. From this we can infer whether the old curve shifts upward (i.e., equilibrium requires a higher r for each X) or downward, or rightward (i.e., equilibrium requires a higher X for each r) or leftward.

SHIFTS IN THE *IS* CURVE

Fiscal policy (G, T) and/or autonomous shifts in private aggregate demand (Z) shift the *IS* curve. In Figures 8.2a and 8.2b, we depict the effects of such shifts on the *IS* curve in both the Keynesian and classical versions of our model.

Fiscal Policy I: A Bond-Financed Change in Government Expenditures (ΔG)

An increase in G shifts the *IS* curve up and to the right in the Keynesian r-X diagram and upward in the classical r-P diagram. Consider the r-X diagram first. Assume r_0, X_0 (point a) is a combination of r and X consistent with commodity market equilibrium for the given values of T, Z, and G. If G increases, what must happen to X to maintain commodity market equilibrium at the initial r? An increase in G increases demand so that point a is now a position of excess demand.[1] To

---

[1] If $X_0 = C(X_0 - \bar{T}) + I(r_0) + \bar{Z} + \bar{G}$, then $X_0 < C(X_0 - \bar{T}) + I(r_0) + \bar{Z} + \bar{G}'$ (excess demand) if $\bar{G}' > \bar{G}$.

restore equilibrium at the initial r, output (X) must increase relative to the demand for output. Of course, as X increases, the supply and demand for output *both* increase. But given that $C_y < 1$, the demand for output increases by less than the supply of output. Therefore, an increase in X reduces the excess demand gap, and a large enough increase in X restores equilibrium at the initial r; e.g., an increase from X_0 to X_1 in Figure 8.2a. The magnitude of the change in X required to restore equilibrium at the initial r is determined by the simple Keynesian multiplier derived in the simplest Keynesian cross model in Chapter 6; i.e.,[2]

$$\left.\frac{\Delta X}{\Delta G}\right|_{\bar{r}} = \frac{1}{1 - C_y}. \tag{8.4}$$

We refer to this as the magnitude of the horizontal shift in the *IS* curve.[3]

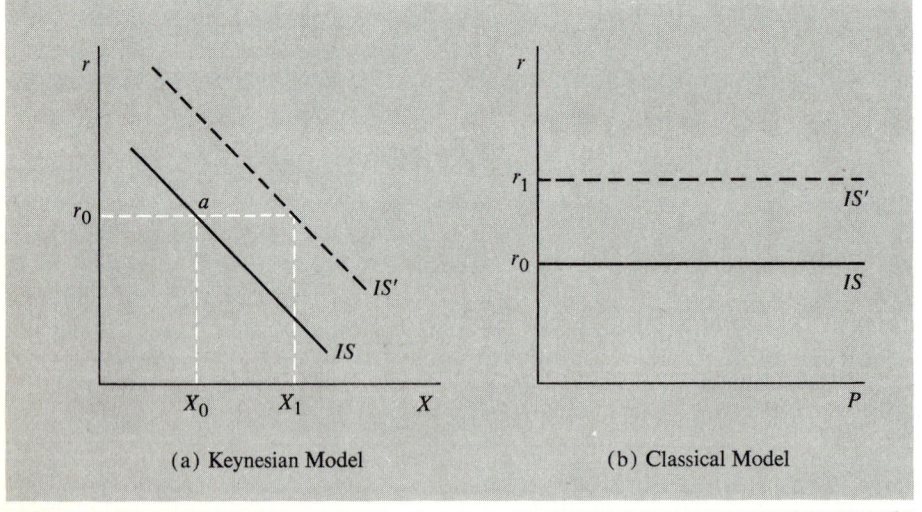

FIGURE 8.2
Shifts in the *IS* Curve

In the r-P diagram, an increase in G shifts the horizontal *IS* curve upward. An increase in G increases aggregate demand above the fixed full employment level of

---

[2] $\left.\frac{\Delta X}{\Delta G}\right|_{\bar{r}}$ indicates the ΔX required to restore equilibrium at the unchanged r following the change in G. Holding r constant is like making I exogenous; this is why the horizontal shift is precisely the same as the multiplier in the Keynesian cross model.

[3] To derive the horizontal shift, we first solve the *IS* curve for X. $X = \frac{1}{1-C_y}\bar{G} + \frac{1}{1-C_y}\bar{Z} - \frac{C_y}{1-C_y}\bar{T} + \frac{I_r}{1-C_y}r$. Taking first differences and setting $\Delta r = 0$, we obtain $\Delta X = \frac{1}{1-C_y}\Delta\bar{G} + \frac{1}{1-C_y}\Delta\bar{Z} - \frac{C_y}{1-C_y}\Delta\bar{T}$. The coefficients of ΔG, ΔZ, and ΔT indicate the magnitude of the horizontal shift in the *IS* curve for one-dollar changes in G, Z, and T, respectively.

output. To restore equilibrium in the commodity market, r must rise. A sufficient rise in r will reduce investment until the demand for output again just equals $\overline{X}_f$.[4]

○ Fiscal Policy II: A Bond-Financed Change in Net Taxes

A bond-financed *decrease* in net taxes is qualitatively like a bond-financed increase in government expenditures; i.e., in both cases the *IS* curve shifts up along a fixed *LM* curve. However, the two policies differ in quantitative effects, with a tax-financed decrease in net taxes generating a smaller shift. In the Keynesian case, for example, the increase in X at the initial r is

$$\left.\frac{\Delta X}{\Delta T}\right|_{\bar{r}} = \frac{-C_y}{1-C_y}. \tag{8.5}$$

Thus, the tax shift (in absolute value) is only C_y of the shift for government expenditures where $1 > C_y > 0$.

A similar result holds in the classical version. The rise in r required to reequilibrate the commodity market is smaller for a decrease in net taxes than for an equal dollar increase in G.[5]

○ Fiscal Policy III: A Balanced-Budget Fiscal Policy

Equal increases in G and T leave the deficit unchanged but nevertheless shift the *IS* curve. The reason balanced-budget fiscal operations affect aggregate demand is, of course, the differential quantitative impacts of equal changes in G and T. Equal changes in G and T have offsetting effects on aggregate demand; however, given that a change in G has a larger quantitative effect than an equal-sized change in T, equal increases in G and T increase aggregate demand and therefore shift the *IS* curve up and to the right in the Keynesian model and up in the classical model.[6]

In Figures 8.3a and 8.3b we compare the magnitude of the shift in the *IS* curve for the three cases of fiscal policy. Both a decrease in taxes and equal increases in taxes and government expenditures are unambiguously less potent than an increase in government expenditures. Assuming $C_y > .5$ (it is usually estimated at .7 to .9), a decrease in taxes is more potent than equal increases in taxes and government expenditures.

---

[4] To determine the magnitude of the vertical shift in the *IS* curve, we first solve for r in terms of G, Z, T, and $\overline{X}_f$. $r = -\frac{1}{I_r}\overline{G} - \frac{1}{I_r}\overline{Z} + \frac{C_y}{I_r}\overline{T} + \frac{1-C_y}{I_r}\overline{X}_f$. We then take first differences and assume $\Delta \overline{X}_f = 0$. $\Delta r = \frac{-1}{I_r}\Delta \overline{G} - \frac{1}{I_r}\Delta \overline{Z} + \frac{C_y}{I_r}\Delta \overline{T}$. The coefficients of ΔG, ΔZ, and ΔT indicate the magnitude of the increase in r required to restore commodity market equilibrium in response to changes in G, Z, or T, respectively.

[5] For taxes, the vertical shift is $\frac{\Delta r}{\Delta T} = \frac{C_y}{I_r}$; for a change in G, the vertical shift is $\frac{\Delta r}{\Delta G} = -\frac{1}{I_r}$.

[6] The horizontal shift in the Keynesian case is $\left.\frac{\Delta X}{\Delta G}\right|_{\bar{r}} = \frac{1-C_y}{1-C_y} = 1$ where $\Delta G = \Delta T$. The vertical shift in the classical case is $\frac{\Delta r}{\Delta G} = \frac{1-C_y}{I_r}$ where $\Delta G = \Delta T$.

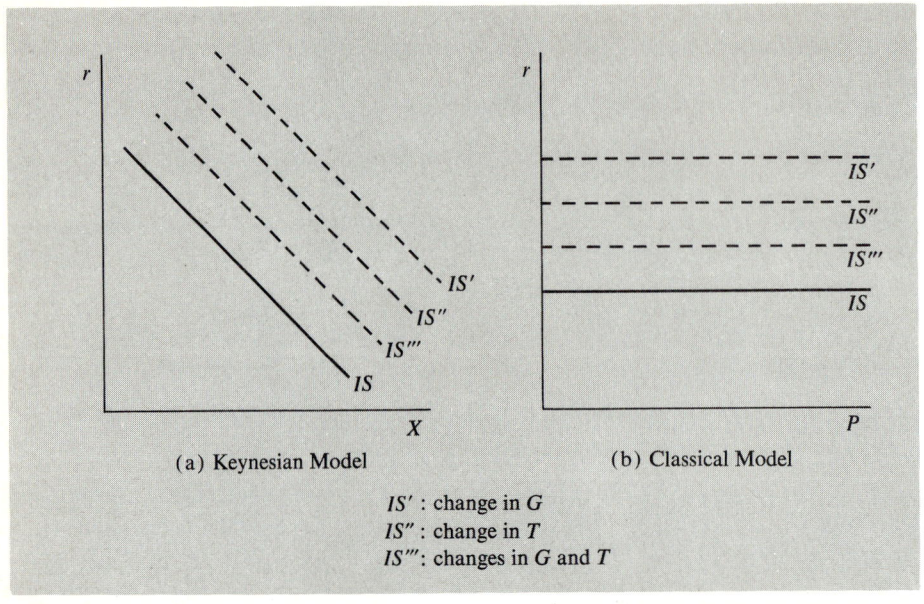

FIGURE 8.3
Comparing the Shifts in the *IS* Curve for
Alternative Fiscal Policies

○ An Autonomous Change in Private Aggregate Demand

A change in Z has an equivalent (quantitative as well as qualitative) effect to a (bond-financed) change in G in our models. Thus, Figures 8.3a and 8.3b can be used to depict the effect of an increase in Z on the *IS* curve in the Keynesian and classical versions of our model.

○ SHIFTS IN THE *LM* CURVE

Changes in the money supply associated with monetary policy or autonomous changes in the demand for money shift the *LM* curve in both the Keynesian and classical models.

○ Monetary Policy: Open Market Operations

Monetary policy is conducted in our models exclusively via open market operations. If the policy authority wants to increase the money supply, it purchases government securities in the open market (i.e., from the stock of securities held by households); this is referred to as an *open market purchase*. If the policy authority wishes to reduce the money supply, it sells government securities to households (referred to as an *open market sale*) and takes the money out of circulation.

The money supply is the single instrument of monetary policy in the current specification of our models. This does not, however, prevent the policy authority from conducting policy exclusively in terms of interest rates. To do so, the policy authority must manipulate the money supply via open market operations to maintain the interest rate at its targeted level. The relative merits of a strategy which focuses directly on the money supply and one which focuses on interest rates will be discussed in detail in Chapter 24. Until that time we describe monetary policy exclusively in terms of changes in the money supply.

The effect of an increase in the money supply is depicted in Figures 8.4a and 8.4b. In the Keynesian model an increase in the nominal money supply increases the real money supply by an equivalent amount because the price level is fixed. In the classical model the effect of a change in nominal money supply on real money supply depends on what happens to the price level. Thus, we treat the real money supply as exogenous in the Keynesian model and the nominal money supply as exogenous in the classical model.

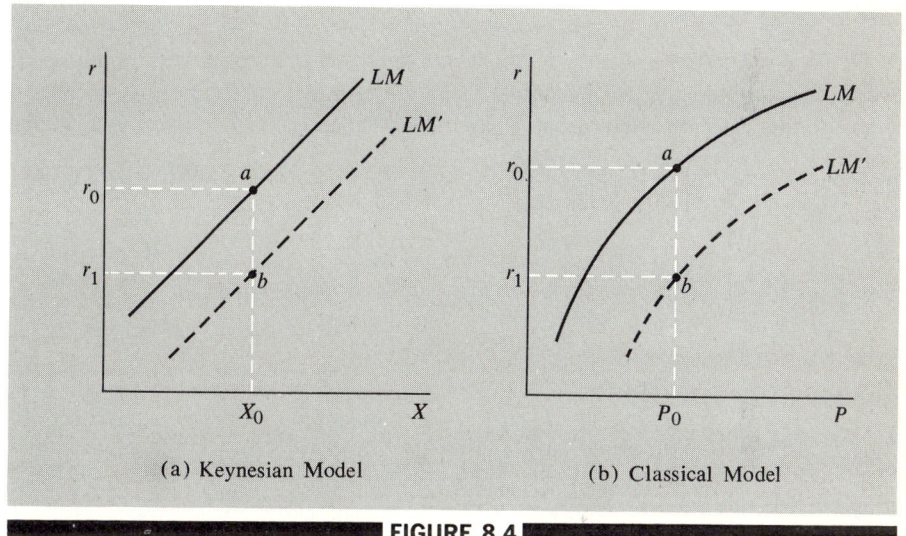

FIGURE 8.4

Shift in the *LM* Curve Due to an Increase in the Money Supply

In each case, we can determine the direction of the shift in the *LM* curve by considering how the interest rate must change to restore money market equilibrium at the initial level of X (in the Keynesian model) or P (in the classical model). Assume the money market is initially in equilibrium at point a in either diagram. If the money supply increases, point a becomes a position of excess supply in the money market.[7] What must happen to r to restore money market equilibrium at the initial X or P? An increase in r reduces the demand for money, given that $L_r < 0$. To increase the demand for money, therefore, r must fall.

---

[7] In the Keynesian model, for example, if $\bar{m}_1 = L(r_0, X_0)$, then $\bar{m}_2 > L(r_0, X_0)$ if $\bar{m}_2 > \bar{m}_1$. That is, for $m = m_1$, r_0 and X_0 are an equilibrium combination of r and X, while for $m = m_2$, r_0 and X_0 result in excess supply in the money market.

Part II • Comparative Static Analysis with the Basic Model

How much must r fall (i.e., what is the magnitude of the vertical shift)? A one percentage-point increase in the interest rate reduces the demand for money by L_r dollars. To increase the demand for money by one dollar, therefore, interest rate must fall $1/L_r$ percentage points. Thus, the vertical shift is equal to $1/L_r$.[8]

○ An Autonomous Change in the Demand for Money

An autonomous decrease in the demand for money is qualitatively equivalent in its effect to an increase in the money supply in both models. A decrease in $\bar{L}$ results initially in excess supply in the money market, requiring a decline in r to restore equilibrium. Thus, a decrease in $\bar{L}$ shifts the LM curve down in each case.[9]

○ MONEY-FINANCED FISCAL POLICY—SHIFTS IN BOTH THE *IS* AND *LM* CURVES

We have not considered money-financed changes in taxes or government expenditures in this chapter and we will not consider this policy in the next two chapters. We ignore this case for two reasons. The first is that in the U.S., government deficits

---

[8] To compute the vertical shift for the Keynesian model, we first solve the LM curve for r.

$$r = \frac{1}{L_r}\bar{m} - \frac{1}{L_r}\bar{L} - \frac{L_x}{L_r}X.$$

Then we take first differences and set $\Delta X = 0$.

$$\Delta r = \frac{1}{L_r}\Delta \bar{m} - \frac{1}{L_r}\Delta \bar{L}$$

The coefficients of Δm and $\Delta \bar{L}$ are the magnitude of the vertical shifts in the LM curve corresponding to one-dollar increases in m and $\bar{L}$, respectively.

The derivation for the classical model is complicated by the fact that the LM curve is nonlinear in this case. We can still derive the vertical shift. But to do so we must use calculus. Solving for dr/dM, holding P constant, yields

$$\left.\frac{dr}{dM}\right|_{\bar{P}} = \frac{1}{P}\frac{1}{L_r}.$$

Note that the vertical shift in this case depends on the price level which varies along the horizontal axis. The higher the price, therefore, the smaller the vertical shift.

[9] In the Keynesian model, the vertical shift for a change in $\bar{L}$ is identical in absolute value but of opposite sign to the shift for a shift in m. In the classical case, however, the vertical shift for a change in $\bar{L}$ is

$$\left.\frac{dr}{d\bar{L}}\right|_{\bar{P}} = \frac{1}{L_r}$$

and is thus, unlike the case of a shift in M, independent of the price level.

are financed exclusively via bond sales to private sector units. When the Treasury sells bonds to finance a deficit, it initially reduces the money supply; i.e., private sector units purchase the bonds by transferring an equivalent sum of money to the government. But this money is then used by the government to purchase goods. When the entire operation is completed (the sale of bonds *and* the government expenditures), government expenditures and the supply of government bonds have increased but there has been no net change in the money supply. The Treasury is not currently empowered to issue new money. The Federal Reserve System does so via open market operations. Thus, fiscal policy refers to either balanced-budget changes in G and T or bond-financed changes in G and T. Nevertheless, we can get a result which appears similar to a money-financed change in G if we combine a bond-financed change in G and an open market purchase. Indeed, it is often suggested that the Fed help the Treasury to market its new bonds by buying old bonds in the market at the same time the Treasury is issuing new bonds. In this case, the fiscal policy would shift the *IS* curve up and the subsequent monetary policy would shift the *LM* curve down.[10]

By the government financing constraint discussed above, however, the increase in G will lead to a deficit which must be financed not only in the period in which the increase is initiated but in all future periods as long as the deficit persists. This does not create a problem in our simple specification when we assume the deficit is financed by bond sales because the supply of bonds does not directly affect either *IS* or *LM* curves. Therefore, the increases in the supply of bonds in subsequent periods do not alter the equilibrium determined by the change in G.[11]

Increases in the money supply do affect the system by shifting the *LM* curve. If deficits are financed by money issue in subsequent periods as well as in the current period, the *LM* curve will continue to shift over time and there will be no well-defined equilibrium for the system. We return in Chapter 22 to the problem of long-run equilibrium analysis of deficit-financed fiscal policy. Until then, deficits are assumed to be financed exclusively by bonds. We can combine such a policy with an open market purchase *in the initial period* to generate the result generally associated in the literature with a money-financed fiscal policy—once-and-for-all shifts in both *IS* and *LM* curves.

● REVIEW QUESTIONS

1. What is the distinction between policy instruments, nonpolicy disturbances, and endogenous variables?

---

[10] The Fed is limited in the amount of bonds it can purchase directly from the Treasury. If the Treasury could sell bonds to the Fed whenever it wished to, it would be equivalent to the power to issue new money directly.

[11] It is clear from the specification of the model that the supply of bonds does not enter either the *LM* or *IS* curve as long as $L_a = 0$ and $C_a = 0$. To clarify why an increase in the supply of government bonds does not result in an excess supply of bonds in this case, recall that $L_a = 0$ implies that $B_a = 1$. Increases in the supply of government bonds via deficit financing increase the supply *and* demand for bonds by the same amount as long as wealth owners want to hold all increments in wealth in the form of bonds.

2. Distinguish between monetary and fiscal policies.

3. Distinguish between the various types of fiscal policy.

4. Explain in what sense decisions about policy instruments are interdependent.

5. When the government carries out a bond-financed increase in government expenditures, what happens to the money supply? Explain.

6. Explain the nature of the shift in the *LM* curve (in either Keynesian or classical cases) associated with an increase in the money supply.

7. Explain the nature of the shift of the *IS* curve (in either Keynesian or classical cases) associated with an increase in government expenditures.

8. What is the relation between the magnitude of the horizontal shifts in the *IS* curve associated with changes in G, Z, and T in the Keynesian model and the $\Delta X/\Delta G$, $\Delta X/\Delta Z$, and $\Delta X/\Delta T$ multipliers in the Keynesian cross model? Explain carefully.

● PROBLEMS

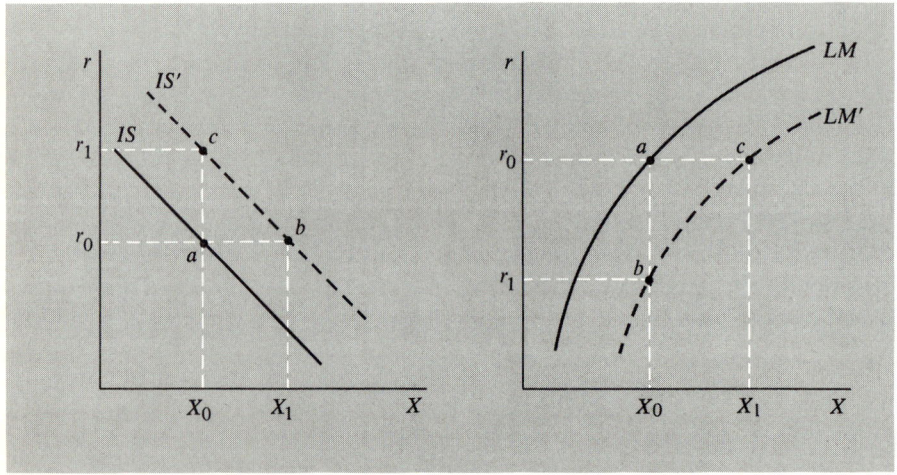

FIGURE 1   **FIGURE 2**

1. What could move the *IS* curve from *IS* to *IS'* in Figure 1? If $C_y = .8$ and $I_r = -20$, find the value of $X_1 - X_0$ and $r_1 - r_0$ for a $10 billion change in one of the variables that could have been responsible for the shift.

2. What could shift the *LM* curve from *LM* to *LM'* in Figure 2? If $L_r = -20$, find the value of $r_0 - r_1$ for a $10 billion change in a variable that could cause the shift.

3. Using the Keynesian *IS* curve $X = .8Y - 20r + \bar{G} + \bar{Z}$ where $Y \equiv X - \bar{T}$, find the horizontal shifts of the *IS* curve associated with a $10 billion increase in G and a $10 billion reduction in T. How do these compare to the increases in income that would occur in the Keynesian cross model?

Chapter 8 • Sources of Disturbances and Shifts in *IS* and *LM* Curves

4. An increase in the money supply initially reduces the interest rate; the decline in interest rate over time increases aggregate demand and income. The decline in the interest rate required to restore money market equilibrium at the original level of output is generally called the *liquidity effect* of the monetary change. Calculate the liquidity effect associated with a $1 billion increase in the money supply for the *LM* curve given by

$$\bar{m} = .2X - 20r + \bar{L}.$$

5. The classical *IS* curve immediately yields the equilibrium interest rate. Use the *IS* curve given in problem 3 to solve for the equilibrium interest rate when $\bar{T} = 150$, $\bar{G} = 200$, autonomous private demand, $\bar{Z}$, is 200, and $\bar{X}_f = 1000$.

6. The only role of the classical *LM* curve is to determine the price level. *X* is assumed to be fixed at the full employment level and *r* is uniquely determined by real sector forces (the *IS* curve). Use the *LM* curve

$$\frac{\bar{M}}{P} = .2X - 25r + \bar{L}$$

to determine the price level associated with the full employment level of income of $1,000 billion and the equilibrium interest rate determined in problem 4 ($\bar{L} = 0$ and $\bar{M} = 100$).

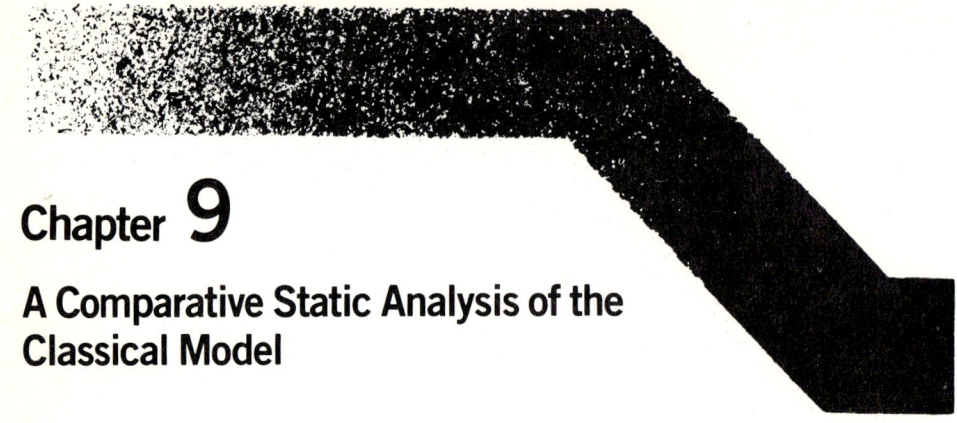

Chapter 9
A Comparative Static Analysis of the Classical Model

The purpose of this chapter is to explore the determination of the price level and nominal and real interest rates using the classical version of our basic model. The classical version is useful in understanding price and interest rate determination in two types of circumstances. The first is when we wish to consider the *long-run* response of the economy to disturbances. The economy does not always satisfy the classical assumption of full employment. The path of output over time is depicted in Figure 9.1, where the solid line depicts the path of actual output (X) and the dashed line depicts the trend growth in potential or full employment output (X_f). At times, actual output falls below potential output. But the long-run growth of

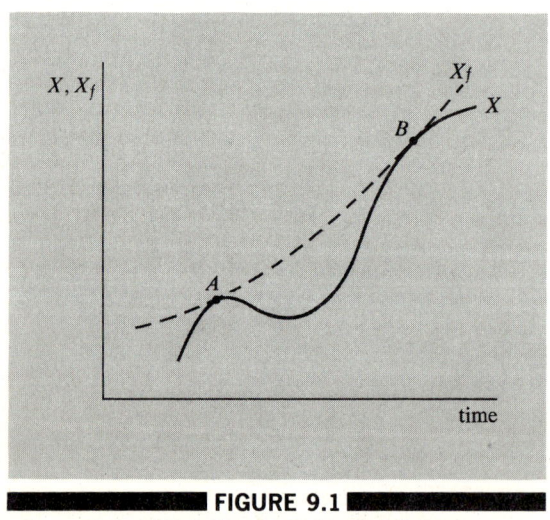

FIGURE 9.1
Actual Relative to Potential Output

the economy can be described in terms of the growth of potential output; i.e., in terms of movement between points like A and B in Figure 9.1. The classical model is useful in determining why prices and interest rates might differ at point B compared to point A. Of course, our model is static so that potential output is constant rather than growing over time. This does not, however, alter the usefulness of the framework for studying the long-run response of price and interest rates to disturbances.

The second situation in which the classical version is relevant is one where the economy's initial conditions conform to those of the classical model; i.e., the economy is at full employment. Even though prices may not be very flexible in the downward direction, prices are certainly flexible upward. Thus, we can use the classical model to determine the consequences of disturbances which increase aggregate demand—disturbances such as increases in either government expenditures or the money supply when the economy begins from full employment. The model will give the "equilibrium" response of P and r to such disturbances and this will provide useful insight into the direction of movement in r and P during even a relatively short period, such as the first year following the disturbance.[1]

In the first section of this chapter we consider the adjustment mechanism in the classical model whereby the economy always returns to full employment equilibrium following any disturbance. Then we discuss the conditions under which the mechanism might fail to operate. In the third section we introduce the distinction between nominal and real interest rates. We begin our comparative static analysis in the fourth section by considering the effects of the various disturbances on the IS and LM curves and hence on the equilibrium price level and the interest rate. We end the chapter with a discussion of the important properties of the classical version, based on our previous analysis. Here we consider such properties as neutrality, dichotomy, and the quantity theory of money, and we discuss such important issues as the sources of inflation, the crowding-out of private expenditures by government expenditures, and the response of nominal and real interest rates to monetary change.

THE ADJUSTMENT MECHANISM IN THE CLASSICAL MODEL

The classical model assumes that there is a unique equilibrium level of output (X_f) and that there exists an adjustment mechanism which tends to drive actual output back to this unique equilibrium following any disturbance. The purpose of this section is to make this adjustment mechanism explicit. Consider an autonomous decline in aggregate demand. In the Keynesian version where prices are assumed to be rigid in the downward direction, this disturbance would result in a multiplied reduction in aggregate demand and income. In the classical version, on the other hand, downward *flexibility of prices* operates to counter the demand disturbance and return the system to full employment equilibrium.

We can summarize the classical adjustment mechanism by equations (9.1) and (9.2) which specify the response of the price level and interest rate to market disequilibrium.

---

[1] Of course, if we believed that prices were very flexible in both directions so that equilibrium would be quickly restored following any disturbance, the model would provide insight into the short-run movement in prices and interest rates in response to any disturbance.

Part II • Comparative Static Analysis with the Basic Model

$$\dot{P} = \alpha(X^d - X_f) \qquad (9.1)$$

$$\dot{r} = \beta\left(L - \frac{\overline{M}}{P}\right) \qquad (9.2)$$

The dot over the P and r denotes the rate of change in each variable over time; i.e., $\dot{P}$ and $\dot{r}$ are the rates of change in the price level and the interest rate, respectively. We initially introduced this type of an equation in our Keynesian cross model in Chapter 6. There we viewed output as responding to excess demand in the commodity market. In the classical model, on the other hand, the price level rather than output responds to commodity market disequilibrium. Beginning from full employment, an increase in aggregate demand results in excess demand for output, and, according to equation (9.1), prices rise as economic agents bid for the limited supply of output. According to the second disequilibrium assumption, given by equation (9.2), the interest rate responds directly to the excess demand for money. If there is an excess demand for money, economic agents will attempt to increase their money holdings by selling bonds. The sale of bonds will put downward pressure on the price of bonds and upward pressure on the interest rate.[2]

Now let us consider the response to the demand disturbance based on our disequilibrium assumptions summarized by equations (9.1) and (9.2). The adjustment mechanism in response to a decline in demand is pictured symbolically in Figure 9.2 where each link in the adjustment mechanism is numbered ($A1$ through $A3$). The initial impact of the demand disturbance is to cause the price level to begin falling via equation (9.1); this link is referred to as $A1$ in Figure 9.2. The decline in the price level, in turn, increases the real money supply, given the exogenous nominal money stock ($\overline{M}$). The increase in real money balances relative to the as yet unchanged demand for real money balances generates a decline in the interest rate via equation (9.2); i.e., wealth owners attempt to rid themselves of excess real balances by purchasing

$$X^d \neq X_f \xrightarrow{A1} \Delta P \rightarrow \Delta\left(\frac{\overline{M}}{P}\right) \xrightarrow{A2} \Delta r \xrightarrow{A3} \Delta I \rightarrow \Delta X^d \rightarrow X_f$$

FIGURE 9.2
The Classical Adjustment Mechanism

---

[2] Note that money market disequilibrium is a reflection of imbalance in the *composition* of portfolios: too little money *relative to wealth*. Therefore, wealth owners are viewed as responding to such disequilibrium by attempts to rearrange the composition of their portfolios; i.e., to increase their money holdings relative to wealth by reducing their bond holdings relative to wealth. Equation (9.2) is sometimes referred to as the liquidity preference approach: interest rates respond to money market disequilibrium. This view is generally associated with Keynes. An alternative view, called the *loanable funds approach*, holds that interest rates respond directly to bond market disequilibrium. There has been a long controversy about the relative merits of these two approaches (and indeed about whether they are even different in any meaningful way). We will not discuss this controversy and make use of the liquidity preference approach because it simplifies the exposition, given our use of *IS-LM* analysis.

bonds, and this drives up bond prices and depresses the interest rate on bonds. This link is referred to as $A2$ in Figure 9.2. The decline in the interest rate then feeds back to aggregate demand via its impact on investment;[3] as the interest rate declines, investment and hence aggregate demand increase. This is link $A3$ in Figure 9.2. As long as aggregate demand is below X_f, the price level and the interest rate are falling, and hence investment and aggregate demand are rising. Ultimately, the price level and the interest rate adjust sufficiently to restore aggregate demand to a level consistent with the economy's productive capacity (X_f).

Similarly, any upward disturbance to aggregate demand would initially raise the price level. The increase in the price level would, in turn, induce a rise in the interest rate in response to an excess demand for real money balances. The rise in the interest rate would depress investment and hence aggregate demand. The process would continue until aggregate demand returned to balance with X_f.

In depicting the effects of changes in the exogenous variables in the classical model we will use two diagrams—the r-P and the r-X diagrams used in the previous two chapters. The r-X diagram is particularly useful in depicting the classical adjustment mechanism. To employ the r-X diagram in the classical model, we must introduce a third curve depicting the unique equilibrium level of output. This is the vertical line $X = X_f$ in Figure 9.3. The intersection of the IS curve and the $X = X_f$ line depicts the combinations of r and X consistent with commodity market equilibrium; i.e., given G, T, and Z (the position of the IS curve), there is a unique equilibrium interest rate in the classical model.

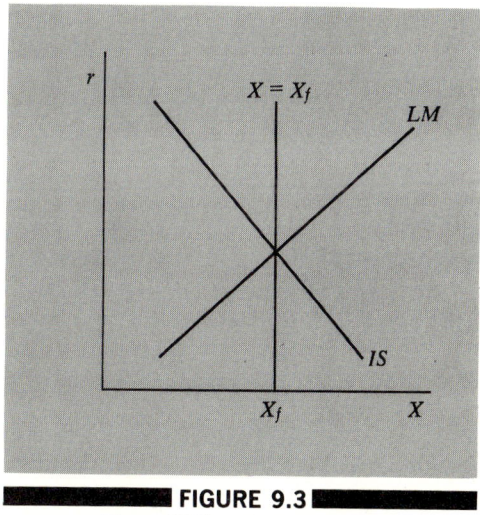

FIGURE 9.3
The *r-X* Classical Diagram

---

[3] Classical economists generally viewed saving as being responsible to the interest rate. Therefore, a decline in the interest rate would stimulate aggregate demand both by stimulating investment and discouraging saving (encouraging consumption).

The LM and IS curves shift for all the reasons discussed in Chapter 8. Note however that the LM curve is drawn for a given price level in the r-X case. Changes in the real money supply (one determinant of the position of the LM curve in the r-X diagram), in this case, result from either changes in the nominal money supply or changes in the price level; i.e., an increase in the price level shifts the LM curve up and to the left in the r-X diagram.

Consider the classical adjustment mechanism using the r-X diagram. An autonomous decline in private aggregate demand (decline in Z) shifts the IS curve leftward in Figure 9.4. Point b however cannot be an equilibrium point because the demand for commodities is below X_f. The resulting excess supply in the commodity market induces a decline in the price level. This in turn increases the real money supply shifting the LM curve down. This reduces the interest rate and increases investment and aggregate demand. As long as $X^d < X_f$, the price level is falling, the LM curve is shifting down, and aggregate demand is increasing. Ultimately, aggregate demand is reequated to X_f at point c and equilibrium is restored.

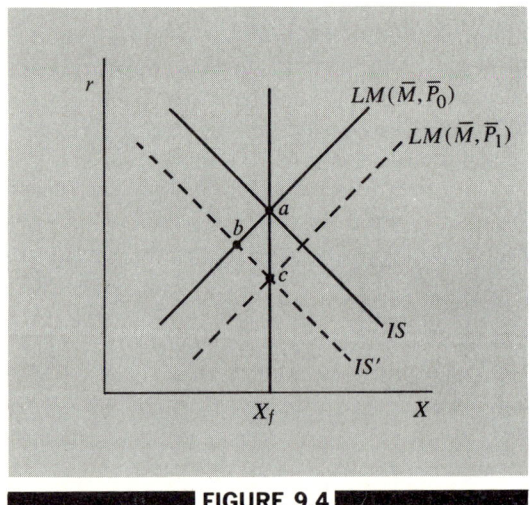

FIGURE 9.4
The Classical Adjustment Mechanism

CONDITIONS UNDER WHICH THE CLASSICAL ADJUSTMENT MECHANISM BREAKS DOWN

Throughout the remainder of this chapter we will assume that the adjustment mechanism described above is effective in returning output to full employment following any disturbance. However, we may gain additional insight into the nature of the adjustment process if we consider in this section the conditions under which the mechanism breaks down. We consider four cases: (1) inflexible prices which immobilize the first link, (2) critical values of the model's parameters which result in the failure of the second and/or third links in the mechanism, (3) destabilizing price expectations, and (4) widespread bankruptcies and financial collapse. The first two sources of the breakdown in the adjustment mechanism result from failure of one of the three links to operate as described above. The second two sources of failure result from additional impacts of price declines on aggregate demand, impacts which are not incorporated in our basic model and which have effects that tend to counter or offset those described above in the adjustment mechanism.

○ Inflexible Prices

Inflexible prices, of course, immobilize the adjustment mechanism. Keynes, in the *General Theory*, emphasized that the requirement of flexible prices was a weak link in the classical adjustment mechanism. But Keynes also noted that, even if prices were flexible, the classical mechanism might still fail to operate as described above.[4]

○ Critical Parameters and the Breakdown of the Interest Rate Link (Links $A2$ and $A3$)

Interest rate flexibility is a critical part of the adjustment mechanism. This link in the adjustment mechanism can break down in two ways: (a) if the interest rate is inflexible (link $A2$) and (b) if aggregate demand is unresponsive to the interest rate (link $A3$).

The interest rate mechanism is activated by the increase in real money supply relative to real money demand. When $-\infty < L_r < 0$, wealth owners get rid of excess money balances by buying bonds and the increased demand for bonds drives down the interest rate. However, if $L_r = -\infty$ (the "liquidity trap"), wealth owners are *indifferent between holding money and bonds* and the increase in real money is absorbed into portfolios at an unchanged interest rate. In this case, the interest rate becomes rigid (at least downward) and the adjustment mechanism breaks down. This is depicted in Figure 9.5 where the autonomous decline in aggregate demand does not lower interest rates so output declines from X_f to X_1.[5] At r_0, X_1 (point b in Figure 9.5) there is excess supply, prices continue to fall, but the price level decline leaves the interest rate and hence aggregate demand unaffected.

---

[4] Some have interpreted Keynes as suggesting that policy be directed at preventing a cumulative decline in prices because the price declines either will not help or may even further depress aggregate demand. The reasons for this are considered next.

[5] Recall from Chapter 7 that the slope of the LM curve in the r-X diagram is $-L_x/L_r$. As L_r increases (in absolute value), the slope declines. The limiting value of the slope is 0 as L_r approaches minus infinity. Also, recall from Chapter 8 that the vertical shift of the LM curve in response to a change in the real money supply in the r-X diagram is given by

$$\frac{\Delta r}{\Delta m}\bigg|_{\bar{X}} = \frac{1}{L_r}.$$

Thus, the vertical shift of the LM curve also approaches 0 as L_r approaches infinity. Reductions in the price level increase the real money supply and ordinarily shift the LM curve downward in the r-X diagram, reducing the interest rate; in the liquidity trap case, however, price declines leave the LM curve and the interest rate unchanged. The liquidity trap is discussed in more detail in Chapters 19 and 21.

Part II · Comparative Static Analysis with the Basic Model

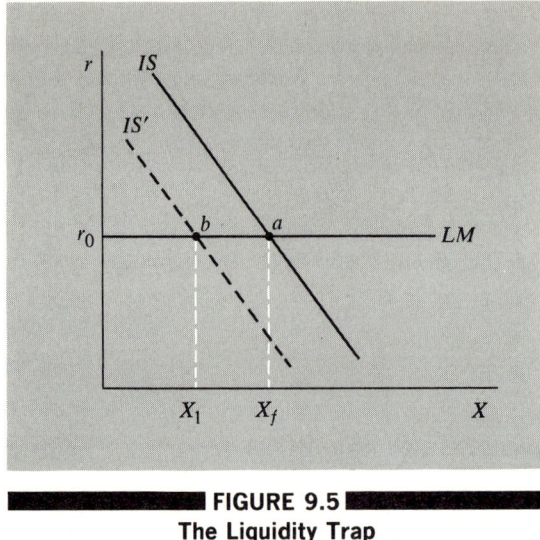

FIGURE 9.5
The Liquidity Trap

Even if the interest rate declines, aggregate demand may be unresponsive; i.e., $I_r = 0$ in our model. This is depicted in Figure 9.6. A leftward shift in the IS curve in this case cannot be offset by a price-decline-induced rightward shift in the LM curve. Output declines from X_f to X_1 and the price level declines, but this movement in P and r is ineffective in altering aggregate demand and hence output remains at X_1.[6]

Pigou and others are said to have "rehabilitated" the classical adjustment mechanism by adding an additional equilibrating mechanism that is immune to the two

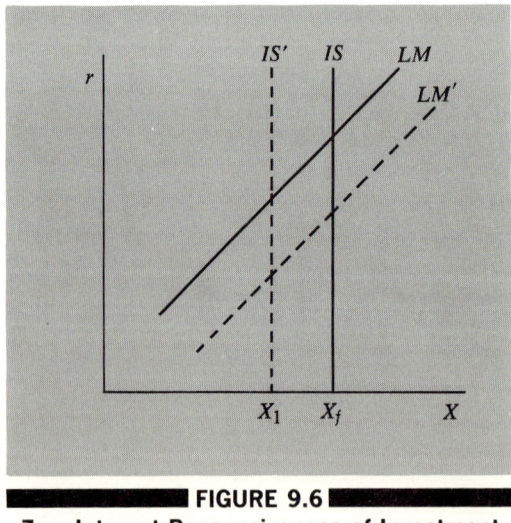

FIGURE 9.6
Zero-Interest Responsiveness of Investment

---

[6] The slope of the IS curve in the r-X diagram is $(1 - C_y)/I_r$; as $I_r \to 0$, the slope becomes steeper and approaches (minus) infinity.

special cases just discussed. This involves introducing a wealth effect into the consumption function where the real value of household net wealth depends on the price level as discussed in Chapter 4.[7] A decline in the price level in this case increases the real value of household wealth and increases consumption. The wealth effect will be discussed further in Chapters 12 and 13. The additional factors discussed below, however, operate to disrupt the adjustment mechanism even when the wealth effect is incorporated into the model.

○ Destabilizing Price Expectations

Even if the interest rate and wealth effects are both operative, their expansionary impact may be more than offset by the *intertemporal substitution effect*. This effect arises from expectations that prices will differ in the future and spending units speed up or postpone expenditures, accordingly. *Static price expectations* exist when spending units expect the current price level to persist. The model of the response to price flexibility in the first section implicitly assumed static price expectations. This is, of course, unrealistic, given that the continuing, downward price movement continuously contradicts this assumption. If spending units expect future prices to be lower than current prices, they may *postpone* expenditures to take advantage of even lower prices in the future. In this case, the intertemporal substitution effect offsets, at least in part, the interest rate and wealth impacts of lower prices and may even result in the price decline being, on net, an additional depressing influence on real aggregate demand.

○ Bankruptcies and Financial Collapse

Contracts are typically written in nominal terms so that contractually committed payments increase in real terms as prices fall. For firms or households with high debt, this means that as nominal dollar income from wages or sales declines with declining prices, their repayments of principal and interest payments on outstanding debt remain fixed in dollar terms and thus become increasingly burdensome. While this makes debtors worse off, it makes creditors better off. It is often assumed that this simply nets out for all inside assets in the private sector. If deflation persists, however, widespread default may result. When a unit becomes bankrupt, the creditor may lose the entire value of its loan. Thus, there is an important discontinuity. As the price level declines, the real value of the loan increases until the borrower is forced into bankruptcy; at that point, the real value of the loan to the issuer (creditor) may fall to zero. The price decline has now harmed both debtor and creditor. This is likely to disrupt the entire financial mechanism.[8] The net result of such bankruptcies

---

[7] A. C. Pigou, "The Classical Stationary State," *Economic Journal*, Vol. 53 (1943), pp. 343–351. A still earlier reference to the role of the wealth effect in the classical adjustment mechanism is Gottfried Haberler, *Prosperity and Depression* (3d ed.; New York: Columbia University Press, 1941), pp. 242, 389, and 403. For an excellent analysis of the role of and limitations of price flexibility in maintaining full employment, see Don Patinkin, "Price Flexibility and Full Employment," *American Economic Review*, Vol. 38 (1948), pp. 543–564.

[8] We might formally integrate this into our model by including the ratio of nominally fixed contractual commitments to nominal income as an argument in expenditure functions. As this ratio increases, private aggregate demand declines. In this case, the effect of price declines on aggregate demand is ambiguous.

and financial collapse is *further* declines in aggregate demand reinforcing the initial disturbance.

REAL VS. NOMINAL RATES

Another important consequence of abandoning the assumption of static price expectations is the necessity of distinguishing nominal from real interest rates. The definition of the real interest rate, introduced in Chapter 2, is

$$i = r - \rho \tag{9.3}$$

where i = real interest rate, r = nominal rate, and $\rho = \dfrac{\dot{P}e}{P}$ = the expected rate of inflation in output prices.[9] Investment is rewritten as a function of the real interest rate.

$$I = I(i) = I(r - \rho) \tag{9.4}$$

The demand for money and bonds, however, still depends on the nominal rate.[10]

ρ is treated as an exogenous variable in the model. Thus, the *IS* curve in the r-P diagram now assumes a given value for ρ as well as given values of T, G, and Z. Assume initially that $\rho = 0$ so that $r_0 = i$ in Figure 9.7. If the rate of expected inflation increases to x percent per year, the *IS* curve will shift upward. When spending units expect prices to increase by x percent per year, they will find that given the prevailing nominal rate (r_0), the expected real interest rate has declined by x percentage points. This in turn will induce an increase in investment and hence aggregate demand

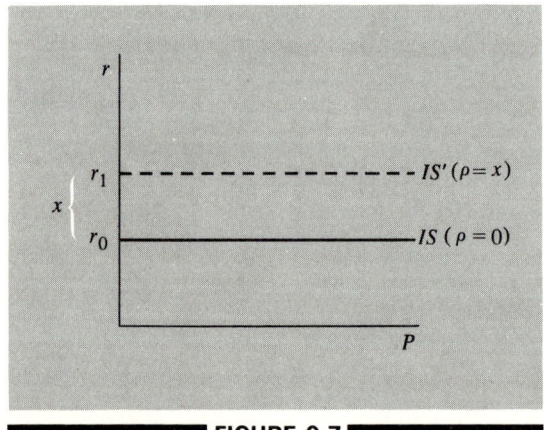

FIGURE 9.7
A Change in the Expected Inflation Rate

---

[9] We are using the approximation to the precise formula, ignoring the interaction term.
[10] Money and bonds both have returns stipulated in nominal terms and are thus both affected symmetrically by inflation. Thus, the differential between bonds (r) and money (o) in nominal terms is $r - o = r$ and in real terms $(r - \rho) - (-\rho) = r$. Therefore, the current specification remains accurate for money and bond equations.

Chapter 9 • A Comparative Static Analysis of the Classical Model

as reflected by the upward shift in the *IS* curve in Figure 9.5. Given that there is a *unique equilibrium real interest rate* given *G, Z,* and *T* in the classical model,[11] the nominal rate must rise by exactly x percentage points.[12] The new nominal interest rate, r_1, is said to include an *inflation premium* equal to x percentage points. As the nominal rate rises, both the real rate and investment return to their initial levels.[13]

RESPONSE OF THE CLASSICAL SYSTEM TO VARIOUS DISTURBANCES

In this section we present a comparative static analysis of the response of the price level and the interest rate to various disturbances in the classical system. We consider changes in (1) the supply of money, (2) the demand for money, (3) government expenditures financed by bonds, and (4) autonomous private demand for output. In the following section we will use these results to develop a better understanding of the properties of the classical system.

Monetary Policy: A Change in the Money Supply (ΔM)

The effect of a change in the money supply is depicted in Figures 9.8a and 9.8b. A change in the money supply *shifts only the LM* curve in each diagram. The *r-P* diagram makes it clear that the equilibrium rate of interest is uniquely determined by the real sector forces (i.e., by the position of the *IS* curve in that diagram). An increase in the money supply, therefore, shifts the *LM* curve rightward along the fixed *IS* curve, generating an increase in the price level at an unchanged interest rate.

---

[11] This property is discussed in more detail below.

[12] The vertical shift in the *IS* curve can be derived by solving the *IS* curve for the nominal interest rate. The *IS* curve is written as

$$\bar{X} = C_y(\bar{X} - \bar{T}) + I_i(r - \rho) + \bar{Z} + \bar{G}.$$

Solving for r yields

$$r = \frac{(1 - C_y)}{I_i}\bar{X} - \frac{C_y}{I_i}\bar{T} + \rho - \frac{1}{I_i}\bar{Z} - \frac{1}{I_i}\bar{G}.$$

Taking first differences and assuming $\Delta X = \Delta T = \Delta Z = \Delta G = 0$, we derive the vertical shift in the *IS* curve due to an increase in ρ.

$$\frac{\Delta r}{\Delta \rho} = 1$$

[13] If the nominal rates are slow to adjust, as Keynes believed, the initial response to an increase in the rate of *deflation* will be an *increase* in the real rate. This is another way in which the classical mechanism might fail to operate smoothly to restore full employment equilibrium. This point has been recently reemphasized by James Tobin, "Keynesian Models of Recession and Depression," *American Economic Review Papers and Proceedings,* Vol. 65 (May, 1975), pp. 195–202.

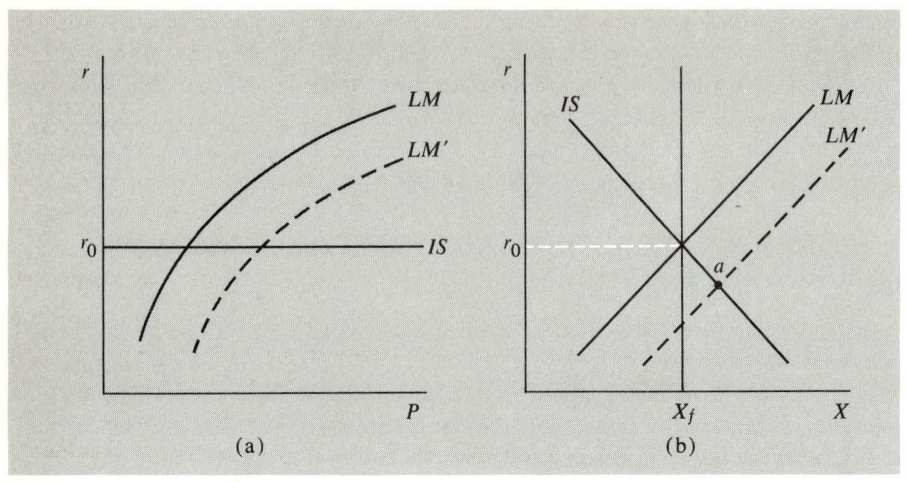

FIGURE 9.8
Monetary Policy in the Classical Model

The r-X approach of Figure 9.8b clarifies the process of adjustment to the change in the money supply. The increase in M initially shifts the LM curve rightward; this depresses the rate of interest and increases the level of aggregate demand. The intersection of IS and LM' at point a cannot represent an equilibrium solution because aggregate demand for output exceeds the maximum feasible aggregate supply (X_f); prices rise, shifting the LM curve leftward. How much must the price level rise? It must rise until the LM curve is restored to its initial position; only then will there be neither excess demand nor excess supply in the output market.

○ An Autonomous Change in the Demand for Money ($\Delta \bar{L}$)

Figures 9.8a and 9.8b can also be used to determine the response to a change in the demand for money (i.e., an autonomous change in the shift parameter $\bar{L}$ in the money demand function). In our simple classical model a *decrease* in the demand for money has an identical effect to an increase in the supply of money. Given that an increase in the supply of money increases the price level but leaves the interest rate unchanged, the same result must follow for a decrease in the demand for money.

○ Fiscal Policy I: An Increase in Government Expenditures Financed by the Sale of Government Bonds

The classical model assumes that the economy is maintained at the full employment level of output by price and wage adjustments. Government fiscal policy is not required to combat unemployment. We can still investigate what happens if the government decides to increase its share of total output. Again, we consider both the r-P and r-X diagram, Figures 9.9a and 9.9b. A bond-financed increase in G shifts *only the IS curve* in this model. An increase in G shifts the IS curve upward in each diagram. In the r-P diagram, there is a unique equilibrium r that can be solved for from the IS curve. An increase in G increases the interest rate which equilibrates

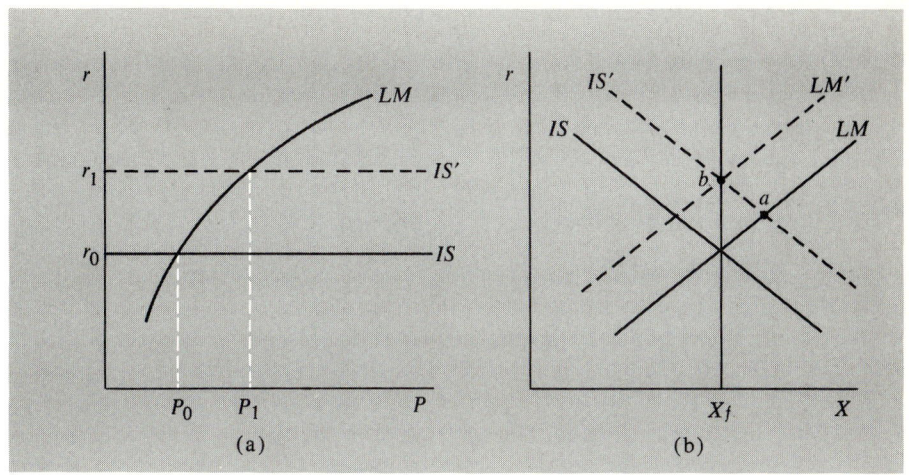

FIGURE 9.9
Bond-Financed Fiscal Policy in the Classical Model

the output market. Therefore, the *IS* curve shifts upward and as a consequence, both r and P increase.

This result can also be shown using the r-X diagram. An increase in G shifts the *IS* curve rightward; at point a, there is excess demand in the output market so prices rise, shifting the *LM* curve leftward. The final equilibrium will be at point b, where r and P are both higher than at the initial equilibrium. The change in P is part of the adjustment process by which resources are released from the private sector. The increase in G increases aggregate demand relative to X_f. As the government bids for resources controlled by the private sector, the price level is bid up. In the present model, the bidding-up of the price level does not directly tend to restrict private demand; real private demand depends on only r and X. The increase in P indirectly reduces private demand by reducing the real money supply relative to the real demand for money, putting upward pressure on the rate of interest. The increase in r reduces private demand until private demand has decreased by precisely the amount of the increase in G.

The impacts of bond-financed changes in net tax receipts and of equal increases in G and T are qualitatively identical to the case of bond-financed increases in G. The diagramatic analysis is therefore the same as in Figures 9.9a and 9.9b. The three fiscal operations have different quantitative impacts as discussed in Chapter 8; the change in G yields the largest shift in the *IS* curve (and therefore the largest increase in both r and P) and balanced-budget fiscal policy yields the smallest shift in the *IS* curve.

○ An Increase in the Autonomous Component of Private Demand

The results of this change are identical to those derived for an increase in G. This reflects the fact that G and Z enter the present model in precisely the same way, as autonomous components of aggregate demand. Thus, an increase in desired saving (i.e., a reduction in desired consumption) or a decrease in desired investment results in reductions in both r and P.

Part II · Comparative Static Analysis with the Basic Model

IMPORTANT PROPOSITIONS BASED ON THE CLASSICAL MODEL

Our first two comparative static experiments in the previous section uncovered an interesting property of the classical model. We found that *real variables in the economy were invariant with respect to changes in the supply of or demand for money.* The real variables in our model are X, C, I, and i. The key nominal variable is P.

The Existence of Neutrality and Dichotomy

Neutrality obtains when the equilibrium values of the real variables of the economy are invariant with respect to changes in the money supply. To test for neutrality, we alter M and observe changes in the real variables (X and i). By assumption, the equilibrium value of X remains unchanged. Our first comparative static experiment indicated that i also remained unchanged. Thus, neutrality holds.

Dichotomy holds when the equilibrium values of the real variables are invariant with respect to both changes in the supply of money and changes in the demand for money. Thus, dichotomy is a more inclusive concept than neutrality. Neutrality may hold without dichotomy holding. But the existence of dichotomy implies that neutrality also holds.

To test for dichotomy, we must consider the response of the equilibrium real variables to both changes in the money supply and changes in the demand for money. From the first two experiments in the previous section, we know dichotomy obtains in our simple classical model.

When dichotomy holds, we can solve our real sector for all the equilibrium values of the real variables independent of the equations in the financial sector. This is the sense of the term "dichotomy": the model is dichotomous, composed of two subsectors. The money sector cannot influence real variables (at least in the long run, when the classical model is relevant). Given the equilibrium values of the real variables, the role of the financial sector is to determine the equilibrium value of the *nominal* variables, in our case the price level.[14]

It follows that the *equilibrium real interest rate is exclusively a real phenomenon* in the classical model, meaning that the equilibrium real interest rate depends exclusively on real sector decisions such as saving and investment along with government budget decisions. The money supply cannot affect the equilibrium real interest rate although the rate of change in the money supply can affect the inflation premium in nominal rates.[15]

---

[14] The structure of our model is *recursive.* Unknowns in subsector 1 (real sector) can be determined without knowledge of the equations in subsector 2 (financial sector). Once we have solved for the equilibrium values of real variables in subsector 1, we use these in subsector 2 to determine *the equilibrium values of nominal variables.*

This aspect of the classical model can also be seen mathematically by observing that the equilibrium condition in the commodity market can be written as one equation in one unknown, the interest rate. There is only one value of the interest rate that is consistent with equilibrium in the commodity market, given values of $\bar{T}$, $\bar{G}$, and $\bar{Z}$.

This can also be seen clearly from the r-P diagram. The equilibrium interest rate is uniquely determined by the position of the (horizontal) *IS* curve and is thus completely independent of the position of the *LM* curve (and thus of the supply of or demand for money).

[15] Although the *equilibrium* value of the interest rate is determined exclusively by real variables, its short-run movements are due exclusively to *disequilibrium in the financial sector* according to the disequilibrium assumptions we have adopted.

○ Inflation and the Quantity Theory of Money

Inflation refers to a situation in which there are *continuing* and appreciable increases in the price of output. It is important to distinguish between the *temporary inflation* associated with the adjustment to a once-and-for-all disturbance which increases the equilibrium price level and the *continuing inflation* associated with continuing movements in one or more of the exogenous variables and, therefore, with continuing increases in the *equilibrium* price level.

A once-and-for-all increase in an exogenous variable can, at most, generate an increase in the equilibrium price level and a temporary burst of inflation as the economy moves from one price level to the other. To clarify why a once-and-for-all disturbance can only generate a once-and-for-all change in the equilibrium price as opposed to a continuing inflation, consider the response to an increase in autonomous private aggregate demand. This demand disturbance results in excess demand in the commodity market and this in turn induces increases in the price level. But the price level increases cannot continue indefinitely. The rising price level induces a rise in the interest rate[16] and the increase in the interest rate, in turn, decreases aggregate demand. Thus, as the price level rises, the excess demand gap declines, the inflation rate slows, and eventually, excess demand is eliminated and the price level is stabilized.

A similar result follows for a once-and-for-all change in the money supply. This initially reduces the interest rate, stimulating investment. The resulting excess demand gap on the commodity market induces a rise in the price level. The rise in the price level, in turn, induces a rise in the interest rate until the interest rate and aggregate demand return to their initial levels, excess demand is eliminated, and the price level is stabilized. Note that this result is a reflection of the classical adjustment mechanism which operates to eliminate any disequilibrium in the economy. The adjustment mechanism chokes off any inflation resulting from a once-and-for-all change in an exogenous variable by eliminating the source of inflation, the excess demand in the commodity market. Thus, inflation induced by a once-and-for-all change in an exogenous variable *cures itself* as the rising prices eliminate the excess demand in the commodity market.

In this model once-and-for-all increases in M, G, or Z or a once-and-for-all decrease in $\bar{L}$ or T can equally well increase the equilibrium price level. Furthermore, *continuing* increases in M, G, or Z or *continuing* decreases in $\bar{L}$ or T can fuel a continuing inflation. There is one major difference, however. Inflations associated with continuing increases in G or Z or continuing decreases in T are accompanied by continuing increases in *both* the real and nominal interest rate. Inflations associated with either continuing increases in M or continuing decreases in $\bar{L}$, on the other hand, can occur at an unchanged real interest rate and at constant nominal rates after the initial upward adjustment to incorporate the inflationary premium in the nominal interest rate.

There is, however, an important case when continuous increases in autonomous expenditures cannot be the source of inflation. This is when $L_r = 0$, as in the crude quantity theory where $M^d = kPY$. In this case, increases in G or Z shift the *IS*

---

[16] The rise in the price level reduces the real money supply generating excess demand for money, and interest rates rise as wealth owners attempt to move out of bonds into money.

curve upward along the vertical *LM* curve (as in Figure 9.10), raising the interest rate but not the price level. In this case the quantity theorists' motto that *"inflation is always and everywhere a monetary phenomenon"* is valid. But in general, although the interest rate is purely a real phenomenon, *the price level is not a purely monetary phenomenon*; i.e., the interest rate is determined uniquely by the *IS* curve (real sector), but unless $L_r = 0$, the price level is jointly determined by the *IS* and *LM* curves (real and monetary sectors).[17]

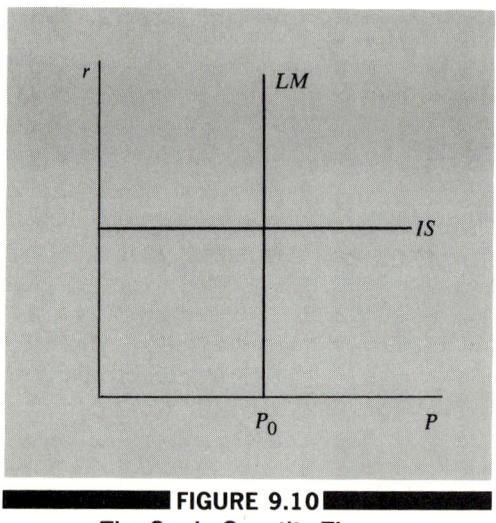

FIGURE 9.10
The Crude Quantity Theory

The *quantity theory of money (QT)* refers to the proposition that *changes in the price level are proportional to changes in the money supply*. In the present model, prices change in proportion to changes in the money supply but prices may also change in response to changes in the other exogenous variables. Only when $L_r = 0$ (or $I_r = -\infty$) and $\bar{L}$ remains fixed is the strict form of the *QT* valid: prices are proportional to the money supply.[18]

These propositions can be clarified by considering the classical model's *LM* curve.

$$\frac{\bar{M}}{P} = L_r r + L_x X + \bar{L} \tag{9.5}$$

Note that X and $\bar{L}$ are fixed (there is a unique equilibrium value of X, and $\bar{L}$ is exogenous). By neutrality, the equilibrium r is determined by the real sector. Therefore, the real demand for money [the right-hand side of equation (9.5)] is independent of

---

[17] The same result follows if $I_r = -\infty$. In this case the *IS* curve does not shift when G, Z, or T change, so these real sector disturbances cannot be a source of inflation.

[18] When $L_r < 0$, $\eta_{PM} = \frac{\Delta P}{\Delta M} \frac{M}{P} = 1$ (changes in M result in proportional changes in P) but $\frac{\Delta P}{\Delta G}$ and $\frac{\Delta P}{\Delta Z}$ are both positive (changes in real sector variables can also affect P).

the nominal money supply. If M doubles, the only way to restore money market equilibrium [equality between the two sides of equation (9.5)] is for P to double, restoring the real money supply [the left-hand side of equation (9.5)] to its original level.[19] Note that changes in G, T, or Z alter the equilibrium interest rate and therefore require a change in the price level to maintain money market equilibrium as long as changes in the interest rate affect the demand for money. When $L_r = 0$, however, changes in r leave the demand for money unchanged; therefore, P also remains unchanged.

○ The Response of Interest Rates to Monetary Change

In considering the response of interest rates to monetary change, it is crucial to distinguish between a once-and-for-all change in the money supply and a sustained change in the rate of growth of the money supply.

A Once-and-for-All Increase in M. We know from the analysis above that money is neutral so that the (real) interest rate is independent of the money supply. However, it is useful to trace out the sequence of events likely to follow an increase in the money supply. The time pattern of the response of interest rates to monetary change is depicted in Figure 9.11.

The initial impact of an increase in M is to *lower* interest rates as excess supply of money results in an attempt to buy bonds to restore portfolio balance. This initial decline in interest rates is usually referred to as the *liquidity effect*. As r falls, investment demand and hence aggregate demand increase, putting upward pressure on prices as demand for output exceeds the economy's productive capacity. As prices rise, the real money supply falls, eventually tending to return the money market to equilibrium at the original interest rate.

An Increase in the Rate of Growth of the Money Supply. We can use our analysis above to determine the impact of a change in the *rate of growth* of the money supply on the nominal interest rate.

---

[19] The key property that insures the proportionality of changes in P to changes in M is the *absence of money illusion* in both the money demand function and the real sector equations; i.e., real consumption and real investment demand as well as the real demand for money depend exclusively on real variables. We will find in subsequent chapters, however, that the introduction of wealth effects can also alter the proportionality result.

If we write the nominal demand for money as a function of r, X, and P,

$$\bar{M} = L(r, X, P),$$

the absence of money illusion implies that the partial elasticity of the demand for money with respect to P is unity.

$$\epsilon_{LP} = L_P \frac{P}{M} = 1$$

Given that r, X, and $\bar{L}$ will be unaffected by a change in M, P must change proportionately to restore money market equilibrium. Writing the demand for money in real terms as we have done imposes the restriction that $\epsilon_{LP} = 1$.

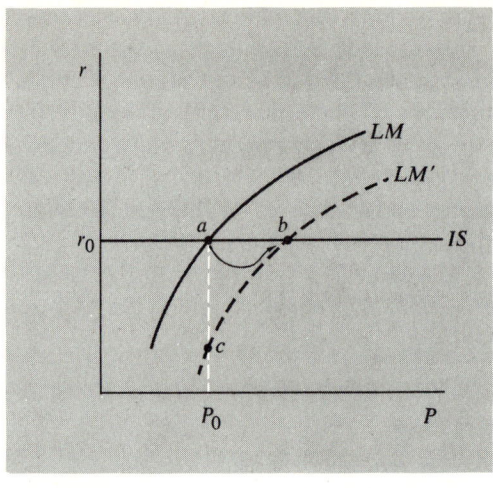

FIGURE 9.11
The Time Pattern of Response of Interest Rates to an Increase in the Money Supply

Assume we begin with M fixed (zero growth rate) and an equilibrium at point a in Figure 9.12 where the nominal and real interest rate is r_0 and the price level is P_0. Assume the growth of the money supply is increased to x percent per year. The initial response is still likely to be a decline in nominal rates, reflecting the liquidity effect of an increase in the money supply. As aggregate demand increases, prices are bid up. The upward pressure on prices begins to push the interest rate back toward r_0, as in the case of a once-and-for-all increase in M.

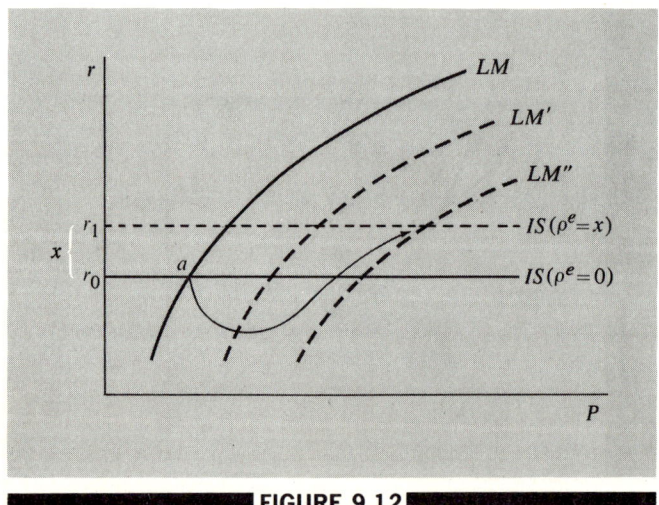

FIGURE 9.12
The Time Pattern of Response of Interest Rates to an Increase in the Rate of Monetary Growth

In addition, however, the increase in the rate of monetary growth will alter the rate of price change and hence the rate of expected inflation. We assume that the rate of expected inflation responds to current and past actual inflation rates and that the expected rate will ultimately converge to the actual rate after the actual rate has been maintained at some level for a period of time. We present a more formal discussion of the formulation of expectations in Appendix B at the end of Chapter 18. For now, the results that we need to complete this analysis are (1) that the actual inflation rate ($\dot{P}$) will equal the rate of growth of the money supply ($\dot{M}$) via the quantity theory of money results derived above; and (2) that the expected inflation rate will converge to this actual rate ($\dot{P}^e = \dot{P}$) so that $\dot{P}^e = \dot{P} = \dot{M}$.[20]

We are now prepared to complete the analysis of the response to a sustained increase in the rate of growth of the money supply. The increase in the expected rate of inflation, ultimately equal to the increase in $\dot{M}$, x percentage points, ultimately shifts the IS curve upward by exactly x percentage points. We derived this result previously in this chapter. The LM curve shifts out over time in response to the constant rate of monetary growth. Thus, we get both a once-and-for-all shift in the IS curve (reflecting the incorporation of the inflationary premium in nominal rates) and continuing shifts in the LM curve. The net result is that the nominal interest rate rises by x percentage points above its initial level and remains there so long as $\dot{M} = x$. This in turn implies that although the real rate may initially decline (due both to the initial decline in nominal rates and the failure of $\dot{P}^e$ to adjust immediately to the increase in the actual inflation rate), in equilibrium the real rate is unchanged by the monetary expansion.[21] This analysis forms the basis of the view, often associated with *monetarists*, that an increase in the rate of monetary growth increases rather than reduces the nominal interest rate.[22]

○ Crowding-Out

Crowding-out refers to the decline in private expenditures in response to an increase in government expenditures. When crowding-out is complete, private expenditures decline by the exact amount of the increase in government expenditures. In the classical model crowding-out in real terms is built in by the assumption of a fixed, unique

---

[20] Here and in subsequent discussions we use $\dot{P}$, $\dot{P}^e$, and $\dot{M}$ to refer to *percentage* changes in P and M over time.

[21] The distinction is often made between *neutrality* (invariance of the real variables with respect to the *level* of the money supply) and *superneutrality* (invariance of real variables with respect to the *rate of growth* of the money supply). In the simple framework employed in this chapter, both neutrality and superneutrality hold.

[22] This view is widely accepted as applying to a long-run analysis of the economy's response to changes in the rate of monetary expansion. Differences relate primarily to how long the long run is. Gibson, for example, suggests that interest rates decline only briefly in response to an increase in the money supply, returning to their initial level within *three months*. See William Gibson, "Interest Rates and Monetary Policy," *Journal of Political Economy*, Vol. 78, No. 3 (May–June, 1970), pp. 431–435. Friedman suggests it takes 18 months to get back to the initial level and 10–20 years to fully respond to the price expectations effect. See Milton Friedman, "Factors Affecting the Level of Interest Rates," in *Savings and Residential Financing*, 1968 Conference Proceedings, pp. 11–27. We will find in the next chapter that when the economy is at a position below full employment and prices and wages are rigid or very sluggish in the downward direction, increases in the money supply will lead to a sustained decline in the interest rate. We will have more to say about the dynamics of interest rate response to monetary change in Chapters 10 and 15.

equilibrium level of output. If government expenditures are specified in real terms, as we have assumed, an increase in the share of real output controlled by the government can only occur if real resources are bid away from the private sector.

The process by which these real resources are released by the private sector is depicted in Figure 9.13. An increase in G shifts out the IS curve. The increase in aggregate demand puts upward pressure on the price level P. Thus, point b in Figure 9.13 is not feasible because the output at b exceeds X_f. The excess demand for output at b generates an increase in P which in turn shifts the LM curve up or backward. This decline in real money balances induced by a rise in P results in bidding up the interest rate. As long as excess demand persists, P and r rise; but as long as P and r rise, the excess demand gap declines until a new equilibrium is achieved at c where P and r are higher than initially but X remains at X_f. Given that consumption depends only on X_f, it too remains unchanged but investment declines in response to the rise in the interest rate. Thus, the increase in G has been offset by an equivalent decline in I. The decline in I has released the resources to permit the increase in G to be obtained.

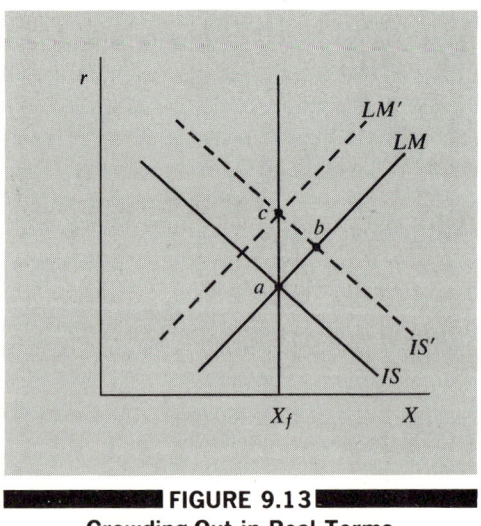

FIGURE 9.13
Crowding-Out in Real Terms

Some economists have suggested that a bond-financed increase in government expenditures does not affect either the level of output or the price level. We refer to this situation as *nominal crowding-out*: an increase in government expenditures does not affect real or nominal income.[23] This is a stricter and less likely proposition

---

[23] See, for example, Friedman's discussion of fiscal policy in Milton Friedman and Walter W. Heller, *Monetary vs. Fiscal Policy: A Dialogue* (New York: W. W. Norton & Company, Inc., 1969), pp. 50–51. Here Friedman argues that fiscal policy has no "significant effect" on nominal income or inflation; i.e., it affects neither real income nor the price level. The only thing fiscal policy can affect is the fraction of total output controlled by the government (the share of G in GNP) and interest rates. This passage is one of the reasons many associate Friedman with the view that $L_r = 0$; this parameter restriction would be consistent with nominal crowding-out in the classical model. We discuss Friedman's views on L_r and crowding-out further in Chapter 21.

than real crowding-out. Indeed, one of the key mechanisms through which real crowding-out occurs is the increase in the price level in response to the increase in government spending. The two cases in which nominal crowding-out can occur are depicted in Figures 9.14a and 9.14b and Figures 9.15a and 9.15b. The first case is where $I_r = -\infty$. In this case the IS curve does not shift when G increases.[24] Therefore, r and

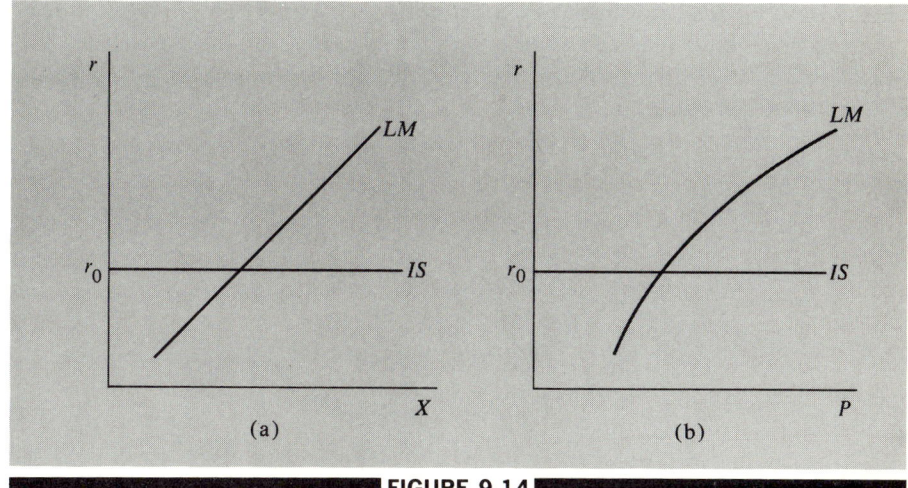

FIGURE 9.14
Nominal Crowding-Out When $I_r = -\infty$

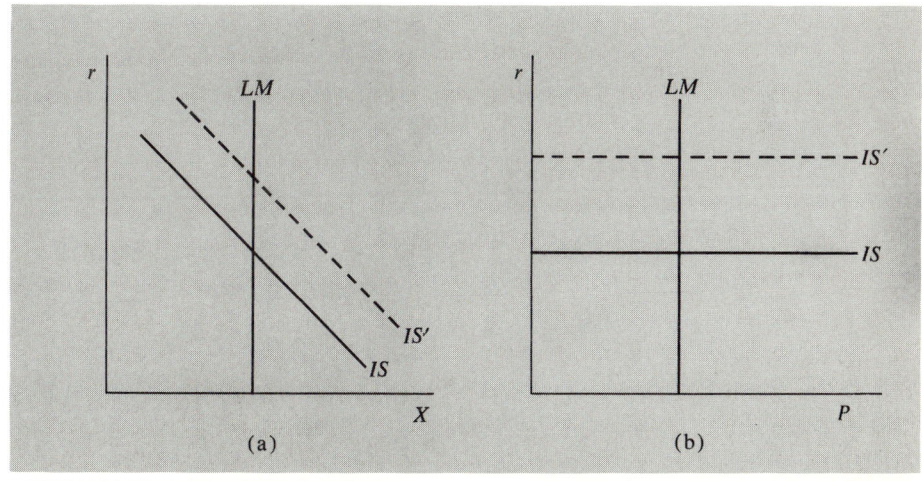

FIGURE 9.15
Nominal Crowding-Out When $L_r = 0$

---

[24] Recall that the vertical shift in the IS curve is

$$\frac{\Delta r}{\Delta G} = -\frac{1}{I_r}$$

in both r-P and r-X cases. If $I_r = -\infty$, then $\frac{\Delta r}{\Delta G} = 0$.

P remain unchanged. The increase in G puts upward pressure on aggregate demand and hence on prices and then the interest rate. But given the infinite interest responsiveness of investment, the smallest increase in the interest rate reduces aggregate demand until prices and interest rates return to their initial level and investment declines by the precise amount of the increase in G.

In the second case, $L_r = 0$ so that the *LM* curve is vertical.[25] An increase in G shifts the *IS* curve upward along the vertical *LM* curve. This induces a rise in the interest rate which continues until investment declines by the precise amount of the increase in G so that equilibrium is reestablished at the original price level but at a higher interest rate.

---

[25] If $L_r = 0$, a change in r cannot affect the demand for money. Therefore, equilibrium in the money market is independent of the interest rate.

APPENDIX

Mathematical Derivation of the Multipliers for the Classical Model

The general functional form of the *IS* and *LM* curves is given by equations (9A.1) and (9A.2).

$$\bar{X} = C(\bar{X} - \bar{T}) + I(r) + \bar{Z} + \bar{G} \tag{9A.1}$$

$$\frac{\bar{M}}{P} = L(r, \bar{X}) + \bar{L} \tag{9A.2}$$

To derive the interest rate multipliers, note that the *IS* curve alone, equation (9A.1), uniquely determines the equilibrium value of the interest rate; i.e., there is a single endogenous variable, and therefore equation (9A.1) is a system of one equation and one unknown which can generally be solved for a unique value of the unknown. The multipliers for changes in M and $\bar{L}$ must be zero, given that M and $\bar{L}$ do not appear as arguments in the *IS* curve.

$$\frac{dr}{dM} = 0 \tag{9A.3}$$

$$\frac{dr}{d\bar{L}} = 0 \tag{9A.4}$$

The multipliers for G, T, and Z can be derived by taking total derivatives of equation (9A.1) and solving for dr/dG when $dT = dZ = 0$, and then solving for dr/dT when $dG = dZ = 0$, etc.

$$\frac{dr}{dG} = -\frac{1}{I_r} \tag{9A.5}$$

$$\frac{dr}{dT} = \frac{C_y}{I_r} \tag{9A.6}$$

$$\frac{dr}{dZ} = -\frac{1}{I_r} \tag{9A.7}$$

To derive the multipliers for changes in P in response to changes in M or $\bar{L}$, we can disregard the *IS* function. Its role is to fix the interest rate in the *LM* function. Given r, X, and $\bar{L}$ we can totally differentiate equation (9A.1) and solve for dP/dM (where $dr = dX = d\bar{L} = 0$).

$$\frac{dP}{dM} = \frac{P}{M} \tag{9A.8}$$

Defining the elasticity of prices with respect to changes in the money supply as

$$\eta_{PM} = \frac{dP}{dM}\frac{M}{P}, \tag{9A.9}$$

we can observe from equation (9A.8) that

$$\eta_{PM} = 1. \tag{9A.10}$$

This confirms the *quantity theory of money*.

The multiplier for a change in $\bar{L}$ is

$$\frac{dP}{d\bar{L}} = \frac{P^2}{M} \tag{9A.11}$$

and is derived by the same procedure used to find dP/dM.

To derive the dP/dG, dP/dZ, and dP/dT multipliers, we must use both equations (9A.1) and (9A.2). Using Cramer's rule,[1] we first totally differentiate equations (9A.1) and (9A.2) with respect to G, Z, or T. For the dP/dG multiplier, for example, we get

$$0 - I_r \frac{dr}{dG} + 1$$
$$-\frac{M}{P^2}\frac{dP}{dG} = L_r \frac{dr}{dG}$$

Rearranging terms so that we form columns for terms unrelated to dP/dG and dr/dG on the left and columns for dP/dG and dr/dG on the right, we obtain

$$-1 = 0 + I_r \frac{dr}{dG}$$
$$0 = +\frac{M}{P^2}\frac{dP}{dG} + L_r \frac{dr}{dG}.$$

Solving, using Cramer's rule, we get

$$\frac{dP}{dG} = \frac{\begin{vmatrix} -1 & I_r \\ 0 & L_r \end{vmatrix}}{\begin{vmatrix} 0 & I_r \\ M/P^2 & L_r \end{vmatrix}}$$

$$\frac{dP}{dG} = \frac{-L_r}{-I_r \dfrac{M}{P^2}} > 0. \tag{9A.12}$$

Note, from equation (9A.12), it follows that if $L_r = 0$ or $I_r = -\infty$, $dP/dG = 0$. The multiplier

---

[1] For a discussion of the use of Cramer's rule in this type of model, see Thomas F. Dernburg and Judith D. Dernburg, *Macroeconomic Analysis: An Introduction to Comparative Statics and Dynamics* (Reading, Mass.: Addison-Wesley Publishing Company, Inc., 1969), Chapter 3 and the appendix to Chapter 3.

for dP/dZ is identical to equation (9A.12) and the multiplier for dP/dT is

$$\frac{dP}{dT} = -\frac{-C_y L_r}{I_r \frac{M}{P^2}}.$$ (9A.13)

● REVIEW QUESTIONS

1. Define neutrality, dichotomy, and the quantity theory of money.
2. Why is the interest rate referred to as a "real" phenomenon in the classical model?
3. Summarize the classical adjustment mechanism and identify the possible reasons why it may operate slowly or even break down entirely.
4. Why is the introduction of the wealth effect into the consumption function said to have rehabilitated classical macroeconomics from Keynes's critique? Does the existence of a wealth effect in the consumption function guarantee that the classical adjustment mechanism will be effective?

● PROBLEMS

1. Use the classical model to verify or reject each of the following propositions. Use graphs or refer to specific equations in each case.

    (a) An increase in government expenditures will reduce investment by an equivalent amount.

    (b) An increase in the rate of growth of the money supply will leave both real and nominal interest rates unchanged.

    (c) Inflation associated with any once-and-for-all increase in an exogenous variable eventually cures itself.

    (d) An equal increase in government expenditures and taxes has no effect.

    (e) An autonomous increase in saving will increase investment.

    (f) The government can encourage investment by running a budget surplus (i.e., by government saving).

    (g) Although the real interest rate is independent of the supply and demand for money, the price level is affected by both real and monetary forces.

    (h) The paradox of thrift holds.

2. Are either or both of the following quotes valid in the classical model? Can they be reconciled with each other?

(a) "Even though the demand for money depends on the interest rate, the interest rate does not depend on the amount of money."

(b) "A higher rate of monetary expansion will result in a *higher* rather than a lower level of interest rates, compared to what otherwise would have prevailed."

3. "If there is money illusion in the demand for money, neither neutrality nor the quantity theory of money holds." To introduce money illusion, respecify the *LM* curve as

$$\bar{M} = L(r, X, P)$$

where $L_p > 0$ but the elasticity of the demand for money with respect to the price level (ϵ_{LP}) is less than one. Use this *LM* curve to evaluate the quote.

4. "Crowding-out always occurs in real terms in the classical model, but only under special cases will it occur in nominal terms as well." What is the distinction between real and nominal crowding-out? Use classical *IS-LM* analysis to verify the quote. What are the special cases referred to in the quote?

5. "Inflation is always and everywhere a monetary phenomenon." Is this true in the classical model? Is it only true under special assumptions? If so, what are the assumptions?

6. Assume $X_f = 2000$, $T = 250$, and $G + Z = 700$; $P = 1.0$ and $M = 300$ initially; and $L_r = -10$, $I_r = -20$, $C_y = .8$, and $L_x = .2$. If M increases to 600, find the equilibrium response of r and P.

7. Using the parameter values and initial conditions given above, solve for the equilibrium value of the interest rate.

8. Using the same parameters and initial conditions as above, determine what happens to the interest rate and investment when government expenditures increase by $10 billion.

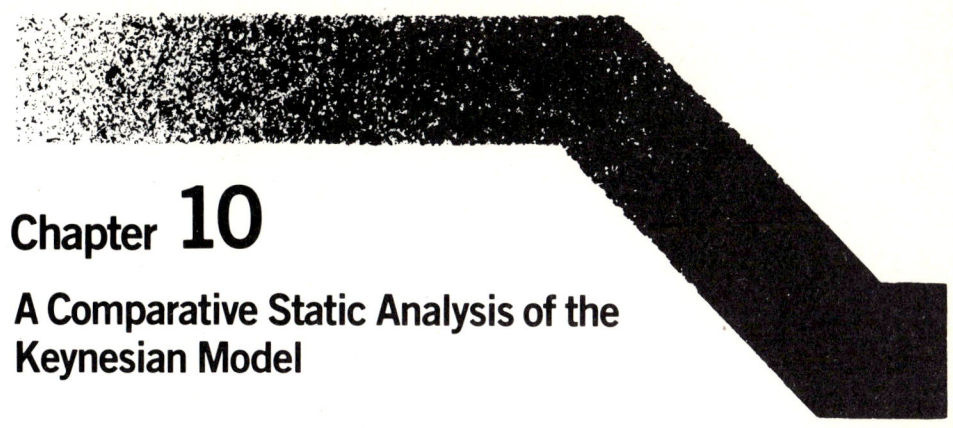

Chapter 10
A Comparative Static Analysis of the Keynesian Model

In this chapter we consider the determination of output and interest rates in the Keynesian version of the basic model. In the Keynesian version prices are assumed to be predetermined and changes in aggregate demand therefore affect output but not the price level. This model provides useful insight into output and interest rate determination in the *short run* when there is slack in the economy so that upward movements in aggregate demand do not press upon the economy's productive capacity. Even if the economy is initially at full employment, the Keynesian model provides insight into the short-run response to downward disturbances to aggregate demand.

The key assumption is that prices are rigid in the downward direction and inflexible upward as well, as long as aggregate demand is below the level of potential output. But the model remains useful for short-run analysis as long as the classical adjustment mechanism discussed in the previous section operates slowly to restore aggregate demand to full employment when aggregate demand is below the level of potential (full employment) output. In this case, aggregate demand can remain below potential output for an extended period, and the actual level of output will respond in the short run along the general lines suggested in the Keynesian version. This model can thus be used to determine the response of *actual* output and interest rates in the short run as opposed to full equilibrium values of those variables in the long run associated with the classical model. Nevertheless, the assumption of wage-price rigidity needs to be relaxed at a later stage in the analysis to permit a more precise modeling of the short-run response of output to policy changes and nonpolicy disturbances. We will introduce a model with both variable output and variable prices in the next chapter and devote Part IV to introducing variable prices and wages into short-run macroeconomic analysis.

In this chapter we first review the disequilibrium assumptions in the Keynesian model. We use these assumptions to describe the *sequence* of events in response to disturbances; e.g., the response of interest rates over time to monetary change. Next, we derive the explicit reduced form for the Keynesian model and then interpret the multipliers. Then we use *IS* and *LM* curves as well as the reduced form for income to present a comparative static analysis of the response of output and interest rates to (1) a change in government expenditures financed by bond issuance or retirement, (2) a change in tax receipts involving bond issuance or retirement, (3) a change in *G* and *T* of equal amounts, (4) a change in the money supply, (5) an autonomous change in the demand for money, and (6) an autonomous change in private aggregate demand. In the final section we review important properties of the Keynesian model uncovered by the previous analysis. Here we consider the influence of real and monetary changes on interest rates, the crowding-out of private expenditures by government expenditures, the conditions under which monetary policy becomes ineffective as a stabilization device, and the determinants of the relative effectiveness of monetary and fiscal policies.

DISEQUILIBRIUM ASSUMPTIONS FOR THE KEYNESIAN MODEL

Implicit in our discussion below of the sequence of events following changes in exogenous variables will be a set of disequilibrium assumptions which specify how economic agents respond to market disequilibrium. The comparative static results themselves do not depend on the specific disequilibrium assumptions except that comparative statics is a valid methodology only if the system is stable and the stability of the system depends on the specification of the disequilibrium assumptions. The description of how variables move between equilibrium positions, on the other hand, does depend explicitly on the disequilibrium assumptions.

We assume that output responds directly to commodity market disequilibrium (as in the Keynesian cross model of Chapter 6)

$$\dot{X} = \alpha(X^d - X) \tag{10.1}$$

where X^d is the level of aggregate demand and the interest rate responds directly to money market disequilibrium:[1]

$$\dot{r} = \beta(L - m). \tag{10.2}$$

Equations (10.1) and (10.2) correspond to the disequilibrium assumptions in the classical model except that output rather than prices responds to commodity market disequilibrium. If demand for output exceeds current production, there will be an involuntary decumulation of inventories and producers will respond by increasing production to accommodate demand. Thus, *production responds to accommodate changes in the demand for output in the Keynesian model.* Note that equation (10.2) is identical to the disequilibrium equation employed in the classical model, equation (9.2).

---

[1] This is the same assumption we employed in our discussion of the classical adjustment mechanism. The qualification in footnote 2 in Chapter 9 applies here also.

Chapter 10 • A Comparative Static Analysis of the Keynesian Model

DERIVING THE REDUCED FORMS FOR THE KEYNESIAN MODEL

The *IS* and *LM* curves for the Keynesian model are given by

$$X = C_y(X - \bar{T}) + I_r r + \bar{G} + \bar{Z} \tag{10.3}$$

and

$$\bar{m} = L_r r + L_x X + \bar{L}. \tag{10.4}$$

The endogenous variables are r and X and the exogenous variables are the policy instruments G, T, and m and the shift parameters Z and $\bar{L}$.

To derive the reduced forms for X and r, equations (10.3) and (10.4) must be solved by substitution for X and r, respectively.

We can rewrite equation (10.4) as

$$L_r r = \bar{m} - L_x X - \bar{L}$$

or

$$r = \frac{1}{L_r}\bar{m} - \frac{L_x}{L_r}X - \frac{1}{L_r}\bar{L}$$

and use this result to substitute for r in equation (10.3). This substitution yields

$$X = C_y X - C_y \bar{T} + I_r \left\{ \frac{1}{L_r}\bar{m} - \frac{L_x}{L_r}X - \frac{1}{L_r}\bar{L} \right\} + \bar{Z} + \bar{G}.$$

Collecting terms in X on the left, we obtain

$$X - C_y X + (L_x/L_r)I_r X = -C_y \bar{T} + (I_r/L_r)\bar{m} - (I_r/L_r)\bar{L} + \bar{Z} + \bar{G}$$

or

$$\{1 - C_y + (L_x/L_r)I_r\}X = -C_y \bar{T} + (I_r/L_r)\bar{m} - (I_r/L_r)\bar{L} + \bar{Z} + \bar{G}.$$

Dividing through by the bracketed term on the left, we get the reduced-form equation for output:

$$X = \frac{1}{D}\bar{G} + \frac{1}{D}\bar{Z} - \frac{C_y}{D}\bar{T} + \frac{I_r/L_r}{D}\bar{m} - \frac{I_r/L_r}{D}\bar{L} \tag{10.5}$$

where

$$D = 1 - C_y + (L_x/L_r)I_r. \tag{10.6}$$

The coefficients of the exogenous variables in a reduced-form equation are referred to as *multipliers*. Thus, the multipliers in equation (10.5) describe the response of output to changes in each of the exogenous variables. The multiplier for the response of output to a change in government expenditures, for example, is $\Delta X/\Delta G = 1/D$; and the multiplier for a change in the money supply is $\Delta X/\Delta m = (I_r/L_r)/D$.

INTERPRETING MULTIPLIERS—DIRECT IMPACTS AND FEEDBACK RESPONSES

Each multiplier indicates the role of each parameter in conditioning the response of output to a given disturbance. The response of output to any policy action or nonpolicy disturbance reflects the interaction of *direct impacts* and the *basic model multiplier*, and the basic multiplier, in turn, reflects the interaction of *positive* and *negative feedback responses*. The direct impact refers to the initial effect of the exogenous change on aggregate demand and hence on output and income. The basic multiplier summarizes the *income-induced* responses which then augment or dampen (i.e., multiply) the initial effect on income.

An increase in G, for example, has a direct impact (which we refer to as the *direct fiscal impact*) because G is a component of aggregate demand. As output responds to the increase in aggregate demand, two indirect or feedback responses become operative. The first is the *positive feedback effect* due to simple Keynesian multiplier. As output (and thus income) expands, there is an induced increase in consumption which reinforces the impact of the increase in G on aggregate demand and further stimulates output. In our model, the positive feedback depends exclusively on C_y; *the larger C_y, the greater the positive feedback and the larger the basic model multiplier.*

The second income-induced effect is the *negative feedback effect* which operates via the financial sector. As income rises due to the direct fiscal impact and the consumption-multiplier response, the demand for money increases relative to the fixed supply. As wealth owners attempt to increase money holdings relative to bond holdings by selling bonds, they drive up the rate of interest. The increase in the rate of interest dampens, and in extreme cases may completely crowd out, the impact on output of the increase in G. The magnitude of the negative feedback depends on the values of L_x, L_r, and I_r. The larger the L_x, the greater the negative feedback response. L_x controls the size of the disequilibrium in the money market generated by the rise in output initiated by the change in G and the multiplier; the larger the L_x, the greater the disequilibrium due to any given change in X and the larger the change in r required to restore portfolio balance. L_r controls the size of the change in r required to eliminate a given gap between money demand and supply; the smaller the L_r, the smaller the change in the demand for money for any given change in r and the larger the change in r required to restore portfolio balance for any given portfolio disequilibrium. I_r controls the influence of a change in r on aggregate demand (via investment); the larger the I_r, the greater the negative effect on investment and aggregate demand resulting from the income-induced rise in r.

The operation of the negative feedback and the interaction of direct impacts and feedback responses are depicted symbolically in Figures 10.1 and 10.2.

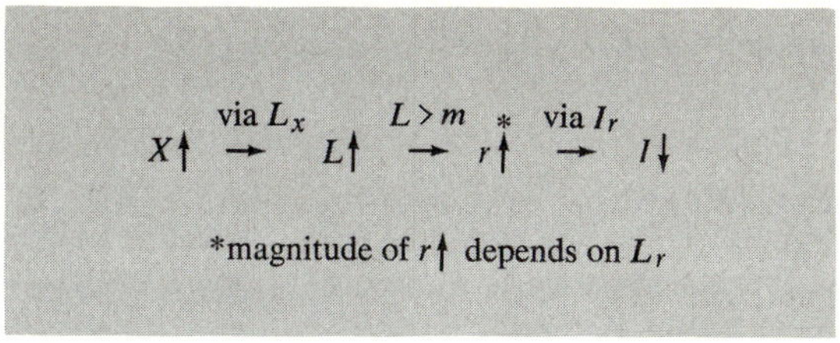

Chapter 10 · A Comparative Static Analysis of the Keynesian Model

$$X\uparrow \xrightarrow{\text{via } L_x} L\uparrow \xrightarrow{L > m} r\uparrow \xrightarrow{\text{via } I_r} I\downarrow$$

*magnitude of $r\uparrow$ depends on L_r

FIGURE 10.1
Negative Feedback

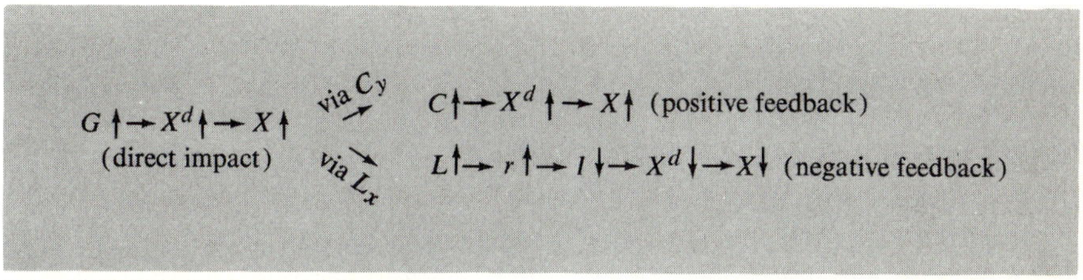

$$G\uparrow \rightarrow X^d\uparrow \rightarrow X\uparrow \quad \begin{array}{c}\text{via } C_y \\ \nearrow \\ \searrow \\ \text{via } L_x\end{array} \quad \begin{array}{l} C\uparrow \rightarrow X^d\uparrow \rightarrow X\uparrow \text{ (positive feedback)} \\ L\uparrow \rightarrow r\uparrow \rightarrow I\downarrow \rightarrow X^d\downarrow \rightarrow X\downarrow \text{ (negative feedback)} \end{array}$$
(direct impact)

FIGURE 10.2
Direct Impacts and Feedback Responses

The multipliers are always written so that the parameters that control the direct impact are in the numerator and the parameters that control the feedback responses are in the denominator; e.g.,

$$\frac{\Delta X}{\Delta ?} = \frac{DI}{1 - PF + NF} \qquad (10.7)$$

where DI = parameters that control the magnitude of the direct impact, PF = parameters that control the size of the positive feedback, and NF = the parameters that control the size of the negative feedback. One over the denominator of each of the multipliers is therefore the basic model multiplier [$1/D$ in equation (10.5)]. This reflects the fact that the income-induced or feedback responses are the same for all disturbances. Therefore, the various reduced-form multipliers differ only in their direct impacts (numerators).

COMPARATIVE STATIC RESULTS

Fiscal Policy I: Bond-Financed Changes in Government Expenditures

A bond-financed increase in G shifts the IS curve rightward but leaves the LM curve unchanged in this model.[2] The result is an increase in both output X and the interest rate, r. This is illustrated in Figure 10.3. The multiplier, as noted in the previous section, is

---

[2] In the current specifications, changes in the supply of bonds do not directly affect either IS or LM curves. This assumption will be relaxed in later chapters.

$$\frac{\Delta X}{\Delta G} = \frac{1}{D} = \frac{1}{1 - C_y + \frac{L_x}{L_r} I_r}. \tag{10.8}$$

The numerator describes the direct impact of the fiscal operation. G is a component of aggregate demand; an increase in G, therefore, directly increases aggregate demand and hence income dollar-for-dollar. The final outcome then reflects the multiplier process as income-induced or feedback responses are activated. The positive feedback via the consumption function tends to further increase aggregate demand and hence income while the negative feedback, activated by the income-induced rise in interest rates, tends to dampen the impact on aggregate demand and income.

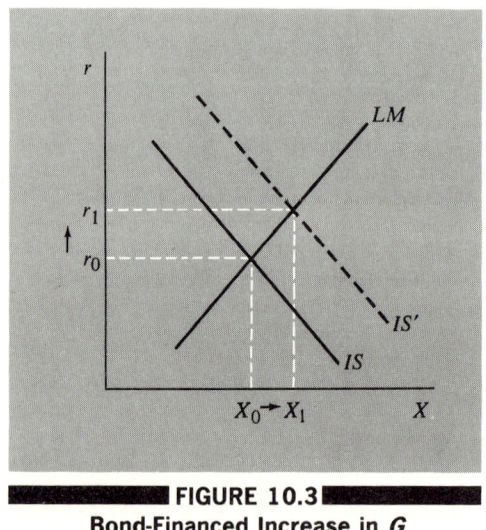

FIGURE 10.3
Bond-Financed Increase in G

○ **Fiscal Policy II: Bond-Financed Changes in Taxes or Transfers**

A bond-financed increase in transfer payments or decrease in tax receipts (ΔT) shifts the IS curve rightward (by a smaller amount than in the case of a bond-financed increase in government expenditures) but again leaves the LM curve unchanged. Thus, Figure 10.3 can also be used to show the results of this operation—an increase in both output and the interest rate.

The multiplier for a bond-financed change in taxes or transfers is

$$\frac{\Delta X}{\Delta T} = \frac{-C_y}{D}. \tag{10.9}$$

The direct impact of a one-dollar increase in tax receipts on aggregate demand is $-C_y$. The one-dollar increase in tax receipts reduces disposable income (Y) by one dollar and this, in turn, reduces consumption and hence aggregate demand by C_y dollars (e.g., by 80 cents where $C_y = .8$). The multiplier process operates exactly as described in the previous case.

Fiscal Policy III: A Change in Government Expenditures Financed by a Change in Tax Receipts (Balanced-Budget Fiscal Policy)

Increases in G and T of equal amounts have offsetting impacts on the IS curve; however, because an increase in G tends to shift the IS curve rightward by a larger amount $(1/1 - C_y)$ than an increase in T tends to shift the IS curve leftward $(-C_y/1 - C_y)$ where $C_y < 1$, the net effect is a small rightward shift of the IS curve (by $1 - C_y/1 - C_y$ or 1). As a consequence, there is an increase in X by less than the increase in G and T; e.g., $\Delta X < \Delta G$ in Figure 10.4. Thus, the balanced-budget multiplier is less than one in the simple Keynesian IS-LM model.

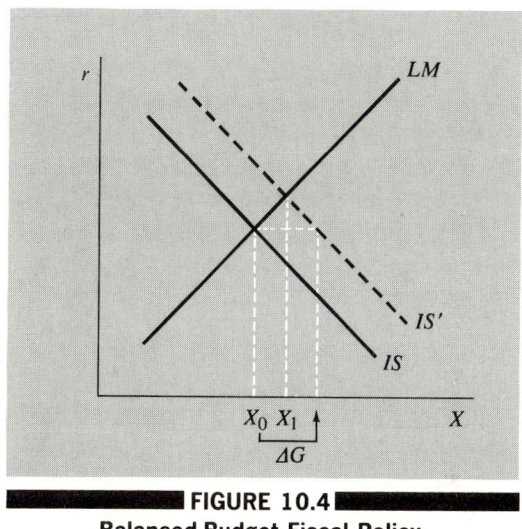

FIGURE 10.4
Balanced-Budget Fiscal Policy

This result can also be seen from the multiplier for this operation.

$$\frac{\Delta X}{\Delta G = \Delta T} = \frac{1 - C_y}{1 - C_y + \frac{L_x}{L_r} I_r} = \frac{1}{1 + \frac{L_x}{L_r} \frac{I_r}{1 - C_y}} < 1 \qquad (10.10)$$

The direct impact is $1 - C_y$: the 1 for the direct impact of the increase in G and $-C_y$ for the direct impact of the increase in T. The direct impact and positive feedback response associated with balanced-budget fiscal policy is the same in the Keynesian cross and IS-LM models; in the latter case, however, there is also negative feedback due to the income-induced rise in the interest rate. The multiplier is therefore smaller in the IS-LM framework.

Monetary Policy: Open Market Operations

In this model we consider the (real) money supply (m) as the policy instrument under the direct control of the policy authorities. We assume changes in the money supply are engineered via open market operations (purchase or sale of government bonds by the policy authority in exchange for money). In a subsequent chapter we will introduce a banking system, converting the money supply to an endogenous variable, and reconsider the operation of monetary policy.

The effect of an open market operation (*OMO*) is depicted in Figure 10.5. An increase in the money supply via an *OMO* shifts the *LM* curve down (to the right) along a fixed *IS* curve. The net effect is to depress the interest rate and increase output.

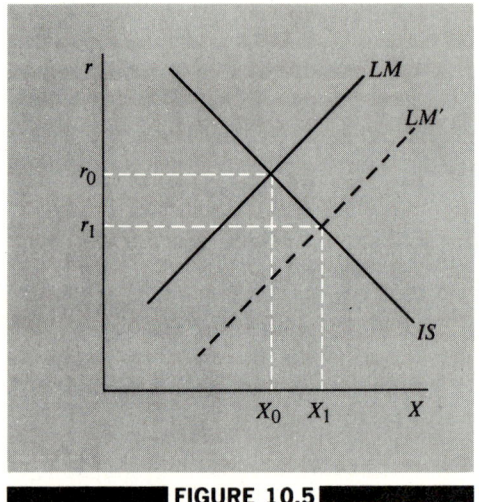

FIGURE 10.5
Monetary Policy: An Open Market Purchase

The multiplier for an *OMO* is given by

$$\frac{\Delta X}{\Delta m} = \frac{I_r/L_r}{D}. \tag{10.11}$$

The numerator specifies the parameters that control the direct impact (initial impact of the operation on aggregate demand) of an *OMO*. $1/L_r$ describes the effect of a one-dollar increase in the money supply on interest rates at an unchanged level of output; i.e., L_r is the change in the demand for money for a given change in the interest rate, so $1/L_r$ is the size of the decline in r required to raise the demand for money by one dollar. Thus, $1/L_r$ describes the change in r required to reequilibrate the money market at an unchanged output level following a one-dollar increase in the money supply. I_r/L_r describes the initial impact of the operation on aggregate demand as the decline in r stimulates investment. The income-induced feedback effects summarized in D are the same as for fiscal policy.

○ An Autonomous Change in the Demand for Money ($\Delta \overline{L}$)

An autonomous decline in the demand for money (a decline in the shift parameter $\overline{L}$) has an equivalent effect to an increase in the money supply in this model. Thus,

Figure 10.5 can also be used to describe the effects of an autonomous decrease in the demand for money—a decrease in the interest rate and an increase in output.

The multiplier, of course, is also identical in magnitude, although of opposite sign, to the $\Delta X/\Delta m$ multiplier.

$$\frac{\Delta X}{\Delta \bar{L}} = \frac{-I_r/L_r}{D} \qquad (10.12)$$

When there is a decline in the demand for money, wealth owners attempt to move out of money into bonds.[3] This drives up the price of bonds, or equivalently, depresses the interest rate. The decline in the interest rate stimulates investment. At this point the income-induced effects are activated as the general multiplier process begins.

An Autonomous Change in Private Aggregate Demand (ΔZ)

G and Z enter the model in an identical way (as exogenous components of aggregate demand). Hence, changes in Z and G have identical effects and Figure 10.3 can be used to depict the effects of an increase in Z—an increase in both interest rates and output.

The multiplier for a change in Z is also identical to the $\Delta X/\Delta G$ multiplier.

$$\frac{\Delta X}{\Delta Z} = \frac{1}{D} \qquad (10.13)$$

IMPORTANT PROPERTIES OF THE KEYNESIAN MODEL

In this section we will use the comparative static results derived in the previous section to draw some conclusions about the nature of the Keynesian model. First, we consider the forces that determine interest rates. Whereas the equilibrium interest rate in the classical model is determined exclusively by real forces, we find that the interest rate is jointly determined in the Keynesian model by real and monetary forces. Then we consider the response of interest rates to monetary change in the Keynesian model and contrast the results with those we found for the classical model. We next consider the conditions under which government expenditures crowd out an equivalent amount of private expenditures and then the conditions under which monetary policy becomes powerless. We conclude with a discussion of the parameters influencing the relative effectiveness of monetary and fiscal policies.

Real and Monetary Influences on the Interest Rate

In the classical model we found that the equilibrium interest rate was exclusively a real phenomenon. In the Keynesian version, on the other hand, any disturbance,

---

[3] We always consider a change in the demand for money as a change in desired portfolio composition and therefore as a movement between money and bonds. A change in desired wealth is introduced by an autonomous change in desired saving, i.e., via a change in Z.

real or financial, can alter the equilibrium interest rate.[4]

These seemingly conflicting results can be reconciled by recognizing that the classical and Keynesian models are really complementary rather than competitive models of interest rate, price, and output determination. Which model is appropriate for predicting the response of interest rates to disturbances depends on the *initial conditions* (position of the economy relative to full employment) and the *time horizon* being considered (short run or long run). The Keynesian model is relevant to short-run movements in interest rate and output in response to disturbances when the economy is operating below full employment. The classical model is relevant to long-run responses to disturbances and to short-run movements when the economy is at full employment. The change in the interest rate in response to monetary change in the Keynesian model can therefore be interpreted as the short-run disequilibrium movement that initially occurs in the classical model.

○ The Response of Interest Rates to Monetary Change

Even within the short-run horizon of the Keynesian model, there is a time pattern of interest rate movement in response to monetary change. The initial impact of an *OMO* is exclusively on the interest rate; i.e., at the initial level of output, the increase in the money supply depresses the interest rate. Assuming the money market is re-equilibrated before output begins to respond to the decline in r, the initial decline in r is from r_0 to r_1 in Figure 10.6. This decline is referred to as the *liquidity effect*.

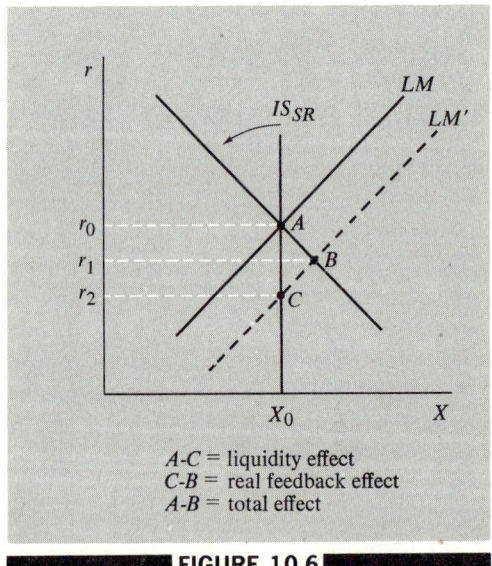

$A\text{-}C$ = liquidity effect
$C\text{-}B$ = real feedback effect
$A\text{-}B$ = total effect

FIGURE 10.6
The Response of Interest Rates
to Monetary Change

---

[4] There is in fact a special case, the liquidity trap, in which the interest rate is said to be a purely monetary phenomenon in that it is uniquely determined by the position of the *LM* curve. However, in a liquidity trap the interest rate is determined exclusively by interest rate expectations and is independent of changes in either real or monetary variables in the economy.

The very short-run *IS* curve may be vertical (IS_{SR} in Figure 10.6), reflecting the fact that aggregate demand does not initially respond to interest rates. Over time, as aggregate demand responds to the decline in interest rates, the *IS* curve rotates and the interest rate begins to move upward again. But the upward income-induced movement in the interest rate (referred to as the *real feedback response*) stops short of the initial interest rate (unless $I_r = -\infty$). The net result is that interest rates decline, although more in the short run than in the longer run. Thus, economists who believe that the Keynesian model is relevant to describing the response of interest rate to monetary change emphasize this *inverse* relationship between the money supply and the interest rate. Those who believe that the classical model is more relevant either expect the interest rate to return to its initial level (for a once-and-for-all change) or expect nominal interest rates to rise (in response to an increase in the growth rate for the money supply). As we noted just above, however, the nature of the initial conditions and the time period of the analysis determine which model is appropriate.

○ Crowding-Out

In this model, investment declines when government expenditures increase. However, the decline in investment is generally smaller than the increase in government expenditures, with the net result that income increases.[5] There are, on the other hand, two special cases in which the decline in investment just matches the increase in *G* so that income remains unchanged. These cases are associated with extreme values of the L_r and I_r parameters—with $L_r = 0$ and/or $I_r = -\infty$.

Crowding-out of investment occurs in this model exclusively due to the negative feedback response; i.e., due to the *income-induced* rise in interest rates. Therefore, only in extreme situations can the rise in *r* completely offset the rise in output associated with the increase in *G* (because it is the rise in output which puts upward pressure on *r*), and it is impossible for the negative feedback response to cause income to decline in response to an increase in *G*.

The conditions under which crowding-out will be complete can be determined by looking at the $\Delta X/\Delta G$ multiplier.

$$\frac{\Delta X}{\Delta G} = \frac{1}{1 - C_y + \frac{L_x}{L_r}I_r} \qquad (10.14)$$

Crowding-out will be complete ($\Delta X/\Delta G = 0$) when the denominator is infinite. The two cases which have received much attention are where $L_r = 0$ or $I_r = -\infty$. In either case, the negative feedback term becomes infinitely large and the full multiplier goes to zero.

---

[5] This is only our initial look at the crowding-out phenomenon. The oversimplifying assumptions that $L_a = C_a = 0$ eliminate any impact of bond financing on the outcome. In later chapters (and particularly in Chapter 22) we will consider the implications of a number of modifications of the model for the nature and magnitude of crowding-out. We will summarize the results in Chapter 25 on fiscal policy.

Crowding-Out When $I_r = -\infty$. In this case, the smallest increase in income and the associated income-induced rise in the interest rate generates a reduction in investment sufficient to restore the initial levels of r and X. This case is depicted in Figure 10.7. Note that when $I_r = -\infty$, the slope of the *IS* curve is zero (i.e., the *IS* curve is horizontal) and the *IS* curve does not shift when G changes.[6]

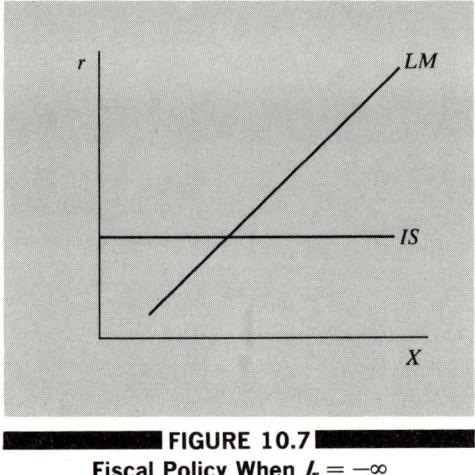

FIGURE 10.7
Fiscal Policy When $I_r = -\infty$

Crowding-Out When $L_r = 0$. In this case, the initial increase in X in response to an increase in G generates an upward movement in r which continues until investment declines by an amount just equal to the increase in G and total output is returned to its original level. As X increases, the demand for money increases, inducing wealth owners to sell bonds. When $L_r < 0$, the rise in r induced by the sale of bonds reduces the demand for money; portfolios can be in equilibrium at a higher X and a higher r. But when $L_r = 0$, the rise in r in response to the selling of bonds does not help to restore portfolio equilibrium. As long as X is higher than initially, excess demand for money prevails and wealth owners continue attempts to unload bonds. The rate

---

[6] The slope of the *IS* curve is

$$\left.\frac{\Delta r}{\Delta X}\right|_{IS} = \frac{1-C_y}{I_r}.$$

Thus, when $I_r \to -\infty$, $\left.\frac{dr}{dX}\right|_{IS} \to 0$. The vertical shift in the *IS* curve in response to a ΔG is

$$\left.\frac{\Delta r}{\Delta G}\right|_{IS} = -\frac{1}{I_r}.$$

When $I_r \to -\infty$, $\left.\frac{dr}{dG}\right|_{IS} \to 0$.

of interest rises until it crowds out an amount of private demand just equal to the change in G; output is then returned to its original level where portfolios are again in equilibrium. This case is pictured in Figure 10.8.

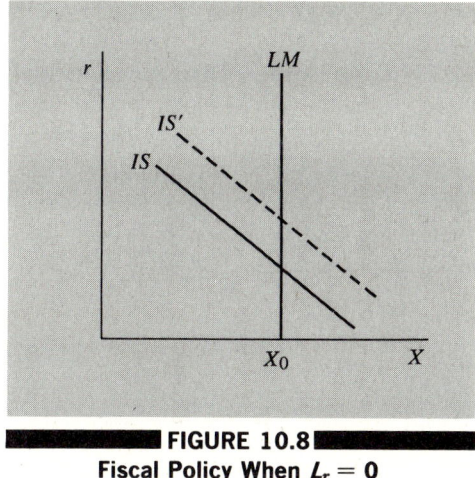

FIGURE 10.8
Fiscal Policy When $L_r = 0$

○ Conditions Under Which Monetary Policy Is Powerless

An increase in the money supply generally lowers interest rates and stimulates investment in the Keynesian model. There are two major links in the transmission of changes in the money supply to aggregate demand: the decline in the interest rate due to the increase in the money supply[7] and the increase in investment due to the decline in the interest rate.[8] If either of these two links fails to operate, monetary policy becomes impotent.

The key parameters can be seen from the $\Delta X/\Delta m$ multiplier. Dividing the numerator and denominator of the $\Delta X/\Delta m$ multiplier, equation (10.11), by I_r/L_r we get

$$\frac{\Delta X}{\Delta m} = \frac{1}{(1 - C_y)\frac{L_r}{I_r} + L_x}. \tag{10.15}$$

---

[7] We only have a single nonmoney financial asset and a single interest rate in this version of the model. The channels of monetary policy become more complicated when we distinguish short-term and long-term bonds as well as bonds and equities in Chapters 20 and 22.

[8] We have confined the influence of interest rates to investment. We will relax this restriction later on. In Chapter 13, for example, we will introduce the interest rate in the consumption function. Monetarists have often criticized income-expenditure models (like the present one) for restricting the influence of monetary change to a small component of total expenditures instead of allowing monetary policy to affect a wide class of expenditures. See, for example, Milton Friedman and Anna Schwartz, "Money and Business Cycles," *Review of Economics and Statistics*, Vol. 45 (Feb., 1963), pp. 32–78. Including r in the investment function allows for influence on plant and equipment spending, inventory investment, and residential construction. None of the qualitative conclusions are altered, however, by including the interest rate as an argument in the consumption function.

$\Delta X/\Delta m$ goes to zero when the denominator of equation (10.15) goes to infinity. The two cases which have generally been emphasized are $L_r = -\infty$ or $I_r = 0$. Note that in terms of the original form of the multiplier, either of these extreme values causes the direct impact of the monetary operation (I_r/L_r) to become zero.

Monetary Policy When $L_r = -\infty$. In this case, monetary policy loses control over the interest rate. As noted in the previous chapter, wealth owners become indifferent between money and bonds. If the policy authority wishes to purchase bonds, wealth owners passively respond by selling their bonds without requiring the usual inducement of an increase in the price of the bond (decline in the interest rate).

This case is pictured in Figure 10.9. When $L_r = -\infty$, the slope of the LM curve is zero and changes in m cannot shift the LM curve.[9]

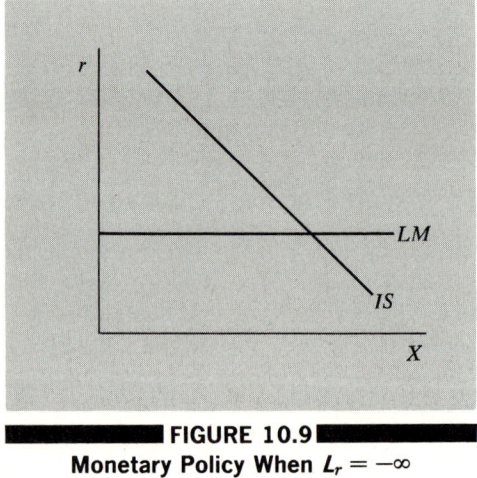

FIGURE 10.9
Monetary Policy When $L_r = -\infty$

Monetary Policy When $I_r = 0$. In this case, the decline in interest rate associated with an increase in the money supply leaves investment, and hence aggregate demand and income, unchanged. This case is depicted in Figure 10.10.

---

[9] The vertical shift in the LM curve is

$$\left.\frac{\Delta r}{\Delta m}\right|_{\bar{X}} = \frac{1}{L_r}.$$

When $L_r \to -\infty$

$$\left.\frac{\Delta r}{\Delta m}\right|_{\bar{X}} \to 0.$$

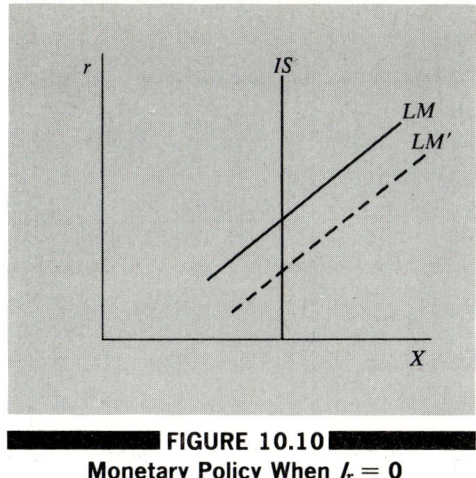

FIGURE 10.10
Monetary Policy When $I_r = 0$

THE RELATIVE EFFECTIVENESS OF MONETARY AND FISCAL POLICIES

Now we are ready to consider the determinants of the relative effectiveness of monetary and fiscal policies.

The Income Parameters (C_y and L_x)

The income parameters affect both policies symmetrically. C_y affects all policies via the positive feedback response. *The larger C_y, the larger the positive feedback response and the larger all the multipliers in the model.* L_x, on the other hand, affects all policies exclusively via the negative feedback response. L_x determines the size of the income-induced increase in demand for money and interest rate. *The larger L_x, the larger the negative feedback response to all disturbances and the smaller all the multipliers.*

The Interest Rate Parameters (L_r and I_r)

The interest rate parameters affect the two policies asymmetrically. The two critical parameters for determining the relative effectiveness of monetary and fiscal policies are L_r and I_r. The smaller L_r and the larger I_r (in absolute value), the more effective is monetary policy and the less effective is fiscal policy.

L_r affects monetary policy via the direct impact.[10] The smaller the L_r (in absolute value), the larger the decline in r associated with an increase in m and the larger the $\Delta X/\Delta m$ multiplier. L_r affects fiscal policy only through the negative feedback response. The smaller the L_r, the larger the income-induced change in r, the larger the negative feedback response, and the smaller the $\Delta X/\Delta G$ multiplier.

---

[10] L_r and I_r affect monetary policy through both the direct impact and negative feedback effects. The dominant effect on the full multiplier can always be judged by considering the influence on the direct impact.

I_r affects the direct impact of monetary policy. The larger the I_r, the larger the direct impact of an *OMO* and the larger the $\Delta X/\Delta m$ multiplier. I_r affects fiscal policy via the negative feedback response. The larger the I_r, the larger the decline in investment induced by an income-induced rise in interest rates, the larger the negative feedback response, and the smaller the $\Delta X/\Delta G$ multiplier.

Each of these results can be seen clearly from the way L_r and I_r enter the $\Delta X/\Delta m$ and $\Delta X/\Delta G$ multipliers. It is also possible to show these results graphically. Consider the effect of L_r on monetary and fiscal policies. To demonstrate how the value of L_r affects the multipliers, we draw two *LM* curves which assume different values of L_r. In Figure 10.11, LM_1 assumes a larger L_r (in absolute value) than LM_2. The slope of the *LM* curve is $-L_x/L_r$; therefore, the larger the L_r, the flatter the slope of the *LM* curve. Now consider how the impact of an increase in G depends on the shape of the *LM* curve. An increase in G shifts the *IS* curve rightward in Figure 10.11; the effect on output is greater along the flatter *LM* curve. Thus, *the larger L_r, the greater the impact of fiscal policy.*

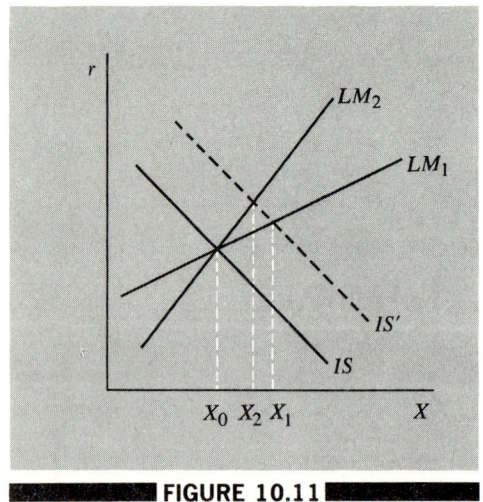

FIGURE 10.11
L_r and the Response to Fiscal Policy

The graphical analysis of the impact of the magnitude of L_r on the magnitude of the monetary policy multiplier is more complicated. The problem is how an increase in money shifts the two *LM* curves. Equally, of course. But, given that the curves have different slopes, they can shift by equal amounts in only *one direction*. The horizontal shift in the *LM* curve depends on L_x and the vertical shift on L_r. Therefore, the two curves must shift by equal amounts in the horizontal direction and unequal amounts in the vertical direction. In Figure 10.12 we see that *an increase in m has a larger impact on income for the smaller value of L_r.*[11]

---

[11] You may find it useful to review the discussion of horizontal and vertical shifts of the *IS* and *LM* curves in Chapter 8. See footnotes 3 and 7 in that chapter.

Chapter 10 • A Comparative Static Analysis of the Keynesian Model

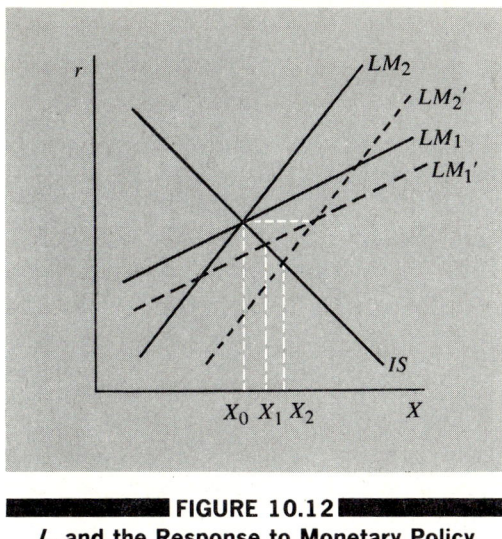

FIGURE 10.12
L_r and the Response to Monetary Policy

A similar analysis can be applied to different values of I_r. In Figure 10.13 there are two IS curves which differ only in the value of I_r. IS_1 assumes a smaller value (in absolute value) of I_r than IS_2. *An increase in the money supply has a greater impact on income, the larger the value of I_r.*

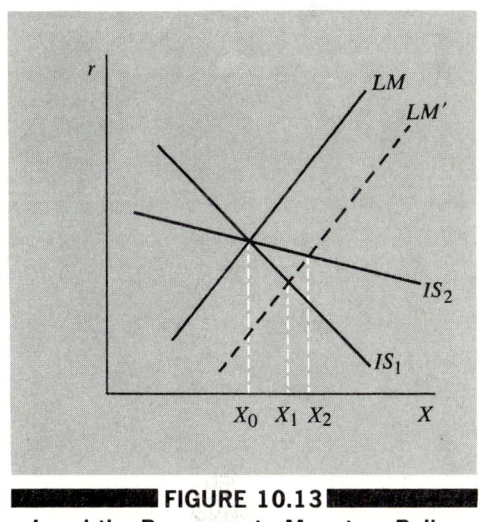

FIGURE 10.13
I_r and the Response to Monetary Policy

An increase in G shifts the two IS curves by equal amounts in the horizontal direction. *The larger I_r (in absolute value), the smaller the impact of an increase in G on income* (see Figure 10.14).

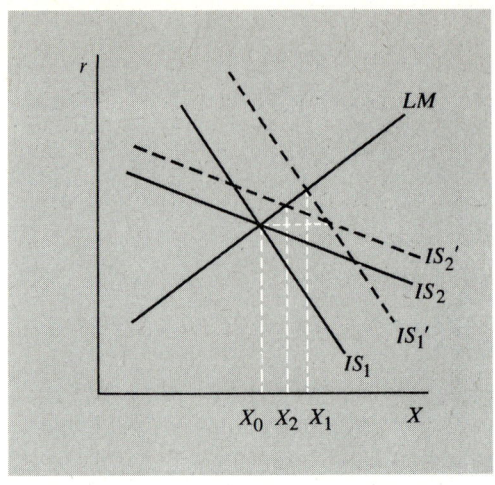

FIGURE 10.14
I_r and the Response to Fiscal Policy

APPENDIX

A Numerical Example of Income Determination in the Keynesian Model

In this appendix we derive quantitative values for the multipliers of the Keynesian model based on assumed values of model parameters.

Model Parameters

The values of C_y, I_r, L_x, and I_r assumed in this example are reported in Table 10A.1.

$$C_y = 0.8$$
$$I_r = -20$$
$$L_x = 0.15$$
$$L_r = -10$$

TABLE 10A.1
Assumed Parameter Values

The values of the parameters were chosen primarily to approximate empirical estimates and secondarily to generate a denominator which divides easily into one! We will discuss the empirical evidence on which our choices were based in subsequent chapters. The value of C_y is generally found to be 0.7–0.8 in econometric estimates of the consumption function (see Chapter 12). We use 0.8 to insure "round" answers for the multipliers. Much of the evidence is based on estimated values of elasticities. For example, ϵ_{LX} is generally found to be about 0.7. Given that $\epsilon_{LX} = \frac{\Delta L}{\Delta X}\frac{X}{M}$, we set $L_x = \frac{\Delta L}{\Delta X} = \epsilon_{LX}(M/X)$ where the values of M and X are the values of real output and real money supply in 1977. Similarly, we based the values of L_r on empirical estimates of ϵ_{Lr} (see Chapter 19); $L_r = \epsilon_{Lr}(M/r)$ where we assumed $r = 5.0$ percent and $\epsilon_{Lr} = -0.2$. The value of I_r is based on the βk_r term in the stock adjustment model of investment where k_r is based on the relevant elasticity (see Chapter 15).

The Reduced Forms

Based on the assumed parameter values, the reduced forms for income are given by equation (10A.1)

$$X = 2.0\bar{Z} + 2.0\bar{G} - 1.6\bar{T} + 4.0\bar{m} - 4.0\bar{L} \tag{10A.1}$$

The basic income multiplier ($1/D$) is therefore 2.0. Given that $I_r/L_r = 2$, monetary policy has a multiplier double that for bond-financed changes in G, G and Z have identical multipliers while the multiplier of T is of the opposite sign and smaller in absolute value. Table 10A.2 summarizes the various income multipliers.

Policy/Disturbance	Income Multipliers
Bond-Financed ΔG	2.0
Bond-Financed ΔT	−1.6
Balanced-Budget $\Delta G, \Delta T$	−0.4
Open Market Operation	4.0
Autonomous ΔZ	2.0
Autonomous ΔL	−4.0

TABLE 10A.2
Income Multipliers

● REVIEW QUESTIONS

1. Explain the role of each of the parameters in the basic model multiplier; i.e., explain how the parameter affects the positive and/or negative feedback responses.

2. Explain verbally why (a) increasing C_y increases all model multipliers; (b) increasing L_x decreases all model multipliers; and (c) increasing L_r or I_r has asymmetric effects on monetary policy and government expenditure multipliers.

● PROBLEMS

1. Use graphical or mathematical analysis of the Keynesian model to verify or reject each of the following propositions:

    (a) The balanced-budget multiplier is unity.

    (b) The paradox of thrift holds. (An autonomous increase in saving decreases aggregate saving.)

    (c) Bond-financed increases in government expenditures reduce private spending but increase output.

    (d) The rise in interest rates associated with a bond-financed increase in G reflects the effect of an increase in the supply of bonds on the interest rate.

    (e) One way of increasing capital spending is to provide an incentive for increased saving.

2. The values of the parameters in the Keynesian IS-LM model employed in the appendix are repeated below, along with the value of the government expenditure and monetary policy multipliers corresponding to the parameter values. In this problem you will derive the impact on these multipliers of changes in the parameters.

Parameter Values				Multipliers	
C_y	L_x	I_r	L_r	$\Delta X/\Delta G$	2.0
.8	.15	−20	−10	$\Delta X/\Delta m$	4.0

(a) Variation in I_r—Calculate the value of the multipliers for a high value (-100), a low value (-10), and two extreme cases (0 and $-\infty$).

(b) Variation in L_r—Calculate the multipliers for a high value (-50), a low value (-5), and the two extreme cases (0 and $-\infty$).

(c) Now compute the multipliers for (1) the high value of I_r and the low value of L_r (-100 and -5, respectively) and (2) the low value of I_r and the high value of L_r (-10 and -50, respectively). Compare the size of the two multipliers under the two sets of assumptions.

3. Assume the *GNP* gap is $50 billion. Calculate the size of open market operations, bond-financed changes in G, bond-financed changes in T, and money-financed changes in G and T required to close the gap. Use the same parameter value as in the appendix.

4. Assume $C_y = 1.2$; all other parameters take on the values in the appendix. Calculate the multiplier for an increase in autonomous private demand (Z). Compare with the multiplier in the appendix and the Keynesian cross multiplier when $C_y = 1.2$. Explain the differences.

5. Assume the economy is initially at full employment. Using the same parameter values as in the appendix, find the size of open market operations required to offset (a) a $20 billion decline in autonomous private demand and (b) a $10 billion autonomous increase in the demand for money.

Chapter 11

Aggregate Supply and Demand Analysis

The two versions of *IS-LM* employed in Chapters 9 and 10 assumed that either output or the price level was exogenous. This simplified the analysis, yet permitted us to develop some of the basic elements of income and price level determination. However, we need to develop models with less restrictive assumptions in order to be able to explain the simultaneous existence of recession and inflation experienced during the latter 1960s and 1970s. In this chapter we make a modest beginning in this direction by developing two simple models allowing for variation in both prices and output. We begin by modeling the effect of the price level on the supply and demand for output. In the first section we develop two alternative specifications of the aggregate supply curve, the relation between the price level and the supply of goods. The first specification allows for flexible price level but assumes that the nominal wage rate is inflexible in the downward direction. The second specification allows for flexibility in both wages and prices but assumes that the supply of labor depends on the nominal rather than the real wage rate. In the second section we combine the *IS* and *LM* curves to yield a relation between the price level and the *demand* for output, called the aggregate demand curve. Then we bring together the aggregate demand and aggregate supply curves to investigate the response of output and prices to both demand and supply disturbances.

THE AGGREGATE SUPPLY CURVE

In the Keynesian and classical versions of the *IS-LM* model, either the price level or the level of output is assumed to be fixed. We now turn to models in which prices and output are both variable. We will develop such a model in two alternative ways. In the first approach, we assume that although prices are flexible, the nominal wage rate is inflexible in the downward direction. A second model that yields variable prices and output is one in which workers exhibit money illusion in their labor supply decision; i.e., the supply of labor depends on the nominal rather than the real wage rate.

○ The Aggregate Supply Curve I: Rigid Nominal Wages and Variable Prices

We assume that wages are rigid in the downward direction but prices are flexible in both directions. Both the supply and demand for labor depend on the real wage rate, as in previous chapters. Although firms always operate on their labor demand curve, workers are often off their labor supply curve. Despite the resulting excess supply of labor, nominal wages fail to decline.

The Derivation of the Aggregate Supply Curve. To derive the relation between the price level and the supply of output, we begin with the marginal condition for the profit-maximizing demand for labor,

$$W = PF_N \qquad (11.1)$$

where F_N is the marginal physical product of labor (the increase in output associated with a unit increase in labor input). According to equation (11.1), the profit-maximizing demand for labor occurs at the point where the marginal cost of hiring another unit of labor (the wage rate, assuming a competitive labor market) equals the marginal revenue associated with another unit of labor (the marginal product of labor times the price of output, assuming a competitive output market). Equation (11.1) can be rewritten to express the relation between the price level and the wage rate:

$$P = \frac{W}{F_N}. \qquad (11.1')$$

We will initially assume that the nominal wage, W, is fixed; in this case the price level varies inversely with the value of F_N. From the law of diminishing returns, we know that the marginal product of labor, F_N, declines as employment and hence output increases in the short run. Therefore, F_N is a declining function of output, X; given $\overline{W}$, an increase in production (aggregate supply) requires an increase in the price level to offset the rising marginal cost of production. We can express P as a function of W and X:

$$P = \overline{W}S(X) \qquad (11.2)$$

where $S_x > 0$.

According to equation (11.2), the price level is proportional to the wage rate, given the level of output; and P is positively related to X, given the wage rate. This relation is usually referred to as the *aggregate supply function* and is depicted in Figure 11.1. The positive slope of the aggregate supply curve reflects the rising marginal cost of additional output due to the law of diminishing returns and the position of the curve depends on the exogenous nominal wage rate.

The Supply of Labor and the Aggregate Supply Curve. We did not make explicit use of the labor supply curve in deriving the aggregate supply curve. The labor supply

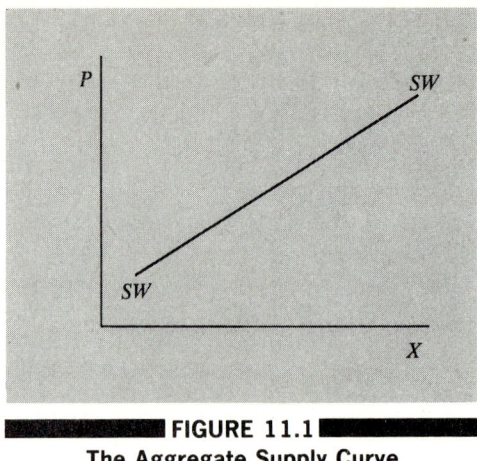

FIGURE 11.1
The Aggregate Supply Curve

curve is only used in this model to define the level of full employment. If the level of employment is less than full employment, there is excess supply without any associated downward pressure on the nominal wage rate. Up to the point at which full employment is achieved, the level of employment adjusts passively to accommodate the demand for labor at the prevailing nominal wage rate as the price level varies. Once full employment is achieved, on the other hand, further increases in the price level induce proportional increases in the nominal wage rate, and employment and output remain fixed at their full employment levels.

The supply and demand curves for labor are depicted in Figure 11.2. At point A, nominal wage is equal to W_0, the price level is P_0, and the level of employment equals N_0. At the prevailing real wage rate (W_0/P_0), there is excess supply of labor but by assumption, no downward pressure on the nominal wage rate. If the price level increases, firms will increase their demand for labor (moving down their labor demand curve). Employment responds passively until full employment (N_f) is achieved. For example, if prices rise to P_1, the real wage falls to W_0/P_1 and labor market equilibrium (full employment) results. Any further increase in the price level would result in *excess demand* for labor. Although the nominal wage is inflexible in the downward direction, it does rise in response to excess demand once full employment has been achieved. Therefore, wages as well as prices respond to increases in demand at full employment and the model reduces to the classical version of *IS-LM* analysis with respect to upward demand disturbances at full employment.

We depict the range in which output and prices vary together in Figure 11.3. The CC curve is the aggregate supply curve in the classical model. Output is fixed at full employment and prices (and wages) are variable. This curve identifies the maximum level of production. The aggregate supply curve in the rigid wage model (the SW curve in Figure 11.3) applies only to the left of the CC curve. Once output reaches X_f, price increases no longer induce increases in production. Instead, wages and prices vary proportionately and employment and output remain at their full employment levels.

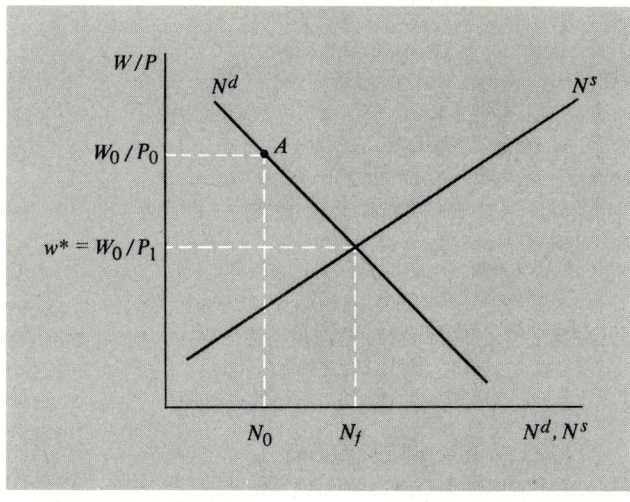

FIGURE 11.2
The Supply and Demand for Labor

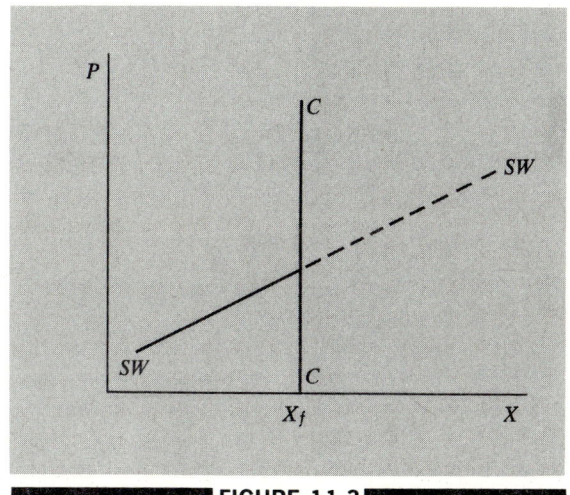

FIGURE 11.3
The Aggregate Supply Curve and Full Employment

○ The Aggregate Supply Curve II: Money Illusion/Misinformation

An alternative specification of the aggregate supply curve follows from the assumption that the supply of labor depends on the nominal instead of the real wage rate. Workers are said to suffer from *money illusion* in this case because their labor supply is influenced by changes in nominal wages and prices which leave the real wage rate unaffected. This view of labor supply has often been associated with Keynes.[1]

---

[1] See, for example, Robert L. Crouch, *Macroeconomics* (New York: Harcourt, Brace Jovanovich, Inc., 1972), pp. 235–245.

More recently this specification has been revived as a model of the *short-run* labor supply decision. Although workers immediately learn of changes in the nominal wage rate, they may require time to process information on changes in the prices of goods. Workers suffer from short-run money illusion in this case, not because of irrational behavior, but because of incomplete information.[2]

In our discussion in this section we will assume that workers only temporarily exhibit money illusion. The short-run labor supply curve can be specified in this case as

$$N^s = N^s(W/\overline{P}) \tag{11.3}$$

where $\overline{P}$ is the initial price level. In the long run, workers correctly perceive the real wage rate and this model collapses to the classical version of *IS-LM* analysis. In the short run, it implies a positively sloped aggregate supply curve and, therefore, the potential for variation in output as well as prices in response to disturbances and policy actions. The supply and demand curves for labor are depicted in Figure 11.4 with the nominal wage on the vertical axis. The position of the demand curve is determined by the price level because the demand for labor is a function of the real wage rate (in both the short run and the long run). An increase in the price level increases the demand for labor at each level of the nominal wage rate; i.e., it shifts the labor demand curve rightward. In Figure 11.4, for example, an increase in the price level from P_0 to P_1 shifts the N^d curve to $N^{d'}$. The position of the labor supply curve, on the other hand, is fixed in the short run, depending on the *initial* price level. If the price level increases, the demand curve shifts rightward along the fixed supply curve, resulting in an increase in the nominal wage rate (inducing an increase in the labor supply) and a decline in the real wage rate (inducing an increase

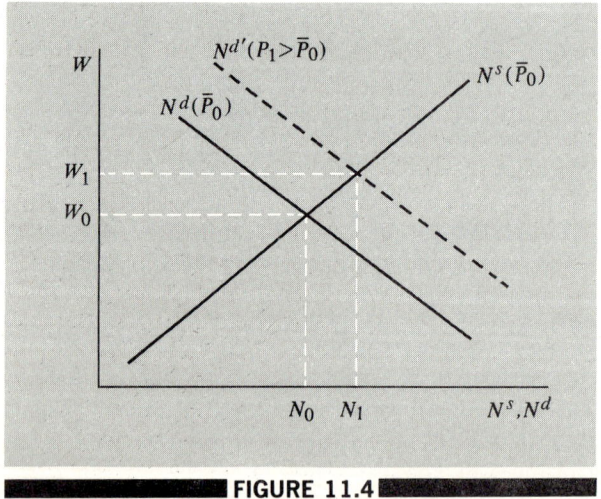

FIGURE 11.4
Money Illusion and Supply and Demand for Labor

---

[2] For an example of this type of model, see Milton Friedman, "The Role of Monetary Policy," *American Economic Review*, Vol. 58 (March, 1968), pp. 1–17.

in the demand for labor).

The higher the price level, the higher the level of employment and production. Therefore, the aggregate supply curve is upward sloping as in the rigid wage case. However, in the money illusion or misinformation case the nominal wage rate also varies along the aggregate supply curve and the supply and demand for labor are always equal.

As we noted above, this specification of the aggregate supply curve is intended as a short-run relationship. In the long run, we assume there is no money illusion in labor supply decisions (workers have had time to acquire and respond to information about prices as well as wages) so that there is again a unique equilibrium level of employment and output as in the classical version of the *IS-LM* model. We depict both the short-run (*SS*) and long-run (*CC*) versions of the aggregate supply curve in Figure 11.5. The essential feature of this model is that it is possible *in the short run* to expand production beyond the level associated with full employment in the long-run model (beyond X_f in Figure 11.5). Thus, unlike the rigid wage case, the upward-sloping aggregate supply curve in Figure 11.5 (*SS*) applies both to the left and to the right of the unique long-run equilibrium level of output (at X_f).

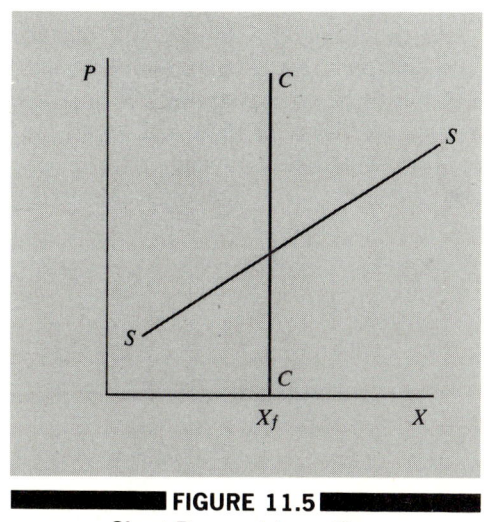

FIGURE 11.5
Short-Run and Long-Run
Aggregate Supply Curves

○ Difference in the Two Specifications of the Aggregate Supply Curve

Both aggregate supply curves are upward sloping, but there are four important differences. First, the money illusion case applies on both sides of the classical curve (at X_f), whereas the rigid wage case applies only to the left of the *CC* curve. Second, the nominal wage is fixed along the rigid wage curve but variable along the money illusion curve. Third, movement along the rigid wage curve is associated with changes in the amount of involuntary unemployment; i.e., as we move up the rigid wage curve toward the full employment level of output, the excess supply of labor is decreasing and $N^d = N^s$ at X_f. In contrast, $N^d = N^s$ all along the money illusion specification

Part II • Comparative Static Analysis with the Basic Model

of the aggregate supply curve. Variations in employment reflect changes in the amount of *voluntary* nonemployment. As the money wage increases, workers increase work *at the expense of leisure*, permitting an increase in employment and production.[3] Finally, the money illusion curve also introduces an essential distinction in the analysis of the response to changes in the price level (and to changes in the rate of inflation): the distinction between *anticipated* and *unanticipated* changes. In the fixed wage specification, the response of output to changes in the price level is independent of whether or not the change is anticipated or unanticipated. In the misinformation case, on the other hand, output responds only to unanticipated price changes; if price changes are anticipated, workers will not be fooled into believing that the rise in the nominal wage rate is also a rise in the real wage rate. We emphasize this distinction here because it is an essential aspect of the modern approach to employment and inflation theory, discussed in more detail in Part V.

THE AGGREGATE DEMAND CURVE

In the previous section we developed two alternative specifications of the relation between the price level and the supply of output. In this section we develop the relation between the price level and the *demand* for output, called the *aggregate demand curve*. It corresponds to the combinations of P and X for which both the money and output markets will be in equilibrium. With X and P both variable, the *IS* and *LM* curves are two equations in three unknowns (r, P, and X). To solve this system for the set of combinations of P and X for which both markets will be in equilibrium, we must first solve each equation in terms of the interest rate. The *LM* curve with a variable P is nonlinear. To simplify the derivation, it is useful to respecify the *LM* curve as a linear relation;[4] e.g.,

$$\bar{M} = L_r r + L_x X + L_p P + \bar{L} \tag{11.4}$$

where $L_p > 0$. Solving the *LM* equation in terms of r yields

$$r = \frac{1}{L_r}\bar{M} - \frac{L_x}{L_r}X - \frac{L_p}{L_r}P - \frac{1}{L_r}\bar{L}. \tag{11.4'}$$

Similarly, solving the *IS* curve in terms of r yields

$$r = \frac{1}{I_r}X - \frac{C_y}{I_r}(X - \bar{T}) - \frac{1}{I_r}(\bar{Z} + \bar{G}). \tag{11.5}$$

---

[3] We will have another complementary explanation for this increase in employment in Chapter 17. There we discuss the recent literature on search theory which suggests that money illusion induces workers to search for a shorter duration when wages and prices are rising. In this case, workers substitute employment for search along the aggregate supply curve.

[4] In the linear specification given by equation (11.4), the elasticity of nominal demand for money with respect to the price level is no longer constrained to unity (and indeed is not even constant). We use this specification only to simplify the derivation and exposition of the aggregate demand curve.

Equating equations (11.5) and (11.4') (since they both equal r), we obtain

$$X = \frac{I_r/L_r}{D}\bar{M} - \frac{(I_r/L_r)L_p}{D}P - \frac{I_r/L_r}{D}\bar{L} + \frac{1}{D}(\bar{Z}+\bar{G}) - \frac{C_y}{D}\bar{T} \qquad (11.6)$$

where $D = 1 - C_y + (L_x/L_r)I_r$, the basic denominator derived for the Keynesian model in Chapter 10. Equation (11.6) is the equation for the aggregate demand curve, the combinations of X and P for which money and commodity markets are both in equilibrium. Note that if P is constant, the change in X required to reequilibrate the money and commodity markets following changes in M, $\bar{L}$, Z, G, or T are identical to the multipliers derived in Chapter 10.

The slope of the aggregate demand curve, depicted in Figure 11.6, is

$$\frac{\Delta P}{\Delta X} = \frac{-D}{(I_r/L_r)L_p} < 0 \qquad (11.7)$$

and is unambiguously negative. To clarify the negative slope, assume the money and commodity markets are initially in equilibrium at point a (X_0, P_0). Consider the balance between supply and demand in the two markets at point b, where X is the same but P is higher than at a. The output market is still in equilibrium because P is not an argument in the IS function.[5] But there is excess demand in the money market because the increase in P reduces the real money supply relative to the real demand for money (or alternatively, increases the nominal demand relative to the fixed nominal supply). Excess demand in the money market puts upward pressure

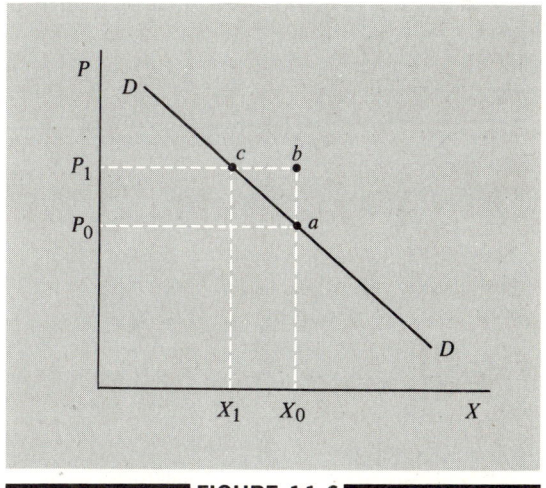

FIGURE 11.6
The Aggregate Demand Curve

---

[5] A similar but more complicated argument applies if we allow for changes in P to affect aggregate demand via the wealth effect in the consumption function.

on the interest rate as wealth owners attempt to sell bonds to acquire additional money balances. This in turn reduces investment and results in excess supply in the commodity market. To restore the commodity market to equilibrium at the higher r, X must decline. Thus, a new equilibrium will be at point c where the higher P is offset by a lower X; therefore, the DD curve must be downward sloping.

In the next two sections we will use the aggregate supply and demand curves to analyze the response of the economy to demand and supply disturbances and compare the results with those derived in the Keynesian and classical versions of the *IS-LM* model. In this section we consider the response of output to demand disturbances. In the next section we consider the price level response to demand and supply disturbances.

THE AGGREGATE SUPPLY CURVE AND THE RESPONSE OF OUTPUT TO DEMAND DISTURBANCES

The upward-sloping supply curve is an intermediate case between classical and Keynesian models. In response to demand disturbances (shifts in the aggregate demand curve), output increases by more than in the classical model but by less than in the Keynesian model, and prices respond by more than in the Keynesian model but by less than in the classical model. These results are depicted in Figure 11.7. KK is the aggregate supply curve in the Keynesian case: both P and W are fixed, but X is variable. CC is the aggregate supply curve in the classical case: X is fixed at its full employment level but P is variable. SS, SW is the rising aggregate supply curve with both P and X variable; we use it to illustrate both the SS and SW curves developed above. In Figure 11.7 we compare the response to an increase in aggregate demand, a shift in the aggregate demand curve from DD to $D'D'$, when the economy begins from the full employment level of output.

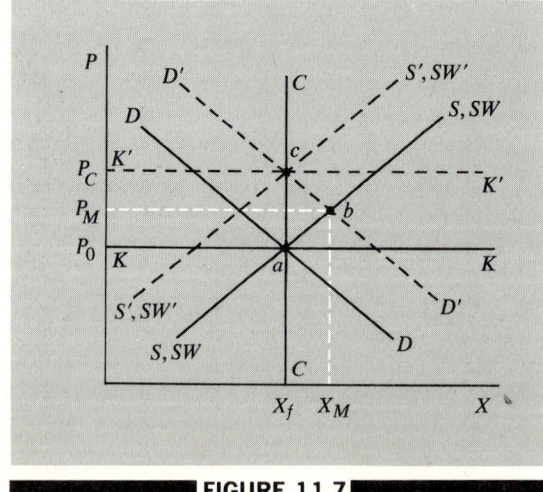

FIGURE 11.7
The Response to a Demand Disturbance (I)

Initially the economy is at point a, with the price level equal to P_0 and output at X_f. Only in the money illusion case does output respond to the increase in aggregate demand; in this case, the economy moves from point a to point b. Neither the Keynesian nor the fixed wage aggregate supply curves apply beyond the full employment level of output. In response to an increase in demand, therefore, the system moves from point a to point c if there is no money illusion. Wages as well as prices increase and output and employment remain unchanged. The KK and SW curves, therefore, shift upward: the KK curve directly in response to the increase in P and the SW curve in response to the increase in W, which in turn increases P. Given that money illusion is a temporary phenomenon, the SS curve will eventually also shift backward and intersect the $D'D'$ curve at point c. But the importance of the money illusion assumption is the possibility of the temporary increase in output beyond X_f.

Now let's consider the response to demand disturbances when the Keynesian and fixed wage aggregate supply curves allow for output response. So that we can also compare the results to the classical case, we again begin from full employment but consider the response to a decline in aggregate demand. In Figure 11.8 the economy begins from point a and we show the response to a downward shift in the DD curve. The output response is smallest (zero) and the price response largest (from P_0 to P_C) in the classical case; the new equilibrium is at point b. The output response is greatest (from X_f to X_k) and the price response smallest (zero) in the Keynesian case; in this case, the new equilibrium is at point d. The two rising aggregate supply curves give intermediate results; the SS curve could be either of the two aggregate supply curves (fixed wage or money illusion cases). Output declines from X_f to X_s and prices fall from P_0 to P_s as the economy moves from point a to point c. In the money illusion case, the output response is temporary; ultimately as money illusion disappears, the SS curve shifts to $S'S'$ and the economy ends up at point b along the classical CC curve.

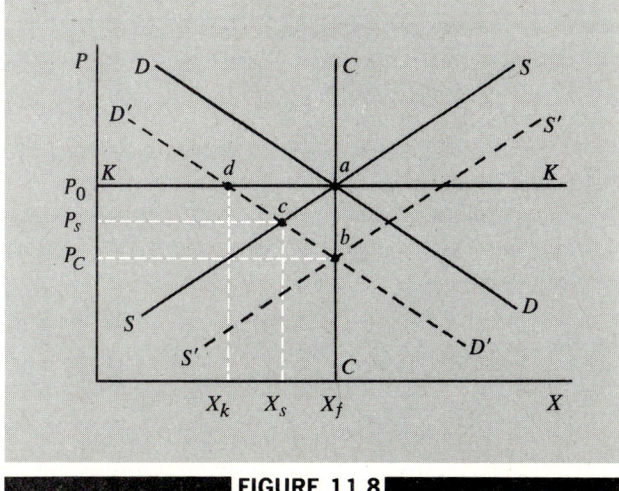

FIGURE 11.8
The Response to Demand Disturbances (II)

The smaller output response along the *SS* curve (at least in the short run) compared to the *KK* curve reflects the added negative feedback when prices vary positively with output. From our discussion of the slope of the aggregate demand curve we know that the price level and aggregate demand are inversely related. The decline in aggregate demand, due for example to an autonomous decline in private aggregate demand, would result in a decline in output equal to $(1/D)\Delta Z$ in the Keynesian case. This would be the size of the horizontal shift in the *DD* curve in response to a change in *Z*. When the aggregate supply curve is positively sloped, however, the decline in *X* is associated with a decline in the price level and the decline in the price level stimulates aggregate demand and therefore dampens the decline in output. The price flexibility increases the negative feedback to demand disturbances. As output declines, the income-induced decline in interest rates now reflects both the decline in real demand for money balances (via L_x) and the increase in real money supply (due to the decline in *P*).

THE RESPONSE OF THE PRICE LEVEL TO DEMAND AND SUPPLY DISTURBANCES

Inflation initiated by shifts in the aggregate demand curve is generally referred to as *demand-pull inflation,* and inflation originating in shifts in the aggregate supply curve is called *cost-push inflation.* Demand-pull inflation is sometimes further decomposed by the source of the demand disturbances. The quantity theory or monetarist approach generally associates inflation with monetary disturbances. Keynesians have sometimes been interpreted as associating inflation with real demand disturbances (changes in *G, T,* or *Z*). Another distinction between varieties of demand-pull inflation is between *diminishing returns inflation,* associated with shifts in the aggregate demand curve along the rigid wage aggregate supply curve prior to full employment, and *classical excess demand inflation,* associated with shifts in the aggregate demand curve at full employment.

Cost-push inflations are often attributed to the exercise of market power by firms and/or unions. Another source of supply-induced inflation is increases in prices that are unrelated to either changes in nominal wages or in the level of economic activity. For example, increases in agricultural prices due to the effect of bad weather on crops or increases in the price of petroleum due to pricing decisions by the Organization of Petroleum Exporting Countries (OPEC) can be incorporated into this model as shifts in the aggregate supply curve. These types of disturbances are often referred to as *exogenous supply shocks,* although that expression would fit all exogenous shifts in the aggregate supply curve.

Demand Inflation

The propositions about the nature of inflation we developed in Chapter 9 remain valid. Inflation is self-liquidating unless fed by continuing disturbances or accommodated by policy. Any once-and-for-all shift in the aggregate demand curve results in a once-and-for-all increase in the *price level* and only a temporary burst of inflation as the economy moves from the initial to the new price level. Inflation can, in principle, occur in response to continuing monetary or continuing real disturbances. But it should be recalled that inflations associated with real and money disturbances have dramatically different effects. One problem with the aggregate supply and demand curve framework is that it masks this difference; in *IS-LM* analysis, on the other hand, this distinction is quite evident. Inflations associated with continuing real disturbances are accompanied by rising real interest rates and continuing changes in the composition of output. Inflations associated with continuing monetary disturbances may occur at unchanged real interest rates and without disturbing the composition of real output.

Supply Inflation

Up to the point of full employment in the rigid wage case and in the short run in the money illusion case, shifts in the aggregate demand curve result in movements in the price level and output in the same direction. For example, in Figure 11.9a the shift in the aggregate demand curve from *DD* to *D'D'* moves the equilibrium from point *a* to point *b*: both prices and output increase. This corresponds to diminishing returns inflation discussed above. Further increases in demand, such as a shift from *D'D'* to *D"D"*, result in increases in price without further increases in output, as the demand curve moves up along the classical aggregate supply curve (*CC*) from point *b* to point *c*.

Shifts in the aggregate supply curve, on the other hand, may result in opposite movements in the price level and output. For example, in Figure 11.9b, the upward shift in the aggregate supply curve from *SW* to *SW'* moves the system from point *a* to point *b*: prices increase but output declines. Thus, exogenous supply shocks can be a source of *simultaneous inflation and recession*.

This of course assumes downward rigidity in the nominal wage rate. If wages are perfectly flexible, autonomous increases in some prices that induced a decline in

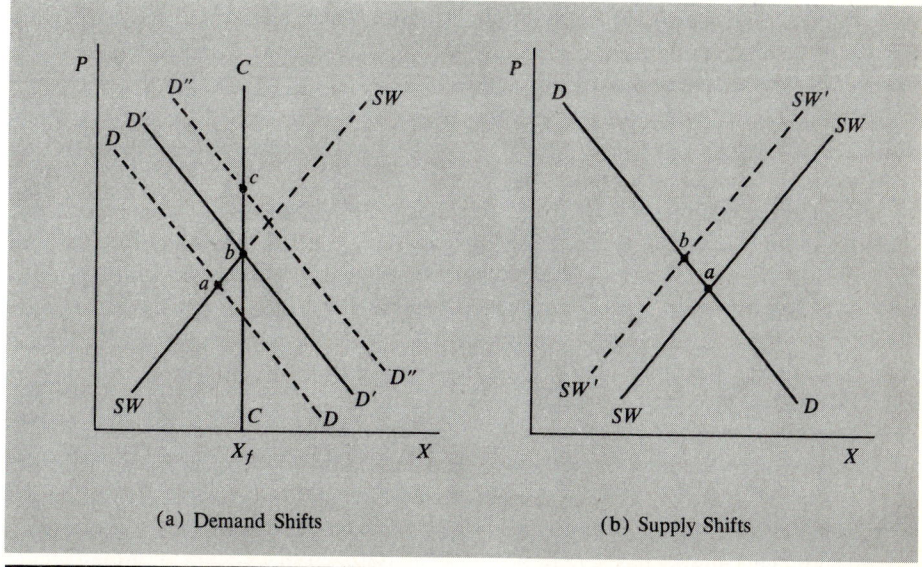

FIGURE 11.9
Demand and Supply Shifts as Sources of Inflation

aggregate demand would result in wage and price declines which would fully offset the impact of the autonomous increase in the price level. In this case, the shift to SW' would be only temporary and the economy would soon return to point a. We must also be careful, as in the case of demand inflation, to distinguish between once-and-for-all and continuing shifts in the aggregate supply curve. A once-and-for-all shift in the aggregate supply curve can only result in a once-and-for-all increase in the price level and a temporary burst of inflation in the process of moving from one price level to a higher one.

Wage-Push, Profit-Push, and Incomes Inflation. One set of influences on the aggregate supply curve is the exercise of market power by firms and/or unions. The existence of market power by firms and/or unions may result in higher prices and/or wages. A monopolist, for example, sets a profit-maximizing price proportional to marginal cost where the proportionality factor depends on the elasticity of demand. The more inelastic is the demand curve facing the monopolist, the higher will the price level be relative to costs. In addition, the degree of market power exercised by a firm (or union) may vary with demand. For example, if elasticity of demand declines as demand increases, the monopolist will raise prices as demand increases both to cover the higher marginal cost and to exploit the additional monopoly power. This provides a further rationale for the upward-sloping aggregate supply curve and simply another case of a demand-induced increase in the price level.

What we want to explore in this section is the possibility of price rises induced by *autonomous* shifts in the aggregate supply curve. One scenario is that unions refuse to settle for less than 7 percent a year nominal wage gains, while productivity increases by only 2.5 percent a year; in this case, unit labor costs, and hence prices, will rise 5.5 percent a year. The problem with this description of market power induced inflation is that it does not allow for any feedback from the effect of higher prices on aggregate demand and from aggregate demand to market power. Recall from our aggregate demand curve analysis that a rising price level tends to reduce aggregate demand (assuming an unchanged nominal money supply). If the market power of unions declines as unemployment increases, there will be a limit to how long this market power induced inflation can persist. And once we relate the market power to the balance between supply and demand for labor and output, we have reverted again to demand- rather than supply-initiated inflation.

To generate changes in the price level unrelated to the level of economic activity, there must be exogenous increases either in the degree of market power or in the degree to which firms and/or unions exploit existing market power. To induce inflation from such supply shifts, there must be continuing changes in market power or in the degree to which existing power is utilized. However, even a once-and-for-all increase in market power results in a temporary burst of inflation which may persist for a couple of years as the system moves from the initial to the new equilibrium price level.

To formalize this analysis, we might view firms as setting prices by some markup over unit labor costs (wages adjusted for the level of labor productivity). The markup may itself depend on the overall level of economic activity, yielding the upward-sloping aggregate supply curve. The aggregate supply curve will shift if unions succeed in obtaining wage demands in excess of productivity gains. The result is usually referred to as *wage-push inflation* (or increases in the price level for once-and-for-all increases in the nominal wage rate). Firms, on the other hand, may exogenously increase their markup of prices over unit labor costs, perhaps in response to an exogenous increase in market power. This results in *profit-push* or *markup inflation*. Finally, if workers and firms have irreconcilable differences concerning the share of income that should go to wages and profits, their nominal demands can only be reconciled by price level increases which expand the total nominal income to be divided. This is called *incomes inflation*. The general rise in wages and prices frustrates both firms and workers but is unlikely to continue indefinitely without policy accommodation because the rise in prices and wages is accompanied by declines in output and employment.

Assume we begin from point a in Figure 11.10. An increase in the market power or exercise of the market power of firms or unions shifts the aggregate supply curve upward from SW_1 to SW_2 and moves the economy from point a to b. Any once-and-for-all shift in SW results in a once-and-for-all change in the price level. Unions and/or firms are unlikely to continue the upward push on prices and/or wages indefinitely because, given the level of the policy instruments, each upward shift in the SW curve reduces output and employment, and this presumably erodes the market power of both firms and unions.

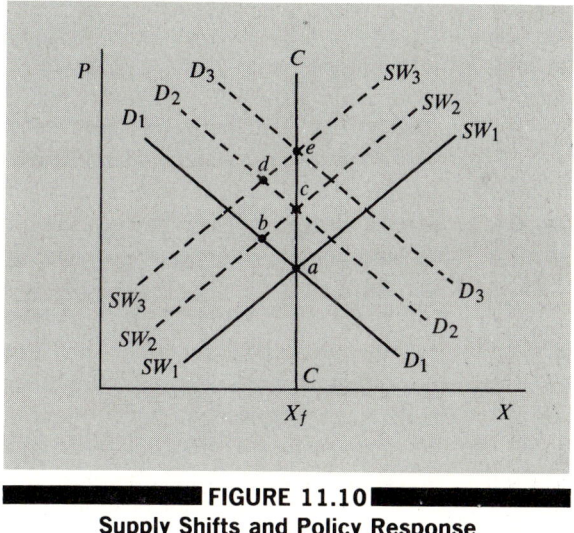

FIGURE 11.10
Supply Shifts and Policy Response

We can explain inflation initiated by such once-and-for-all increases in market power if we assume that the policy authorities have committed themselves to maintaining full employment. They respond to the decline in output with stimulative policy, shifting the aggregate demand curve out until point c is reached, at a still higher price level but back at full employment. At point c wages and prices are both higher than at point a, and unions and/or firms may feel their aims have been frustrated by the general rise in wages and prices. So they try again, shifting the SW curve to SW_3. This process may continue with prices and wages rising at full employment.

Exogenous Supply Shocks. Increases in prices whose movements are largely exogenous to wages and the overall level of economic activity are another source of supply inflation. Once again, once-and-for-all exogenous supply shocks result in only temporary bursts of inflation. Nevertheless, if the supply shocks are large, they can dominate inflation rates over a period of a year or two. These types of supply shifts also pose a dilemma for policy authorities. If they do not respond at all, output and employment will decline, at least temporarily. On the other hand, if policy is used to insulate output from any effect of the supply disturbance, the increase in the price level will be magnified.

During 1973 and 1974, the inflation rate accelerated sharply, and at least part of this jump in the inflation rate was attributed to a series of supply shocks. During 1960–1965, the rate of inflation remained in the 1–2 percent range. In the second half of the 1960s, however, stimulative fiscal and monetary policies associated with financing both the Vietnam War and various social programs generated a classical excess demand inflation. By 1970, the inflation rate had accelerated to the 5–6 percent range. When the 1969–1970 recession failed to bring about a substantial deceleration in the rate of inflation, President Nixon imposed a freeze on wages and prices in August, 1971, and followed this with a series of price-wage control programs during 1972 and 1973. We will discuss the rationale and experience with wage-price controls in Chapter 26. Under the control programs (but also in response to unemployment rates in the 5.5–6 percent range), inflation decelerated at the end of 1971 and into 1972. Expansionary monetary and fiscal policies in 1972, exogenous supply shocks in 1973 and 1974, and the phasing out of the control program in 1974 resulted in a new acceleration in inflation in 1973 and 1974.

The exogenous supply shocks that contributed to the acceleration of inflation in 1973 and 1974 included a tripling in the price of oil following the formation of the OPEC (Organization of Petroleum Exporting Countries) cartel and sharp increases in the price of food due to adverse weather conditions and in the price of industrial raw materials due to a worldwide boom in aggregate demand. In this section we will focus on the effect of the tripling of oil prices. During the fourth quarter of 1973, the price of imported oil rose from $3.50 to $10.00 a barrel. This exogenous price increase can be captured in the aggregate demand and supply analysis as a backward shift of the aggregate supply curve. This development could therefore have been expected both to reduce the aggregate demand and to increase the equilibrium price level. However, such a once-and-for-all increase in the price of oil imports cannot have a permanent effect on the rate of inflation. On the other hand, the movement to the higher price level can be expected to be distributed over time so that inflation could be expected to accelerate for some period. A study by James Pierce and Jared Enzler using simulations with the *FMP* model suggests that the increase in oil prices increased the inflation rate by almost 4.5 percentage points in the quarter following the jump in oil prices, but that the effect on the inflation rate was rapidly dissipated within four or five quarters.[6] Therefore, the oil price increase contributed importantly to the acceleration in inflation in 1974 compared to 1973,

---

[6] James L. Pierce and Jared J. Enzler, "The Effects of External Inflationary Shocks," *Brookings Papers on Economic Activity* (1974), pp. 13–61.

and the dissipation of its effect on the inflation rate also helps to explain the deceleration in the inflation rate in 1975 compared to 1974.

○ Demand Shift Inflation

Even if market power is not directly a source of increases in prices and/or wages, it may explain why the overall level of wages and prices rise without generalized excess demand for commodities. If there is excess demand in some sectors, for example, prices will rise there while market power in other sectors prevents prices from declining in spite of excess supply. The demand shift model was initially set forth as an explanation of the acceleration of inflation during the 1955–1957 period. The *CPI* increased by only .4 percent in 1955 (measured from December to December), then jumped by 2.9 and 3.0 percent in 1956 and 1957, respectively, while the unemployment rate remained in the 4.0 to 4.5 percent range. The acceleration in the rate of inflation did not seem attributable to either excess aggregate demand or to autonomous increases in administered wages and prices. In a classic study of inflation, C. L. Schultze concluded that the inflation during this period resulted from increases in demand in some sectors of the economy (particularly the capital goods sector) combined with administered wage and price setting behavior in other sectors.[7]

This asymmetry in the response of wages to excess demand and excess supply was an important element in our rigid wage version of the aggregate supply curve developed above and will be an essential feature of our development of the Phillips curve model of wage determination in Chapter 18. If demand increases and results in excess demand in some sectors, wages and prices will rise in those sectors. If excess demand in some sectors is counterbalanced by excess supply elsewhere, under classical model assumptions, wages and prices should fall in the excess supply sectors. If wages and prices are rigid downward, on the other hand, the wage and price increases in the excess demand sectors will increase the aggregate level of wages and prices. Therefore, the aggregate price level will rise as long as there is excess demand in at least some sectors of the economy.

With administered prices based on a markup over costs and administered wages, the wage and price increases in the excess demand sector tend to spread to sectors with supply-demand balance or even excess supply. This occurs as excess demand in some sectors raises the prices of materials used in excess supply sectors and as wage gains in excess demand sectors spill over into excess supply sectors in response to union attempts to maintain traditional wage differentials among sectors. In this model, inflation is initiated by increases in demand in some sectors, but aggregate excess demand is unnecessary to cause the price level to rise; and wages rise in response to both the excess demand in some sectors and the diffusion of wage gains through union attempts to maintain traditional wage patterns. In the excess supply sectors, inflation will appear to be of the cost-push variety. Nevertheless, the inflation has its roots in demand increases.

---

[7] C. L. Schultze, "Recent Inflation in the United States," Study Paper No. 1, *Study of Employment Growth, and Price Levels* (Joint Economics Committee, 86th Congress, 1st session, 1959).

Part II • Comparative Static Analysis with the Basic Model

● REVIEW QUESTIONS

1. What are the different assumptions underlying the two alternative upward-sloping aggregate supply curves developed in this chapter?

2. How do the two curves differ in terms of (a) their applicability to the right of the full employment point, (b) the behavior of the nominal wage along the aggregate supply curve, and (c) the source of the change in employment along the curve?

3. Explain verbally why prices and output are inversely related along the aggregate demand curve.

4. What is the distinction between (a) demand-pull and cost-push inflation and between (b) diminishing returns and classical excess demand inflation?

5. What is the limitation of market power explanations of inflation?

● PROBLEMS

1. Assume the labor supply curve is $N^s = N^s(W)$, where W is the nominal wage rate. Contrast this with the labor supply curves employed in this chapter. Then derive the aggregate supply curve based on it and consider how its implications compare with those associated with the SW and SS curves in the chapter.

2. Classical economists believed that wage and price flexibility would be able to maintain full employment; i.e., any decline in demand would induce wage and price declines which would offset the decline in demand. Keynes argued that it was possible that declines in nominal wages in response to an excess supply of labor would only result in proportional declines in prices and no increases in aggregate demand. Evaluate the classical and Keynesian arguments using aggregate supply and demand analysis. Does the validity of Keynesian and classical cases depend on certain parameter values? If so, which ones? Explain why. (Hint: You can determine the effects of wage flexibility by assuming that the wage rate declines as long as $X < X_f$ and then by analyzing the implications of wage declines using the SW curve).

3. "The *IS-LM* model fails to do justice to Keynes's insights in the *General Theory* because it fails to allow for the aggregate supply curve. Keynes assumed fixed wages but variable prices, not fixed wages and fixed prices." Discuss the differences in the results associated with the fixed wage, fixed price *IS-LM* model of Chapter 10 and with the fixed wage, variable price aggregate supply and demand curve analysis developed in this chapter. Comment on the quote.

4. "The monetarist view that inflation is exclusively a product of excessive monetary growth neglects the possibility of inflation associated with inconsistent income claims. Such inflation can continue indefinitely in the absence of monetary accommodation as each faction finds its negotiated income claims eroded by inflation." Comment.

Part III

Refinements of the Real Sector: Aggregate Demand

Chapter 12. Consumption
13. The Implications of the Life Cycle Hypothesis
14. Investment
15. The Implications of Alternative Specifications of the Investment Function

Chapter 12

Consumption

This chapter develops the theoretical foundation for the simple consumption function employed above in our macroeconomic models and then refines the specification of the consumption function so that its properties are consistent with the empirical evidence. We begin by developing a demand function for consumption goods from a standard utility-maximizing model of household behavior and then develop the relation between income and consumption. Next, we consider the properties of the simple Keynesian specification of the consumption function in which consumption is a linear function of income. This is the specification used in Part II. The empirical evidence presented in the third section is only partially consistent with the simple Keynesian specification. We therefore develop an alternative, refined specification—the life cycle hypothesis—and consider its consistency with the empirical evidence presented earlier in the chapter.

INCOME AND CONSUMPTION

We begin by deriving a demand equation for consumption goods from a simple utility-maximizing model of consumer behavior. In our initial formulation we find that consumption depends on the real wage rate rather than on income. Then we develop the conditions under which income rather than the real wage rate becomes the appropriate argument in the consumption function.

The Notional Consumption Function

The consumption decision is based on utility maximization subject to constraints. Households derive utility (U) both from the consumption of goods (C) and from leisure (L). We can therefore write a utility function for households in which consumption and leisure enter as arguments.

$$U = U(C, L) \tag{12.1}$$

Households maximize utility subject to constraints on available hours (T)

$$T \equiv H + L \tag{12.2}$$

where $H =$ hours worked, and on a given real wage rate (w). Households are assumed to be able to supply as much labor as they would like at the prevailing real wage rate. Household income[1] is defined as

$$Y = wH. \tag{12.3}$$

The supply of hours of work and the demand for commodities can be simultaneously determined by maximizing equation (12.1) subject to both equations (12.2) and (12.3). Both will depend on the real wage rate.

$$H = H(w) \tag{12.4}$$

$$C = C(w) \tag{12.5}$$

This formulation illustrates the simultaneous nature of the labor supply and consumption decisions; i.e., given the real wage rate, the household simultaneously selects its labor supply (and therefore its income) and its consumption. Thus, income is a *choice* variable, not an exogenous constraint. Equation (12.5) is referred to as the *notional household demand function for commodities*. It gives the relationship between the real wage rate and demand for commodities *under the assumption that households can supply as much labor (up to T) as they wish at the prevailing real wage rate.*

○ The Income-Constrained Consumption Function

Assume, however, that there is excess supply in the labor market and as a consequence, households cannot supply as much labor as they would like at the prevailing real wage rate. For example, if the real wage is w_1 above the equilibrium wage rate w_0 as in Figure 12.1, actual employment will be N_1 while labor supply is N_2. In this case, the appropriate specification of the consumption function is

$$C = C(Y) \tag{12.6}$$

where Y is household income ($w_1 N_1$ is this case). Equation (12.6) is referred to as the household's *income-constrained or effective demand for commodities*.[2] This illustrates an important property of disequilibrium analysis. Disequilibrium in one market (the labor market in this case) generally affects supplies and/or demands in other markets (the demand for consumption goods in this case). The effect of disequilibrium in one market on supplies and/or demands in other markets is referred to as a *spillover*

---

[1] To simplify, we initially assume that all household income takes the form of labor income.
[2] The distinction between notional and effective demand for commodities was introduced by Robert Clower, "The Keynesian Counter-Revolution: A Theoretical Appraisal" in Frank Brechling and Frank Hahn (eds.), *The Theory of Interest Rates* (London: Macmillan & Co., Ltd., 1965), pp. 103–125.

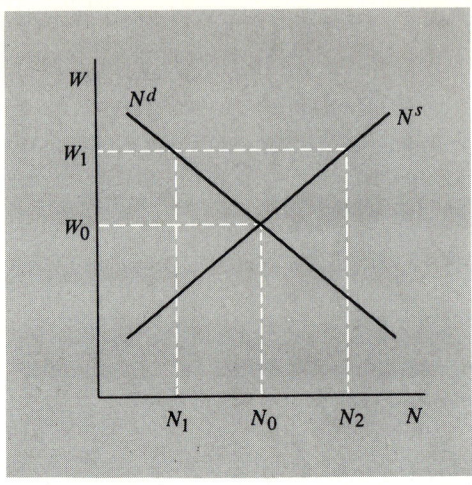

FIGURE 12.1
Disequilibrium in the Labor Market and the Effective Demand for Commodities

effect. The general way in which disequilibrium spills over into other markets is by altering the constraint on supplies and/or demands. In this case, income rather than the real wage rate becomes the effective constraint on the demand for commodities by households (consumption expenditures).

Note that consumption can always be written as a function of income. In the classical model, however, hours of work and therefore household income can be expressed as a function of the real wage rate so that consumption can also be expressed as a function of the real wage rate. In the Keynesian model, on the other hand, consumption can be related to income but the relation between consumption and real wage breaks down. While equation (12.5) would be suitable for the classical model, it is clearly inappropriate for use in the Keynesian model. Equation (12.6), on the other hand, can be used in either model.

THE ABSOLUTE INCOME HYPOTHESIS (*AIH*)

The income-constrained consumption function was introduced by Keynes.[3] It is generally written in linear form as

$$C = \bar{C} + C_y Y \qquad (12.7)$$

where Y is disposable (total) income, $\bar{C}$ is autonomous consumption, and C_y is the constant *marginal propensity to consume* (*MPC*). Both consumption and income are in real terms.[4] This specification is generally referred to as the *absolute income hypothe-*

---

[3] John Maynard Keynes, *The General Theory of Employment, Interest and Money* (New York: Harcourt, Brace and World, Inc., 1936), Book III.
[4] Recall from Chapter 4 that we generally write supply and demand functions in *real* terms, reflecting the assumption of the absence of money illusion.

sis (AIH) to distinguish it from the alternative specifications that we will consider below. C_y cannot exceed unity, because if it did, the household would continually spend in excess of income. $\bar{C}$ is assumed to be positive. The *average propensity to consume (APC)*,

$$APC = \frac{C}{Y} = \frac{\bar{C}}{Y} + C_y, \tag{12.8}$$

declines as income increases and is greater than the *MPC*.

The relationship between the *APC* and *MPC* is depicted in Figure 12.2. The vertical axis intercept of the consumption function is the autonomous component of consumption, $\bar{C}$. The slope is the $MPC = \Delta C/\Delta Y$. The slope is constant; therefore, the function is a straight line. The $APC = C/Y$ at any Y is the slope of the straight line from the origin to the point on the consumption function corresponding to that level of Y. For example, the *APC* at Y_0 is the slope of the line OA and the *APC* at Y_1 is the slope of the line OB. As Y increases, the slope of the line from the origin to the consumption function declines; i.e., *the APC declines as Y increases.*

To summarize, the key properties of the *AIH* are: (1) constant *MPC*, (2) an *APC* which declines with income, and (3) *APC > MPC*.

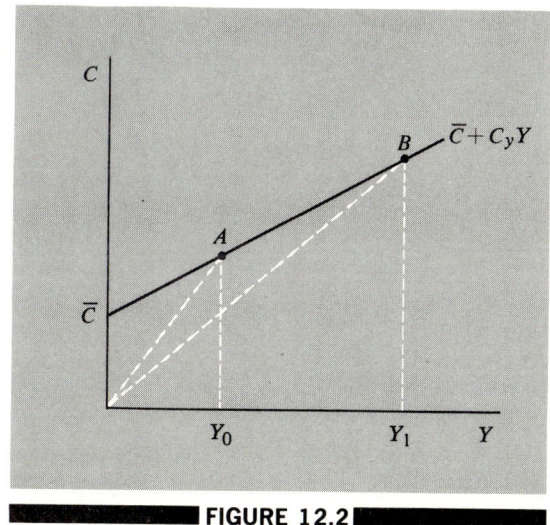

FIGURE 12.2
The Properties of the *AIH*

◯ EMPIRICAL EVIDENCE

Estimation of short-run aggregate consumption functions using time series data (aggregate data for consumption and income over a period of time) tend to confirm the *AIH*. Such short-run functions are estimated using quarterly or annual data over a period of about ten years. The results generally show an *MPC* of approximately

.7 and a positive constant term. Therefore, *MPC* is constant, $APC > MPC$, and the *APC* varies inversely with income.[5]

○ The Instability of the Short-Run Consumption Function

In spite of the fact that such short-run functions appear to fit the data well within the period over which they are estimated, they have not proved to be very accurate in predicting consumption outside the sample period. In particular, such short-run functions systematically *underpredict* future consumption.

For example, assume SR_1 in Figure 12.3 is the short-run consumption function estimated over the period t_0 to t_1. If it were used to predict consumption over t_1 to t_2, predicted consumption would be systematically lower than actual consumption over that period. If a new short-run function were estimated using data over the period t_1 to t_2, it would again fit the data quite well, but its predicted values of consumption over the period t_1 to t_2 would be systematically higher than the predictions made with the first short-run function. One interpretation of this is that the short-run consumption function is shifting up over time.

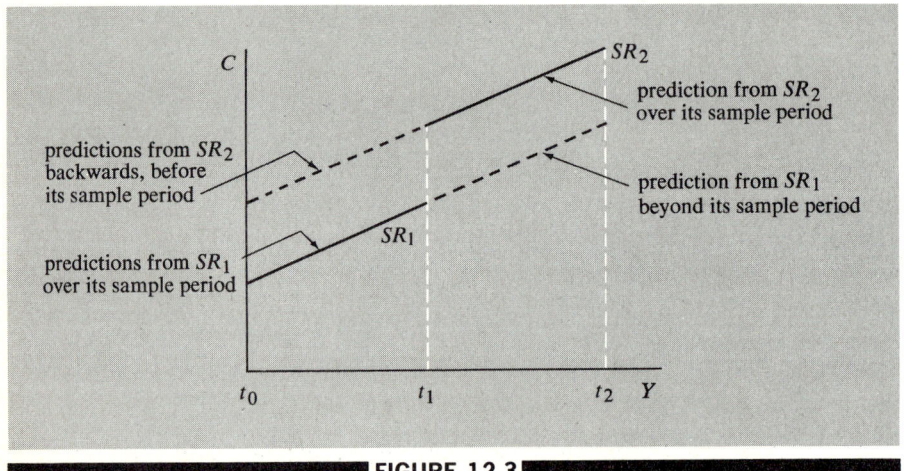

FIGURE 12.3
Upward Instability of the Short-Run Consumption Function

○ The Conflict Between the Short-Run and Long-Run Evidence

Evidence derived from long-run aggregate consumption functions appears to contradict the short-run evidence. Long-run consumption functions are estimated by using averages of *C* and *Y* over a full business cycle or over long enough periods that the cyclical properties of the series are averaged out (e.g., over decades). Long-run consumption functions estimated in this manner yield a *proportional* relationship

---

[5] For an empirical analysis of the consumption function, see Daniel Suits, "The Determinants of Consumer Expenditures: A Review of Present Knowledge," from the Commission on Money and Credit, *Impacts of Monetary Policy* (Englewood Cliffs, N.J.: Prentice-Hall, Inc., 1963), pp. 1–53.

between C and Y.[6]

$$C = bY \tag{12.9}$$

In this case, $MPC = b$ is constant but $APC = MPC$ and is also constant. Furthermore, the estimate of b is approximately .9, significantly higher than the estimates of the MPC from the short-run consumption function.

The relationship between the short-run and long-run consumption functions is depicted in Figure 12.4. SR_1 is estimated over t_0 to t_1, SR_2 over t_1 to t_2, and SR_3 over t_2 to t_3. Point A is the coordinates of the average consumption and the average income over t_0 to t_1; points B and C are the coordinates of the average consumption and income over the periods t_1 to t_2 and t_2 to t_3, respectively. Points A, B, and C form the long-run consumption function and fall along a straight line from the origin.

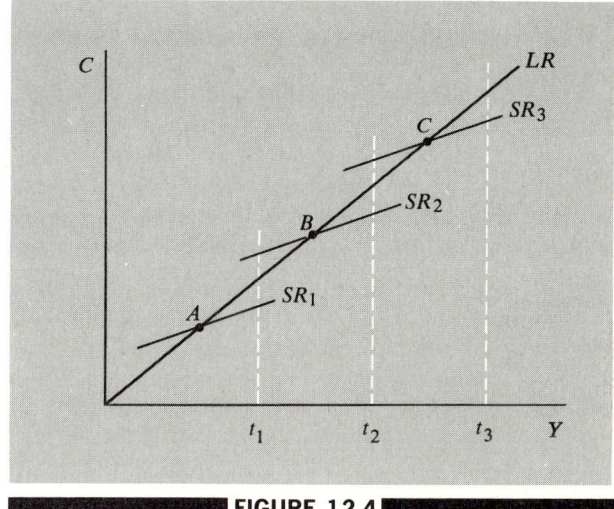

FIGURE 12.4
The Relation Between Short-Run and Long-Run Consumption Functions

We conclude from the empirical evidence that: (1) in the short run, MPC is constant, $APC > MPC$, and APC varies inversely with income; (2) in the long run, MPC is constant, $APC = MPC$ and is also constant; (3) the short-run $MPC <$ the long-run MPC; and (4) the short-run consumption function shifts upward over time.

The contradictory evidence from short-run and long-run time series analysis provided the impetus for the development of a series of consumption theories designed to reconcile this evidence. The initial effort, however, was on saving and the absolute income hypothesis via a series of *ad hoc* modifications. According to this approach,

---

[6] The early evidence on the long-run consumption function was based on estimates of national income and consumption for overlapping decades from 1869 to 1938 published by Kuznets in 1946. See Simon Kuznets, *National Product Since 1869* (New York: National Bureau of Economic Research, Inc., 1946).

the basic relationship between C and Y is nonproportional (as suggested by the short-run evidence), but the vertical axis intercept shifts upward over time at a rate which results in a long-run proportional association between C and Y.[7] This can be captured by introducing a time trend (t) into the consumption function:

$$C = \bar{C} + C_y Y + \delta t \tag{12.10}$$

where δ is the rate at which the consumption function intercept is shifting upward. The short-run function is

$$C = (\bar{C} + \delta t) + C_y Y \tag{12.11}$$

and the long-run function just happens to be

$$C = bY \tag{12.12}$$

where $b > C_y$.

A series of secular trends capable of explaining the upward drift of the intercept has been suggested, including increases in wealth, increased urbanization (assuming that the *MPC* for an urban population exceeds *MPC* for a rural population), increased percentage of older people in the population (assuming older people have higher *MPC*s), and the rapid introduction of new products. This attempt to reconcile the short-run and long-run evidence has been criticized for involving *appeal to coincidence*. Although it explains why the short-run function may be shifting up over time, it does not provide an explanation of why the shifting (nonproportional) short-run function should trace out a proportional long-run function.

Three alternative consumption hypotheses were specifically developed to reconcile the short-run and long-run evidence: (1) the relative income hypothesis (*RIH*), (2) the permanent income hypothesis (*PIH*), and (3) the life cycle hypothesis (*LCH*). In the next section we develop the life cycle hypothesis and in the following chapter we consider the implications of the life cycle hypothesis for the way the economy responds to disturbances. The other two specifications are developed in Appendices B and C at the end of this chapter. We concentrate on the life cycle hypothesis because we find it the most attractive of the three approaches; particularly important, in this respect, is the fact that it explicitly incorporates net household wealth along with income as a determinant of consumption.

LIFE CYCLE HYPOTHESIS (*LCH*)

The *life cycle hypothesis*, developed by Franco Modigliani, Richard Brumberg, and Albert Ando,[8] assumes that households maximize an *intertemporal* utility function

---

[7] For an example of this approach, see A. Smithies, "Forecasting Postwar Demand: I," *Econometrica*, Vol. 14 (January, 1945), pp. 1–14.

[8] Franco Modigliani and Richard Brumberg, "Utility Analysis and the Consumption Function: An Interpretation of Cross Section Data," in K. K. Kurihara (ed.), *Post-Keynesian Economics* (New Brunswick, NJ: Rutgers University Press, 1954), pp. 388–436; and Albert Ando and Franco Modigliani, "The Life Cycle Hypothesis of Saving: Aggregate Implications and Tests," *American Economic Review*, Vol. 53 (March, 1963), pp. 55–84.

subject to the constraint of *lifetime* resources (R).[9] Thus, it views the consumption decision as part of a long-run plan. Each period's consumption is not constrained by that period's income but reflects the way in which households desire to allocate their lifetime resources to consumption. Assuming diminishing marginal utility from consumption in each period, households are assumed to smooth their consumption path relative to the path of income. This smoothing of consumption relative to income provides the motivation for saving/dissaving in the *LCH*; i.e., households save to transfer current resources to future consumption.

According to the *LCH*, household utility is specified as a function of consumption in current and future periods.

$$U = U(C_0, C_1, \ldots, C_T) \tag{12.13}$$

Lifetime resources are the sum of current and discounted future labor income and current wealth:

$$R_t = \sum_{t=0}^{N} \frac{Y_{Lt}}{(1+r)^t} + \bar{a} \tag{12.14}$$

where Y_{Lt} is labor income in period t, $\bar{a}$ is current wealth (beginning-of-period wealth in a discrete formulation), and N is the date of retirement from the labor force. Note that the income concept is (disposable) labor income, not total income. The present value of property income is already included in the wealth term. Maximizing intertemporal utility subject to lifetime resources yields a demand function in which consumption in period t depends on lifetime resources. Specifically, Ando and Modigliani assume that consumption is directly *proportional* to R.

$$C_t = \alpha R_t \tag{12.15}$$

For any unit, the proportionality factor depends on the specific form of the utility function, the rate of return on assets, and the stage of the life cycle; but α does not depend on R.

○ A Two-Period Example

Consider a two-period example. The utility function describes preferences between consumption in period 1 (C_1) and consumption in period 2 (C_2). These preferences are depicted in the indifference curves in Figure 12.5. The budget line requires that the present value of lifetime consumption equals the present value of lifetime resources.

$$C_1 + \frac{C_2}{(1+r)} = Y_{L1} + \frac{Y_{L2}}{(1+r)} + \bar{a} \tag{12.16}$$

---

[9] This simple specification assumes that the unit does not intend to make a bequest and that future income as well as life span is known with certainty. Relaxing these assumptions does not, however, alter the thrust of the analysis. Also, the consumption variable used in the *LCH* differs from that used in the *AIH*. In the *AIH* the consumption variable is total consumer expenditures. In the *LCH* the consumption variable is consumption expenditures on nondurables and services and consumption of services on durable goods. See Appendix A for further details.

Part III • Refinements of the Real Sector: Aggregate Demand

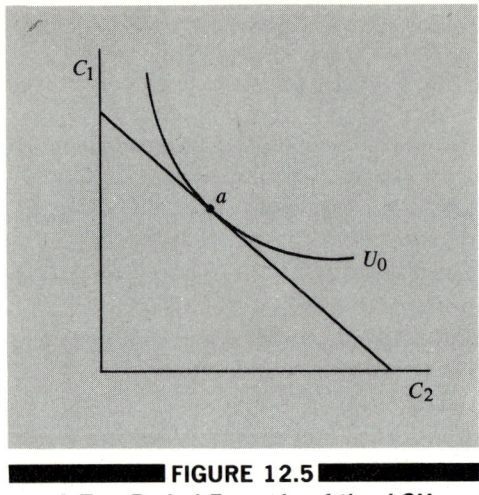

FIGURE 12.5
A Two-Period Example of the *LCH*

The vertical axis intercept of the budget line, $C_1^{max} = Y_{L1} + \frac{Y_{L2}}{1+r} + \bar{a}$, is the maximum consumption in period 1. It occurs if the household spends its first period income and initial wealth and $\frac{1}{1+r}$ times its second period income in period 1. It borrows $\frac{Y_{L2}}{1+r}$ in period 1 and uses its second period income to repay this loan with interest; i.e., $Y_{L2} = \left(\frac{Y_{L2}}{1+r}\right)(1+r)$. The horizontal axis intercept is $C_2^{max} = (1+r)Y_{L1} + Y_{L2} + (1+r)\bar{a}$. If the household lends its first period income and initial wealth for period 1, this is the sum it will have to consume in period 2.

The slope of the budget line is $-1/(1+r)$. This represents the rate at which C_2 can be converted into C_1. The budget line identifies all attainable or feasible combinations of C_1 and C_2 such that the unit exhausts its entire lifetime resources between C_1 and C_2. Which combination the unit choose depends on its preferences between C_1 and C_2 as reflected by its indifference curves. In Figure 12.5 the equilibrium is achieved at point *a*, where the consumer has reached the highest indifference curve possible with the given lifetime resources.

The essential property of the *LCH*, captured in this simple two-period model, is that decisions about consumption in the current period are not made exclusively on the basis of income in the same period but on the basis of income prospects over a longer period. Thus, the consumption decision is *forward looking*, made on the basis of both current income and future values of income.

○ The Relation Between the Propensities to Consume Out of Income and Wealth

The life cycle model provides the theoretical basis for the specification of the consumption function introduced in Chapter 4. There we noted that consumption should respond by more to a sustained change in income (a recurring flow) than to a once-and-for-all increase in wealth (an exhaustible stock). This relation between C_y and C_a is implied in the life cycle model developed above. To derive the relation between C_y and C_a explicitly, we assume that the income of some unit is expected to remain constant over the unit's remaining years in the work force. At age T, the unit has $N - T$ years remaining in the labor force, where N is the age at retirement. Assuming a zero interest rate, total resources can be expressed as

$$R = (N - T)Y + a. \tag{12.17}$$

Consumption is proportional to R. The proportionality factor must be related to the remaining life span of the unit, $L - T$, where L is the age at which the unit dies. If the unit does not wish to leave a bequest, it will arrange its lifetime consumption pattern to just exhaust its lifetime income. At age T, there are $L - T$ years remaining, so the unit consumes $1/(L - T)$ of its resources each period. These assumptions yield the following consumption function:

$$C = \alpha R = \frac{1}{L - T}[(N - T)Y + a]. \tag{12.18}$$

The *MPC* out of income, assuming the change is expected to be maintained over the rest of the earning period, is

$$C_y = \frac{N - T}{L - T}, \tag{12.19a}$$

while the *MPC* out of an increase in wealth is

$$C_a = \frac{1}{L - T}. \tag{12.19b}$$

If the unit is 45, plans to work to 60, and live to 70, $C_y = .6$ and $C_a = .04$. Note, however, a *temporary* increase in income (due, for example, to a temporary tax cut) has exactly the same effect as an increase in wealth. This accounts for the large differences we expect to be associated with permanent versus temporary tax cuts.

○ **Time Patterns of Consumption and Savings Over the Life Cycle**

Income is generally not constant over the years in the labor force, nor does it generally fall to zero upon retirement. Instead, income is generally relatively low for an individual immediately following entry into the labor force, then tends to rise throughout the working years, falling off as the unit approaches then passes retirement. This pattern of income presumably reflects changes in productivity over the life cycle. According to the *absolute income hypothesis*, consumption should follow a similar pattern over the life cycle. The *life cycle hypothesis*, on the other hand, suggests that households pursue a time pattern of consumption quite different from the time pattern of income. The only constraint that must be met is that the present values of the consumption and income streams over the life cycle be equal. In particular, in the simple model developed above, consumption was *constant* over the life cycle.

Figure 12.6 depicts life cycle consumption, saving, and income. Household income is depicted as rising steadily from entry in the labor force at time E to retirement at time N; at retirement, income falls to Y' based on social security and other pension benefits. Consumption is constant at $\tilde{C}$ throughout the life span beginning with entry in the labor force at time E to death at time L. In the early years (from E to M in Figure 12.6) the unit dissaves, presumably by borrowing, to permit consumption to exceed current income. During the middle years (M to N), the unit saves to repay the borrowing during the initial period and to accumulate enough wealth to permit dissaving during the retirement years N to L.

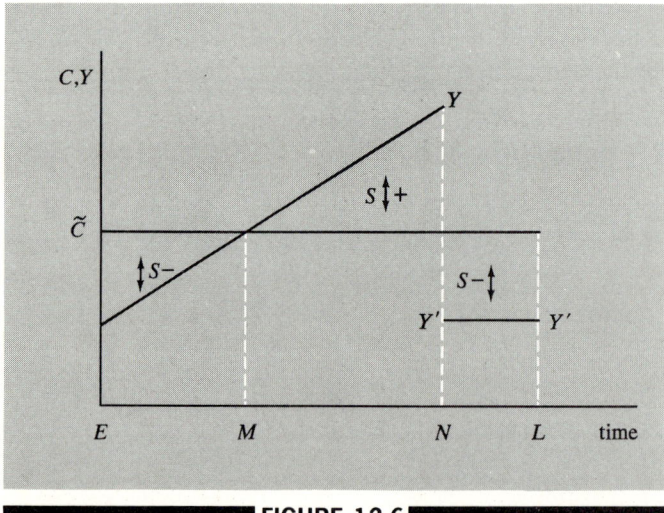

FIGURE 12.6
The Life Cycle Pattern of Consumption, Saving, and Income

○ Liquidity Constraints[10]

The *LCH* indicates how spending units would like to allocate consumption over their life when constrained only by the requirement that the present value of consumption equal the present value of income. In fact, however, households may find it impossible to smooth out consumption as much as the *LCH* suggests would be optimal. This is particularly true for young workers who may be unable to borrow sufficiently to achieve the optimal smoothing of consumption. For example, it may be impossible to incur a negative net worth; i.e., the additional restriction that $a \geq 0$ for all households may be imposed. This puts a kink in the budget line at point l in Figure 12.7. C_1^{**} = $Y_1 + \bar{a}$ is the maximum consumption that can be achieved in period 1. The budget line is therefore $C_1^{**}la$. The household prefers the consumption pattern C_1^*, C_2^* (point

---

[10] This section is based on James Tobin and Walter C. Dolde, "Wealth, Liquidity, and Consumption," *Consumer Spending and Monetary Policy: The Linkages* (Boston: Federal Reserve Bank of Boston, 1971), pp. 99–146.

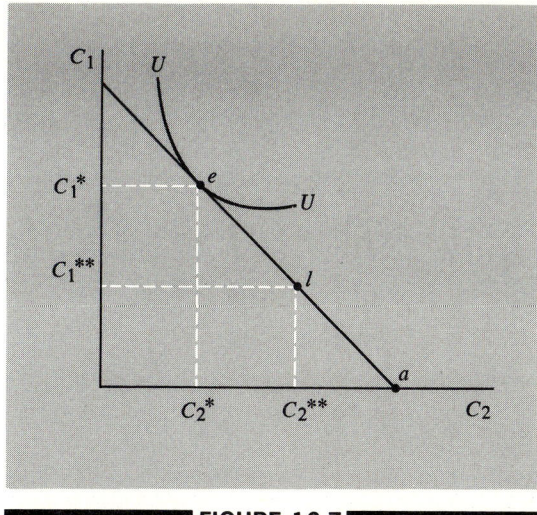

FIGURE 12.7
The Effect of Liquidity Constraints

e), but has to settle for C_1^{**}, C_2^{**} because of the inability to borrow against expected future income. This is an example of a liquidity constraint. *Liquidity* refers to the speed with which units can convert assets into cash without appreciable loss in the principal value of the asset. If we view R as the total wealth of the unit, the component associated with expected future income is extremely illiquid. The assets included in the nonhuman wealth component, a, may also vary in liquidity.

○ Deriving a Testable Specification of the *LCH*

The life cycle hypothesis implies that aggregate consumption depends on current and expected future labor income and current wealth. Ando and Modigliani employ average expected future labor income ($\overline{Y}_{Lt}^e$), along with current labor income and wealth, as the arguments of the aggregate consumption function:

$$C_t = \alpha_1 Y_{Lt} + \alpha_2 \overline{Y}_{Lt}^e + \alpha_3 \bar{a} \qquad (12.20)$$

where $\overline{Y}_{Lt}^e$ is defined, for a given individual, as the present value of future labor income divided by the number of future years of life. Note that the wealth variable is the *beginning-of-period* value of wealth. End-of-period wealth depends on saving and hence income over the current period. The end-of-period specification of wealth would therefore involve a double-counting of the resources available to households since the current income is already included once in the income term. If some of the income is saved, wealth will increase, and the increase in wealth will affect consumption next period. The purpose of saving, after all, is to redistribute consumption from current to future periods.[11] We consider two specifications of expected income

---

[11] While we consider both beginning- and end-of-period specifications of asset supplies and demands, we allow only the beginning-of-period specification of wealth in the consumption function. End-of-period planned wealth is the appropriate constraint on *end-of-period* asset demands but is not a reasonable constraint on consumption expenditures *over the period* when current income is also included in the consumption function.

in which expected income is a function of either current income or current and *past* levels of income. These specifications reflect the conventional practice in economics of relating expected values of variables to current and past actual values.[12] This approach, however, transforms a model which is in theory forward looking to one which is in practice backward looking. This is the price we pay for using a theory that relies on unobservable expected future values as an important explanatory variable.

Expected Income Is Proportional to Current Income. In their early work, Ando and Modigliani assumed that average expected future labor income was simply proportional to current labor income

$$\bar{Y}^e_{Lt} = \beta Y_{Lt} \tag{12.21}$$

so that equation (12.20) could be rewritten as

$$C_t = \alpha_4 Y_{Lt} + \alpha_3 \bar{a} \tag{12.22}$$

where $\alpha_4 = \alpha_1 + \beta\alpha_2$. They estimated this equation and derived the following estimates of α_4 and α_3:

$$C_t = 0.7 Y_{Lt} + .06 \bar{a}.^{13} \tag{12.22'}$$

Expected Income as a Function of Current and Past Levels of Actual Income. In more recent empirical applications of the *LCH*, consumption is specified as a function of current income and two years of past income along with beginning-of-period wealth. In addition, *total* disposable income is employed rather than disposable *labor* income. This modification reflects absence of data on disposable labor income which remains the theoretically preferred measure.

The form of *LCH* thus becomes

$$C_t = \sum_{i=0}^{2} \alpha_i Y_{t-1} + \alpha_3 \bar{a}. \tag{12.23}$$

The estimates of this equation from the *FMP* model[14] indicate that $\sum_{i=0}^{2} \alpha_i = .67$ and $\alpha_3 = .05.$[15]

---

[12] This approach was introduced in Chapter 9 when we discussed the relation between actual and expected rates of inflation.

[13] This equation is reported in Ando and Modigliani, "The Life Cycle Hypothesis of Saving: Aggregate Implications and Tests," *American Economic Review*, Vol. 53 (March, 1963), p. 77.

[14] The Federal Reserve—MIT—Penn (*FMP*) model is a large-scale econometric model developed by economists at MIT, the University of Pennsylvania, and the Federal Reserve Board. We will refer to estimates of parameters and model multipliers based on the *FMP* model on occasion throughout the text. For a discussion of the main features of the *FMP* model, see Frank de Leeuw and Edward Gramlich, "The Federal Reserve—MIT Econometric Model," *Federal Reserve Bulletin* (January, 1963), pp. 11–40.

[15] These results are reported in Franco Modigliani, "Monetary Policy and Consumption," *Consumer Spending and Monetary Policy: The Linkages* (Boston: Federal Reserve Bank of Boston, June, 1971), pp. 9–84. The consumption variable is total consumption. The wealth coefficient was also estimated using current and lagged values, but we only report the sum of the coefficients (current and three-lagged quarters). The equation was estimated using quarterly data and current and eleven-lagged values of disposable income.

◯ Reconciliation of Short-Run and Long-Run Evidence

Equation (12.22) can be used to reconcile the short-run and long-run evidence. The life cycle consumption function is plotted in Figure 12.8. The vertical axis intercept is positive $(\alpha_3 \bar{a})$ so that in the short run $APC > MPC$ and is inversely related to Y_L. Note also that the short-run function will shift up over time as wealth accumulates. To derive the long-run relationship between consumption and income, we divide equation (12.22) through by Y_L.

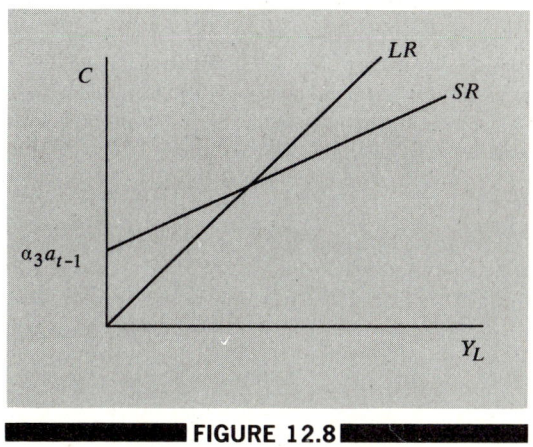

FIGURE 12.8
The Short-Run and Long-Run
Consumption Functions

$$\frac{C}{Y_L} = \alpha_4 + \alpha_3 \frac{a}{Y_L} \tag{12.24}$$

C/Y_L will be constant in the long run if a/Y_L is. In addition, the ratio of consumption to total disposable income (C/Y) will be constant in the long run if both the a/Y_L and Y_L/Y ratios are constant.

$$\frac{C}{Y} = \frac{C}{Y_L}\left(\frac{Y_L}{Y}\right) \tag{12.25}$$

Both ratios are in fact relatively constant in the long run, so that the *LCH* is consistent with both the short-run and long-run evidence.

APPENDIX

A The Definition of Consumption

According to the *AIH*, there is a stable relationship between consumption and income. In this appendix we will consider in greater detail the appropriate definition of consumption.

The variable employed in the absolute income hypothesis is total consumer expenditures (C). There are two basic components of C: expenditures on nondurable goods and services (CN) and expenditures on durables (CD). An alternative definition, employed in many of the modern theories of consumption including the life cycle and permanent income approaches, is consumption (CON): expenditures on nondurables and services plus consumption of the services of durable goods (CSD). The two definitions are:

$$C \equiv CN + CD \tag{12A.1}$$

and

$$CON \equiv CN + CSD. \tag{12A.2}$$

Thus,

$$CON \equiv C - CD + CSD. \tag{12A.3}$$

The rationale for using CON is that the argument in the utility function should be the *services* provided by the consumption goods, not the expenditures; i.e., the basic decision variable for the household is consumption, not consumption expenditures.

On the other hand, we are trying to explain the determination of income and therefore must also explain consumption expenditures. Once we determine CON, we can determine C from equation (12A.3) (i.e., $C = CON + CD - CSD$) if we can find CD and CSD. The services of consumer durables can be measured by the opportunity cost of using the durable good. This has two components. One is the reduction in the value of the durable due to use or time; i.e., depreciation of the durable good (δ_D). The other is the opportunity cost of the funds tied up in the durables or the explicit borrowing cost on the loan used to purchase the durable (r). The services provided by durables are given by

$$CSD = (\delta_D + r) P_D K_D \tag{12A.4}$$

where $P_D K_D$ is the value of consumer durables. (P_D is the price index of consumer durables and K_D is the stock of consumer durables.)

The discussion of the determinants of expenditures on consumer durables is postponed until we have discussed the theory of investment because of the similarity of the two approaches. In our models we will continue to use consumer expenditure (C) as our basic consumption variable.

APPENDIX

B The Relative Income Hypothesis

The *relative income hypothesis* developed by Duesenberry was one of the early efforts to develop a model which was consistent with both the short-run and long-run evidence.[1] According to the *RIH*, the basic relationship between C and Y is proportional, as in the long-run relationship. Duesenberry explains the short-run nonproportionality in terms of the *irreversibility* of consumption patterns. Once units have become accustomed to a certain standard of consumption, they attempt to maintain it even if income temporarily declines. To capture the effect of *habit persistence*, Duesenberry makes the APC depend on the ratio of actual to peak level income.

$$\frac{C}{Y} = a - c\frac{Y}{Y_0} \qquad (12B.1)$$

where Y_0 is the previous peak level of Y. Income increases over time so that in the long run $Y = Y_0$ and

$$\frac{C}{Y} = a - c = b. \qquad (12B.2)$$

In the long run, therefore, $MPC = APC = b$. In the short run, however, $Y \leq Y_0$. When $Y \leq Y_0$, APC varies inversely with Y. From equation (12B.1), the short-run function can be written as

$$C = aY - c\frac{Y^2}{Y_0}. \qquad (12B.3)$$

The short-run MPC is

$$\frac{dC}{dY} = a - 2c\frac{Y}{Y_0}. \qquad (12B.4)$$

Duesenberry's estimates for equation (12B.1) are

$$\frac{C}{Y} = 1.2 - .25\frac{Y}{Y_0} \qquad (12B.5)$$

Therefore, the long-run $MPC = APC = .95$. The short-run MPC is not constant in this case. For Y close to Y_0, the short-run MPC will be approximately $1.2 - 2(.25) = .7$ and the short-run MPC will increase as Y declines relative to Y_0. The short-run $MPC <$ the long-run MPC, and the values of each are consistent with the short-run and long-run evidence. In addition, the short-run function shifts upward over time as Y_0 increases.[2] Duesenberry's short-run and

---

[1] James Duesenberry, *Income, Saving and the Theory of Consumer Behavior* (Cambridge, Mass.: Harvard University Press, 1949).

[2] Modigliani presented a similar approach. See Franco Modigliani, "Fluctuations in the Saving-Income Ratio: A Problem in Economic Forecasting," in *Studies in Income and Wealth*, Vol. 11 (New York:

continued, p. 226.

long-run consumption functions are depicted in Figure 12B.1. The long-run function is proportional; the slope equals $b = MPC = APC$. As income expands to new peaks, consumption rises proportionately to income. Assume the economy reaches Y_0 and then income declines. Consumers will not retreat along the long-run function, but rather along the much flatter short-run function, SR_0, as they attempt to maintain the consumption standard they had become accustomed to at Y_0. Therefore, the short-run MPC will be smaller than the long-run MPC as consumers reduce consumption less than in proportion to the decline in income. As income increases during the recovery stage, the consumers move back along the short-run function until Y_0 is reached. Once at Y_0, consumers will again increase consumption in proportion to increases in income. If another recession occurs at Y_1, consumers will move back along SR_1. Thus, the short-run relationship is nonproportional, the short-run $MPC <$ the long-run MPC, and the short-run function shifts upward over time.

Duesenberry's theory reconciles the short-run and long-run evidence. Yet it has serious limitations, and as a result, has not received as much attention as the two other hypotheses we develop. According to the relative income theory, C and Y always change in the same

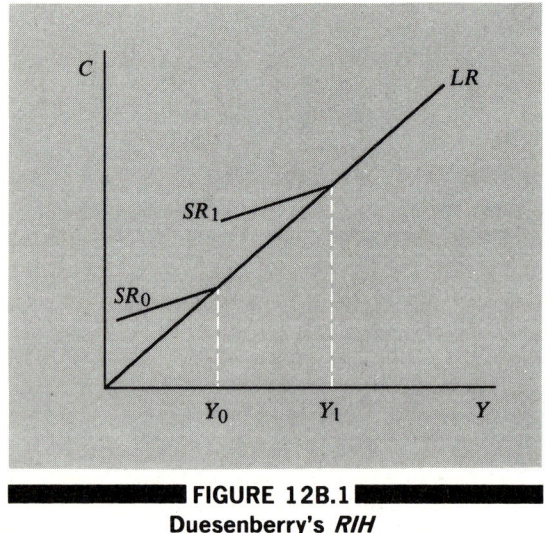

FIGURE 12B.1
Duesenberry's *RIH*

National Bureau of Economic Research, 1949). His consumption function is

(a) $\dfrac{C}{Y} = .9 - 0.125 \dfrac{Y - Y_0}{Y}$

where Y_0 is the previous peak income. The long-run consumption function is derived by setting $Y = Y_0$.

(b) $C = .9Y$

Thus, the long-run $MPC = APC = .9$. The short-run function is derived by multiplying equation (a) through by Y and solving:

(c) $C = .775Y + 0.125Y_0$.

The short-run $MPC = .755$ and the APC varies inversely with Y. The short-run $MPC <$ the long-run MPC, and the short-run consumption function shifts upward over time as Y_0 rises.

direction. But consumption often continues to rise during mild recessions. Secondly, we would not expect consumption standards to be irreversible, only slowly reversible. If a lower income level were maintained indefinitely, we would expect the consumers to gradually adjust their standards.

APPENDIX

The Permanent Income Theory

Friedman's *permanent income theory* (*PIT*), like the *LCH*, emphasizes the role of the present value of current and discounted future income in the consumption function.[1] Consumption depends on permanent income (Y_p) rather than measured income (Y).

The Theoretical Definition of Permanent Income

Friedman defines *permanent income* as the amount a unit could consume (or believes it could) while maintaining its wealth unchanged. Total wealth (a^*) can be written as the sum of human wealth (a_h) and nonhuman wealth (a).

$$a^* = a_h + a \tag{12C.1}$$

Human wealth is the present value of current and discounted future labor income

$$a_h = Y_{Lt} + \sum_{t=0}^{N} \frac{Y_{Lt}}{(1+r)^t} \tag{12C.2}$$

Note that human wealth (a_h) corresponds to the first term in equation (12.14), the definition of lifetime resources in the *LCH*. Total wealth (a^*) corresponds to the entire expression for R_t in equation (12.14). However, instead of relating consumption to lifetime resources as in the *LCH*, Friedman relates consumption to permanent income, defined as

$$Y_p = ra^* \tag{12C.3}$$

where r is the rate of return on total wealth. Thus, permanent income corresponds to income earned on the unit's total wealth.

The Basic Assumptions

The basic hypothesis associated with the *PIT* is that permanent consumption (C_p) is a function of permanent income (Y_p). Permanent consumption reflects planned consumption.

---

[1] Milton Friedman, *Theory of the Consumption Function* (Princeton, N.J.: Princeton University Press, 1957).

Like the *LCH*, consumption rather than consumption expenditures is the dependent variable. The basic definitions and assumptions underlying *PIT* are, in addition to equations (12C.1), (12C.2), and (12C.3),

$$Y = Y_p + Y_t \qquad (12C.4)$$

$$C = C_p + C_t \qquad (12C.5)$$

$$\rho(Y_p, Y_t) = 0 \qquad (12C.6)$$

$$\rho(C_p, C_t) = 0 \qquad (12C.7)$$

$$\rho(C_t, Y_t) = 0. \qquad (12C.8)$$

Equation (12C.4) defines *measured income* as the sum of the permanent and transitory income. Y_p can be thought of as the expected value of a probability distribution. Y_t reflects accidental or chance occurrences, such as illness, and is called *transitory income*. Equation (12C.5) defines *measured consumption* as the sum of permanent and transitory consumption. *Permanent consumption* reflects planned consumption. *Transitory consumption* is unplanned, due to an unexpected illness, cold spell, or unusual opportunity to purchase consumption services. Conditions (12C.6) and (12C.7) are virtually derived from the definitions of Y_p and Y_t and C_p and C_t; the correlation between Y_p and Y_t and between C_p and C_t is zero. The permanent components are systematic, the transitory components random and unrelated to the permanent components. Condition (12C.8) is perhaps the most controversial assumption in the *PIT*. It asserts that there is zero correlation between transitory consumption and transitory income; i.e., the *MPC* out of transitory income is zero. Note, however, that the purchase of a durable good is defined as an act of saving, not consumption, according to the *PIT*.

The basic equation is

$$C_p = k(r, w, u) Y_p. \qquad (12C.9)$$

This specification adds an additional assumption to the ones previously set forth: proportionality. C_p is proportional to Y_p. The factor of proportionality depends on a series of variables but not on Y_p. k depends on the interest rate, r (determinant of the slope of the budget line in our two-period example above). w is the ratio of nonhuman wealth to total wealth. One reason households save is to provide an emergency reserve in a world of uncertainty. The composition as well as total value of a^* affects the size of the emergency reserve. Households cannot sell or borrow against a_h and thus realize its value for immediate use. Nonhuman wealth, on the other hand, can be sold and borrowed against, although even here the composition of nonhuman wealth may affect its usefulness as an emergency reserve. The larger the w (the larger the proportion of nonhuman wealth in total wealth), the higher the C_p for any value of Y_p. u is a "portmanteau variable" reflecting tastes and preferences of consuming units and life cycle considerations (number of members in unit, their ages, etc.). In most empirical tests of the *PIT*, k is treated as a constant.

The Operational Definition of Permanent Income

In empirical applications of the *PIT* no attempt is made to directly transform the definition of Y_p given by equation (12C.3) into operational form. Friedman argues that it is not necessary to decide in advance the precise meaning that should be attached to the permanent and transitory components of income. Instead, Friedman suggests letting the data itself dictate the precise definition of permanent income. The typical approach is to ignore the distinction between measured and permanent consumption and to specify permanent income as a distributed lag of current and past values of measured income, like the treatment of income in equation (12.23).

Reconciliation of the Short-Run and Long-Run Evidence

According to the *PIT*, the basic relationship between consumption and income is proportional. In the long run, $Y = Y_p$ because if income is averaged over a long period (i.e., a decade or a cycle), the transitory component averages out to zero. Therefore, the *PIT* predicts $APC = MPC$ in the long run. The *PIT* is also consistent with the short-run evidence. In a boom $Y > Y_p$ because $Y_t > 0$; therefore, $C/Y < k$. In a recession $Y < Y_p$ because $Y_t < 0$; therefore, $C/Y > k$. Also, the short-run $MPC <$ the long-run MPC according to the *PIT*.

● REVIEW QUESTIONS

1. What are the key properties of the absolute income hypothesis?

2. What is the conflict between evidence based on short-run and long-run consumption functions?

3. How does the life cycle hypothesis reconcile the evidence based on short-run and long-run consumption functions?

4. Explain how lifetime resources are defined in the life cycle hypothesis.

5. Expected income is unobservable. How is expected income specified in econometric models?

6. What is the distinction between consumption and consumption expenditures?

● PROBLEMS

1. Does the following consumption function satisfy the properties associated with the absolute income hypothesis? Explain.

$$C = -100 + .8\,Y$$

2. Using the consumption function given below, find the *MPC* and the *APC* when income is 1000, 1500, and 2000, respectively. Is the relation between *APC* and *MPC* and income consistent with the *AIH*?

$$C = 150 + .8\,Y$$

3. Now consider the following dynamic specification of the consumption function.

$$C_t = 75 + .4Y_t + .5C_{t-1}$$

(a) Show how this specification implies that consumption depends on current and past levels of income.
(b) What is the rationale for the specification?
(c) Assume income increases by $1,000; what will happen to consumption in the period in which income increases?
(d) What will happen in the second and third periods?
(e) What will the equilibrium response be?

4. Use the life cycle model to compare the short-run and long-run values of the *MPC* (out of labor income).

$$C_t = a_1 Y_{Lt} + a_3 a_t + a_2 \overline{Y}^e_{Lt}$$

Assume that $\overline{Y}^e_{Lt} = \beta Y_{Lt}$ and that the ratio of wealth to labor income is *w*.

5. Assume there is a $1,000 tax cut. Find the first-period response in consumption for the consumption functions used in problems 2 and 3. Which consumption function yields a more powerful short-run multiplier? Explain why.

6. Assume the tax cut in problem 5 is a temporary one, scheduled to last only one period. Contrast the way in which consumption would respond under the simple *AIH*, the consumption function in problem 3, and the *LCH*.

7. Compare the implications of the *AIH* and *LCH* for the response of consumption to temporary and permanent tax cuts. Assume $C_y = .7$ in the *AIH* specification. For the *LCH*, use equation (12.18) and assume the current age (*T*) is 45, the retirement age (*N*) is 60, and the life expectancy (*L*) is 70. First, calculate the response in consumption to a $1,000 temporary (one-year) tax cut and then to a $1,000 permanent tax cut.

8. Compare the implications of the theoretical specification of the *LCH* [equation (12.18)] and the empirical specification [equation (12.20)] where $a_0 = .37$, $a_1 = .22$, and $a_3 = .08$] to the temporary and permanent tax cuts.

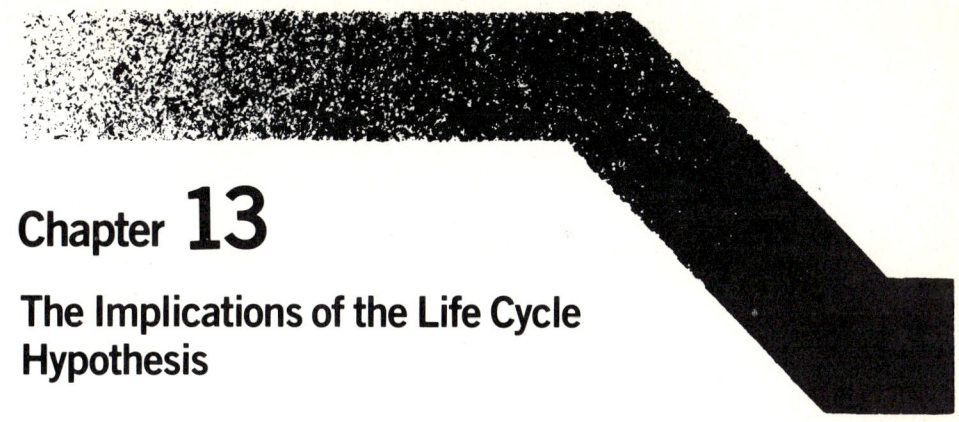

Chapter 13

The Implications of the Life Cycle Hypothesis

In this chapter we consider the implications of the life cycle hypothesis for the response of the interest rate and output to disturbances. There are two features of the life cycle hypothesis which must be integrated into our models: the dependence of consumption on lagged as well as current values of income and on wealth as well as income. In the first section we consider the implications of the dependence of consumption on lagged income. Then we consider the implications of the wealth effect. We begin our discussion of the wealth effect by identifying two alternative approaches to modeling changes in wealth, then classify the various ways in which wealth can change, and conclude with a discussion of the implications of the various types of wealth effects.

CONSUMPTION AS A FUNCTION OF CURRENT AND LAGGED VALUES OF INCOME

In this section, we ignore the wealth effect. We write consumption as a function of Y^* where Y^* is defined as a weighted average of current and lagged income over a given horizon (n periods); i.e.,

$$C_t = C_y Y_t^* \qquad (13.1)$$

where

$$Y_t^* = \sum_{i=0}^{n} w_i Y_{t-i} \qquad (13.2)$$

where w_i = the weight associated with the income level lagged i periods and Y_{t-i} is the value of income lagged i periods. The Y_t^* variable captures the role of current

231

and expected future income in the life cycle model; i.e., we collapse the Y and $\bar{Y}^e$ variables included in the LCH specification in the previous chapter into a single variable, Y^*, in this chapter.

○ The Weighting Pattern

The weighting pattern should have the following two properties: (1) *The weights should decline as the lag increases.* Y^* is a measure of *expected* income. The declining pattern of weights reflects the presumption that households' expectations about future income depend on past experience, and the more recent experience exerts more influence on their appraisal of the future than experience further in the past. (2) *The sum of the weights should equal one*; i.e., $\Sigma w_i = 1$. This restriction is required to insure that expected income converge to actual income if actual income remains constant for n periods.[1] This restriction implies that the long-run equilibrium results will be identical for consumption functions with Y or Y^* as the explanatory variable.[2] Therefore, the introduction of the dependence of consumption on current and lagged values of income in our model can only affect the dynamic response of income to disturbances, not the equilibrium response. We consider two forms of weighting patterns that fulfill these restrictions.

The Koyck Lag Distribution. A simple weighting pattern which has these properties is the geometric or Koyck-distributed lag. It is specified as

$$w_i = (1-w)w^i \tag{13.3}$$

where w is a constant between zero and one and the horizon, n, is infinity. The weights decline geometrically and the sum of the weights equals unity.[3] If consumption depends on Y^* and Y^* is formed using a Koyck lag, consumption can also be written as a function of current income and lagged consumption.

---

[1] If $Y_{t-i} = \bar{Y}$ for n periods and $\sum_{i=0}^{n} w_i = 1$,

$$Y^* = \sum_{i=0}^{n} w_i Y_{t-i} = \bar{Y}.$$

[2] Long-run equilibrium requires that Y remain constant over time when exogenous variables remain constant. If Y_{t-i} is not equal to $\bar{Y}$ for n periods, Y^* will change over time; therefore, C, Y, and other endogenous variables cannot remain constant. In the life cycle model, equilibrium requires $Y_t = Y_{t-1} = \ldots = Y_{t-n}$; in this case, Y^* will remain constant permitting constant values for C, Y, and other endogenous variables. In equilibrium, therefore, $Y^* = Y$ so equilibrium results do not differ when consumption depends on Y or Y^*.

[3] The weight on current income (period 0) is $1 - w$. The weight on income lagged one period is $(1-w)w$ which is less than $1-w$ when $1 > w > 0$. The weights on income lagged two, three, and n periods are $(1-w)w^2$, $(1-w)w^3$, and $(1-w)w^n$, respectively. Thus, the weights decline as the constant is raised to higher and higher powers; this is referred to as a *geometrically declining series*. Note also that $\sum_{i=0}^{\infty}(1-w)w^i = 1$.

$$C_t = C_y(1-w)Y_t + wC_{t-1}.^4 \tag{13.4}$$

This form of the relation highlights the inertia in the consumption decision. Current consumption depends on past consumption and changes only gradually in response to changes in income.

A Three-Period Lag Distribution. Alternatively, we may assume the horizon is some *finite* period. In econometric studies, the period is generally found to be about three years; i.e., consumption depends on current income and two years of lagged values of income. Treating the unit time interval in our model as one year, Y^* can be written as

$$Y^* = w_0 Y_t + w_1 Y_{t-1} + w_2 Y_{t-2} \tag{13.5}$$

where $w_0 + w_1 + w_2 = 1$ and $w_2 < w_1 < w_0$. Based on the estimates in the *FMP* model, $C_y = .67$, $w_0 = .55$, $w_1 = .33$, and $w_2 = .12$.[5]

○ Impact and Equilibrium Multipliers

When we introduce lagged values of income, our model becomes *dynamic* rather than static; i.e., time now enters explicitly into the analysis. When we consider the response of the economy to a disturbance, we must now distinguish between the initial or first-period effect, referred to as the *impact* effect, and the long-run or *equilibrium* effect. As we noted above, *the equilibrium response to disturbances in this model is identical to the multiplier effects in our static model in Chapter 9*.[6] In the remainder of this section we therefore concentrate on the influence of the respecification of the consumption function on the *impact multipliers*.

---

[4] To derive this, we substitute equation (13.2) into equation (13.1) and rewrite the consumption function as:

$$C_t = C_y(1-w)Y_t + C_y(1-w)wY_{t-1} + C_y(1-w)w^2 Y_{t-2} + \ldots + C_y(1-w)w^{n-1} Y_{t-n-1}.$$

Lagging all variables by one period and multiplying all terms by w yields

$$wC_{t-1} = C_y(1-w)wY_{t-1} + C_y(1-w)w^2 Y_{t-2} + \ldots + C_y(1-w)w^{n-1} Y_{t-n-1} + C_y(1-w)w^n Y_{t-1}.$$

Subtracting the last equation from the previous one yields

$$C_t - wC_{t-1} = C_y(1-w)Y_t - C_y(1-w)w^n Y_{t-1}.$$

For large values of n, w^n approaches zero; i.e., $\lim_{n\to\infty} w^n = 0$. For the Koyck lag distribution where $n = \infty$, $w^n = 0$. The last term can therefore be ignored. Rearranging terms, we obtain equation (13.4).

[5] Franco Modigliani, "Monetary Policy and Consumption," *Consumer Spending and Monetary Policy: The Linkages* (Boston: Federal Reserve Bank of Boston, 1971), p. 75.

[6] The static model yields only the equilibrium response.

Employing the finite horizon specification of Y^*, the *IS* and *LM* curves in the Keynesian model can be written as

$$X_t = C_y w_0 Y_t + I_r r_t + C_y w_1 Y_{t-1} + C_y w_2 Y_{t-2} + \bar{Z}_t + \bar{G}_t \qquad (13.6)$$

$$m_t = L_r r_t + L_x X_t + \bar{L}_t. \qquad (13.7)$$

We assume the demand for money depends exclusively on current values of r and X and that investment depends exclusively on the current value of r. In this way we isolate the effect of consumption depending on current and lagged values of income. To determine the current values of X_t and r_t, we treat Y_{t-1} and Y_{t-2} as *predetermined* variables; i.e., they are exogenous like Z and G in that changes in the current values of X_t and r_t cannot affect their values. The solution for the reduced form for X_t now includes Y_{t-1} and Y_{t-2} as exogenous variables. In addition, wherever C_y appeared before, $w_0 C_y$ now appears. Solving equation (13.7) for r_t, using this to substitute for r_t in equation (13.6), and solving for X_t, we obtain

$$X_t = \frac{1}{D_1}\bar{G}_t + \frac{1}{D_1}\bar{Z}_t - \frac{w_0 C_y}{D_1}\bar{T}_t + \frac{I_r/L_r}{D_1}\bar{m}_t - \frac{I_r/L_r}{D_1}\bar{L}_t + \frac{w_1 C_y}{D_1} Y_{t-1} \qquad (13.8a)$$

$$+ \frac{w_2 C_y}{D_1} Y_{t-2}$$

where

$$D_1 = 1 - w_0 C_y + (L_x/L_r) I_r. \qquad (13.8b)$$

Given that $w_0 < 1$, $w_0 C_y < C_y$; therefore, $D_1 > D$ (derived in Chapter 9) and $(1/D_1) < (1/D)$; i.e., *the basic impact multiplier is smaller when consumption depends on current and past values of income*. According to the *LCH*, consumption responds gradually to income changes so that consumption is less responsive to changes in current income than in the *AIH*. Therefore, the model's positive feedback via the consumption income relation is smaller initially, and all model impact multipliers are smaller in the short run under the *LCH*.[7]

In Figure 13.1 we compare the short-run response to an open market operation (shift in the *LM* curve) under the *LCH* and the *AIH*. The IS_i curve is the short-run *IS* curve under the *LCH*; it corresponds to equation (13.6). The IS_e curve is the long-run *IS* curve under the *LCH*; it also corresponds to the *IS* curve under

---

[7] The long-run multiplier is found by assuming $Y_t = Y_{t-1} = Y_{t-2}$. This is a condition for equilibrium; i.e., given values of G, Z, T, m, and $\bar{L}$, X must settle down to a constant value. Imposing this assumption, the long-run consumption function becomes

$$C = C_y Y.$$

This equation is identical (except for the absence of a constant term, $\bar{C}$) to the *AIH* and to the one used in our static specification. Therefore, as noted above, the *LCH* does not alter the equilibrium multipliers in our model.

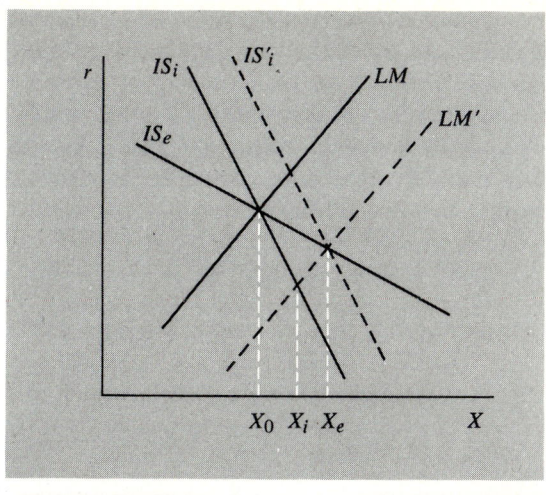

FIGURE 13.1
The Short-Run Response to Monetary Changes: AIH vs. LCH

the AIH where there is no distinction between short run and long run because there are no lagged effects. The IS_e curve corresponds to the curve we have been using in earlier chapters with a slope of $(1 - C_y)/I_r$. The IS_i curve is steeper; its slope is $(1 - w_0 C_y)/I_r$ where $w_0 < 1$. A shift in the LM curve results in an increase in income from X_0 to X_i in the first period under the LCH, compared to an increase from X_0 to X_e in the long run under the LCH and in the short run and long run under the AIH. Under the LCH the IS curve appears to rotate over time; more precisely, the short-run curve shifts (e.g., from IS_i to IS'_i) until the short-run curve intersects the LM' curve at the same r and X as the long-run IS curve (IS_e).[8]

We conclude that if consumption depends on current and lagged values of income, the *short-run or impact multipliers will be smaller* for all disturbances than if consumption depended only on current income. Because this modification affects only the positive feedback, it has a symmetric effect on all multipliers. This modification does not, on the other hand, alter the long-run equilibrium results. It affects the time path of the response, not the ultimate equilibrium response.

Problems with the Operational Specification of the *LCH*

The assumption that expected income depends on current and past levels of income is common to virtually all econometric specifications of consumption. But this specification implies that consumption will respond to the same degree and with the same lags to all changes in income, independent of the source of the change.

---

[8] Y_{t-1} and Y_{t-2} are arguments in the short-run IS curve. As Y_{t-1} and Y_{t-2} increase, the IS curve shifts upward; i.e.,

$$\frac{\Delta r}{\Delta X_{t-1}}\bigg|_{IS_i, \bar{X}} = \frac{-w_1 C_y}{I_r} > 0.$$

These models cannot distinguish between the response to a temporary tax surcharge (as in 1968) or tax rebate (as in 1975) and a permanent tax cut (as in 1964). There is, however, persuasive evidence that the former variety of tax policy has a substantially smaller effect than the latter and these results are, of course, consistent with the implications of the life cycle model presented in the previous chapter. The life cycle model implies a *larger* initial response to a permanent tax change and a *smaller* response to a temporary tax change than the $w_0 C_y$ term in the typical operational specification of the consumption function. Franco Modigliani and Charles Steindel found some evidence that the 1964 tax act, which was widely understood at the time to be a permanent tax change, had a stronger effect on consumption than suggested by the conventional life cycle equation.[9] Okun and Modigliani and Steindel found that the temporary tax surcharge of 1968 had only half the effect on consumption predicted by the conventional equation.[10] And Modigliani and Steindel also found that the 1975 tax rebate had a much more modest effect than suggested by the conventional equation.

A second deficiency of the conventional equation is the failure to take liquidity constraints into account. The impact of tax changes depends on the extent to which households have been prevented from increasing consumption by liquidity constraints such as prohibition of borrowing against expected future income. When liquidity constraints are restricting current consumption, tax cuts may yield a *larger* response; indeed, for units that are perfectly liquidity constrained, the *MPC* associated with tax cuts will be one for temporary or permanent tax cuts. There is not much evidence about the importance of liquidity constraints.

WEALTH EFFECTS

In this section we consider the implications of introducing wealth into the consumption function. To allow us to concentrate on the role of wealth, we ignore the role of expected income and write the consumption function as

$$C = C_y Y + C_a \bar{a} \tag{13.9}$$

where C_a = propensity to consume out of wealth and $\bar{a}$ = beginning-of-period net wealth of households.

Defining Wealth

There are two equivalent approaches that can be used to define wealth: the *sum of the assets approach* and the *perpetual inventory approach*.

The Sum of the Assets Approach. We can define a as the sum of the assets minus the sum of the liabilities in household-sector portfolios. In our simple models, households have no liabilities and their assets consist of money and government and private bonds;

---

[9] Franco Modigliani and Charles Steindel, "Is a Tax Rebate an Effective Tool for Stabilization Policy," *Brookings Papers on Economic Activity* (1977:1), pp. 175–209.

[10] Arthur Okun, "The Personal Tax Surcharge and Consumer Demand, 1968–70," *Brookings Papers on Economic Activity* (1971:1), pp. 167–204.

$$a \equiv m + b + d \tag{13.10}$$

where m, b, and d are real values of money and government and private bonds held by households. The money supply is a policy variable while changes in the supplies of government and private bonds are determined via the government and business sector financing constraints, respectively.

The Perpetual Inventory Approach. End-of-period wealth (a) can also be defined as beginning-of-period wealth ($\bar{a}$) plus current period saving (S).[11]

$$a \equiv \bar{a} + S \tag{13.11}$$

This is the approach usually employed in econometric models. To demonstrate the equivalence of the two approaches, note that we can write saving as the sum of the government deficit (D) and investment.

$$S \equiv D + I \tag{13.12}$$

where $D = G - T$.[12] The deficit equals the sum of change in the supplies of money and government bonds via the government financing constraint (GFC) and investment equals the change in the supply of private bonds via the investment financing constraint (IFC). Thus, saving equals the sum of new issues of money and government and private bonds, and the two approaches yield identical results.

○ Direct and Indirect Wealth Effects

Changes in wealth are associated either with changes in the number of units of money and/or bonds outstanding or with revaluations of existing units of wealth. We refer to the effect of changes in wealth due to changes in the number of units of assets as *direct wealth effects*. Wealth effects due to revaluations of existing units of assets are referred to as *indirect wealth effects*. There are two types of indirect wealth effects: *price-induced* and *interest-induced wealth effects*.

Direct Wealth Effects. When we introduce wealth into our macro model, we must be careful about the dating of that variable. We noted in the previous chapter that it was inappropriate to employ an end-of-period specification of wealth in the consumption function because this would involve a double-counting of the resources available to households and because the purpose of saving in the life cycle model is to postpone consumption, to transfer resources to other periods. Ignoring indirect wealth effects, we would use a beginning-of-period specification of wealth in the consumption function and relate beginning-of-period wealth to the *BOP* wealth in the previous period via the perpetual inventory definition of wealth,

$$\bar{a} = \bar{a}_{-1} + S_{-1}.$$

---

[11] For the moment, we ignore capital gains and losses.
[12] To derive this identity, note that income can be defined as $X \equiv C + I + G$ and as $X \equiv C + S + T$. It follows that $C + S + T \equiv C + I + G$ and that $S \equiv I + (G - T) \equiv I + D$.

Thus, direct wealth effects via induced saving affect income only in subsequent periods, not in the period the induced saving increases wealth. However, later in the chapter when we model the implications of direct wealth effects, we will collapse the direct wealth effect into the first period in order to show their effect within the simple one-period framework.

The Price-Induced Wealth Effect. We will model the effect of each of the indirect wealth effects as occurring within the period in which the changes in wealth occur. The *price-induced wealth effect* refers to the effect of changes in wealth activated by changes in the price of output. In the classical model, for example, money and government bonds have fixed nominal values; their real values therefore vary inversely with the price level. An increase in the price level lowers the real value of money and government bonds. If consumption depends on real wealth, the increase in the price level will reduce consumption.[13]

The real value of private bonds also varies in the short run with changes in the price level. The classical model, however, is really a long-run framework. The increase in the price level will increase the nominal value of the capital stock; in the long run, as capital wears out and is replaced, firms will have to issue a larger nominal volume of bonds to finance the same real capital stock. If we introduced equities instead of private bonds, an increase in the price level would immediately increase the nominal value of firms' residual income and therefore result in an immediate upward valuation in the nominal value of equities outstanding.

This illustrates an important difference between real assets, such as capital, and financial assets, such as money and government bonds. While financial assets have fixed nominal values and real values that are inversely related to the price level, real assets have fixed real values and nominal values that are proportional to the price level. Given this distinction between capital on the one hand and money and government bonds on the other hand, it is convenient to respecify the sum of the assets definition of wealth as

$$a \equiv \frac{M + B_g}{P} + K \tag{13.13}$$

for use in the classical model, where K is the real value of the stock of capital.

The Interest-Induced Wealth Effect. Up to this point we have been assuming that all bonds were of the *fixed price-variable coupon* variety. For such bonds, changes in the interest rate do not affect the market value of the bond. Now we introduce the *fixed coupon-variable price bond*.[14] The simplest form of this type of bond to

---

[13] The price-induced change in wealth is

$$\frac{da}{dP} = -\frac{M + B_g}{P^2}$$

and the price-induced wealth effect is $\frac{dC}{dP} = -C_a \frac{M + B_g}{P^2}$.

[14] The distinction between fixed price-variable coupon and fixed coupon-variable price bonds was introduced in Chapter 2.

incorporate into our model is a *perpetuity,* a bond which carries a promise to pay a fixed dollar coupon per period forever. Assume the coupon per bond is one dollar. From Chapter 2, recall that the market value of perpetuities is given by b/r where b is now the value of coupons on outstanding bonds (and also the number of bonds outstanding). Treating both government and private bonds as perpetuities, $b = b_g + b_p$ where b_g is the number of government bonds and b_p the number of private bonds outstanding. The government and private sector financing constraints must now be rewritten as

$$\frac{\Delta b_g}{r} = G - T - \Delta m \tag{13.14a}$$

and

$$\frac{\Delta b_p}{r} = I(r). \tag{13.14b}$$

Thus, the number of bonds that must be issued to finance deficits and investment depends on the prevailing interest rate. We will investigate the interest-induced wealth effect in the Keynesian version of our model; therefore, the b/r terms refer to the real value of bonds outstanding.[15] Using the sum of the assets definition of wealth and the beginning-of-period specification of wealth (in the sense that direct wealth effects will affect consumption only in later periods), we can define the wealth variable as

$$a \equiv \overline{m} + \overline{b}/r \tag{13.15a}$$

where $\overline{m}$ and $\overline{b}$ are money and bonds outstanding at the beginning of the period. An increase in the interest rate reduces the market value of bonds and hence wealth and therefore reduces consumption.[16,17]

---

[15] If we included the interest-induced wealth effect in the classical model, we would write the real value of bonds as B/rP where B is the number of bonds paying fixed *nominal* coupons of one dollar.

[16] The decline in the real value of wealth due to an increase in the interest rate is given by

$$\frac{da}{dr} = -\frac{b}{r^2}$$

and the interest-induced decline in consumption by

$$\frac{dC}{dr} = -C_a \frac{b}{r^2}$$

[17] The interest-induced wealth effect operates through fixed coupon-variable price bonds in our model; the major source of interest-induced movements in wealth in the economy are actually associated with movements in the price of equities. We have not explicitly included equities in our model, although the private bonds can be viewed as corresponding to equities. In terms of equation (13.13), the interest-induced wealth effect applies both to government bonds and the market value of the existing capital stock. We noted in Chapter 3 that the market value of the capital stock is given by the value of private bonds and equities outstanding. In terms of household net worth, the interest-induced wealth effect operates on government and private bonds as well as on equities. But the effect on equities is the dominant one.

Alternatively, we could define the wealth variable as beginning-of-period wealth ($\bar{a}$) plus capital gains (CG).

$$a \equiv \bar{a} + CG \tag{13.15b}$$

Captial gains are increases in the market value of existing units of wealth; the indirect wealth effects therefore operate through the CG term.[18] To allow for the interest-induced wealth effect, we specify capital gains as a function of the interest rate

$$CG = g_r r \tag{13.16}$$

where $g_r < 0$. An increase in the interest rate imposes capital losses on bonds, reducing the real value of wealth.

○ The Price-Induced Wealth Effect and the Classical Adjustment Mechanism

The price-induced wealth effect was introduced in Chapter 9 as a part of the classical adjustment mechanism. Figures 13.2a and 13.2b depict the operation of the price-induced wealth effect following an autonomous decline in aggregate demand

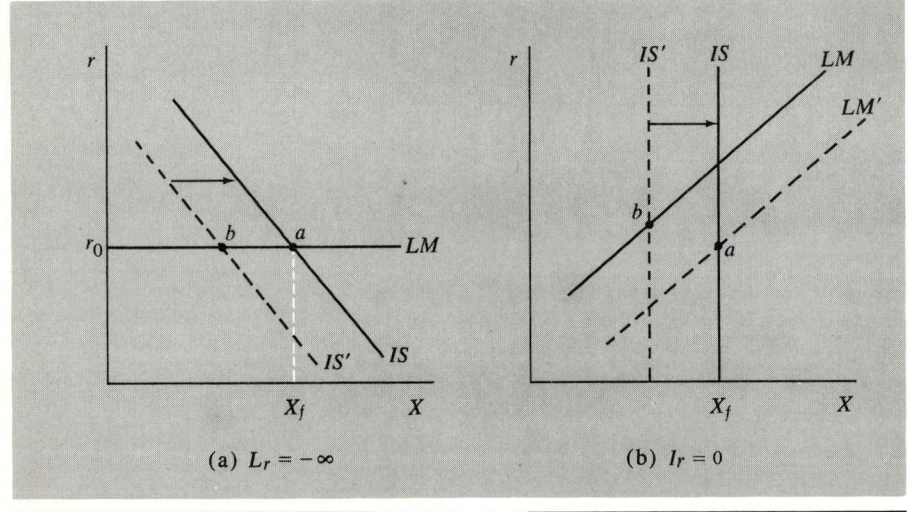

FIGURE 13.2
The Wealth Effect and the Classical Adjustment Mechanism

---

[18] The price-induced wealth effect can also be introduced by making the capital gains function depend on P as well as r; i.e.,

$$CG = g(r, P)$$

where $g_p < 0$.

(i.e., a shift from *IS* to *IS'*) in the two cases where the interest rate mechanism breaks down.

If $L_r = -\infty$ (liquidity trap), the decline in *P* associated with excess supply in the commodity market (at point *b* in Figure 13.2a) will not reduce *r* and increase investment. However, the price-induced wealth effect will generate increased consumption demand and will eventually restore equilibrium at full employment. When there is a price-induced wealth effect, the *IS* curve in the *r-X* diagram depends on the price level; the decline in *P* shifts the *IS* curve upward until the *IS* curve is returned to its original level in Figure 13.2a.

If $I_r = 0$, as depicted in Figure 13.2b, the decline in *P* induced by excess supply in the commodity market at point *b* lowers *r* (via a shift in the *LM* curve) but the decline in *r* does not stimulate aggregate demand. However, the price-induced wealth effect again shifts the *IS* curve rightward until the original position of the *IS* curve and hence equilibrium at full employment is restored. Where $L_r > -\infty$ and $I_r < 0$, the price-induced wealth effect *reinforces* the interest rate effect in the classical adjustment process.

○ The Wealth Effect and the Existence of Neutrality, Dichotomy, and the Quantity Theory of Money

The wealth effect greatly complicates the analysis of the classical model. The existence of neutrality and the quantity theory of money may depend in this case on the composition of assets in the economy. Nevertheless, it generally is agreed that the wealth effect should not cause great departures from neutrality and the quantity theory of money so that the analysis given in Chapter 9 remains essentially correct.[19]

○ Direct Wealth Effects and the Effectiveness of Monetary and Fiscal Policies

In this section we use the saving approach to define wealth because it provides the simplest method of identifying direct wealth effects. Because we are employing the Keynesian model with a fixed price level, there is no price-induced wealth effect. To simplify, we also ignore the interest-induced wealth effect. We will consider the implications of the latter in the next section.

We noted above that direct wealth effects (increases in wealth associated with saving) affect consumption in subsequent periods, not in the period in which the saving occurs. In order to simplify our analysis of the implications of direct wealth effects, we will collapse the effect of direct wealth effects into the first period. The *IS* curve is now written as

---

[19] For discussions of neutrality, dichotomy, and the quantity theory when there are wealth effects, see Franco Modigliani, "The Monetary Mechanism and Its Interaction with Real Phenomena," *The Review of Economics and Statistics*, Vol. 45 (February, 1963), Supplement, pp. 79–107; Warren L. Smith, "A Graphical Exposition of the Complete Keynesian System," *Southern Economic Journal*, Vol. 23 (October, 1956), pp. 115–125; and Don Patinkin, *Money, Interest, and Prices* (2d ed.; New York: Harper and Row, Publishers, 1965).

$$X = C_y(X - \bar{T}) + C_a[\bar{a} + X - C_y(X - \bar{T})] + I_r r + \bar{Z} + \bar{G} \qquad (13.17)$$

where the bracketed term following C_a is the perpetual inventory definition of end-of-period wealth. The reduced-form equation for income becomes

$$X = \frac{1}{D_2}\bar{G} + \frac{1}{D_2}\bar{Z} - \frac{(1 - C_a)C_y}{D_2}\bar{T} + \frac{1}{D_2}\bar{m} - \frac{1}{D_2}\bar{L} \qquad (13.18)$$

where

$$D_2 = 1 - C_y - C_a(1 - C_y) + (L_x/L_r)I_r. \qquad (13.19)$$

Note that $D_2 < D$ where D, derived in Chapter 9, is equal to $1 - C_y + (L_x/L_r)I_r$. D_2 contains an additional negative term, $-C_a(1 - C_y)$. We assume that $C_y + C_a(1 - C_y) < 1$ since this term is now the full income-induced increase in consumption. The denominator therefore remains unambiguously positive. But the negative term in D_2 results in D_2 being smaller than D. Hence, $1/D_2 > 1/D$ so that the *existence of direct wealth effects increases the size of the model's basic multiplier.* Note also that the direct wealth effect enters as part of the positive feedback (i.e., income-induced) response. As income increases, part is saved, wealth increases, and the increase in wealth further stimulates aggregate demand. The increase in positive feedback explains the fact that the model's basic multiplier increases. We now consider the implications of direct wealth effects for the monetary and fiscal policy multipliers.

Monetary Policy and Direct Wealth Effects. Open market operations involve an exchange between money and government bonds; therefore, there is no wealth effect initially. However, as income increases in response to an open market purchase, the associated increase in saving increases wealth. This increased wealth takes the form of an increase in household holdings of private sector bonds, reflecting the effect of the open market purchase on the capital stock via investment. This can be clarified by considering the change in wealth by the sum of the assets approach: $\Delta a = \Delta m + \Delta b_g + \Delta b_p$. For an *OMO*, $\Delta m = -\Delta b_g$. But the change in the interest rate alters investment and this results in a change in the supply of private bonds (Δb_p).

The graphical analysis, depicted in Figure 13.3, employs two *IS* curves: IS_1 excludes the direct wealth effect and IS_2 includes it. IS_2 is flatter than IS_1.[20] An increase in the money supply results in a larger increase in income when there is a wealth effect; this is illustrated in Figure 13.3 by the fact that X_2 corresponding to the intersection of the new *LM* curve and the *IS* curve incorporating direct wealth effects exceeds X_1.

---

[20]
$$\left.\frac{\Delta r}{\Delta X}\right|_{IS_1} = \frac{1 - C_y}{I_r}$$

$$\left.\frac{\Delta r}{\Delta X}\right|_{IS_2} = \frac{1 - C_y - (1 - C_y)C_a}{I_r}$$

Assuming $1 - C_y - (1 - C_y)C_a > 0$, both curves are negatively sloped and the slope of IS_2 is smaller in absolute value than the slope of IS_1.

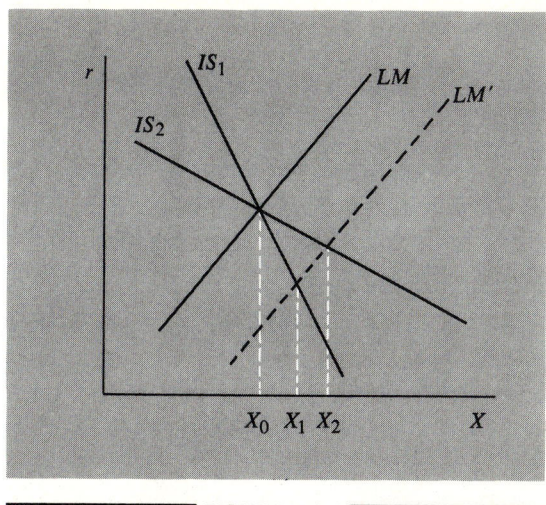

FIGURE 13.3
Direct Wealth Effects and
Open Market Operations

Fiscal Policy and Direct Wealth Effects. Direct wealth effects also increase the fiscal policy multipliers for bond-financed changes in G or T but *decrease* the multiplier for balanced-budget fiscal policy.

Debt-Financed Fiscal Policy. An increase in G increases income and hence saving; the resulting increase in wealth further increases aggregate demand and enlarges the multiplier. From the sum of the assets approach we can see that debt-financed fiscal policy increases household-sector holdings of government securities and *decreases* household holdings of private securities. The reduction in private-sector bonds is a reflection of the crowding-out phenomenon. The increase in government expenditures crowds out some private securities by discouraging investment. Given that income and saving increase, it is clear in the present model that *private securities decline by less than government securities increase* (a reflection of the fact that the increase in G exceeds the decline in I). Hence, on balance, wealth increases and the introduction of a wealth effect in the consumption function increases the debt-financed fiscal multipliers.[21]

Balanced-Budget Fiscal Policy. A balanced-budget increase in G leaves the deficit and hence the supply of government bonds unchanged. The rise in the interest rates reduces investment and hence the supply of private bonds. Therefore, although *GNP* increases, wealth declines so that the introduction of the wealth effect decreases the multiplier for balanced-budget fiscal policy. This result can also be explained in terms of the perpetual inventory definition of wealth. Income increases by less than the increase in G and T in this specification of the model. Therefore, disposable income,

---

[21] The role of the bond market in fiscal policy is discussed in detail in Chapter 25.

saving, and hence wealth decline.[22]

○ The Interest-Induced Wealth Effect and the Effectiveness of Monetary and Fiscal Policies

To introduce the interest-induced wealth effect, we add a capital gains term to the *BOP* definition of wealth and specify capital gains as a function of the interest rate; the explicit equation for wealth is given by equations (13.15b) and (13.16) above. The alternative sum of the assets approach [equation (13.15a)] yields equivalent results.

Increases in the interest rate now reduce wealth and therefore consumption. The interest-induced wealth effect thus makes consumption inversely related to the interest rate. The interest responsiveness of consumption simply increases the overall interest responsiveness of aggregate demand; thus, the results of incorporating the interest-induced wealth effect are precisely the same as increasing I_r (in absolute value).

The reduced form becomes

$$X = \frac{1}{D_3}\bar{G} + \frac{1}{D_3}\bar{Z} - \frac{-C_y}{D_3}\bar{T} + \frac{(I_r + C_a g_r)L_r}{D_3}\bar{m} - \frac{(I_r + C_a g_r)/L_r}{D_3}\bar{L} \qquad (13.20)$$

where

$$D_3 = 1 - C_y + (L_x/L_r)(I_r + C_a g_r). \qquad (13.21)$$

Wherever I_r appeared in our initial multiplier (1/D), $I_r + C_a g_r$ now appears. The interest responsiveness of aggregate demand is now the sum of the interest responsiveness of investment (I_r) and the interest responsiveness of consumption ($C_a g_r$). The increased interest responsiveness of aggregate demand increases the direct impact of monetary policy. The increased interest responsiveness of aggregate demand also increases the size of the negative feedback and therefore reduces the size of all fiscal policy multipliers. Therefore, the *interest-induced wealth effect increases the potency of monetary policy and reduces the potency of fiscal policy.*

The graphical analysis is presented in Figures 13.4a and 13.4b. The interest-induced wealth effect reduces the slope of the *IS* curve; i.e., IS_2 includes the interest-induced wealth effect while IS_1 does not.[23] An increase in the money supply, depicted

---

[22] As long as saving is positive, wealth will increase; but this would be true even in the absence of changes in G and T (or other exogenous variables). What is relevant to our multiplier analysis is that wealth declines relative to what it would have been in the absence of the change in G and T. Similarly, the supply of bonds declines relative to what it would have been in the absence of changes in G and T; as long as investment remains positive, the supply of bonds will increase over the period.

[23] $\left.\dfrac{\Delta r}{\Delta X}\right|_{IS} = \dfrac{1 - C_y}{I_r + C_a g_r}$. Thus, if $g_r = 0$, the slope of the *IS* curve is higher (in absolute value) than if $g_r < 0$.

in Figure 13.4a, can be seen to increase income more when there is an interest-induced wealth effect (i.e., $X_2 > X_1$), and an increase in government expenditures, in Figure 13.4b, increases income by less when there is an interest-induced wealth effect (i.e., $X_1 > X_2$).

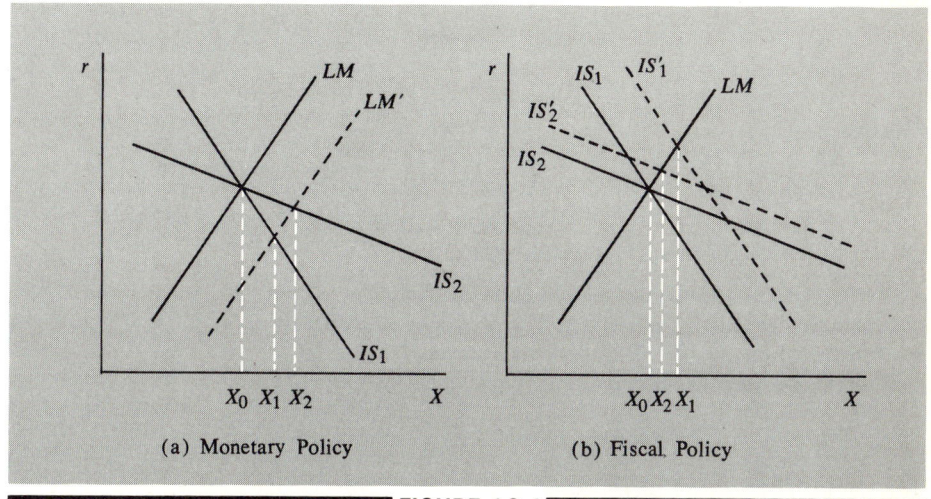

FIGURE 13.4
The Implications of the Interest-Induced Wealth Effect

○ Empirical Evidence on the Importance of the Interest-Induced Wealth Effect

Modigliani ran policy simulations with the *FMP* model to determine the quantitative importance of an interest-induced wealth effect.[24] He found that in the absence of the interest-induced wealth effect, the real income multiplier for an increase in government expenditures reaches a peak of 3 after three years. The introduction of the interest-induced wealth effects both reduces the peak value of the multiplier and increases the speed with which the multiplier peaks and begins to decline. The peak multiplier falls to 2 and occurs in the fifth quarter following the increase in *G*.

The monetary policy simulations also confirm the theoretical results developed above. Without the interest-induced wealth effect, the effect of an increase in the money supply is modest and slow, reaching 2 by the end of two years. With the interest-induced wealth effect, the multiplier reaches 3 by the fifth quarter; at this point, the interest-induced wealth effect accounts for one half of the effect of monetary policy.

● REVIEW QUESTIONS

1. Describe the operational specification of expected income.

[24] Franco Modigliani, "Monetary Policy and Consumption," *Consumer Spending and Monetary Policy: The Linkages* (Boston: Federal Reserve Bank of Boston, 1971).

2. What is the difference between impact and equilibrium multipliers?

3. Distinguish between direct and indirect wealth effects.

4. What is the most important implication of the price-induced wealth effect in the classical model?

● PROBLEMS

1. Compare the implications of the theoretical model of the life cycle hypothesis presented in Chapter 12 and those of the operational specification presented in this chapter for the relative response of consumption to permanent versus temporary tax changes.

2. The effect of specifying consumption as a function of expected income rather than current income on model multipliers can be described in terms of a change in the value of one of the basic model parameters (C_y, L_x, L_r, or I_r). Which one? Explain how this helps to understand the implications of the LCH.

3. The effect of introducing the interest-induced wealth into the model is also analogous to a change in the value of one of the basic model parameters. Which one? Explain how this helps to understand the implications of the interest-induced wealth effect.

Chapter 14
Investment

The inherently dynamic nature of the investment decision makes it particularly difficult to derive the investment function from microeconomic theory and to integrate it into a simple macroeconomic model. Net investment occurs only when firms want to alter their capital stock; in this sense, it is a disequilibrium phenomenon. Once firms have fully responded to any change which affects their demand for capital, net investment falls to zero. To develop the nature of the investment decision, we must therefore consider both the determinants of the firm's desired capital stock and the factors which determine the rate at which firms respond to changes in the variables that alter their desired capital stock.

We begin with a presentation of a simple model of the demand for inputs by a profit-maximizing firm. Next, we consider the implications of time, uncertainty, and disequilibrium for the nature of the demand for capital and discuss two alternative decision rules which indicate when it is profitable to undertake additional investment.

We then turn to a more thorough treatment of investment as opposed to the demand for capital. First, we introduce the stock adjustment model, widely used in econometric studies of investment. Next, we consider an alternative approach which develops the investment decision more directly from profit-maximizing behavior of firms. We conclude the section on models of investment with a discussion of the simple accelerator model and the role of profits in the investment decision.

Gross domestic investment, as defined in the national income accounts, includes business expenditure on plant and equipment (*IPE*), the change in business inventories (*II*), and residential construction (*RC*). This chapter concentrates on the determinants of business fixed investment (business expenditures on plant and equipment); indeed, throughout the chapter we will use the term *investment* to refer to business fixed investment. In an appendix at the end of the chapter, we apply the models developed in the chapter to the explanation of the other components of gross domestic investment (residential construction and inventory investment) as well as to the explanation of expenditures on consumer durables.

Part III • Refinements of the Real Sector: Aggregate Demand

Much of the disagreement among those who have studied investment behavior reflects different assumptions about the nature of the production function. In the final section we therefore develop the implications of the production function for the degree of short-run and long-run substitutability between capital and labor.

THE MICROFOUNDATIONS OF THE DEMAND FOR CAPITAL

In this section, we develop the determinants of the firm's profit-maximizing capital stock. The model is thoroughly static and therefore applies in its simple form only under extremely unrealistic assumptions. Nevertheless, it provides a useful point of departure. First, we derive the marginal rule for profit maximization for a perfectly competitive firm when capital is the only variable input. We use this to specify the least-cost rule when all inputs are variable. Based on this analysis, we identify the determinants of the firm's desired capital stock.

Capital as the Only Variable Input

Profits (π) are equal to revenue (PQ) minus costs:

$$\Pi = PQ - WN - cK \tag{14.1}$$

where P is the price of output, Q is the level of output, W is the wage rate, N is the level of employment, K is the capital stock, and c is the cost of capital.

Recall from our discussion in Chapter 4 that the cost of capital, c, includes two components. When the firm purchases a capital good, it pays the purchase price, P_I, at the time of purchase. However, since the capital good lasts for many periods, the firm does not charge this sum as a cost in the period in which it purchases the capital good. Rather, it *amortizes* the purchase of the capital good; i.e., it charges the cost off over a period of time. In particular, it charges the cost off at the rate it uses up the capital good. Therefore, one element in the cost of capital over a given period will be the decline in the value of the capital over the period, equal to δP_I where δ is the rate of depreciation.

In addition to the explicit cost of the capital good itself, there is also an opportunity cost for the funds used to purchase the capital good. If the capital good is purchased from internal funds, this is an *implicit or imputed cost*: the income foregone because the firm's funds were tied up in the capital good. If the firm borrows the money to purchase the capital good, the second cost element is the *explicit borrowing cost*. In either case, it can be measured by some rate of interest times the funds tied up: rP_I. Thus, the cost of capital is

$$c = (r + \delta)P_I. \tag{14.2}$$

Note that if the firm were to rent the capital good rather than to purchase it, the rental price would be equal to the cost of capital, c.

The firm maximizes profits subject to a production function,

$$Q = F(K, N). \tag{14.3}$$

The dependent variable, Q, is a flow: units of output per period. The arguments of the production function, N and K, should also be flows: the number of person-hours per period and the rate of capital services per period. N is a flow, person-hours per period; but K is a stock. However, the traditional assumption is that capital services are proportional to the stock. By a suitable choice of units, this proportionality factor can be set equal to one. Therefore, the capital stock appears as an argument in the production function.

The condition for the optimal (profit-maximizing) capital stock, derived by maximizing profits subject to the production function, is the requirement that the marginal revenue product of capital per period (MRP_K) be equal to the marginal resource cost of capital (c), the fixed cost per unit of capital services per period. The marginal revenue product is the marginal physical product of capital (F_K) times the price of output (assuming the firm is a perfect competitor in its product market). Therefore, we can write the condition for profit maximization as

$$PF_K = c.[1] \qquad (14.4)$$

Figure 14.1 depicts the firm's *marginal revenue product curve*; this curve gives the demand for capital corresponding to each value of the cost of capital services.

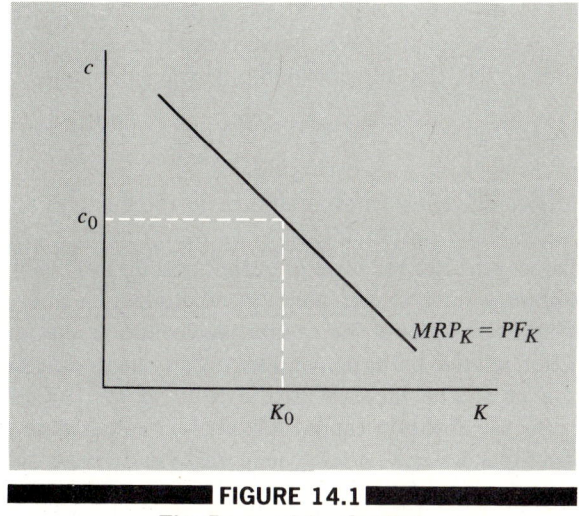

FIGURE 14.1
The Demand for Capital

---

[1] To derive this condition, we substitute equation (14.3) into equation (14.1),

$$\Pi = PF(K,N) - W\bar{N} - cK,$$

assume N is given, and set the derivative Π with respect to K equal to zero:

$$\frac{\delta \Pi}{\delta K} = PF_K - c = 0.$$

This yields the condition given by equation (14.4) above.

If $PF_K > c$, the additional revenue a firm can earn by expanding its capital stock exceeds the additional costs thereby incurred, indicating that profits can be increased by expanding K. As K increases, F_K declines due to the law of diminishing returns; therefore, increases in K will eventually restore equality between PF_K and c.

○ The Long-Run Profit-Maximizing Level of the Capital Stock

Labor is the variable input and the capital stock a fixed input in the short run. Therefore, the rule just derived is of limited relevance by itself. A similar rule can be derived for the case of labor as the only variable input; this condition was discussed in Chapter 5. It requires that the marginal revenue product of labor (PF_N) be equal to the wage rate (W). Given $PF_K = c$ and $PF_N = W$, it follows that

$$\frac{F_N}{W} = \frac{F_K}{c}. \tag{14.5}$$

This is the familiar rule for the least-cost combination of two variable inputs: the marginal product per last dollar spent on each input must be equal. If the marginal product per last dollar were unequal for the two factors, the firm could increase output and therefore revenue and profit by transferring a dollar from the factor with a lower ratio to the factor with a higher ratio. As this process continued, the ratios would eventually be equated. We conclude that the demand for capital depends on the production function, the cost of capital, the wage rate, and the price of output.

$$K^* = K(c/P, W/P) \tag{14.6}$$

Note that output does not enter as an argument in the demand for capital. As long as the firm can sell all the output it desires at the prevailing price level, the firm simultaneously chooses the desired level of output and desired levels of factor inputs. A decline in the interest rate lowers the cost of production and expands both the supply of output and the demand for capital. A decline in the interest rate lowers the cost of production relative to the demand for output, increasing the profit-maximizing output for the firm. The increase in the demand for capital involves both a *substitution effect* (firms substitute capital for labor in response to the decline in the relative cost of capital) and a *scale effect* (the increase in demand for inputs associated with the increase in the rate of production).[2]

○ TIME, UNCERTAINTY, DISEQUILIBRIUM, AND THE DEMAND FOR CAPITAL

The simple micro model of the firm's demand for capital discussed above highlights the role of relative input prices and the price of output in the investment decision but misses some of the essential features of the decision to acquire capital goods.

---

[2] The scale effect on the demand for inputs is not necessarily positive, but normally the scale effect reinforces the substitution effect in this case.

In particular, the treatment above fails to deal explicitly with the element of time, the problem of uncertainty, and the effects of disequilibrium in the output market on the demand for capital.

○ Owning and Renting and the Irreversibility of Investment Decisions

Time does not enter explicitly in the micro model of the previous section. But one of the essential features of the investment decision is that it commits the firm to an increase in its capital stock over a long period of time. This reflects the highly *irreversible* nature of investment. Investment is *perfectly reversible* if the firm can always sell the capital good at a price that differs from the purchase price only by an adjustment for the loss in value of the capital good due to depreciation. The purchase of the capital good is then identical to the renting of a capital good (with the rental price equal to $c per period). In either case, the firm needs to consider only current values of input and output prices in its decision to acquire capital.

Investment decisions, however, are highly irreversible. Capital goods tend to be highly specialized, tailored to the needs of the particular firm, and also involve large costs of installation (and of removal). Therefore, capital goods are generally purchased rather than rented and are not readily saleable if the firm subsequently prefers a smaller stock of capital. This irreversibility implies that the maximum rate at which firms can reduce their capital stock equals the rate of depreciation; i.e., gross investment must be nonnegative ($I \geq 0$). This is certainly true for the economy as a whole; for individual firms, investment decisions may not be perfectly irreversible, but the costs of reversing investment decisions may be sufficiently large that firms make every effort to avoid making investment decisions they subsequently regret.

In order to assess the profitability of a purchase of a unit of capital, the firm must therefore estimate the return expected to be associated with the capital over a fairly long period. The marginal product of capital (a purely technological concept) is relevant to this forecast, but the firm must also forecast demand (and hence price and quantity produced) as well as costs of other inputs. This suggests that the variables that enter the demand for capital are not simply the current values of input prices and the output price, but also the expected future values of these variables. As in the life cycle model developed in Chapters 12 and 13, we face the problem of specifying the formation of expectations about future values of input and output prices. In econometric work, expected future values of a given variable are generally specified as a function of either current values of the variable (as in one specification of the expected income term on the life cycle model discussed in Chapter 12) or as a function of current and past values of that variable (the adaptive expectations model). We could follow either of these approaches—either using current values of W, P, and c or current and past values of W, P, and c, respectively. Of course, this specification of expectations makes investment decisions backward- rather than forward-looking. Without defending the adequacy of this approach, it nevertheless serves to remind us that the demand for capital may not be very responsive to current period changes in variables unless these changes are expected to persist.[3]

---

[3] See Robert Eisner, "Econometric Studies of Investment Behavior: A Comment," *Economic Inquiry*, Vol. XII (March, 1974), pp. 91–104 for a discussion of the importance of adequately treating expectations in investment equations.

Uncertainty and the Demand for Capital

The basic determinants of the demand for capital are the net income flow associated with the use of the capital good (what Keynes called the *prospective yield* on the capital good), the price of the capital good, and the rate of interest. While the firm pays the purchase price as a lump sum at the time of purchase, the net income flow is distributed over a long number of years and is therefore subject to considerable uncertainty. To calculate the expected net income flow, the firm must estimate the gross expected income flow and then subtract all costs expected to be associated with the use of the machine, including labor services and raw materials, but excluding any interest costs. According to Keynes,

> The outstanding fact is the extreme precariousness of the basis of knowledge on which our estimates of prospective yield have to be made. Our knowledge of the factors which will govern the yield of an investment some years hence is usually very slight and often negligible.[4]

The firm is uncertain about the gross income per period since this depends not only on the physical productivity of the machine but also on the ability to sell all the output that the machine can produce (or the price at which it can sell the output). In addition, there is uncertainty about the cost of using the machine (particularly in later periods), about the expected life of the machine, and about the prices of other inputs that will be used with the machine.

One implication of the uncertainty associated with the future returns on capital, and the one greatly emphasized by Keynes, is the likelihood of sharp changes in the assessment of the prospective yield on capital and the importance of the resulting swing in investment for the explanation of the business cycle. For example, Keynes noted that,

> It is important to understand the dependence of the marginal efficiency of a given capital stock on changes in expectations, because it is chiefly this dependence which renders the marginal efficiency of capital subject to somewhat violent fluctuations which are the explanation of the Trade Cycle.[5]

In this quote, Keynes is using the term *marginal efficiency of capital* to refer to the expected rate of return on the capital good. We will define this term more precisely in the next section.

The existence of uncertainty about the future returns also suggests that firms will require an expected rate of return in excess of that on safe assets (such as government debt) in order to induce the firms to purchase capital goods rather than hold the safe assets. Alternatively, the discount rate that firms use to determine the present value of the future net returns will include a *risk premium* over the rate available on safe assets. Similarly, households and financial intermediaries that lend to firms will require a rate of interest in excess of the rate available on safe assets to compensate for the greater risk associated with lending to firms. The risk premium will vary with the perceived degree of uncertainty surrounding future economic developments.

---

[4] John Maynard Keynes, *The General Theory of Employment, Interest and Money* (New York: Harcourt, Brace and World, Inc., 1936), p. 149.
[5] *Ibid.*, pp. 143–144.

Exogenous shifts in the perception of risk or willingness to bear risk can be an important source of economic instability. But the risk premium may also have an endogenous component. A period of high and relatively stable output and employment, for example, may tend to reduce the risk premium and therefore generate additional investment. Similarly, a period of unexpected declines in output and employment may cause upward revisions in the risk premium, reducing investment and aggravating the decline in economic activity.[6]

○ Disequilibrium and the Accelerator

In our discussion of the demand for capital, we have assumed that firms were able to sell as much output as they desired at the prevailing price level for output. This, after all, is the standard assumption in the analysis of a perfectly competitive firm. In this case, we noted that output does not appear explicitly as an argument in the firm's demand for capital. Instead, the firm simultaneously chooses desired values for output, labor input, and capital, given the cost of capital, the wage rate, and the price level [as in equation (14.6)]. If it is assumed, on the other hand, that firms are limited in the amount they can sell at the prevailing price level, as must be the case when there is excess supply in the output market, then the capital stock decision becomes output constrained. In this case, the demand for capital depends on the input prices and the demand for output:

$$K = K(c/P, W/P, X). \tag{14.7}$$

Note, however, that we can always express the relationship between capital, output, and input prices in terms of equation (14.7). When the firm can sell all the output it wants at the prevailing price of output, X will also be a function of W and c as well as of P so that equation (14.7) can be written as a function of c/P and W/P alone. When demand is output constrained, on the other hand, the demand for capital must be expressed using equation (14.7) rather than equation (14.6).

When we use the output-constrained demand for capital in the Keynesian version of our model, W/P is treated as a predetermined variable; in addition, the only variable component of c is the interest rate. Therefore, we can write the demand for capital in this case as simply

$$K = K(r, X) \tag{14.7'}$$

where $K_r < 0$ and $K_x > 0$.[7]

The output-constrained demand for capital provides the theoretical basis for the *accelerator principle*. According to the accelerator, net investment depends on the change (acceleration) in the level of output. Given that the demand for capital depends on the level of output in equation (14.7), net investment (the change in the capital stock) will depend on the change in output.

---

[6] The endogeneity of the risk premium has been emphasized by Minsky. See, for example, Chapter 6 in Hyman P. Minsky, *John Maynard Keynes* (New York: Columbia University Press, 1975).

[7] For an elegant derivation of the role of output in the investment function, see Herschel Grossman, "A Choice Theoretic Model of An Income-Investment Accelerator," *American Economic Review*, Vol. LXII (September, 1972), pp. 630–641.

THE INTERNAL RATE OF RETURN AND PRESENT VALUE RULES: TOWARD A THEORY OF NET INVESTMENT

We can now develop two alternative decision rules that combine information about expected net income flow, the purchase price of the capital good, and the risk-adjusted rate of interest to determine whether or not the firm should undertake additional investment. The two alternative rules reflect two alternative interpretations of the role of the rate of interest in determining the profitability of investment. One interpretation is that the rate of interest is the relevant opportunity cost or explicit borrowing cost of funds tied up in the capital good. The higher the interest rate, the fewer the investment prospects that will be profitable to undertake.

The second interpretation of the interest rate is that it is the discount rate applied to determine the present value of the expected future returns. As we noted above, an essential feature of the purchase of a capital good is that the purchase price is paid immediately in one lump sum while the return (the expected net income flow) is spread over a number of years. We need a way of comparing the price of the capital good and the value of the expected net income flow. Recall from Chapter 2 that a dollar today is worth more than a dollar tomorrow. To find the present value of a stream of dollars to be received in the future, we must "discount" the dollars expected in the future. The second interpretation of the rate of interest is as the discount factor used to calculate the present value of expected future net income.

The Internal Rate of Return Rule (*i* Rule)

An investment should be undertaken if the expected rate of return on the capital good (the internal rate of return or the marginal efficiency of capital) exceeds the (risk-adjusted) market rate of interest (r). The internal rate of return (i) is defined by the following expression:

$$P_I = \frac{R_1}{(1+i)} + \frac{R_2}{(1+i)^2} + \cdots + \frac{R_n}{(1+i)^n} \tag{14.8}$$

where P_I is the purchase price of the capital good, the R_n are the expected net income flows in periods 1, 2, $\cdots$, n, and i is the internal rate of return. As can be seen from this equation, the internal rate of return is the discount rate which would just make the present value of the expected net income flows equal to the purchase price of the capital good; it is a measure of the rate of return on the capital good. This rule states that if $i > r$, the investment should be undertaken. The firm ranks investment projects in decreasing order of i. The optimal capital stock is achieved when investment has been undertaken to the point where $i = r$.

The Present Value Rule (*PV* Rule)

An alternative rule compares the purchase price (P_I) and the present value of the expected net income flow (PV). The present value of the expected net income flow is given by

$$PV = \frac{R_1}{1+r} + \frac{R_2}{(1+r)^2} + \cdots + \frac{R_n}{(1+r)^n}. \tag{14.9}$$

This rule states that an investment should be undertaken if $PV > P_I$. It permits projects to be ranked in terms of contribution to the present value of the firm, $PV - P_I$. All projects that make a contribution to the present value of the firm should be undertaken; i.e., all those with $PV - P_I > 0$. Thus, the optimal capital stock is achieved when investment has been undertaken to the point where $P_I = PV$ for the next best investment project. In simple cases, the i rule and the PV rule yield identical results; in more complicated situations, the PV rule is superior. A comparison of the internal rate of return and present value rules is presented in Appendix A.

○ The Interest Rate vs. "q" as an Argument in the Investment Function

The i and PV rules are the source of two competing formulations of the investment equation. The traditional specification derives from the i rule. Investment occurs when $i > r$; therefore, the investment function might be written as

$$I_N = I(i - r). \tag{14.8'}$$

The rate of net investment is a function of the incentive to expand the capital stock, the gap between i and r. An alternative specification emerges from the PV rule. Investment responds to the ratio of the present value of the expected returns to the purchase price of a new capital good

$$I_N = I(PV/P_I). \tag{14.9'}$$

The problem with this specification is the necessity of obtaining an operational measure of the present value term. The approach suggested by James Tobin and William Brainard is to use the valuation of capital in the bond and equity markets to measure the markets' valuation of the net returns to the existing capital stock.[8] Recall from Chapter 2 that we noted that the market valuation of the capital stock, K, could be measured by the market value of bonds and equities outstanding ($B_p + E$). The denominator of the PV/P_I ratio is the cost of replacing the capital stock, equal to the price per unit of new capital goods times the number of units of capital ($P_I K$). The ratio of the market value of the existing capital stock to its replacement cost has been labelled "q" by Tobin and Brainard.[9]

$$q = \frac{B_p + E}{P_I} \tag{14.10}$$

The q variable differs from the PV/P_I ratio in an important respect. PV/P_I is supposed to reflect the returns and cost associated with the *marginal* unit of capital (e.g., the purchase of one additional unit); q, on the other hand, is an average measure, applying to the returns and replacement cost of the existing capital stock. The q

---

[8] See James Tobin and William C. Brainard, "Pitfalls in Financial Model Building," *American Economic Review, Papers and Proceedings*, Vol. 58 (May, 1968), pp. 99–122 and James Tobin and William C. Brainard, "Asset Markets and the Cost of Capital," in *Economic Progress, Private Values, and Public Policy*, Essays in Honor of William Fellner (North Holland Publishing Co., 1977), pp. 235–262.

[9] James Tobin and William C. Brainard, "Pitfalls in Financial Model Building," *American Economic Review, Papers and Proceedings*, Vol. 58 (May, 1968), pp. 99–122.

variable has an important advantage. The numerator summarizes all the information about expected returns and discount rates needed to determine the present value of returns to the existing capital stock. We do not have a direct measure of i. Therefore, when we begin from the i rule, we have to include in our investment equation the determinants of i; current and expected future values of wages, output prices, and output. This advantage of q in explaining investment unfortunately does not carry over when we include the investment equation in a complete macro model. For now we must explain the q variable within the model and this is a most difficult task, involving explanation of movements in equity prices. Now we are back to having to know the R's, and the advantage of the q variable is no longer so clear-cut.

The q version of the investment equation can be written as

$$I_N = I(q-1) \tag{14.11}$$

so that $I_N = 0$ when $q = 1$ (the firm is in equilibrium, at its desired capital stock), and $I_N > 0$ when $q > 1$ (when $PV > P_I$).

The investment equations discussed above [equations (14.8′), (14.9′), and (14.11)] presumed that net investment responded gradually to discrepancies between r and i or PV and P_I. But we didn't explain why firms would not move immediately to the desired capital stock. Yet this is the essential aspect of investment theory: the determinants of the speed with which firms move to the new desired capital stock in response to a change in i or r (or PV or P_I). We turn to this question in the next section.

ALTERNATIVE MODELS OF INVESTMENT

In this section we present several alternative models of net investment. The first model is the stock adjustment approach, the most widely used model in econometric studies of investment.[10] It is, however, quite *ad hoc* and without any explicit relation to the profit-maximizing behavior of firms. Next, we consider the role of adjustment costs, costs which are an increasing function of the rate of investment, in inducing profit-maximizing firms to respond gradually to changes in variables which affect their demand for capital. We conclude the section with a discussion of two more specialized explanations of investment: the simple accelerator model and a model in which investment is related to current profits.

Recall from Chapter 2 that gross investment (I) is the sum of net investment (equal to the change in the capital stock over the unit interval of the analysis) and replacement investment (I_R). The conventional treatment of replacement investment is to assume a constant, technologically imposed rate of depreciation (δ) and therefore, replacement needs proportional to the existing capital stock,

$$I_R = \delta \overline{K}, \tag{14.12}$$

where $\overline{K}$ is the beginning-of-period value of the capital stock. This specification, referred

---

[10] For a survey of econometric studies of investment, see Dale Jorgenson, "Econometric Studies of Investment Behavior: A Survey," *Journal of Economic Literature*, Vol. 9 (December, 1971), pp. 1111–1147.

to as the *proportional replacement hypothesis*, will be assumed as one component of the explanation of gross investment. Below we will concentrate on the explanation of net investment.

○ The Stock Adjustment Model of Investment

The essential properties of the *stock adjustment model* are that the desired capital stock depends on long-run considerations (the factors that determine i or PV) and that net investment is determined by a distributed lag function of the arguments that enter the demand function for capital. The model can allow for a wide range of variables to influence the desired capital stock (K^*). The simplest specification is one in which net investment is proportional to the gap between the desired and actual (beginning-of-period) capital stocks:

$$I_N = \beta(K^* - \bar{K}) \tag{14.13}$$

where β is the speed of adjustment coefficient, the proportion of the gap between the desired and actual capital stock that firms plan to close in a given period. The determinants of the speed of adjustment are not explicit in this approach. Whatever the causes of noninstantaneous adjustment, an empirical estimate of this equation will yield the value of the speed of adjustment.

Slow adjustment may reflect the implementation lag of the investing firm and/or the production lag in the capital goods supplying firms. Once firms have decided on their desired capital stock, they still must decide where to purchase it and how to finance it. Since capital goods are typically made to order rather than sold out of inventory, it is necessary to allow for a production lag, the gestation period of a capital good. In addition, the capacity of the capital goods supplying industry limits the speed with which capital goods using firms can move to their desired capital stocks. Furthermore, where there is uncertainty, firms may choose to proceed cautiously.

The desired capital stock depends on i and r (or PV and P_I). Given that i is not observable, the desired capital stock is usually related to r and the factors that determine i (the R's and P_I); given that the profitability of any investment depends crucially on the overall level of economic activity, the main additional argument is generally the current and expected future levels of aggregate demand (output) in the economy. This yields a typical specification of

$$I_N = \beta[K(r^*, X^*) - \bar{K}] \tag{14.14}$$

where the r^* and X^* represent a measure of the current and expected future values of r and X. Often only the current values of r and X are included in K^*, but this is only appropriate if the current r and X serve as the best way to proxy the expected future values.

○ Adjustment Costs and the Theory of Investment

The stock adjustment specification rests on the existence of production and delivery lags which prevent the firm from achieving its desired capital stock on a period-by-period basis. An alternative approach to investment is to explain the gradual response to changes in the variables that affect the demand for capital by the existence of *adjustment costs*, costs that vary with the speed at which firms acquire capital. Given the existence of adjustment costs, firms find it profitable to respond gradually to changes in interest rates and output. Although firms respond gradually, as in the stock adjustment approach, they increase their capital stock each period by an amount consistent with profit maximization.

There are two different types of adjustment costs. *External adjustment costs* reflect the cost conditions of the capital goods producing firms. These adjustment costs are associated with the rising supply curve of the capital goods producing firms; the higher the rate of investment, the higher the rate of production of capital goods and the higher the price per unit for the capital goods. Firms can lower the average price they pay for capital goods by spreading their purchases over time. *Internal adjustment costs* are costs associated with the installation of new capital goods by the firms demanding the goods. If these costs also rise with the speed at which firms acquire new capital goods, firms will again have an incentive to spread out their purchases over the time even if the price charged by capital goods supplying firms is independent of the rate of production.[11]

We present a model with rising supply curves of capital goods producers (external adjustment costs) in Appendix C to explain the determinants of residential construction. In this section we explicitly integrate the internal adjustment costs into our treatment of investment. We define a new measure of the price of new capital goods which includes the cost of integrating the new capital goods into the firm. We call this the *effective price* of new capital goods, P_I^*; and write it as

$$P_I^* = P_I + AC. \tag{14.15}$$

To isolate the role of internal adjustment costs, we assume firms can purchase capital goods at a constant price from capital goods producing firms; in Figure 14.2a we depict the supply curve of the capital goods producing firms as a horizontal line at the prevailing price of new capital goods $\overline{P_I}$. In Figure 14.2b, we depict the relationship between internal adjustment costs (AC) and the rate of investment. We assume adjustment costs are a constant amount per unit of replacement investment but a rising function of net investment. Figure 14.2c depicts the relation between investment and the effective price of capital goods; it is a vertical summation of the P_I and AC curves.

We now integrate this rising effective price of capital goods schedule into our analysis of the optimal capital stock. We noted above that the demand for capital depends on the price of capital goods, the rate of interest, and the expected quasi rents. In Figure 14.3a, we have drawn the demand curve for capital for the effective price that would prevail if firms were just meeting replacement needs ($\overline{P_I} + \overline{AC}$). We begin with the desired and actual capital stock equal to K_0 and a market interest

---

[11] The role of adjustment costs in the theory of investment is discussed by Robert Eisner and Robert Strotz, "Determinants of Business Investment," in Commission on Money and Credit, *Impacts of Monetary Policy* (Englewood Cliffs, N.J.: Prentice-Hall, Inc., 1964), pp. 61–337; and J. P. Gould, "Adjustment Costs in the Theory of Investment of the Firm," *Review of Economic Studies*, Vol. 35 (January, 1968), pp. 447–466.

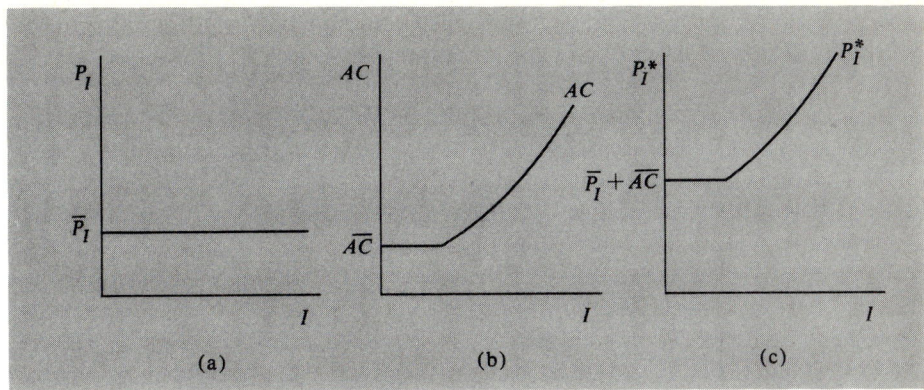

FIGURE 14.2
Internal Adjustment Costs
and the Effective Price of New Capital Goods

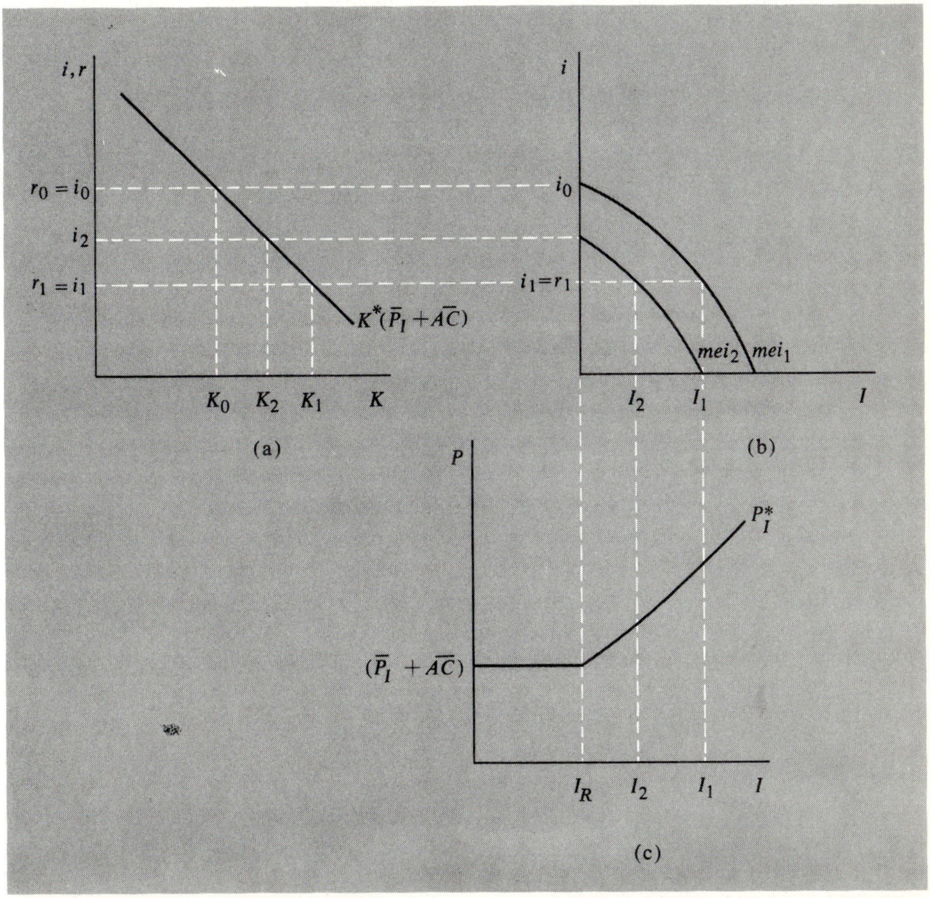

FIGURE 14.3
Internal Adjustment Costs and Investment

rate of i_0. Gross investment just equals replacement investment and net investment is zero. The firm is in equilibrium, and the internal rate of return must therefore be equal to the prevailing interest rate.

Now assume that the market rate of interest falls to r_1. At r_1, $i > r$ and the new desired capital stock is apparently K_1. Why doesn't the firm immediately move to K_1? The more rapid the adjustment, the higher the internal adjustment costs incurred by firms, and the higher the effective price that firms will have to pay for their new capital goods. As firms expand more rapidly, their internal rates of return decline in response to the increase in the effective price of capital goods. (Review the formula for the internal rate of return.) Instead of shifting the K^* curve in response to changes in the effective price of capital, we hold the curve fixed for the effective price of capital associated with replacement investment $(\overline{P_I} + \overline{AC})$ and we use this curve to identify the capital stock to which firms will ultimately move. In Figure 14.3b, we relate the internal rate of return to the rate of investment. The larger the rate of investment, the smaller the internal rate of return. The downward slope of the marginal efficiency of investment (*mei*) curve reflects both the downward slope of the K^* curve in Figure 14.3a and the rising effective price of capital depicted in Figure 14.3c. The *mei* schedule begins on the vertical axis at the internal rate of return (i_0) associated with an initial capital stock of K_0 and a price of P_0. As K and P_I^* rise, the internal rate of return declines. Firms should continue to invest as long as the internal rate of return exceeds the interest rate. Therefore, the optimal rate of investment is the point along the *mei* schedule at which $i = r$. From Figure 14.3b, we find that the optimal rate of investment in the first period is I_1, where $r_1 = i_1$. Therefore, the profit-maximizing capital stock for the initial period is not K_1, but K_2.

At the end of the first period, the firm's capital stock is $K_2 = K_0 - \delta K_0 + I_1$. At K_2, if the firm just replaces worn-out capital during the next period, the internal rate of return associated with the relevant effective price of capital goods, $\overline{P_I} + \overline{AC}$, will still be greater than the market rate of interest. This implies that the desired capital stock in the second period is greater than K_2. Thus, positive net investment will occur in the second period also. The relevant *mei* schedule (mei_2) now begins on the vertical axis at the internal rate of return associated with a capital stock of $K_2(i_2)$. As $K_2 > K_0$, mei_2 begins at a lower point on the vertical axis than mei_1. Again, the optimal rate of investment is that at which the internal rate of return is just equated to the interest rate. This occurs at I_2. This augments the capital stock and sets up the initial conditions for the investment decision in period 3. The process continues until the firm reaches K_1. But at each period along the way, the firm was at its desired capital stock.

○ The Accelerator Model

A simple specification of the investment equation is based on the assumption of a fixed-coefficients production function and constant returns to scale. This implies a constant capital-output ratio, v,

$$v = \frac{K}{Q}, \tag{14.16}$$

so that the desired capital stock is proportional to output.

$$K^* = vQ \tag{14.16'}$$

Assuming that firms always utilize all units of capital (i.e., no excess capacity), the equation for net investment is simply

$$I_N = \Delta K = v\Delta Q. \tag{14.17}$$

Therefore, net investment depends on the change (acceleration) in the level of output, not the level of output itself.[12]

The Flexible Accelerator. The rigid form of the accelerator, given by equation (14.17), fails to take into account the highly irreversible nature of the investment decision. The irreversibility of investment requires a modification of equation (14.17) for two reasons. First, it implies that firms should not respond to current changes in demand without regard to their expected duration. Firms can initially meet increases in sales out of inventories and gradually respond to changes in demand by increasing their capital stock. Secondly, the irreversibility of investment implies that a reduction in sales and production will initially result in excess capacity (idle machines). When sales subsequently increase, the firm will initially be able to meet the demand by reactivating the idle capital so that net investment does not have to respond rigidly to changes in production.

These considerations suggest that net investment should be less responsive to movements in current output, even under the restrictive fixed-proportions production function assumed in the accelerator model. To allow for gradual response of net investment to changes in output, the stock adjustment model is employed with the desired capital stock specified as vQ, the capital stock firms would require to produce Q when there is no excess capacity and the firm is neither increasing nor decreasing its inventories:

$$I_N = \beta(vQ - \bar{K}) \tag{14.18}$$

where β is the speed with which investment responds to changes in output. This is usually referred to as the *flexible accelerator model.*[13]

The Permanent Accelerator. Another way to respecify the rigid accelerator to avoid the implication that firms respond to every increase in demand as if it were permanent is to relate net investment to "permanent" changes in output. Robert Eisner has developed a modification of the fixed accelerator model based on Friedman's permanent income theory of consumption, discussed in Appendix C to Chapter 12.[14] Eisner measures permanent changes in output as a distributed lag on current and past changes

---

[12] The simple accelerator model was suggested by J. M. Clark, "Business Acceleration and the Law of Demand," *Journal of Political Economy,* Vol. 25 (March, 1917), pp. 217–235.

[13] The flexible accelerator was suggested by Hollis B. Chenery, "Overcapacity and the Acceleration Principle," *Econometrica,* Vol. 20 (January, 1952), pp. 1–28.

[14] Robert Eisner, "A Permanent Income Theory of Investment," *American Economic Review,* Vol. 57 (June, 1967), pp. 363–390.

in output. Using an n period distributed lag, the permanent accelerator model can be expressed as

$$I_N = v \sum_{i=0}^{n} w_i \Delta Q_{t-i} \tag{14.19}$$

where w_i's decline and $\sum_{t=0}^{n} w_i = 1$.

○ Profits and Internal Funds

Investment is undertaken if it is expected to be profitable. Therefore, the optimal capital stock depends on *expected profitability* of further additions, not on *actual profits*. Moreover, a high level of current profits indicates the profitability of past investment projects, not the profitability of future ones. Is there any basis, then, for investment depending on actual profits? One rationale for the role of the actual level of profits is that current profits may be used as a guide to expected profits from additions to the capital stock. A second explanation of the relevance of profits, or more correctly internal funds (retained earnings plus depreciation allowances), is the low cost of internal funds relative to the cost of external finance.[15]

Firms may be unwilling to invest such internal funds in other firms even if such an investment promised a higher expected return than the firm's own investment. This of course denies the assumption that firms are profit maximizers. An alternative assumption about firm motivation which is consistent with such behavior is that firms are sales maximizers (subject to some minimum profit constraint), interested in increasing the size of the firm rather than maximizing profits.

Even if current profits are not a proxy for the expected profitability associated with the purchase of capital goods, they may still exert an important influence on the actual rate of investment. Some firms may not have access to external financing, particularly small or new firms. In this case, the availability of internal funds will limit the rate at which firms can expand their capital stock.

The profit theory is one basis for the view that investment is related to the *level* of income. The level of profits is closely related to the level of aggregate demand or output:

$$\Pi = \Pi(X). \tag{14.20}$$

Therefore, the profits theory

$$I = I(\Pi) \tag{14.21}$$

---

[15] Part of a firm's net revenue can be deducted in computing a firm's taxable net income to reflect the cost associated with the depreciation of the firm's capital stock; this is called the *depreciation allowance*. The remaining net income is the firm's profits. A certain portion must be paid in taxes; another portion is paid out in dividends to stockholders. The remaining sum out of profits is called *retained earnings*. The sum of depreciation allowances and retained earnings is called *internal funds*. *External financing* refers to funds raised by borrowing (i.e., selling bonds) or issuing equities.

implies that the investment function can be expressed as

$$I = I(X) \tag{14.21'}$$

where $I_r > 0$.

THE PRODUCTION FUNCTION, THE DEMAND FOR CAPITAL, AND INVESTMENT

Many of the empirical disagreements about the investment equation relate to the specific properties of the production functions employed in various studies. The nature of the production function determines both the degree of the long-run substitutability between capital and other inputs and the speed with which firms are able to respond to changes in the desired capital intensity of production. Both aspects of the production function have important implications for the short-run interest responsiveness of investment (I_r in our models) and therefore for the response of the economy to both policy changes and nonpolicy disturbances. First, we consider the long-run substitutability between capital and labor and then the short-run substitutability in the case where there is some degree of long-run substitutability.

The Production Function and the Demand for Capital

The production function determines the degree of substitutability among inputs in the long run. In the case of the fixed-coefficients production function, for example, there is no possibility of substitution among inputs. To produce a given output, the firm must have a fixed amount of capital, and there is no possibility of compensating for somewhat less capital by hiring additional units of labor.

The greater the degree of substitutability among inputs, the greater the responsiveness of the demand for capital to changes in relative input costs. A measure of the degree of long-run substitutability is the elasticity of substitution, σ,

$$\sigma = \frac{\%\Delta(K/N)}{\%\Delta(W/c)}, \tag{14.22}$$

the percentage change in the capital-labor ratio in response to a given percentage change in relative input prices. In the fixed coefficient model $\sigma = 0$. The most widely used production function in models of the demand for capital is the Cobb Douglas production function, which assumes $\sigma = 1$. Thus, imposing the assumption of a *Cobb Douglas (CD)* production function automatically results in the prediction of a high degree of long-run substitutability and therefore, a large long-run response of the demand for capital to changes in the rate of interest. An alternative production function employed in investment studies is the *constant elasticity of substitution (CES)* production function. The *CD* production function is a special case of the *CES* in which $\sigma = 1$. In the general specification of the *CES* model, σ is free to take on other values, and when freely estimated, σ is generally found to be less than one, although often fairly close to one.[16]

The Cobb Douglas Production Function and the Demand for Capital. The Cobb Douglas production function yields a simple specification of the demand for capital:

$$K^* = \left(\frac{P}{c}Q\right) \tag{14.23}$$

where P is the price of output, Q is the level of output, and c is the cost of capital. The elasticity of the demand for capital with respect to a change in the cost of capital equals -1 in this case ($\epsilon_{Kc} = -1$). For a derivation of the equation, see Appendix B.

The CES Production Function and the Demand for Capital. The CES production function yields a specification in which ϵ_{Kc} is free to take on values other than minus one.[17]

$$K^* = \beta(P/c)^\sigma Q \tag{14.24}$$

In this case, $\epsilon_{Kc} = -\sigma$, and σ generally is found to be less than one.[18] Note also that the response to changes in the cost of capital can now be smaller than the response to a change in output.

○ The Production Function and Investment

The nature of the production function also determines how rapidly firms will be able to achieve a change in the desired capital intensity of production, induced, for example, by a decline in the cost of capital. We consider three alternative forms of a production function: putty-putty, putty-clay, and clay-clay. The terminology refers to the *ex ante* and *ex post* possibilities for substituting capital for labor. A *putty* capital good is *malleable*; i.e., it can be used with varying amounts of labor. A *clay* capital good must use capital and labor in fixed proportions. *Ex ante substitutability* means that alternative production techniques of varying capital intensity are

---

[16] The principal advocates of the use of the Cobb Douglas production function in the derivation of investment equations are Dale Jorgenson and Robert Hall. See, for example, Dale Jorgenson, "Econometric Studies of Investment Behavior: A Survey," and Robert E. Hall, "Investment, Interest Rates, and the Effects of Stabilization Policies," *Brookings Papers on Economic Activity* (1977:1), pp. 51–103. The principal advocate of the *CES* is Charles Bischoff. See, for example, "Business Investment in the 1970's: A Comparison of Models," *Brookings Papers on Economic Activity* (1971:1), pp. 13–58. For a skeptical view of the wisdom of imposing restrictive assumptions about the nature of the production function in the derivation of investment equations, see L. R. Klein, "Issues in Econometric Studies of Investment Behavior," *Journal of Economic Literature*, Vol. XII (March, 1974), pp. 43–49.

[17] For a derivation of the demand for capital from the *CES* production, see David J. Ott, Attiat F. Ott, and Jang H. Yoo, *Macroeconomic Theory* (New York: McGraw-Hill Book Co., 1975), pp. 99–100.

[18] L. R. Klein's judgement from his own empirical work is that, although the elasticity of substitution in many lines of economic activity is somewhat less than unity, the Cobb Douglas form may be a "tolerably good approximation." See L. R. Klein, "Issues in Econometric Studies of Investment Behavior," *Journal of Economic Literature*, Vol. XIII (March, 1974), p. 43–49. Eisner, on the other hand, finds evidence that "the price elasticity of the demand for capital goods [is] considerably closer to zero than unity. . . ." See Robert Eisner, "Econometric Studies of Investment Behavior: A Comment," *Economic Inquiry*, Vol. XII (March, 1974), p. 94.

available to the firm before (*ex ante*) a particular capital good is purchased. *Ex post substitutability* means that, even after a particular capital good has been purchased, the capital intensity of production can be altered by varying the amount of labor used with it. A *putty-putty* technology is one in which there is both *ex ante* and *ex post* substitutability. A *putty-clay* technology is one in which there is *ex ante* substitutability but no *ex post* substitutability. A *clay-clay* technology is one in which there is neither *ex ante* nor *ex post* substitutability.

It is the *ex ante* substitutability that determines the long-run possibilities for substituting capital for labor. The fixed-proportions technology allows no *ex ante* substitution, while the Cobb Douglas and *CES* production functions allow varying degrees of *ex ante* substitutability. In this section we are concerned with the possibilities of *ex post* substitutability for production functions that allow *ex ante* (and therefore long-run) substitutability. Thus, we are interested in the distinction between putty-putty and putty-clay production functions.[19]

Putty-Putty Technology. This is the type of technology we have implicitly been assuming above. Firms can vary the capital intensity of their production both with respect to old machines and newly purchased machines. A decline in the interest rate increases the desired capital intensity of production, and firms achieve this both by using existing machines with fewer laborers and by purchasing new machines. Investment responds rapidly to a change in the interest rate.

Putty-Clay Technology. In the putty-putty case, there are a variety of capital intensities available in new machines, but once a machine has been purchased, it must always be used with a fixed capital-labor ratio. If the interest rate declines, the firm's desired capital intensity increases as in the previous case; however, the firm can only increase the capital intensity of its production process as it replaces worn-out capital or as it expands its output. It cannot alter the capital-labor ratios for existing machines. Therefore, it will take longer for the firm to reach its desired capital intensity. Only when all the old machines have worn out will the firm have achieved the full adjustment. Therefore, there will be a smaller interest responsiveness of investment in early periods, and the adjustment to the desired capital stock will take longer.

---

[19] The principal proponents of the putty-putty model are Dale Jorgenson and Robert Hall, same references as in footnote 16. The principal advocate of the putty-clay model is Charles Bischoff, same reference as in footnote 16. Thus, Jorgenson and Hall combine the Cobb Douglas and putty-putty specifications to generate high short-run interest elasticities. Bischoff combines the *CES* and putty-clay (for equipment), and therefore finds smaller short- and long-run interest rate elasticities.

APPENDIX

A A Comparison of the *i* and *PV* Rules

The *PV* and *i* rules can be illustrated graphically. The vertical axis of Figure 14A.1 is the net present value of a project (*NPV*) defined as

$$NPV = PV - P_I. \tag{14A.1}$$

The horizontal axis measures the rate of interest used to discount future cash flows (r) and the discount rate (i) which makes $NPV = 0$. Consider the desirability of undertaking project A. The *PV* and *i* rules yield the same conclusion: if $r < r_0$, accept the project; but if $r > r_0$, reject it. In terms of the *i* rule, the internal rate of return is i_A (the horizontal axis intercept of the NPV_A schedule). If $i_A > r$, the project is profitable; if $i_A < r$, it is not. The net present value of the schedule depends on the interest rate. If $r < r_0$, $NPV_A > 0$, and the project should be undertaken. If $r > r_0$, $NPV_A < 0$, and the project should be rejected.

The *PV* and *i* rules are not identical in all cases, however, and may even give contradictory results when ranking mutually exclusive projects.

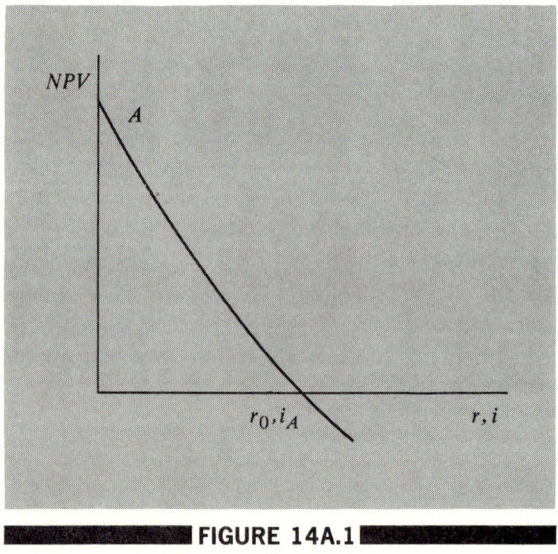

FIGURE 14A.1
The *i* and *PV* Rules

Mutually Exclusive Projects with Different Time Paths of Net Return

Assume there are two mutually exclusive investment projects, A and B, with different time profiles of net income flows. For example, assume each requires an initial outlay of $25.[1] Project A yields a net revenue stream of $5 per year (obtained at the beginning of

---

[1] The numerical example and diagram are taken from A. A. Alchian, "The Rate of Interest, Fisher's Rate of Return Over Costs and Keynes' Internal Rate of Return," *The American Economic Review*, Vol. 45 (December, 1945), pp. 938–943.

each year) for ten years. Project B yields $1, $2, $3, etc., up to $10 over the ten years. Figure 14A.2 depicts the net present value of the two projects. The net present value of each project depends on the interest rate (measured on the horizontal axis) used to discount the future net income flows. The internal rate of return for projects A and B is that rate of return which just equates the present value of the net income flows to the initial outlay; i.e., the rate that makes the net present value of the project equal to zero. In Figure 14A.2, therefore, i_A and i_B are the horizontal axis intercepts of the net present value schedules for A and B. In terms of the numerical example, $i_A = 0.17$ and $i_B = 0.125$. On the basis of the i rule, therefore, project A ranks ahead of project B.

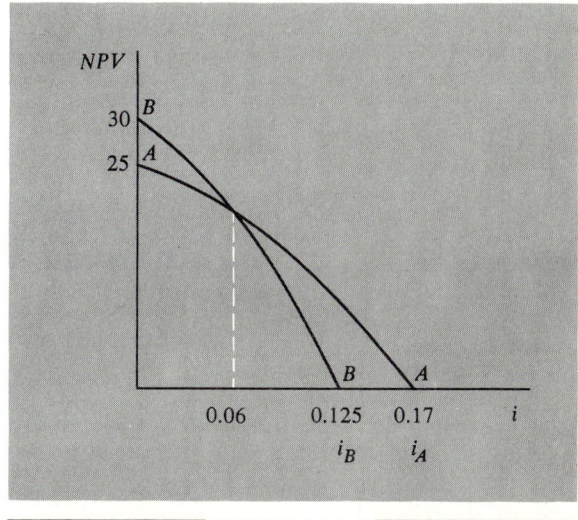

FIGURE 14A.2
Mutually Exclusive Projects

However, the relative net present value for the two projects depends on the rate of interest. At $r = 0.06$, $NPV_A = NPV_B$, implying that the two projects are equally desirable. But if $r < 0.06$, $NPV_A < NPV_B$ so that project B ranks ahead of project A, whereas if $r > 0.06$, $NPV_A > NPV_B$ so that the ranking is reversed.

The PV rule should be followed in this case. The ranking according to *the PV rule takes into account the interest rate and therefore appropriately discounts the future cash flows*; the rankings according to the i rule do not make use of the interest rate at all.

Projects of Different Size

The i rule is also misleading when comparing mutually exclusive projects of different sizes. Assume project A is small compared to project B and that $i_A > i_B$. The i rule would recommend project A over project B. The excess of present value of expected net income over price of the capital good may be much greater, however, for project B than project A. The present value rule would therefore correctly select B over A.

Multiple Values of *i*

A further deficiency of the i rule is that there may not be a unique internal rate of return for a project if the signs of the net income flow alternate over time. Negative net income flows can arise, for example, from major overhauls to the capital good at various intervals. Figure 14A.3 provides an example of a project with multiple internal rates of return.

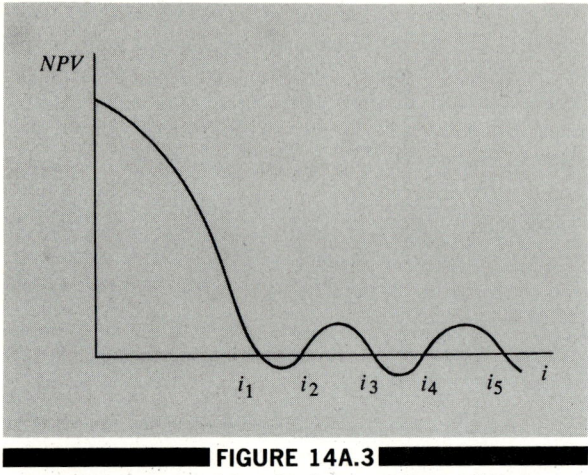

FIGURE 14A.3
Multiple Solutions for the Internal Rate of Return

Variable Rate of Interest

If the interest rate is expected to vary over the life of the project, the calculation of the present value and comparison with P_I is no more difficult than in the case of a constant interest rate. But the i rule can no longer be applied.

APPENDIX

B A Simplified Derivation of Jorgenson's Model of Optimal Capital Accumulation

The classic treatment of the theory of optimal capital accumulation is that of Dale Jorgenson.[1] Jorgenson sets up his model as one of maximizing the present value of the firm's net income over time. We can derive the same expression for the optimal capital stock, however, using a simpler static framework.

The firm is assumed to maximize profits subject to a Cobb Douglas production function

$$Q = AN^\alpha K^{1-\alpha}. \tag{14B.1}$$

The marginal condition for profit maximization is that the marginal product of capital (F_K) be equated to the ratio of the cost of capital services to the price level

---

[1] Dale W. Jorgenson, "The Theory of Investment Behavior," in R. Ferber (ed.), *Determinants of Investment Behavior* (New York: Columbia University Press, 1967).

$$F_K = \frac{c}{P}. \tag{14B.2}$$

From equation (14B.1), we can derive an explicit expression for the marginal product of capital

$$F_K = \frac{\partial Q}{\partial K} = \frac{A(1-\alpha)N^\alpha K^{1-\alpha}}{K} = A(1-\alpha)\frac{Q}{K}. \tag{14B.3}$$

Substituting this into equation (14B.2) and solving for K yields an expression for the profit-maximizing capital stock

$$K^* = A(1-\alpha)Q\frac{P}{c}. \tag{14B.4}$$

Thus, the optimal capital stock varies directly with the level of output and inversely with respect to the cost of capital services.

APPENDIX

Applications to Other Components of Aggregate Demand

In this appendix we use the investment models developed above to explain residential construction, inventory investment, and expenditures on consumer durables. Each of these decisions shares a common theme with the fixed business investment decision: the importance of the demand for the durable stock (of equipment, plant, housing stock, inventories, consumer durables) and the necessity of explaining why economic agents do not adjust their stocks immediately to changes in the determinants of the demand for the particular durable good.

Residential Construction

The q (dual price) model of investment introduced previously is particularly useful in explaining residential construction.[1] We will also introduce external adjustment costs via a rising supply curve for producers of new housing units in this model.[2]

Unlike the market for business capital goods, there is frequent trading in the existing physical capital stock in the housing market. Therefore, the market valuation of the capital stock is a direct valuation of the existing physical units rather than an indirect valuation via the market in which financial claims on the capital stock are traded.

---

[1] For a discussion of a model of residential construction that uses this approach, see Frank deLeeuw and Edward Gramlich, "The Federal Reserve-MIT Econometric Model," *Federal Reserve Bulletin*, Vol. 54 (January, 1968), pp. 11–40.

[2] The role of the rising supply curve of capital goods producers is developed in James G. Witte, "The Microfoundations of the Social Investment Function," *Journal of Political Economy*, Vol. LXXI (October, 1963), pp. 441–456.

The price of the existing housing stock (PH) is determined by the supply and demand for existing houses. In Figure 14C.1a we depict the supply and demand curves for existing houses and in Figure 14C.1b we depict the supply curve for new housing units (residential construction). The demand for the existing housing stock (KH^d) depends on the population, the level of the interest rate, and the price of houses.

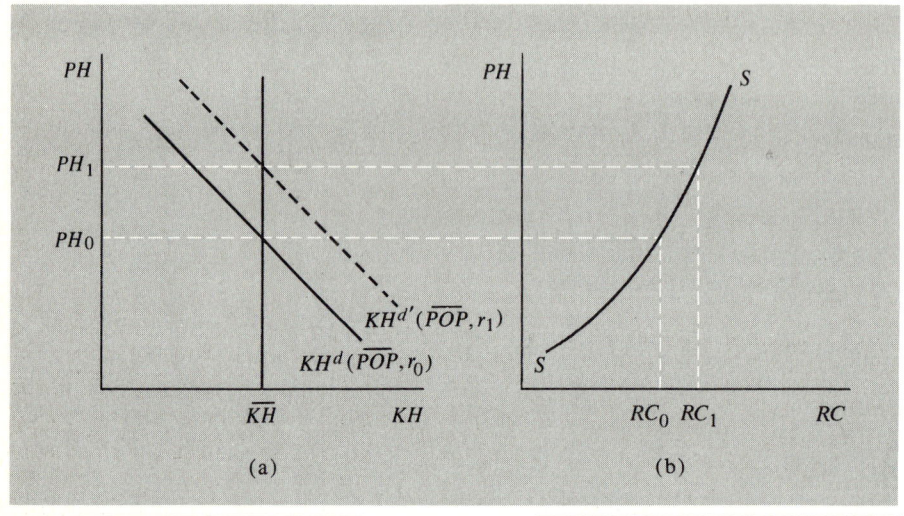

FIGURE 14C.1
Residential Construction

$$KH^d = KH^d(POP, r, PH) \tag{14C.1}$$

where $KH^d_{POP} > 0$, $KH^d_r < 0$, and $KH^d_{PH} < 0$. Population is an important determinant of the housing stock in the long run. The interest rate can be interpreted either as the opportunity cost of funds tied up in the housing stock or as the explicit borrowing cost of externally financing the purchase of a house (e.g., the mortgage rate). The supply of existing houses (KH^s) is fixed at any moment.

$$KH^s = \overline{KH} \tag{14C.2}$$

Equilibrium in the housing market requires equality of supply and demand for the existing housing stock.

$$KH^s = KH^d \tag{14C.3}$$

Substituting equations (14C.1) and (14C.2) into equation (14C.3) yields

$$\overline{KH} = KH^d(POP, r, PH). \tag{14C.3'}$$

Given $\overline{KH}$, POP, and r, equation (14C.3') determines the price of the existing housing stock PH.

$$PH = PH(POP, r, \overline{KH}) \tag{14C.4}$$

The price of existing houses relative to the cost curves of construction firms determines the rate at which construction firms build new homes. The supply of new housing units (residential construction, RC) is a rising function of PH, reflecting the rising cost curves of construction firms.

$$RC = RC(PH) \tag{14C.5}$$

This corresponds to the supply curve for producers of capital goods in Figure 14C.1b.

A decrease in the interest rate from r_0 to r_1 increases the demand for houses and shifts up the KH^d curve *to* $KH^{d\prime}$ in Figure 14C.1a, bidding up the price of existing houses from PH_0 to PH_1. This in turn induces increased production of new houses from RC_0 to RC_1.

The residential construction each period gets added to the beginning-of-period stock.

$$KH = \overline{KH} + RC \tag{14C.6}$$

We ignore depreciation to simplify the model. The increase in the supply of existing units reduces the price of existing units until that price is driven to a level at which residential construction is no longer profitable so the stock of houses is constant. Thus, we get residential construction in response to a decline in the interest rate only until the stock of houses has risen to a level consistent with the new lower interest rate. And we get a gradual increase in the housing stock in response to changes in the arguments in the demand function for houses due to the existence of (external) adjustment costs.

Residential construction is highly responsive to variations in interest rates. This is not due exclusively to a high interest responsiveness of the demand for housing. Housing purchases are financed by mortgages. Savings institutions, particularly savings and loan associations, are the dominant suppliers of mortgage financing. The source of mortgage funds to savings institutions is savings deposits placed with these institutions by households. The rates paid on savings deposits are relatively inflexible compared with open market rates on competing instruments such as government securities. The inflexibility of rates on savings deposits in turn reflects the fact that savings institutions' earnings on their holdings of mortgages varies relatively little with changes in the interest rate due to the long term of mortgages and the fixed interest nature of the mortgage contract. Mortgages are typically written for 20 to 30 years and the interest rate is fixed at the time the mortgage is written and does not vary with open market rates. Higher open market rates permit higher mortgage rates only on newly issued mortgages.[3] In addition, usury laws limit the rate that can be charged on mortgages, and interest rate ceilings limit the rate that can be offered on savings deposits.

If open market rates rise and rates on savings deposits lag, savings will flow out of savings institutions, reducing the availability of mortgage financing. Sharp increases in mortgage rates would be required to balance the supply and demand for mortgages. Usury laws and government-imposed interest rate ceilings prevent this adjustment. Savings institutions are forced to ration credit by nonprice techniques; e.g., by outright denials of credit to prospective borrowers. To capture the sensitivity of residential construction to the availability of mortgage financing, some proxy for credit rationing or availability of mortgage financing is usually included along

---

[3] Several states, however, have recently enacted legislation allowing variable rates on home mortgages.

with mortgage rates in housing equations. Alternatively, we can include a more flexible open market rate in the housing equation instead of the sluggish mortgage rate. The high sensitivity of residential construction to changes in this open market rate will reflect the combined explicit interest rate effect and the availability effect that operates indirectly via changes in open market rates.

Inventory Investment

Firms maintain inventories of raw materials, intermediate products, and finished products to facilitate production and sales. Firms' demand for the stock of inventories (KI) depends primarily on their level of sales (X). A rigid version of this relationship, corresponding to our fixed accelerator model of fixed business investment, is

$$KI = \alpha X \tag{14C.7}$$

and

$$II = \alpha \Delta X \tag{14C.8}$$

where $II = \Delta KI$ is inventory investment. Note that the inventory investment equation is an adjustment or disequilibrium relation indicating the rate at which firms move to their desired stock of inventories. The simple fixed accelerator version assumes the adjustment occurs within a single period.

The fixed accelerator can be modified to allow for lagged adjustment (yielding a flexible accelerator model) and to allow for a variable relationship between the desired stock and sales (yielding a variable accelerator model). For example, the desired stock of inventories may be inversely related to the interest rate (the opportunity cost of funds tied up in holding inventories or the explicit borrowing cost of external financing of inventory holdings). However, empirical studies have not generally found the interest rate to be a significant explanatory variable.

Inventory investment has fluctuated more than any other component of GNP in the postwar period and is considered a principal source of postwar recessions (often referred to as *inventory recessions*). In the next chapter we will show the way such accelerator relations can generate cyclical responses to disturbances.

Consumer Durable Expenditures[4]

The decision concerning expenditures on consumer durables is similar to the decision concerning fixed business investment, inventory investment, and residential construction in that the basic decision concerns the desired stock and the expenditure decision is a decision

---

[4] The model developed in this section is based on the consumption sector in the *FMP* model. For the specific equations and a more complete discussion, see Franco Modigliani, "Monetary Policy and Consumption," in *Consumer Spending and Monetary Policy: The Linkages* (Boston: Federal Reserve Bank of Boston, 1971), p. 75.

about the rate at which the actual stock moves to the desired stock. The desired stock of consumer durables depends on the desired flow of consumer services (*CON*) and the relative cost of using durable goods and nondurable goods. The cost of using durable goods in consumption (*cd*) is analogous to the cost of using capital goods in production. It has two components: the interest rate (opportunity cost of funds tied up or explicit borrowing cost) and the depreciation rate (reflecting the using up of the durable good).

$$cd = (r + \delta_d) PCD \tag{14C.9}$$

where δ_d is the depreciation rate on the consumer durable and *PCD* is the price index for consumer durables. The cost of nondurables is measured by the price index for nondurables, *PCN*.

$$KCD^* = KCD^d \left(CON, \frac{cd}{PCN} \right) \tag{14C.10}$$

CON in turn depends upon disposable income and wealth so that equation (14C.10) can also be written as

$$KCD^* = KCD^d \left(Y, a, \frac{cd}{PCN} \right). \tag{14C.10'}$$

The rate of expenditures on consumer durables (*CD*) is usually modelled as a stock adjustment process

$$CD = \gamma (KCD^* - KCD) \tag{14C.11}$$

where γ is the speed of adjustment.

We can now demonstrate how total consumer expenditures can be derived from a model specified in terms of consumption. The model includes the following equations:

$$CON = CON(Y, a) \tag{14C.12}$$

$$KCD = KCD^d \left(CON, \frac{cd}{PCN} \right) \tag{14C.13}$$

$$CD = \gamma (KCD^* - KCD) \tag{14C.14}$$

$$C = CON - CSD + CD \tag{14C.15}$$

$$CSD = (r + \delta_D) PCD. \tag{14C.16}$$

The basic decision variable is *CON*, determined via the life cycle hypothesis. Consumption is related to consumer expenditures via the identity given by equation (14C.15). Thus, to get to *C* from *CON* we must first determine expenditures on consumer durables (*CD*) and consumption of services of durables (*CSD*). Equations (14C.13) and (14C.14) determine *CD* and equation (14C.16) determines *CSD*.

Part III • Refinements of the Real Sector: Aggregate Demand

● REVIEW QUESTIONS

1. In what sense is investment more difficult to model than consumption or money demand equations?

2. What does the irreversibility of investment decisions mean and what are its implications for the specification of investment demand functions?

3. What are adjustment costs and how do they help to explain the gradual response to changes in the arguments of the demand for capital?

4. Define *ex ante* and *ex post* substitutability and explain the nature of putty-putty and putty-clay technologies. Which technology yields the more rapid response of investment to changes in the interest rate? Explain.

5. "A change in the interest rate generates investment but in the long run there is no systematic relation between investment and the interest rate." Comment.

6. Discuss the relevance of the Tobin-type model to the explanation of residential construction.

7. Explain the role of institutional factors in increasing the sensitivity of residential construction to monetary policy.

● PROBLEM

Investment is usually viewed as being inversely related to the interest rate. Yet this is inconsistent with the tendency of investment and interest rates to rise together during expansions and fall during recessions. Can you explain these observations without abandoning the inverse relation between investment and the interest rate in the investment function?

Chapter 15

The Implications of Alternative Specifications of the Investment Function

In this chapter we will investigate the implications of the alternative specifications of the investment function introduced in Chapter 14. In the first two sections we consider the implications of induced investment and the accelerator, respectively. In the final section we discuss the implications of various assumptions about the speed with which investment responds to changes in the interest rate. A discussion of the implications of the "q" model of investment is postponed until we introduce a three-asset model of the financial sector in the appendices to Chapters 20 and 22.

◯ INDUCED INVESTMENT

In this section we introduce the level of income as an argument in the investment function. This can be rationalized in two alternative ways. First, it could reflect the view that profits or internal funds are a determinant of the level of investment. We considered this possibility in the previous chapter and noted there that both profits and internal funds are closely related to the overall level of economic activity. Although our model does not explicitly allow for internal financing of investment by firms, we will nevertheless allow the income variable to serve as a proxy for the role of profits or internal funds in our investment function. A second explanation for the role of current income is the accelerator, also introduced in the previous chapter. According to the accelerator principle, investment depends on the *change* in income. In our one-period solution, a disturbance or policy action which affects current income activates the accelerator. We will consider the accelerator in more detail in the following section. Here it simply provides a second rationale for the influence of current income in our short-run model.

If investment depends on the level of income, the *IS* curve is respecified as[1]

$$X = C_y(X - \bar{T}) + I_r r + I_x X + \bar{Z} + \bar{G} \qquad (15.1)$$

and the reduced form becomes

$$X = \frac{1}{D_4}\bar{Z} + \frac{1}{D_4}\bar{G} - \frac{C_y}{D_4}\bar{T} + \frac{I_r/L_r}{D_4}\bar{m} - \frac{I_r/L_r}{D_4}\bar{L} \qquad (15.2)$$

where $D_4 = 1 - C_y - I_x + (L_x/L_r)I_r$. Thus, the basic multiplier $1/D_4$ appears larger than in the model without induced investment ($1/D$). Note, however, that D_4 may be *negative* in this case (even if $C_y < 1$, as we have assumed throughout); if $D_4 < 0$, the model is *unstable* and comparative statics is not a valid methodology for determining the response of endogenous variables to disturbances. Before we consider the implications of induced investment for the various multipliers, we derive the condition that must be met to insure that the *IS-LM* model is stable. We have saved this discussion of the stability of the *IS-LM* model until this point because the introduction of induced investment may result in an unstable system.

○ Stability Analysis of the *IS-LM* Model

To study the stability conditions in the Keynesian model, we must use the disequilibrium assumptions introduced in Chapter 10. We assume that interest rate flexibility maintains the money market in continuous equilibrium; i.e., the speed of adjustment in this market is so rapid that supply and demand are always equal. This is a simplification that greatly aids the graphical analysis of stability; it requires that the economy is always on the *LM* curve. In the commodity market, output responds over time to excess demand. The disequilibrium response of output depicted in Figure 15.1 is for the case without induced investment. Points to the left of the *IS* curve correspond to positions of excess demand in the commodity market; therefore, if the economy is to the left of the *IS* curve, output is rising. If, on the other hand, the economy is at a point to the right of the *IS* curve, output is falling in response to excess supply in the output market.[2]

---

[1] If the role of income reflects the accelerator, the precise specification of the *IS* curve is

$$X = C_y(X - \bar{T}) + I_r r + I_x(X - X_{-1}) + \bar{Z} + \bar{G}$$

or $\quad X = C_y(X - \bar{T}) + I_r r + I_x X + I_x X_{-1} + \bar{Z} + \bar{G}.$

In our one-period solution, X_{-1} is a predetermined variable that does not influence the one-period response of income and interest rate to disturbances.

[2] We previously discussed the relation of disequilibrium in the commodity market to the *IS* curve in Chapter 7.

Chapter 15 • Alternative Specifications of the Investment Function

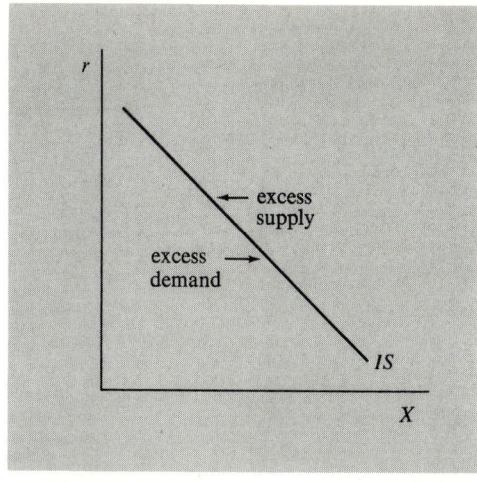

FIGURE 15.1
Disequilibrium in the Commodity Market

The Stability of the Simple Keynesian Model. We can now determine whether or not the simple specification of the *IS-LM* model we employed in Chapter 10 is stable. A model is stable if the time path of the endogenous variables is such that they move *from their initial equilibrium to the new equilibrium* in response to some disturbance. Consider the response to an increase in autonomous private demand. The *IS* curve shifts to *IS'*. Point *a* in Figure 15.2 is now a position of excess demand for output. Output begins to rise and this immediately induces an increase in the interest rate to maintain money market equilibrium. The movement of the system is therefore

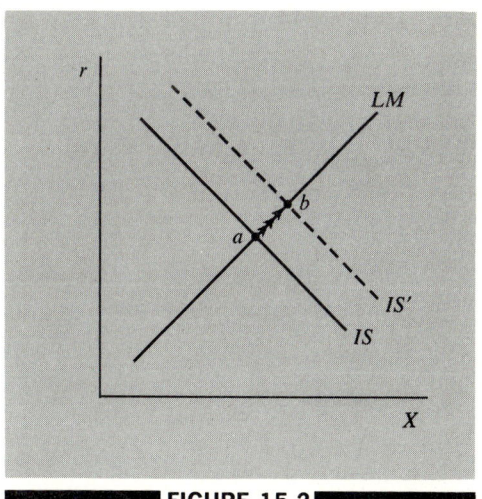

FIGURE 15.2
Response to a Shift in the *IS* Curve:
The Stable Case

upward along the *LM* curve from *a* to *b*, from the initial to the new equilibrium. The system is stable.

The Stability of the Keynesian Model with Induced Investment. If investment depends on income, the sign of the slope of the *IS* curve

$$\left.\frac{\Delta r}{\Delta X}\right|_{IS} = \frac{1-C_y-I_x}{I_r} \tag{15.3}$$

is ambiguous. If $1 - C_y - I_x > 0$, the *IS* curve remains negatively sloped and the analysis of stability is unchanged. However, if $1 - C_y - I_x < 0$, the *IS* curve is positively sloped. *Stability now depends on the relative slopes of the IS and LM curves.*

If the *IS* curve is positively sloped, as in Figure 15.3, points to the left of the *IS* curve are now positions of excess supply and points to the right are positions of excess demand. To see this, consider points *a* and *b* in Figure 15.3. Point *a* is on the *IS* curve and is therefore, by definition, an equilibrium point. At point *b*, *X* is greater than at *a*, but *r* is the same. The type of disequilibrium at *b* depends on whether the demand for or supply of output increases by more when *X* increases. Because the *IS* curve is upward sloping, we know $1 - C_y - I_x < 0$ or $C_y + I_x > 1$. An increase in *X* is an increase in the supply of output. The condition $C_y + I_x > 1$ means that each dollar increase in income increases the demand for output by more than one dollar. Therefore, an increase in *X* at an unchanged *r* results in excess demand in the commodity market. It follows that point *b* is a position of excess demand in the commodity market. The potential for instability is evident from Figure 15.3. At point *b*, the excess demand is driving the economy further *away* from the *IS* curve; i.e., the excess demand for output is inducing an increase in production.

In the Keynesian cross framework, the condition that $C_y + I_x > 1$ would immediately imply an unstable economy. The Keynesian cross model is equivalent to the

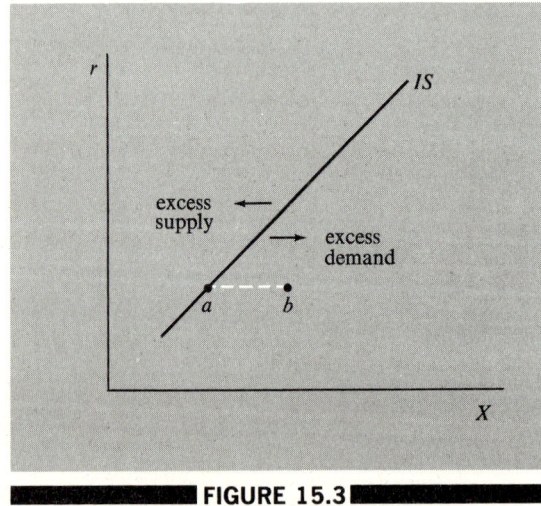

FIGURE 15.3
The Positively Sloped *IS* Curve

IS-LM model when the interest rate is fixed either by monetary authorities or by a liquidity trap. Consider the response to an increase in autonomous expenditures in this case, pictured in Figure 15.4. Point *a* is an equilibrium position. An increase in autonomous private demand (*Z*) shifts the *IS* curve upward, to *IS'* in Figure 15.4.[3] According to our disequilibrium assumption, excess demand in the commodity market generates an increase in output. Thus, at point *a*, output is increasing and therefore moving progressively further away from equilibrium. The system is unstable.

In *IS-LM* analysis where the money supply is controlled by the policy authority and there is no liquidity trap, the *LM* curve is upward sloping. This implies that increases in income, such as in response to an increase in *Z*, put upward pressure on the interest rate. This negative feedback response is a *built-in stabilizer* in the economy, so that the *IS-LM* model *may* be stable even though the commodity market alone (at constant *r*) is unstable. There are two cases to consider, depending on the relative magnitude of the stabilizing negative feedback (associated with the slope of the *LM* curve) and the destabilizing influence of the condition $C_y + I_x > 1$ (associated with the slope of the *IS* curve).

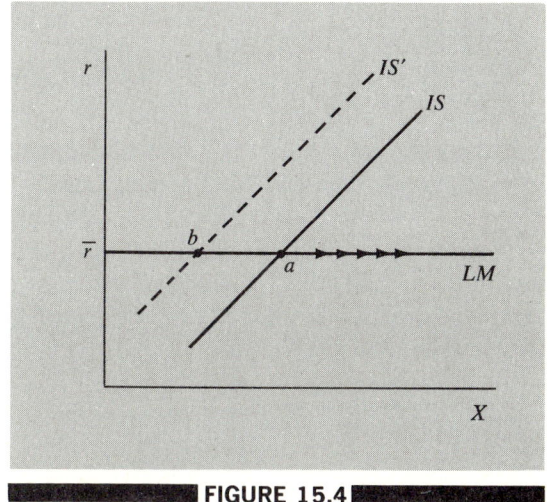

FIGURE 15.4
The Positively Sloped *IS* Curve with $r = \bar{r}$

---

[3] Recall that the vertical shift in the *IS* curve is

$$\left.\frac{\Delta r}{\Delta Z}\right|_{\bar{X}} = \frac{-1}{I_r} > 0.$$

To clarify the leftward horizontal shift, note that an increase in *Z* increases aggregate demand; point *a* is now a position of excess demand. To restore commodity market equilibrium at an unchanged *r*, *X* must fall because a decline in *X* reduces demand by more than supply in this case. As *X* declines, the excess demand gap declines until equilibrium is achieved at point *b*.

1. *IS* Steeper than *LM*. This case is depicted in Figure 15.5. Consider the effect of an increase in Z. The excess demand in the output market increases output and puts upward pressure on the interest rate. The system moves upward along the *LM* curve away from the new equilibrium (at point *b*). Thus, the system is unstable. As output increases, demand increases by more than supply (even allowing for negative feedback) so that the excess demand gap increases and output rises indefinitely.

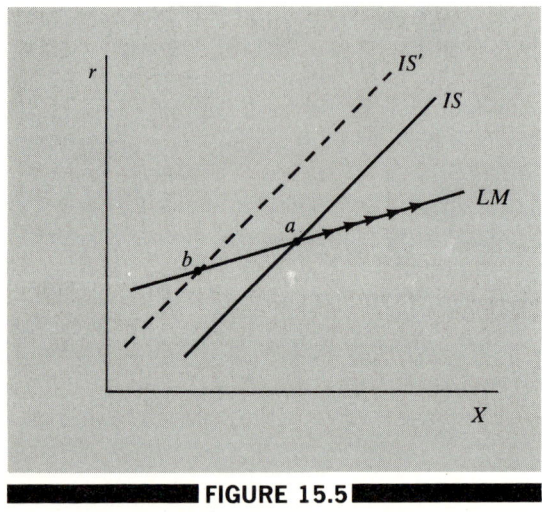

FIGURE 15.5
IS Steeper than *LM*: The Unstable Case

2. *LM* Steeper than *IS*. In this case, pictured in Figure 15.6, an increase in Z results in an increase in both r and X and a new equilibrium at point *b*. The model is therefore stable. Here the negative feedback is sufficiently great to offset the destabilizing influence of $C_y + I_x > 1$.

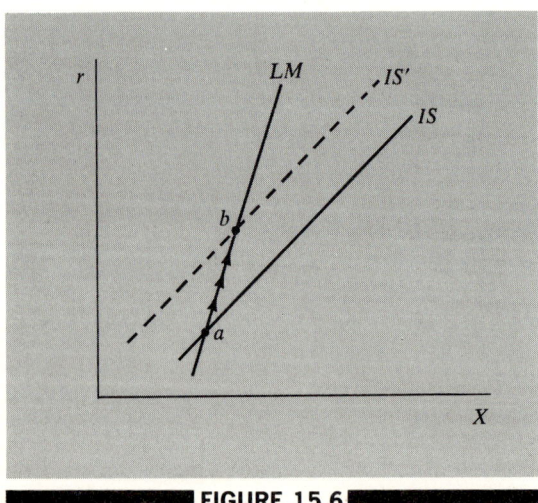

FIGURE 15.6
The Positively Sloped *IS* Curve: The Stable Case

From these results we can infer that the *stability of the model requires that the slope of the LM curve exceed the slope of the IS curve*; i.e.,

$$\left.\frac{\Delta r}{\Delta X}\right|_{LM} > \left.\frac{\Delta r}{\Delta X}\right|_{IS}. \tag{15.4}$$

When $I_x = 0$, the *IS* curve is negatively sloped and the *LM* curve is positively sloped; therefore, condition (15.4) must be satisfied. However, if $I_x > 0$, the *IS* curve may be positively sloped and condition (15.4) may be violated. Condition (15.4) may be rewritten as a restriction on the parameters in the model:

$$-\underbrace{\frac{L_x}{L_r}}_{\text{slope of } LM} > \underbrace{\frac{1-C_y-I_x}{I_r}}_{\text{slope of } IS} \tag{15.4'}$$

or

$$\overbrace{1 - C_y - I_x + \frac{L_x}{L_r} I_r}^{D_4} > 0. \tag{15.4''}$$

The left-hand side of the inequality is the denominator of the reduced-form multipliers (D_4). Thus, *the stability condition requires that the denominator be positive*. This restriction on the sign of the denominator remains valid for all specifications of our model. Whenever the denominator is qualitatively ambiguous (i.e., cannot be signed on the basis of information about the signs of the various parameters), the model is potentially unstable. The model is nevertheless stable, and comparative statics therefore remains valid if the quantitative values of the parameters result in the denominator being positive.

○ The Implications of Induced Investment When the Model Is Stable

We can now consider the implications of induced investment in the case where the model remains stable (i.e., where the *IS* curve remains negatively sloped, or if positively sloped, the *IS* curve is less steep than the *LM* curve). First, we consider the effect of induced investment on the model multipliers. Then we consider some interesting implications for the economy's response to increases in government expenditures and to open market operations.

The Implications for Model Multipliers. The effect of induced investment is obvious once we realize that its only effect is to *increase the positive feedback in the economy*. The income-induced rise in aggregate demand will be larger and therefore *all the multipliers will be larger* when $I_x > 0$. Interpreting induced investment as reflecting the initial response of the accelerator mechanism, we find that the interaction of the multiplier and accelerator increases the short-run response of income to disturbances.

The implications of induced investment for the response of income to monetary change are depicted in Figure 15.7. IS_1 is the IS curve when $I_x = 0$. When $I_x > 0$ but $1 - C_y - I_x > 0$, IS_2 results; when $I_x > 0$ and is sufficiently large so that $1 - C_y - I_x < 0$, IS_3 results (assuming the model remains stable). From Figure 15.7 we can see that the increase in income is larger when $I_x > 0$ (X_2 is greater than X_1), and of course larger the greater the size of I_x (X_3 is greater than X_2). Similar results hold for fiscal policy but the diagram is more complicated due to the fact that all three IS curves must shift by equal amounts in the vertical direction in response to an increase in G.[4] The results for fiscal policy are depicted in Figure 15.8.

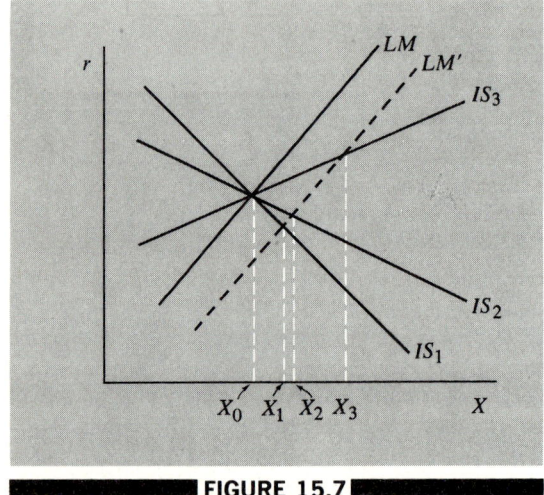

FIGURE 15.7
Monetary Policy and Income-Induced Investment

Induced Investment and Pulling-In. Another implication of induced investment is that fiscal policy may now stimulate rather than crowd out investment.[5] The investment function is now

$$I = \overline{I} + I_r r + I_x X. \tag{15.5}$$

The interest rate rises in response to expansionary fiscal policy, putting downward pressure on investment. But output rises, and when $I_x > 0$, the increase in output stimulates investment. The net effect on investment of the increase in both r and X associated with fiscal policy is ambiguous, but it is now possible that fiscal policy will stimulate investment.

---

[4] The vertical shift in the IS curve is $\left.\dfrac{\Delta r}{\Delta G}\right|_{\overline{X}} = \dfrac{-1}{I_r}$. Given that I_r is assumed to be the same for all three IS curves, they all must shift by the same amount in the vertical direction.

[5] This possibility is discussed in Patric Hendershott, "A Tax Cut In A Multiple Security Model: Crowding-Out, Pulling-In and the Term Structure of Interest Rates," *Journal of Finance*, Vol. 31 (September, 1976), pp. 1185–1199.

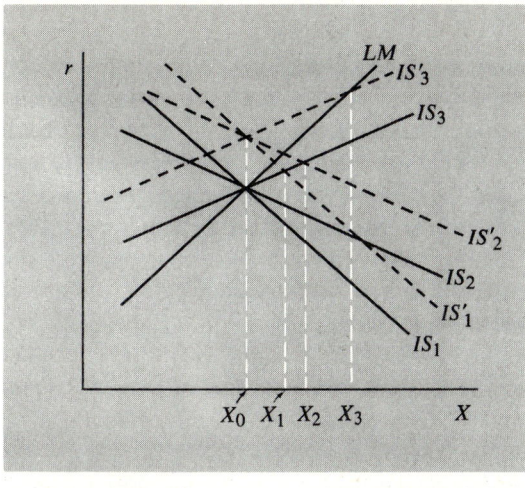

FIGURE 15.8
Fiscal Policy and Income-Induced Investment

The Response of the Interest Rate to Monetary Change. We considered the response of interest rates to monetary change in Chapters 9 and 10 and found that the (nominal) interest rate might fall, remain unchanged, or even increase, depending on initial conditions, the time period considered, and the nature of the monetary change. In the short-run Keynesian version of the model, we found that the interest rate declined in response to monetary change. When we add income-induced investment to the Keynesian model, however, interest rates may rise in response to monetary change, even though the price level and the expected inflation rate are unchanged. This is the result whenever induced investment results in a positively sloped *IS* curve. In Figure 15.7, for example, monetary change increases the interest rate if the *IS* curve is IS_3. We will return to this possibility in the next section when we discuss the implications of the accelerator.

THE ACCELERATOR

We now explicitly introduce the accelerator. To do so we develop an explicitly dynamic version of the Keynesian fixed price model. We will use the dynamic *IS-LM* model to analyze the response of income and interest rates to policy actions and nonpolicy disturbances over a number of periods. We found in the previous section that the introduction of the accelerator increases the initial response of income to disturbances. When we expand the time period under consideration in this section, we find that the accelerator may also result in an oscillatory or cyclical response of the endogenous variables. In this section we will first introduce the dynamic version of our model and then consider the role of this model in the explanation of business cycles and the implications of the model for the economy's response to fiscal and monetary policies.

The Dynamic *IS-LM* Model

We specify consumption as depending on income lagged one period and investment as depending on the change in income lagged one period and on the lagged interest rate. The precise specification of the lag pattern between consumption and income and between investment and the change in income will affect the nature of the dynamic response of the endogenous variables to disturbances. We have selected lag relationships for our *IS* curve that correspond to the traditional multiplier accelerator model introduced by Paul Samuelson.[6] This model, although quite simple, is capable of generating a wide range of dynamic responses depending on the values of the parameters assumed. The *IS* curve is specified as

$$X_t = C_y(X_{t-1} - \bar{T}_{t-1}) + I_x(X_{t-1} - X_{t-2}) + I_r r_{t-1} + \bar{Z}_t + \bar{G}_t. \tag{15.6}$$

We assume the demand for money depends on the current values of r and X.

$$\bar{m}_t = L_r r_t + L_x X_t + \bar{L}_t \tag{15.7}$$

Solving for the reduced form for X_t, we obtain

$$X_t = \bar{Z}_t + \bar{G}_t - C_y \bar{T}_{t-1} + \frac{I_r}{L_r} \bar{m}_{t-1} - \frac{I_r}{L_r} \bar{L}_{t-1} \tag{15.8}$$

$$+ \left(C_y + I_x - \frac{L_x}{L_r} I_r \right) X_{t-1} - I_x X_{t-2}.$$

This type of equation is referred to as a *second order difference equation with constant coefficients*. A *difference equation* is an equation in which X_t and lagged values of X, X_{t-i}, appear. The longest lag determines the order of the equation. Thus, equation (15.8) is a second order equation. Difference equations of order 2 or more are capable of generating oscillatory responses to disturbances. Difference equations in which exogenous variables or shift parameters are stochastic and therefore provide random shocks to the system form the core of models designed to explain business cycles.

Comparative Statics

Before exploring the dynamic properties of this model, we will show that its longer run or equilibrium response will be the same as the simple Keynesian *IS-LM* model we have been using in previous chapters, provided that the dynamic specification does not cause the model to become unstable. For the moment, we simply assume the model remains stable and solve it for the equilibrium response of income to disturbances. To solve for the equilibrium value of X associated with given values of the exogenous variables, we must set $X_t = X_{t-1} = X_{t-2} = \tilde{X}$ where $\tilde{X}$ is the

---

[6] Paul Samuelson, "The Interaction of the Multiplier and the Principle of Acceleration," *Review of Economics and Statistics*, Vol. 21 (May, 1939), pp. 75–78.

equilibrium value of X, the value of X at which the system will settle down and remain until displaced by some exogenous change. Because the equilibrium is defined for fixed values of the exogenous variables, we set $\bar{m}_{t-1} = \bar{m}$, $\bar{G}_t = \bar{G}$, $\bar{T}_{t-1} = \bar{T}$, $\bar{Z}_t = \bar{Z}$, and $\bar{L}_{t-1} = \bar{L}$ for all t. Solving for $\tilde{X}$, we obtain

$$\tilde{X} = \frac{1}{D}\bar{G} + \frac{1}{D}\bar{Z} - \frac{C_y}{D}\bar{T} + \frac{I_r/L_r}{D}\bar{m} - \frac{I_r/L_r}{D}\bar{L} \tag{15.9}$$

where D is the denominator in the basic *IS-LM* model of Chapter 10. Thus, the accelerator does not alter the equilibrium response of income or the interest rate.

This should not be surprising, given that the accelerator relates investment to the change in income (ΔX), and in equilibrium, X settles down to a constant level so that $\Delta X = 0$. The accelerator term therefore completely drops out of the model when it is solved for the equilibrium response. However, the accelerator may cause the model to become unstable, and in this case, the model does not move to the new equilibrium values in response to a disturbance. And even if the model is stable, the accelerator may cause a cyclical response to disturbances. We turn now to a discussion of the dynamic properties of the model.

○ Dynamic Properties of the Model

This model is capable of generating oscillatory or monotonic and stable or unstable responses to disturbances depending on numerical values of the parameters. An *oscillatory response* is one in which variables *cycle* or increase, then decrease over time. A *monotonic response* is one in which the variables continue to move in a single direction following a disturbance. If the model is *stable*, the movement of the endogenous variables takes them to the new equilibrium following a disturbance. If an oscillatory response takes the system to the new equilibrium, it is said to be a *damped oscillatory response*. If the oscillatory response takes the variables further and further from their new equilibrium values, it is said to be an *explosive oscillatory response*.

The four different cases are depicted in Figures 15.9a through 15.9d. X_0 is the initial equilibrium and X_1 is the new equilibrium following a diturbance at time $t = 0$. Each diagram shows the time path of income in response to the disturbance. The two most interesting possibilities are the cases of damped oscillations (Figure 15.9a) and explosive montonic movement (Figure 15.9d). These two cases form the basis of the formal models of the business cycle to which we now turn.

Properties of Business Cycles. We noted in Chapter 2 that historically, output follows a cyclical pattern—rising an average of three years, then declining an average of one year. Models without lagged relations could only explain this cyclical phenomenon by an unexplained corresponding cyclical pattern in the exogenous variables. Models of endogenous business fluctuations must therefore be explicitly dynamic and the accelerator has been the main ingredient in formal models of business cycles. Before discussing the role of the accelerator in business cycle theory, we review the important regularities among broad economic aggregates observed during business cycles so that we can judge whether the accelerator-type models are broadly consistent with

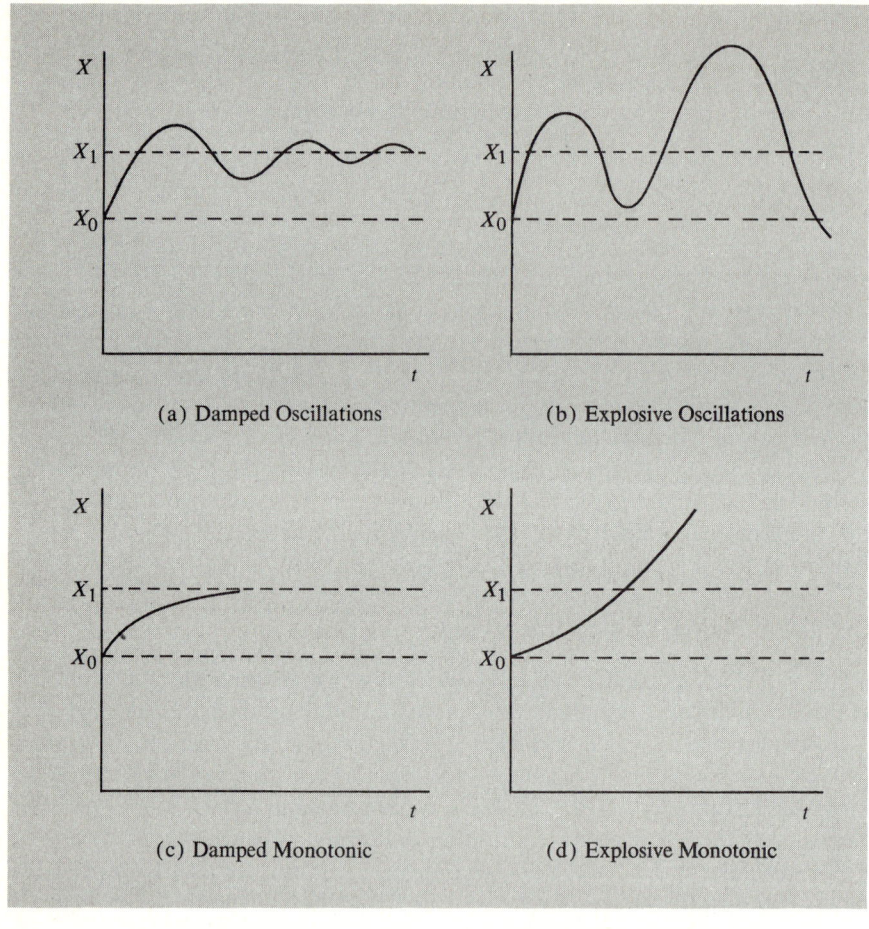

FIGURE 15.9
Time Paths of Income in Response to a Disturbance

the observed regularities.[7] First, various components of output tend to move together over the cycle, but durable goods (both consumer durables and plant and equipment production) tend to exhibit greater amplitude than other components of output. Prices and interest rates tend to exhibit procyclical movements. The dynamic *IS-LM* model discussed in this section is capable of generating the movements in output and interest rates observed in business cycles. We would have to add a Phillips curve (or some alternative relation between price change and commodity market disequilibrium) to account for the procyclical variation in the price level.

---

[7] For discussions of the observed regularities among broad economic aggregates that characterize business cycles, see Arthur F. Burns and Wesley C. Mitchell, *Measuring Business Cycles* (New York: National Bureau of Economic Research, 1946); Robert A. Gordon, "The Stability of the U.S. Economy," in Martin Bronfenbrenner (ed.), *Is the Business Cycle Obsolete?* (New York: Wiley-Interscience, 1969), pp. 3–33; and Victor Zarnowitz, "The Business Today: An Introduction," in Victor Zarnowitz (ed.), *The Business Cycle Today* (New York: National Bureau of Economic Research, 1972), pp. 1–38.

Chapter 15 • Alternative Specifications of the Investment Function

There are two basic approaches to modelling the role of the accelerator in business fluctuations.

Damped Oscillations with Random Disturbances. Depending on assumed parameter values, it is possible to generate any of the four time paths of endogenous variables depicted in Figures 15.9a through 15.9d. One approach to business cycle theory presumes that parameter values result in *damped oscillatory* responses to disturbances, as in Figure 15.9a. This was the approach suggested by Ragnar Frisch in his classic article on business cycles and modelled by Paul Samuelson in his famous article on the interaction of the multiplier and the accelerator.[8] Continuing random disturbances set off and continue the cyclical pattern in the endogenous variables.

Explosive Responses with External Boundaries. An alternative cyclical model results if the values of system parameters result in an explosive response to disturbances, such as in Figure 15.9d.[9] To convert such explosive movements into cycles requires the existence of boundaries or constraints (ceilings and floors). The ceiling is simply potential output; i.e., an explosive upward movement in real output will eventually hit and perhaps bounce off the ceiling imposed by the existence of physical limitations on production. When the ceiling is hit and the system cannot follow the time path dictated by the system equations, a new set of initial conditions emerges and these may result in a reversal of direction and an explosive downward movement. In John Hicks's model of this genre, the decline is qualitatively different from the expansion phase. Gross investment cannot be negative. Thus, when income begins to decline and the induced component of gross investment goes to zero, the accelerator becomes inoperative and the decline in income proceeds via the multiplier until income equals the autonomous component of investment times the multiplier.

These models yield cyclical variation in both consumption and investment and procyclical variation in interest rates when the disturbances originate in the real sector. In this case, cycles originate with shifts in the *IS* curve; the accelerator transforms the initial disturbance to a series of oscillations in which income and interest rates tend to move together.

◯ Policy Simulations with Numerical Values of the Parameters

An analytical treatment of this model would require us to develop the properties of second order linear difference equations with constant coefficients. However, we can also investigate the basic properties of the model by specifying numerical values for the model parameters and iteratively solving the reduced form for X_t, X_{t+1}, etc. This is the approach we follow in this section.

The values of the model parameters we will assume are presented in Table 15.1. As in the appendix to Chapter 10, the numerical values were chosen to approximate

---

[8] Ragnar Frisch, "Propagation Problems and Impulse Problems in Dynamic Economics," in *Economic Essays in Honour of Gustav Cassel* (London: George Allen and Unwin, Ltd., 1933); Paul Samuelson, "The Interaction of the Multiplier and the Principle of Acceleration," *Review of Economics and Statistics*, Vol. 21 (May, 1939), pp. 75–78.

[9] Models of this type include N. Kaldor, "A Model of the Trade Cycle," *Economic Journal*, Vol. L (March, 1940), pp. 78–92; and John R. Hicks, *A Contribution to the Theory of the Trade Cycle* (London: Oxford University Press, 1950).

Part III • Refinements of the Real Sector: Aggregate Demand

values estimated in empirical studies; in addition, we chose the values to insure oscillations of uniform amplitude.[10]

C_y	=	0.9
I_x	=	1.0
I_r	=	−20.0
L_r	=	−15.0
L_x	=	0.2

TABLE 15.1
Parameter Values for the Dynamic *IS-LM* Model

To *simulate* the model, we must also specify a time path of the exogenous variables and *initial conditions*. Note that to determine the values of income in period t from the reduced form, equation (15.7), we need values of income in the two previous periods (X_{t-1}, X_{t-2}) as well as values of exogenous variables in the current period.

For values of the exogenous variables, we took actual values of the money supply for m and added $160 billion to actual federal government expenditures on goods and services to get our series for G; this made our exogenous variables and equilibrium multipliers compatible with actual *GNP* in 1967. As initial conditions we took the actual values of *GNP* in the first two quarters of 1967. Thus, the first period for which we calculate income takes values of actual money supply and actual G plus $160 billion in the third quarter of 1967. We solve for income (X_t) and then use that value to determine income in the next period; i.e., X_t and X_{t-1} are needed to solve for X_{t+1}. This procedure is used to derive 32 periods of response of income to disturbances.

Using the values of the parameters, the values of the exogenous variables, and the initial conditions assumed above, we first simulate the model to derive a time path of income corresponding to the assumed actual values for m and G. This is referred to as the *base run*. We then alter the value of one exogenous variable; e.g., we increase G by $10 billion beginning in 1967 III and maintain it at its new value throughout the 32 periods of the analysis. A new time path of income is derived and this simulation is referred to as the *policy run*. The difference in the value of income between the base run and the policy run is a measure of the response of income to a maintained change in G. The cumulative dynamic multiplier is defined as

$$\frac{\Delta X(t)}{\Delta G} = \frac{X^P(t) - X^B(t)}{\Delta G} \tag{15.10}$$

where $X^P(t)$ is the value of income in the policy run and $X^B(t)$ is its value in the base run. The same approach can be used to derive the dynamic multipliers for a

---

[10] The amplitude of an oscillatory response refers to the magnitude of the change in the endogenous variable from its peak value to its next trough value. If the amplitude declines over time, the oscillatory response is damped and the model is stable. If the amplitude increases, the oscillatory response is explosive and the model is unstable. If the amplitude is constant, as we have assumed in this section, the model continues to oscillate around the equilibrium values of the endogenous variables, neither moving closer nor further away over time.

change in the money supply or to derive the response of interest rates to changes in m or G.

Below we employ this approach to investigate the implications of the accelerator for the response of income to fiscal policy and the response of interest rates to monetary change.

Crowding-Out and the Accelerator. The structure of the model allows for crowding-out exclusively through the negative feedback response. Given that neither L_r nor I_r take on extreme values, the comparative statics indicate a positive equilibrium response. Based on the values of the parameters assumed above,

$$\frac{\Delta X}{\Delta G} = 2.7. \qquad (15.11)$$

However, because the income response is oscillatory, the multiplier will oscillate.

The values of the multipliers are plotted in Figure 15.10. The value of the multiplier builds from a first-quarter value of 1.0 to 5.5 in the fifth quarter. Thereafter, the multiplier begins to decline and becomes negative in the tenth quarter. The pattern over the ten quarters follows very closely the pattern suggested by monetarists: an

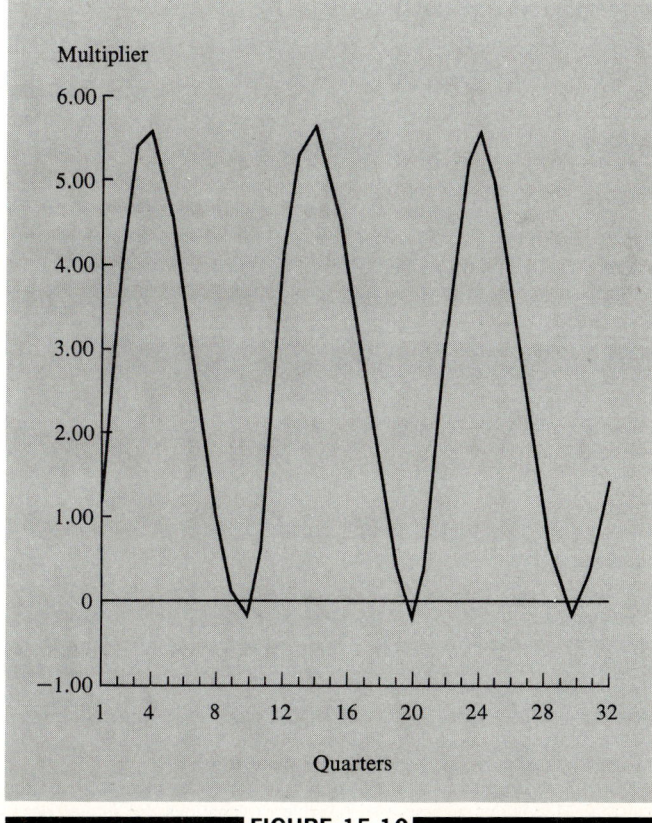

FIGURE 15.10
Response of Income to a Change in Government Expenditures

Part III • Refinements of the Real Sector: Aggregate Demand

initial positive impact which soon disappears and may even become negative. The pattern has little or nothing to do, however, with the traditional crowding-out mechanism—the negative feedback determined by the values of L_x, L_r, and I_r, and the direct impact of the increased supply of bonds.

The dynamic multipliers in the *MPS* model for the response of real *GNP* to an increase in governmental expenditures exhibit these general features.[11] The accelerator substantially increases the multipliers over the first couple of years, but by the third year the accelerator is responsible for the cumulative multiplier declining and by the end of the third or fourth year the cumulative multiplier has been reduced to zero. However, this is not the end of the response to the increase in *G*. Output now oscillates and the cumulative multiplier generally becomes negative at a time during this oscillatory response. This negative multiplier is not a product of the usual crowding-out mechanisms stressed by monetarists, but simply part of the dynamic oscillatory response associated with the accelerator.

Interest Rate Snapback and the Accelerator. Monetarists expect monetary expansion to raise rather than lower interest rates. We found in Chapter 9 that an increase in the rate of monetary growth could generate a rise in the nominal interest rate due to the role of inflation expectations. However, some monetarists have suggested that the interest rate "snaps back" beyond its original level over a period too short to reflect the rate of inflation expectations.[12]

The comparative static analysis of our model suggests that the interest rate should decline in response to an increase in the money supply.

$$\frac{\Delta r}{\Delta m} = -0.02 \qquad (15.12)$$

A $10 billion increase in the money supply will lower the equilibrium short-term rate by 20 basis points. To investigate the dynamic response in our model, we simulate the effect of a money supply increase. The simulation results are depicted in Figure 15.11. We ran a base version with the value of the money supply taking on its historical value and a policy run in which the money supply is increased by $5 billion throughout the run. The dynamic multiplier is computed as:

$$\frac{\Delta r(t)}{\Delta m} = \frac{r^P(t) - r^B(t)}{\Delta m} \qquad (15.13)$$

where $r^P(t)$ is the value of r in the policy run and $r^B(t)$ is its value in the base run.

Again, the pattern over the first two years corresponds to the monetarist view

---

[11] The *MPS* simulations discussed in this and the next section were reported by Albert Ando in "Short-Run Dynamic Responses and the Stability Characteristics of the *MPS* Model," mimeo.

[12] See, for example, Burton Zwick, " 'Snap Back' and 'Crowding Out' in Monetary and Fiscal Policy: Explanation and Interpretation," *Journal of Money, Credit and Banking*, Vol. VI (November, 1974), pp. 559–566; David Meiselman "Comment" in *Controlling Monetary Aggregates* (Boston: Federal Reserve Bank of Boston, June, 1969), pp. 15–19; and William Gibson, "Interest Rates and Monetary Policy," *Journal of Political Economy*, Vol. 78 (May–June, 1970), pp. 431–435.

Zwick suggests that the accelerator mechanism can generate the snapback pattern. Our results in this section confirm this. Meiselman suggests two possible explanations: (a) monetary change may have a direct impact on aggregate demand (i.e., *m* may appear as an argument in our *IS* curve) and/or (b) income-induced investment may result in an upward-sloping *IS* curve.

Chapter 15 • Alternative Specifications of the Investment Function

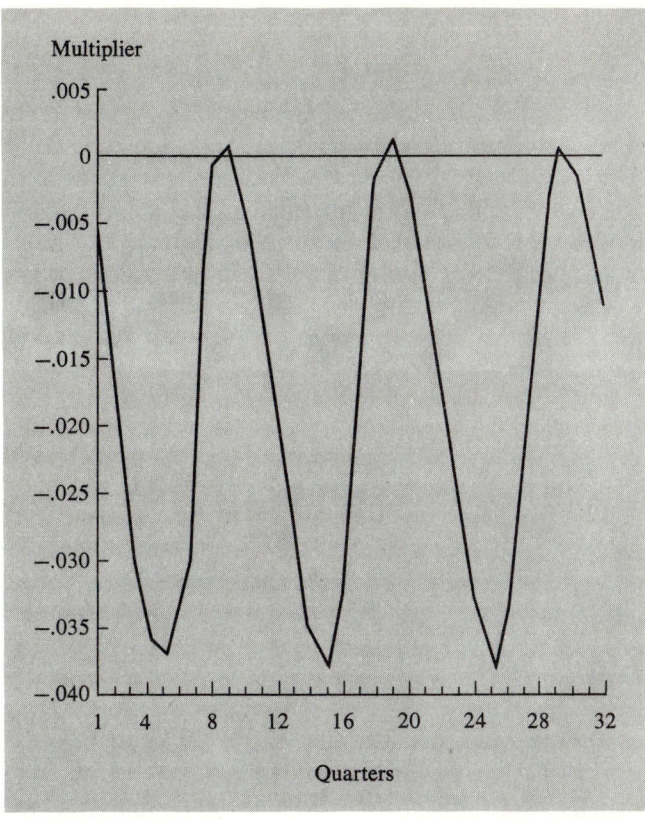

FIGURE 15.11
Multiplier for Response of Interest Rates to Monetary Change

that the interest rate initially declines, then increases, eventually rising to or beyond its initial level. The cumulative decline increases during the first five quarters. Thereafter, the interest rate begins to rise, and by the tenth quarter it is higher than it would have been in the absence of the monetary change. This result has nothing to do with any direct impact of monetary change nor the role of inflationary expectations; the price level is fixed throughout the simulation. The results are due exclusively to the dynamics associated with the accelerator mechanism.

Simulations with the *MPS* model again yield a similar pattern. For example, Albert Ando reports simulations of an increase in the money supply on the Treasury bill rate in a version of the *MPS* model in which the price expectations mechanism was rendered inoperative to eliminate this source of upward pressure on interest rates following an increase in the money supply. Initially, the bill rate declines but the cumulative negative multiplier progressively becomes smaller in absolute value, and after five years the interest rate is *higher* than it would have been in the absence of the monetary change. Although this is quite a bit longer than the period monetarists suggest as being required for "snapback," the simulation if ended at this point generally conforms to the snapback view. However, if the simulation is extended beyond five years, the interest rate multiplier turns negative again.

Conclusion. The internal dynamics of large scale econometric models typically result in their displaying stable or unstable oscillatory responses to disturbances. If simulations are ended prior to the point at which the oscillatory nature of the response has become evident, the results might be interpreted as suggesting something very different from what is apparent in the longer period simulations results. In this section we considered two examples in which short-period results appeared to confirm monetarist conclusions about the response of income to fiscal policy and the response of interest rates to monetary change. The longer period simulations, however, demonstrated that the negative income multiplier for fiscal policy and the positive interest rate multipliers for monetary policy were transitory and reflected the cyclical response of the model to disturbances rather than the forces monetarists typically rely upon as sources for such results.

LAGGED ADJUSTMENT OF INVESTMENT TO A CHANGE IN THE INTEREST RATE

In Chapter 13 we considered the implications of a gradual response of consumption to changes in income. The most important element of gradual response to disturbances is usually considered to be associated with the response of investment to changes in the interest rate.

Survey evidence on the lags associated with decisions to construct new plants or plant additions suggests an average lag of six months from the drawing of plans to the beginning of construction, and an average lag of five quarters from the beginning of construction to completion, yielding a total lag of seven quarters from the decision to invest to the completion of the project.[13] Econometric evidence generally suggests even longer lags. In this section we consider the implications of the gradual adjustment of investment for the short-run model multipliers.

In the previous chapter we noted that the stock adjustment model is the specification of investment often employed in econometric models. Ignoring depreciation, we write investment as

$$I = \beta(K_r r - \bar{K}) \tag{15.14}$$

where the desired capital stock is assumed to depend on the interest rate. If $\beta = 1$, then the full adjustment is assumed to occur in the unit interval of the analysis; one year is the unit interval we have generally assumed. The econometric estimates of ϵ_{Kc} generally fall in the range of -0.5 to -1.0 where ϵ_{Kc}, the elasticity of the optimal capital stock with respect to the cost of capital, is

$$\epsilon_{Kc} = \frac{\Delta K}{\Delta c} \frac{c}{K} = K_c \frac{c}{K}. \tag{15.15}$$

---

[13] See, for example, Thomas Mayer, "The Inflexibility of Monetary Policy," *Review of Economic Statistics*, Vol. 40 (November, 1958), pp. 358–374, and "Plant and Equipment Lead Times," *Journal of Business*, Vol. 33 (April, 1960), pp. 127–132.

Assuming $\epsilon_{Kc} = -1.0$, $K_c = -K/c = -K/P_I(r + \delta)$. The value of K is taken to be the real value of fixed business capital stock of the business sector in 1976 IV (about \$1,000 billion) and $r + \delta$ is assumed to be 20.0;[14] assuming $\Delta c = \Delta r$, $K_c = K_r = -50$. If all adjustment occurs in the first period, $I_r = K_r = -50$. However, if only a fraction of the full response occurs in the first period, $I_r = \beta K_r$. There is substantial disagreement about the speed with which investment responds to changes in interest rates and these disagreements result in substantial differences in model multipliers.[15]

In Table 15.2 we assume $C_y = .4$, the value associated with the response of consumption over the first year to a change in income in the *LCH* in Chapter 13. We continue to assume $L_x = .2$ and $L_r = -25$. We compute the government expenditure and monetary policy multipliers for different values of β and hence I_r, assuming $K_r = -50$. From Table 15.2 we see that variations in I_r have a powerful effect on the relative effectiveness of fiscal and monetary policies. If all adjustment to a change in interest rate occurs in a single period ($\beta = 1$), the one-period monetary policy multiplier is 2.0, double the size of the fiscal policy multiplier. On the other hand, if only one quarter of the investment response occurs in the first period ($\beta = .25$), the monetary policy multiplier falls to less than half of its value when $\beta = 1$ and the fiscal policy multiplier is double the monetary policy multiplier.

β	I_r	$\Delta X/\Delta G$	$\Delta X/\Delta m$
1.0	−50	1.0	2.0
.5	−25	1.25	1.25
.25	−12.50	1.41	.7
.10	−6.25	1.65	.4

TABLE 15.2
The Implications of Lags in Response of
Investment for Policy Multipliers

The pattern of the cumulative multipliers depends on the pattern of lagged response of investment to a change in the interest rate in the present model. In the stock adjustment specification of investment, the parameter on lagged interest rates declines geometrically. This implies that the largest increase in investment occurs initially and thereafter investment declines until the new desired capital stock is achieved. In this case the cumulative income multipliers would decline over time. The empirical evidence, however, generally suggests a small initial increase in investment, then rising investment for a while, followed by declines until the new desired capital stock is achieved.[16] This implies small initial money multipliers followed by

---

[14] This is the value used by Robert Hall in "Investment, Interest Rates, and the Effects of Stabilization Policy," *Brookings Papers on Economic Activity* (1977:1), pp. 66–103. Hall computes K_r differently and finds it is −83.5. Also he used an extremely low value of L_r, −2.0.

[15] For a discussion of the response of investment to changes in interest rates and the implications for monetary and fiscal policies, see Robert Hall, "Investment, Interest Rates, and the Effects of Stabilization Policy," *Brookings Paper on Economic* Activity (1977:1), pp. 66–103.

[16] See Dale Jorgenson, "Econometric Studies of Investment Behavior: A Survey," *Journal of Economic Literature*, Vol. 9 (December, 1971), pp. 1111–1147, for a survey of econometric evidence on lags in investment response.

increases for a while, and then by declines. Of course, this is just one of the important dynamic responses in the economy, and the actual cumulative response of output to monetary change also depends on the life cycle consumption function, the accelerator, and the Phillips curve.

● REVIEW QUESTIONS

1. How does the accelerator affect the time path of response of income to fiscal policy and interest rates to monetary policy?

2. Explain why lags in the adjustment of capital to changes in the interest rate have asymmetric effects on the results for monetary and fiscal policies.

3. Explain why $C_y > 1$ is sufficient to generate instability in the Keynesian cross model but may be consistent with stability in the *IS-LM* model.

● PROBLEMS

1. "The introduction of induced investment makes the comparative static multipliers ambiguous in sign. Thus, both increases in the money supply and government expenditures may increase or decrease income in this case." Comment.

2. "Income in the investment function can reflect either income-induced investment or the accelerator. The main implications are identical for these two rationales for introducing income, so it does not really matter which explanation we employ." Comment.

Part IV

Refinements of the Real Sector: Aggregate Supply

Chapter 16. The Demand for and Supply of Labor
17. The Response of Output and Employment to Aggregate Demand
18. The Phillips Curve

Chapter 16

The Demand for and Supply of Labor

The labor market has a peculiar and important role in the macroeconomic models we have developed above. The key feature differentiating the classical and Keynesian models analyzed in Part II was the assumption made about the adjustment of the wage rate to labor market disequilibrium. The classical and Keynesian assumptions about price-wage flexibility introduced in Chapter 5 permitted us to drop the labor market from explicit treatment in the fixed price and fixed output versions of *IS-LM* analysis. In Part IV we refine our treatment of the labor market and the response of the wage rate to labor market disequilibrium. In this chapter we begin by refining our analysis of the demand for and supply of labor and considering the relation between unemployment, full employment, and the supply and demand for labor. In the following two chapters we refine our treatment of employment and inflation theory and investigate the short-run response of output, prices, and wages to nonpolicy disturbances and policy actions with special emphasis on the role of the specification of labor market supply and demand.

THE DEMAND FOR LABOR

The important distinction in the macroeconomic approach to the demand for labor, introduced initially in Chapter 4, is between the notional demand and the output-constrained or effective demand for labor. First, we consider this distinction in more detail and then we discuss the dynamics of the response of labor demand to changes in the demand for output.

The Notional Demand Curve

Assume that firms maximize profits in competitive factor and product markets subject to a production function and a fixed capital stock. The production function,

$$X = F(\bar{K}, N), \tag{16.1}$$

is a technical relationship describing the alternative ways in which capital and labor can be combined to produce output. The firm faces a given price level for output, P, at which it can sell as much output as it desires, and a given nominal wage, W, at which it can purchase as much labor as it desires. How much labor should the firm demand?

Define profits as

$$\Pi = PX - NW. \tag{16.2}$$

PX is the revenue and NW is the variable costs. We neglect the fixed costs associated with the capital stock because only the variable costs are relevant to determining the profit-maximizing labor input. The firm maximizes equation (16.2) subject to equation (16.1). This yields the following marginal conditions for profit maximization: the marginal revenue product of labor (MRP_N) must equal the marginal resource cost of labor (MRC_N). The marginal revenue product of labor equals the marginal physical product of labor (F_N) times the price of output (P). The marginal resource cost of labor is simply the nominal wage rate (W). Thus, profit maximization requires that firms hire labor services up to the point where the marginal revenue product of labor equals the nominal wage rate.

$$PF_N = W.[1] \tag{16.3}$$

If the additional revenue from hiring an additional worker ($MRP_N = PF_N$) exceeds the cost of hiring an additional unit of labor ($MRC_N = W$), the firm will increase its profits by increasing its labor input; as it expands employment, the marginal product of labor (F_N) will decline due to the law of diminishing returns so that eventually $MRP_N = MRC_N$ and profits are at a maximum.

The shape of the marginal revenue product of labor curve reflects the law of diminishing returns. Given the fixed capital stock, equal increments in labor services will be associated with smaller and smaller increments in output; i.e., the marginal physical product of labor diminishes as the amount of labor is increased. As the price of output is constant for the firm, the revenue generated by hiring an additional unit of labor services also declines. Given the price level and the capital stock (the determinants of the position of the MRP_N curve in Figure 16.1), firms will require a reduction in the wage rate to expand their use of labor services. Thus, a decline in the wage rate from W_0 to W_1 will increase the demand for labor from N_0^d to N_1^d.

An increase in the price level shifts the MRP_N schedule up and to the right. This is pictured in Figure 16.2 where $P_1 > P_0$. At the initial wage rate, W_0, the

---

[1] Substituting equation (16.1) into equation (16.2) and setting the derivative with respect to N equal to zero,

$$\frac{\partial \Pi}{\partial N} = PF_N - W = 0,$$

we get condition (16.3).

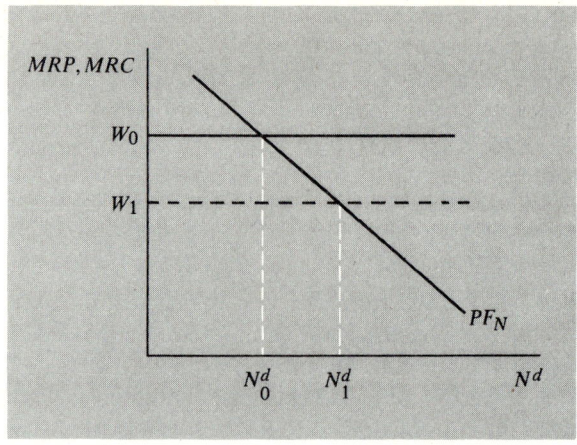

FIGURE 16.1
The Effect of an Increase in the Wage Rate

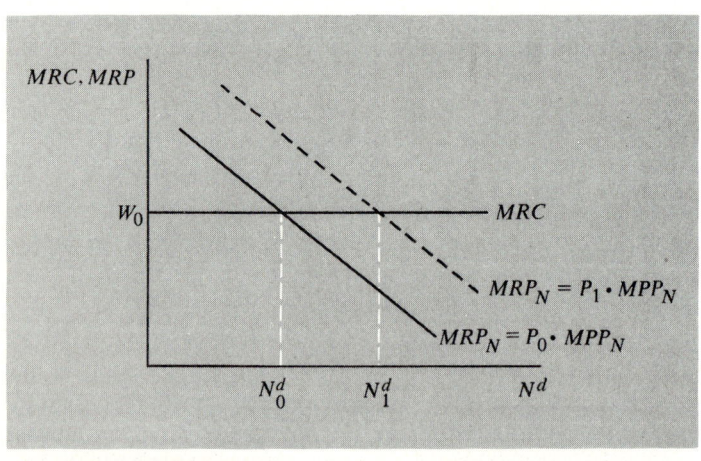

FIGURE 16.2
The Effect of an Increase in the Price of Output

MRP_N now exceeds the marginal resource cost. Therefore, firms can increase profits by hiring additional labor. The profit-maximizing level of labor services is where $MRP_N = W$, at N_1^d.

An alternative statement of the marginal condition is that firms should hire labor services to the point where the marginal physical product of labor (F_N) equals the real wage rate (W/P).

$$F_N = \frac{W}{P} \tag{16.3'}$$

This specification, pictured in Figure 16.3, relates the real wage rate to the F_N curve to determine the profit-maximizing level of labor input. A reduction in the real wage

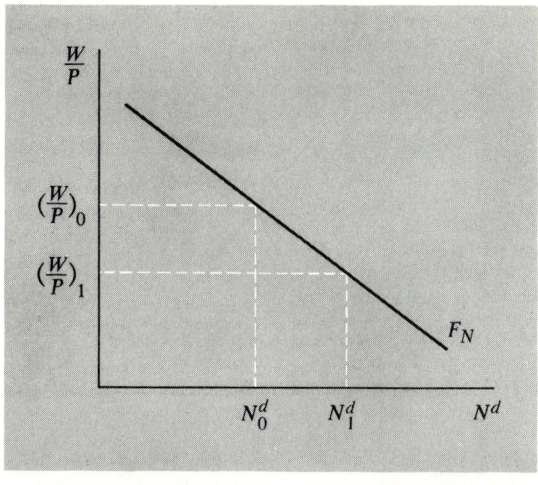

FIGURE 16.3
The Notional Demand Curve for Labor

rate due either to a drop in the nominal wage or an increase in the price level will increase the quantity of labor demanded.

The labor demand function pictured in Figure 16.3 is called the *classical* or *notional demand curve for labor*. Note that output does not appear as an argument in the notional demand curve. The demand for output does not constrain the firm's production under the assumption embodied in the notional demand curve: *firms can sell all the output they desire at the prevailing price level*. This assumption is derived from the more fundamental assumption of perfect competition in the commodity market.

○ Income-Constrained Demand Curve

Labor input also appears as an argument in the production function. The production function can be solved to yield an expression for the amount of labor input required to produce a given level of output, given the fixed capital stock:

$$N = F^*(X, \bar{K}) \tag{16.4}$$

Equation (16.4) is called the *labor requirements function*. It implies that the smaller the demand for output, the smaller the labor requirements. How can this be reconciled with the notional demand curve?

Figure 16.4a pictures the production function and the labor requirements function and Figure 16.4b pictures the notional demand and income-constrained demand curves. As long as firms find they can sell all the output they desire, the notional demand curve is relevant. For example, assume that with a real wage rate of $(W/P)_0$ and a level of aggregate demand of X_0, firms can sell all the output they produce when they hire N_0 units of labor services. Notional demand and labor requirements are both N_0. Now assume that aggregate demand declines to X_1, and as a consequence, firms find they cannot sell all they produce with N_0 units of labor.

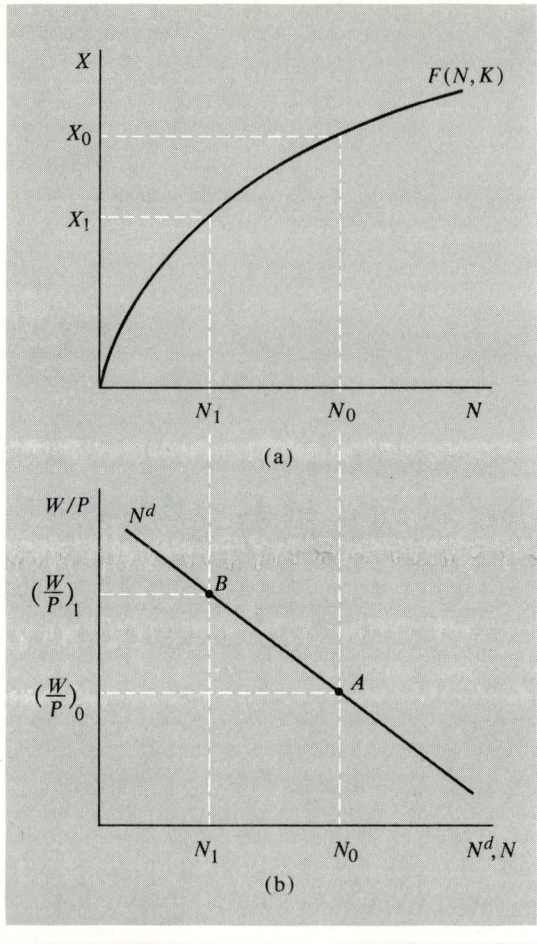

FIGURE 16.4
The Production Function and the Effective Demand for Labor

Since aggregate demand is less than the level of production, unwanted inventory accumulation is taking place; i.e., $X_1 - X_0$ of unwanted inventories will accumulate each period that production and aggregate demand remain at X_0 and X_1, respectively. The notional demand curve is no longer relevant to determining the demand for labor because one of its assumptions has been violated; i.e., an insufficient level of aggregate demand is incompatible with the assumption that each firm believes it has an unlimited market at the prevailing price.

Firms respond to the rising level of unwanted inventories by cutting back production and, therefore, employment. The firms' demand for labor under conditions of inadequate aggregate demand is given by N^dBN_1 in Figure 16.4b. This is called the *income-constrained demand curve*. Firms will not hire more than N_1 workers if their sales will be limited to X_1. But if the real wage rises above $(W/P)_1$, firms will be willing to employ even fewer than N_1 units of labor services. As long as the real wage rate is at or below $(W/P)_1$, firms will employ N_1 units of labor services.[2]

The Response of Employment and Hours to Changes in the Demand for Labor

The labor variable in the production function is not the stock of workers (employment), but rather the services provided by labor over the period used to define production, *person-hours* of labor services. We can measure this variable as the product of employment (E) and average hours per worker (h):

$$N = \frac{N}{E} \cdot E = hE. \tag{16.5}$$

Although employment and average hours per worker generally move together over the cycle, they also tend to exhibit a distinct pattern relative to each other. In particular, hours tend to respond quickly to changes in production, whereas employment responds only as firms become convinced that the output change will be of sufficient duration to warrant the added costs associated with firing and then rehiring workers.

Adjustment Costs and Cyclical Variation in Hours. We discussed the role of adjustment costs in the theory of investment in Chapter 14. There are also adjustment costs associated with varying labor services, particularly with changes in the number of employees. These adjustment costs take the form of expenses associated with hiring and training new workers and affect the profit-maximizing response to variations in the demand for output. The total cost of employment includes both a variable cost element (the wage bill, based on hours of work) and a fixed cost component. The fixed cost component, in turn, consists of costs associated with hiring and training workers. Hiring costs include the cost of searching for or recruiting workers and processing payroll records. These costs are related to the number of *new* workers, not to the flow of labor services (hours of work). Training expenses are costs associated with improving the productivity of workers.[3]

The existence of this fixed cost component of the cost of labor services makes firms reluctant to vary the number of employees in response to fluctuations in demand that they may perceive as being of short duration. A lower cost method of responding to temporary changes in demand is to vary average hours per worker. Because adjustment costs are even greater for changes in the capital stock, the dynamic response of the firm to changes in demand will be to first vary average hours per worker, then number of employees, and last of all, the size of the capital stock. Average hours do in fact display the procyclical pattern this analysis suggests, falling during

---

[2] The distinction between the notional and effective demand curves for labor was suggested by Don Patinkin in Chapter 13 of *Money, Interest, and Prices* (2d ed.; New York: Harper & Row, Publishers, 1965). See also Robert Barro and Herschel Grossman, "A General Disequilibrium Model of Income and Employment," *American Economic Review*, Vol. 61 (March, 1971), pp. 82–93.

[3] It is useful to distinguish between specific and general training. *Specific training* increases the productivity of a worker in a particular firm without increasing the worker's productivity in alternative employments. An example would be acquainting workers with the specifics of a firm's production process. *General training*, on the other hand, increases the workers productivity in both the current and alternative employments. Firms limit their training to specific training; workers must generally acquire general training at their own expense.

the initial stages of a recession as overtime is reduced and as workers are forced into part-time employment and then rising during expansions.[4]

Labor Hoarding and Cyclical Variation in Productivity. The existence of adjustment costs also has important implications for cyclical movements in labor productivity (output per person-hour of labor input). We noted in the previous section that firms will be reluctant to lay off workers to meet cyclical variation in demand for their product. This applies particularly to those workers in whom the firm has invested heavily in the form of training. During a cyclical decline in demand, firms will cut back production but retain those workers in whom they have heavily invested. This practice is sometimes referred to as *labor hoarding*. For example, they may lay off production line workers but retain supervisory personnel. The existence of labor hoarding results in a procyclical pattern of labor productivity (output per person-hour). Person-hours fall less than in proportion to output during cyclical declines in demand; therefore, output per person-hour (productivity) falls. During the recovery as demand increases, production increases relative to employment so that output per person-hour rises. We will discuss the implications of the pattern of average hours and productivity over the cycle in an appendix to the next chapter.[5]

THE SUPPLY OF LABOR

Like the decision about the demand for labor services, the supply decision can be broken down into an employment and hours decision. The supply of labor (N^s) is a flow, person-hours of labor services; it involves a decision about whether or not to seek employment (the employment or participation decision) and a decision concerning the number of hours to work.

Labor Force Participation

We define β as the proportion of the population (*POP*) that is in the labor force (*LF*); i.e., working or actively seeking work:

$$LF = \beta\ POP. \tag{16.6}$$

β is called the *labor force participation rate*. Labor force participation depends on a variety of life cycle, cultural, and economic factors. It has an important secular as well as cyclical pattern.

The cyclical pattern involves the response of the participation rate to the overall level of economic activity. However, the precise relationship between the participation

---

[4] The classic discussion of the fixed cost component of employment is Walter Oi, "Labor as a Quasi-Fixed Factor," *Journal of Political Economy*, Vol. 70 (December, 1962), pp. 538–555. For a discussion of the implications of adjustment costs for the hours and employment decisions, see M. Ishag Nadiri and Sherwin Rosen, "Interrelated Factor Demand Decisions," *American Economic Review*, Vol. LIX (September, 1969), pp. 459–471.

[5] For an empirical analysis of cyclical movements in productivity, see George Perry, "Potential Output and Productivity," *Brookings Papers on Economic Activity* (1977:1), pp. 11–47. Perry also provides evidence on the cyclical and secular patterns of average hours per worker.

rate and the level of economic activity was long a source of controversy. There are two competing hypotheses.

The Additional Worker Hypothesis. If economic activity is high and unemployment low, secondary workers in the family may drop out of the labor force. If economic activity declines and unemployment rises, on the other hand, secondary (additional) workers may enter the labor force to compensate for the decline in income earned by the primary worker. This hypothesis implies that the unemployment rate *overstates* the increase in employment required to reach full employment. As employment increases, primary workers are reemployed and secondary workers drop out of the labor force. Thus, N increases and LF decreases during an expansion, sharply reducing the unemployment rate $\left(\frac{LF-N}{LF}\right)$.

The Discouraged Worker Hypothesis. An alternative hypothesis is that secondary workers enter the labor force only when they believe there is a high probability of finding a suitable job. This probability increases with the level of economic activity. When unemployment increases, some workers are discouraged from looking for a job, believing the probability of finding a suitable one is too low to warrant continued search. This hypothesis implies that the unemployment rate *understates* the increase in employment required to restore full employment. During an expansion, N and LF both rise; assuming N rises by more than LF, each additional person employed reduces the number of persons unemployed *by less than one.*

The two hypotheses are not mutually exclusive. Both identify patterns of behavior observed in the labor market. The question relevant here is which dominates. The evidence suggests that at least during moderate recessions, the discouraged worker effect dominates the additional worker effect so that both N and LF fall during the downturn and rise during recovery. There remains some controversy about the magnitude of this effect. In the early 1960s researchers regarded the discouraged worker effect as being of major magnitude, but Jacob Mincer's classical and convincing critique suggests a more minor role for it.[6]

The participation rate also varies over time independently of the rate of unemployment. For example, the participation rate among women has been increasing over the entire postwar period. In the early postwar years, only about one third of adult women were in the labor force. During the 1970s, about one half of adult women were in the labor force, and the secular increase in the participation rate among women seems to have accelerated. The participation rate among teenagers has also been increasing.[7]

To capture the cyclical and secular variation in the participation rate, we write β as a function of both the unemployment rate (u) and time (t).[8]

---

[6] Jacob Mincer, "Labor Force Participation and Unemployment: A Review of Recent Evidence," Robert A. and Margaret S. Gordon, (eds.), *Prosperity and Unemployment* (New York: John Wiley & Sons, Inc., 1966), pp. 73–112.

[7] Perry has emphasized the effects of these changes in the composition of the labor force on productivity and aggregate unemployment. See George Perry, "Labor Force Structure, Potential Output, and Productivity," *Brookings Papers on Economic Activity* (1971:3), pp. 533–565.

[8] β should also be a function of the real wage rate. We develop the role of the real wage rate in our discussion in this chapter of the determinants of hours of work.

$$\beta = \beta(u,t) \tag{16.7}$$

The additional worker hypothesis suggests $\beta_u > 0$, while the discouraged worker hypothesis suggests $\beta_u < 0$. Mincer's estimate of the relationship yields a value of $\beta_u = -.2$; i.e., a one percentage-point increase in the unemployment rate will reduce the labor force participation rate by .2 percentage points. At a given unemployment rate, the participation rate has been increasing over the 1970s; therefore, $\beta_t > 0$.

○ Hours of Work

The labor supply decision reflects utility maximization by households subject to constraints. Household utility (U) is assumed to depend upon consumption of goods and services (C) and leisure (L).

$$U = U(C, L) \tag{16.8}$$

Households maximize U subject to the constraint that total time (T) must be exhausted between work (H) and leisure (L)

$$T = H + L \tag{16.9}$$

and that household income, used to purchase goods and services, is positively related to work,

$$Y_L = wH, \tag{16.10}$$

where w is the hourly wage rate and Y_L is income from labor.

The analysis of the labor supply decision can be depicted in terms of indifference curves. The vertical axis of Figure 16.5 represents income and the horizontal axis,

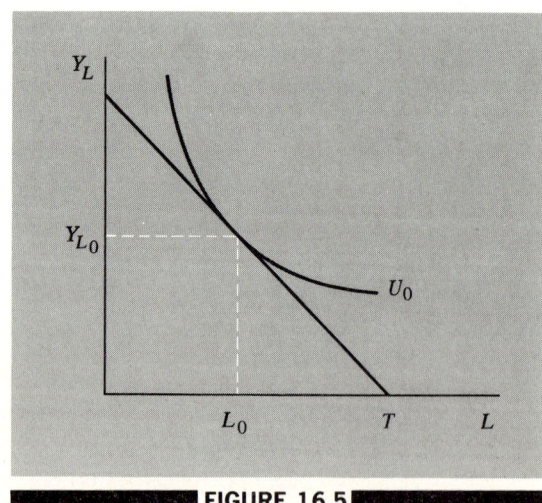

FIGURE 16.5
The Labor-Leisure Decision

leisure. The indifference curves picture preferences between consumption (purchased with income from work) and leisure. The budget line pictures the opportunities for trading off leisure for income.

The equation for the budget line is

$$Y_L = w(T - L). \qquad (16.11)$$

The vertical axis intercept is the labor income if all time is allocated to work. The horizontal axis is the maximum amount of leisure that can be consumed, equal to T. And the slope is the change in labor income associated with consuming an extra hour of leisure, equal to minus the wage rate.

The indifference curves depict combinations of income and leisure among which the unit is indifferent. Given that households like both leisure and income, the indifference curves are downward sloping; i.e., if leisure increases, income must fall to maintain the households' level of total utility unchanged. The indifference curves are convex to the origin because of the presumption that households will be willing to give up less and less income for each additional increment in leisure; therefore, the slope, $\Delta Y_L/\Delta L$, declines. Tangency between the indifference curve and budget line represents the utility-maximizing combination of Y_L and L subject to the constraint of given wage rate and available time.

The analysis immediately yields a supply function for hours of labor services offered which depends on the real wage rate.

$$N^s = N^s(w) \qquad (16.12)$$

To determine the influence of changes in the wage rate on labor supply, we alter w, rotating the budget line as shown in Figure 16.6 where $w_1 > w_0$. An increase in w rotates the budget line from Tw_0T to Tw_1T. The influence of change in w, however,

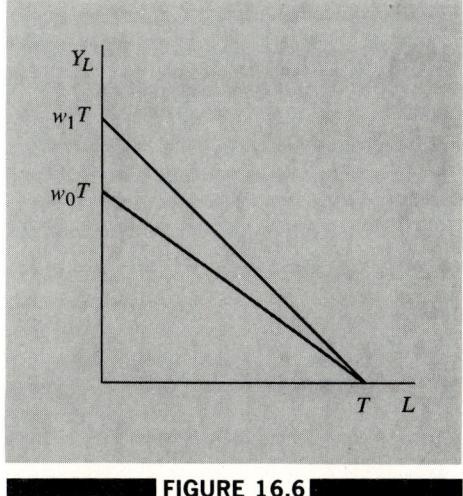

FIGURE 16.6
A Change in the Wage Rate

is ambiguous due to the interaction of income and substitution effects. w is the opportunity cost of leisure, and income and leisure are alternative ways of generating utility. An increase in w increases the cost of leisure, and the substitution effect is to decrease the demand for leisure and increase the supply of labor. Assuming leisure is a normal good (i.e., a good for which demand increases as income goes up), the increase in real income associated with the increase in w will be used to purchase both more Y_L and more L. In this case, the impact on L is ambiguous. Therefore, the slope of the labor supply schedule is ambiguous. The traditional assumption in macroeconomic models is that labor supply is a positive function of the real wage rate; i.e., that the substitution effect outweighs the income effect. This case is pictured in Figure 16.7. However, there is some empirical evidence which suggests that, at least over some range of real wage rates, the labor supply curve is negatively sloped.[9] As long as we assume that the labor supply curve is steeper (less elastic) than the labor demand curve, a (backward-bending) negatively sloped labor supply curve will not alter any of the qualitative results based on our analysis of the labor market. Indeed, our overall judgment of the effect of changes in the real wage on labor supply is that the effect, whichever way it goes, is quite small.[10]

There has been a secular decline in average hours per worker. However, after the 40-hour work week was achieved in manufacturing in the mid 1950s, this decline has been very gradual.

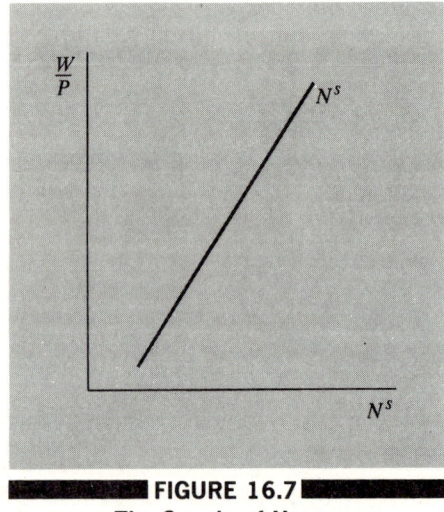

FIGURE 16.7
The Supply of Hours

---

[9] See, for example, T. Aldrich Finegan, "Hours of Work in the United States: A Cross Sectional Analysis," *The Journal of Political Economy*, Vol. 70 (October, 1962), pp. 452–470.

[10] For a summary of evidence on income and substitution effects, see Glen G. Cain and Harold W. Watts, "Toward a Summary and Synthesis of the Evidence," in Glen G. Cain and Howard W. Watts, *Income Maintenance and Labor Supply: Econometric Studies* (Chicago: Rand McNally College Publishing Co., 1973), pp. 328–367.

in the real wage and therefore induce a decrease in desired labor supply. Therefore, this model allows for money illusion in the short run. As long as the weights sum to one ($\Sigma w_i = 1$), workers will ultimately correctly perceive the real wage rate and therefore will not suffer from money illusion in the long run.

The short-run money illusion in this case reflects lags in processing information on prices, not irrational behavior. Workers directly observe their wage rates but must infer the price level by sampling prices in the goods market. Given that it is costly to acquire information about prices, it is not irrational for workers to make decisions without complete information about prices. As information is obtained about current prices, the worker updates the estimate of the overall price level, and the perceived price level converges to the actual if the actual remains constant for some period.

The Search Model. An alternative approach which also allows for temporary money illusion is the search model.[14] This model differs from the continuous auction model in that workers do not know the prevailing wage rates available to them. The essential proposition in the search model is that information is costly to acquire. Workers do not find it advantageous to acquire complete information on all possible job opportunities. Therefore, it is possible for employers to post different wage rates for workers with the same qualifications. Such differentials are competed away only when information is costless to acquire. Where information is costly, on the other hand, there is not a prevailing wage rate for workers of given qualifications, but rather a *distribution* of wage offers. Workers are uncertain about what wage offers will be forthcoming over any given period and must therefore develop a search strategy.

In such an environment, search is productive as well as costly. If workers simply accepted the first wage offer, they might receive a wage well below the wage possible with a longer search. The cost of search involves both explicit costs of travel, telephone, etc., and the implicit or opportunity cost associated with passing up wage offers to continue searching for better offers. The cost of search is assumed to be smaller when workers are unemployed. Therefore, unemployment is productive when used to acquire information about employment opportunities.

Unemployed workers sample employment opportunities and accept or reject wage offers depending on whether or not they exceed a predetermined reservation or acceptance wage. The *reservation wage rate* is set to balance the cost of continued search (the opportunity cost of remaining unemployed until receiving an acceptable wage offer along with explicit costs involved in search) against the cost of accepting too low a wage offer (the present value of the difference between the current wage offer and a better one available by continued search over a relevant time horizon).[15]

If the worker knows the probability distribution governing the wage offers, he or she sets the reservation wage in relation to the distribution so as to balance the cost of continued search against the cost of accepting too low a wage offer. The worker then simply samples wage offers until receiving one at or above his or her reservation rate.

---

[14] The search model is developed in a series of papers in Edmund S. Phelps *et al.*, *Microeconomic Foundations of Employment and Inflation Theory* (New York: W. W. Norton & Company, Inc., 1970). See also J. J. McCall, "Economics of Information and Job Search," *Quarterly Journal of Economics*, Vol. LXXXIV (February, 1970), pp. 113–126.

[15] For an excellent discussion of the cost and benefits of search, see Armen A. Alchian, "Information Costs, Pricing, and Resource Unemployment," in Phelps, *et al., ibid.*, pp. 27–52.

○ Labor Supply and Money Illusion

We noted in Chapter 11 that workers have often been viewed as suf[fering from] either permanent or temporary money illusion. *Money illusion* refers to [situations] in which economic agents make decisions about real variables (e.g., supp[ly of] services) based on nominal rather than real variables (e.g., the nominal r[ather than] the real wage rate). If workers suffer from permanent money illusion, the lab[or supply] function must be respecified as

$$N^s = N^s(W)$$

where W is the nominal wage rate. The assumption of permanent money i[llusion is] difficult to accept because it implies chronic irrational behavior on the part of [workers]. A more reasonable view is that workers temporarily suffer from money ill[usion in] response to changes in nominal wages and prices because of the time req[uired to] obtain information about these changes. There are two basic versions of this te[mporary] *misinformation* view: the continuous auction and search models.[11]

The Continuous Auction Model. In this model, introduced by Milton Friedman[, work]ers know the prevailing nominal wage and all workers who wish to work [at the] prevailing wage can find employment.[12] The essential feature of this model [is that] the supply of labor depends on the *perceived* rather than actual real wage ra[te and] that workers are slow to perceive price level changes and therefore suffer from [money] illusion in the short run following changes in the price level.[13]

To model the effect of temporary misperception of the real wage, we res[pecify] the labor supply function as

$$N^s = N^s\left(\frac{W}{P^*}\right) \qquad (16[.$$

where P^* is a weighted average of current and past price levels,

$$P_t^* = \Sigma w_i P_{t-i}, \qquad (16.$$

and the sum of the weights equals one.

In this specification, workers respond to the perceived real wage (W/P^*) rath[er] than to the actual real wage (W/P). Assuming declining weights which sum to on[e,] an equal percentage decline in W and P would initially result in a perceived reductio[n]

---

[11] For an excellent discussion of these similar but distinct approaches, see Donald Gordon, "A Ne[o]Classical Theory of Keynesian Unemployment," *Economic Inquiry*, Vol. 12 (December, 1974), pp. 431-459.

[12] Milton Friedman, "The Role of Monetary Policy," *American Economic Review*, Vol. 58 (March, 1968), pp. 1–17.

[13] To simplify the presentation, we assume that workers form expectations about the *price level* based on an adaptive expectations model. The models on which this analysis is based, on the other hand, usually assume that workers form expectations about the *inflation rate* based on an adaptive expectations model, and this is the specification we will employ in Chapter 18. The two specifications do not yield identical results about the effect of a steady rate of inflation.

Chapter 16 • The Demand for and Supply of Labor

A more reasonable assumption may be that workers do not know the probability distribution and therefore must develop an estimate of the distribution by sampling wage offers. The worker may form an initial estimate based on the wage in the last job held and then revise it in response to wage offers received. The worker sets the reservation wage rate relative to his or her estimate of the wage distribution. This is referred to as an *adaptive model of job search*.[16]

To formalize this approach, we specify the reservation wage rate (W_R) as a proportion of the estimate of the mean of the distribution of wage offers (W^*),

$$W_R = \alpha W^*, \tag{16.16}$$

and the estimated mean as a weighted average of current and past wage offers,

$$W^* = \sum_{i=0}^{n} v_i W_{-i}, \tag{16.17}$$

where the weights decline as the lag increases and sum to one. This is simply another example of the adaptive expectations model used previously on several occasions.[17] When W increases, W_R also increases but less than in proportion to the change in W in the short run. An increase in W relative to W_R reduces the duration of search and therefore increases the proportion of the labor force employed relative to the proportion searching (unemployed).

Such temporary changes in search and employment induced by increases in W relative to W_R are said to involve *wage illusion*. Workers confuse an increase in the overall distribution of wage offers for a high wage relative to the existing distribution. They are therefore "fooled" into searching for a shorter time. This "illusion" is, however, only temporary; over time, the adaptive process of updating W_R results in a convergence of the estimate of the mean of the distribution to the true value.

1. *Wage Illusion and Participation in the Labor Force.* If the overall level of wages increases relative to reservation wages, workers may choose to enter the labor force and actively seek employment; when actual wage offers decline relative to reservation wages, some may leave the labor force. Thus, this model also predicts a cyclical response of participation rates, rising in response to price increases associated with cyclical increases in aggregate demand. We therefore write the labor supply function as

$$N^s = N^s(W/W^*, W/P). \tag{16.18}$$

The first term captures the impact on the participation rate of temporary wage illusion.

---

[16] For a discussion of optimal search (both when the distribution of wages is known and when it is unknown), see McCall, "Economics of Information and Job Search," *Quarterly Journal of Economics*, Vol. LXXXIV (February, 1970), pp. 113–126.

[17] If wages are rising continuously at a constant rate, this procedure will systematically underestimate the mean of the probability distribution. We could rectify this by specifying the forecasting procedure as applying to the rates of change in wages; of course, this implies that people will systematically underpredict the inflation rate if it is accelerating over time.

In the absence of wage illusion, labor supply depends on the second term, the real wage rate.

2. *Wage Illusion and the Employment Acceptance Decision.* But the important implication of the search model is for the distribution of the labor force between those employed and those unemployed (searching). An increase in W relative to W^* (and hence W_R) increases the probability that a worker will receive a wage offer that meets or exceeds his or her reservation wage rate over any given period. Therefore, an increase in W relative to W^* reduces the expected duration of search and decreases the number of workers unemployed. In order to further refine our treatment of the employment acceptance decision, we need to refine our treatment of the relation of unemployment to the supply and demand for labor. We turn to this problem in the next section.

EQUILIBRIUM IN THE LABOR MARKET AND UNEMPLOYMENT

To develop the implications of wage illusion for the distribution of the labor force between employment and unemployment, it is useful to introduce unemployment explicitly into our labor market analysis. In our treatment of the labor market up to this point, we have defined equilibrium as a situation where supply and demand for labor are equal ($N^d = N^s$), and we have defined actual employment as the minimum of the amount of labor supplied or demanded. In Figure 16.8, introduced previously in Chapter 4, we identified the equilibrium level of employment as the level corresponding to the intersection of the N^d and N^s curves. It seems appropriate to designate the equilibrium level of employment as the "full employment" level of labor input because it appears to be the maximum feasible level of employment. Recall that the actual level of employment is always the minimum of the amount supplied or demanded. At any real wage above or below the equilibrium real wage rate, therefore, the actual level of employment will be lower than N_f.

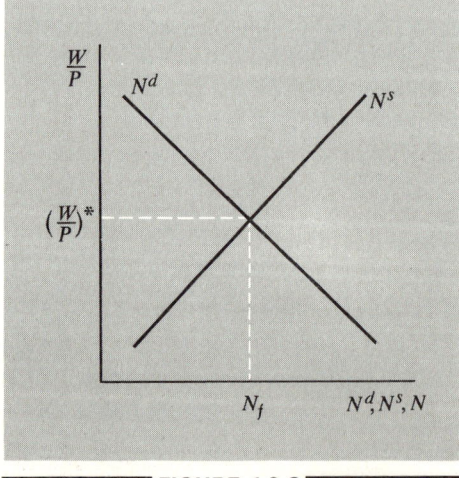

FIGURE 16.8
Equilibrium in the Labor Market and Full Employment

○ Unemployment and Vacancies

This analysis, however, fails to allow for the existence of unemployment when the labor market is in equilibrium. Defining employment (N) as equal to both demand and supply of labor in equilibrium implies that both unemployment (labor supply minus employment) and unfilled jobs or vacancies (demand for labor minus employment) are zero in equilibrium. In fact, however, even when supply and demand for labor are in balance, there are both unemployed persons and vacant jobs.

To introduce unemployment (U) and vacancies (V) explicitly into the analysis, it is useful to define the demand for labor as employment (N) plus vacancies (unsatisfied demand for labor)

$$N^d = N + V, \tag{16.19}$$

and the supply of labor as employment plus unemployment (unsatisfied supply of labor)

$$N^s = N + U. \tag{16.20}$$

The excess demand for labor is therefore

$$N^d - N^s = V - U. \tag{16.21}$$

When supply and demand are equal ($N^d = N^s$), $V = U$. We generally refer to unemployment which is just matched by vacancies as *frictional unemployment*. In this specification, the unemployment at full employment is frictional unemployment. When there is excess supply of labor, unemployment exceeds vacancies; unemployment associated by excess supply (the excess of unemployment over vacancies) reflects inadequate demand relative to supply.[18]

A number of empirical studies of the relation between unemployment and vacancies have found a systematic relation between these variables: as employment increases, vacancies decline.[19] A simple mathematical formulation of this relation is

$$VU = k \tag{16.22}$$

where k is some constant. This equation is depicted in Figure 16.9. V and U are inversely related; as V increases, U falls, and as V falls, U increases.

This relationship between U and V can be used to develop a relation between labor supply, labor demand, and employment; this is the NN curve depicted in Figure 16.10. The NN curve identifies the actual level of employment at each level of the real wage rate. Note that the NN curve is to the left of the N^d and N^s curves; i.e.,

---

[18] For a discussion of the role of vacancies and unemployment in the modeling of labor market equilibrium and disequilibrium, see Bent Hansen, "Excess Demand, Unemployment, Vacancies, and Wages," *Quarterly Journal of Economics*, Vol. 84 (February, 1970), pp. 1–23.

[19] See, for example, J. C. R. Dow and L. A. Dicks-Mireau, "The Excess Demand for Labor: A Study of Conditions in Great Britain, 1946–56," *Oxford Economic Papers*, N.S. 10 (February, 1958), pp. 1–33.

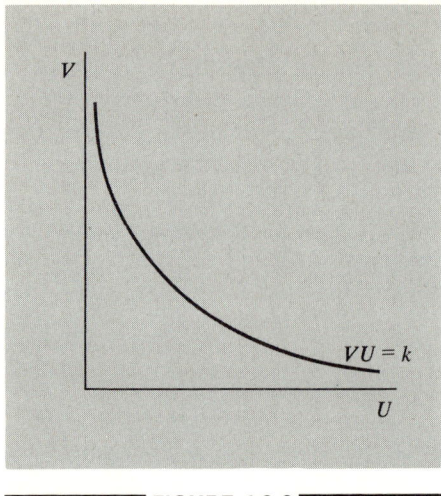

FIGURE 16.9
The Relation Between Vacancies and Unemployment

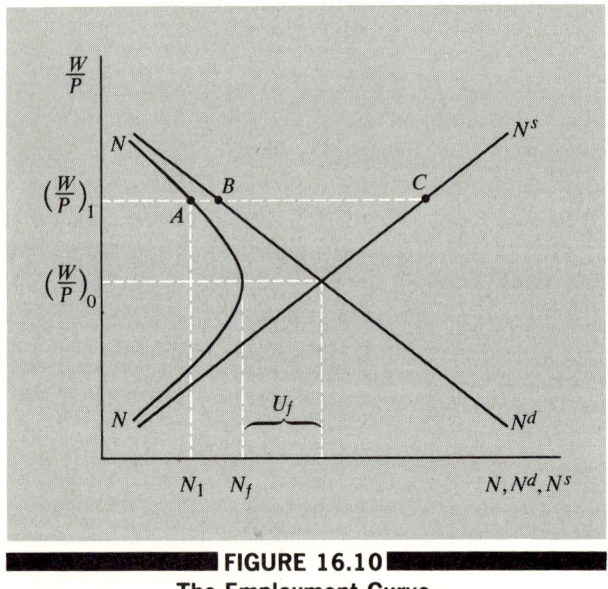

FIGURE 16.10
The Employment Curve

actual employment is always smaller than labor supply and labor demand. This of course reflects the existence of frictional unemployment and vacancies.

This diagram can be used to distinguish frictional versus excess supply unemployment and to illustrate both the level of employment and unemployment at "full employment." At the real wage rate $(W/P)_1$, the level of employment is N_1, read off the NN curve. *Vacancies*, defined as demand for labor minus employment, is the horizontal distance between the N^d and NN curves (AB in Figure 16.10).

Unemployment, defined as the excess of labor supply over employment, is measured by the horizontal distance between the NN and N^s curves (AC in Figure 16.10). Thus, at $(W/P)_1$, unemployment exceeds vacancies; i.e., unemployment exceeds frictional unemployment. In the next chapter we will consider further the nature and sources of unemployment in excess of frictional unemployment. At the equilibrium real wage rate, the level of employment, referred to as the *full employment level of employment*, is N_f, read off the NN curve. The horizontal distance between N_f and the level of both N^s and N^d at the equilibrium real wage rate is equal; i.e., unemployment just equals vacancies at full employment so that all unemployment is of the frictional variety. The level of unemployment is designated as U_f in Figure 16.10.

○ Wage Illusion and Frictional (or Search) Unemployment

We can now introduce the implications of wage illusion on the employment acceptance decision. *Wage illusion will affect the position of the NN curve.* Recall that we specified the relation between vacancies and unemployment as $VU = k$. k is affected by a variety of structural conditions that determine information flows and mobility of workers between jobs and by government programs such as unemployment compensation. The more generous is unemployment compensation (in level and duration), the longer the duration of search that will be optimal and the higher the normal level of frictional unemployment. But the position of the VU curve in Figure 16.11 is also determined by the relation between the reservation wage rate and the mean of the distribution governing wage offers. When workers correctly perceive the distribution of wage offers, k is at its normal value. However, if the overall level of wage offers increases, the mean of the distribution (W) will increase relative to the reservation wage W_R (which is based on the perceived mean W^*). Workers will have to search for a shorter time to obtain an acceptable wage and search unemployment will decline. This can be formalized by specifying k as a function

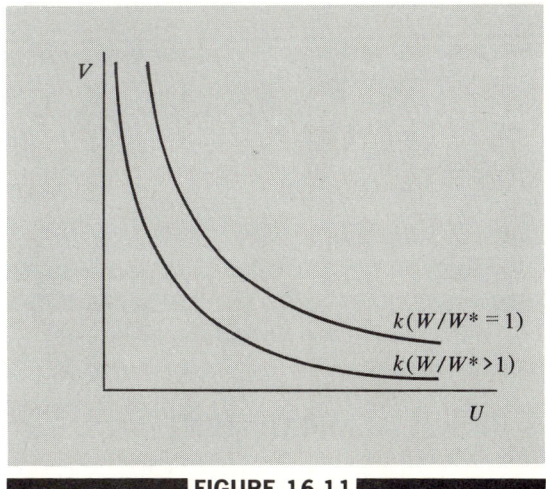

FIGURE 16.11
Wage Illusion and the Level of Unemployment and Vacancies

of structural parameters (s), unemployment compensation and other government policies (g), and W/W^*.

$$k = k(s, g, W/W^*) \qquad (16.23)$$

An increase in W/W^* reduces k and thereby shifts the VU curve leftward, reducing the level of unemployment at each level of vacancies (and reducing the vacancies at each level of unemployment).

We can now relate the changes in the VU curve back to the employment diagram. An increase in the actual relative to perceived mean of the wage distribution will reduce search and therefore frictional unemployment, shifting the NN curve rightward, closer to the N^d and N^s curves. In Figure 16.12, N^*N^* is the NN curve when $W = W^*$ (no wage illusion). This is the "normal" position of the curve, and N_f is the level of "full employment" and U_f is the level of unemployment at full employment. If $W/W^* > 1$, NN shifts rightward to $N'N'$. To simplify the diagram, we have assumed the N^s curve does not shift. Any increase in participation rates would reinforce the effect of wage illusion on employment. The shift in the NN curve results in a decline in search duration, a decline in frictional unemployment (to U_1 from U_f), and an increase in employment (to N_1 from N_f).

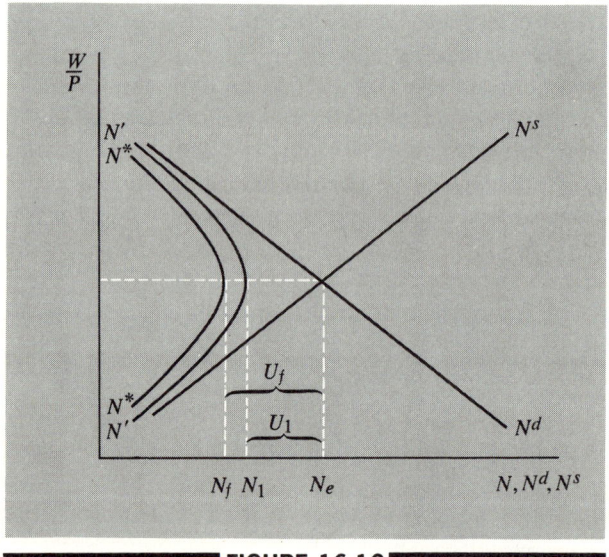

FIGURE 16.12
Wage Illusion and Search Unemployment

○ THE MEANING OF FULL EMPLOYMENT

Up to this point we have identified full employment with equilibrium in the labor market. The problem with this approach is that we cannot directly observe the supply and demand for labor; therefore, we need some procedure for operationally defining the point of full employment.

One possibility, based on our analysis in the previous section, is to define full employment as the point at which unemployment and vacancies are equal. This is certainly a potentially operational approach. However, vacancy statistics are not collected, at least not in the U.S. Therefore, we need an alternative operational approach. In this section we discuss approaches to defining full employment that rely on the observable consequences of labor market disequilibrium to provide an operational definition of labor market equilibrium and full employment.

○ The Noninflationary Rate of Unemployment (NIRU)

Each of the approaches we discuss takes as its point of departure the relation between wage change and labor market disequilibrium (the Phillips curve). We will have a great deal more to say about the Phillips curve in Chapter 18. Here we confine our attention to its usefulness in defining labor market equilibrium and full employment.

We begin with the simple disequilibrium equation in which the rate of change of nominal wages is proportional to the excess demand for labor,

$$\dot{W} = h(N^d - N^s) \tag{16.24}$$

where h is a positive constant, a measure of the speed of adjustment of wages to disequilibrium. Equilibrium can be identified with zero rate of wage change; i.e., $N^d = N^s$ when $\dot{W} = 0$.

Actually, however, wages tend in the long run to rise with increases in labor productivity. The secular rate of increase in labor productivity is about 2.5 percent per year. Therefore, equilibrium in the labor market would be associated with wage rate increases of 2.5 percent rather than zero wage change. As long as wages rise at the same rate as labor productivity, unit labor costs remain unchanged and there is no pressure for prices to rise due to cost increases. Therefore, full employment can be associated with zero rate of price change or 2.5 percent rate of wage change. In the remainder of this section, in order to simplify the analysis, we assume that labor productivity is not changing over time, so that zero wage change is consistent with both price level stability and labor market equilibrium.

Labor market equilibrium can be inferred in this case from the behavior of nominal wages. When the nominal wage rate is constant, the labor market is in equilibrium. Because the excess demand for labor is not directly observable, attempts to estimate equations such as equation (16.24) have proxied the excess demand for labor with the unemployment rate (u). The level of the unemployment rate at which $\dot{W} = 0$ is the noninflationary rate of unemployment (*NIRU*). If equation (16.24) accurately describes the response of the wage rate to labor market equilibrium, the *noninflationary rate of unemployment* corresponds to the rate of unemployment at full employment and provides a target for macroeconomic policy.

○ The Trade-Off Approach

What if the wage equation is

$$\dot{W} = v + h(N^d - N^s) \tag{16.25}$$

instead of equation (16.24) (where v is a positive constant)? We will discuss the theoretical basis for this specification in Chapter 18. For now we simply note its implications. If $N^d = N^s$, wages will still be increasing ($\dot{W} = v$). To achieve wage stability ($\dot{W} = 0$), we must tolerate excess supply of labor and therefore unemployment in excess of vacancies (unemployment in excess of frictional unemployment). Assuming again that unemployment is a proxy for the balance between supply and demand in the labor market, as unemployment increases above its frictional level, the rate of increase in wages declines and ultimately goes to zero. We can still define a noninflationary rate of unemployment, but it may be quite high compared to the amount we might associate with full employment, defined as the situation in which supply and demand for labor are equal. This model also suggests a *trade-off* between inflation and unemployment: lower unemployment can be obtained at the cost of a higher rate of inflation. The target level of unemployment is not necessarily the one at which supply and demand for labor are equal because this requires that we accept the associated rate of inflation. Full employment can be defined in this case with the lowest level of unemployment that can be achieved without imposing an unacceptable rate of inflation. This is, in fact, the basis for the choice of the unemployment rate at "full employment" of 4 percent by the Council of Economic Advisors in 1962.

> . . . the target for stabilization policy is to eliminate the unemployment which results from inadequate aggregate demand without creating a demand-induced inflation. A situation in which this is achieved can appropriately be described as one of "full employment," in the sense that further expansion of expenditures for goods and services, and for labor to produce them, would be met by only minor increases in employment and output, and by major increases in prices and wages. . . . In the existing economic circumstances, an unemployment rate of about 4 percent is a reasonable and prudent full employment target. . . .[20]

The Council Report went on to note that the level of unemployment consistent with price stability or an acceptable rate of inflation need not be constant over time. In particular, it can be reduced by suitable structural policies to improve the flow of information and the mobility of workers. Most evidence suggests, however, that changes in the demographic composition of the labor force over the decade following the selection of the 4 percent target, by increasing frictional unemployment, actually increased the unemployment rate consistent with price stability. For example, George Perry has studied the effect of the changing composition of the labor force on the aggregate unemployment rate.[21] Each demographic group can be viewed as possessing a characteristic rate of frictional unemployment that reflects the stability of their employment experience, which in turn reflects the degree to which they move from job to job or drop out and subsequently reenter the labor force. Women and teenagers experience higher rates of frictional unemployment, for example, than adult males. The increasing representation of women and teenagers in the labor force translates

---

[20] *Economic Report of the President* (Washington: U.S. Government Printing Office, 1962), p. 46.
[21] George Perry, "Labor Force Structure, Potential Output, and Productivity," *Brookings Papers on Economic Activity* (1971:3), pp. 533–565. See also Robert Hall, "Why is the Unemployment Rate So High At Full Employment," *Brookings Papers on Economic Activity* (1970:3), pp. 369–402.

into a higher observed aggregate rate of unemployment for any given degree of overall tightness in the labor market. The Council of Economic Advisors' series for its *benchmark unemployment rate,* the aggregate unemployment rate that corresponds to the same degree of labor market tightness as 4 percent in the 1952–1958 period, is reported in Table 16.1.

1952–1958	4.0%	1970	4.5%
1959–1962	4.1	1971	4.6
1963	4.2	1972	4.7
1964	4.3	1973	4.8
1965	4.4	1974	4.8
1966	4.5	1975	4.8
1967	4.4	1976	4.9
1968	4.5	1977	4.9
1969	4.4		

TABLE 16.1
The CEA's Benchmark Unemployment Rate[22]

○ The Nonaccelerating Inflation Rate of Unemployment (*NAIRU*)

The trade-off model has come under serious attack in recent years. An alternative view holds that there is a *natural rate of unemployment* that corresponds to labor market equilibrium. Like the noninflationary rate of unemployment approach discussed above, the natural rate view holds that there is a unique unemployment rate (at any given time) that corresponds to equilibrium in the labor market and that this "full employment" or natural rate of unemployment is compatible with price level stability. Unlike the noninflationary rate of unemployment view, the natural rate view holds that the equilibrium unemployment rate is also compatible with any *constant rate* of inflation (or deflation). Any attempt to reduce unemployment below the critical rate will result in *accelerating* inflation. Therefore, the *critical rate* is the only one at which inflation is neither accelerating nor decelerating. The critical unemployment rate at which the labor market can be in equilibrium at any constant rate of inflation (including zero) is called the *nonaccelerating inflation rate of unemployment (NAIRU)*. We will develop this approach in detail in Chapter 18.

● REVIEW QUESTIONS

1. What important macroeconomic assumption underlies the classical labor demand function?

2. Explain the source of the cyclical movement in average hours and productivity.

---

[22] *Economic Report of the President,* January, 1978 (Washington: U.S. Government Printing Office, 1978), p. 84.

Part IV • Refinements of the Real Sector: Aggregate Supply

3. What is the participation rate and what are the sources of its cyclical and secular behavior?

4. Define money illusion and explain the source of money illusion in the continuous auction and search models.

5. What is the meaning of the "unemployment rate at full employment" and what determines its level?

● PROBLEMS

1. Compare the implications of the discouraged and secondary worker hypotheses for the responsiveness of the unemployment rate to increases in aggregate demand.

2. Set up the indifference curve model of the labor-leisure choice and show how a change in the wage rate can result in an increase or decrease in the labor supply. Indicate how the labor supply curve can be derived from the indifference curve diagram.

Chapter 17

The Response of Output and Employment to Aggregate Demand

In this chapter we discuss two explanations of the response of output and employment to changes in aggregate demand. The first explanation views movements of output and employment in response to changes in aggregate demand in the context of markets which fail to clear continuously. The second explanation views these movements as responses to demand-induced changes in wages and prices when workers suffer from money illusion. In the appendices at the end of the chapter we further develop the short-run relation of employment to output and discuss the secular relation between employment and output. In Appendix A we analyze the sources of economic growth, drawing upon our discussion in Chapter 16 of the *secular* trends in population, participation rates, average hours, and productivity. In Appendix B we discuss the short-run relation between employment and output, building on our discussion of *cyclical* patterns in participation rates, average hours, and productivity in the previous chapter.

UNEMPLOYMENT AND LABOR MARKET DISEQUILIBRIUM

The labor market is in disequilibrium when $N^d \neq N^s$ at the prevailing real wage rate. We can identify two sources of labor market disequilibrium: the existence of a real wage different from the equilibrium real wage rate and a deficiency of aggregate demand.

Nonequilibrium Real Wage Rate

Assume that the prevailing wage rate is other than $(W/P)^*$; e.g., assume it is $(W/P)_1$ in Figure 17.1. Such a real wage rate could arise as a result of a decline in the price level, a union-imposed increase in the nominal wage rate, or as a consequence of a government-imposed minimum wage rate. Unemployment at $(W/P)_1$ equals the distance ac and exceeds the level associated with frictions in the labor market.

319

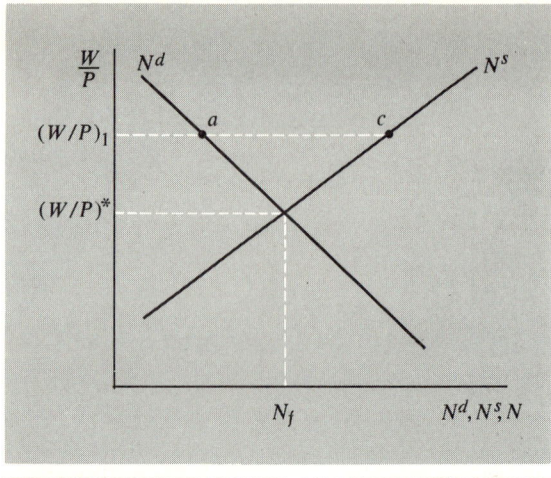

FIGURE 17.1
Disequilibrium Real Wage and Unemployment

○ Deficiency of Aggregate Demand

But disequilibrium unemployment may exist even if the real wage rate is at a level compatible with labor market equilibrium. Assume the economy is initially at full employment; e.g., at point a in Figure 17.2b.[1] Aggregate demand and output are both equal to X_f and employment is N_f. Assume that aggregate demand declines to X_1. If firms continue to hire N_f workers and produce X_f in output, $X_f - X_1$ in output will accumulate as unwanted inventories each period. If firms can only sell X_1 in output, they will reduce employment to N_1 (labor required to produce X_1). Even though the real wage rate remains at a level required for equilibrium in the labor market, the disequilibrium in the commodity market generates disequilibrium in the labor market. Thus, the existence of the equilibrium wage rate is a necessary but not sufficient condition for labor market equilibrium.

Since the ultimate source of the labor market disequilibrium in this case is a deficiency in aggregate demand, adjustments initiated within the labor market will not restore full employment unless they also lead to an increase in the demand for output. The cure for deficiency of demand unemployment is therefore an increase in aggregate demand. The key question becomes whether adjustments initiated within the labor market lead to repercussions in the output market which expand aggregate demand. We will investigate the repercussions of wage adjustments on aggregate demand later in this section. At this point, we simply note that the problem in this case is not the relative price of labor (the real wage rate) but rather the absolute level of wages and prices. The key to the persistence of disequilibrium in this case is the failure of wages and prices to adjust quickly enough to maintain full employment in the face of demand disturbances. Therefore, we turn next to the response of wages to labor market disequilibrium.

---

[1] To simplify the graphical analysis, we ignore the existence of frictional unemployment and vacancies during our discussion of unemployment in disequilibrium. Keep in mind, however, that there is unemployment even at "full" employment.

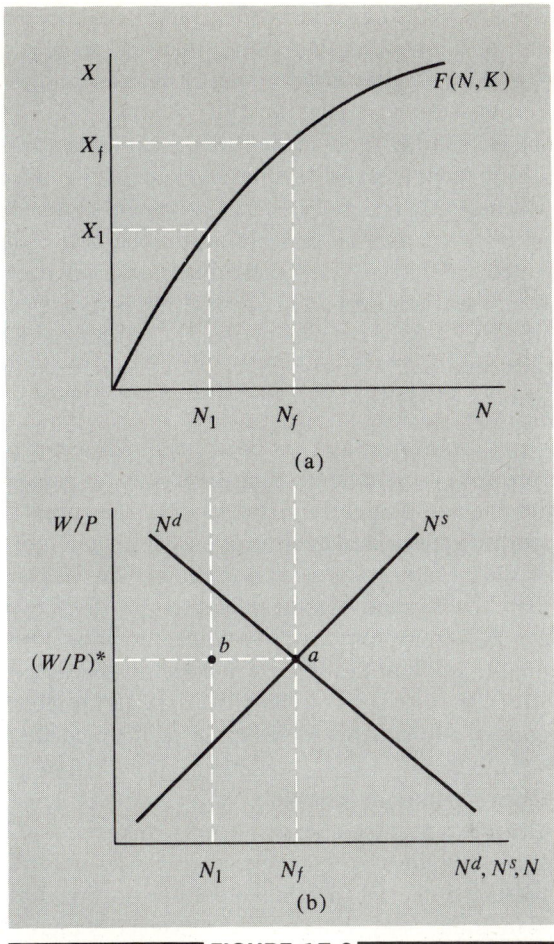

FIGURE 17.2
Demand Deficiency and Disequilibrium Unemployment

○ Price or Quantity Adjustments in Disequilibrium

Assume the labor market is initially in equilibrium at $(W/P)^*$ and N_f in Figure 17.1. Let the price level decline for some reason so that the real wage rate rises above its equilibrium level, say to $(W/P)_1$. At $(W/P)_1$ there is excess supply. What will be the response of market participants to this disequilibrium?

Instantaneous Price Adjustments. One possibility is that instantaneous price (wage) adjustments will occur to maintain the labor market in equilibrium. Consider the real wage rate as the price of labor services. Assume the labor market is run by an auctioneer who sets an initial price, say $(W/P)_1$ in this case, and then calls for offers of supply and demand for labor at that price. If the offers of supply and demand balance at that price, the price is an equilibrium or market clearing price; the auctioneer announces that all offers are accepted and employment equals supply and demand for labor. On the other hand, if there is excess supply or excess demand at the initial price, that price is not compatible with equilibrium, no offers are accepted, and no transactions are allowed at that price. Instead, *recontracting* occurs. The auctioneer sets a new price (higher if there was excess demand at the initial price, lower if there was excess supply) and again calls for offers of supply and demand. The process of price adjustment and recontracting continues until an equilibrium price is achieved. Only then does the auctioneer accept the offers and only then will transactions be permitted to occur. The whole process is assumed to occur instantaneously. Time stops while the auctioneer searches for the new equilibrium.

According to this parable, price (real wage) adjustments will occur instantaneously to restore an equilibrium real wage rate. No quantity adjustments occur. Employment remains at N_f and the real wage rate instantaneously returns to $(W/P)^*$. To sustain the unemployment, disequilibrium must persist. And this in turn implies that prices must fail to move rapidly enough to maintain markets in continuous equilibrium.

The Speed of Wage-Price Adjustment and the Persistence of Disequilibrium. An obvious shortcoming of the previous explanation is that there is no auctioneer! Market participants must search for the new equilibrium, and search takes time. During the period that prices remain out of equilibrium, quantities may bear much or all of the burden of adjustment. Note that it is not necessary to require that wages be perfectly rigid in the downward direction to motivate the usefulness of the Keynesian model. We simply need to reject the assumption that instantaneous price adjustments maintain all markets in continuous equilibrium. Given noninfinite speeds of price adjustment in market disequilibrium, the emphasis on effective demands for labor and commodities and concern for quantity adjustments in response to demand disturbances appears justifiable.

Nevertheless, there remains an unattractive ad hoc character to this rationale for the nonmarket clearing framework. After all, why don't prices fall rapidly enough to maintain continuous equilibrium? To some, even casual observation of the labor and commodity markets is sufficient to validate the nonmarket clearing view. Institutional factors such as minimum wage laws and the existence of unions clearly introduce some inflexibility in wage rates. But there are also a number of explanations for sluggish wage response to disequilibrium that follow more directly from optimizing behavior of economic agents.

1. *Information Costs and the Profitability of Search.* In the previous chapter we discussed the increase in search unemployment in response to a decline in demand when workers have incomplete information about the overall structure of wage offers. The search model therefore suggests a temporary quantity adjustment (decline in employment and output) and slow price adjustment in response to a decline in demand. However, the proponents of search models generally view such increases in unemployment as voluntary (self-employment in order to acquire information) and view labor markets as clearing continuously. We will return to this model in the following section.[2]

---

[2] See, for example, Alchian, "Information Costs, Pricing, and Resource Unemployment," in Phelps et al., *Microeconomic Foundations of Employment and Inflation Theory* (New York: W. W. Norton & Company, Inc., 1970). For a discussion of the search model as an explanation for the persistence of disequilibrium, see Axel Leijonhufvud, *On Keynesian Economics and the Economics of Keynes* (New York: Oxford University Press, 1968), especially Part II.

2. *Explicit and Implicit Contracts.* An obvious source of at least temporary wage inflexibility is the existence of explicit contracts which fix wage rates over some period—generally from one to three years. This is particularly true for union-negotiated contracts, but many nonunion workers also operate under either explicit or implicit contracts which fix wages over some period. Recently there have been a number of attempts to explain why profit-maximizing firms and utility-maximizing workers would find it advantageous to operate under such arrangements.[3] We will briefly sketch out the conditions under which fixed wage contracts can be explained as optimal responses to uncertainty.

The key assumption in these models is that workers are more risk averse than firms. In particular, it is usually assumed that workers are risk averse and firms are risk neutral. If a unit is *risk neutral*, it is concerned only with the expected value of returns and does not care at all about the degree of dispersion of the actual about the expected value of return. If an agent is *risk averse*, it dislikes taking risk and therefore prefers a return of equal expected value but smaller expected dispersion of actual about expected returns. The assumption that workers are risk averse and firms risk neutral can be rationalized in two ways. First, firms have greater opportunity to diversify and can generally reduce risk by diversification. Secondly, the attitude toward risk may be an important factor influencing which individuals work for firms and which individuals own firms.

Risk-averse workers prefer a stable wage to a variable wage of equal expected value. This is true by the definition of risk aversion. Firms, on the other hand, are indifferent between a stable wage and a variable wage of equal expected value; again, this is true by the definition of risk neutrality. Firms can therefore make workers equally well-off with a *lower* fixed wage compared to a variable wage contract with a given expected value. If workers are equally well-off with this fixed wage contract, firms must be better-off; i.e., by lowering their expected wages, they increase their expected profits. Workers can be thought of as paying a premium in the form of a lower wage rate to insure against wage variability.

A similar analysis seems applicable to the employment status of workers. In particular, why don't firms offer a still lower wage at which they also guarantee against layoffs over the duration of the contract? Firms must balance this cost reduction via lower wages against the added cost of carrying workers on their payrolls during periods of below-normal demand. Whether or not a fixed employment contract will be optimal depends on how much of a wage reduction workers will accept to secure such a contract. The wage reduction that workers would accept as a condition for guaranteed employment status depends on the generosity of unemployment compensation and on the utility that workers derive from leisure while unemployed. If unemployment compensation is generous and/or workers derive considerable utility from leisure while unemployed, they will accept only a relatively small decline in their wage to secure a fixed employment contract. On balance, the cost of carrying workers on

---

[3] See, for example, Donald F. Gordon, "A Neo-Classical Theory of Keynesian Unemployment," *Economic Inquiry*, Vol. 12 (December, 1974), pp. 431–459; Martin J. Baily, "Wages and Employment Under Uncertain Demand," *Review of Economic Studies*, Vol. 41 (January, 1974), pp. 37–50; and C. Azariadis, "Implicit Contracts and Underemployment Equilibria," *Journal of Political Economy*, Vol. 83 (October, 1975), pp. 1183–1202.

payrolls during slack periods may outweigh the benefits that can be derived from the wage reduction. Therefore, although it may be optimal to enter into fixed wage contracts, it may nevertheless be profitable to respond to cyclical declines in demand by varying the level of employment.

3. *The Concern about Relative Wages.* Keynes suggested that because workers are concerned with their relative wage rate (i.e., their wage relative to that of other workers), they will resist cuts in their nominal wage rate but would accept equivalent declines in their real wage rate resulting from price level increases.[4] In the latter case, the real wage rate of all workers falls proportionately so that relative wage rates are unaffected. When workers are offered nominal wage cuts, on the other hand, there is no guarantee that all workers' wages will be cut proportionately. A nominal wage cut is therefore both a decline in the real wage and a possible decline in one's relative wage. The existence of unions with strong bargaining power only increases the ability of workers to successfully resist wage cuts.

4. *Adjustment Costs and Nonhomogeneous Workers.* If current employees resist wage reductions, why not replace them with unemployed workers who have an incentive to accept a wage rate below that currently prevailing? One explanation lies in the fixed costs associated with hiring a new worker. In the previous chapter we noted the costs of hiring and training new workers and related these expenses to the concept of adjustment costs in the theory of investment. In the presence of such adjustment costs, the firm has an incentive to encourage a stable work force and will be reluctant to replace existing workers with lower paid recruits from among the unemployed.

A second explanation that reinforces the first one is that employed and unemployed workers are simply not perfectly interchangeable. Workers vary in quality, and the quality of employed workers is likely to exceed that of unemployed workers. If firms reduce wages to encourage workers to quit, they are likely to lose their most qualified employees first. A more efficient procedure is to lay off workers subject to recall when demand recovers. This permits the firm to retain its most qualified workers, and at the same time provides access to other qualified workers when demand increases. Indeed, layoffs rather than quits account for the major portion of increased unemployment during cyclical downturns.[5]

○ The Efficacy of Wage Adjustments

In the preceding section we developed the rationale for gradual wage adjustments in the face of labor market disequilibrium. In this section we investigate the efficacy of wage adjustments, once initiated, in restoring labor market equilibrium. First, we consider the case where disequilibrium is associated with an above equilibrium

---

[4] Keynes, *The General Theory of Employment, Interest and Money* (New York: Harcourt, Brace and World, Inc., 1936), pp. 13–14.

[5] The role of nonhomogeneity in encouraging firms to lay off workers rather than induce them to quit via wage reductions is emphasized by Franco Modigliani, "The Monetarist Controversy, or Should We Forsake Stabilization Policies?" *American Economic Review*, Vol. 67 (March, 1977), pp. 7–8. For a discussion of the role of layoffs, see Martin Feldstein, "Temporary Layoffs in the Theory of Unemployment," *Journal of Political Economy*, Vol. 84 (June, 1976), pp. 937–957.

real wage rate. Then we consider the case where disequilibrium is associated with deficiency of aggregate demand.

Nominal or Real Wage Adjustments in Response to an Above Equilibrium Real Wage Rate. If the source of disequilibrium is exclusively an above equilibrium real wage rate, then the reduction of the real wage rate to its equilibrium value is both a necessary and sufficient condition for the restoration of equilibrium. But exactly how will market participants effect wage adjustments? In particular, will there be a direct reduction in the real wage rate or an attempt to reduce real wage rate via reduction in the nominal wage rate?

1. *Real Wage Rate Adjustment.* Since the real wage rate is the price of labor services, it might appear natural to assume that excess supply in the labor market directly generates reductions in the real wage rate; i.e.,

$$(\dot{W/P}) = j(N^d - N^s). \tag{17.1a}$$

In this case, the direct response of participants in the labor market to disequilibrium can be expected to restore equilibrium.

2. *Nominal Wage Rate Adjustment.* However, as Keynes pointed out, workers traditionally bargain with employers over nominal rather than real wage rates. In this case the appropriate adjustment relationship is

$$\dot{W} = h(N^d - N^s). \tag{17.1b}$$

When there is excess supply, there should be pressure generated within the labor market for the real wage rate to decline. But such pressure can be exerted either by bargaining for a reduction in the nominal wage at a given price level or bargaining directly over the real wage rate.[6] The particular form of the adjustment equation is still important, however. Assume the excess results from a real wage rate above equilibrium. Disequilibrium [equation (17.1a)] immediately suggests that equilibrium will be restored via adjustments within the labor market, assuming the labor market is stable. The result is not as certain if the disequilibrium adjustment is represented by equation (17.1b). We must also determine what is happening to the price level (P) before we are sure that reductions in W will be effective in reducing the real wage rate. If prices fall proportionately with nominal wages, nominal wage declines cannot reduce the real wage rate, and labor market adjustments will be ineffective in restoring labor market equilibrium. This possibility was suggested by Keynes as an explanation for the persistence of unemployment. We will discuss the conditions under which wages and prices will fall proportionately later in this chapter.

---

[6] The spread of "escalator" clauses permits workers to bargain directly over real wage rates. An *escalator clause* guarantees nominal wage increases in response to increases in the price level. If the escalator clause requires nominal wages to change in exact proportion to price changes, then workers are directly bargaining over real wages. However, only a fraction of workers are covered by escalator clauses and most escalators provide only partial protection against price increases (i.e., they require nominal wages to rise less than in proportion to price increases).

Indirect Repercussions of Wage Reduction and the Problem of Demand Deficiency.

The problem of restoring equilibrium via adjustments initiated by market participants is more difficult if the source of the disequilibrium is deficiency of aggregate demand. Assume the labor market is initially in equilibrium at $(W/P)^*$ and N_f in Figure 17.2, and that aggregate demand is just sufficient to sustain employment at N_f.

Consider the consequences of a decline in aggregate demand from X_f to X_1. Labor requirements fall from N_f to N_1. The initial impact of the resulting excess supply is a reduction in employment from N_f to N_1. The resulting excess supply at point b in Figure 17.2 can be expected to put downward pressure on the nominal wage rate as workers attempt to bid down the real wage rate. Note, however, that the prevailing wage rate $(W/P)^*$ is compatible with labor market equilibrium. The source of the disequilibrium is not an excessive real wage rate but a deficient level of aggregate demand. Even if reductions in the nominal wage rate succeed in lowering the real wage rate, employment will not increase unless the demand for output increases. Therefore, adjustments initiated by participants in the labor market in response to disequilibrium may not insure the restoration of equilibrium. Only if those adjustments ultimately generate an increase in the demand for output will they succeed in eliminating the disequilibrium in the labor market. The analysis of disequilibrium must now be undertaken in a multimarket framework. It is the indirect effects of wage reductions on the demand for output that determine the efficacy of wage reductions in restoring labor market equilibrium.

We can analyze the repercussions of money wage cuts using the fixed wage version of the aggregate supply and demand analysis introduced in Chapter 11. The aggregate supply and demand curves are depicted in Figure 17.3. There are two alternative aggregate demand curves: DD, the general case, and $D'D'$, a special case when $L_r = -\infty$ or $I_r = 0$.

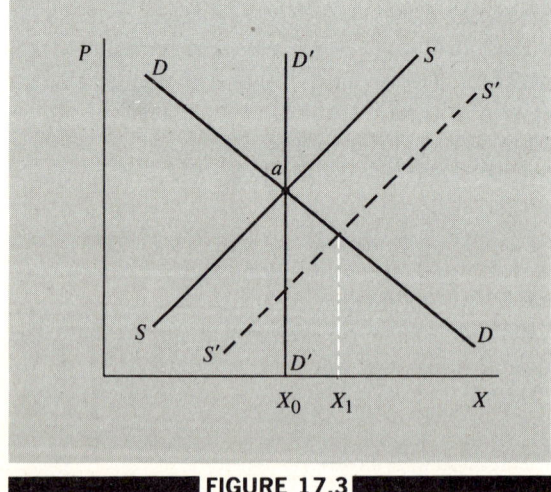

FIGURE 17.3
The Repercussions of Wage Reductions on Aggregate Demand

Assume that the initial level of aggregate demand at point a is below the level associated with full employment; i.e., $X_0 < X_f$. If money wages fall in response to the resulting excess supply of labor, the SS curve will shift downward. The decline in the SS curve will result in a decline in the price level and an increase in aggregate demand. The initial effect of the decline in the nominal wage rate is a decline in the price level via the aggregate supply equation. The decline in the price level, in turn, results in excess supply in the money market and therefore a decline in the interest rate and an increase in investment. Thus, a cut in the money wage rate does generally induce an increase in aggregate demand.

There are, however, conditions under which reductions in the nominal wage rate will not affect aggregate demand. These are, of course, precisely the same restrictions on parameter values that immobilized the classical price adjustment mechanism and were discussed in Chapter 9: $L_r = -\infty$ and $I_r = 0$. In the first case, the excess supply of money resulting from a decline in the price level does not put downward pressure on the interest rate. In the second case, reductions in the interest rate do not stimulate aggregate demand. The aggregate demand curve in either case is vertical. The downward shift in the SS curve therefore reduces prices but leaves output unchanged. From the aggregate supply curve, $P = WS(X)$, it is evident that if wage reductions leave X unchanged, prices must fall proportionately with wages. In either case, however, the efficacy of cuts in nominal wage rates on increasing aggregate demand is restored if we introduce a price-induced wealth effect in the consumption function. On the other hand, we also have to take into account the intertemporal substitution effect and bankruptcies induced by deflation in assessing the usefulness of money wage cuts in restoring full employment. Review the discussion of the classical adjustment mechanism in Chapter 9.

MONEY ILLUSION AND CYCLICAL VARIATION IN EMPLOYMENT AND OUTPUT

In this section we develop an alternative explanation of the response of employment and output to variations in aggregate demand. In contrast to the analysis in the previous section, the approach developed here is consistent with continuous clearing in the labor market and therefore does not allow for involuntary unemployment. Aggregate demand affects employment by inducing changes in both labor supply and frictional unemployment. These models build on the analysis of the labor supply decision under money illusion in the previous chapter.

The Case of Permanent Money Illusion

In Figure 17.4 the supply of and demand for labor are drawn as functions of the nominal wage rate. The demand for labor, however, depends on the real wage rate; therefore, the position of the N^d curve in Figure 17.4 depends on the prevailing price level. An increase in the price level will increase the demand for labor corresponding to each nominal wage rate. Thus, an increase in the price level from P_0 to P_1 shifts the N^d curve from N^d to $N^{d\prime}$ in Figure 17.4. The net result is an increase in the *nominal* wage rate (which induces an increase in the quantity of labor supplied)

Part IV • Refinements of the Real Sector: Aggregate Supply

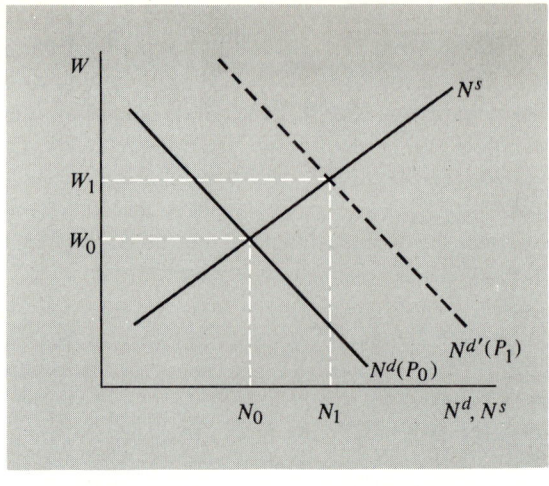

FIGURE 17.4
Money Illusion and the Response to Price Changes

and a decline in the *real* wage rate (which induces an increase in the quantity of labor demanded).[7] This divergence between movements in real and nominal wage rates in response to changes in aggregate demand is the essential feature of the models developed in this section.

The essential implication of this specification of the labor supply function is that *there is no longer a unique equilibrium level of employment.* Equilibrium employment varies with the price level. This specification, based as it is on irrational behavior, is not very plausible, and the main value of presenting it is as a transition to models which allow for money illusion (or misinformation) in the short run but require absence of money illusion (or misinformation) for long-run equilibrium.

○ The Continuous Auction Model

The position of the labor supply curve in the continuous auction model depends on the ratio of the actual to the perceived price level. The effect of changes in aggregate demand in this case is depicted in Figure 17.5. Assume the labor market is initially in full long-run equilibrium at point *a* in Figure 17.5. Long-run equilibrium requires that both $N^d = N^s$ and $P = P^*$. The level of employment in long-run equilibrium is designated as full employment N_f and the corresponding level of unemployment is designated as the natural rate of unemployment.

Consider the effects of an increase in aggregate demand. As the price level begins to rise, the real wage falls and firms increase their demand for labor, putting upward pressure on nominal wage rates. Assume the real wage initially falls to W_1/P_1 in Figure 17.5. If workers correctly perceived the changes in nominal wages and prices, they would respond to the decline in the real wage by offering less labor services

---

[7] From Figure 17.4 it is not obvious that the real wage rate declines. But the labor demand curve, on which Figure 17.4 is based, is an inverse function of the real wage rate. To induce an increase in the quantity of labor demanded, therefore, the real wage must fall.

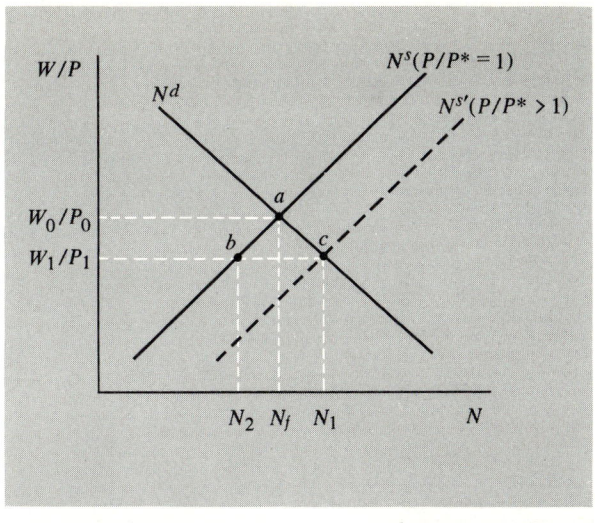

FIGURE 17.5
The Continuous Auction Model

(N_2 at b in Figure 17.5) and the resulting excess supply in the labor market (equal to the horizontal distance between b and c) would immediately drive the real wage back to its initial level at a.

However, workers suffer from short-run money illusion and are therefore *fooled* by the rising nominal wage rate and price level. Instead of recognizing the decline in the real wage, they perceive an increase in the real wage rate; i.e., although W/P falls, W/P^* rises. Thus, workers confuse an increase in the nominal wage for an increase in the real wage. A simple assumption is that workers initially fail to perceive any price level change (the weight on the price level on the current period is zero in the P^* equation); therefore, workers initially evaluate the higher nominal wage at the old price level and believe that the real wage has increased to W_1/P_0. At W_1/P_0 they wish to supply a larger level of labor services (N_1) than at the initial real wage rate. The precise value of W_1 must be such that the labor market continues to clear; i.e., that $N^d = N^s$. We show the short-run market clearing where $P > P^*$ as the intersection of N^d and $N^{s'}$ in Figure 17.5. At point c, the labor market is in short-run equilibrium and in this new equilibrium, employment exceeds N_f.

In the long run, however, P^* must converge to P. As this occurs, the labor supply curve shifts back to its original level and the normal or natural level of employment is restored. This model can also generate declines in employment in response to unanticipated declines in the price level.

○ The Search Model

The search model yields a similar result for cyclical movements in employment, although it also has direct implications for movement in the unemployment rate. Increases in wages associated with cyclical increases in demand result in both increases in participation rates as the labor supply curve shifts out and decreases in search unemployment as the NN curve moves closer to the N^d and N^s curves. These two effects are shown separately in Figures 17.6a and 17.6b.

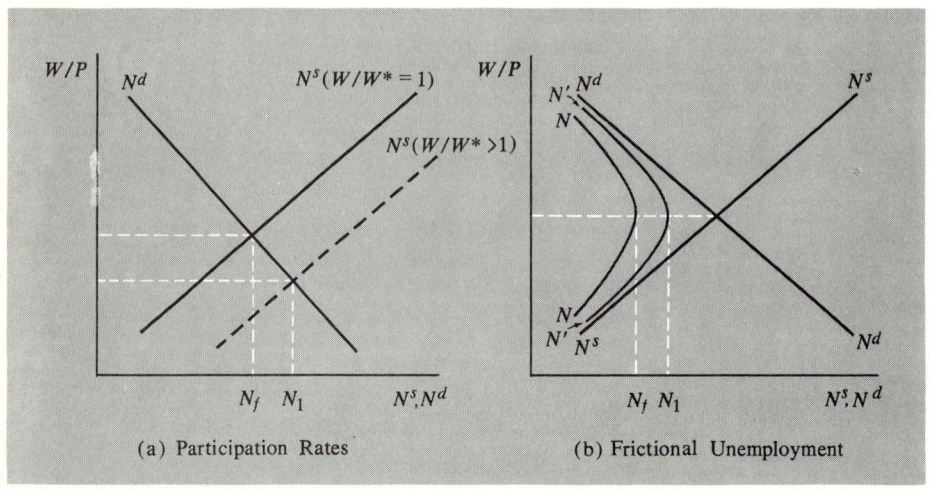

FIGURE 17.6
Search Theory and the Response of Employment to Changes in Aggregate Demand

An increase in aggregate demand puts upward pressure on wages and prices. As wages rise relative to reservation wage rates, some workers enter the labor force and begin to look for work. And the proportion of the labor force searching (unemployed) decreases as workers find that the duration of search required to obtain a wage at or above their reservation wage rate declines. The net result is an increase in employment and a decrease in the rate of frictional unemployment.

These responses in employment and unemployment are only temporary. Workers will eventually adjust their reservation wage rates to correctly reflect the overall level of the distribution of wage offers. When this occurs, participation rates and frictional unemployment will return to their normal levels.

○ Limitations of the Continuous Auction and Search Models

The search model undoubtedly accounts for a great deal of frictional unemployment and probably also explains some of the cyclical variation in unemployment that we observe. But it is not likely to be more than a minor source of the observed cyclical variation in unemployment rates. Both the continuous auction and search models yield predictions which are inconsistent with observed cyclical regularities in labor markets and fail to explain other regularities which appear to be essential to the cyclical behavior of unemployment.[8]

---

[8] For discussions of the limitations of the money illusion approach, see James Tobin, "How Dead is Keynes?" *Economic Inquiry*, Vol. XV (Oct., 1977), pp. 459–468; Herschel Grossman, "Aggregate Demand, Job Search, and Employment," *Journal of Political Economy*, Vol. 81 (November–December, 1973), pp. 1353–1369; and Franco Modigliani, "The Monetarist Controversy, or Should We Forsake Stabilization Policy," *American Economic Review*, Vol. 67 (March, 1977), pp. 1–19.

Chapter 17 • Response of Output and Employment to Aggregate Demand

1. The continuous auction model implies a negative association between changes in real wage rates and employment as the labor supply curve shifts along the fixed labor demand curve. The evidence, however, does not support this negative association.[9]
2. The continuous auction model does not directly explain cyclical variation in unemployment rates; it yields cyclical variation in employment via variation in labor supply rather than via variation in unemployment.
3. Neither the continuous auction nor search models are consistent with the observed *decline* in quits during cyclical increases in unemployment. Both models predict increases in quits in response to declines in aggregate demand.
4. Neither continuous auction nor search models are consistent with the important role of layoffs during cyclical declines in aggregate demand. Cyclical declines in aggregate demand are characterized by layoffs unaccompanied by nominal wage reductions.[10]

---

[9] See the studies by John Dunlop, "The Movement of Real and Money Wage Rates," *Economic Journal*, Vol. 48 (September, 1938), pp. 413–434; and Ronald G. Bodkin, "Real Wages and Cyclical Variations in Employment: A Reexamination of the Evidence," *Canadian Journal of Economics*, Vol. 2 (August, 1969), pp. 353–374.

[10] For evidence on the importance of layoffs, see Martin Feldstein, "Temporary Layoffs in the Theory of Unemployment," *Journal of Political Economy*, Vol. 84 (June, 1976), pp. 937–957.

Part IV • Refinements of the Real Sector: Aggregate Supply

APPENDIX

A The Sources of Economic Growth

We introduced the concept of potential output (X_p) in Chapter 3. We defined potential output as the output the economy could produce if its labor force and capital stock were "fully" employed. Defining full employment as the equilibrium level of employment, we can use the production function to determine the level of output corresponding to the existing capital stock ($\bar{K}$) and level of technology (t) and the full employment level of labor input (N_f):

$$X_p = F(\bar{K}, N_f, t). \tag{17A.1}$$

From this equation, the sources of growth in potential output can be identified: growth in the full employment rate of labor services, growth in the capital stock, and improvement in technology.

To calculate the economy's trend rate of growth in output, we eliminate cyclical movements in output by holding the level of labor force utilization constant at its full employment level. We can then relate the trend rate of growth in output (the rate of growth in potential output) to the rate of growth in the full employment level of labor services, the rate of growth in the capital stock, and the rate of improvement in technology.

The Growth of Full Employment Labor Services

Recall from the previous chapter that we can write person-hours of labor services (N), the labor input variable in the production function, as the product of population (POP); the labor force participation rate (β), the percentage of the population in the labor force; the employment rate (e), the percentage of the labor force employed; and average hours per worker (h).

$$N = h \cdot e \cdot \beta \cdot POP \tag{17A.2}$$

The rate of growth of labor services is equal to the sum of the rates of growth of h, e, β, and POP.

$$\dot{N}/N = \dot{h}/h + \dot{e}/e + \dot{\beta}/\beta + \dot{POP}/POP \tag{17A.3}$$

where $\dot{N}/N$, etc., are the percentage rates of growth in person-hours of labor services, etc.[1]

---

[1] To derive equation (17A.3) from equation (17A.2), take logs of equation (17A.2),

$$\log N = \log h + \log e + \log \beta + \log POP,$$

and then take first differences. The change in the log of a variable is approximately a percentage change. To derive the exact expression, as opposed to approximation, take time derivatives of the logarithmic transformation of equation (17A.2).

e is, of course, simply $1 - u$. We are interested in the rate of growth of potential output; we therefore assume e fixed at $e_f = 1 - u_f$ and calculate trend rates of growth for the remaining variables.[2] As we noted in the previous chapter, the level of the labor force participation rate (β) and of average hours per worker (h) depend on both cyclical and secular forces. We can capture the influence of secular and cyclical factors on the labor force participation rate and average hours by writing each as a function of the unemployment rate and a time trend:

$$\beta = \beta(u,t) \tag{17A.4}$$

$$h = h(u,t). \tag{17A.5}$$

The unemployment rate is a proxy for all cyclical influences on β and h. To isolate the secular trend in these variables, we hold the unemployment variable in the β and h functions at its full employment level and calculate the secular changes in β and h by letting t vary. The main source of increase in full employment labor services has been the growth in the population, about 1.25 percent a year over the last couple of decades.

The Rate of Growth of Labor Productivity

We can complete the determination of the trend rate of growth in output by calculating the rate of growth of the capital stock, determining the rate of improvement in technology, and using an estimated aggregate production function to find the rate of increase in output associated with the growth of inputs and of technology. An alternative approach is to write output as person-hours of labor services times labor productivity (output per person-hour of labor services, $\rho = X/N$)

$$X = N \cdot \rho, \tag{17A.6}$$

and express the rate of growth of output as the sum of the rate of growth of labor services and the rate of growth of productivity:

$$\dot{X}/X = \dot{N}/N + \dot{\rho}/\rho. \tag{17A.6'}$$

This approach is convenient because it makes it unnecessary to estimate the production function itself. Given the lack of agreement on the nature of the production function as well as problems associated with measuring both capital and technological change, this is generally regarded as a considerable advantage. The effects of growth in the capital stock and technical change will be reflected in the growth in productivity. Like β and h, ρ depends on both cyclical and secular forces. Therefore, we can express ρ as a function of u and time:

$$\rho = \rho(u,t). \tag{17A.7}$$

Setting $u = u_f$ and letting t vary, we can calculate the secular trend in ρ from equation (17A.7).

---

[2] To simplify the exposition, we will treat u_f as a constant. As we noted in the previous chapter, however, there is general agreement that secular trends in the demographic composition of the labor force over the last ten years have increased the normal level of frictional unemployment and hence u_f.

The evidence indicates that productivity increased at about a 2.75 percent rate during the 1950s and 1960s, and at a slower 2.5 percent rate since about 1969. There is fairly widespread agreement that potential output grew at a 3.5 percent rate in the 1952–1962 period and at a 3.75 percent rate in the 1963–1968 period, with the increase due to an increase in the rate of growth of labor force. The rate of growth in potential output since 1968 and the prospects over the coming decade are the subject of some controversy, with estimates ranging from 3.25 percent to 4.0 percent.[3]

APPENDIX

B Cyclical Movements in Employment and Output: Okun's Law

We now turn to the cyclical relation between output and employment. We noted above that output can be expressed as the product of person-hours of labor services and labor productivity, and that person-hours of labor services can be expressed as the product of the employment rate, the participation rate, hours per worker, and population. Therefore, we can write output in terms of e, h, β, ρ, and POP

$$X = h \cdot e \cdot \beta \cdot \rho \cdot POP \tag{17B.1}$$

and the rate of change in output as

$$\dot{X}/X = \dot{h}/h + \dot{e}/e + \dot{\beta}/\beta + \dot{\rho}/\rho + \dot{POP}/POP. \tag{17B.1'}$$

We now want to examine the relation between cyclical movements in the unemployment rate and output. It appears from equation (17B.1') that the relation is quite simple: a 1 percent increase in employment (a 1 percentage-point decrease in the unemployment rate) appears to be associated with a 1 percent increase in output. But this assumes that h, β, ρ, and POP are unchanged. In fact, as e varies cyclically, h, β, and ρ also change. Indeed, we expressed each of these variables above as functions of the unemployment rate, and we noted in the previous chapter that the empirical evidence suggests that cyclical declines in the employment rate are associated with declines in labor productivity, participation rates, and hours per worker.

The decline in productivity reflects the fact that firms tend to cut back employment less than in proportion to declines in output during a recession in order to avoid the costs associated with firing and then hiring back the workers when the recession is over. Those workers in whom the firm has made a sizable investment in training, and who might quickly find employment elsewhere if laid off, are the most likely to be retained as output declines. Therefore, productivity declines during recessions (as output falls more rapidly than employment) and rises during expansions. During recessions, moreover, overtime is reduced and the proportion

---

[3] See, for example, the papers by George Perry and Peter Clark in *U.S. Productive Capacity: Estimating the Utilization Gap*, Center for the Study of American Business, Washington University, December, 1977.

of workers forced into part-time work increases, so that h also declines. Finally, during periods when the unemployment rate increases, the difficulty in finding jobs discourages some members of the labor force from continuing to look for work and encourages others not currently in the labor force to delay entry. Therefore, the labor force participation rate declines when u increases and increases when u declines. A decline in e by 1 percent is typically associated with declines in ρ by 1 percent and declines in β and h totalling another 1 percent. Hence, each 1 percent reduction in e relative to e_f is associated with about a 3 percent decline in X relative to X_p.

Arthur Okun has directly estimated this relationship between movements in output and unemployment.[1] He tried a variety of different equations to express this relationship, generally of the form

$$\Delta u = -b \% \Delta X. \tag{17B.2}$$

Okun estimated b to be about .30. This implies that each 1 percentage-point increase in the growth rate of output (relative to potential output) reduces the unemployment rate by a little under one-third of a percentage point. Alternatively, we can write

$$\% \Delta X = -\frac{1}{b}\Delta u; \tag{17B.2'}$$

each 1 percentage-point reduction in the unemployment rate requires about a 3.2 percentage-point increase in the level of output.[2] This relationship between cyclical variation in output and unemployment has become known as *Okun's Law*.

Okun's Law is often expressed as a relation between the *GNP* gap, the percentage difference between potential and actual levels of output, and the difference between actual and full employment rates of unemployment.

$$\frac{X_p - X}{X} = 0.032(u - u_f).\text{[3]} \tag{17B.3}$$

According to this specification, if u exceeds u_f by 2 percentage points, potential output must exceed actual output by 6.4 percent.[4] This specification also highlights the fact that actual output must expand at the rate at which potential output is growing just to maintain the unemployment rate at an unchanged level. If potential output increases at a 4 percent rate per year, unemployment will rise if actual output grows at a rate less than 4 percent. To reduce unemployment by 1 percentage point over a year, output must increase by 7.2 percent: 4 percent to match the growth in potential output and 3.2 percent to allow a 1 percentage-point decline in the unemployment rate.

---

[1] Arthur Okun, "Potential *GNP*: Its Measurement and Significance," *1962 Proceedings* of the Business and Economics Statistics Section of the American Statistical Association.

[2] Okun based the 3.2 figure on evidence from a number of equations of the general form of equation (17B.2').

[3] This equation follows directly from equation (17B.2'). Substitute $(u - u_f)$ for Δu and $(X_p - X)/X$ for $\% \Delta X$.

[4] This equation can in turn be transformed into an expression for the level of potential output in terms of X, u, and u_f; $X_p = X[1 + 0.032(u - u_f)]$, permitting us to calculate the level of X_p, given the values of X and u and the assumed level of u_f.

Part IV • Refinements of the Real Sector: Aggregate Supply

● REVIEW QUESTIONS

1. "Disequilibrium in the labor market is possible even if the real wage is at a level consistent with equilibrium." Explain.

2. Explain the sources of downward wage inflexibility.

3. "The problem of demand deficiency unemployment is not a problem of the failure of relative prices to adjust (the nominal wage relative to the price level) but of the absolute level of (wages and) prices to adjust." Comment.

4. "There can be no systematic relationship between changes in aggregate demand and changes in employment if the labor market clears continuously." Comment.

5. Discuss some of the shortcomings of the money illusion theories of the cyclical variation in unemployment.

*6. What are the major sources of economic growth?

*7. What accounts for the fact that a 1 percent decline in employment reduces output by over 3 percent? Shouldn't there be a one-to-one correspondence between the rate of changes in the employment rate and output?

● PROBLEM

Keynes suggested that wage declines might result in proportional changes in the price level and no increase in employment and output. Use mathematical analysis of aggregate supply and demand curves to derive the multipliers for the response of prices and output to a decline in the nominal wage rate. What restrictions on parameter values are required to obtain the results suggested as a possibility by Keynes? You may use the specification of the aggregate supply and demand curves given by equations (11.2) and (11.6), respectively. Note, however, that the solution requires the use of calculus due to the nonlinear specification of the aggregate supply curve.

---

* The information necessary for solving these problems or questions can be found in the appendices.

Chapter 18
The Phillips Curve

In this chapter we refine our analysis of inflation, building on the analysis of inflation in Chapters 9 and 11 and the labor market analysis in Chapter 16. In the first section we review the theory of inflation implicit in the classical model presented in Chapter 9. This model allows for inflation only when there is excess demand in the commodity market and does not permit any trade-off between unemployment and inflation. Thus, this model cannot explain either the apparent trade-off between unemployment and inflation during the 1950s and 1960s or the simultaneous existence of inflation and high unemployment experienced in our two most recent recessions.

In the second section we develop the theoretical underpinnings and macroeconomic implications of the Phillips curve, the relation between wage change and unemployment, named after A. W. Phillips, who first noted the empirical regularity between inflation and unemployment.[1] According to the "traditional" specification discussed in the second section, there is an inflationary bias in the economy and a stable trade-off between unemployment and inflation. This specification is consistent with the observed relation between inflation and unemployment in the 1950s and 1960s, but breaks down in the 1970s.

In the third section we develop an alternative specification of the Phillips curve, the natural rate version, which introduces inflation expectations as an essential feature of the inflation process. This section develops the implications for the theory of inflation of the continuous auction and search models of labor supply introduced in the previous chapter. Like the classical model, there is a unique equilibrium level of output and employment in the natural rate model. Unlike the classical model, the natural rate model allows for the possibility of a constant rate of inflation at the full employment level of output and employment, and for a temporary trade-off between inflation and unemployment.

---

[1] A. W. Phillips, "The Relation Between Unemployment and the Rate of Change of Money Wage Rates in the United Kingdom, 1862–1957," *Economica*, Vol. 25 (November, 1958), pp. 283–299.

In Appendix A we consider a variety of eclectic specifications which combine features of both the traditional and natural rate versions. In Appendix B we discuss the modeling of expectations. In addition to a more detailed treatment of the adaptive expectations model that we employ in the chapter, we introduce an alternative approach, the rational expectations model.

THE CLASSICAL ADJUSTMENT MECHANISM

The classical adjustment mechanism introduced in Chapter 9 relates the rate of inflation ($\dot{P}$) to excess demand in the commodity market; i.e.,

$$\dot{P} = \alpha(X^d - X_f). \tag{18.1}$$

Equation (18.1) is simply the aggregate version of the disequilibrium mechanism we expect in each of the goods markets in the economy: prices vary in proportion to excess demand. This relation is depicted in Figure 18.1.

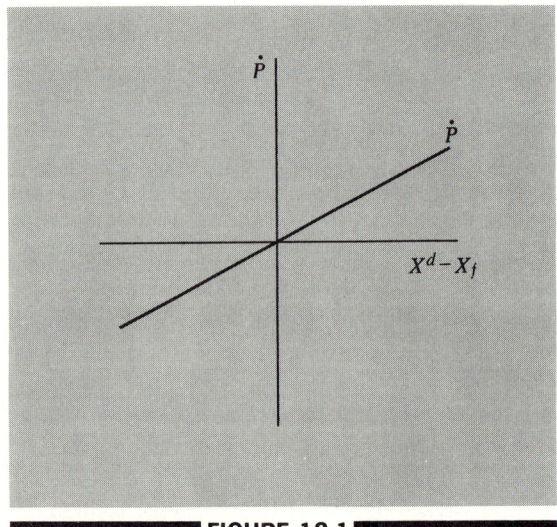

FIGURE 18.1
The Classical Model of Inflation

In the classical model specification, inflation occurs only when the demand for output (X^d) exceeds the productive capacity of the economy (X_f); thus, *inflation requires simultaneous excess demand in the commodity market*. The unique equilibrium level of output (X_f) is compatible with price level stability. If demand exceeds X_f, inflation results, but output cannot expand beyond X_f. Therefore, there is *no trade-off* between inflation and output or employment. Output is at its full employment level (X_f) throughout the range where $\dot{P} > 0$. When aggregate demand falls below X_f, prices fall at a rate proportional to the excess supply. Thus, *inflation cannot exist simultaneously with excess supply* in the commodity and labor markets; the model cannot, therefore, explain recent experiences in which high rates of inflation have been accompanied by substantial economic slack.

Recall from our discussion in Chapter 9 that in the classical model, *inflation cures itself for any once-and-for-all change in an exogenous variable.* The rise in price level lowers the real money supply, raising the real interest rate until aggregate demand declines to the level of potential output where the price level stabilizes. Thus, continuing inflation requires continuing changes in some exogenous variable. We also distinguished inflations associated with continuing monetary and continuing real disturbances. *A rate of monetary growth in excess of the rate of growth in the economy's potential output results in a constant inflation rate at stable interest rates and output.* A 10 percent rate of monetary growth will result in a 10 percent rate of inflation in our model where potential output is constant.[2] This follows from our analysis in Chapter 9 where we found that (1) there is a proportional relation between changes in the money supply and prices (the quantity theory of money) and (2) the real interest rate is invariant with respect to changes in the money supply (neutrality). Nominal rates rise, once-and-for-all, by the increase in the rate of expected inflation and thereafter remain stable.

Continuing changes in real sector variables are also a potential source of inflation. However, the nature of the system's response to continuing real sector disturbances differs dramatically from that associated with continuing monetary change. Whereas the real interest rate and the composition of output remain constant during an inflation generated by monetary change, *the real interest rate rises continuously during an inflation generated by continuing increases in real aggregate demand* and the composition of output continuously changes. This property of an inflation generated by continuing real sector disturbances holds in all the specifications of the Phillips curve that we will consider in this chapter. Hereafter, when discussing the consequences of a continuing inflation, we will focus exclusively on inflation generated by monetary growth.

THE TRADITIONAL SPECIFICATION OF THE PHILLIPS CURVE

In 1958 Phillips noted the negative association between the rate of wage change and the rate of unemployment in the U.K.[3] This relationship, now referred to as the Phillips curve, was verified for the U.S. by Paul Samuelson and Robert Solow,[4] and its theoretical underpinnings were first developed by Robert Lipsey.[5] The Phillips curve is now just as standard a component of large-scale econometric models as the consumption function. In this section we will first discuss the theory underlying

---

[2] If potential output is growing over time, a positive rate of monetary growth will be required to accommodate this real growth at an unchanged price level. The relation between the monetary growth and real growth will depend on the income elasticity of the demand for money.

[3] A. W. Phillips, *loc. cit.*

[4] Paul Samuelson and Robert Solow, "Analytical Aspects of Anti-Inflationary Policy," *American Economic Review,* Vol. 50 (May, 1960), pp. 177–194.

[5] Robert Lipsey, "The Relation Between Unemployment and the Rate of Change of Money Wage Rates in the United Kingdom, 1862–1957: A Further Analysis," *Economica,* Vol. 27 (February, 1960), pp. 1–31.

the Phillips curve and the precise specification of the traditional version, the version that dominated macroeconomic analysis through the 1960s. Then we will appraise the quantitative nature of the trade-off, based on data in the early postwar period, and discuss the macroeconomic implications of this specification of the Phillips curve. We conclude the section by comparing the relation between unemployment and inflation in the 1970s with the relation that prevailed through the mid-1960s.

○ The Specification of the Phillips Curve

The Phillips curve is a hypothesis about the response of the nominal wage rate to labor market disequilibrium, where the latter is proxied by the unemployment rate. In the absence of disequilibrium, nominal wages should increase to reflect the secular rise in labor productivity and to offset the effect of rising prices on the real wage rate. A full specification of the wage adjustment equation should therefore include three elements: a productivity component, a disequilibrium component, and an inflation component. For example,

$$\dot{W} = \rho + h(N^d - N^s) + \dot{P}^e \qquad (18.2)$$

where $\dot{W}$ is the rate of change in the nominal wage rate, ρ is the rate of change in labor productivity, and $\dot{P}^e$ is the expected rate of change in the price level; all the rates of change are percentage rates. Note that, according to equation (18.2), if the labor market is in equilibrium ($N^d = N^s$) and inflation is fully anticipated ($\dot{P} = \dot{P}^e$), then the real wage rate will rise at the rate of increase in labor productivity, provided that $h(0) = 0$.

The precise specification of the function relating labor market disequilibrium to wage changes is the main task of this section. To simplify the discussion, we will assume that labor productivity is constant, permitting us to drop the ρ term in equation (18.2). In addition, we will initially disregard the response of nominal wages to expected increases in the price level. The role of expected inflation will be discussed in detail in the next section. Although early expositions of the Phillips curve often mentioned inflation expectations as an influence on wage changes, both empirical work and discussions of the macro implications of the Phillips curve initially tended to ignore the influence of inflation expectations. In this section, therefore, our point of departure is a simple relation between the rate of change of nominal wages and the degree of excess demand in the labor market:

$$\dot{W} = h(N^d - N^s). \qquad (18.2')$$

Equation (18.2') is simply a market disequilibrium equation; it indicates that the price in this market responds to the market disequilibrium. Up to this point, market disequilibrium equations have always had the following properties: prices (or output) rise when there is excess demand, fall with excess supply, and remain constant when there is equilibrium in the market. This property is generally imposed by making the price or output change strictly proportional to the excess demand gap; in the case of equation (18.2'), h could be specified as a positive constant.[6] In

---

[6] All that is required to obtain the usual implications, however, is that $h(0) = 0$ and $h' > 0$.

this case, $\dot{W} = 0$ when $N^d = N^s$ and $\dot{W} \gtreqless 0$ as $N^d \gtreqless N^s$. The essential feature of the traditional specification is that these properties do not all hold; in particular, the economy has an *inflationary bias* so that wages are increasing when the supply and demand for labor are equal. Two features of the traditional specification account for this inflationary bias: the existence of nonlinear wage adjustment functions in individual labor markets and the aggregation of individual wage adjustment functions when excess demand is not uniformly distributed among the individual labor markets.

Nonlinear Wage Adjustment in Each Labor Market. There are multiple labor markets so that an aggregate wage change equation can only be derived by aggregating the individual wage adjustment functions. Wage behavior in each of these markets is governed by a wage adjustment function which relates the rate of change in the nominal wage rate to disequilibrium in that labor market, and each of these wage adjustment functions is assumed to be nonlinear.[7] If the wage adjustment function is linear, as depicted in Figure 18.2, the rate of change in the nominal wage rate is directly proportional to the level of excess demand. In particular, the rate of increase in the nominal wage rate associated with a given excess demand is exactly the same as the rate of decrease associated with an equivalent sized excess supply; i.e., *wages respond symmetrically to excess supply and demand*. Thus, in Figure 18.2, when excess demand is x, $\dot{W} = y$; when excess demand is $-x$ (excess supply is x), $\dot{W} = -y$.

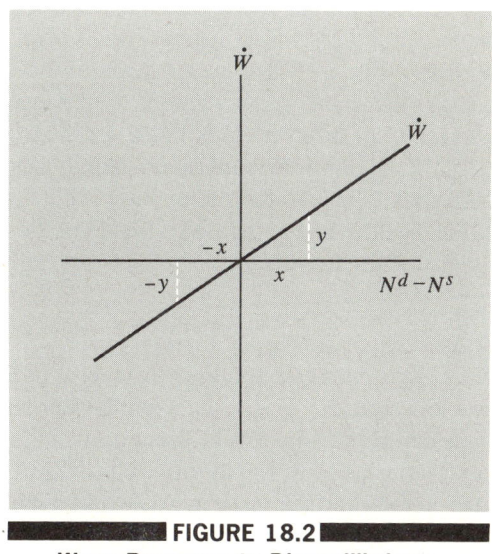

FIGURE 18.2
Wage Response to Disequilibrium: The Symmetric Case

Two specifications of the nonlinear wage adjustment function are depicted in Figures 18.3a and 18.3b. In Figure 18.3a the slope of the wage adjustment function

---

[7] Our treatment differs from Lipsey's in one important respect. Lipsey assumes wages respond linearly to excess demand and introduces the nonlinearity in the relation between unemployment and excess demand for labor. We introduce the nonlinearity immediately in the relation between wage change and excess demand. Although derived with this difference, the essential properties of the resulting Phillips curve are the same as in Lipsey's development.

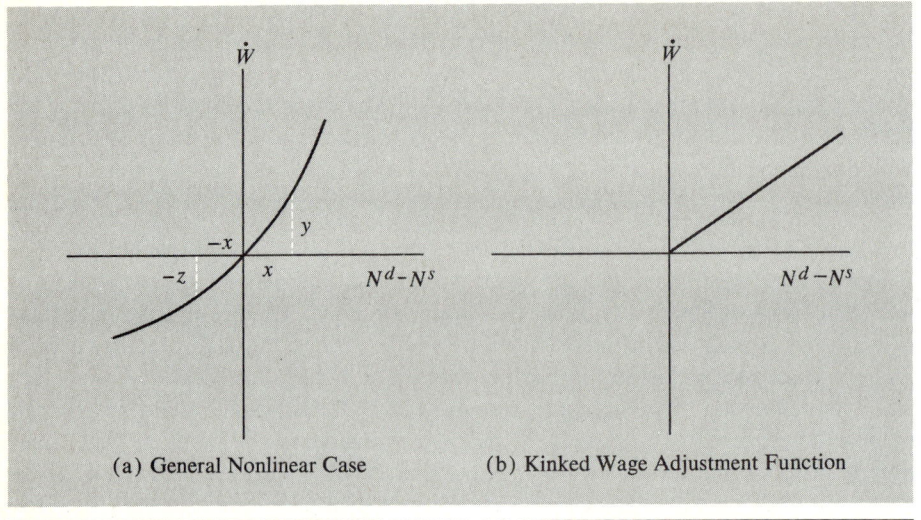

FIGURE 18.3
The Wage Adjustment Relation: The Case of Asymmetries

increases as $N^d - N^s$ increases. Therefore, *wages respond asymmetrically to excess demand and supply*; in particular, wages increase more rapidly in excess demand than they decline in excess supply. When excess demand is x in Figure 18.3a, $\dot{W} = y$; and when excess supply is x, $\dot{W} = -z$ where $z < y$. A special case of nonlinear wage adjustment is where wage adjustment is linear for situations of excess demand and zero for situations of equilibrium and excess supply; this case is depicted in Figure 18.3b and corresponds to the Keynesian case where wages are rigid in the downward direction but flexible in the upward direction. We will refer to this case as the *kinked wage adjustment function*.

Aggregation and the Role of Dispersion of Unemployment Among Individual Labor Markets. Although each labor market is assumed to have a nonlinear wage adjustment function which passes through the origin, aggregation across the individual labor markets yields an aggregate wage adjustment function which is shifted up vertically relative to the individual market adjustment curves, provided that unemployment is not equally distributed among all the labor markets. In Figure 18.4 we depict the aggregate function based on individual functions of the type pictured in Figure 18.3b. The vertical intercept, v, is a function of the dispersion of excess supply throughout the various labor markets. When excess supply is proportionally distributed so that excess supply or demand is the same in all markets, $v = 0$, the aggregate curve passes through the origin, and the aggregate and individual wage adjustment functions are identical. The greater the unevenness of the distribution of excess supply and excess demand, the larger is v, and the greater is the vertical displacement of the aggregate curve relative to the individual curves.

To clarify the derivation of the aggregate relation, assume there are two labor markets, each with a kinked nonlinear wage adjustment function. Assume there is

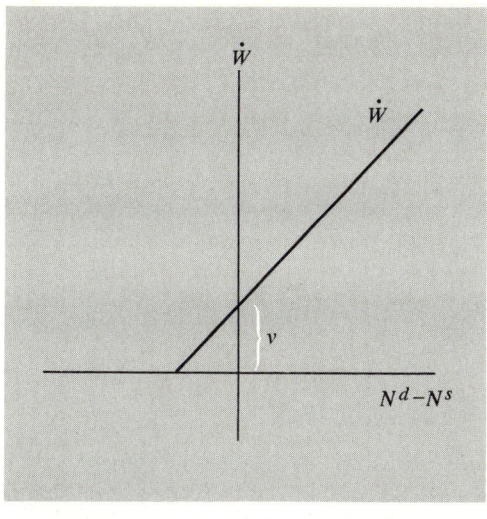

FIGURE 18.4
The Aggregate Wage Adjustment Function

excess demand equal to x in one market and excess supply of x in the other. In the aggregate, there is a balance between supply and demand; i.e., the excess supply (unemployment in excess of vacancies) in one market is just balanced by an excess of unfilled vacancies over unemployment in the other market. In the market where there is excess demand, $\dot{W} = y$; in the market with excess supply, $\dot{W} = 0$. Assuming the two markets are of equal size, in the aggregate, $\dot{W} = v = \frac{1}{2} y > 0$. Thus, wages are increasing even though, in the aggregate, $N^d = N^s$. Note, however, that if excess demand equals x in both markets, the aggregate rate of wage inflation will equal the common rate of wage inflation in both labor markets, y.

We can express this aggregate wage adjustment function as

$$\dot{W} = v + \alpha(N^d - N^s) \tag{18.3}$$

where α is some positive constant and the v term reflects the implication of asymmetry in response of wages to excess demand and supply; if this is derived from kinked wage adjustment functions, then $\dot{W} \geq 0$ is also imposed as a further restriction.

○ The Unemployment Rate as a Proxy for Excess Demand in the Labor Market

The excess demand for labor is not directly observable. Therefore, a proxy must be found for use in empirical studies. In Chapter 16 we noted that excess demand in the labor market could be measured by the difference between vacancies and unemployment; i.e., $N^d - N^s = V - U$. However, data on vacancies are not available either, at least for the U.S. Empirical studies of the Phillips curve usually proxy the excess demand for labor with the unemployment rate (u). This presumes that there is a stable relation between the two variables, which in turn will be true if

Part IV · Refinements of the Real Sector: Aggregate Supply

vacancies and unemployment are systematically related. Recall from Chapter 16 that empirical analysis of the movements of V and U does reveal a systematic inverse relation, which we captured by specifying $VU = k$. Therefore, $V = k/U$ and

$$N^d - N^s = V - U = k/U - U \tag{18.4}$$

so that we can expect a systematic relation between excess demand for labor and the unemployment rate[8] and proxy the excess demand in the labor market with the unemployment rate.

The unemployment specification of the wage adjustment equation can be written as

$$\dot{W} = v + g(u) \tag{18.5}$$

where $g_u < 0$. Thus, a decrease in the unemployment rate is associated with an increase in the rate of wage change. This is the type of equation estimated, for example, by Lipsey and discussed by Samuelson and Solow.

The relationship between excess demand and unemployment should be quite nonlinear, particularly at low rates of unemployment. After all, the minimum possible unemployment rate is zero while excess demand can become indefinitely large. The minimum level of unemployment may be larger than zero. In Figure 18.5 we show the relation between unemployment and excess demand becoming asymptotic to the dashed line at a positive rate of unemployment, $0A$. If we view frictional unemployment as institutionally determined and independent of the demand for labor, the curve in Figure 18.5 would become vertical at point B instead of point A. As it is drawn in Figure 18.5, we have allowed for excess demand to lower the unemployment rate below the frictional level associated with the equality of supply and demand for labor. In this case, we can observe unemployment rates below the level associated with $N^d = N^s(u_f)$ and proxy excess demand by the difference between the unemployment rate at full employment and the actual unemployment rate ($u_f - u$). Note also that even if the relation between wage change and excess demand is linear, the relation between wage change and unemployment will be nonlinear because of the nonlinearity of the relation between excess demand and the unemployment rate.

We will return to the importance of the nonlinearity of the Phillips curve in macroeconomic analysis below. For the moment, we will write the unemployment version of the Phillips curve as a linear relation to enable us to derive a simple expression for the relation between the full employment and noninflationary unemployment rates. Replacing the excess demand gap with the difference between the full employment and actual rates of unemployment and retaining the shift term v, we obtain

---

[8] Using $N^d - N^s \equiv V - U$, we can derive an aggregate Phillips curve with an inflationary bias by assuming that wages respond asymmetrically to vacancies and unemployment; i.e., wages rise more rapidly in response to vacancies than they fall in response to unemployment. This allows us to write

$$\dot{W} = \alpha V - \beta U$$

where $\alpha > \beta$. Note that when $V = U$ ($N^d = N^s$), $\dot{W} = \alpha - \beta > 0$.

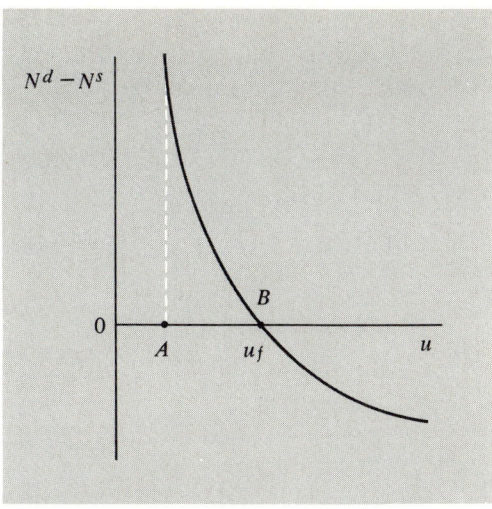

FIGURE 18.5
The Relation Between Excess Demand for Labor and the Unemployment Rate

$$\dot{W} = v + \beta(u_f - u) \tag{18.5'}$$

where we treat β as a positive constant.

We can derive from equation (18.5') the precise value of the unemployment rate required for wage stability by setting $\dot{W} = 0$ and solving for u:

$$u^* = u_f + v/\beta. \tag{18.6}$$

We refer to u^* as the *noninflationary rate of unemployment* (*NIRU*). The essential feature of the traditional Phillips curve is that $u^* > u_f$: wage stability requires an unemployment rate above that associated with full employment. For example, assuming the kinked wage adjustment function, unemployment must increase so that there are no markets in which excess demand prevails. Given the uneven distribution of unemployment, there must be many markets in which there is excess supply, and therefore $u > u_f$.

Given the definition of u^*, we can rewrite the Phillips curve as

$$\dot{W} = \beta(u^* - u) \tag{18.7}$$

where $\dot{W} = 0$ when $u = u^*$, and $\dot{W} \gtreqless 0$ as $u \lesseqgtr u^*$.

○ Completing the Price-Wage Sector: From Wages To Prices

To integrate the Phillips curve into our *IS-LM* framework, we must relate price change to wage change. Alternately, we could use the Phillips curve to endogenize the wage rate in the fixed wage specification of the aggregate supply curve developed in Chapter 11. Recall from our discussion in that chapter that wage change and price change are systematically related: prices either equal wages divided by the marginal product of labor (as in perfect competition) or are proportional to unit labor costs (as in the mark-up model where wages are treated as the only variable cost). In either case, we can specify the inflation rate as

$$\dot{P} = \dot{W} - \rho \tag{18.8}$$

where ρ is the rate of growth in labor productivity, and substitute the Phillips curve [equation (18.5')] for $\dot{W}$ in equation (18.8), yielding

$$\dot{P} = v + \beta(u_f - u) \tag{18.9a}$$

or

$$\dot{P} = \beta(u^* - u), \tag{18.9b}$$

assuming that $\rho = 0$.[9]

○ Early Empirical Evidence

Empirical studies in the early 1960s confirmed the existence of a stable trade-off between unemployment and inflation. The specification of the Phillips curve employed in empirical studies was generally of the form

$$\dot{W} = a + b\frac{1}{u} \tag{18.10}$$

where a and b are positive constants and $\dot{W}$ is the annual percentage change in the wage rate.

Figure 18.6 illustrates the nature of the trade-off suggested by the early postwar empirical evidence. Point A indicates that a 2–3 percent rate of wage change, the rate that just matches the secular rise in labor productivity and therefore is compatible with price level stability, requires a 5–6 percent rate of unemployment.[10] Relating $\dot{W}$ to one over the unemployment rate results in a nonlinear relation between $\dot{W}$ and u, as in Figure 18.6. As unemployment declines, $\dot{W}$ increases more than in proportion to the decline in u. To allow simple manipulation of the Phillips curve equation, we ignored this nonlinearity in our discussion above. However, the nonlinearity is of some importance in macroeconomic analyses employing the Phillips curve. At low unemployment rates, the increase in wage inflation required to reduce the unemployment rate by a given amount becomes quite large. At higher unemployment rates, on the other hand, the decline in wage inflation that can be attained by the

---

[9] Wage change is generally specified as depending on the *trend* rate of growth in labor productivity. Price change, on the other hand, is also influenced by movements in actual relative to trend growth in productivity. For example, during the early phase of cyclical increases in output, productivity tends to rise relative to its trend rate and, as a result, the rate of increase in both unit labor costs and the price level tends to slow relative to the rate of increase in wages.

[10] This is based on the discussion by Samuelson and Solow.

same size increase in the unemployment rate is much smaller. It is this property of the Phillips curve, the increasing sacrifice in terms of increased inflation as the unemployment rate is lowered, that underlies the Council of Economic Advisors' choice of 4 percent as the target unemployment rate in their 1962 annual report. The inflation-unemployment relation suggested by the early postwar evidence is depicted in Figure 18.7, which is adapted from Figure 2 in the Samuelson and Solow paper cited above. Price stability (point *A*) requires an unemployment rate of about 5.5 percent. To reduce the unemployment rate to 3 percent would require tolerating inflation at a rate of 4–5 percent per year. The CEA opted, however, for a target rate of unemployment in between points *A* and *B*: at point *C*, according to Samuelson and Solow, a 4 percent unemployment rate would entail an inflation rate just over 2 percent per year.

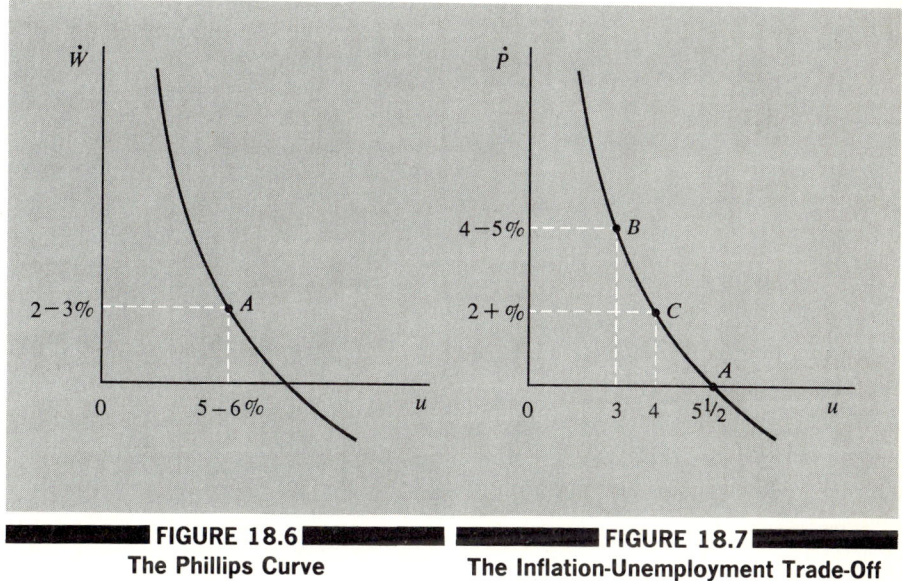

FIGURE 18.6
The Phillips Curve

FIGURE 18.7
The Inflation-Unemployment Trade-Off

Macroeconomic Implications of the Traditional Phillips Curve

The two essential features of the traditional specification of the Phillips curve are the existence of an *inflationary bias* and of a *stable trade-off* between inflation and the rate of unemployment.

The Inflationary Bias. We noted above that the noninflationary unemployment rate, u^*, exceeds the rate associated with full employment in the traditional specification: in particular, $u^* = u_f + v/\beta$ from equation (18.6). This means that there will be a steady rate of inflation when the economy is at full employment; from equation (18.9a), $\dot{P} = v$ when $u = u_f$. This is what we mean by an inflationary bias. The classical model allows for price stability at full employment, while the Phillips curve requires continuing inflation at full employment.

Integrating the Phillips Curve into the IS-LM Framework. To develop the macroeconomic implications of the Phillips curve, it is important to integrate it into our macroeconomic model. We begin with the fixed-price *IS-LM* framework in Figure 18.8a.

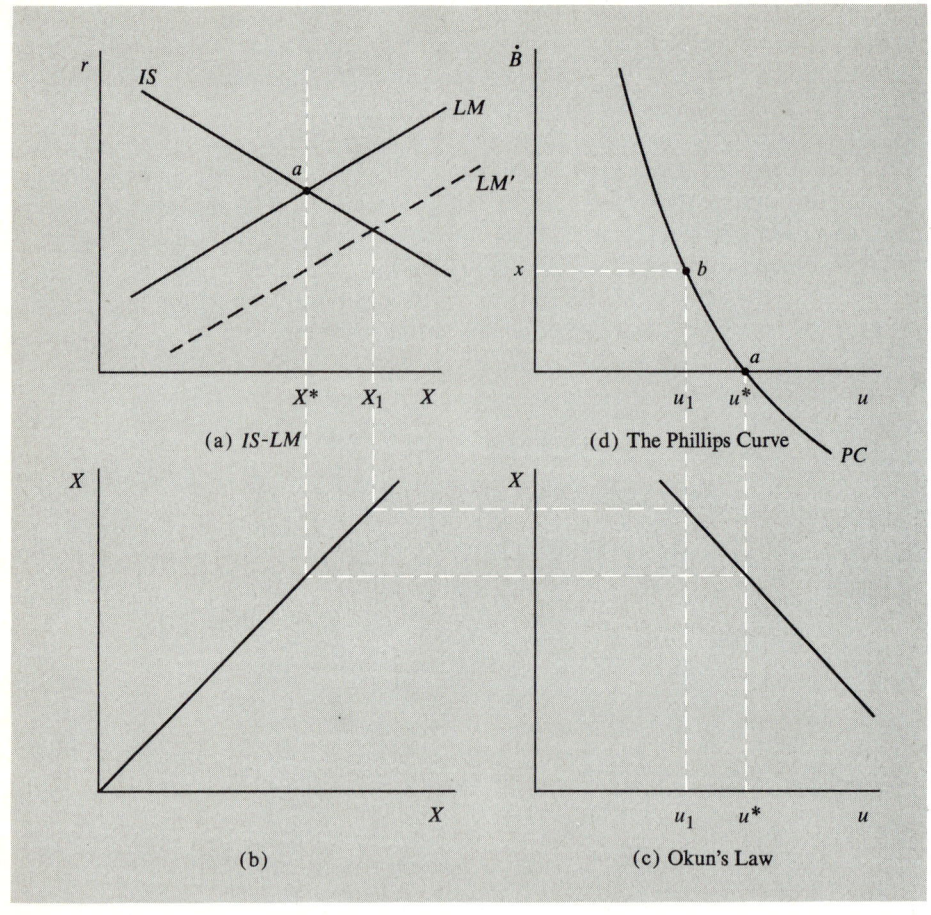

FIGURE 18.8
The Traditional Phillips Curve and *IS-LM* Analysis

Given the price level, the *IS* and *LM* curves determine the level of output. The level of output is in turn associated, via Okun's Law, with some rate of unemployment; this relation is depicted in Figure 18.8c. The Phillips curve in Figure 18.8d indicates the rate of inflation associated with the prevailing unemployment rate. If prices are stable at the prevailing unemployment rate, the *IS* and *LM* curves remain unchanged, and the system remains at the current level of output. This is the case at an output equal to X^* in Figure 18.8a; X^* is the level of output associated with the noninflationary rate of unemployment. If the unemployment rate falls below u^* (or equivalently, if the level of output rises above X^*), inflation will result. For example, if the money supply increases, shifting the *LM* curve to *LM'*, output will increase to X_1, unemployment will fall to u_1, and we will move up the Phillips curve from point *a* to point *b*. At the latter point, prices are rising. If $u_1 = u_f$ (so that $X_1 = X_f$), then the rate of inflation at full employment is x percent per year. This rate of inflation is a measure of the degree of inflationary bias associated with the Phillips curve. Note that some inflation remains as long as the unemployment rate is below u^*. Therefore, *inflation can coexist with excess supply* in the model, another reflection of the economy's inflationary bias.

The Self-Liquidating Nature of Inflation. As is true in the classical case, inflation cures itself for any once-and-for-all change in an exogenous variable. For example, beginning from the intersection of the *IS* and *LM* curves at point *a* in Figure 18.8a, let us sketch the responses to a once-and-for-all increase in the money supply. Initially, aggregate demand and output expand to X_1 and the unemployment rate falls to u_1. The resulting inflation, however, pushes the *LM* backward, and assuming the *IS* curve is unaffected, the *LM* curve will continue to move backward until it returns to its original position and output and the unemployment rate are restored to their noninflationary levels.

The Existence of a Stable Trade-Off. It is possible to maintain unemployment below u^* indefinitely by accepting a steady rate of inflation, and the lower the unemployment rate, the higher the corresponding rate of inflation. Thus, there exists a *stable trade-off between unemployment and inflation*, depicted by the Phillips curve in Figure 18.8d. Note, however, that to sustain this trade-off, inflation must persist at a constant rate. Any once-and-for-all disturbance, however, generates only a temporary reduction in unemployment until the inflation raises unemployment back to u^*. *A constant rate of monetary growth* (*in excess of growth in potential output*), *on the other hand, will produce a steady rate of inflation at constant interest rates, output, and unemployment.* To sustain an unemployment rate of u_1 consistent with X_1, policy must first shift the intersection of the *IS* and *LM* curves to X_1 (e.g., by a shift of the *LM* curve to *LM'* as in Figure 18.8); and then the monetary authorities must permit the money supply to grow at a rate just equal to the rate of inflation associated with u_1, according to Figure 18.8d, thereby maintaining the *LM* curve at *LM'*.

The Policy Dilemma: The Incompatibility of Full Employment and Price Stability. The policymakers would like to obtain *both* full employment and price stability. But the traditional Phillips curve indicates that these objectives cannot be simultaneously achieved. Policymakers must choose among the *feasible* combination of $\dot{P}$ and u, and the Phillips curve is the locus of all such feasible combinations; i.e., the policymakers must select a point along the stable trade-off depicted by the Phillips curve.

We can depict policymakers' preferences between unemployment and inflation by an indifference curve map. Their subjective preference function can be specified as

$$U = U(\dot{P}, u) \tag{18.11}$$

where $U_{\dot{P}}$ and U_u, the changes in utility associated with increased inflation and unemployment, respectively, are both negative; i.e., policymakers dislike both higher rates of inflation and higher unemployment. Therefore, the indifference curves in Figure 18.9 are negatively sloped; a decrease in unemployment increases utility, and to remain on the same indifference curve, inflation must increase.[11]

Note that utility increases as the indifference curves move toward the origin (i.e., toward lower values of inflation *and* unemployment). The concave shape of the indifference curves assumes a decreasing marginal rate of substitution between unemployment and inflation; i.e., the amount of additional inflation that policymakers are willing to accept to reduce the unemployment rate by a given amount declines the lower the unemployment rate and the higher the inflation rate.

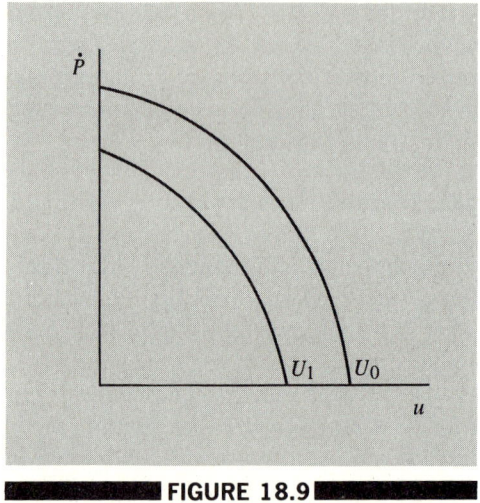

FIGURE 18.9
Indifference Curve Map of Preferences Between Unemployment and Inflation

We can now determine the *optimal trade-off*, given the knowledge of policymakers' preferences. This is depicted in Figure 18.10. Policymakers are assumed to maximize utility subject to the structure of the economy, as reflected in the Phillips curve. To do so, they try to move along the Phillips curve (the locus of all feasible combinations of $\dot{P}$ and u) to the point that is on the highest indifference curve (the indifference curve closest to the origin). As we have noted above, maintaining the economy at a point on the Phillips curve requires continuing policy action as long as $\dot{P} > 0$ (e.g., monetary growth at a rate equal to the desired rate of inflation). The 1962 Annual Report of the CEA indicates that this type of analysis resulted in the solution of a target unemployment rate of 4 percent and a willingness to tolerate the resulting inflation.

---

[11] We can derive the slope using calculus by totally differentiating the equation for an indifference curve,

$$\bar{U} = U(\dot{P}, u),$$

where $\bar{U}$ is a constant level of utility, and solving for $d\dot{P}/du$:

$$\frac{d\dot{P}}{du} = \frac{-U_u}{U_{\dot{P}}} < 0.$$

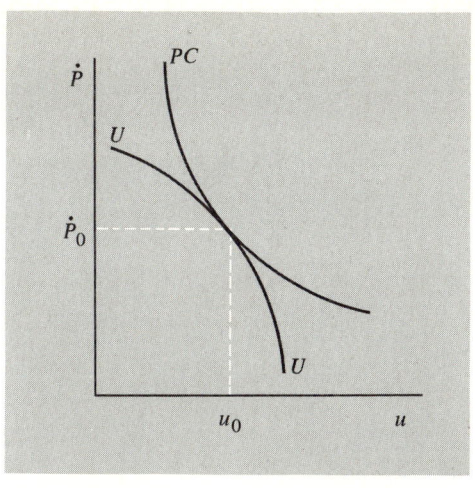

FIGURE 18.10
The Optimal Trade-Off Between Inflation and Unemployment

○ The Breakdown of the Traditional Phillips Curve in the 1970s

Data on inflation and unemployment from the mid-1950s through the late 1970s are plotted in Figure 18.11. The inflation rate is the annual percentage change in the implicit *GNP* price deflator. The curve is drawn freehand and seems to fit the data reasonably well through the 1960s. Thereafter, the simple inverse relation between unemployment and the rate of inflation breaks down. Figure 18.11 dramatically points out the inadequacy of the traditional specification. The natural rate view developed in the following section was developed during the late 1960s while the Phillips curve was performing quite well. This view of the inflation process suggested, however, that the trade-off implied by the traditional specification should turn out to be unstable. The evidence of the 1970s provided immediate confirmation of this prediction. We turn, therefore, to a discussion of the natural rate model.

○ **INFLATION EXPECTATIONS AND THE PHILLIPS CURVE—THE NATURAL RATE VIEW**

When we introduced the wage adjustment equation in the previous section, we noted that it should incorporate three components: the productivity, disequilibrium, and inflationary expectations components. To simplify the exposition, we ignored the productivity component, and we will continue to do so in this section. We also excluded the inflation expectations component and added an additional factor: the vertical shift term reflecting asymmetric wage response. In this section we eliminate the shift term (implicitly assuming symmetrical wage response) and reincorporate the inflation expectations term. The Phillips curve can now be written in the wage change form as

$$\dot{W} = \beta(u_N - u) + \dot{P}^e \qquad (18.12)$$

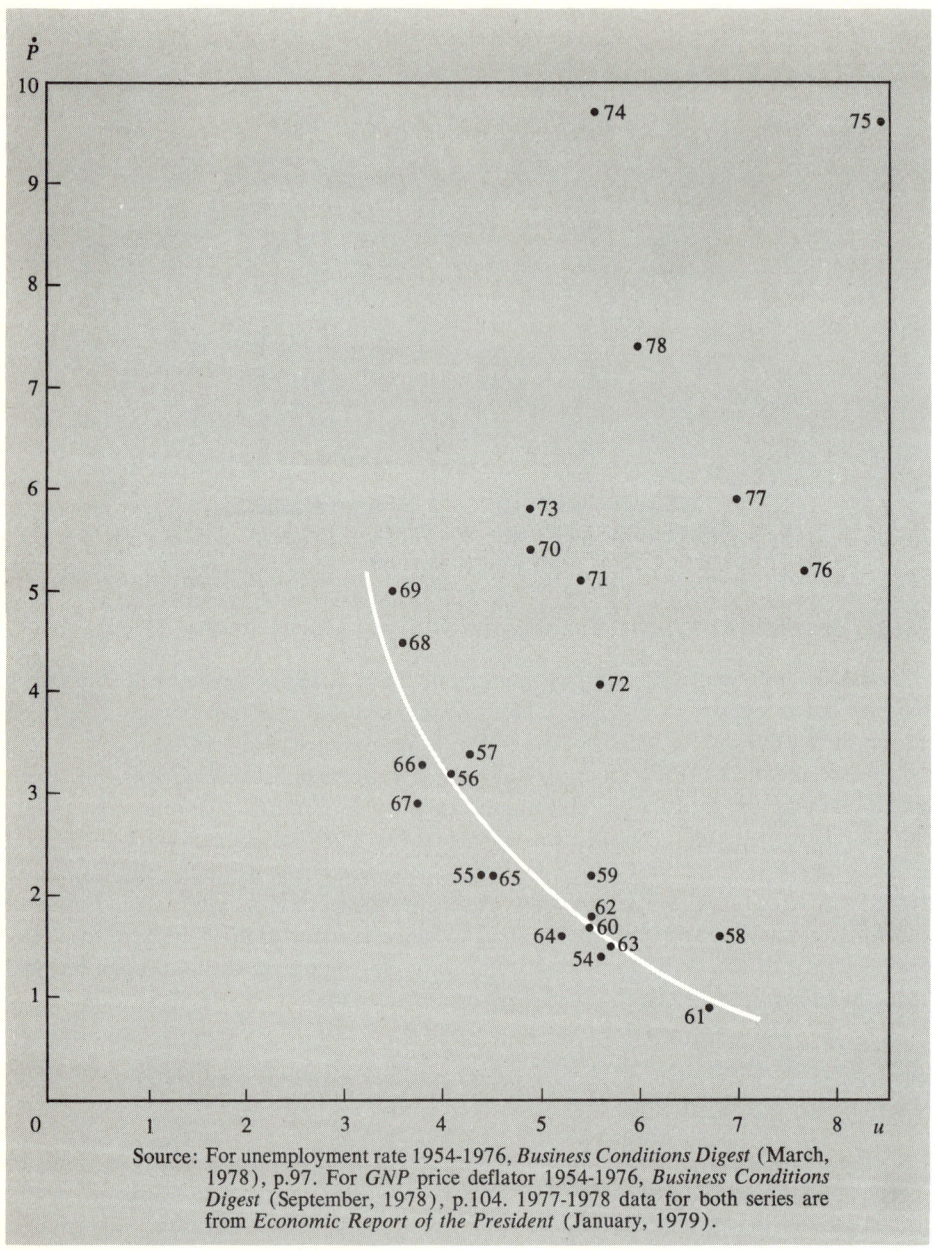

FIGURE 18.11

The Phillips Curve: The Breakdown of the Relation in the 1970s

or in its inflation rate form as

$$\dot{P} = \beta(u_N - u) + \dot{P}^e \qquad (18.13)$$

where we have designated the critical unemployment rate as u_N, the natural rate of unemployment. First, we will discuss the theory underlying this specification and then consider its macroeconomic implications.[12]

The Specification of the Natural Rate Phillips Curve

The essential assumptions underlying the natural rate specification are *symmetric wage responses* to excess supply and demand and the *absence of money illusion*. The first assumption implies the absence of a shift parameter related to the dispersion of unemployment. The second assumption implies both that the nominal wage change should reflect inflation expectations and that the coefficient of expected inflation should equal unity. Our discussion of the natural rate model builds on our discussion of the continuous auction and search models in Chapter 16. However, instead of *price level* expectations, we view economic agents as forming expectations about *inflation rates*.

The Natural Rate of Unemployment. The equilibrium unemployment rate in this model is designated as the *natural rate of unemployment*; this rate is "natural" in that it is determined by the natural forces of supply and demand, unlike the target unemployment rate of 4 percent based on the trade-off model discussed above. The distinguishing feature of the full employment rate we used in the previous section was the absence of excess supply or demand for labor at that rate. In the natural rate model, however, the labor market is viewed as clearing continuously. Although the supply and demand for labor are always equal and all unemployment is frictional, employment varies in response to unanticipated inflation. The distinguishing feature of the natural rate of unemployment is not, therefore, the absence of excess supply and involuntary unemployment, but rather the *absence of unanticipated inflation*. The natural rate is consistent with both sustained price level stability and with constant rates of inflation or deflation. Any other rate of unemployment must either be transitory or must be accompanied by accelerating inflation or deflation. The natural rate is therefore also referred to as the nonaccelerating inflation rate of unemployment (*NAIRU*).

The Influence of Inflation Expectations. We can also view the addition of an inflation expectations term as an extension of the traditional specification. Assuming that both the supply and demand for labor depend on the *real* wage rate, equilibrium in the labor market implies a particular real wage rate, and disequilibrium should put pressure on real wages. The traditional Phillips curve, however, relates nominal wage change to labor market disequilibrium. It is therefore incomplete.

Workers do not generally bargain directly over real wage rates.[13] Instead, they bargain for money wage rates that will apply over discrete intervals. In order to capture the influence of labor market disequilibrium on real wage rates, we must specify the response of nominal wage change to unemployment as being conditional on the expected behavior of prices over the period that the nominal wage will apply.

---

[12] The papers that developed the natural rate specification include: Milton Friedman, "The Role of Monetary Policy," *American Economic Review*, Vol. 58 (March, 1968); and the Phelps and Mortenson papers in Edmund S. Phelps, *et al.*, *Microeconomic Foundations of Employment and Inflation Theory* (New York: W. W. Norton & Company Inc., 1970).

[13] If labor contracts carried complete escalator clauses, then bargaining would relate directly to real wages. Although the proportion of the labor force covered by escalator clauses has increased rapidly, a small minority of workers are covered and the escalator clauses are always partial, allowing for nominal wage gains of only a fraction of price inflation over the life of the contract.

Therefore, we introduce the expected rate of inflation as an argument in the Phillips curve in equation (18.12). The rate of wage change associated with any unemployment rate now depends on the expected rate of inflation; thus, the expected inflation rate is, in effect, a shift parameter in the relation between nominal wage change and unemployment.

The Concept of Money Illusion and the Coefficient on the Rate of Expected Inflation.
The unitary coefficient on the inflation expectations term indicates that the real wage rate will not be affected by the rate of inflation if the inflation is fully anticipated. This means that workers will receive nominal wage gains that fully offset the rate of inflation as long as they correctly anticipate the inflation. This property of the natural rate version reflects the assumption that economic agents are free of money illusion. Decisions about real variables (such as the supply and demand for labor) depend exclusively on real variables (such as the real wage rate). If the coefficient of the expected inflation rate is unity, the real wage will rise by the rate of increase in labor productivity and will be completely independent of fully anticipated inflation.

Adaptive Expectations and Fooling. To complete the specification of the natural rate model, we must specify how economic agents form their expectations about the rate of inflation. The model of expectation formation we will employ is the same one we have employed previously to determine expected income in the life cycle model: the adaptive expectations model.[14]

According to the *adaptive expectations model*, the expected rate of inflation in period t (the rate at which prices are expected to change over the period) depends on a weighted average of past rates of inflation. We can write the expected rate of inflation ($\dot{P}_t^e$) as

$$\dot{P}_t^e = \sum_{i=1}^{n} w_i \dot{P}_{t-i} \qquad (18.14)$$

where w_i is the weight on the actual rate of inflation lagged i periods. The weights should decline with the lag, reflecting the presumption that more recent experience is more important in shaping expectations. The weights should also sum to one, insuring that the expected rate of inflation will ultimately converge to the actual inflation rate. A simple weighting pattern that has this property is the Koyck lag, in which the weights decline geometrically. In this case we can write equation (18.14) as

$$\dot{P}_t^e = \sum_{i=1}^{\infty} w(1-w)^i \dot{P}_{t-i} \qquad (18.14')$$

where w is a constant between zero and one. Although there is no money illusion in the long run (when inflation is fully anticipated), the adaptive expectations model allows for temporary money illusion in response to an increase in the inflation rate.

---

[14] In Appendix B at the end of this chapter, we discuss models of expectation formation in more detail.

This specification of the formation of expectations has two important properties:

1. Workers initially get fooled by an increase in the actual inflation rate. An increase in the actual rate of inflation results in a *gradual* rise in the expected rate of inflation so that a portion of any increase in the rate of inflation will be unanticipated for a period of time. This means that workers will initially fail to bargain for nominal wage gains which offset the actual rate of inflation so that the real wage rate will temporarily decline whenever the inflation rate *increases*. Firms will increase their demand for labor in response to the decline in the real wage rate. Workers, on the other hand, are *fooled* by the increase in nominal wages and prices: they perceive the real wage as rising and therefore increase their supply of labor and/or search for a shorter duration so that search unemployment declines. The net result is that both the demand and supply of labor, and hence employment, temporarily rise in response to an increase in the actual rate of inflation. The fact that real decisions are temporarily affected by nominal variables (i.e., the existence of temporary money illusion) is not attributed to the temporary absence of rational behavior. Instead, it is viewed as reflecting the existence of incomplete information when there are costs of acquiring that information.

2. There will be no unanticipated inflation once the actual rate stabilizes for some period. Because the expected rate of inflation will ultimately converge to the actual rate (given that the weights sum to one), workers will eventually correctly perceive the rate of inflation. When this occurs, all inflation is fully anticipated, and inflation has no effect on the real wage rate and therefore no effect on the supply or demand for labor or employment.

○ Macroeconomic Implications of the Natural Rate Version

The natural rate specification allows for a short-run trade-off between inflation and unemployment but no long-run trade-off. Labor market equilibrium is compatible with any constant rate of fully anticipated inflation, and any attempt to sustain an unemployment rate below the natural rate will result in accelerating inflation.

Labor Market Equilibrium and Fully Anticipated Inflation: The Vertical Phillips Curve. In the natural rate model, full labor market equilibrium requires that inflation be fully anticipated as well as that the supply and demand for labor be equal. This model assumes that the labor market clears continuously so that the supply and demand for labor are always equal. Full equilibrium is therefore identified with the condition that inflation be fully anticipated. Note from equation (18.13) that full equilibrium ($\dot{P} = \dot{P}^e$) can only occur at the natural rate of unemployment ($u = u_N$). Therefore, the combinations of unemployment and (fully anticipated) inflation compatible with full equilibrium are along a vertical line at the natural rate of unemployment in Figure 18.12. This is the long-run Phillips curve (*LRPC*). Because the expected rate will converge to the actual rate of inflation, the vertical long-run Phillips curve indicates there is *no long-run trade-off* between inflation and unemployment. Note, however, that full equilibrium at the natural rate is compatible with any rate of fully anticipated inflation (or deflation). In the long run, therefore, the Phillips curve does not uniquely determine the rate of inflation. This must be determined elsewhere in the model; for example, by the rate of growth in the money supply.

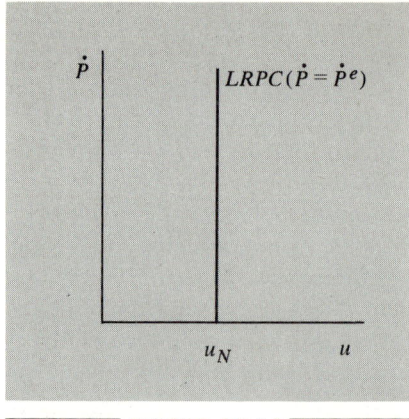

FIGURE 18.12
The Long-Run Phillips Curve Is Vertical

The Short-Run Trade-Off Between Unanticipated Inflation and Unemployment: The Fooling Hypothesis. Although the expected inflation rate ultimately converges to any constant rate of actual inflation, a change in the actual inflation rate will initially result in unanticipated inflation under the adaptive expectations formulation. Unanticipated inflation induces an increase in the supply of labor and/or a reduction in search unemployment, while the resulting decline in the real wage induces an increase in the demand for labor. Therefore, in the short run, an increase in the rate of inflation increases employment and reduces the unemployment rate. Although there is no long-run trade-off between (fully anticipated) inflation and unemployment, there is a short-run trade-off between (unanticipated) inflation and unemployment.

The response to an increase in the rate of inflation is depicted in Figure 18.13.

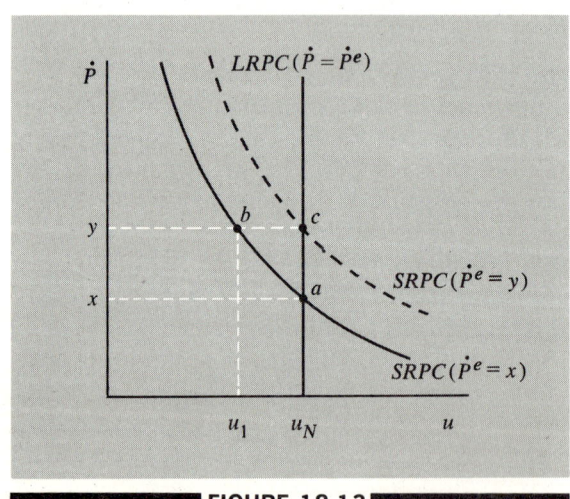

FIGURE 18.13
The Short-Run Trade-Off and
the Vertical Long-Run Phillips Curve

The long-run Phillips curve indicates the relation between the unemployment rate and the rate of inflation when all inflation is fully anticipated; therefore, $\dot{P} = \dot{P}^e$ all along the long-run Phillips curve ($LRPC$). The short-run Phillips curve ($SRPC$), on the other hand, is defined for a specific expected rate of inflation; e.g., all along $SRPC$ in Figure 18.13, $\dot{P}^e = x$. It follows that there is only one point along each $SRPC$ where $\dot{P} = \dot{P}^e$, and this must be at its intersection with the $LRPC$; and that at all other points along the $SRPC$, the expected rate of inflation is either above or below the actual rate.

Assume we are initially at point a in Figure 18.13. This is a point of full equilibrium in the labor market: all inflation is fully anticipated ($\dot{P} = \dot{P}^e = x$) and unemployment equals the natural rate. What will be the response to an increase in the rate of inflation due, for example, to an increase in the rate of monetary growth? Assume, for example, that the inflation rate increases from x to y in Figure 18.13. Initially, we move along the short-run Phillips curve, $SRPC$, from point a in the direction of point b. The reduction in unemployment below u_N reflects the fooling of workers due to unanticipated inflation. Under the adaptive expectations model, the expected rate of inflation will increase over time from x to y. As the expected inflation rate increases, the short-run Phillips curve shifts upward. This is clear from equation (18.13): there is a relation between $\dot{P}$ and u given u_N and $\dot{P}^e$. As $\dot{P}^e$ increases, $\dot{P}$ increases for any value of u. The short-run curve must continue to shift up until $\dot{P}^e$ converges to the actual rate of inflation, y, and the system moves to point c. This is the new equilibrium: once again, $\dot{P} = \dot{P}^e$ and $u = u_N$. However, the inflation rate is higher than initially.

Eradicating Inflation. To eliminate inflation in the traditional Phillips curve or classical models, the policymakers must reduce aggregate demand to a level compatible with the noninflationary rate of unemployment; in the traditional Phillips curve model, the noninflationary rate of unemployment is above the noninflationary rate in the classical model because of the implications of asymmetric wage response. Eradicating inflation in the natural rate model, on the other hand, does not require accepting a permanently higher unemployment rate than would be associated with steady inflation. All that is required is that unemployment rise above the natural rate for a long enough period to induce declines in the actual (and then the expected) inflation rates until price stability is reestablished.

Maintaining Unemployment Below the Natural Rate: The Acceleration Hypothesis. What if the policy authorities attempt to maintain the unemployment rate below the natural rate? To do so, they must impose a certain amount of unanticipated inflation on the economy at all times. Under the adaptive expectations model, the expected rate will converge to the actual rate if the actual rate remains constant. To maintain some unanticipated inflation, the policymakers must constantly increase the actual rate to maintain a constant gap between $\dot{P}$ and $\dot{P}^e$. Therefore, any unemployment rate below u_N will be associated with accelerating inflation, and any unemployment rate above u_N should be associated with accelerating deflation. In Figure 18.14, therefore, the only points at which it is possible to remain lie along the vertical long-run Phillips curve (e.g., point a). At points to the left of this curve (e.g., point b), the inflation rate will be accelerating; at points to the right (e.g., point c), inflation will be declining.

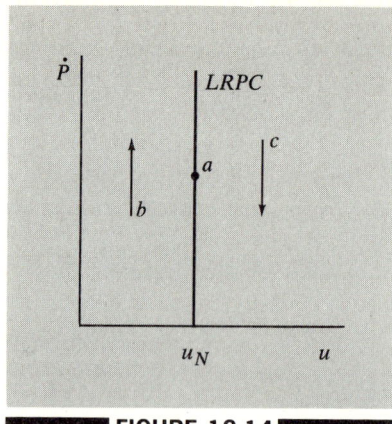

FIGURE 18.14
The Acceleration Hypothesis

Empirical Evidence on the Role of Inflation Expectations

To test the natural rate model, the Phillips curve can be specified as

$$\dot{P}_t = a + b(1/u_t) + e\dot{P}^e_t \qquad (18.15)$$

where $\dot{P}^e_t$ is modeled as a finite distributed lag on past levels of actual inflation rates:

$$\dot{P}^e_t = \sum_{i=1}^{n} w_i \dot{P}_{t-i}. \qquad (18.16)$$

Assume $\dot{P}^e$ depends only on three lagged inflation rates. Then

$$\dot{P}_t = a + b(1/u_t) + ew_1\dot{P}_{t-1} \\ + ew_2\dot{P}_{t-2} \\ + ew_3\dot{P}_{t-3}.$$

This equation can be estimated to obtain values of a, b, ew_1, ew_2, and ew_3. If inflation stabilizes, then $\dot{P}_{t-1} = \dot{P}_{t-2} = \dot{P}_{t-3} = \dot{P}^e_t$ and $\dot{P}_t = a + b(1/u_t) + (ew_1 + ew_2 + ew_3)\dot{P}^e_t$. We cannot separate out the w's and the e's. The usual test for the vertical Phillips curve is that $ew_1 + ew_2 + ew_3 = 1$. We assume that $w_1 + w_2 + w_3 = 1$; this implies that the expected rate converges to the actual rate. Given this assumption, $ew_1 + ew_2 + ew_3 = 1$ implies that $e = 1$.

Early empirical studies which included expected inflation in the Phillips curve found that estimates of e were significantly below unity, generally in the .4 and .6 range.[15] More recent studies using the richer data of the late 1960s and early 1970s generally find estimates of e around unity and thus provide support for a vertical long-run Phillips curve.[16]

---

[15] See, for example, R. M. Solow, *Price Expectations and the Behavior of the Price Level* (Manchester, United Kingdom: Manchester University Press, 1969), and Robert J. Gordon, "Inflation in Recession and Recovery," *Brookings Papers on Economic Activity*, Vol. 2 (1971), pp. 105–158.

[16] See, for example, Robert J. Gordon, "Wage Price Controls and the Shifting Phillips Curve," *Brookings Papers on Economic Activity*, Vol. 3 (1972), pp. 385–421.

APPENDIX

A Eclectic Specifications of the Phillips Curve

The traditional version assumes asymmetrical wage response and no expectations effect, while the natural rate version assumes symmetrical wage response and a unitary coefficient on the expected inflation rate. In this section we discuss three mixed or eclectic specifications which combine aspects of the two models in different ways: (1) symmetric wage response but a coefficient on the expected inflation rate of between zero and one, (2) asymmetric wage response and unitary coefficient on the expected inflation rate, and (3) a two-stage specification in which the coefficient on the expected inflation rate depends on previous inflation experience.

Symmetric Wage Response but a Coefficient Between Zero and One on $\dot{P}^e$ [1]

The Phillips curve is respecified in this case as

$$\dot{W} = \beta(u^* - u) + e\dot{P}^e \tag{18A.1}$$

where $1 > e > 0$. If $\dot{W} = \dot{P}^e = 0$, $u = u^*$ where u^* is the *noninflationary rate of unemployment*. It differs from the natural rate in that, in this model, there is no unique equilibrium unemployment rate. The implications of this specification can be seen more clearly if we transform it into a relation between the inflation rate, excess demand, and expected inflation:

$$\dot{P} = \beta(u^* - u) + e\dot{P}^e. \tag{18A.1'}$$

When $\dot{P} = \dot{P}^e = 0$, $u = u^*$. When $\dot{P} = \dot{P}^e = x > 0$, then

$$u = u^* - \frac{(1-e)}{\beta}x. \tag{18A.2}$$

Thus, this specification permits constant levels of u different from u^* at constant (nonaccelerating) inflation rates. This model has the property of all models that allow for money illusion in the labor market—there is no unique level of "full" employment or equilibrium level of employment and output.

Figure 18A.1 depicts the short- and long-run Phillips curves when $1 > e > 0$. The long-run curve holds for all $\dot{P} = \dot{P}^e$. Each short-run curve corresponds to a particular value of $\dot{P}^e$. As $\dot{P}^e$ increases, the short-run Phillips curve shifts upward.

Assume we are initially at $\dot{P} = \dot{P}_e = 0$ at u^* in Figure 18A.1. Consider the response to a sustained rate of inflation equal to x. Initially the unemployment rate falls to u_1 as the system moves along the initial short-run Phillips curve to point a. As $\dot{P}^e$ increases over time however, the short-run curve shifts upward until $\dot{P}^e$ stabilizes at $\dot{P} = \dot{P}^e = x$ where the unemployment rate, u_2, is higher than the rate achieved in the short run but lower than the noninflationary rate of unemployment, u^*. Thus, there is a stable long-run trade-off between $\dot{P}$ and u, but this long-run trade-off is steeper and therefore less favorable than the short-run trade-off.

---

[1] This model is consistent with the early empirical evidence on the role of inflation expectations. See the articles by Solow and Gordon cited in footnote 15, p. 358.

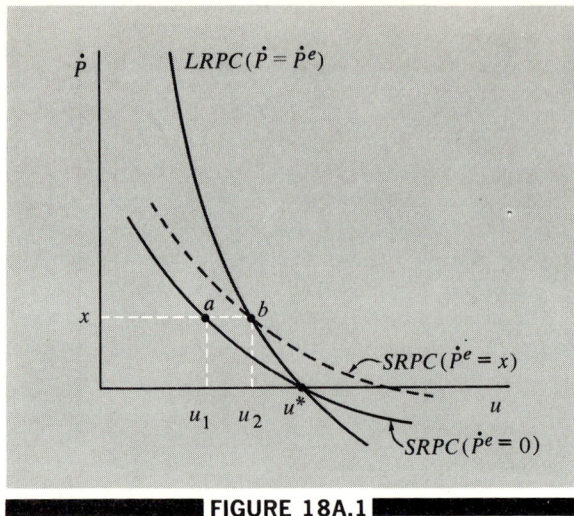

FIGURE 18A.1
The Eclectic Model with Both
Short-Run and Long-Run Trade-Offs

Asymmetric Wage Response but Unitary Coefficient on P^e [2]

The assumption of persistent money illusion in the previous specification makes it theoretically unattractive. On the other hand, the assumption in the natural rate version of symmetric wage response may also be unrealistic. A specification that combines a unitary coefficient on $\dot{P}^e$ and asymmetric wage response is

$$\dot{W} = v + \beta(u_N - u) + \dot{P}^e \tag{18A.3}$$

where $\dot{W} \geq 0$, or

$$\dot{P} = v + \beta(u_N - u) + \dot{P}^e \tag{18A.3'}$$

where $\dot{P} \geq 0$. If we interpret u_N as the unemployment rate consistent with frictional unemployment in each labor market when there is no money illusion (i.e., when $\dot{P} = \dot{P}^e$), the noninflationary aggregate rate of unemployment, u^*, is

$$u^* = u_N + \frac{v}{\beta}. \tag{18A.4}$$

Due to asymmetric wage response, the aggregate (average) unemployment rate required for zero or any other constant but nonaccelerating inflation rate is $u^* > u_N$. The difference between u^* and u_N is deficient demand unemployment.

---

[2] This model is loosely based on James Tobin, "Inflation and Unemployment," *American Economic Review*, Vol. 52 (March, 1972), pp. 1–18. Tobin also suggests the possibility of a two-stage curve, discussed next.

A Two-Stage Phillips Curve

Otto Eckstein and Roger Brinner have suggested another compromise between the traditional and natural rate specifications in which the coefficient on expected inflation is either less than one or equal to one, depending on the recent past history of inflation.[3] The model is specified as

$$\dot{P} = \beta(u_N - u) + e\dot{P}^e \tag{18A.5}$$

where

$$e < 1 \text{ if } \dot{P}_{-1} \leq \dot{P}_c \tag{18A.6a}$$

$$e = 1 \text{ if } \dot{P}_{-1} > \dot{P}_c. \tag{18A.6b}$$

$\dot{P}_c$ is a critical or threshold inflation rate above which wages respond fully to change in expected inflation. In Eckstein and Brinner, $e = 1$ if the average inflation rate over the two previous years exceeds 2.5 percent.

In this model, the long-run Phillips curve is vertical above the critical inflation rate, downward sloping below it. If prices are initially stable, the system begins at the noninflationary rate of unemployment in Figure 18A.2. There will be a stable long-run trade-off between inflation and unemployment between inflation rates of 0 to $\dot{P}_c$. The long-run Phillips curve is steeper than the short-run curve, $SRPC$ ($\dot{P}^e = 0$), but given that $e < 1$, the long-run curve is downward sloping in this range. However, for inflation rates higher than $\dot{P}_c$, $e = 1$ and there is no further long-run trade-off. u_c corresponds to the natural rate of unemployment in that it is consistent with any constant rate of inflation in excess of $\dot{P}_c$, and for $u < u_c$, inflation accelerates indefinitely.

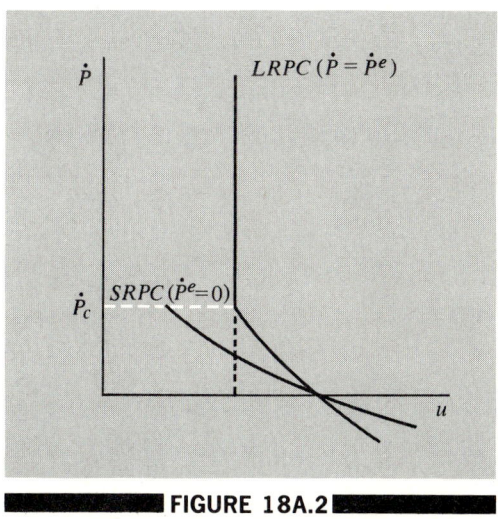

FIGURE 18A.2
The Two-Stage Phillips Curve

[3] Otto Eckstein and Roger Brinner, *The Inflation Process in the United States*, a study prepared for the Joint Economic Committee, 92nd Congress, second session.

Part IV • Refinements of the Real Sector: Aggregate Supply

This model has the considerable advantage that it appears consistent with the observed behavior of unemployment and inflation in both the 1950s and 1960s as well as the 1970s. On the other hand, the assumption that *e* depends on a critical inflation rate is rather implausible and without adequate theoretical justification. The inflation threshold could reasonably be expected to affect the *speed* with which inflation expectations respond to inflation (rather than the degree of response of $\dot{P}^e$ to $\dot{P}$). For low inflation rates, $\dot{P}^e$ may respond sluggishly to a change in $\dot{P}$. But a 2 percent inflation maintained indefinitely would imply continuing money illusion if $e < 1$.

APPENDIX

Models of Expectations Formation

In this appendix we will discuss two formal models that describe the way in which economic agents formulate expectations about the future values of economic variables. The first, the *adaptive expectations* (*AE*) *model,* is the most widely used model of expectations formation and was the basis of our discussion in Chapter 9 of the convergence of the expected inflation rate to the new value of the actual rate in response to a change in the rate of monetary expansion. The adaptive expectations model confines the information upon which economic agents rely in formulating expectations about the future path of a variable to current and past values of that variable. This ignores potentially valuable information available to economic agents. The *rational expectations* (*RE*) *model,* on the other hand, assumes that economic agents use their knowledge about the structure of the economy, and all available information about variables the structure identifies as relevant to form expectations about the future values of those variables.

The Adaptive Expectations Model

According to the *AE* model, the expected value of the inflation rate ($\dot{P}^e$) can be written as a weighted average of the current inflation rate ($\dot{P}$) and the expected rate held last period ($\dot{P}^e_{-1}$):

$$\dot{P}^e = \alpha \dot{P} + (1 - \alpha) \dot{P}^e_{-1} \tag{18B.1a}$$

where $\dot{P}^e$ is the currently held expectation of the value of the inflation rate next period, $\dot{P}$ is the current value of the inflation rate, and $\dot{P}^e_{-1}$ is last period's expected value of the inflation rate for the current period and where $1 > \alpha > 0$. This specification implies that the expected rate is *gradually updated* using information about current inflation rates. The updating of the expected rate may be clearer if we rewrite equation (18B.1a) as

$$\underbrace{\dot{P}^e - \dot{P}^e_{-1}}_{\text{adjustment}} = \alpha \underbrace{(\dot{P} - \dot{P}^e_{-1})}_{\text{error}}. \tag{18B.1b}$$

If economic agents underpredicted the actual inflation rate this period, they adjust their forecast of future inflation rates upward by a fraction of the error. $\dot{P}^e - \dot{P}^e_1$ is the revision of expectations and $\dot{P} - \dot{P}^e_1$ is the error in the forecast of the current inflation rate.

The equation can in turn be rewritten to express the expected inflation rate as a weighted average of current and past values of the actual inflation rate where the weights decline geometrically.

$$\dot{P}^e = \sum_{i=0}^{\infty} \alpha(1-\alpha)^i \dot{P}_{-i}.^1 \tag{18B.1c}$$

The Rational Expectations Model

Economic agents may have additional information beyond past values of the variable in question which they can use to improve their forecasts. According to the rational expectations (*RE*) model, economic agents form their expectations as if they knew the structure of the process which determines the variable in question; i.e., as if they knew the structure of the economy and the probability distributions governing the disturbances to the system. The essential property of expectations formed on this basis is that they are *unbiased predictors* of the future values of the variable being forecast; this does *not* mean that the forecasts are accurate, only that there is no systematic tendency for forecasts to over or underpredict.[2] This provides an important contrast with the adaptive expectations model in which any increase in the actual inflation rate is initially underpredicted.

---

[1] To derive this, begin from equation (18B.1a) and lag all terms one period; this yields

$$\dot{P}^e_1 = \alpha \dot{P}_{-1} + (1-\alpha) \dot{P}^e_2.$$

Substituting this for $\dot{P}^e_1$ in equation (18B.1a), we obtain

$$\dot{P}^e = \alpha \dot{P} + (1-\alpha)[\alpha \dot{P}_{-1} + (1-\alpha) \dot{P}^e_2]$$
$$= \alpha \dot{P} + \alpha(1-\alpha)\dot{P}_{-1} + (1-\alpha)^2 \dot{P}^e_2.$$

We then use equation (18B.1a) to solve for $\dot{P}^e_2$, substitute it for $\dot{P}^e_2$ in the above equation, and continue this process. This gives us

$$\dot{P}^e = \alpha \dot{P} + \alpha(1-\alpha)\dot{P}_{-1} + \alpha(1-\alpha)^2 \dot{P}_{-2}$$
$$+ \ldots + \alpha(1-\alpha)^n \dot{P}_{-n}$$

or

$$\dot{P}^e = \sum_{i=0}^{\infty} \alpha(1-\alpha)^i \dot{P}_{-i}.$$

Since $1 > \alpha > 0$, the sum of the weights equals one; i.e., $\sum_{i=0}^{\infty} \alpha(1-\alpha)^i = 1$. This means that $\dot{P}^e$ will ultimately converge to any steady actual rate of inflation.

[2] The rational expectations model was introduced by John Muth, "Rational Expectations and the Theory of Price Movements," *Econometrica* Vol. 29 (July, 1961), pp. 315–335. For a discussion of its applications to macroeconomics, see Thomas Sargent and Neil Wallace, "Rational Expectations and the Theory of Economic Policy," *Journal of Monetary Economics* Vol. 2 (April, 1976), pp. 169–183. For an interesting collection of papers on the rational expectations challenge to both conventional Phillips curves and conventional macro models, see *After the Phillips Curve: Persistence of High Inflation and High Unemployment* (Boston: Federal Reserve Bank of Boston, 1978).

Part IV • Refinements of the Real Sector: Aggregate Supply

We will illustrate the implications of the rational expectations model in the context of the expectations-augmented Phillips curve. We assume, following the Friedman-Phelps specification, that employment (and hence output) responds to movements in the actual relative to the expected inflation rate. To reflect the line of causation from unanticipated inflation to employment, we rewrite the Phillips curve to express the unemployment rate as a function discrepancy between actual and expected inflation rates.

$$u = u^* + 1/\gamma \, (\dot{P} - \dot{P}^e) \tag{18B.2}$$

We will assume a simple structure for the model determining the inflation rate. The rate of inflation is assumed to depend on the rate of monetary growth ($\dot{M}$) less the rate of increase in the autonomous component of the demand for money (ϵ).

$$\dot{P} = \dot{M} - \epsilon \tag{18B.3}$$

Equation (18B.3) is the reduced form for the inflation rate.

The rate of change in the autonomous component of the demand for money is a random variable; i.e., the value of this variable is governed by the laws of probability. The expected value of this variable is assumed to be zero. There is an equal probability of this variable being above or below zero over any given period; but if we observe this variable over a large number of periods, the average of its realized values will be approximately zero. The rate of monetary growth is determined by the policy authority and is publically announced in advance. Thus, its value is known with certainty.

The expected value of the inflation rate, under the *RE* model, is

$$\dot{P}^e = E(\dot{P}) = E(\dot{M} - \epsilon) = \dot{M} \tag{18B.4}$$

where $E(\,)$ is the expected value operator. The expected value of the actual inflation rate is the expected value of the $\dot{M} - \epsilon$ differential which underlies the inflation process. Given the assumptions above, $E(\dot{M}) = \dot{M}$ and $E(\epsilon) = 0$; hence, $E(\dot{M} - \epsilon) = \dot{M}$.

The rate of unemployment is therefore given by

$$\begin{aligned} u &= u^* + 1/\gamma(\dot{M} - \epsilon - \dot{M}) \\ &= u^* - 1/\gamma(\epsilon). \end{aligned} \tag{18B.5}$$

Thus, in any period, unemployment will deviate from the natural rate in response to realized values of the random variable, ϵ. However, there is no way the government can systematically alter the unemployment rate by varying the rate of monetary growth. An increase in the rate of monetary growth will only raise the rate of inflation. Thus, government policy can have no impact on real variables, unless of course it is random like the autonomous component of the demand for money.

The evolution in views about the ability of the government to influence the unemployment rate has been quite remarkable. Under the traditional specification of the Phillips curve, unemployment can be lowered by accepting a permanently higher inflation rate. Under the natural rate specification (with adaptive expectations), unemployment can be lowered only temporarily by accepting a permanent increase in the inflation rate; the unemployment rate can be maintained below the natural rate only at the cost of accelerating inflation. Under the rational expectations model, government policy cannot systematically influence the unemployment rate.

Limitations of the Rational Expectations Model

We have used the adaptive expectations model as the basis of expectation formation in our modeling of the life cycle hypothesis of consumption in Chapters 12 and 13 and the inflation expectation term in the expectation-augmented Phillips curve in Chapter 18. And we will use it again in our discussion of the term structure of interest rates in Chapter 20.

The powerful conclusions based on the RE model depend in part on its use with the model of output and employment, which allows for the effect of aggregate demand on those variables exclusively via unexpected inflation, induced by shifts in aggregate demand. This presumes that prices and wages are flexible enough to clear the commodity and labor markets continuously. If we believe that prices and wages are insufficiently flexible to achieve this continuous market clearing (due to long-term contracts and/or other reasons cited in Chapter 17), then changes in aggregate demand induce changes in production and employment, independent of the discrepancy between actual and expected inflation rates.

Another limitation of the RE model is that it presumes that it is costless for economic agents to learn the structure of the system and acquire information on variables required for their forecasts. The simpler adaptive expectations approach may be a cost-efficient approach to expectation formation. Thus, economic agents may use new observations to continually update their knowledge of the structure.[3] In this case, the RE model may indicate the long-run tendency of inflation expectations to be an unbiased predictor of future inflation rates, but the adaptive expectations model may nevertheless remain relevant for the short-run response of inflation expectations to economic developments. Nevertheless, it seems certain that the current controversy over rational expectations will at least motivate an improvement in the modeling of expectations even if it fails to bring about a complete revolution in macroeconomic theory.

● REVIEW QUESTIONS

1. We can write the eclectic form of the Phillips curve as

   $$\dot{W} = v + h(u^* - u) + e\dot{P}^e.$$

   Discuss how this can be transformed into various special cases by selecting alternative combinations of values for v and e.

2. What is the meaning of nonlinear wage adjustment and why is it an important assumption underlying the traditional specification of the Phillips curve?

3. Discuss the relationship between the unemployment rate associated with the absence of involuntary unemployment and the noninflationary rate of unemployment in the traditional specification.

4. There remains a short-run trade-off in the expectation-augmented vertical long-run Phillips curve. Contrast the nature of the trade-off in this case with the trade-off associated with the traditional specification.

---

[3] Benjamin Friedman, "Optimal Expectations and the Extreme Information Assumptions of 'Rational Expectations' Macromodels," *Journal of Monetary Economics,* Vol. 5 (January, 1979), pp. 23–41.

5. Contrast the nature of the policy required to eradicate inflation in the classical model and in the traditional and natural rate specifications of the Phillips curve.

6. Why is the natural rate model also referred to as the "accelerationist" model?

*7. What is the difference between the adaptive and rational models of expectation formation?

● PROBLEMS

1. "The obvious limitation of the Phillips curve approach to modeling inflation is its total failure to take into account the single most important source of inflation—the rate of monetary growth. Something might be saved of the Phillips curve approach by including the rate of monetary growth as one of the explanatory variables in the Phillips curve equation." Comment.

*2. "The unemployment consistent with zero inflation is not wholly voluntary. Indeed, when there is no involuntary unemployment there will be accelerating inflation. To maintain zero (or any constant rate of) inflation, we must accept some involuntary unemployment. Thus, the choice is between involuntary unemployment and accelerating inflation." Is this consistent with the traditional or natural rate specifications of the Phillips curve? If not, what are the key features of the Phillips curve consistent with this quote?

*3. "The natural rate specification was an improvement over the traditional specification in that it recognized that only unanticipated inflation affected unemployment; hence, there can be, at most, a short-run trade-off between unemployment and inflation and no long-run trade-off. However, this relation between unemployment and unanticipated inflation cannot be systematically exploited by the government to affect the unemployment rate, even in the short run." Contrast the implications of the natural rate model under the adaptive and rational models of expectation formation and comment on the above quote.

---

* The information necessary for solving these problems or questions can be found in the appendices.

Part V

Refinements of the Financial Sector

Chapter 19. The Demand for Money
20. The Supply and Demand for Bonds and the Term Structure of Interest Rates
21. The Implications of Alternative Specifications of the Demand for Money
22. The Bond Market and Crowding-Out
23. A Model of the Money Supply Process and the Implications of an Endogenous Money Supply

Chapter 19

The Demand for Money

In Part V we refine our treatment of the financial sector of our model. We begin in Chapter 19 by developing the theory of the demand for money. Here we discuss both the Baumol-Tobin model of transactions demand and alternative models of the asset demand for money. In Chapter 20 we discuss the demand for and supply of bonds, consider implications of the balance sheet identity for the demand for bonds and of the government and business sector financing constraints for the supply of bonds, and develop the theory of the term structure of interest rates. Chapters 21 and 22 discuss the implications of the refinements introduced in the previous two chapters. Chapter 21 develops the implications of extreme values of the interest responsiveness of the demand for money and of the introduction of wealth in the money demand function. Chapter 22 discusses the implications of the financing constraints and of other refinements of the financial sector introduced in Chapter 20 for the effectiveness of fiscal policy. In Chapter 23 we introduce a banking system and develop the implications of an endogenous money supply.

THE FUNCTIONS OF MONEY AND THE CENTRAL ISSUE IN THE THEORY OF THE DEMAND FOR MONEY

In Chapter 2 we presented hypothetical sectoral balance sheets indicating the variety of forms in which wealth owners can hold their wealth. In our formal models, on the other hand, we have imposed a more restricted menu of assets while confining attention to the portfolio behavior of households: households can hold noninterest-bearing money or a single type of interest earning asset, a bond.[1] Whether we include

---

[1] The simple structure of our model removes any possible ambiguity about what assets should be included in the definition of "money." In Appendix A at the end of the chapter we discuss the problems that arise in defining money when we allow for the larger variety of financial assets that we observe in the economy. Throughout the chapter we assume that money yields no interest. We note in Appendix A the recent trend toward interest-bearing deposits which can be used as a means of payment. If these deposits are included in the definition of money, the portfolio decision is between interest-bearing money and bonds which offer higher (expected) yields than "money."

a wide array of assets or just two assets, the decision concerning the desired holding of money is really the decision concerning desired portfolio composition; i.e., the desired allocation of a given stock of wealth among competing assets. In the two-asset case, of course, the demand for money completely defines the portfolio composition choice.

○ The Functions of Money

In attempting to understand why people hold money as part of their portfolios, a useful starting point is to identify the functions of money.

Medium of Exchange. Money serves as a means of payment or a medium of exchange. The use of money as a generally acceptable means of payment for goods and services facilitates exchange by greatly reducing the time and effort necessary to complete trades. An economy without money is called a *barter economy*. Exchange takes place in barter economies primarily by direct trades of goods and services. Direct exchange requires a *double coincidence of wants*: if A has X and wants Y, A must find someone else who has Y and wants X. Alternatively, A could engage in a series of indirect exchanges: if B has Z but wants X, and C has Y and wants Z, A can trade X to B for Z, then Z to C for Y. By eliminating the necessity of a double coincidence of wants or still more complicated indirect barter exchanges, the use of money greatly reduces transactions costs associated with making exchanges. By reducing time devoted to exchange, it increases the amount of leisure and/or production.[2]

The use of money in transactions also economizes on the cost of acquiring information about the quality and/or attributes of goods available for exchange.[3] Money is a good that has a low "recognition" cost; i.e., a low cost of identifying its qualities and/or attributes. The fact that nonmoney goods differ in quality provides an incentive for nonexperts in each such good to deal only with experts who, in turn, have developed reputations of reliability. Trades therefore tend to take place by the exchange of money for goods or services provided by experts. The cost of carrying out two exchanges using money rather than a single (double coincidence of wants) exchange as in a barter situation is more than offset by the opportunity to economize on the cost of acquiring information about the quality of the good bought and of the good sold (as well as on the cost associated with searching for the double coincidence of wants).

The fact that the use of money in carrying out exchanges economizes on the costs of making such exchanges, however, explains why money is *used* in such transactions (the evolution of a money economy) but does not completely explain why money is *held* in between transactions (the demand for money balances as part of wealth owners' portfolios). We will develop the rationale for holding money *in between* transactions below.

---

[2] For a particularly insightful discussion of the distinction between money and barter economies, see Robert Clower, "A Reconsideration of the Microfoundations of Monetary Theory," *Western Economic Journal*, Vol. VI (December, 1967), pp. 1–8.

[3] This view of the role of money is developed in Karl Brunner and Alan Meltzer, "The Uses of Money: Money in the Theory of An Exchange Economy," *American Economic Review*, Vol. 61 (December, 1971), pp. 784–805; and A. Alchian, "Why Money?" *Journal of Money, Credit and Banking*, Vol. 9 (February, 1977), pp. 133–140.

Part V · Refinements of the Financial Sector

Store of Value. Money also serves as a store of value, permitting units to transfer command over goods and services through time. Units could also accumulate wealth by storing durable goods or by holding nonmonetary financial assets such as bonds. The advantage of money over goods is that storage costs are much lower and that changes in tastes or technology which drastically lowered the value of some good would not much affect the purchasing power of money. The advantage of money relative to nonmonetary financial assets is that money is perfectly safe in the sense that its nominal price is fixed, that it is immediately available to satisfy unanticipated expenditures, and that the zero nominal holding period yield on money may exceed the expected holding period yield on alternative assets.[4] We will discuss the asset demand for money in detail below.

○ The Central Issue in the Demand for Money

J. R. Hicks stated the central issue in the theory of the demand for money in his well-known 1935 paper.[5] Why do units hold wealth in noninterest-bearing money when they could be holding interest-earning assets? The various models of the demand for money we present below represent attempts to answer this question. Each begins from some aspect of the functions performed by money, i.e., from the role of money as a means of payment or as a store of value with special desirable properties. The two basic approaches to the demand for money were both initially sketched by Hicks in his 1935 article: (1) the utility approach to the asset demand for money and (2) the role of exchange costs and the transactions demand for money.[6]

The Utility Approach. The *utility approach* to the asset demand for money views money as yielding a nonpecuniary return in the form of a flow of services reflecting the convenience, flexibility, and security afforded by holding money. A unit's demand for money, according to this approach, depends on the size of its portfolio (i.e., its total wealth) and on the rates of return on alternative assets.

The Transactions Approach. According to the *transactions approach*, the unique, distinctive feature of money is that it serves as a means of payment. There are other assets which are highly liquid, equally safe, and pay a positive rate of return; e.g., default-free, fixed price-variable coupon bonds (savings accounts) issued by insured banks and nonbank financial intermediaries. These assets *dominate* money as a store of value; i.e., they are equally safe but pay a positive return. Therefore, wealth owners would not choose to hold money as part of their permanent or investment portfolio. Although the role of money as a medium of exchange explains its *use* in carrying out exchanges, we must still explain why wealth owners choose to *hold money in between exchanges*, instead of investing all income receipts in bonds and coordinating the sale of the bonds over the period between income receipts to precisely match the pattern of desired payments for goods. The explanation, as Hicks suggested, lies

---

[4] Money also serves as a unit of value and standard for deferred payment. However, the latter two functions are not a source of demand for money as part of wealth owners' portfolios.

[5] J. R. Hicks, "A Suggestion for Simplifying the Theory of Money," *Economica*, No. 5 (February, 1935), pp. 1–19.

[6] Hicks, however, has changed his mind about the usefulness of these approaches. For his current thinking, see Chapter 1, *Critical Essays in Monetary Theory* (Oxford: The Clarendon Press, 1967), pp. 1–16.

in the existence of exchange costs associated with movements out of money into bonds and back into money. Modigliani has summarized this approach as follows: ". . . the basic reason for holding idle cash balances is not that they provide a useful service but simply that it does not pay to shed them."[7] According to this view, people hold money when the cost of moving temporarily out of money into bonds and then back into money to make purchases exceeds the interest that could be earned by temporarily investing in earning assets. In the next two sections we develop formal models of both the transactions demand and asset demand approaches to money holdings.

THE TRANSACTIONS DEMAND FOR MONEY

The transactions demand for money has a long tradition in economics. Classical economists, for example, based their formulations of the demand for money on the necessity of accumulating pools of money in order to carry out purchases of goods and services during the intervals between income payments (called the *payment period*). Their models, however, were generally excessively mechanical and inadequately derived from maximizing behavior.[8] The modern theory of the transactions demand was motivated by models of optimal inventory behavior by firms, and the resulting models are therefore referred to as *inventory theoretic models of the demand for money*.[9]

The Assumptions Underlying the Inventory Model

The inventory model assumes that households receive periodic income receipts and make expenditures evenly over the period between income receipts. To simplify, it is generally assumed that the expenditures over the period just exhaust the income payments. In this case, the income receipt at the beginning of the period is the initial value of the transactions portfolio, the sum that will be needed to make payments over the period. In Figure 19.1 the payment period is depicted as the distance between

---

[7] Franco Modigliani, "Liquidity Preference," *International Encyclopedia of the Social Sciences* (New York: The Macmillan Co., 1968), p. 399.

[8] The two most well-known classical formulations of the demand for money are associated with Irving Fisher, *The Purchasing Power of Money* (New York: Macmillan Co., 1911); and A. C. Pigou, "The Value of Money," *Quarterly Journal of Economics*, Vol. 37 (November, 1917), pp. 38–65. Fisher's point of departure was his well-known equation of exchange, $MV \equiv PX$. V, the velocity of money, is defined as PX/M, the number of times money turns over in making income transactions. The equation of exchange is an identity. But it can be used to derive an expression for the demand for money by making an assumption about the determinants of V. Fisher assumed that V was determined by institutional factors, such as the time period between income receipts, and that it changed slowly if at all over time; in particular, V was independent of the level of nominal income, PX. Given V, the equation of exchange can be used to compute the amount of money required to carry out the planned nominal amount of transactions.

Pigou's Cambridge cash balances approach was less mechanical but its conclusions were virtually identical to the Fisherian theory. Pigou viewed the demand for money as a portfolio decision by wealth owners. Although Pigou mentioned both interest rates and wealth as possible influences on the demand for money, the demand for money was usually written as a function of income alone; e.g., $M^d = kPX$ where k was influenced by the same factors that determined V.

[9] The two papers that initially set out this approach are William J. Baumol, "The Transactions Demand for Cash: An Inventory Theoretic Approach," *Quarterly Journal of Economics*, Vol. 66 (November, 1952), pp. 545–556; and James Tobin, "The Interest Elasticity of the Transactions Demand for Cash," *Review of Economics and Statistics*, Vol. 38 (August, 1956), pp. 241–247. Our presentation follows Baumol's treatment.

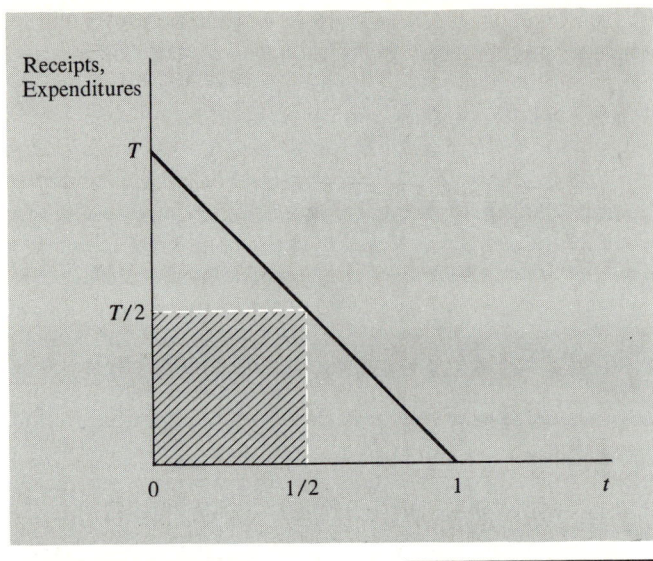

FIGURE 19.1
Receipts, Expenditures, and the Composition
of the Transactions Portfolio

0 and 1 on the horizontal axis. The income payment is received at $t = 0$ and equals T, the value of transactions over the period. The transactions portfolio declines continuously over the period as the expenditures are made. This is shown by the line beginning at T at $t = 0$ and going to 0 at $t = 1$ in Figure 19.1. The household must decide on the *composition* of the transactions portfolio, how much of the income receipts to hold in money and how much in bonds at the beginning of the period, and how to schedule bond sales over the period.

It is obvious that the household does not need to hold all the transaction balances in money to carry out its purchases of goods over the period. Half of the money balances, for example, remain idle for half the period. This is depicted by the shaded area in Figure 19.1. Therefore, the household can purchase bonds with half its income ($T/2$) at $t = 0$, spend the remaining money balances (also $T/2$) over the first half of the period, then sell the bonds and use the resulting money balances for goods purchases over the second half of the period. The incentive to hold a portion of transaction balances in bonds is the interest that can be earned. In the case just discussed the household held $T/2$ of bonds for $1/2$ the period and therefore could have earned $(T/4) \cdot r$ in interest where r is the periodic interest rate. The larger the initial bond purchase and the larger the number of bond sales over the period, the larger are the average bondholdings, the smaller the average money holdings, and the larger the interest earnings on the transactions portfolio over the period.

If it were costless to buy and sell bonds, it would pay to purchase bonds with the entire income received at the beginning of the period and sell the bonds continuously over the period to generate the money balances to make payments for goods. However, bond purchases and sales are not costless; indeed, it is the existence of such exchange costs that provide the rationale for limiting the number of bond sales. Exchange costs include both explicit brokerage fees for buying and selling bonds, implicit costs associated with the time exhausted in executing such exchanges, and the phone and gas bills and psychic costs incurred. In the formal model presented below we assume these costs are a fixed amount (E) per exchange, although the qualitative results would not be changed by allowing also for costs proportional to the value of bonds bought and sold. The decision about how much money to hold requires balancing the interest that can be earned by holding bonds against the exchange costs incurred by the larger number of exchanges required when bondholdings are increased.

○ A Formal Model of the Transactions Demand for Money

Households attempt to maximize the interest earnings net of transaction costs, or alternatively, to minimize the costs associated with their transactions portfolios. The costs associated with the transactions portfolio (C) consist of both the opportunity cost due to interest foregone by holding money and the exchange cost arising from movements between money and bonds. Interest foregone can be computed by finding average cash balance over the period and multiplying it by the periodic interest rate (r). The decision variable in the model is the value of bonds converted into money each time such an exchange occurs (B). Average cash balances will be equal to $B/2$[10] and the number of exchanges between money and bonds will be T/B, where T is the level of income receipts and the value of transactions over the period.[11]

We can write the total cost of managing the transactions portfolio (C) as the sum of foregone interest (the interest rate times average money holdings) and exchange costs [the cost per exchange (E) times the number of exchanges]:

$$C = r \cdot \frac{B}{2} + E\frac{T}{B}. \tag{19.1}$$

We must solve this equation for the value of B which minimizes C.[12] This requires

---

[10] Each subperiod, the unit begins with B dollars in money balances and ends up with zero dollars, and the money balances decline from B to 0 evenly over the interval. Therefore, average money holdings are $B/2$ for each subperiod and therefore also $B/2$ for the whole period. For example, if $B = T/2$ as assumed in Figure 19.1, the unit begins with cash balances of $T/2$. Average cash balances were $B/2$ or $T/4$ over the first half of the period. The unit then sells B dollars of bonds ($T/2$) and begins the second half of the period with B of money balances and ends up at $t = 1$ with zero cash balances again. Therefore, average cash balances equal $B/2 = T/4$ each half period and therefore $B/2 = T/4$ for the whole period.

[11] If each transfer involves B dollars and exchanges are made until the entire stock of bonds in the transactions portfolio is exhausted, T/B exchanges will be required. For example, if the unit receives income of $1,000 in the beginning of the period, it purchases $500 worth of bonds, using the remaining $500 to carry out exchanges. When the $500 in cash is exhausted, the unit sells the $500 in bonds and uses the $500 to complete its goods transactions over the period. Therefore, the unit makes two moves between money and bonds; i.e., $T/B = 1000/500 = 2$.

[12] The Baumol model assumes that bond sales are symmetric over the period so that B is a constant. Tobin derives this result from maximizing behavior of households. Tobin demonstrates that it always pays to purchase any bonds at the beginning of the period, to sell bonds only when money balances have been exhausted, and to schedule bond sales evenly over the period.

the use of calculus.[13] Taking the derivative of C with respect to B, setting the result equal to zero, and solving for B yields

$$\frac{\partial C}{\partial B} = \frac{r}{2} - \frac{ET}{B^2} = 0$$

$$B^* = \sqrt{\frac{2ET}{r}}$$

(19.2)

where B^* is the optimal (cost minimizing) value of B. To convert this to an expression for the demand for money, recall that average money holding is simply $B/2$. Therefore, the nominal demand for money (M^d) is

$$M^d = \frac{B^*}{2} = \sqrt{\frac{ET}{2r}}.$$

(19.2′)

From equation (19.2′) it is evident that the demand for money is inversely related to the interest rate; i.e., the higher the opportunity cost associated with holding money, the smaller is B^*. It is positively related to the level of transactions (T) and to the cost of moving between money and bonds (E). Note also that if $E=0$, $M^d=0$; i.e., without any cost of exchanging money for bonds, it would pay to synchronize bond sales perfectly with the purchase of goods. In this case, money would not be held in between transactions, only at the instant that bonds are sold by the purchaser of goods and transferred to the seller of goods.

Equation (19.2′) is an example of a multiplicative specification (discussed in Chapter 1) in which the parameters are the constant elasticities; i.e., it can be written as

$$M^d = \alpha T^{1/2} \cdot E^{1/2} \cdot r^{-1/2}.$$

(19.2″)

Thus, the elasticities of the demand for money with respect to the rate of transactions and exchange costs is ½ and with respect to the interest rate is $-½$.[14]

Nominal transactions (T) equal $X \cdot P$ where X is the real value of transactions and P is the price level, and nominal exchange costs equal $e \cdot P$ where e is real exchange costs. Therefore, we can write equation (19.2″) as

---

[13] Note, however, that the use of calculus permits the solution for the cost-minimizing value for B to take on noninteger values (such as 2.3 transactions). The only economically meaningful solutions are integer values equal to or greater than two. One exchange allows only for the purchase of bonds but not for their subsequent sale to rebuild money balances to carry out spending plans, and noninteger values simply are not meaningful. In addition, for given values of the interest rate and exchange costs, there will be a minimum level of transactions required to justify active management of cash balances. If transactions are below this threshold, the unit holds all transactions balances in money. The implications of imposing an integer constraint on the solution are considered in more detail in Appendix B at the end of the chapter.

[14] These results are modified in Appendix B where we consider the implications of imposing an integer constraint on the solution to the optimal number of exchanges between money and bonds.

$$M^d = \sqrt{\frac{e \cdot PX \cdot P}{2r}} = \sqrt{\frac{eX}{2r}} \cdot P$$

so that

$$\frac{M^d}{P} = \sqrt{\frac{eX}{2r}}. \tag{19.3}$$

Thus, our transactions model is consistent with our specification of the demand for money in previous chapters, as the demand for real cash balances as a function of the interest rate and the level of real income.

We can now summarize the implications of our analysis of the transactions demand for money. The usual specification is log linear [following from the multiplicative form of equation (19.2″)], and the dependent variable is the demand for real money balances.

$$\ln\left(\frac{M}{P}\right) = \alpha + \epsilon_{Lr} \ln r + \epsilon_{LX} \ln X \tag{19.4}$$

Real exchange costs are assumed to be constant and are absorbed into the constant term, α. The coefficients of $\ln r$ and $\ln X$ are the elasticities of the demand for money with respect to r and X, respectively. The interest rate should be a rate on some short-term liquid asset such as savings accounts or Treasury bills; often both are included. The transactions variable is generally real *GNP*. To simplify the solution of our model, however, we continue to assume that the money demand function is linear rather than log linear.

THE ASSET DEMAND FOR MONEY

Before we consider empirical evidence, we will discuss alternative theoretical models of the demand for money. Each of the theories developed in this section can be characterized as an asset demand approach. The first two are *partial* theories of the demand for money that can be employed along with the transactions demand for money. A portion of a unit's wealth is not expected to be used for transactions purposes. We refer to this portion as the unit's permanent or investment portfolio. The first two theories provide a rationale for holding money in the investment portfolio. We conclude, however, that neither of these models adequately explains an asset demand for money, although both models are important in understanding the demand for short-term liquid interest-bearing assets such as savings accounts and short-term government debt. The third model, on the other hand, is intended as a complete theory of the demand for money and as an alternative to the transactions demand for money. Its point of departure is Hicks's suggestion that wealth owners hold money because money yields some form of utility.

The Speculative Demand for Money

The concept of the speculative demand for money was introduced by Keynes and formalized by Tobin.[15] The important feature of money according to this approach is that money is perfectly safe (in nominal terms). It has zero yield; but a zero yield is higher than a negative yield. If the alternative to money is a fixed coupon-variable price bond which is expected to earn a negative yield, then a unit will maximize the return on its investment portfolio by holding its wealth in money rather than in bonds. Recall that the price of fixed coupon-variable price bonds varies inversely with the market rate of interest. An increase in the interest rate would cause the price of the bond to fall, imposing capital losses on the holder. If the capital losses are sufficiently large to outweigh the coupon earned on the bond, the bondholder will suffer a negative return by holding the bond. He or she would have been better off holding money.

Wealth owners are assumed to hold expectations about the future course of interest rates. These are based on the perception of some normal level of the interest rate; we refer to this level as the *expected interest rate* (r_e). If the prevailing interest rate is above the expected rate, the wealth owner expects the interest rate to decline; this will generate capital gains so that the expected holding period yield will be in excess of the coupon yield. If the prevailing interest rate is below the expected rate, on the other hand, the wealth owner expects the interest rate to increase; this will impose capital losses on the unit, so that the expected holding period yield will be less than the coupon yield. If the expected interest rate increase is sufficiently large, the unit will expect to suffer a negative holding period yield on bonds. Each wealth owner decides whether to hold money or bonds based on the relationship between the prevailing interest rate (r) and his or her own subjective view of the rate expected at the end of some relevant holding period (r_e); i.e., based on whether the expected holding period yield on bonds is greater or less than zero (the holding period return on money).

The model can be formalized as follows:[16]

R = coupon
P = market price of bond
r = market rate of interest
r_e = expected rate of interest
y_e = expected holding period yield

Assuming the bond is a perpetuity, the relationship between R, P, and r is

$$P = \frac{R}{r} . \tag{19.5}$$

---

[15] J. M. Keynes, *The General Theory of Employment, Interest and Money* (New York: Harcourt, Brace and World, Inc., 1936); and James Tobin, "Liquidity Preference as Behavior Toward Risk," *Review of Economic Studies*, Vol. 25 (February, 1958), pp. 65–68.

[16] Our treatment is based on Tobin's analysis in "Liquidity Preference as Behavior Toward Risk," ibid.

The expected holding period yield is

$$y_e = \frac{R}{P} + \frac{\Delta P^e}{P} \tag{19.6}$$

The first term is the coupon yield (market interest rate) and the second is the expected percentage change in the price of the bond. This can be rewritten as

$$y_e = \frac{R + \left(\frac{R}{r_e} - \frac{R}{r}\right)}{\frac{R}{r}} = r + \left(\frac{r}{r_e} - 1\right) \tag{19.6'}$$

making use of equation (19.5). The *critical interest rate*, r_c, is the market rate which, given r_e, would yield a zero expected holding period yield for bonds ($y_e = 0$). Thus, setting y_e equal to zero in equation (19.6') and solving for r, we obtain

$$r_c = \frac{r_e}{1 + r_e}. \tag{19.7}$$

If $r > r_c$, then $y_e > 0$ and the wealth owner will hold all bonds, no money. If $r < r_c$, then $y_e < 0$ and the wealth owner will hold all money, no bonds. The money demand function is, therefore, discontinuous at the critical rate as depicted in Figure 19.2. The size of the portfolio to be allocated between money and bonds is a. If $r < r_c$, $m^d = a$; if $r > r_c$, $m^d = 0$.

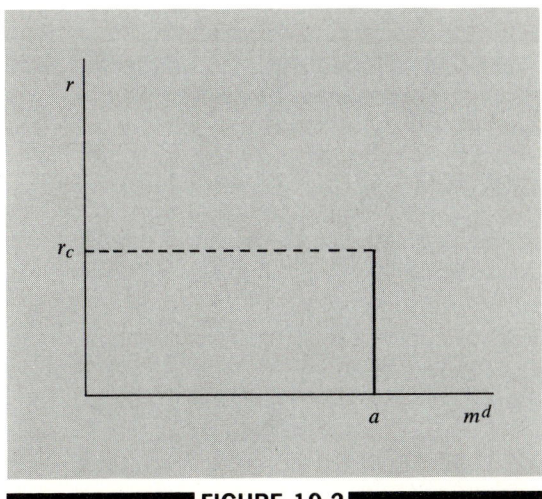

FIGURE 19.2
The Portfolio Decision: All Money or All Bonds

To derive the aggregate money demand function, we simply sum the individual money demand functions. Assuming a large number of individuals and differences in opinion about r_e, this summation can generate a smooth relation between m^d and r as depicted in Figure 19.3. The aggregate function is derived by summing the wealth of all wealth-owning units whose critical rate is above the prevailing interest rate. As the market rate falls, more and more wealth owners find that the market rate is below their critical rate and therefore want to hold money rather than bonds. Therefore, as the interest rate declines, the demand for money increases. Note that above the maximum r_c, $m^d = 0$ (everyone wants to hold bonds) and below the minimum r_c, $m^d = a$ (everyone believes the holding period yield on bonds will be negative). In between, there is a smooth relation between m^d and r.

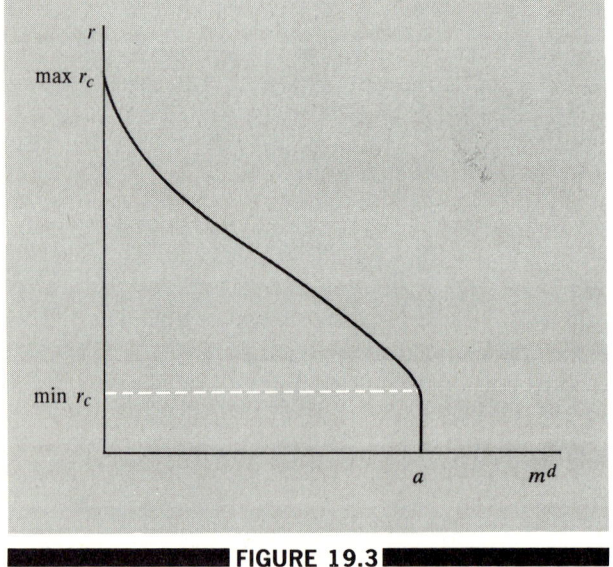

FIGURE 19.3
The Aggregate Demand for Money

An important special case arises if everyone agrees on the critical interest rate or if the interest rate declines to the minimum critical rate. This situation is called a *liquidity trap*. If a liquidity trap exists, the monetary authorities will either completely lose control of the interest rate or will be unable to depress the interest rate below some minimum rate. A principle innovation of Keynes's in the *General Theory* was his discussion of the possibility of a liquidity trap and of the implications of a liquidity trap for the efficacy of monetary policy.

If opinions about r_c converge, the aggregate money demand schedule looks like the individual schedule, Figure 19.2, and becomes discontinuous at the agreed upon r_c. In this case the interest rate will be driven precisely to r_c. If $r > r_c$, everyone wants to hold bonds. Wealth owners who are holding money attempt to purchase bonds, driving up bond prices until the interest rate is depressed to r_c. At this point, wealth owners are just indifferent between holding money and bonds. Therefore, the monetary authorities can buy or sell bonds without affecting the price of bonds or the market interest rate. We will discuss the implications of the liquidity trap further in Chapter 21.

○ Uncertainty, Risk Aversion, and the Asset Demand for Money[17]

The previous section did not explicitly introduce uncertainty. Each wealth-owning unit made its portfolio decision based on its judgment about the expected interest rate over the holding period. This expectation, however, was in effect held with complete certainty. We now explicitly take into account the fact that the holding period yield on fixed coupon bonds is uncertain.

In the previous section we found that wealth owners would prefer to hold all bonds and no money when the expected holding period yield on bonds was positive. When we introduce uncertainty, however, we find wealth owners may prefer to diversify their portfolios, to hold some money as well as some bonds, even when bonds have a positive expected holding period yield. The explanation for the desire to hold money in this case is that, given the uncertainty about the actual holding period yield, there is still a chance that the actual yield will be negative, even though the best estimate of the yield, its expected value, is positive. If wealth owners dislike to take risk, they may prefer to accept some reduction in expected return by holding some of the safe asset, money, in their portfolios.

Assume there is a subjective probability distribution associated with the holding period yield on bonds, y. Define the expected value of y as

$$E(y) = y_e. \tag{19.8}$$

Assume the portfolio is one dollar. The return on the portfolio, R, will then be

$$R = \alpha y \tag{19.9}$$

where α is the proportion of the portfolio held in bonds. The expected value of the return, E, is

$$E = E(R) = E(\alpha y) = \alpha E(y) = \alpha y_e. \tag{19.10}$$

The risk associated with a given portfolio can be measured by the standard deviation of the return on the portfolio, σ. This is a measure of the degree of dispersion of the actual return on the portfolio, R, around the expected value of the return on the portfolio, E:

$$\sigma = \sqrt{E(\alpha y - \alpha y_e)^2} = \alpha \sigma_y \tag{19.11}$$

where σ_y is the standard deviation of the holding period yield on bonds, the measure of the dispersion of the holding period yield on bonds around its expected value.

The utility derived from a portfolio is presumed to depend on the expected return and standard deviation of the portfolio.

---

[17] The model in this section is also based on Tobin's treatment in "Liquidity Preference as Behavior Toward Risk," *ibid.*

$$U = U(E, \sigma) \tag{19.12}$$

Wealth owners must choose among various combinations of E and σ that are available in the market by combining money and bonds in different proportions. To derive the available combinations of E and σ, we use equations (19.10) and (19.11). Solving equation (19.10) for α and substituting this for α in equation (19.11), we get

$$E = \frac{y_e}{\sigma_y} \sigma \tag{19.13}$$

as the equation of the opportunity locus. Assuming $y_e > 0$, this is a positively sloped line through the origin, OC in Figure 19.4. This line depicts all the available combinations of expected return and risk that wealth owners can obtain by varying the amount of money relative to bonds in their portfolios.

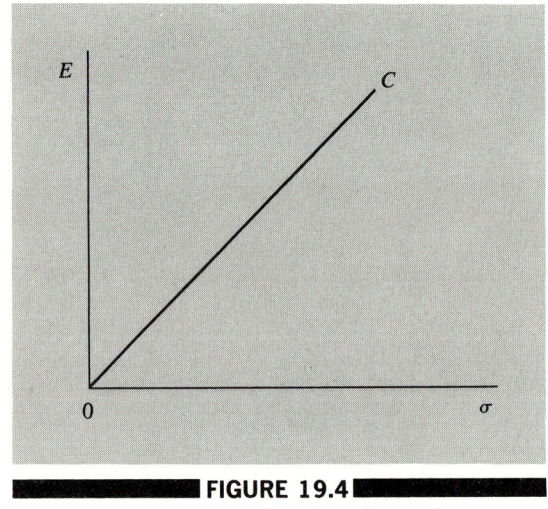

FIGURE 19.4
The Feasible Combinations of Expected Return and Risk

The preferences between E and σ can be depicted as a map of risk-expectation indifference curves, each of which represents combinations of E and σ which provide a constant amount of expected utility. The equation for such an indifference curve is

$$\bar{U} = U(E, \sigma) \tag{19.14}$$

where $\bar{U}$ is some level of expected utility. The slope of an indifference curve is

$$\left. \frac{dE}{d\sigma} \right|_{\bar{U}} = -\frac{U_\sigma}{U_E}. \tag{19.15}$$

$U_E > 0$ but the sign of U_σ can be either positive or negative. If $U_\sigma < 0$, the unit is called a *risk averter*. A risk averter likes expected return but dislikes risk. This is the assumption generally employed in portfolio models. The slope of the indifference curve in this case is positive. The nature of the utility-maximizing combination of money and bonds for risk averters depends on whether their indifference curve is concave or convex. If the curve is concave from above, the unit is called a *diversifier*.[18] A *concave curve* is one whose slope increases as σ becomes larger. This means that the larger the return (and risk), the larger the increase in return required to induce the unit to accept another unit of risk. This seems like the most plausible assumption to make for a risk averter. If the unit is a diversifier, an interior maximum is possible; i.e., the unit may maximize utility by holding both money and bonds, by diversifying the portfolio. The asset demand for money is rationalized in this case as an attempt by wealth owners to adjust the overall riskiness of their portfolios by combining the holding of a safe asset along with the holding of a risky asset with higher expected yield. The expected utility maximum for a diversifier is depicted in Figure 19.5. The wealth owner selects the expected return, risk combination given by E^* and σ^*; this implies the proportion of the portfolio to be held in bonds is $\alpha = \sigma^*/\sigma_y$.

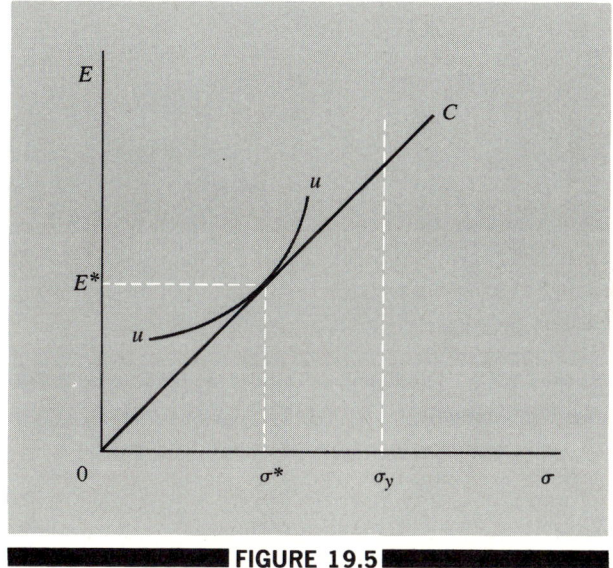

FIGURE 19.5
The Demand for Money:
The Implications of Risk Aversion

This model, generally referred to as the *mean-variance model* of portfolio behavior, demonstrates that uncertainty can induce wealth owners to hold money balances; e.g., if wealth owners are risk averters and diversifiers.[19] In this case, the proportion of money wealth owners desire to hold in portfolios depends on the interest rate as

---

[18] The other cases (where units are risk averters but the indifference curves are convex from above, and where units are *risk lovers*) will be considered as problems at the end of the chapter.
[19] The variance of a variable is σ^2 where σ is the standard deviation.

in the typical money demand function. A change in the expected holding period yield rotates the opportunity locus; e.g., if y_e increases, OC rotates to OC' as in Figure 19.6. As should be expected in any indifference curve type analysis, the result of such a rotation of the opportunity locus on desired money balances is ambiguous, reflecting the usual conflict between substitution and income effects. An increase in y_e increases the expected return on bonds relative to money, inducing wealth owners to substitute in favor of bonds; this is the *substitution effect*. On the other hand, a higher rate of return on bonds provides the opportunity for the unit to enjoy both a higher return *and* additional security by increasing money holdings; this is the *income effect*. Thus, while the model suggests that the demand for money should depend upon the interest rate, it does not yield an unambiguous relationship between the demand for money and the interest rate.

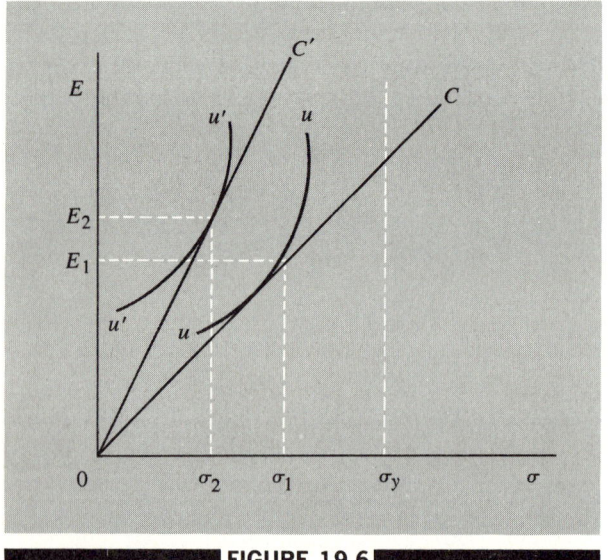

FIGURE 19.6
The Response to a Change in the Interest Rate

The two models of the asset demand for money developed above are subject to the same criticism: they do not apply to the demand for money in an economy in which there exists highly liquid, default-free short-term debt, such as savings deposits at insured commercial banks and thrift institutions and short-term debt issued by the government. Such assets are said to *dominate* money; i.e., they are equally safe but pay a certain positive return. Wealth owners who expect negative holding period yields on variable price bonds or who prefer to reduce the risk associated with their portfolio by mixing a safe asset with holdings of a risky asset will prefer to hold the liquid interest-earning asset that dominates money, not money. Therefore, the models of asset demand discussed above are really models of the demand for liquid, short-term debt rather than money.

The Application of the Portfolio Approach to Asset Holdings to the Demand for Money

Despite these objections to the speculative demand and mean-variance models, many students of the demand for money continue to prefer an asset demand approach.[20] The point of departure for this approach is Hicks's suggestion that one explanation for a demand for noninterest-bearing money is that money yields a nonpecuniary "utility" yield.

The Portfolio Demand for Money. According to this view, money is like a consumer durable good which yields a flow of services in kind. For money, this service flow takes the form of security, convenience, and flexibility, and it is this return in kind that corresponds to the rate of return on money balances. Once we have identified a rate of return on money, we can treat the demand for money like the demand for any other asset, depending on wealth (the size of the portfolio to be allocated among alternative assets) and relative rates of return.

The portfolio approach to asset demands is analogous to the theory of consumer choice. The objects of choice, however, are asset stocks rather than commodity flows, the relative prices are the relative rates of return, and the constraint is wealth rather than income. The demand for any asset is assumed to depend on its rate of return and the rate of return on alternative assets and on the stock of wealth:

$$a_i^d = f(r, a) \tag{19.16}$$

where a_i^d is the demand for the ith asset, r is the vector of rates of return on the various assets, and a is the net wealth of the unit. The influence of a change in the rate of return on the jth asset on the demand for the ith asset depends on whether the ith and j^{th} assets are gross complements or gross substitutes. It is often assumed that all assets are *gross substitutes*. This means that an increase in the rate of return on one asset increases the demand for that asset and decreases the demand for all other assets. Another assumption usually made is that all assets are *normal* with respect to wealth; i.e., an increase in wealth increases the demand for all assets.

This application of the general theory of portfolio selection to the demand for money is intended as a complete explanation of the demand for money, not as a partial theory (such as the speculative demand and mean-variance approaches), relevant only to decisions regarding the investment as opposed to transactions portfolios. In the general portfolio approach, no distinction is made between investment and transactions portfolios. The usefulness of money in facilitating transactions, nevertheless, is one of the key factors which result in a flow of nonpecuniary services from

---

[20] Among those who have contributed to the development and empirical estimation of the asset demand approach are Milton Friedman, "The Quantity Theory of Money—A Restatement" in Milton Friedman (ed.), *Essays in the Quantity Theory of Money* (Chicago: The University of Chicago Press, 1956), pp. 3–21; Alan Meltzer, "The Demand for Money: Evidence from the Time Series," *Journal of Political Economy,* Vol. 71 (June, 1963), pp. 219–246; Karl Brunner and Alan Meltzer, "Predicting Velocity: Implications for Theory and Policy," *Journal of Finance,* Vol. 18 (May, 1963), pp. 319–354; and David Laidler, "Some Evidence on the Demand for Money," *Journal of Political Economy,* Vol. 74 (June, 1966), pp. 55–68.

holding money. Another property associated with the service flow of money is the security afforded by holding money, compared to risky assets. Thus, the general portfolio approach combines some aspects of both transactions, speculative and mean-variance approaches.

Operational Specification of the Portfolio Approach. The wealth variable employed in such formulations is either nonhuman wealth—corresponding to the wealth variable in our models (although it should also include consumer durable goods as well as financial assets) or permanent income, which is the return on total (human plus nonhuman) wealth. The rates of return generally include rates on bonds (long term as well as short term), equities, and goods. The *dividend price ratio* (the ratio of dividend payments to the price of equities) is generally used as a measure of the rate of return on equities, and the expected rate of inflation is often included as a measure of the expected nominal rate of return on durable goods held in portfolios. Thus, the demand for money according to the general portfolio approach can be specified as

$$\frac{M^d}{P} = L(r,\ i,\ e,\ \dot{P}^e/P,\ X_P,\ \text{or}\ a) \tag{19.16'}$$

where r is the short-term bond rate, i is the long-term bond rate, e is the dividend price yield, $\dot{P}^e/P$ is the expected inflation rate, X_P is permanent income, and a is nonhuman wealth.

It has generally been difficult to get both long- and short-term rates to enter significantly into money demand equations. Transaction approaches invariably opt for the short rate, since short-term assets are the only type of assets that can be expected to be included in the transactions portfolio. Empirical specifications of the portfolio approach generally have included long-term rates. We have not distinguished bonds of differing maturities, so this issue never had to be considered. In the next chapter we will introduce bonds of differing maturities and therefore distinguish between short-term and long-term interest rates. In applications of our model where there is a single interest-earning financial asset, the three rates included in equation (19.16') reduce to the single rate, r. We do not explicitly allow for real assets in portfolios, so we also exclude the expected inflation rate; estimated money demand functions also have generally not included the expected inflation rate.

Income is sometimes included along with wealth in portfolio models of the demand for money to capture the special role of money as a medium of exchange.[21] Generalizing the portfolio demand for money to include both wealth and income, and specializing our specification to include a single interest rate and to exclude the expected inflation rate, we rewrite our basic money demand function as

$$\frac{M^d}{P} = L(r,X,a) \tag{19.17}$$

---

[21] See, for example, Duncan Foley and Miguel Sidrauski, *Monetary and Fiscal Policy in a Growing Economy* (New York: Macmillan Co., 1971); and Milton Friedman, "The Quantity Theory of Money—A Restatement," in Milton Friedman (ed.), *Essays in the Quantity Theory of Money* (Chicago: The University of Chicago Press, 1956).

where $L_r < 0$, $L_x > 0$, and $1 > L_a \geq 0$. In Chapter 21 we will investigate the implications of $L_a > 0$ and compare the role of the money demand function in macro models when $L_x > 0$ but $L_a = 0$, referred to as the *pure transactions approach*, and when $L_a > 0$ but $L_x = 0$, called the *pure wealth approach*.

EMPIRICAL EVIDENCE

In this section we consider the empirical evidence on the demand for money. First, we discuss the evidence in support of the asset approach. Then we turn to Stephen Goldfeld's extensive empirical study of the demand for money[22] which provides considerable support for the transactions approach.

The Evidence on the Asset Demand for Money

The empirical evidence in support of the asset approach includes both casual comparisons of money holdings and income and econometric analyses of money demand functions using income and wealth as alternative scale variables. Milton Friedman and Anna Schwartz support their preference for the vaguer portfolio approach over the more explicit but narrower transactions approach with evidence that the narrow transactions approach simply cannot account for the size of observed household money holdings.[23] Friedman and Schwartz note that households hold about three weeks of income in currency and two months of income in demand deposits. These amounts are simply too large to represent transaction needs. According to the inventory models, households should hold on average, at most, one half of their regular income receipts as money balances; this amounts to one half of weekly income for those who get paid weekly or one half of monthly income for those who get paid monthly. This evidence suggests that the transactions demand approach does not fully capture the range of motives for holding money by households. Friedman and Schwartz, on the other hand, accept the inventory model as an adequate explanation of the business demand for money. They conclude from a similarly casual look at data on money holdings and transactions that the inventory model is capable of accounting for the observed size of business money balances.[24]

Early econometric results also provided support for the asset demand approach. Karl Brunner, Alan Meltzer, and David Laidler found that either nonhuman wealth or permanent income performed better than measured income in money demand functions using annual data.[25] However, more recent evidence using quarterly data,

---

[22] Stephen Goldfeld, "The Demand for Money Revisited," *Brookings Papers on Economic Activity* (1973:3), pp. 577–646.

[23] Milton Friedman and Anna Schwartz, *Monetary Statistics of the United States: Estimates, Sources, Methods* (New York: National Bureau of Economic Research, 1970).

[24] In contrast to the conclusions of Friedman and Schwartz, Case Sprenkle found that the simple inventory models substantially underpredict money balances held by firms. See Case M. Sprenkle, "The Uselessness of Transactions Demand Models," *Journal of Finance*, Vol. 24 (December, 1969) pp. 835–847.

[25] These articles are referenced in footnote 20 in this chapter.

such as Goldfeld's empirical study of the demand for money, suggests that income performs better than wealth in the money demand function.[26]

○ Goldfeld's Empirical Results

Goldfeld's study generally supports the transactions model of the demand for money. In particular, it supports the role of income rather than wealth; it supports the role of short-term interest rates rather than long-term rates; and it rejects a separate role for inflationary expectations (other than through the effect of inflationary expectations on nominal short-term interest rates).[27]

Goldfeld's basic equation is

$$\ln \frac{M}{P} = \alpha + \epsilon_{LRCP} \ln RCP + \epsilon_{LRTD} \ln RTD + \epsilon_{LX} \ln GNP. \qquad (19.18)$$

Two short-term interest rates are employed: the commercial paper rate (RCP) and the passbook rate on time deposits at commercial banks (RTD). The former is an *open market* rate—one determined on a day-to-day basis by supply and demand forces. The latter is an *administered rate*—set by commercial banks and changed quite infrequently. The income variable is real GNP. And the real money supply is computed by deflating the nominal money supply by the GNP price deflator. Quarterly data from 1952 II through 1972 IV was used to estimate the parameters. The equation estimated by Goldfeld allowed for lagged adjustment of the demand for money to changes in interest rates and income. Letting equation (19.18) represent the target or long-run money demand function, the short-run money demand function is given by

$$\Delta \ln \left(\frac{M}{P}\right)_t = \beta \left[\ln \left(\frac{M}{P}\right)^*_t - \ln \left(\frac{M}{P}\right)_{t-1}\right] \qquad (19.19)$$

where $\ln \left(\frac{M}{P}\right)^*_t$ is the long-run demand for money given by equation (19.18). According to equation (19.19), the change in the demand for money is proportional to the gap between desired and actual money balances. β is the speed of the adjustment coefficient, indicating the percentage of the gap closed per quarter. This coefficient is estimated to be about 0.3 so that 30 percent of the gap is closed in the first quarter. This implies that the adjustment is nearly complete within a year. Given that our models

---

[26] It should be noted, however, that Goldfeld's equation was estimated using a stock adjustment specification; i.e., assuming that there are lags in the adjustment of actual to desired money balances. This specification implies that the demand for money can be expressed as a function of a distributed lag on both income and interest rates. The operational specification of permanent income, in turn, is generally a distributed lag on current and past values of measured income. Therefore, it is difficult to determine whether the implicit distributed lag on income is capturing lagged adjustment or the formation of expectations concerning permanent income.

[27] Goldfeld's results are not so overwhelming, however, as to close out debate on these issues. There was some evidence, for example, that wealth might be included as a separate variable along with income. Particularly in light of the recent breakdown in the performance of most money demand equations, these issues should be considered quite unsettled. For my own part, I admit to a strong preference for the transactions model.

are intended to represent the response over a one- to three-year period following a disturbance, we only consider the equilibrium or long-run values of the elasticities.

The long-run elasticities based on Goldfeld's study are presented in Table 19.1; they conform to the expectations based on the transactions demand model, at least when that model is solved subject to an integer constraint. The interest elasticity of the demand for money is between zero and -0.5. If both interest rates change, the interest elasticity is the sum of ϵ_{LRCP} and ϵ_{LRTD}, -0.227. However, if only the open market rate changes, the interest elasticity is a slim -0.06. The simple inventory theoretic model developed above suggested an interest elasticity of -0.5. But in Appendix B we demonstrate that requiring an integer solution lowers the expected elasticity to between 0 and -0.5. The real income elasticity is 0.68, between 0.5 and 1.0 as expected. The simple inventory theoretic model suggests a real income elasticity of 0.5. But allowing only for integer solutions, the expected value of this parameter is between 0.5 and 1.0. The elasticity of nominal demand for money with respect to the price level is unity; this result however was imposed as an assumption rather than estimated. However, empirical tests reported by Goldfeld support this assumption.

$$\left.\begin{array}{l}\epsilon_{LRCP} = -0.067\\ \epsilon_{LRTD} = -0.16\end{array}\right\} -0.227$$

$$\epsilon_{LX} = 0.68$$

TABLE 19.1
Long-Run Elasticities

APPENDIX

A The Definition of Money

The model we have been employing includes two financial assets: a noninterest-bearing asset which we have called *money* and a single-earning asset (issued by both government and business sectors) which we have referred to as a *bond* (although it really includes both bonds and equities). We have assumed the money supply is controlled by the government and have not explicitly introduced a banking system. Therefore, *money* in the model corresponds to currency issued by the government. In the next chapter we will introduce a commercial banking sector and redefine the money supply as the sum of the public's holdings of currency and *demand deposits*, checking accounts issued by commercial banks. This definition of money has become known as $M1$ and has long been identified as the money concept most closely corresponding to the means of payment; it has uniformly been the definition employed by those who accepted a transactions approach to the demand for money.

Those accepting the alternative asset approach to the demand for money have sometimes employed broader definitions of money—including savings and time deposits (other than large-scale negotiable certificates of deposits, called *CD*'s) at commercial banks, and perhaps also, such deposits at thrift institutions (mutual savings banks, savings and loan associations, and credit unions). These broader definitions are referred to as $M2$ and $M3$, respectively. *Savings deposits* (or shares) are mostly passbook accounts. Although commercial banks and thrift institutions must reserve the right to require at least 30 days written notice before withdrawal, in practice, withdrawals are honored on demand. *Time deposits*, unlike savings deposits, explicitly specify a maturity but are redeemable prior to maturity with some sacrifice of interest.

Recently there has been growing concern that developments in financial practices over the postwar period and in financial instruments and technology over the last few years have reduced the importance of the narrowly defined money stock ($M1$) in the financial system and have blurred the distinction between $M1$ and savings and time deposits at both commercial banks and thrift institutions. In particular, the introduction in New England of *negotiable order of withdrawal* (*NOW*) *accounts* (which in effect allow checking privileges on interest-bearing savings accounts), expanded third-party payment privileges from savings accounts, telephone transfers between savings and demand deposit accounts, and noninterest-bearing checking accounts at state-chartered thrift institutions in some states has made the association of $M1$ with the means of payment increasingly less compelling. The most recent development has been the introduction of *automatic transfers from savings to demand deposits* (*ATS*) *accounts* permitting commercial banks, in effect, to convert savings deposits into interest-bearing checking accounts. In response to these developments, the Federal Reserve System has been experimenting with a new definition of money, called $M1+$, which includes all checkable deposits (demand deposits, *NOW* accounts, checking deposits at thrift institutions) and savings accounts at commercial banks, and has proposed a new set of definitions for $M1$, $M2$, and $M3$.[1]

The net effect of these developments is that the appropriate definition of money remains an unsettled issue. For our purposes it is not critical which of the several definitions discussed

---

[1] See "A Proposal for Redefining the Monetary Aggregates," in *Federal Reserve Bulletin*, Vol. 65 (January, 1979), pp. 13–42. $M1$ would be redefined to include all transactions-related savings deposits at commercial banks and thrift institutions (e.g., *NOW* accounts, *ATS* accounts, and demand deposits at thrift institutions). $M2$ would add all other savings deposits at commercial banks and thrift institutions; and $M3$ would add all time deposits at commercial banks and thrift institutions.

above is employed. The particular definition will not dramatically affect our conclusions.[2] If we move to an $M1+$ or broader definition of money, we must view the interest rate term in our money demand equation as the difference between the interest rate on bonds and the interest rate earned on money balances. The resulting models would be a bit more complicated but would not contradict any of the basic insights developed throughout our analysis.

APPENDIX

B The Implications of the Integer Constraint in the Transactions Model of the Demand for Money

In the previous chapter we used calculus to solve the formal model of the transactions demand for money for the cost-minimizing value of B, the value of bonds converted into money each time such an exchange takes place. This procedure permitted us to derive an explicit solution for the optimal value of B in terms of the interest rate (r), the total value of transactions (T), and the cost per exchange between money and bonds (E). However, allowing B to take on any value fails to impose a necessary restriction on T/B^*, the optimal number of exchanges; the number of exchanges must be an *integer* greater than or equal to two. One exchange allows only for the purchase of bonds, not for the sale of bonds necessary to generate the money ultimately required to carry out spending plans. And 2.3 exchanges has no meaning. In this appendix, we consider the implications of the integer restriction for the demand for money.[3]

The Demand for Money by Noncash Managers

The first implication of the integer restriction is that if it is not profitable to make at least two exchanges, the unit should hold its transactions balances entirely in the form of money. It will be profitable to make two exchanges only if the interest earned on bonds in this case exceeds the exchange costs associated with two exchanges. If two exchanges are made, $T/B = 2$ and exchange costs are $2E$. If $T/B = 2$, $B = T/2$, and average bond holdings equal $T/4$ ($1/2 \cdot T/2$). This was the case illustrated in Figure 19.1. Therefore, it is profitable to make two exchanges only if

---

[2] On the other hand, the evolution of the appropriate definition of money through the effects of financial innovations increases the uncertainty of policymakers about the structure of the economy and thus greatly complicates the formulation and execution of macroeconomic policy. In addition, these developments may explain, at least in part, why empirical money demand functions using the conventional definition of $M1$ (and to a lesser extent, equations using the conventional definitions of broader aggregates such as $M2$) have markedly deteriorated in quality (as judged by both in-sample "fit" and out-of-sample "predictive" performance). For a discussion of the deterioration in estimated money demand functions and an assortment of attempted but largely unsuccessful remedies, see Stephen Goldfeld, "The Case of the Missing Money," *Brookings Papers on Economic Activity* (1976:3).

[3] The implications of the integer constraint are discussed in Robert Barro, "Integral Constraints and Aggregation in an Inventory Model of Money Demand," *Journal of Finance*, Vol. 31 (March, 1976), pp. 77–88.

Part V · Refinements of the Financial Sector

$$r(T/4) > 2E$$

or

$$T > \frac{8E}{r}. \tag{19B.1}$$

This is the threshold level of income below which active cash management will not be profitable. For example, if the interest rate is 6 percent per year ($r = .06/12$) and the exchange cost is $1 per exchange ($E = 1$), the threshold level of monthly transactions is $1,600 ($19,200 per year). If T is less than $1,600, the unit should hold all its transactions balances in money.[4] Such units are called *noncash managers*.

The demand for money equation for noncash managers can easily be derived. They begin the period with money balances equal to income receipts. They spend the money evenly over the period. Their average cash balance is therefore

$$M^N = \frac{T^N}{2} \tag{19B.2}$$

where M^N is the demand for money by noncash managers and T^N is the value of transactions by such units.

The Implications of Integer Solutions for the Behavior of Active Cash Managers

The restriction of the number of exchanges to integers equal to or greater than two also has important implications for active cash managers. A change in E or r will affect the demand for money *only* if it affects the optimal number of exchanges (T/B). Therefore, small changes in E and r will not affect the demand for money by active cash managers. In addition, small changes in X will result in proportional changes in the demand for money (at an unchanged number of exchanges between money and bonds).

The implication of integer constraints therefore is to reduce the interest elasticity to between 0 and $-1/2$ and to increase the income (transactions) elasticity to between 1/2 and 1.

● REVIEW QUESTIONS

1. Explain the economic gains associated with the evolution from a barter to a money economy.

2. Compare the theoretical predictions concerning the signs and magnitudes of the parameters in the inventory theoretic specification of the money demand function with the empirical evidence.

---

[4] For a household, the relevant transactions measure is total expenditures rather than income and is therefore net of saving and taxes.

3. The speculative demand and mean-variance models demand for money both provide a rationale for an asset demand for money. How do these models differ? What are their limitations?

● PROBLEMS

1. Draw the risk-return indifference map for risk-averse portfolio owners if the indifference curves are (a) concave from above and (b) convex from above. Discuss the behavior implied by each case. Then show a typical solution for the utility-maximizing combination of risk and return in each case; to do so, impose budget constraints on each diagram and find the point of utility maximization. Then explain why units with concave curves are called *diversifiers* and those with convex curves are called *plungers*.

2. Draw the indifference map for risk lovers. Then impose a budget constraint and find the utility-maximizing solution. Explain the result.

3. Assume a unit receives periodic income payments of $1,500. Exchange costs are $2 per exchange and the interest rate is 1 percent per period. What is the unit's demand for money, based on the inventory theoretic approach? Explain.

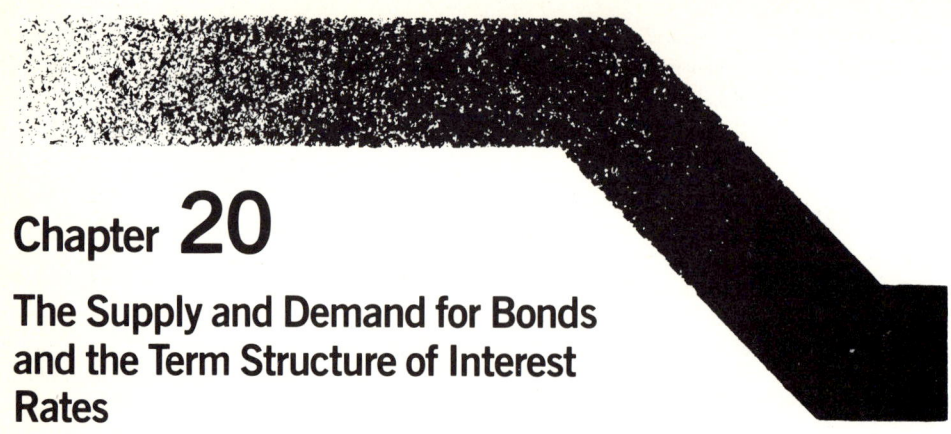

Chapter 20

The Supply and Demand for Bonds and the Term Structure of Interest Rates

Up to this point we have treated the bond market as the "redundant" market. All graphical and mathematical analysis has been carried out in terms of the commodity and the money markets. In this chapter we will examine the bond market explicitly. Bonds have two roles in our model: as an alternative asset to money in household portfolios and as a source of finance for government deficits and business investment. In the first section we discuss the demand for bonds and develop restrictions on the money and bond demand equations required to insure internal consistency in portfolio transactions. In the second section we make explicit the relation of the supply of bonds by the government and business sectors to the financing of government expenditures and private investment. This completes the specification of the end-of-period form of the financial market equations.

In the previous chapters, we have assumed that there was a single nonmoney financial asset issued by both government and business firms and therefore a single interest rate. In this chapter we relax this assumption in two different ways. First, we allow for bonds differing in term to maturity by introducing a term structure equation. In Appendix B at the end of the chapter we introduce an explicit three-asset model that includes equities as well as money and bonds. This extension of the financial sector to include the determination of the price of equities completes the modeling of the dual price theory of investment, introduced in Chapter 14.

○ THE BALANCE SHEET IDENTITY AND THE DEMAND FOR BONDS

We begin by assuming that there are two financial assets that can be held in household portfolios: money and bonds. In Chapter 19 we discussed the specification of the demand for money. The household balance sheet constraint (BSC) permits us to derive the specification of the demand for bonds implicit in the specification of the demand for money. This analysis follows the warning of James Tobin and William Brainard to always look at the implied specification of the missing asset demand equation; if it appears unreasonable, then the specification of the explicit asset demand equation must also be unreasonable.[1]

The precise application of the *BSC* depends on the specification of the stocks in the model. We will employ a continuous framework in this section in which asset stocks and hence wealth are fixed at time t. This simplifies the use and interpretation of the *BSC*, but the basic restrictions on asset demand equations are unchanged in the more complicated discrete end-of-period specification discussed in Appendix A.

Wealth (a) is exogenously fixed as the sum of exogenously supplied money, government, and private bonds in this case;

$$a \equiv m + b \tag{20.1}$$

where $b = b_g + b_p$, the sum of government and private bonds. Equation (20.1) is the household balance sheet identity (*BSI*). For our purposes, a related identity, referred to as the balance sheet constraint (*BSC*), is most useful. The *BSC* requires that the sum of wealth owners' demands for money and bonds exhaust the total amount of wealth; i.e., households must want to hold their existing wealth in either money or bonds. The *BSC* is written as

$$a \equiv L(\ ) + B(\ ) \tag{20.2}$$

where $L(\ )$ and $B(\ )$ represent the demands for money and bonds, respectively. Note that the *BSC*, like the *BSI*, is an identity. It is not a conditional relationship that applies only in equilibrium, despite the fact that the *BSI* and *BSC* differ from each other only in that the demands for money and bonds in the *BSC* replace the actual supplies in the *BSI*. The *BSC* is a logical proposition about the relationship among asset demands and wealth. It requires that household demands for assets just exhaust existing wealth; i.e., households must want to hold their wealth in some combination of available assets. Whatever they do not want to hold in money, they must want to hold in bonds.

The *BSC* implies that *the specification of the demand for bonds is implicit in the specification of the demand for money*. We can derive the implied form of the bond demand equation from the *BSC* and the explicit money demand equation. Assume the money demand function is given by

$$L(\ ) \equiv \bar{L} + L_x X + L_r r. \tag{20.3}$$

The bond demand function must be given by

$$B(\ ) \equiv a - L(\ ) \tag{20.4}$$

or

$$B(\ ) \equiv -\bar{L} - L_x X - L_r r + a$$

---

[1] James Tobin and William Brainard, "Pitfalls in Financial Model Building," *American Economic Review*, Papers and Proceedings, Vol. LVIII (May, 1968), pp. 99–122.

or

$$B(\ ) = \bar{B} + B_x X + B_r r + B_a a$$

where $\bar{B} = -\bar{L}$, $B_x = -L_x$, $B_r = -L_r$, and $B_a = 1$. In Appendix A we discuss these restrictions in more detail. At this point, though, we want to show how the *BSC* may aid us in specifying the form of the explicit asset demand functions in our model.

The assumption that $B_a = 1$ is a very powerful one. It implies, for example, that any increase in government bonds associated with financing a deficit will not introduce any excess supply into the bond market; the demand for bonds will increase dollar-for-dollar with the increase in the supply of bonds (i.e., with the increase in wealth, the sum of money and bonds outstanding). This might well be an assumption that we are unwilling to make and indeed would not make if we were explicitly specifying the bond demand function. Yet we did make this assumption implicitly when we specified the money demand function so that $L_a = 0$. In the next two chapters we will consider the implications of allowing $1 > L_a > 0$ and hence $0 < B_a < 1$. For now, we simply note that the use of the *BSC* can aid in the specification of the form of the included asset demand functions by permitting us to consider the plausibility of the implied specification of the redundant asset demand function.

FINANCING CONSTRAINTS AND THE SUPPLY OF BONDS

The supply of bonds is intimately related to the decision to purchase goods. In this section we develop supply functions for both government and private bonds; in each case, the supply function is explicitly related to the relevant spending decision.

The introduction of the financing constraints completes the end-of-period specification of the model by determining the change in the supply of bonds over the period. Although the financing constraints are not relevant to the determination of the initial response of income, the price level, or the interest rate to disturbances in the beginning-of-period specification, financing constraints link the periods, so that the long-run analysis of the model is unaffected by the choice of beginning- or end-of-period specification of stocks.

The Government Financing Constraint

The government must finance its current expenditures on goods and services (G) and transfer payments (Tr) by some combination of tax receipts (Tx) and issue of money and/or bonds (ΔM, ΔB_g). To simplify the analysis, assume that prices are fixed so that we can treat the issue of money and bonds in real terms (Δm, Δb_g).[2] The government financing constraint (*GFC*) can be written as

$$G + Tr \equiv Tx + \Delta m + \Delta b_g. \tag{20.5}$$

---

[2] When prices are variable, the amount of the change in nominal supplies of money and/or bonds required to finance a deficit will depend on the price level.

To further simplify, we define taxes net of transfers, T, as $T \equiv Tx - Tr$ so that

$$G \equiv T + \Delta m + \Delta b_g. \tag{20.5'}$$

The *GFC* has two important implications which we have discussed previously: it implies that the government's policy instruments cannot be set independently and it implies that full equilibrium requires that the government's budget be balanced.

The Interdependence of Fiscal Instruments and the Supply of Government Bonds. The government can select independently only three of the four instruments; the fourth must be set so as to be consistent with the *GFC*. It is a matter of taste and convenience which of the four instruments we treat as depending on decisions about the remaining three. But we find it most useful to view Δb_g as being determined by decisions concerning G, T, and Δm. G and T decisions are the core of fiscal policy; if $G = T$, then the budget is balanced and $\Delta m + \Delta b_g = 0$. If $G \neq T$, then a deficit (surplus) is being run and a decision about financing the deficit (surplus) must be made. Under our institutional arrangements, the government does not issue money; this is the responsibility of the Federal Reserve System (Fed). The Fed issues money by purchasing government securities for its own portfolio. Thus, the *GFC* as specified above represents a consolidated financing constraint that applies to the government plus the Fed. Writing it with bond supply as the dependent variable

$$\Delta b_g \equiv \underbrace{G - T}_{\text{fiscal}} - \underbrace{\Delta m}_{\text{OMO}} \tag{20.5''}$$

allows us to identify decisions about G and T (with appropriate Δb_g of course) as *fiscal decisions* and decisions about Δm (accompanied of course by appropriate Δb_g) as *monetary policy decisions* (open market operations).

We can rewrite this in a form that will permit us to introduce this relation into our model. Government expenditures (G) equal last period's government expenditures (G_{-1}) plus the change in government expenditures from last period to the current one; thus, $G \equiv G_{-1} + \Delta G$. Similarly, $T \equiv T_{-1} + \Delta T$ where T_{-1} is last period's net tax receipts and ΔT is the change in net tax receipts from last period to the current one. Substituting these relations into equation (20.5″) yields

$$\Delta b_g \equiv G_{-1} - T_{-1} + \Delta G - \Delta T - \Delta m$$

or

$$\Delta b_g \equiv D_{-1} + \Delta G - \Delta T - \Delta m \tag{20.5'''}$$

where $D_{-1} \equiv G_{-1} - T_{-1}$, last period's deficit.

The Cumulative vs. Impact Effects of Changes in Fiscal Instruments. This form of the *GFC* is convenient for pointing out that government bonds may be increased even if government expenditures and taxes remain unchanged in a given period; i.e., bonds must be issued to finance not only current changes in G and T, but also past changes as reflected in the deficit inherited from the previous period. Assume, for example, that the budget is initially balanced and $\Delta m = 0$. If G is increased, then in the first period $\Delta b_g = \Delta G$. If G remains indefinitely at its new value, $\Delta G = 0$ in future periods but each period will inherit a deficit from the previous period. Therefore, $\Delta b_g = \Delta G$ in the first period and $\Delta b_g = D_{-1}$, the deficit inherited from the previous period (and always equal to the first period's ΔG under assumptions that T is exogenous), in all future periods. Even if there are no lags in consumption, investment, and money demand functions, the response of the economy to a once-and-for-all change in G will evolve *over time* as bonds are issued to finance a deficit initiated in some previous period. This reflects the basic dynamic element in all stock-flow models: short-run stock-flow equilibrium is upset by the changes in stocks associated with financing the flows. A full stock-flow equilibrium requires that households, businesses, and government run balanced budgets so that no asset accumulation or liability emission occurs to upset the equilibrium. We will return to this problem in the next chapter when we consider the long-run response of the economy to fiscal policy.

○ The Investment Financing Constraint and the Supply of Private Bonds

A similar analysis applies to the supply of private bonds, but most macro models ignore the private sector counterpart to the *GFC*. Businesses supply bonds to finance the acquisition of capital. We will model this process in a particularly simple manner. We assume that all capital is financed by sale of bonds to households. There is no internal finance; i.e., firms do not use retained earnings to purchase capital goods. The problem with this approach is that such bonds should really be treated more properly as equities, claims on the residual earnings of the firm; i.e., earnings after payment of all factor costs. If firms do not retain earnings, they must pay out all residual income (profits) to their owners. The present value of such residual income would be an asset in wealth owners' portfolios. The equities that reflect this claim to residual income would differ from a bond in a number of ways. Bonds have coupons fixed in nominal terms; equities have variable coupons, coupons that can be expected to vary with both the price level and the level of real economic activity. Despite all this, we will assume that the private bonds issued by firms to finance investment are perfect substitutes for government bonds in order that we can retain our two-asset framework. In Appendix B we will expand our model to a three-asset case and explicitly introduce equities along with bonds.

We write the investment financing constraint as

$$\Delta b_p \equiv I(\ ) \tag{20.6}$$

where Δb_p is the change in the supply of private (business-issued) bonds and $I(\ )$ is desired investment. $I(\ )$ can be written as last period's investment (I_{-1}) plus the desired change in investment from last period to the current period (ΔI); i.e., $I \equiv I_{-1} + \Delta I$. And ΔI can be expressed in terms of the interest rate from our basic investment function $(\Delta I = I_r \Delta r)$. Thus, the *IFC* gives us the endogenous change in the supply of private bonds:

$$\Delta b_p = I_{-1} + I_r \Delta r \qquad (20.6')$$

Capital and Household Portfolio Behavior

The conventional specification of macroeconomic models assumes the capital stock is fixed although net investment is occurring. The capital stock affects both the level of the economy's potential output and the stock of assets which must be absorbed into portfolios. In Keynesian models where there is an assumed gap between actual and potential output, we can ignore any effect of changes in potential output. However, the introduction of the financing constraint permits us to incorporate the mechanism by which new capital is absorbed into portfolios.

To maintain a simple framework, we have allowed only households to make meaningful portfolio decisions, in the sense of decisions about the *composition* of assets (or liabilities). Our firms are allowed to hold physical units of capital and issue bonds. Their portfolio decision is confined to matching liability issue to asset acquisition; i.e., they must finance their position in capital. Firms of course hold financial assets as well as capital and issue short- and long-term bonds as well as equities. However, we are going to continue to ignore firm portfolio decisions concerning composition of assets and composition of liabilities.

Nevertheless, we are able to improve the modeling of the absorption of capital into portfolios. Firms, after all, are artificial entities. They do not "own" capital. Households own firms and hence indirectly own the economy's capital. The value of the economy's capital is reflected in household portfolios by the market value of household holdings of business bonds and equities.[3] In the present framework, we require via the *IFC* that all investment be financed by issue of bonds: $I \equiv \Delta b_p$. The capital stock is the summation of past net investments (assuming no depreciation)

$$K_t \equiv \sum_{i=0}^{\infty} I_{t-i} \qquad (20.7a)$$

and the outstanding stock of bonds is the summation of past changes in the supply of bonds

$$b_p \equiv \sum_{i=0}^{\infty} \Delta b_{pt-i}. \qquad (20.7b)$$

Therefore, the value of the capital stock is reflected in household portfolios in the value of business bonds.

$$K \equiv b_p \qquad (20.8)$$

THE TERM STRUCTURE OF INTEREST RATES

We have been assuming that government and business bonds are considered to be perfect substitutes in household portfolios so that there is a single bond market

---

[3] Recall our discussion of sectoral balance sheets in Chapter 2. There we showed that the market value of capital was given by the sum of business bonds and equity.

and a single interest rate on financial assets in the economy. In this section we relax this restrictive treatment by introducing relations among bonds of different maturity and risk. The *maturity of a bond* refers to the date at which the principal amount of the loan is due to be repaid. The *term structure of interest rates* refers to the relation among the interest rates on bonds that differ only in the length of time (term) to maturity.[4] The approach used in this section to allow for multiple bonds and interest rates is the one generally used in econometric models. An alternative approach would be to specify separate supply and demand functions for each type of bond, similar to our analysis in Appendix B.

○ The Expectations Theory of the Term Structure[5]

Let us begin by assuming that there are two maturities of bonds—a one-year and a two-year maturity—and by ignoring risk associated with the possibility of default. The following notation will be useful:

$_tR_n$ = the rate on an n-year bond in period t; for the case of a one-year bond, $_tR_1$, for a two-year bond, $_tR_2$.

$_{t+j}r_n$ = the expected interest rate on an n-year bond, j years from now; e.g., $_{t+1}r_1$ is the rate expected on a one-year bond in one year.

The *pure expectations hypothesis* assumes that there are no transactions costs of moving between bonds, that there is no uncertainty, and that investors are profit-maximizers and therefore select the security that yields the highest return over the period for which funds are to be invested.

Assume that the relevant holding period is two years. The investor has the option of investing in a two-year bond or in two successive one-year bonds. The sum available at the end of two years if the investor purchases a two-year bond is

$$W(2) = (1 + {_tR_2})^2 \qquad (20.9)$$

where $_tR_2$ is the one-year rate on a two-year bond and we have assumed that the return in year one is reinvested at that rate. If, on the other hand, the investor purchases a one-year bond and uses the sum available at maturity to purchase another one-year bond, the sum available at the end of two years is

$$W(1,1) = (1 + {_tR_1})(1 + {_{t+1}r_1}). \qquad (20.10)$$

In equilibrium, the two end-of-period sums, $W(2)$ and $W(1,1)$, must be equal. If $W(2) > W(1,1)$, investors would move out of the short-term bond into the long-

---

[4] Bonds can also differ due to differences in the probability of default. Thus, bonds issued by private sector units (e.g., business firms) must bear a higher rate of return than default-free government bonds to compensate for the greater risk of default. In addition, the riskiness of private bonds may vary over the business cycle, increasing during recessions and falling during expansions. Bonds may also differ in tax treatment and administrative costs.

[5] An excellent introduction to the term structure theory can be found in Burton Malkiel, *The Term Structure of Interest Rates: Theory, Empirical Evidence, and Applications* (Morristown, N.J.: General Learning Press, 1970). Our notation and treatment follow his.

term bond, raising the short-term yield and lowering the long-term rate until the two were equal. Therefore,

$$(1 + {}_tR_2)^2 = (1 + {}_tR_1)(1 + {}_{t+1}r_1) \tag{20.11}$$

or

$$1 + {}_tR_2 = \sqrt{(1 + {}_tR_1)(1 + {}_{t+1}r_1)}. \tag{20.11'}$$

We can generalize this to the n-period maturity bond

$$1 + {}_tR_n = [(1 + {}_tR_1)(1 + {}_{t+1}r_1)(1 + {}_{t+2}r_1) \cdots (1 + {}_{t+n}r_1)]^{1/n}. \tag{20.12}$$

Thus, according to the expectations approach, the long-term rate is a geometric average of current and expected future short-term rates. If short-term rates are expected to rise, the long-term rate must be above the current short-term rate; the rate of return that can be earned by holding a series of short-term bonds is higher than the current short-term rate, and it is this average rate that must be equated to the long-term rate. Symmetrically, the long-term rate should be below the current short-term rate when expected future short-term rates are lower than the current short-term rate.

One way to test this approach is to take a survey of interest rate expectations and determine whether the yield curve (the curve depicting the relationship among rates on various maturities) is consistent with the expectations theory. Survey results reported by Edward Kane and Burton Malkiel confirm the expectations view.[6] A July, 1966, survey of major institutional investors, for example, indicated widespread expectations that short-term rates would fall in the future. In this case the longer term bond rates should be lower than shorter term rates, resulting in a negatively sloped yield curve. Indeed, this was the shape of the yield curve during the period; this case is depicted by the yy curve in Figure 20.1. If rates were expected to rise, the expectations model predicts that the yield curve will be upward sloping, as depicted by the $y'y'$ curve in Figure 20.1.

○ Liquidity Premiums

The expectations model is widely accepted as the basic explanation of the term structure. However, one assumption of the pure expectations model that is often relaxed is the assumption of perfect certainty. In this section and the next we consider two implications of introducing uncertainty into the expectations model. First, we discuss the existence of liquidity premiums on long-term bonds. Then we discuss how risk-averse behavior can result in the preference of some investors for particular maturities and thereby permits the relative supply of different maturities to affect the term structure.

---

[6] Edward J. Kane and Burton G. Malkiel, "The Term Structure of Interest Rates: An Analysis of a Survey of Interest Rate Expectations," *Review of Economics and Statistics,* Vol. 49 (August, 1967), pp. 343–355.

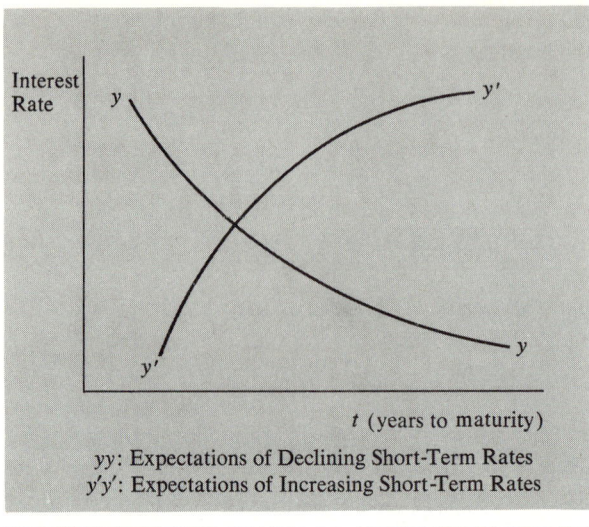

FIGURE 20.1
Yield Curves

Short-term bonds have an advantage that is not accounted for in the pure expectations approach: they are more "liquid." The concept of liquidity is a rather difficult one to define precisely. *Liquidity* refers to the speed with which assets can be converted into cash with no appreciable loss in principal value. Thus, liquidity has two dimensions: time (speed with which the asset can be sold) and percentage of principal value obtained. And both of these dimensions for long-term assets may be uncertain. Short-term bonds, particularly fixed price-variable coupon instruments such as saving deposits, have high liquidity since they can be quickly converted into cash without any loss in principal value. This is a convenient property when transactions are uncertain. This precautionary demand for liquid assets is analogous to the precautionary demand for money. The possibility of unexpected spending requirements or unusual opportunities for spending or investing induce wealth owners to prefer short-term (highly liquid) assets to longer term (less liquid) assets.

If investors are to be indifferent between holding short- and long-term bonds, long-term bonds must pay a premium over the yield on short-term bonds to compensate for the greater liquidity of short-term bonds. To derive the relation required between the returns on a two-year bond versus two successive one-year bonds, we add a liquidity premium to year two's forecasted one-year rate:

$$(1 + {}_tR_2) = \sqrt{1 + {}_tR_1(1 + {}_{t+1}r_1 + \rho(2)} \tag{20.13}$$

where $\rho(2)$ is the liquidity premium in the two-year bond yield. Assuming liquidity premiums increase with the maturity of the bond, the existence of liquidity premiums implies that the yield curve will be upward sloping even when short-term rates are expected to remain constant and may be upward sloping (or at least less downward sloping) when short-term rates are expected to fall.

Risk Aversion and the "Preferred Habitat" Theory[7]

It is an oversimplification, however, to view short-term bonds as safe and long-term bonds as risky. The riskiness of alternative maturities depends on the dates on which the holder expects to spend the funds as well as on the liquidity of the asset. For example, assume the unit is accumulating wealth for retirement in 20 years. The safest investment is a 20-year bond, in the sense that this is the only way to know precisely the yield that will be realized over the 20 years. If the unit chooses to invest in 20 successive one-year bonds, on the other hand, the return is uncertain because at the current moment only the first one-year rate is known.

Consider the example of a life insurance company that is committed to an actuarially determined flow of payments over a long horizon. If the insurance company invests in long-term assets, it will lock in a known cash flow of coupons over this long horizon. If it chooses to invest in short-term bonds, on the other hand, its return will be uncertain. If the company is risk averse, it will prefer to match its cash flow commitments to its investment returns and will therefore exhibit a preference for long-term bonds in its asset portfolio. Other financial institutions, such as commercial banks, prefer short-term assets. Banks specialize in making short-term loans to businesses and take in demand deposits and relatively short-term time deposits. Again, the desire to match the maturity of its assets to the maturity of the liabilities suggests that banks will have a preference for short-term bonds.

Such maturity preferences reduce the substitutability among different maturities. The extreme form of the preference for specific maturities makes short- and long-term markets completely *segmented*. The short- and long-term rates are then determined by the supply and demand for the particular maturity and there is no connection between the two markets due to interest rate expectations. This is unrealistic, however, because such preferences for maturities are not absolute (i.e., they can be overcome by sufficient yield differentials) and because there exist units without such maturity preference who buy and sell in a number of different maturities and thereby interconnect the markets for different maturities. A more realistic version is the Modigliani-Sutch preferred habitat theory which introduces relative asset supply effects into the expectations framework model; i.e., long-term rates depend on both current and expected short-term rates and on the relative supplies of short- and long-term debt.

Term Structure Theory and the Interest Rate Trap

As we have previously noted in our discussion of the liquidity trap, the evidence does not suggest a near-infinite interest elasticity of the demand for money, even at low interest rates. Therefore, the extreme Keynesian case of $L_r = -\infty$ is not considered realistic. The deficiency of the Keynesian speculative demand for the money model that provided the rationale for the $L_r = -\infty$ assumption in Chapter 19 is its failure to take into account the implications of the existence of assets which dominate money.

---

[7] The preferred habitat model is developed in Franco Modigliani and Richard Sutch, "Innovations in Interest Rate Policy," *American Economic Review, Papers and Proceedings,* Vol. 56 (May, 1966), pp. 178–197; and "Debt Management and the Term Structure of Interest Rates: An Empirical Analysis," *Journal of Political Economy,* Vol. 75 (August, 1967), Supplement, pp. 569–589.

Given the existence of short-term, liquid, default-free assets, there will be no speculative demand for money and therefore no liquidity trap (short of a zero interest rate). The speculative demand concept, however, is meaningfully applied to the demand for the short-term liquid assets that dominate money, and the concept of an interest rate trap therefore applies to the term structure of interest rates, to the relation between short- and long-term interest rates. Indeed, Keynes suggests in the *General Theory* that, although the central bank can move the short-term rate at will by buying and selling short-term bonds, it might lose control of the long-term rate.[8]

To illustrate the interest rate trap arising out of the term structure model, we consider the relation between the 20-year bond yield and the 90-day Treasury bill rate. The key to the term structure version of the interest rate trap (as in the case of the liquidity trap) is the assumption that wealth owners hold expectations about future short-term rates which are quite inelastic with respect to current short-term rates; this corresponds to the normal level of the interest rate that was so important in the speculative demand model. The central bank can drive the short-term bond rate down to near zero by aggressively purchasing short-term bonds. But as long as wealth owners believe that interest rates will not long remain below normal levels, the long-term rate will get trapped at a level well above the current short-term rate; i.e., even if the short-term rate is driven to near zero, interest rate expectations will result in a floor for the long-term rate. Thus, the key implication of the liquidity trap, the potential for the central bank to lose the ability to affect the real sector via monetary policy, is preserved in this long-term interest rate trap.

○ Operational Specification of the Term Structure Approach

The problem with testing the expectations model is that we do not directly observe expected future interest rates. Of course, if we assume the pure expectations theory is correct, we can compute the implicit expected future rates (called *forward rates*) from the observed yield curve. For example, if we assume

$$(1 + {}_tR_2) = \sqrt{(1 + {}_tR_1)(1 + {}_{t+1}r_1)}$$

we can compute the expected one-year rate one year hence, ${}_{t+1}r_1$, given that we know both the current one- and two-year rates (${}_tR_1$ and ${}_tR_2$). Given "knowledge" of the expected one-year rate one year hence along with the current three-year and one-year rates, we can compute the expected one-year rate two years hence, and so on. One simple test would be to compare the actual one-year rate in a given year with the expected one-year rate one year ago. But this is only a test of the *accuracy* of forecasts and not a test of the expectations model itself.

The approach taken in most econometric models is to assume that expected future short-term rates are related to *current* and *past* short-term rates. The basic form of the term structure equation, abstracting for the moment from liquidity premiums and relative supply effects, is

---

[8] J. M. Keynes, *The General Theory of Employment, Interest and Money* (New York: Harcourt, Brace and World, Inc., 1936), p. 203.

$$i = \sum_{j=0}^{n} \alpha_j r_{-j} \qquad (20.14)$$

where i is the long-term rate and r_{-j} is the short-term rate j periods prior to the current period.[9]

To take into account the effect of liquidity premiums and relative supplies, we can add a constant term to reflect the liquidity premium[10] and a relative supply term to take into account preferences for maturities:

$$i = \rho + \sum_{j=0}^{n} \alpha_j r_{-j} + \beta(b_s/b_L) \qquad (20.14')$$

where b_s/b_L is the ratio of the supply of short-term bonds to the supply of long-term bonds and β is assumed to be negative. Modigliani and Sutch estimated a term structure model corresponding to this equation. Their equation, estimated using quarterly data over the period 1952 I to 1961 I, is

$$i_t = 1.2 + 0.32\, r_t + \sum_{j=1}^{16} \alpha_j r_{t-j} \qquad (20.15)$$

where i = the long-term government bond rate and r = the Treasury bill rate.[11] The effect of an increase in the short-term bond rate of 100 basis points (one full percentage point) would be a 32 basis-point increase in the long-term rate in the first quarter. If the short-term rate remained at the new higher level, the long-term rate would rise 40 basis points over the first year and a full 100 basis points over three years according to the estimated lag distribution (the values of the α_j). The constant term reflects the risk premium on the long-term bond relative to the short-term bond; i.e., the long-term rate has to be higher than the short-term rate on average by 1.2 percentage points to compensate for the greater liquidity of the short-term bond. Attempts to include the relative supply of short- and long-term bonds were unsuccessful.[12]

---

[9] If the two bonds were a perpetuity and a one-day bond, there would be two and only two clear-cut maturities. In fact, there is a continuum of maturities. A thirty-year bond becomes a twenty-nine-year bond next year, etc. In the term structure approach we typically relate some specific short-term maturity (e.g., 90-day Treasury bill) to some average rate on long-term maturities (e.g., average rate on bonds maturing in over 20 years).

[10] Of course, the liquidity premiums need not be constant. However, empirical efforts to predict movements in liquidity premiums have not generally proved successful, and they are therefore usually treated as constant.

[11] Modigliani and Sutch, "Innovations in Interest Rate Policy," *op. cit.*, p. 189.

[12] The specification of the term structure equation given by equations (20.14) or (20.14') has recently been criticized for being inconsistent with rational expectations (since it presumes that interest rate expectations are formed exclusively on the basis of current and *past* values of interest rates). See, for example, William Poole, "Rational Expectations in the Macro Model," *Brookings Papers on Economic Activity* (1976:2), pp. 463–505; and Frederic S. Mishkin, "Efficient-Markets Theory: Implications for Monetary Policy," *Brookings Papers on Economic Activity* (1978:3), pp. 707–752. While equations such as equation (20.14) continue to dominate empirical macro models, there appears to be a growing uneasiness about their adequacy and no consensus has developed concerning the appropriate respecification.

Part V · Refinements of the Financial Sector

APPENDIX

A The Equivalence of the Adding-Up Restrictions in the Continuous and Period Specifications

The adding-up restrictions are identical in the continuous (or *BOP*) and *EOP* specifications. The derivation and interpretation of the results in the *EOP* case are somewhat more complicated. First, we discuss the interpretation of the adding-up restrictions in the continuous (or *BOP*) case and then derive and interpret the restrictions in the *EOP* case and compare them with those derived in the continuous (*BOP*) case.

The Continuous or *BOP* Case

The *BSC* imposes restrictions or *adding-up requirements* on the parameters of the asset demand functions. These restrictions were derived for the continuous (or *BOP*) case in the preceding chapter:

$$L_x + B_x \equiv 0 \tag{20A.1a}$$

$$L_r + B_r \equiv 0 \tag{20A.1b}$$

$$L_a + B_a \equiv 1. \tag{20A.1c}$$

These restrictions enforce consistent behavior on wealth owners. For example, if wealth increases, condition (20A.1a) requires that wealth owners absorb the increased wealth into their portfolios in some combination of increased desired holdings of money and bonds. Again, wealth must be held in some form. Asset demand functions determine desired *composition* of asset holdings. But the sum of desired asset holdings must always exhaust the wealth owners' total wealth.

The other two restrictions require that, *given wealth,* any change which increases the demand for one asset must simultaneously reduce the demand of the other asset by an equivalent amount. For example, an increase in the interest rate on bonds increases the demand for bonds; but if wealth owners want to hold more bonds, given wealth, they must want to hold less money. Thus, a change in r induces a change in desired portfolio composition.

The restriction on the income parameters is the most difficult to grasp. The key is that in the continuous (or *BOP*) specification of asset markets, we do not allow income flows to increment wealth via saving at the moment (during the period) to which these equations apply. The interest rate is determined by supply and demand at the moment t (at the beginning of the period in the *BOP* case); income and saving will alter the supplies of assets *over time* (at the beginning of the *next* period). If the rate of income flow increases, wealth owners will want to adjust their portfolios at the moment t (at the beginning of the period) to permit them to carry out a larger volume of transactions. Therefore, they increase the demand for money; at the moment t (at the beginning of the period), wealth is fixed so that this can only be accomplished by a reduction in desired bondholdings.

The End-of-Period Specification

In the end-of-period specification, the *BSC* requires that end-of-period demands for assets sum to end-of-period planned wealth. End-of-period planned wealth equals beginning-of-period

Chapter 20 · The Supply and Demand for Bonds

wealth ($\bar{a}$) plus desired wealth accumulation over the period. Households accumulate wealth via savings.[1] Thus, end-of-period planned wealth equals beginning-of-period wealth plus desired saving.

$$a \equiv \bar{a} + S(\ ) \qquad (20A.2)$$

where $S(\ )$ denotes desired saving over the period. Note that saving is defined as dollars of saving over the unit period of the analysis. The demand for money and bonds is also specified as of the end of the period and therefore depends on (desired) end-of-period wealth. The household BSC now is written as

$$a \equiv L(r, X, a) + B(r, X, a) \qquad (20A.3)$$

or

$$\bar{a} + S(\ ) \equiv L[r, X, \bar{a} + S(\ )] + B[r, X, \bar{a} + S(\ )]. \qquad (20A.3')$$

The adding-up restrictions turn out in this case to be identical to those derived in the previous section.[2] To show this, note that an increase in $\bar{a}$ must be absorbed into desired money or bondholdings; thus, $L_a + B_a \equiv 1$ as in the beginning-of-period specification. We assume that an increase in the interest rate does not affect desired saving; therefore, a change in the interest rate leaves end-of-period wealth unaffected and $L_r + B_r \equiv 0$. An increase in income, however, affects both desired accumulation (and hence desired end-of-period wealth) and desired portfolio composition. To derive the full impact of an increase in income, rewrite the BSC as

$$\bar{a} + S_y Y \equiv L_r r + L_x X + L_a(\bar{a} + S_y Y) + \bar{L} + B_r r + B_x X$$
$$+ B_a(\bar{a} + S_y Y) + \bar{B}. \qquad (20A.3'')$$

Taking first differences, assuming $\Delta \bar{a} = \Delta r = 0$, yields

$$S_y \equiv L_y + L_a S_y + B_y + S_y B_a. \qquad (20A.4)$$

S_y is the change in end-of-period wealth associated with a change in income. The change in money and bond demands each has two components: the effect of a change in income, assuming wealth is constant (L_x, B_x), and the effect of the change in wealth due to the income-induced change in saving ($L_a S_y$, $B_a S_y$). We can rewrite equation (20A.4) as

$$S_y(1 - L_a - B_a) \equiv L_x + B_x. \qquad (20A.4')$$

Given that $1 \equiv L_a + B_a$, this reduces to

$$0 \equiv L_y + B_y.$$

Thus, the adding-up restrictions on the parameters are the same as in the previous section. The only difference is that the influence on portfolios of a change in income is restricted by the adding-up restrictions on both the income and wealth parameters.

---

[1] Household wealth also can change due to capital gains or losses on existing assets. To simplify, we ignore the possibility of such capital gains and losses.

[2] This section is based on Laurence H. Meyer, "The Demand for Money and Bonds in Continuous Time Models: A Comment," *Journal of Economic Theory*, Vol. 15 (June, 1977), pp. 220–224.

APPENDIX

B A Three-Asset Model

A more explicit approach to including multiple financial assets is to introduce supply and demand functions for each distinct financial asset. To develop the implications of multiple financial assets, we introduce a three-asset model of the financial sector in this appendix.[1] The two nonmoney financial assets could be short-term and long-term bonds, government and private bonds, or bonds and equities. Our treatment involves bonds and equities. This is the model that is needed to complete the dual price model of investment discussed in Chapter 14. We will employ a beginning-of-period formulation to simplify the analysis.

The Specification of the Asset Demands

Each asset demand is assumed to depend on the rate of return on bonds, the rate of return on equities, income, and wealth:

$$m = L_r r + L_i i + L_x X + L_a a \qquad (20\text{B}.1)$$

$$b = B_r r + B_i i + B_x X + B_a a \qquad (20\text{B}.2)$$

$$qE = E_r r + E_i i + E_x X + E_a a \qquad (20\text{B}.3)$$

where i is the rate of return on equities, E is the number of units of equities outstanding, and q is the price per unit of equities. Note that m, b, and qE are all defined in real terms; therefore, q is the *price of equities relative to goods*, a relative price rather than an absolute price of equities. The q variable then is a ratio of the two prices that were the key variables in the dual price theory of investment discussed in Chapter 14: it is the asset market valuation of a unit of capital relative to the cost of producing a new unit of capital.[2]

The financial sector is completed with the definition of wealth and the relation between the price of equities and the rate of return on equities:

$$a \equiv m + b + qE \qquad (20\text{B}.4)$$

$$q = \frac{R}{i} \qquad (20\text{B}.5)$$

where R is the residual income of the firm, the quasi rents; the price of equities is simply the present value of these quasi rents. To simplify, we have treated R as fixed and equities

---

[1] This analysis is based on James Tobin, "An Essay on the Principles of Debt Management," in Commission on Money and Credit, *Fiscal and Debt Management Policies* (Englewood Cliffs, N.J.: Prentice-Hall, Inc., 1963), pp. 143–218; and James Tobin, "A General Equilibrium Approach to Monetary Theory," *Journal of Money, Credit and Banking*, Vol. 1 (1969), pp. 15–29.

[2] This variable is often referred to as "Tobin's q" because of the importance of Tobin's contributions to modeling both the determination of q and the role of q in transmitting financial sector influences to the real sector. See the articles listed in the previous footnote.

as analogous to perpetuities. In a more complete model, R would be related to the overall level of economic activity, X.

We assume, as in the general portfolio model introduced in Chapter 19, that all assets are gross substitutes and normal with respect to wealth. This implies that $L_r < 0$, $L_i < 0$, $L_a > 0$, $B_r > 0$, $B_i < 0$, $B_a > 0$, $E_r < 0$, $E_i > 0$, and $E_a > 0$.

The Financial Market Impact of Changes in the Supply of Money and Bonds

In this section we discuss the financial market impact of changes in the supply of money via open market operations and changes in the supply of government bonds associated with the financing of last period's deficit.

Open Market Operations. Consider the effect of an open market operation—an increase in money in exchange for an equivalent amount of government bonds; i.e., $\Delta m = -\Delta b$. The attempt by the central bank to purchase bonds drives down the interest rate on bonds, and this in turn induces households to exchange bonds for money. The decrease in the rate on bonds then increases the demand for equities as wealth owners attempt to move out of bonds into equities to take advantage of the increase in the return on equities relative to bonds. The increase in the demand for equities drives up the price of equities (reduces the rate of return on equities). Thus, the multipliers for the effect of an *OMP* on r and i are both negative while the multiplier for the effect of an *OMP* on q is positive. Thus, open market purchases unambiguously reduce the interest rate on bonds and raise the price of equities.

An Increase in the Supply of Bonds. Now consider the effect of an increase in the supply of bonds associated with the financing of the previous period's deficit; in this case, $\Delta b = \Delta a$.[3] Wealth and therefore the demand for bonds increase. But the increase in wealth is all in the form of bonds, and wealth owners prefer to hold a portion of any increase in wealth in money and equities; therefore, the supply of bonds increases by more than the demand for bonds and the increase in bond supply generates excess demands in the money and equity markets as well as excess supply for bonds. The excess demand for equities puts upward pressure on the price of equities. But the excess supply of bonds puts upward pressure on the bond rate which in turn reduces the demand for equities and puts downward pressure on the price of equities. The net effect of the interaction of wealth and substitution effects is therefore ambiguous. This means that an increase in the supply of bonds, although it puts upward pressure on the bond rate, may nevertheless stimulate investment by putting upward pressure on the price of equities.[4]

---

[3] This is true only if we ignore the investment financing constraint (*IFC*). However, the analysis in this section develops an important aspect of portfolio response to financial market disturbances which carries over to more complicated models that incorporate the *IFC*.

[4] This analysis can be extended to the case where there is more than one maturity of bond. Assume there are short- and long-term bonds, for example, that the government can finance deficits in either maturity, and that firms finance investment only in the long-term market. An increase in the supply of government debt in the long-term market will unambiguously drive up the long-term rate and discourage investment. But an increase in the supply of short-term government debt will have an ambiguous effect on the long-term rate; it may lower the long-term rate and thereby stimulate investment. This of course implies that relative supply effects are important and would have to be included in the term structure equation relating short- and long-term rates. For a model allowing for differential effects associated with the choice of short- or long-term bond financing of deficits, see Patric Hendershott, "A Tax Cut in a Multiple Security Model: Crowding-Out, Pulling-In, and the Term Structure of Interest Rates," *Journal of Finance*, Vol. 31 (September, 1976), pp. 1185–1199.

Part V • Refinements of the Financial Sector

● REVIEW QUESTIONS

1. "The balance sheet constraint only applies when money and bond markets are in equilibrium. This is clear from its derivation; i.e., it is derived by substituting the demands for money and bonds for the exogenous supplies in the balance sheet identity." Comment.

2. Explain the interdependence of decisions involving government expenditures, tax revenues, and money and bond supplies.

3. Explain how interest rate expectations affect the slope of the curve relating interest rates to term maturities in Figure 20.1.

● PROBLEMS

1. If there are two assets held in household portfolios (e.g., money and bonds), the demand function for one of the assets can be derived from the specification of the other demand function. Explain why and give an example.

2. According to the government financing constraint, the supply of bonds will increase in response to a deficit inherited from a previous period. When we derive the multiplier for the response of income to a change in government expenditures, what allowance, if any, is made for the effect of increases in the supply of bonds to finance any inherited deficit?

3. "The pattern of interest rate expectations can be read off the yield curve." Comment.

*4. Derive the multipliers for the response of the price of equities to (a) an open market operation and (b) an increase in the supply of government bonds.

---

* The information necessary for solving these problems or questions can be found in the appendices.

Chapter 21

The Implications of Alternative Specifications of the Demand for Money

In this chapter we discuss the macroeconomic implications of the alternative specifications of the demand for money introduced in Chapter 19. In the first section we consider the implications of extreme assumptions about the interest-responsiveness of the demand for money. First, we consider the implications of a zero interest elasticity and the relation of this parameter restriction to monetarism. Then we consider the implications of an interest-responsive demand for money and assess the importance Keynes attached to this parameter in his attack on classical macroeconomics. In the second section we consider the implications for the effectiveness of fiscal policy of introducing wealth as an argument in the money demand function and then contrast the implications of the pure transactions approach to the demand for money ($L_x > 0$, $L_a = 0$) and the pure wealth approach ($L_x = 0$, $L_a > 0$).

THE IMPLICATIONS OF EXTREME VALUES OF THE INTEREST RESPONSIVENESS OF THE DEMAND FOR MONEY

Despite the voluminous empirical evidence that the interest elasticity of the demand for money is negative but quite small,[1] the assumption that this parameter takes on an extreme value (either zero or minus infinity) has generally received a great deal of attention in macroeconomics and has often been the source of considerable controversy. In this section we consider the implications of the two extreme assumptions about the value of the interest responsiveness of the demand for money: $L_r = 0$ and $L_r = -\infty$. The first assumption is generally associated with the classical view of the demand for money but is also attributed at times to monetarists. The second is often attributed to Keynes and sometimes to modern Keynesians. It is not clear that *any* of these attributions are valid. Classical economists often listed the foregone

---

[1] The empirical evidence is consistent with the inventory model of the demand for money which suggests that the interest elasticity of the demand for money is less than one half. See Chapter 19.

interest as a possible determinant of money holdings; on the other hand, their macroeconomic analysis often implicitly or explicitly assumed $L_r = 0$. Friedman is often accused of believing that $L_r = 0$; however, he has explicitly rejected this extreme position and claims to have been misinterpreted.[2] Keynes mentioned the possibility of a liquidity trap but also noted he could not think of a case when it had actually occurred.[3] Keynesians today generally agree that the interest responsiveness of the demand for money is modest.

The Crude Quantity Theory ($L_r = 0$)

The *LM* curve has often been viewed as directly providing a model of income determination, permitting predictions about the response of income to money and other exogenous changes independent of real sector developments (as summarized in the *IS* curve). The situation in which the *LM* curve can yield direct predictions about income is generally associated with $L_r = 0$. In this section we consider the precise restrictions on the *LM* curve required for it to permit direct income predictions. Then we discuss the role of velocity as a link between money and income and develop some aspects of the monetarist approach to macroeconomic analysis.

The LM Curve and Income Determination. We need *three* assumptions to allow the *LM* curve to directly predict prices, output, or nominal income.[4] We begin with the general specification of the *LM* curve,

$$\frac{M}{P} = L(r, X). \tag{21.1}$$

The three assumptions are:

1. *The Nominal Money Supply (M) Is Exogenous.* In this case equation (21.1) still includes three unknowns (r, P, and X), so it cannot in general be solved for any of the unknowns or the value of any multipliers.

2. $L_r = 0$. In this case the *LM* curve becomes

$$\frac{\bar{M}}{P} = L(X). \tag{21.2}$$

We now have one equation and two unknowns. We still require one further restriction to permit us to derive model multipliers from the *LM* curve alone. Otherwise we will still need additional equations to permit us to solve for X and P. Any of the following three restrictions are sufficient, given the first two restrictions:

---

[2] For an excellent discussion of the theoretical implications of $L_r = 0$ and his own views on L_r, see Milton Friedman, "Interest Rates and The Demand for Money," *Journal of Law and Economics*, Vol. 9 (October, 1966), pp. 71–85.

[3] J. M. Keynes, *The General Theory of Employment, Interest and Money* (New York: Harcourt, Brace and World, Inc., 1936), p. 3.

[4] These are discussed by Friedman, *loc. cit.*

3a. *X Is Exogenous.* For example, we are at full employment and want to predict the impact of an increase in M. In this case P will change proportionately with M. To see this, note that the right-hand side of equation (21.2) is now a constant. There is only one value of the real money supply consistent with money market equilibrium; i.e., $\bar{M}/P = L(\bar{X})$. Therefore, any increase in M requires an equiproportionate change in P to restore equilibrium. This case is depicted graphically in Figure 21.1. The LM curve is a vertical line in the r-P plane when $L_r = 0$. It uniquely determines P without reference to the shape or position of the IS curve.

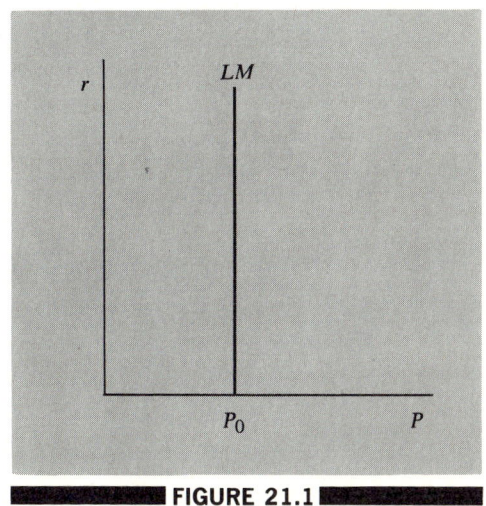

FIGURE 21.1
Price Level Determination
when $L_r = 0$ and $X = \bar{X}$

3b. *P Is Exogenous.* For example, there is slack in the economy and we want to predict the response of income to changes in the money supply (or other disturbances) over a period sufficiently short that prices can be treated as given exogenously. In this case we can treat the real money supply, m, as exogenous and write the LM curve as

$$\bar{m} = L(X). \tag{21.3}$$

Again, we have one equation in one unknown. The only way money market equilibrium can be restored in response to an increase in m is at a higher level of X (assuming $L_x > 0$); i.e., an increase in the money supply must be matched by an increase in money demand and this requires, given that X is the only argument in the money demand function, an increase in X.

Assuming a linear specification of the money demand function and exogenous real money supply, the LM curve can be written as

$$\bar{m} = L_x X + \bar{L} \tag{21.3'}$$

and the reduced form for income is now given by

$$X = \frac{1}{L_x}\bar{m} - \frac{1}{L_x}\bar{L}. \tag{21.4}$$

According to equation (21.4), the reduced-form multipliers depend exclusively on the parameters in the money demand function. The determination of income in this case is depicted in Figure 21.2 where the *LM* curve is vertical in *r-X* space.

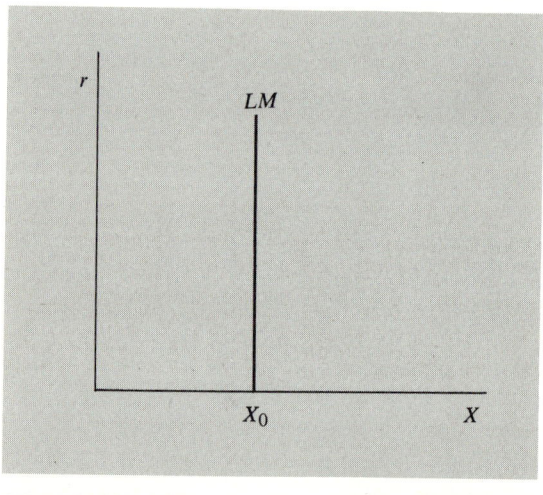

FIGURE 21.2
Income Determination when $L_r = 0$ and $P = \bar{P}$

3c. *The Real Income Elasticity of the Demand for Money (ϵ_{LX}) Must Be Unity.* $\epsilon_{LX} = 1$ means that a given percentage increase in X induces an equal percentage change in the real demand for money.[5] In this case the *LM* curve can be respecified as

$$\frac{M}{P} = L_x X; \tag{21.5}$$

i.e., the demand for real balances is linear in X and without a constant term.[6] In this case the *LM* curve can also be written as

$$\bar{M} = L_x(PX) = L_x X\$ \tag{21.5'}$$

where $X\$ = PX =$ nominal income. Thus, if M is exogenous, $L_r = 0$ and $\epsilon_{LX} = 1$, *nominal income* is uniquely determined by the level of nominal money supply. The

---

[5] $\epsilon_{LX} = \dfrac{\%\Delta \text{money demand}}{\%\Delta X} = \dfrac{\Delta \text{money demand}}{\Delta X} \cdot \dfrac{X}{M} = L_x \dfrac{X}{M}$

[6] If $m^d = L_x X$, then $\dfrac{\Delta m^d}{\Delta X} = L_x$ and $\epsilon_{LX} = L_x \dfrac{X}{m^d}$. But $\dfrac{X}{m^d} = \dfrac{1}{L_x}$ so that $\epsilon_{LX} = 1$.

LM equation, under the above assumptions, permits us to determine the impact of monetary change on nominal income; additional information would still be required to decompose the change in nominal income into change in real income and prices. Under the assumptions discussed above, the *LM* curve uniquely determines output, prices, or money income; the effects of monetary changes on output, prices, or money income can be predicted without knowledge of the real sector equations, and output, prices, or money income is unaffected by real sector variables such as government spending.

Velocity, the Demand for Money, and the Monetarist Approach. The discussion of the macroeconomic implications of alternative specifications of the money demand function provides an opportune point to develop one of the important distinctions between the Keynesian and monetarist models of income determination—their respective points of departure in analyzing the process of income determination. The point of departure in the Keynesian model is the *GNP* identity ($X \equiv C + I + G$). In order to explain the total flow of goods and services, the Keynesian approach disaggregates the total into component flows (e.g., *C, I, G*), each of which is either exogenous (*G*) or is represented by a structural equation (*C* and *I*). Furthermore, other flows are typically key variables in the explanation of the component flows (e.g., the principal determinant of consumption is disposable income). The financial sector is by no means ignored in the income expenditure approach; the purpose and scope of the financial sector, however, is determined by the necessity of explaining the financial variables which appear as arguments in the equations for the component expenditure flows. These are typically confined to one or a small number of market rates of interest.

Monetarists tend to emphasize the role of stocks, especially the stock of money, and the importance of portfolio relations, particularly the demand for money. The velocity concept, therefore, provides a useful point of departure for monetarist analysis. *Velocity* (*V*) is defined as the number of times money "turns over" in income payments during the period of analysis; i.e.,

$$V \equiv \frac{X\$}{M}. \qquad (21.6)$$

We can rewrite the velocity equation so that nominal income is expressed as the product of velocity and the nominal stock of money; i.e., velocity is the link between money and income.

$$X\$ \equiv VM \qquad (21.6')$$

Monetarists are generally less concerned with the structure of the economy, the precise channels of monetary influence, than with the reduced form of the economy. And under restrictive conditions, equation (21.6′) is the reduced-form equation for income. Those restrictions are that *M* is exogenous, $L_r = 0$, and $\epsilon_{LX} = 1$—precisely the restrictions discussed in the previous section. This is the reduced form often associated with monetarism.[7]

---

[7] See, for example, the reduced-form results presented by Leonall C. Andersen and Jerry Jordan, "Monetary and Fiscal Actions: A Test of Their Relative Importance in Economic Stabilization," Federal Reserve Bank of St. Louis, *Review* (November, 1968), pp. 11–24.

The velocity concept is closely related to the demand for money. It describes the behavior of money relative to income; assuming that the money supply is exogenous, the demand for money determines the behavior of velocity. Under the restrictive assumptions discussed above (assumptions 1, 2, and 3c)

$$\bar{M} = L_x X\$ \tag{21.7}$$

so that

$$\frac{X\$}{M} = V = \frac{1}{L_x}. \tag{21.8}$$

Thus, the reduced form can be written either as equation (21.6′) where V is constant or, as

$$X\$ = \frac{1}{L_x} M. \tag{21.8′}$$

If, on the other hand, L_r is not equal to zero, then V depends on r. For example, if

$$\bar{M} = L(r) X\$ \tag{21.9}$$

then

$$\frac{X\$}{M} = \frac{1}{L(r)} = V(r) \tag{21.10}$$

and

$$X\$ = V(r) M. \tag{21.10′}$$

An interest elastic money demand breaks the unique link between the money supply and nominal income. We can no longer use the money demand function alone to predict the effects of monetary and other disturbances on money income. Nonmonetary disturbances may now affect nominal income if they alter velocity via the interest rate. In such a case, predicting the consequences of both financial and real disturbances requires us to specify the real sector equations (the *IS* curve and perhaps the aggregate supply equations as well) along with the *LM* curve. On the other hand, as long as velocity is a stable function of the interest rate and the interest rate responds predictably to monetary changes, equation (21.10′) suggests a stable relation between changes in income and money. However, the view that there is a stable relation between changes in money and income does not imply that $L_r = 0$ and monetarists, in general, do not contend that $L_r = 0$, although many of the key propositions associated with monetarism would indeed follow directly from this parameter restriction (e.g., large multipliers for monetary change and zero multipliers for fiscal policy instruments).

Friedman, for example, has summarized his position as follows: "I know of no empirical student of the demand for money who denies that interest rates affect the real quantity of money demanded—though others have misinterpreted me as so asserting."[8] We will not therefore identify $L_r = 0$ with monetarism. But this leaves us with the task of explaining the monetarist's skepticism about the potency of fiscal policy. One element of this explanation is the low interest responsiveness of the demand for money; while allowing for $L_r < 0$, the view that L_r is quite small remains an important element in the monetarist argument that fiscal policy multipliers are extremely small. This is not, however, the only reason monetarists view fiscal policy as having only a minor effect. Our discussion of "crowding-out" in this and the next chapter and in Chapter 25 will help to further clarify the monetarist view of fiscal policy.[9]

○ Interest-Responsive Demand for Money and the Classical Adjustment Mechanism

In the next section we will consider the implications of infinite interest responsiveness of the demand for money ($L_r = -\infty$). But Keynes placed great importance on simply the noninfinite interest responsiveness of money demand ($-\infty < L_r < 0$) in his attack on classical macroeconomics. To understand the role of $L_r < 0$ in Keynes's attack on classical macroeconomics, we consider the introduction of an interest responsive money demand function in the classical flexible price model; i.e., we ask what differences would result from assuming $L_r < 0$ instead of $L_r = 0$ in such a model. This modification of the classical model does not affect the existence of the neutrality of money or of the quantity theory of money. Neither does it affect the existence of a full employment equilibrium. These are some of the conclusions of what is referred to as the *Keynesian counterrevolution*; according to this view, the basic innovations Keynes introduced, such as the consumption-income relation and the interest-responsive demand for money, can be introduced into an otherwise classical model without altering the basic equilibrium conclusions. Under this interpretation, Keynes becomes identified either with the assumption of wage-price rigidity or extreme values of parameters such as $L_r = -\infty$ or $I_r = 0$.[10]

Recently emphasis has been placed on the importance of understanding Keynes's analysis as disequilibrium rather than equilibrium analysis.[11] Although an interest-responsive demand for money does not alter the qualitative comparative static conclusions of the classical model, it does play an important role in the nature of the adjustment required to restore full employment following a downward demand disturbance. In particular, it determines the degree of downward price flexibility required for the classical adjustment mechanism to offset demand disturbances. And given

---

[8] Milton Friedman, "Interest Rates and the Demand for Money," *Journal of Law and Economics*, Vol. 9 (October, 1966), p. 72.

[9] For discussions of the monetarist approach, see Robert J. Gordon (ed.), *Milton Friedman's Monetary Framework: A Debate with His Critics* (Chicago: The University of Chicago Press, 1970); and Jerome Stein (ed.), *Monetarism* (New York: Elsevier: North Holland Pub. Co., 1976).

[10] For a discussion and critique of the Keynesian counterrevolution, see Robert Clower, "The Keynesian Counter-Revolution: A Theoretical Appraisal," in F. Hahn and F. Brechling (eds.), *The Theory of Interest Rates* (London: Collier-Macmillan, Ltd., 1965).

[11] For example, see Axel Leijonhufvud, *On Keynesian Economics and The Economics of Keynes* (New York: Oxford University Press, Inc., 1968); and Hyman P. Minsky, *John Maynard Keynes* (New York: Columbia University Press, 1975).

that prices and wages respond slowly at best to excess supply in the output and labor markets, the greater the decline in prices and wages required to restore equilibrium, the longer the period during which the decline in demand may be reflected in lower output and employment.

In Figures 21.3a and 21.3b, we depict the classical version of the *IS-LM* model using both the *r-X* diagram (Figure 21.3a) and the *r-P* diagram (Figure 21.3b). Two *LM* equations are depicted in each case—LM_1 where $L_r = 0$ and LM_2 where $-\infty < L_r < 0$. We can use these diagrams to develop the role of L_r in the response to a demand disturbance; e.g., a decline in autonomous private demand (Z), shifting the *IS* curve to *IS'*. We begin at full employment (i.e., in equilibrium) at point *a* in each diagram. Following the shift in the *IS* curve, point *a* becomes a position of excess supply in the commodity market. Note that if $L_r = 0$, it is possible for equilibrium to be restored at full employment by a decline in the interest rate *without any movement in the price level*; i.e., in each case the system moves along the fixed *LM* curve from point *a* to point *b*. Classical economists often appeared to view interest rate movements as a response to disequilibrium between saving and investment (or, equivalently, to disequilibrium in the output market); i.e.,

$$\dot{r} = \alpha[I(r) + \bar{Z} - S(X)]. \tag{21.11}$$

In this case, the decline in Z sets off a decline in r (along the *LM* curve) which increases aggregate demand until equilibrium is restored without ever moving away from full employment.

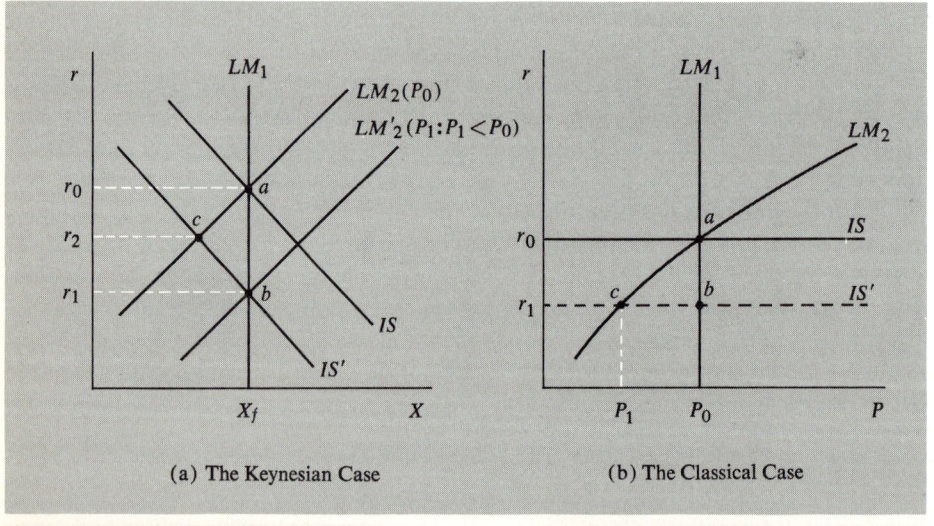

(a) The Keynesian Case

(b) The Classical Case

FIGURE 21.3

L_r and the Response to Shifts in Aggregate Demand

Note, however, that if $L_r < 0$, there is no decline in the interest rate that can restore both markets to equilibrium at full employment and the original price level. In this case the shift in the *IS* curve initially moves the system from point *a* to point c in Figure 21.3a. To return to full employment, prices must fall, shifting the LM_2 curve until point b is reached. The effect of the decline in Z on the equilibrium price level is immediately evident in Figure 21.3b; here the system moves from point a to point c in response to the shift in the IS curve.

Thus, if $L_r < 0$, pressure is put on the weak link in the classical adjustment mechanism—wage-price flexibility. It is not necessary to assume that wages and prices are rigid, only that they do not adjust instantaneously (or even rapidly). In the short run, given the failure of prices to fall fast enough to immediately reestablish equilibrium at full employment by shifting the LM_2 curve to LM_2' in Figure 21.3a, there is pressure on output to fall as unwanted inventories signal the fact that production exceeds demand.

The role of price flexibility in reestablishing equilibrium at full employment in response to a demand disturbance also depends on the nature of the adjustment of prices and interest rates to disequilibrium. Keynes strongly objected to the classical assumption summarized by our equation (21.11). He held that interest rates do not adjust to equilibrate saving and investment but rather to equilibrate the supply and demand for money while movements in prices and/or output respond to commodity market disequilibrium. In our judgment, this *reversal of disequilibrium assumptions* was one of Keynes's fundamental points; this reversal implies that demand disturbances *immediately* put pressure on prices rather than interest rates. With prices failing to decline instantaneously, production is cut back and only then do financial markets respond with declining interest rates. If prices fail to decline, interest rates decline only until output falls enough to equilibrate the supply and demand for output. Interest rates get trapped in this case at r_1 in Figure 21.3a, well above the r_2 level required to increase aggregate demand to X_f. In addition, as output declines, the multiplier process results in intensifying the disequilibrium, the gap between actual and full employment output. If prices decline, ultimately full employment may be restored, but the speed has been affected by $L_r < 0$ and the Keynesian disequilibrium assumptions.

Under these "Keynesian" disequilibrium assumptions, the failure of r to enter the demand for money function does not alter the basic disequilibrium response. As demand declines, prices and/or output decline and the resulting excess supply of money puts downward pressure on the interest rate as wealth owners attempt to reduce money balances by buying bonds. However, if $L_r = 0$, the smallest decline in output would set off a decline in the interest rate sufficient to restore equilibrium. As long as prices or output were below their initial level, the excess supply in the money market would be driving down the interest rate. The decline in the interest rate however cannot directly affect money market equilibrium since $L_r = 0$. But it indirectly increases the demand for money by increasing aggregate demand and hence prices and/or output. The interest rate continues to fall in this case until prices and/or output are restored to their initial levels. If $L_r < 0$, on the other hand, money market equilibrium can be achieved at a lower level of both output and the interest rate (as at point c in Figure 21.3a). We conclude that an interest-responsive demand for money increases the flexibility in wages and prices required for the automatic adjustment process to function and it increases the decline in output during the period in which the slow response of prices and wages to disequilibrium puts downward pressure on output and employment.

○ The Liquidity Trap ($L_r = -\infty$)

If $L_r = 0$ is associated with the *crude* quantity theory, then $L_r = -\infty$ should symmetrically be identified with *crude* Keynesianism. While there are few if any economists that believe $L_r = -\infty$, this assumption was at least implicit in much of the early postwar macroeconomic analysis, particularly early econometric model building. Whereas $L_r = 0$ (combined with the other assumptions discussed above) implies that monetary change has a powerful effect on prices and/or output and real sector disturbances affect neither prices nor output, $L_r = -\infty$ implies that monetary change has no effect on prices or output and real sector disturbances have powerful effects on prices and/or output.[12] Note that in this case, the $\Delta X/\Delta G$ multiplier equals the simple Keynesian cross consumption multiplier $[1/(1 - C_y)]$, because with r fixed in the liquidity trap, there can be no income-induced rises in the interest rate (i.e., no negative feedback).

We should be careful to recognize that the liquidity trap is only expected to exist at *low* interest rates. The liquidity trap view therefore holds that the demand for money is *nonlinear* so that the response of the demand for money to a change in the interest rate varies with the level of the interest rate; in particular, that L_r becomes very large (in absolute value) as the level of r declines. Tests for the existence of the liquidity trap therefore must involve more than simply estimating L_r (i.e., estimating an average level of L_r); tests must investigate whether L_r varies with r and how large (in absolute value) L_r becomes at low values of r. Tests designed to investigate the nonlinearity of the demand for money have not supported the existence of a low interest rate liquidity trap.[13]

In this section we will develop more fully the nature and consequences of such a liquidity trap. One motivation for this analysis, given that evidence suggests to the contrary that L_r is quite modest and does not become extremely large even at low interest rates, is that a similar analysis may apply to the demand for short-term bonds, even if it does not appear theoretically or empirically relevant to the demand for money. We noted this possibility in the previous chapter. Figures 21.4a and 21.5a are repeated from the discussion of Tobin's formalization of Keynes's speculative demand for money in Chapter 19. r_c is the critical rate at which money and bonds yield equal expected holding period yields. When there is disagreement about this critical rate among wealth owners, there will be a smooth relation between the interest rate and the demand for money as depicted in Figure 21.4a.

When the economy is in the downward-sloping region of the money demand curve in Figure 21.4a and the monetary authorities wish to increase the money supply by purchasing bonds from the private sector, they have to offer a price for the bonds above that prevailing in the market. At the prevailing price of bonds (and associated market interest rate), wealth owners are just content with their money and bondholdings. To induce some wealth owners who are holding bonds to part with them in

---

[12] Friedman, in "Interest Rates and the Demand for Money," notes that the only value of L_r which is of theoretical significance is $L_r = -\infty$. As we saw above, even if $L_r = 0$, other assumptions are still required to permit us to infer the impact of disturbances from knowledge of the *LM* curve alone. If $L_r = -\infty$, on the other hand, we immediately know that the interest rate is unaffected by disturbances so that the $\Delta X/\Delta m$ multiplier is zero.

[13] See David Laidler, *The Demand for Money: Theories and Evidence* (New York: Thomas Y. Crowell, Co., 1977), pp. 130–133, for a summary of evidence on the liquidity trap.

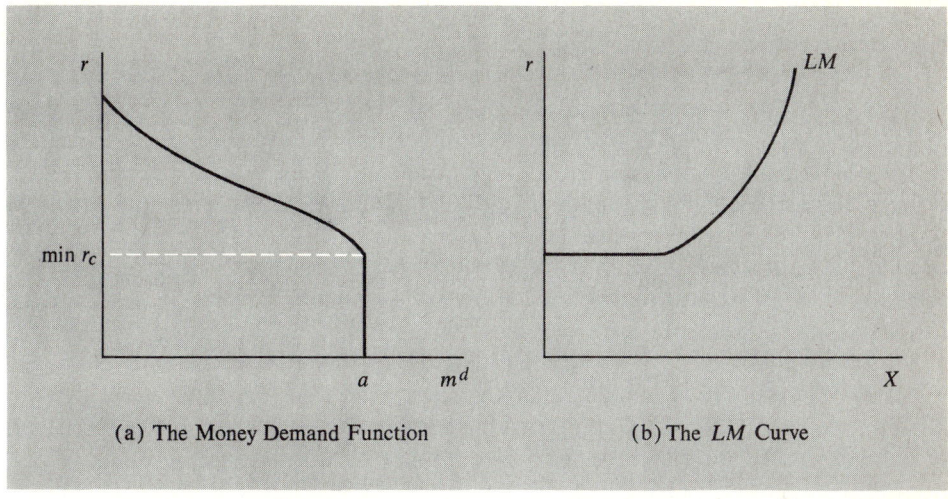

FIGURE 21.4
The Liquidity Trap at the Minimum Critical Rate

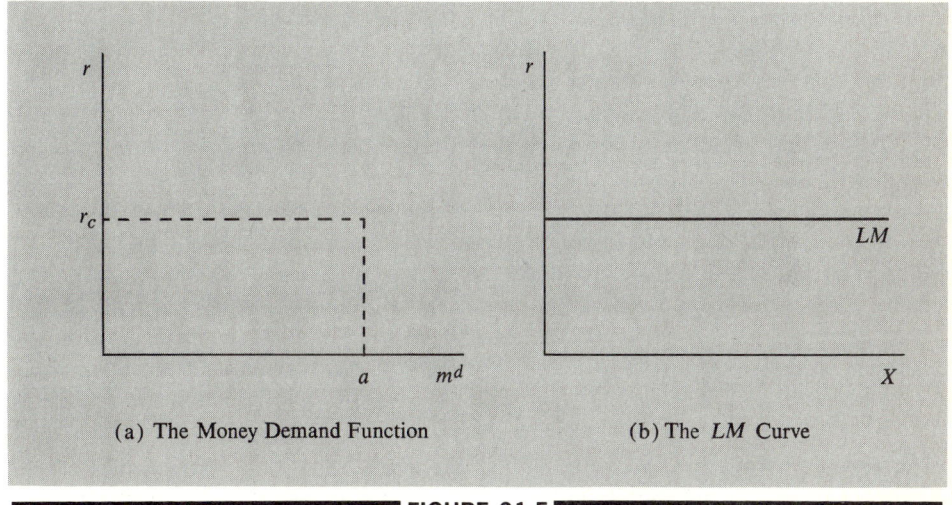

FIGURE 21.5
The Liquidity Trap: Convergence of Views
About the Expected Interest Rate

exchange for money, the monetary authorities must offer a price for bonds in excess of that prevailing in the market (i.e., they must lower the market interest rate). However, in the liquidity trap case depicted in Figure 21.5, wealth owners are *indifferent* between holding money and bonds (given they have equal expected holding period yields) and will passively accept any composition of wealth initiated by the monetary authorities without requiring the usual inducement of an increase in bond prices to sell bonds or a decrease in bond prices to buy bonds. The monetary authorities can buy or sell bonds at the prevailing interest rate, but bond purchases and sales have no effect on the market rate of interest which remains "trapped" at the universally held critical interest rate. In this case the *LM* curve is a horizontal line at the universally held critical interest rate as in Figure 21.5b.

We can demonstrate that in the latter case the interest rate will always tend toward this critical interest rate. If the prevailing rate were higher than r_c in Figure 21.5b, *everyone* would prefer to hold bonds rather than money because the expected holding period yield on bonds would be perceived as being positive by all wealth owners. As wealth owners attempt to get out of money into bonds, they bid up bond prices, reducing the market rate until it equals r_c. Only then are wealth owners content with the available mix of money and bonds. And of course at that point, they would be content with *any* mix of money and bonds. If, on the other hand, the prevailing interest rate were below r_c, then all wealth owners would prefer to hold money and attempts to get out of bonds would drive up the interest rate to r_c.

Even if wealth owners hold different views about the critical interest rate, a liquidity trap will exist at the minimum critical rate in the economy. This case can be illustrated in terms of Figures 21.4a and 21.4b. This case differs in several respects from the previous one. First of all, the interest rate will not be automatically driven down to the minimum critical interest rate. Consider what happens if the monetary authorities drive r down to the minimum r_c through bond purchases. At the minimum r_c, many wealth owners prefer to hold money (those whose $r_c >$ minimum r_c) and some (those whose $r_c =$ minimum r_c) are just indifferent between holding money and bonds. Here again, the monetary authorities will be unable to depress the interest rate any further. They can buy bonds only from those whose $r_c =$ minimum r_c. These wealth owners are indifferent between money and bond holdings; they will sell bonds without demanding the normal inducement of a higher price (lower market rate). However, this case differs from the previous one in that by lowering the price of bonds (raising the market interest rate), the monetary authorities can induce some wealth owners who are holding money to accept bonds in exchange. Therefore, if r falls to the minimum r_c, the monetary authorities can raise the interest rate but cannot lower it. This is reflected in the shape of the *LM* curve in Figure 21.5b where there is a floor to the interest rate at the minimum r_c, but it is possible to raise interest rates above that level by sufficiently vigorous open market sales.

THE IMPLICATIONS OF WEALTH IN THE MONEY DEMAND FUNCTION

In Chapter 19 we noted that there remains some disagreement about whether wealth is an argument in the money demand function. In our use of our basic model in previous chapters, however, we have assumed that wealth did not enter as an argument in the money demand function. In this section we explore the macro implications of introducing wealth into the money demand function. First, we consider the implications of the wealth effect in the money demand function for the short-run response to bond-financed fiscal policy. Then we compare the way in which the financial sector introduces negative feedback in response to real disturbances under the pure transactions and pure wealth approaches to the demand for money.

○ The Wealth Effect in the Money Demand Function and "Crowding-Out"

We have previously discussed the "crowding-out" of private expenditures by increased government expenditures in Chapters 9 and 10. We found that in the Keynesian fixed price model, crowding-out is only partial as long as no parameters take on extreme values. However, the model used to derive this result did not include wealth as an argument in the money demand function. In the previous chapter we demonstrated that the assumption of $L_a = 0$ (assumed throughout the analysis in Chapters 9 and 10) implies that $B_a = 1$, which in turn implies that increases in the supply of bonds (to finance government expenditures) will increase the demand for bonds by an equivalent amount. It follows that if $L_a = 0$, increases in the supply of government bonds to finance an increase in government spending do not result in an excess supply of bonds and therefore do not put upward pressure on the interest rate and contribute to "crowding-out." We did find in Chapters 9 and 10, however, that the interest rate does rise in response to a bond-financed increase in government spending. But the rise in the interest rate in this case results entirely from the income-induced increase in the demand for money; i.e., the interest rate rises to maintain portfolio equilibrium as the rise in income induces an increase in the demand for money ($L_x > 0$) and a corresponding decline in the demand for bonds ($B_x < 0$). *This income-induced rise in the interest rate is independent of any change in the supply of bonds.* The excess supply of bonds in this case reflects the income-induced decline in the demand for bonds, not the increase in the supply of bonds.

The controversy about the effectiveness of fiscal policy, on the other hand, generally focuses on the effects of increases in the supply of government bonds on interest rates. To allow for this effect in our one-period multiplier analysis, we must both introduce wealth as an argument in the money demand function (i.e., we must assume $L_a > 0$) and use the end-of-period (*EOP*) specification of our model. In the beginning-of-period specification, wealth and the supplies of government and private debt are fixed at their beginning-of-period values. In the end-of-period specification, the supply of government and private debt is linked directly to the government deficit and investment during the period being analyzed. This increase in the supply of government debt over the period must be absorbed into (end-of-period) household portfolios. From the perspective of the sum of the assets definition of wealth ($a = m + b_g + b_p$), there are two ways in which this can occur: increases in wealth (*a*) and/or reductions in private bondholdings (b_p). Households accumulate wealth via saving; this is reflected in the perpetual inventory definition of wealth according to which end-of-period wealth equals beginning-of-period wealth plus saving ($a = \bar{a} + S$). Thus, the increase in government debt associated with a bond-financed increase in government spending must be absorbed into private portfolios by some combination of increased saving induced by the operation or by displacing private debt. The counterpart of the crowding-out of private expenditures by government expenditures is therefore the crowding-out of private borrowing by government borrowing.

The model now consists of the *IS* and *LM* curves [equations (21.12) and (21.13), respectively], the definitions of disposable income and wealth [equations (21.14) and

(21.15), respectively], and the saving function [equation (21.16)]. We assume consumption and therefore saving are proportional to disposable income. The money supply, government expenditures, and net taxes are exogenous.

$$X = C_y Y + I_r r + \bar{Z} + \bar{G} \tag{21.12}$$

$$\bar{m} = \bar{L} + L_r r + L_x X + L_a a \tag{21.13}$$

$$Y \equiv X - \bar{T} \tag{21.14}$$

$$a \equiv \bar{a} + S \tag{21.15}$$

$$S = Y - C_y Y = S_y Y \tag{21.16}$$

To derive the multiplier for the response of income to a bond-financed increase in government expenditures, substitute for S in the definition of wealth, then substitute for a and Y in the IS and LM curves, take first differences assuming $\Delta \bar{Z} = \Delta \bar{L} = \Delta \bar{m} = 0$, and solve for $\Delta X/\Delta G$.

$$\frac{\Delta X}{\Delta G} = \frac{1}{1 - C_y + \{[L_x + L_a(1 - C_y)]/L_r\} I_r} \tag{21.17}$$

If we ignored the increment in wealth associated with saving (as in the beginning-of-period specification of the model) or assumed that $L_a = 0$, the multiplier would collapse to the standard textbook result, derived in Chapter 10 and repeated below.

$$\frac{\Delta X}{\Delta G} = \frac{1}{1 - C_y + (L_x/L_r)I_r} \tag{21.17'}$$

This multiplier takes into account the income generating effect of the increase in G but ignores the effect on portfolios of the increase in the supply of government bonds associated with deficit financing. Note that the multiplier given by equation (21.17), although also unambiguously positive, is smaller than the multiplier given by equation (21.17'). The additional term in the denominator in equation (21.17), $L_a(1 - C_y)$, reflects the effect of the increased wealth (via saving) on the demand for money. The money supply is unchanged; *all the increased wealth, therefore, is implicitly in the form of bonds.* To induce the private sector to increase its holdings of bonds relative to money, the government must offer an inducement in the form of a higher interest rate. Of course, if $L_a = 0$ so that households want to hold all increments of their wealth in bonds, no inducement of a higher rate is required and equation (21.17) reduces to equation (21.17').

○ Saving and the Unambiguous $\Delta X/\Delta G$ Multiplier

The result of this analysis, that bond-financed fiscal policy has an unambiguously positive short-run effect even when we take into account the offsetting effect of the increase in the supply of government bonds, is probably not one that is immediately obvious. After all, the increase in the supply of government bonds puts upward pressure on the interest rate and depresses investment. Why isn't it possible for this restrictive impact of the increase in the supply of bonds to offset completely the expansionary effect of the increase in the flow of government expenditures? The answer is that the wealth effect that controls the rise in interest rates associated with the increase in the supply of government bonds can *only occur if income increases*; i.e., the fiscal operation increases wealth only if it increases income and hence saving. Indeed, the multiplier, equation (21.17), indicates that there is really a *single direct impact*, the direct fiscal impact, associated with the increase in G. As income rises, there is the usual positive feedback via C_y, but the negative feedback is now larger. It includes the usual attempt to increase the demand for money for transactions purposes out of initial wealth; this is captured via the L_x term. But it now also includes the increase in the demand for money associated with the income-induced increase in wealth; this is captured by the $(1 - C_y)L_a$ term. As income and hence wealth increase, wealth owners attempt to increase demands for both money and bonds; the increase in wealth, however, is entirely in the form of bonds, so this attempt to increase the demand for money puts upward pressure on the interest rate until wealth owners are content to hold all their increase in wealth in bonds. The increase in the interest rate in this model is entirely *income induced*, and we know that an income-induced rise in interest rates can never reverse the rise in income. Fiscal policy has an unambiguously positive short-run income multiplier. We will clarify this result further when we consider the effect of the fiscal operation in the bond market in the next chapter. Remember also that this result applies only to the one-period multiplier. We will consider the longer run effects of bond-financed fiscal policy in the next chapter.

○ Comparison of the Pure Transactions and Pure Wealth Models of the Demand for Money

The models used in Chapters 9 and 10 employed the pure transactions approach (*PTA*) to the demand for money ($L_x > 0$ and $L_a = 0$). We found that the role of the L_x parameter was to activate the negative feedback response; as income increased, the demand for money increased (and the demand for bonds declined), and the resulting excess demand for money (excess supply of bonds) generated upward pressure on interest rates which in turn dampened the rise in income. In this section we will contrast this with the way the economy responds to disturbances if the demand for money depends on wealth but not income ($L_a > 0$, $L_x = 0$)—the pure wealth approach (*PWA*).

The Pure Wealth Approach with Beginning-of-Period Equilibrium. We begin by specifying asset market equilibrium in terms of beginning-of-period supplies and demands. In this case the wealth model yields quite different results from the pure transactions model. However, when we consider the end-of-period specification of asset market equilibrium, the two approaches yield qualitatively similar results.

The *LM* curve under the *PWA* is

$$\bar{m} = L_r r + L_a a + \bar{L}. \qquad (21.18)$$

Applying the beginning-of-period specification of asset equilibrium, we treat the supply of money and bonds as exogenously determined. Therefore, a is also exogenous. In Figure 21.6, the LM curve is a horizontal line in the r-X plane, given that X does not affect the supply of or demand for money. An increase in the autonomous component of private aggregate demand (Z) shifts the IS curve along the horizontal LM curve. The change in income in this case is equal to the horizontal shift in the IS curve which is simply the Keynesian consumption multiplier; i.e.,

$$\frac{\Delta X}{\Delta Z} = \frac{1}{1 - C_y}. \tag{21.19}$$

The increase in income no longer increases the demand for money so there is no income-induced rise in interest rate—*no negative feedback.*

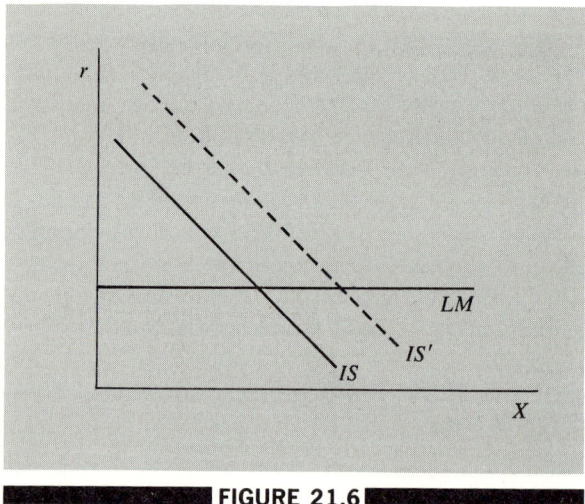

FIGURE 21.6
The Pure Wealth Approach: The *BOP* Case

The Pure Wealth Approach with End-of-Period Equilibrium. However, when we employ the end-of-period specification of asset market equilibrium, the *PWA* and *PTA* yield qualitatively similar responses to disturbances; in particular, there are both positive and negative feedbacks in response to disturbances.

The model consists of the *PWA* version of the *LM* equation, the basic *IS* equation, and the perpetual inventory definition of wealth. The *LM* curve can be written as

$$\bar{m} = \bar{L} + L_r r + L_a(\bar{a} + S_y Y) \tag{21.20}$$

where the wealth variable is end-of-period planned wealth, $a = \bar{a} + S_y Y$. Thus, the *LM* curve once again depends on income. The slope of the *LM* curve

$$\left.\frac{\Delta r}{\Delta X}\right|_{LM} = \frac{-S_y L_a}{L_r} > 0 \tag{21.21}$$

is again positive, as in the *PTA* version. An increase in income generates wealth accumulation via saving, and given that $L_a > 0$, the demand for money increases. To maintain the demand for money equal to the unchanged money supply, the interest rate must rise.

The $\Delta X/\Delta Z$ multiplier now becomes

$$\frac{\Delta X}{\Delta Z} = \frac{1}{1 - C_y + \frac{L_a S_y}{L_r} I_r}. \tag{21.22}$$

The last set of terms in the denominator is once again the negative feedback in the economy. Assume there is an autonomous increase in investment. It must be financed. Firms increase the supply of bonds. The increase in income induces an increase in saving. Ex post, the increase in saving will just balance the increase in investment so that wealth increases by the same amount as the increase in the supply of bonds. But households do not want to hold all the addition to wealth in bonds at the prevailing interest rate. Therefore, the increase in investment generates an excess supply in the bond market and upward pressure on the interest rate.[14] The increase in the interest rate dampens aggregate demand via I_r, and if there is an interest-induced wealth effect, via C_a.[15]

Note, however, the difference in the nature of the negative feedback in the *PTA* and *PWA* versions. In the *PTA* version, the income-induced excess supply of bonds (excess demand for money) results from the *decline in the demand for bonds* as wealth owners shift wealth into transactions balances. In the *PWA* version, the income-induced excess supply of bonds results from an *increase in the supply of bonds* which is only partially offset by an increase in the demand for bonds.

● REVIEW QUESTIONS

1. "The money demand function reduces to a single equation model of income determination if $L_r = 0$." Comment.

---

[14] The bond market may be in disequilibrium for two reasons: (1) the desired increase in wealth via saving may not equal the desired increase in the supply of private bonds; and (2) even if desired wealth accumulation were sufficient to absorb the desired increase in the supply of bonds, households may prefer to diversify their portfolios and therefore increase their demand for bonds by less than their desired increase in wealth. The view that interest rates respond directly to bond market disequilibrium is referred to as the *loanable funds* approach. We have generally viewed the interest rate as responding directly to money market disequilibrium; this is generally referred to as the *liquidity preference* approach and identified with Keynes. Note that in the end-of-period specification of the model, the loanable funds view of interest rate determination gives saving and investment important roles in generating changes in the interest rate through their effects on the demand for and supply of bonds over the period being analyzed.

[15] The sharp distinction between the results associated with the *BOP* and *EOP* specifications of asset equilibrium holds only for the one-period multipliers. Over time (e.g., in the *next* period), saving increases wealth and activates the negative feedback in the *BOP* specification.

Part V • Refinements of the Financial Sector

2. Define velocity and discuss its relation to the demand for money.

3. "The money demand function is the critical behavioral relation in monetarist models the way the consumption function is in income expenditure models." Comment.

4. "Introducing an interest-responsive demand for money in no way alters the equilibrium properties of the classical model. Therefore, Keynes must have greatly overplayed the importance of this innovation in his critique of classical macroeconomics." Comment.

5. "Introducing wealth into the money demand function in a short-run macroeconomic model cannot affect short-run multipliers, because in the short run, wealth should be treated as fixed." Comment.

6. Compare the nature of the income-induced movements in the interest rate under the pure transactions and pure wealth specifications of the demand for money.

● PROBLEMS

1. Milton Friedman has suggested that permanent rather than money income belongs in the money demand function. Using the Keynesian fixed price model, compare the short-run and long-run multipliers for monetary and fiscal policies under the following two alternative specifications of the money demand function:

$$m^d = \bar{L} + L_r r + L_x X$$

$$m^d = \bar{L} + L_r r + L_{x_p} X_p$$

where X_p is permanent income. Use the specification of the expected income component in the life cycle model for the permanent income variable. Assume consumption depends on actual income.

2. Compare your results in problem 1 with the implications of permanent income in the consumption function.

3. What can you conclude about the implications of permanent income in both consumption and money demand functions for the effectiveness of monetary and fiscal policies?

4. We noted in this chapter that the increment in saving will generally absorb only a portion of the increase in the supply of government bonds associated with bond financing. Derive the multiplier for the response of saving to a bond-financed fiscal policy and demonstrate that it must be less than one unless some parameters take on extreme values. What is the multiplier if $I_r = 0$? Explain why.

Chapter 22
The Bond Market and Crowding-Out

In this chapter we further refine the analysis of bond-financed fiscal policy. In the first section we indicate how the multiplier for a bond-financed increase in government expenditures can be derived using the bond market equilibrium condition in place of the money market equilibrium curve. This permits us to make explicit the role of the government and investment financing constraints. In the second section we discuss the implications of the term structure equation for the short-run response to fiscal policy. In the last section of the chapter we discuss the implications of the government financing constraint for the long-run response of income to fiscal policy. In an appendix at the end of the chapter we develop the implications of a three-asset model for fiscal policy.

THE BOND MARKET AND CROWDING-OUT

In the previous chapter we derived the one-period multiplier for a bond-financed increase in government expenditures. Although we allowed for the effect of the increase in the supply of government bonds in the model, we did not explicitly use either the government financing constraint (*GFC*) or the investment financing constraint (*IFC*) in the derivation of the multiplier. The only role of the *GFC* and *IFC* in our model is to relate the end-of-period *supply of bonds* to government and business spending decisions. Because the bond market was treated as the redundant market in the derivation in Chapter 21, neither the *GFC* nor the *IFC* were explicitly involved in the solution of the model. In this section we discuss two ways of solving the model that make explicit use of the *GFC* and *IFC* and further clarify the explanation of the unambiguous nature of the one-period multiplier for bond-financed fiscal policy.

One way to make explicit the role of the *GFC* and *IFC* is to solve the model using the bond market equilibrium curve along with the equilibrium condition in either of the other two markets (money or commodity). The bond market equilibrium curve (the *BB* curve) is given by

Part V · Refinements of the Financial Sector

$$b^s = \bar{B} + B_r r + B_x X + B_a a. \tag{22.1}$$

Taking first differences,

$$\Delta b^s = B_r \Delta r + B_x \Delta X + B_a \Delta a. \tag{22.1'}$$

We can now use the *GFC* and *IFC*, equations (22.2) and (22.3), respectively,

$$\Delta b_g \equiv D_{-1} + \Delta G - \Delta T - \Delta m \tag{22.2}$$

$$\Delta b_p \equiv I_{-1} + I_r \Delta r \tag{22.3}$$

(where D_{-1} and I_{-1} are the government deficit and investment over the previous period) to determine the change in the supply of bonds (Δb^s) and the perpetual inventory definition of wealth to determine Δa.

$$\Delta a = S_y \Delta Y \tag{22.4}$$

The *IS* and *BB* curves (or the *LM* and *BB* curves) can now be solved for the $\Delta X/\Delta G$ multiplier. This is left as a problem at the end of the chapter. By making use of the adding-up restrictions on the parameters of the money and bond demand equations (discussed in Chapter 20), you can demonstrate that the resulting multipliers are identical to the one derived in Chapter 21.

This illustrates the role of the *GFC* and *IFC* in the modeling of fiscal policy but does not yield further insight concerning the unambiguous nature of the one-period multiplier. However, there is an additional way of deriving the multiplier that does further clarify the result. We return to the specifications of the *LM* and *IS* curves employed in Chapter 21 but now use the sum of the assets definition of wealth.

$$a \equiv m + b_g + b_p \tag{22.5}$$

We take first differences of equation (22.5) and use the *GFC* and *IFC* to determine Δb_g and Δb_p, respectively. Taking first differences of the *IS* and *LM* curves and substituting for ΔY and Δa, we solve again for $\Delta X/\Delta G$.

$$\frac{\Delta X}{\Delta G} = \frac{1 - [L_a/(L_r + L_a I_r)] I_r}{1 - C_y + [L_x/(L_r + L_a I_r)] I_r} \tag{22.6}$$

Not only does this multiplier not look identical to that given by equation (21.17), but it also *looks* ambiguous. But it is identical to equation (21.17) and unambiguously positive.[1] One attractive feature of this way of writing the multiplier is that the

---

[1] Equation (22.6) is identical to equation (21.17), even though it does not look that way! Multiply and divide both the numerator and denominator of equation (22.6) by $L_r + L_a I_r$. The numerators of each of the resulting ratios will be the numerator and denominator of equation (21.17); the denominators of the two ratios cancel.

numerator includes terms for both the direct fiscal and direct portfolio impacts of the fiscal operation. The first term in the numerator is the direct fiscal impact: aggregate demand increases initially dollar-for-dollar with the increase in G. The second term is the direct portfolio impact of the increase in the supply of government bonds. Under the sum of the assets definition of wealth, the increase in the supply of government bonds associated with the financing of the increase in government spending increases wealth and generates an increase in the demand for money (via L_a) and upward pressure on the interest rate. Note that the second term can also be written as $L_a I_r/(L_r + L_a I_r)$; the denominator is larger (in absolute value) than the numerator so the ratio is less than one. Therefore, the numerator of equation (22.6) is unambiguously positive; the increase in G exceeds the decline in investment due to the increase in the interest rate directly associated with the increase in the supply of government bonds.

This approach provides another perspective on understanding why the short-run $\Delta X/\Delta G$ multiplier must be positive. The numerator of equation (22.6) describes the impact of the fiscal operation on income without allowing for income-induced feedback responses. This permits us to trace through the relation between the increase in G and interest-induced decline in investment ignoring the income-induced responses in the denominator. The increase in G increases aggregate demand dollar-for-dollar. The associated increase in the supply of bonds results in an excess supply of bonds, upward pressure on the interest rate, and a decline in investment. *But this decline in investment cannot exceed the increase in G.* If it did, the supply of private bonds would fall by more than the increase in the supply of government bonds. But this is impossible! If the decline in b_p exceeded the increase in b_g, the total supply of bonds ($b_g + b_p$) would fall. The decline in the supply of bonds would put *downward* rather than upward pressure on the interest rate, *encouraging* rather than discouraging investment. This of course involves a contradiction, because we know the only reason b_p declined was because the interest rate rose. Therefore, the interest-induced decline in the supply of private bonds can dampen but never reverse the direction of movement in the interest rate.

We conclude that *the short-run response to bond-financed fiscal policy is unambiguously positive.* This does not guarantee that the multiplier is large, of course. The size of the multiplier depends on the interaction of direct impacts and feedback responses discussed above. We will summarize the evidence on the size of the multiplier in our discussion of fiscal policy in Chapter 25. But the impact of the increase in the supply of government bonds on the interest rate when $L_a > 0$ unambiguously reduces the size of the one-period fiscal multiplier.

IMPLICATIONS OF THE TERM STRUCTURE EQUATION FOR FISCAL AND MONETARY POLICY MULTIPLIERS

We now assume that there are two types of bonds—short term and long term. Firms are assumed to finance their investment entirely through the issue of long-term bonds while the government finances its deficit and conducts open market operations exclusively in the short-term market. These assumptions are reasonable approximations since firms finance their plant and equipment expenditures primarily in long-term rather than short-term markets and government finances the major portion of its deficit and conducts most of its open market operations with relatively short-term bonds. The model now consists of *IS* and *LM* curves and a term structure equation. The *LM* curve, equation (22.7), includes the short-term rate, r, in the money demand function (based on the transactions approach to the demand for money) and the *IS* curve, equation (22.8), contains only the long-term rate, i, (based on the assumption that investment depends on the long-term rate). The term structure relation, equation (22.9), links the short-term rate in the *LM* function with the long-term rate in the *IS* function. The model is completed with the definitions of wealth, saving, and disposable income. We employ the perpetual inventory definition of wealth.

$$\bar{m} = L_r r + L_x X + L_a a \tag{22.7}$$

$$X = C_y Y + I_i i + \bar{Z} + \bar{G} \tag{22.8}$$

$$i = \beta + \alpha r \tag{22.9}$$

The specification of the term structure (*TS*) equation requires further explanation. Recall from Chapter 20 that the basic form of the *TS* equation is

$$i_t = \Sigma \alpha_j r_{t-j}; \tag{22.9'}$$

i.e., the long-term rate is a weighted average of current and past short-term rates. The Modigliani-Sutch empirical results discussed in Chapter 20 indicate that by the end of the first year, the long-term rate has risen by about 40 percent of the initial rise in the short-term rate.[2] The full response, which takes four years to occur, is an equal change in long- and short-term rates; i.e., the sum of the weights in equation (22.9') is equal to about one. We are interested here in the short-run, say one year, response to fiscal policy. The α parameter in equation (22.9) is therefore interpreted as giving the response of long-term rates to a change in the short-term rate over a year; the constant term reflects the other items in the *TS* equation which only affect the longer run response of the long-term rate.

An increase in the supply of short-term government bonds (as well as the income-induced increases in the demand for money relative to short-term government bonds via the L_x parameter) puts upward pressure on the short-term rate. The short-run effect of an increase in the short-term rate is to raise the long-term rate by only a fraction, α, of the increase in the short-term rate (and by the same fraction of the long-run response in the long-term rate). The effect of the *TS* equation is therefore to generate a gradual rise in the long-term rate so that the short-run effect of bond-financed fiscal policy is larger than the longer run response which allows for full adjustment of the long-term rate.[3]

The explicit multiplier in this case is

---

[2] Modigliani and Sutch, "Innovation in Interest Rate Policy," *American Economic Review, Papers and Proceedings*, Vol. 56 (May, 1966), pp. 178-197.

[3] Of course, in the longer run there will also be additional bond financing and this may reinforce the tendency of the cumulative multiplier to decline after the first period.

$$\frac{\Delta X}{\Delta G} = \frac{1}{1 - C_y + \{[L_x + L_a(1 - C_y)]/L_r\}\alpha I_i} \qquad (22.10)$$

It differs from the result in the previous section only in that αI_i replaces I_r in the denominator. The smaller is α, the larger the short-run response of income to fiscal policy.

The multiplier for an open market operation (a purchase of short-term government bonds) is

$$\frac{\Delta X}{\Delta m} = \frac{\alpha I_r / L_r}{D5} \qquad (22.11)$$

where $D5$ is the same as the denominator in equation (22.10). The term structure equation implies that open market operations in short-term bonds have a gradual effect on the long-term rate and therefore on investment. This means that unlike fiscal policy, monetary policy has a smaller short-run effect due to the term structure relation.

THE GOVERNMENT BUDGET CONSTRAINT AND THE LONG-RUN EFFECT OF FISCAL POLICY

Up to this point, the analysis of fiscal policy has been confined to the short-run (i.e., one period) response of output to fiscal changes. In this section we turn to the implications of the *GFC* for the longer run response to fiscal policy.

The Long-Run Response when Taxes Are Exogenous

Except for a brief section in Chapter 6, we have maintained the simplifying assumption that (net) tax revenues (T) are exogenous. In this case, a once-and-for-all increase in G will result in a deficit in the initial period and all future periods as long as G and T remain unchanged. The long-run response to the increase in G will depend on the response to the financing of the resulting deficit in future periods. If the financing has a positive effect on income, as it certainly will if deficits are financed by issuing additional money, income will continue to increase indefinitely. There is no well-defined long-run equilibrium response in this case and the cumulative $\Delta X/\Delta G$ multiplier increases indefinitely. If the effect of the financing is to reduce income, as may be the case when the deficits are financed by issuing additional government bonds, income will decline indefinitely. The key then is the sign of the response of income to deficit financing in subsequent periods. There is no question about the response to money-financed deficits, so we confine our analysis to the effect of increases in government bonds.

The key feature of the model underlying this analysis is the existence of wealth effects in both the consumption and money demand functions ($C_a > 0$ and $L_a > 0$). Once again we have the two alternative approaches to defining wealth. The usual approach is the sum of the assets definition. According to this perspective, increases in the supply of government bonds to finance inherited deficits increase wealth and consumption but also raise the interest rate and discourage investment. The net effect of the wealth-induced increase in consumption and the interest-induced decline in investment is ambiguous, and therefore the effect of the fiscal operation in future periods is also ambiguous.[4] In Appendix A we demonstrate that if we expand the model to the three-asset case discussed in the appendix to Chapter 20, the portfolio impact of bond financing becomes ambiguous. Thus, it is more likely that the net effect of bond financing is expansionary in the three-asset case than in the two-asset case. In Appendix B we derive the multiplier for the response of output to bond financing of inherited deficits in the two-asset case.

○ The Long-Run Response to Fiscal Policy with Endogenous Tax Revenues[5]

We found above that as long as the budget is unbalanced, either the supply of money or government bonds is changing, and this in turn will affect income. Thus, a *condition for full equilibrium is a balanced government budget*. If taxes are endogenous, say proportional to income, then the condition of a balanced government budget permits us to determine the long-run equilibrium response to policy changes and nonpolicy disturbances, and these long-run multipliers are independent of all the other relations in the economy. To see this, write the balanced-budget condition as

$$G - tX = 0 \qquad (22.12)$$

and solve for the implied reduced form for X:

$$X = \frac{1}{t} G. \qquad (22.12')$$

According to this equation, the long-run multiplier for a change in G is $\frac{1}{t}$, and all other policy changes (other than a change in t) and all nonpolicy disturbances have zero multipliers!

Consider first the response to an increase in G. This initially results in a deficit which must be financed by the issue of money or bonds. Assume that the response to the fiscal action is positive both in the initial period and in succeeding periods; this will certainly be the case if the deficit is financed by money issue and may be the case with bond finance. Consider the money-financed case. As long as the budget is in deficit, the money supply and therefore income are increasing. Income continues to increase until tax revenues rise sufficiently to balance the budget. At this point, money issue stops and income stabilizes. Consider the response to any other disturbance; for example, an increase in autonomous private spending will increase income,

---

[4] In terms of the perpetual inventory definition of wealth, the wealth-induced increase in consumption would derive from the first-period increase in income and any subsequent increases in income that occur if the wealth-induced increase in consumption in subsequent periods exceeds the interest-induced decline in investment.

[5] This section is based on Alan S. Blinder and Robert M. Solow, "Does Fiscal Policy Matter?" *Journal of Public Economics*, Vol. 2 (November, 1973), pp. 318–337.

pushing the budget into a surplus. This will induce a decline in the money supply that will continue as long as there is a surplus. The decline in the money supply will reduce income until tax revenues and income fall to their original levels. Hence, the long-run multiplier for an autonomous increase in private spending is zero.

Refining the Analysis to Include Interest Payments on the Outstanding Debt. The analysis above ignored interest payments on the outstanding stock of government bonds. Indeed, we have not separately considered this component of government transfer payments in the models we developed previously; implicitly we assumed that other transfers were reduced or taxes increased to maintain net tax revenue (T) unchanged. But now we are assuming that the other components of net tax revenues are proportional to income; this would be an inappropriate assumption for government interest payments so we include interest payments on the government debt as a separate component of government spending. Government interest payments on the outstanding stock of government bonds (T_i) equal the coupon payment per bond times the outstanding stock of bonds. To simplify, we assume that bonds are perpetuities paying coupons of one dollar each; the sum of the coupons is then simply the number of bonds outstanding (b)

$$T_i = b \qquad (22.13)$$

and the balanced-budget condition is rewritten as

$$G + (1-t)b - tX = 0. \qquad (22.14)$$

assuming that taxes are paid on interest on government bonds. This modification yields some further surprising results: bond-financed fiscal policy is more powerful than money-financed fiscal policy and open market purchases are restrictive.

The Relative Effect of Money and Bond Financing. To derive the income multiplier for this case, take first differences of equation (22.14) and solve for $\Delta X / \Delta G$.

$$\frac{\Delta X}{\Delta G} = \frac{1 + (1-t)\frac{\Delta b}{\Delta G}}{t} \qquad (22.15)$$

For a bond-financed increase in G, $\Delta b / \Delta G > 0$, while for the money-financed case, $\Delta b / \Delta G = 0$; therefore, the multiplier is greater in the bond-financed case. When the deficit is financed by bonds, the increase in G also results in an increase in government debt and therefore government interest payments; income must now rise by enough to generate tax revenues to cover the increase in both components of government spending. In the money-financed case, government debt and hence interest payments are unaffected; therefore, the budget can be rebalanced with a smaller increase in income.

The Effect of an Open Market Operation. An open market purchase involves a reduction in the outstanding stock of government bonds and hence a decline in government interest payments. To rebalance the budget, tax revenues and therefore income must decline.

○ Stability of the Model

The correspondence principle warns us that a comparative static result, such as the $\Delta X/\Delta G$ multiplier derived above, is meaningful only if the system is stable. Although the equilibrium multipliers derived above do not depend on the *IS* and *LM* curves, the stability of the system does. The stability of the model depends on whether the effect of deficit financing is to increase or reduce income. Assume, for example, that in response to the increase in G and the associated deficit financing, income increases. Then, as long as the deficit continues, income increases and this generates a rise in tax revenues which eventually closes the deficit. In this case the model is clearly stable. This will certainly apply to the situation in which deficits are financed by money issue. However, the economy is not necessarily stable when deficits are financed by bond issue. In our discussion of the response to bond financing in the exogenous tax revenue case, we concluded that the long-run response to bond-financed deficits might be ambiguous. If bond financing ultimately causes income to decline, the model will be unstable (unless the initial increase in income is just sufficient to close the deficit). As income declines in future periods, the deficit will become larger; the larger deficit, in turn, means progressively larger increases in the supply of government debt which in turn induces progressively larger declines in income. Thus, we conclude that for the case of bond financing, the response of income in initial and future periods is positive until the budget is rebalanced or the system is unstable.

Chapter 22 • The Bond Market and Crowding-Out

APPENDIX

A Implications of a Three-Asset Model

The term structure equation is a simple way of introducing differences among bonds due exclusively to differences in term to maturity. But government bonds also differ from private bonds in terms of risk of default, and bonds differ from equities as well. An alternative approach to allowing for more than one nonmoney asset is to include explicit supply and demand functions for each asset.[1] In this appendix we consider a model with three assets: money, a bond issued by the government, and equities issued by firms. This analysis builds on the three-asset model introduced in Appendix B to Chapter 20 and the interaction of substitution and wealth effects discussed there. An increase in the supply of government bonds has two effects on the equity market. The increase in the interest rate on government bonds puts downward pressure on the price of equities via the substitution effect. The increase in wealth associated with the fiscal operation, on the other hand, puts upward pressure on the price of equities. The net effect of the interaction of substitution and wealth effects on the price of equities is ambiguous. It is possible therefore that a bond-financed increase in government expenditures can increase investment.

Fiscal Policy in the Three-Asset Model

The model now includes three asset market equilibrium conditions, an *IS* curve in which investment is a function of q (the price of equities relative to newly produced capital goods), and the definitions of income, q, and wealth. The explicit solution is left as a problem at the end of this chapter. The implications of the three-asset model follow easily from the results developed in Appendix B to Chapter 20. An increase in government expenditures financed by the sale of bonds has an unambiguous positive income multiplier (as in the two-asset case developed in Chapters 21 and 22); the effect on investment, however, is ambiguous. The increase in the supply of bonds has offsetting wealth and substitution effects on the demand for equities. In addition, as income rises, there are further offsetting influences on the price of equities. The increase in income may drive up bond interest rates, putting downward pressure on the price of equities, but the increase in income will also increase quasi-rents, and this puts upward pressure on the price of equities. Therefore, the effect of the operation on q and hence investment is ambiguous. Bond-financed fiscal policy may encourage investment, at least in the short run.[2]

---

[1] Note that by redundant market analysis as developed in Chapter 5, it is necessary to include explicit equations for all but one of the assets included in the model.

[2] The ambiguity of the financial market impact of an increase in the supply of bonds on the price of equities can be removed by imposing restrictions on values of parameters in the asset demand functions. One set of restrictions which removes the ambiguity is associated with the pure transactions approach (*PTA*) to the demand for money. According to the *PTA*, the demand for money depends only on the short-term bond rate (r) and income. To develop the *financial market* response to an increase in the supply of bonds in this case, we treat both m and X as being fixed; therefore, the *LM* curve uniquely determines r, independently of the supply of bonds. Given that an increase in the supply of bonds cannot increase the bond rate, there will be *no substitution effect* operating on the equity market. The wealth effect is still operative, however, so that equity prices must unambiguously rise in response to an increase in the supply of bonds.

Part V • Refinements of the Financial Sector

Additional Implications of the Three-Asset Model

q not r Measures the Financial Market Effect of Policies. The key feature of this model is that the effect of policies on the market interest rate (r) is not an accurate guide to their influence on the real sector; i.e., policies which reduce r may nevertheless have a restrictive impact on aggregate demand. The explanation of the failure of r to reflect the financial market impact on the real sector is that it is q and not r that is the critical financial variable in real sector spending decisions.

It is movements in q not r which determine changes in the market value of household wealth. If we allowed for long-term bonds as well as equities, variations in both the long-term bond rate and q would affect the market value of wealth. Nevertheless, quantitatively, it is movement in the price of equities that generates the major source of capital gains/losses in household portfolios. And according to the dual price models of investment, it is q, not r, which enters as an argument in the investment function.

There is No Unique Relation Between r and q. If q were a simple function of r, it would nevertheless be possible to write consumption and investment functions in terms of r. This is not, however, the case in this model. The response of q to a change in r depends on the source of the change in r. An open market purchase (an exchange of money for bonds) unambiguously lowers the bond rate and raises the price of equities; i.e., r falls and q rises. Thus, an *OMP* is unambiguously expansionary. An increase in the supply of bonds, on the other hand, has an ambiguous impact on q. This reflects the offsetting influence of the wealth and substitution effects. This means that r and q do not always move in the opposite directions. *Changes in r are therefore a potentially misleading indicator of the effect of financial policies on the real sector.*

If bonds and equities are close substitutes, the substitution effect will be powerful, and r and q will generally move in opposite directions. In this case, aggregating bonds and equities into a single financial asset and including only a single interest rate in the model do not seriously distort the qualitative conclusions that the model will yield.

APPENDIX

 The Effect of Bond Financing after the Initial Period

In this chapter we derived both the one-period multiplier and the long-run equilibrium multiplier for the response of income to a change in government expenditures. We noted that the effects on income after the first period and indeed the stability of the system depend on the response to the financing of the deficits inherited in subsequent periods. In this appendix we derive the explicit multiplier for the response to increases in the supply of government bonds associated with the financing of deficits associated with some prior change in government expenditures or taxes. We employ an end-of-period specification consisting of *IS* and *LM* curves with wealth effects, the sum of the assets definition of wealth, and the *GFC* and *IFC*

to define the end-of-period supply of bonds. Substitute the *GFC* and *IFC* into the wealth definition and the wealth definition into the *IS* and *LM* curves, and solve for the multiplier for an increase in the supply of bonds associated with financing an inherited deficit ($\Delta X/\Delta b_g$).[1]

The multiplier is

$$\frac{\Delta X}{\Delta b_g} = \frac{C_a - [L_a/(L_r + L_a I_r)] \, I_r(1 + C_a)}{1 - (1-t)C_y + [L_x/(L_r + L_a I_r)] \, I_r(1 + C_a)}. \tag{22B.1}$$

The numerator is ambiguous. The first term is the wealth effect via the consumption function and is positive. The second set of terms is the portfolio impact of the increase in the supply of bonds and is negative. The denominator is positive. Therefore, the multiplier is positive if the wealth effect in the consumption function dominates and negative if the portfolio impact dominates.

● REVIEW QUESTIONS

1. Identify the role of the government and investment financing constraints in the *EOP* specification of the model and explain how it is possible to derive the model multipliers without explicit use of the financing constraint.

2. Interpret the multiplier given by equation (22.6). Why must it be positive?

3. Why does the assumption that both *G* and *T* are exogenous rule out a well-defined comparative static (equilibrium) government expenditure multiplier for the money-financed case?

4. "The long-run response to an increase in government expenditures is independent of the specification of the consumption, investment, and money demand functions." Comment.

5. Explain how the stability of the model may depend on the source of deficit financing assumed.

● PROBLEMS

1. Solve for the one-period $\Delta X/\Delta G$ multiplier for the bond-financed case using the bond and commodity market equilibrium conditions. Demonstrate the equivalence of this multiplier to the one derived using the money and commodity market equilibrium conditions in Chapter 21.

---

[1] The wealth definition is now $a \equiv \bar{m} + \bar{b} + D_{-1} + \Delta G - \Delta T + I_{-1} + I_r r$. The change in government bonds due to the inherited deficit is $D_{-1} = \Delta b_g$. $\Delta m = \Delta G = \Delta T = 0$. Therefore, $\Delta a = \Delta b_g + I_r \Delta r$.

Part V • Refinements of the Financial Sector

2. Derive the multiplier given by equation (22.6). Rearrange terms to demonstrate that it is (a) unambiguously positive and (b) equivalent to the multiplier derived in question 1.

3. Consider the following model: The *IS* and *LM* curves are given by equations (21.12) and (21.13). Disposable income is defined as in equation (21.14) and wealth is defined as

$$a = \bar{m} + \bar{b}_g$$

where $\bar{m}$ and $\bar{b}_g$ are the stock of money and government bonds outstanding. The supply of government bonds is determined via the government financing constraint,

$$\Delta b_g \equiv D_{-1} + \Delta G - \Delta T - \Delta m$$

where D_{-1} is the deficit inherited from the previous period. Use this model to derive the multiplier for a bond-financed increase in government expenditures. Compare this multiplier to those given by equations (21.17) and (21.17′) and explain the difference.

4. "Adding the term structure equation is equivalent to assuming lagged response of investment to the interest rate." Comment.

5. Solve the three-asset model for the response of income to bond-financed fiscal policy.

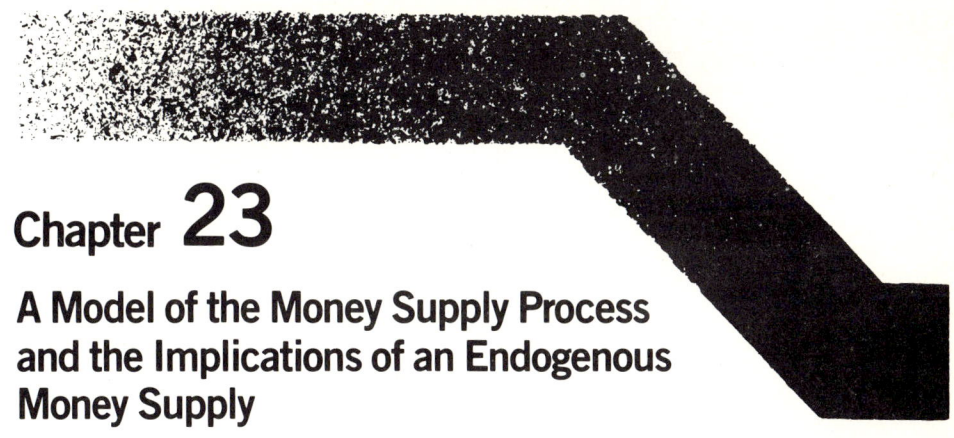

Chapter 23

A Model of the Money Supply Process and the Implications of an Endogenous Money Supply

Up to this point, we have assumed that the money supply was determined directly by the government. In this chapter we introduce the Federal Reserve System and the commercial bank sector and develop a model of the money supply process in which the money supply is jointly determined by the behavior of the nonbank public, the commercial banks, and the Federal Reserve System. We begin by discussing the balance sheet of the Federal Reserve, commercial bank, and nonbank public sectors and then develop hypotheses about the behavior of each of these units. We then develop a series of money supply models of increasing complexity and conclude with a discussion of the implications of an endogenous money supply for the economy's response to disturbances and policy actions.

THE FEDERAL RESERVE SYSTEM, COMMERCIAL BANKS, AND THE MONEY SUPPLY PROCESS

The Federal Reserve System (FRS) is the nation's central bank. At this point we will not discuss the institutional structure of the Federal Reserve System (e.g., the relation between the twelve regional Federal Reserve Banks and the Board of Governors of the Federal Reserve System). We will simply view the FRS as a unified policy authority and central bank. The institutional structure of the FRS will be discussed in the next chapter. The FRS carries out monetary policy, supervises the member banks, and provides services to its member banks, such as check clearing, loans, and provision of currency.

Balance Sheets of the FRS, Commercial Banks, and Nonbank Public

A useful starting point is the balance sheets of the Federal Reserve System, commercial banks, and the nonbank public, presented in Tables 23.1a, 23.1b, and

440

Part V • Refinements of the Financial Sector

23.1c. We have simplified the accounts by assuming that all banks are members of the FRS and that banks issue only demand deposits.[1] We will maintain these simplifying assumptions throughout the chapter to allow us to develop a simple model of the money supply process. In the problems at the end of the chapter you will have the opportunity to develop the implications of relaxing them.

(a) Federal Reserve System	
Government Securities (B_g^F)	Member Bank Deposits (MBD)
	Currency ($CURR$)
Loans to Member Banks ($BORR$)	

(b) Commercial Banks	
Reserves (R) $\begin{cases} \text{Deposits at the FRS } (MBD) \\ \text{Currency in Vaults } (C^B) \end{cases}$	Demand Deposits (D)
	Borrowing from FRS ($BORR$)
Government Securities (B_g^B)	
Business Loans (B_p^B)	

(c) Nonbank Public	
Demand Deposits (D)	Private securities (B_P)
Currency (C^H)	
Government Securities (B_g^P)	
Private Securities (B_p^P)	
Capital Stock (K)	

TABLE 23.1
The Balance Sheets of the FRS,
Commercial Banks, and Households

The money supply (M) is defined as the sum of nonbank public holdings of currency (C^H) and demand deposits (D) issued by commercial banks.[2]

$$M \equiv C^H + D \tag{23.1}$$

---

[1] Note that private securities are issued by firms (part of the nonbank public) and held by both commercial banks (as bank loans) and households (also part of the nonbank public). The nonbank public's balance sheet is shown in nonconsolidated form, with gross liabilities equal to the total issue of private securities and gross assets including the sector's holdings of those securities. The assets of the nonbank public also include the capital stock which in turn is balanced by the financial claims issued to acquire the capital stock on the liability side. To simplify, we have not explicitly included household holdings of capital goods (consumer durables including houses) or the liabilities issued by households to finance the acquisition of these assets. Finally, we have not included the financial claims (equities) issued by banks and held by the nonbank public.

[2] The money supply excludes both currency and demand deposits held by the government. To simplify, we will assume government does not hold money balances. When an asset is held by more than one unit we use a superscript to identify the holder; e.g., C^B is currency held by banks and C^H is currency held by households. When a liability is issued by more than one unit, we identify the issuing unit by subscripts; e.g., B_g and B_p are bonds issued by government and private sector units, respectively.

Commercial banks issue demand deposits. They are prohibited from paying explicit interest on demand deposits, but must stand ready to convert their own deposits into currency on demand and accept deposits of other banks' demand deposits at par (i.e., at face value, without discount).[3] Banks hold three types of assets: reserves (R), investments, and loans to business. Members of the Federal Reserve System are required to hold reserves against their deposit liabilities in the form of either deposits with the FRS (MBD) or currency in their own vaults (C^B); these reserves are called *required reserves* (R_r). Banks may also hold reserves in excess of the amount required by the FRS; these are naturally called *excess reserves* (R_e). Total bank reserves (R) are the sum of required reserves and excess reserves:

$$R \equiv R_r + R_e. \tag{23.2}$$

Commercial bank earning assets include both investments (mainly government securities) and loans to business. We treat their investment portfolio as commercial bank holdings of government securities (B_g^B) and their loans to business as commercial bank holdings of bonds issued by business (B_p^B).

The Federal Reserve carries out monetary policy primarily by buying and selling government bonds from its own portfolio (B_g^F). It pays for purchases with checks drawn against itself and thereby increases member bank deposits at the FRS. The FRS will convert member bank deposits with it into currency on demand. Therefore, the Fed really controls the sum of member bank deposits and currency outstanding, called *high-powered money* or the *monetary base* (MB):

$$MB \equiv MBD + CURR. \tag{23.3}$$

A more convenient way of writing this is to combine member bank deposits at the FRS and currency held by the commercial banks into bank reserves

$$R \equiv MBD + C^B \tag{23.4}$$

and write the monetary base as the sum of reserves plus currency held by the nonbank public.

$$MB \equiv R + C^H \tag{23.3'}$$

The FRS holds other assets in addition to government securities. For simplicity, we will include only one other asset in our model in this chapter, loans from the FRS to commercial banks ($BORR$). We can also write the monetary base as the sum of FRS assets (the source base).

$$MB \equiv B_g^F + BORR \tag{23.3''}$$

---

[3] There are, however, checking accounts on which interest is paid. These include the *NOW* accounts in New England and the *ATS* accounts authorized by the Federal Reserve on November 1, 1978. Both types of accounts were discussed in Appendix A at the end of Chapter 19. These accounts are technically classified as savings accounts rather than demand deposit accounts. However, they both would be included in the revised narrow (transactions-related) definition of the money supply recently proposed by the FRS.

Commercial Bank Portfolio Behavior

Our model of commercial banks at this point only allows for a single deposit liability, demand deposits. Bank portfolio behavior in our simple model consists primarily of *asset management*. We noted above that banks must hold some required reserves. The amount of required reserves is simply the level of demand deposits times the reserve requirement ratio.

$$R_r = dD \tag{23.5}$$

The required reserves provide only a limited buffer against changes in a bank's demand deposits. For example, if $d=.2$ and a bank's demand deposits decline by $10,000, its required reserves fall by only $2,000 (.2 times $10,000) and the remainder of the decline in demand deposits must be offset by either a decline in other bank assets or by borrowing from the FRS. Banks are generally viewed as being reluctant to borrow from the FRS. First of all, the Fed is quick to remind banks that borrowing from the Fed is a privilege, not a right. The Fed maintains a borrowing rate (called the *discount rate*, r_d) but does not promise to meet all demand for loans at that rate. In particular, it discourages certain types of borrowing; e.g., continuing borrowing to take advantage of the spread between the discount rate and the rate on bank earning assets. The purpose of borrowing is to ease the adjustment to unforeseen deposit losses or unexpected increases in loan demand. It is therefore expected to be infrequent and of short duration. The reluctance to take advantage of this source of borrowing is reinforced by the way in which the FRS exercises surveillance over those banks that borrow from the FRS. The Fed is more likely in such cases to look over the management of the bank and make unsolicited suggestions about bank portfolio management.

The amount of borrowing from the Fed (*BORR*) depends on both the rate on such borrowing (the discount rate) and the rate on earning assets. The higher the rate on earning assets, the lower the excess reserves the bank will want to hold and the greater the likelihood that unforeseen reserve needs will have to be met by borrowing. The rate on earning assets also reflects the return on securities held by banks. An alternative means of meeting reserve deficiencies is the sale of securities. The higher this rate, the more costly it is to meet reserve needs by selling securities, and the greater the use of borrowing. Thus,

$$BORR = B(r, r_d) \tag{23.6}$$

where $B_r > 0$ and $B_{r_d} < 0$.[4]

Alternative means of meeting unexpected deposit withdrawals or loan opportunities are reducing excess reserves and selling securities. Excess reserves are analogous to a precautionary demand for money. The demand for excess reserves depends on the rate on earning assets (the opportunity cost of holding excess reserves) and the

---

[4] For a discussion of the determinants of member bank borrowing, see Murray E. Polakoff, "Reluctance Elasticity, Least Cost, and Member-Bank Borrowing: A Suggested Integration," *Journal of Finance*, Vol. 15 (March, 1960), pp. 1–18.

discount rate (the rate associated with an alternative source of funds to meet unforeseen contingencies).

$$R_e = E(r, r_d) \tag{23.7}$$

where $E_r < 0$ and $E_{r_d} > 0$.

○ The Behavior of the Public

The nonbank public holds both currency and demand deposits. To maintain a simple specification of the nonbank public's portfolio behavior, we will assume that their demand for currency (C^H) is simply proportional to their demand for demand deposits.

$$C^H = cD \tag{23.8}$$

○ The Behavior of the FRS

The Fed controls the discount rate (r_d), the reserve requirement ratio (d), and its portfolio of government securities (B_g^F). For the remainder of the chapter we will treat the required reserve ratio and the discount rate as fixed and view monetary policy as variations in the portfolio of government securities (open market operations). Although borrowing is a privilege rather than a right, it nevertheless varies with interest rates on earning assets and is therefore endogenous. This means that one component of the monetary base, *BORR*, is endogenous. This does not necessarily imply that the monetary base itself is endogenous because the Fed could immediately offset changes in borrowing with open market operations to keep the monetary base independent of the amount of borrowing. If the Fed does not act to offset the borrowing, however, the monetary base will be endogenous. In this case, the policy-controlled variable is the monetary base net of member bank borrowing, called the *net source base* or *nonborrowed monetary base* (*NMB*):

$$NMB \equiv MB - BORR. \tag{23.9}$$

The uses of the nonborrowed base are reserves and currency, but because we have excluded borrowed reserves, the nonborrowed base is the sum of nonborrowed reserves (R^u) and currency held by the nonbank public.

$$NMB \equiv R^u + C^H \tag{23.9'}$$

○ MODELS OF THE MONEY SUPPLY PROCESS

In this section we develop a series of models of the money supply process, building upon the analysis in the previous section. We begin by developing the nature of the multiple expansion of deposits in response to increases in reserves available to the banking system. To isolate the response of deposits, we initially assume that currency holdings are constant. Next, we reintroduce currency demand and then the demand for free reserves and derive the money supply equation in each case.[5]

○ A Simple Model of Multiple Expansion of Deposits

To develop the nature of the multiple expansion of deposits in response to a change in the reserve base, we begin with a simple model in which we assume that currency holdings by the nonbank public are constant and that banks hold no excess reserves and do not borrow from the FRS. The reserve base available to banks is therefore fixed directly by the FRS, equal to the monetary base minus currency held by the nonbank public.

$$\bar{R} \equiv \overline{MB} - \bar{C}^H \qquad (23.10)$$

We assume initially that the required reserve ratio is 1.0; i.e., banks must hold 100 percent reserves against deposits. The balance sheet of the commercial banking sector is depicted in Table 23.2 in this case.

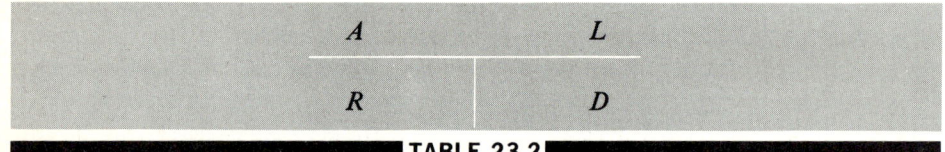

TABLE 23.2
The Balance Sheet of the Commercial Banking System when $d = 1$

Under 100 percent reserves, banks hold a dollar of monetary base as reserves for each dollar of demand deposits outstanding and therefore cannot invest any portion of their deposit inflows. Assume now that the reserve requirement ratio is reduced below one; e.g., from 1.0 to 0.2. When this happens, banks find they have *surplus* reserves: reserves in excess of the amount they desire to hold. In the present case, in which desired excess reserves are zero, surplus reserves are simply total reserves minus required reserves (or excess reserves).

$$R^s = R - R_r \qquad (23.11)$$

Banks use their surplus reserves to purchase earning assets (i.e., to purchase securities and make loans). Banks pay for the security or make the loan by writing a check against themselves. Therefore, as banks dispose of surplus reserves, they increase both their earning assets and deposits. In order to develop the dynamics of the response of deposits to an increase in surplus reserves, we will introduce an explicit dynamic model of bank response to surplus reserves: banks increase earning assets (EA) and

---

[5] For an excellent development of the interaction on commercial banks and the public in the money supply process, see Warren L. Smith, "Time Deposits, Free Reserves, and Monetary Policy," in G. Pontecorvo, R. P. Shay, and A. G. Hart (eds.), *Issues in Banking and Monetary Analysis* (New York: Holt, Rinehart & Winston, Inc., 1967), pp. 79–113; and Albert E. Burger, *The Money Supply Process* (Belmont, California: Wadsworth Publishing Company, Inc., 1971).

deposits by the amount of surplus reserves in the previous period.

$$\Delta EA = \Delta D = R^s_1 \qquad (23.12)$$

Although the deposits generated in this process cannot leave the banking system, each bank expects to lose the deposits it generates by purchasing earning assets and therefore must limit its purchases to its surplus reserves. However, since deposits remain in the system, the surplus reserves decline only by the increase in required reserves associated with the increase in deposits. The expansion of deposits continues until the total stock of reserves is absorbed into required reserves. Required reserves are $R_r = dD$; therefore, equilibrium in the market for bank reserves implies

$$R = dD \qquad (23.13)$$

which in turn determines the equilibrium level of demand deposits.

$$D = \frac{1}{d} R \qquad (23.13')$$

This is the simple formulation of multiple expansion of deposits. If $d = .2$, each \$1 increase in the reserve base induces a \$5 increase in the level of demand deposits. $1/d$ is called the deposit expansion or reserve multiplier.

We describe the time path of required and surplus reserves and deposits in Table 23.3. Initially (period 0) $D_0 = \bar{R}$ (100 percent reserves), $R_r = \bar{R}$, and $R^s = 0$. In period 1, d is reduced below unity and $R_{r_1} = dD_0 = d\bar{R}$ and $R^s_1 = (1-d)D_0 = (1-d)\bar{R}$. Commercial banks thus find themselves with surplus reserves which they use to purchase earning assets. In period 2 banks therefore lend out their surplus reserves from period 1. The change in earning assets in period 2 is

$$\Delta EA_2 = (1-d)\bar{R}$$

and the increase in required reserves associated with the accompanying increase in deposits is

$$\Delta R_{r_2} = d\Delta D_2 = d(1-d)\bar{R}.$$

The surplus reserves in period 2 are therefore

$$R^s_2 = R^s_1 - \Delta R_{r_2} = (1-d)\bar{R} - d(1-d)\bar{R} = (1-d)^2 \bar{R}.$$

Banks lend out R^s_2 in period 3, increasing required reserves and decreasing surplus reserves. This process continues until all reserves have been absorbed into required reserves. The sum of the deposit changes is

$$\sum_{t=1}^{\infty} \Delta D_t = \sum_{t=1}^{\infty} (1-d)^t \bar{R} = \frac{1-d}{d} \bar{R}. \qquad (23.14a)$$

Part V • Refinements of the Financial Sector

Period	Required Reserves	Surplus Reserves	Deposits
0	$\bar{R}$	0	$D_0 = \bar{R}$
1	$dD_0 = d\bar{R}$	$(1-d)D_0 = (1-d)\bar{R}$	$D_0 = \bar{R}$
2	$d\bar{R} + d(1-d)\bar{R}$	$(1-d)(1-d)\bar{R}$	$\bar{R} + (1-d)\bar{R}$
3	$d\bar{R} + d(1-d)\bar{R} + d(1-d)^2\bar{R}$	$(1-d)^3\bar{R}$	$\bar{R} + (1-d)\bar{R} + (1-d)^2\bar{R}$
∞	$\bar{R}$	0	$\bar{R} + \sum_{t=2}^{\infty}(1-d)^t\bar{R}$

TABLE 23.3
Time Path of Required and Surplus
Reserves and Deposits

Deposits in the initial period were equal to $\bar{R}$. Therefore, total deposits are

$$D = \bar{R} + \frac{1-d}{d}\bar{R} = \frac{1}{d}\bar{R}. \tag{23.14b}$$

Thus, the multiplier $1/d$ is the result of a sequential process of lending out surplus reserves until surplus reserves are eliminated. This dynamic model of the reserve multiplier process is of course analogous to the consumption multiplier process developed in Chapter 6.

○ Currency Holdings and the Money Supply Process

We continue to assume that banks do not wish to hold excess reserves and that there is no borrowing from the FRS. We now reintroduce the demand for currency into the model and develop the implications of currency holdings for the money supply process. The demand for currency is assumed to be proportional to the demand for demand deposits, as in equation (23.8) above. The reserve base available to the banking system is no longer determined uniquely by the FRS. It also depends on the demand for currency by the nonbank public; an increase in currency reduces the amount of the monetary base available to the banking system as reserves and therefore reduces the amount of demand deposits that can be issued by commercial banks. We view the FRS as controlling the size of the monetary base and the nonbank public and the banking system as determining the division of the base between reserves and currency.

The demand for the monetary base equals the sum of required reserves of banks ($R_r = dD$) and currency holdings of nonbank public ($C^H = cD$)

$$MB^d \equiv R_r + C^H = dD + cD = (c+d)D. \tag{23.15}$$

The supply of demand deposits depends on the interaction of the supply and demand for the monetary base. Equilibrium exists when the exogenous (policy-controlled) supply of high-powered money ($\overline{MB}$) equals the demand for high-powered money (MB^d).

$$\overline{MB} = \overline{MB}^d \tag{23.16}$$

or

$$\overline{MB} = (c+d)\,D. \tag{23.16'}$$

We can solve (23.16') for the equilibrium level of the supply of demand deposits as a function of the level of the exogenous monetary base.

$$D = \frac{1}{c+d}\,\overline{MB} \tag{23.16''}$$

Currency holdings reduce the amount of demand deposits that the banking system can generate from any given monetary base. As banks lend out surplus reserves, the increase in deposits absorbs some surplus reserves into required reserves and some into currency holdings.

The money supply is the sum of currency and demand deposits. The equilibrium level of currency holdings is

$$C^H = cD = \frac{c}{c+d}\,\overline{MB} \tag{23.17}$$

and the equilibrium money supply is

$$M = C^H + D = \frac{1+c}{c+d}\,\overline{MB}. \tag{23.18}$$

The supply of money now depends on the behavior of the public (the demand for currency relative to demand deposits, c), the required reserve ratio (d), and the supply of base money ($\overline{MB}$). An increase in the demand for currency relative to demand deposits decreases the money supply. An increase in currency demanded matched by a reduction in demand deposits decreases the amount of the monetary base available as reserves to support demand deposits. As long as $d < 1$, the decrease in reserves will reduce demand deposits by a multiple of the decline in reserves and therefore the net effect will be a reduction in the money supply.

○ Adding Excess Reserves and Borrowing

To allow for excess reserves and borrowing, it is useful to define a new concept, *free reserves* (R_f).

$$R_f = R_e - BORR \tag{23.19}$$

Banks with sufficient excess reserves meet deposit withdrawals by reducing excess reserves while banks without sufficient excess reserves may meet deposit withdrawals by borrowing from the *FRS*. In either case (a reduction in excess reserves or an increase in borrowing) the result will be a decline in free reserves. The demand for free reserves depends on both the interest rate on bank earning assets and the discount rate on member bank borrowing. The higher the rate on bank earning assets, the lower the demand for excess reserves and the higher the demand for borrowing. The higher the rate on borrowing, the higher the demand for excess reserves and the lower the demand for borrowing. Therefore, the demand for free reserves is inversely related to the yield on earning assets and positively related to the discount rate:

$$R_f^d = F(r, \overline{rd}) \tag{23.20}$$

where $F_r < 0$ and $F_{rd} > 0$.

With the introduction of member bank borrowing, we treat the nonborrowed monetary base (*NMB*) as the variable directly controlled by the Fed. The nonborrowed base can be expressed as the sum of reserves and currency held by the nonbank public less member bank borrowing.

$$NMB \equiv R + C^H - BORR \tag{23.21}$$

Total reserves (R) are the sum of the excess and required reserves. Therefore, we can write

$$NMB = R_r + C^H + R_f \tag{23.21'}$$

where $R_f = R_e - BORR$.

Equilibrium in the market for the nonborrowed base requires equality of the supply and demand for the nonborrowed base:

$$\overline{NMB} = cD + dD + F(\ ) \tag{23.22}$$

where $F(\ )$ is the demand for free reserves. Therefore,

$$D = \frac{1}{c+d}[\overline{NMB} - F(\ )] \tag{23.22'}$$

and

$$M = \frac{1+c}{c+d}[\overline{NMB} - F(\ )]. \tag{23.22''}$$

The money supply now depends on the interest rate. The higher the interest rate, the smaller the demand for free reserves (the lower the demand for excess reserves and the greater the demand for borrowing from the FRS) and therefore the higher the money supply.

THE IMPLICATIONS OF AN ENDOGENOUS MONEY SUPPLY

In this section we consider the implications of the endogenous nature of the money supply for the response of interest rates and income to disturbances. First, we integrate our money supply sector into an extended *LM* curve. Then we compare the response to disturbances when the money supply is exogenous and endogenous.

The Extended *LM* Curve

There are two alternative interpretations of the *LM* curve in the model with a banking sector. The first interpretation is the equilibrium condition in the money market; we simply replace the exogenous money supply with the money supply equation derived above.

$$\overbrace{\frac{1+c}{c+d}}^{m}[\overline{nmb} - F(\ )] = L(\ ) \tag{23.23}$$

where $\overline{nmb}$ and $F(\ )$ are, like $L(\ )$, in real terms. Alternatively, we could interpret the *LM* curve as the equilibrium condition in the market for the nonborrowed monetary base. Rearranging equation (23.23), we get

$$\overline{nmb} = \frac{c+d}{1+c}L(\ ) + F(\ ). \tag{23.23'}$$

The right-hand side of this equation is the demand for the nonborrowed base. To see this, recall that $C^H = cD$ so that $M = C^H + D = (1+c)D$ and $D = \frac{1}{1+c}M$. Therefore, the first term on the right is simply $(c+d)D$, the sum of the demand for the nonborrowed base as required reserves and currency. The second term is the demand for free reserves.

There are two ways to compare the implications of adding the banking sector. First, we could compare regimes with and without a banking system. Second, we could compare regimes with banking systems but with and without an interest-responsive supply of money. The *LM* curves corresponding to the three different regimes are given in equations (23.24a), (23.24b) and (23.24c): equation (23.24a) is the *LM* curve with no banking system, equation (23.24b) is the *LM* curve with a banking system but assuming a zero interest responsiveness of the money supply, and equation (23.24c) is the *LM* curve when there is a banking system and an interest-responsive money supply.

$$\overline{m} = L(\ ) \tag{23.24a}$$

$$\frac{1+c}{c+d}(\overline{nmb}) = L(\ ) \tag{23.24b}$$

$$\frac{1+c}{c+d}[nmb - F(r, r_d)] = L(\ ) \tag{23.24c}$$

○ The Implications of a Banking System

The LM curves with and without a banking system [equations (23.24a) and (23.24b), respectively] have identical slopes and therefore respond identically to real disturbances. The only difference is that open market operations now have a larger effect because the increase in the nonborrowed base results in a multiple expansion in the money stock.

○ The Implications of an Interest-Responsive Money Supply

To determine the implications of an interest-responsive money supply, we consider the LM curves given by equations (23.24b) and (23.24c): each assumes a banking system, but only the latter curve allows for an interest-responsive money supply.

The slope of the LM curve given by equation (23.24c) is easily derived, assuming both the money demand and free reserves demand functions are linear. Take first differences where $\Delta nmb = \Delta r_d = 0$ and solve for Δr; the coefficient of ΔX is the slope of the LM curve:

$$\left.\frac{\Delta r}{\Delta X}\right|_{LM} = \frac{L_x}{L_r + \dfrac{1+c}{c+d}F_r}$$

Note that if $F_r = 0$, the money supply is not interest responsive and the slope is the same as in the case of the two other LM curves. When $F_r < 0$, on the other hand, the slope is smaller in absolute value and therefore the LM curve is flatter than when $F_r = 0$. The LM curves corresponding to $F_r = 0$ and $F_r < 0$ are depicted in Figure 23.1.

Assume the economy is initially at point a, a point of money market equilibrium in both regimes. An increase in X (movement from point a to point b) increases the demand for money and induces an identical excess demand gap for both regimes at point b. To restore equilibrium at the new, higher level of X, the interest rate must rise, but by less when the money supply depends on the interest rate (from point b to point d). When the money supply is positively related to the interest rate, a given rise in the interest rate has a greater effect on the excess demand for money because the rise in the interest rate not only decreases the demand for money, it also increases the supply of money. Therefore, the interest rate must rise by a smaller amount to close a given excess demand gap.[6]

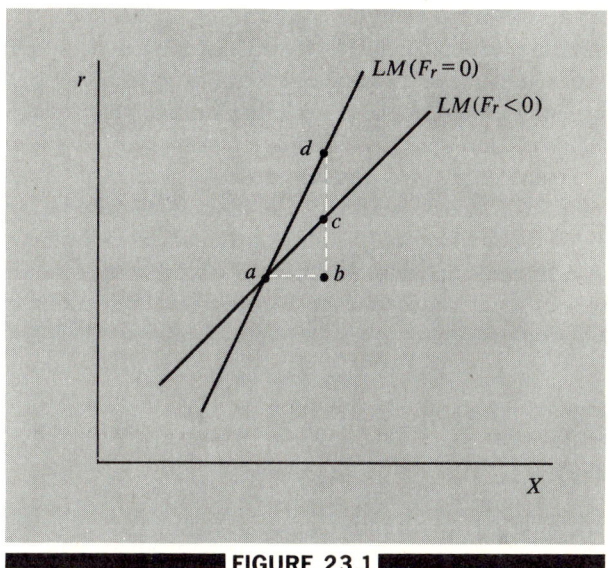

FIGURE 23.1
The *LM* Curve With and Without an Interest-Responsive Money Supply

To derive the implications of an interest-responsive money supply, we consider the response to real and monetary disturbances in the two regimes. The key insight is that the addition of an interest-responsive free reserves function is analogous to an increase in the interest responsiveness of the demand for money: everywhere L_r appears in our basic model, $L_r + \dfrac{1+c}{c+d}F_r$ now appears. Recall from Chapter 10 that changes in L_r have an asymmetrical effect on multipliers associated with real-sector and financial-sector disturbances: the larger the L_r (in absolute value), the smaller the monetary policy and the greater the fiscal policy multipliers. This is precisely the conclusion concerning the implications of introducing an interest-responsive money supply: it makes monetary policy (and nonpolicy financial disturbances) less powerful and fiscal policy (and all real-sector nonpolicy disturbances) more powerful.

---

[6] Viewing the *LM* curve as the equilibrium condition in the market for high-powered money, an interest-responsive demand for free reserves increases the interest responsiveness of the demand for high-powered money so that a smaller change in r is required to reequilibrate the market for high-powered money when it is disturbed.

The diagrams for this analysis are those given by Figures 10.11 and 10.12 in Chapter 10. The flatter *LM* curve is the one with the interest-responsive money supply. The flatter the *LM* curve, the greater the effect of a fiscal change on income. An interest-responsive money supply weakens the negative feedback in the economy; as income rises, the interest rate has to rise by less to maintain money market equilibrium so there is less of a rise in the interest rate and fall in investment in response to real-sector disturbances.

Increases in high-powered money (shifts in the *LM* curve) have a smaller effect on income when the money supply is interest responsive. This is because an interest-responsive money supply weakens the direct impact of monetary policy on the interest rate and investment; because the interest rate has to fall by less to eliminate a given excess supply, a given change in the nonborrowed base will have a smaller effect on the interest rate when the money supply is interest responsive.

This analysis of the implications of an endogenous money supply presumes that the Federal Reserve System carries out its policy by setting a value for the nonborrowed base. In this case the money supply will vary in response to real and financial disturbances. In an appendix to the next chapter we will discuss alternative strategies for carrying out monetary policy in which the Fed attempts to maintain the interest rate or the money supply at values believed to be consistent with its target values of income and then varies its level of nonborrowed reserves to maintain the interest rate or money supply at its predetermined value. If the Fed chooses to control the money supply and does so effectively, then the relevant model is again our simple *IS-LM* framework in which the money supply is treated as being set by the Fed.

● REVIEW QUESTIONS

1. Identify the sources and uses of the monetary base.
2. In what form do (member) banks hold their reserves?
3. Why are banks said to be "reluctant" to borrow from the FRS?
4. What is the distinction between the monetary base and the nonborrowed base and which is more meaningful as a measure of the instrument under the direct control of the FRS?

● PROBLEMS

1. "The existence of required reserves is essential in insuring that there is a limit to the money supply that banks can generate from a given monetary base." Comment.

2. The Federal Reserve System has expressed concern about the implications of the erosion of membership in the Federal Reserve System for the efficacy of monetary policy. Amend the money supply sector developed in this chapter to investigate the implications of a dual banking system—one with both members and nonmembers of the FRS. Make the following assumptions:

(a) Member banks hold required reserves at the Fed in proportion to their total demand deposits which are now the sum of public deposits (D_{MB}^P) and nonmember bank deposits (D_{MB}^{NMB}).

(b) The public holds a proportion of its total deposits (m) at member banks.

(c) Nonmember banks hold all their reserves at member banks; their required reserve ratio is q.

(d) Member banks hold free reserves but nonmembers hold only required reserves.

(e) The money supply is the sum of the public's deposits at member and nonmember banks ($M = D_{MB}^P + D_{NMB}^P$).

Write out the structural equations of the model and solve for the new *LM* curve. Then investigate the implications of including nonmember banks by comparing monetary policy multipliers with and without member banks and determining the implications of shifts in public deposits between member and nonmember banks.

3. Using the model developed in the previous question, consider the implications of the following reforms: (a) equalizing reserve requirements ($d = q$) but permitting nonmember banks to continue holding reserves at member banks, (b) requiring nonmember banks to hold reserves at the Fed but allowing $q < d$, and (c) equalizing reserve requirements *and* requiring nonmembers to hold reserves at the Fed.

4. Banks issue savings and time deposits (T) as well as demand deposits. Denote the interest rate on time deposits as r_t. This rate generally moves with the level of interest rates on earning assets, although some types of savings and time deposits are subject to interest ceilings which limit their response to movements in the rate on earning assets.

Assume initially that the interest rate on time deposits is fixed. Assume that the public's demand for time deposits depends on the interest rates on both time deposits and open market securities (r):

$$T = T(r, r_t)$$

where $T_r < 0$ and $T_{r_t} > 0$. Banks must hold reserves against time deposits, but the required reserve ratio against time deposits (t) is less than that against demand deposits. Find the new *LM* curve by adding to the equation developed in this chapter for the demand for the nonborrowed base the banks demand for required reserves on time deposits (tT) where the level of T is determined by the demand for time deposits. Compare the response to open market operations with and without time deposits in the model.

Part V • Refinements of the Financial Sector

5. Now assume that banks vary their interest rate on time deposits in response to changes in the rate on their earning assets; i.e.,

$$r_t = \bar{g} + g_r r.$$

Compare the response to open market operations in this case with the two cases analyzed in the previous question.

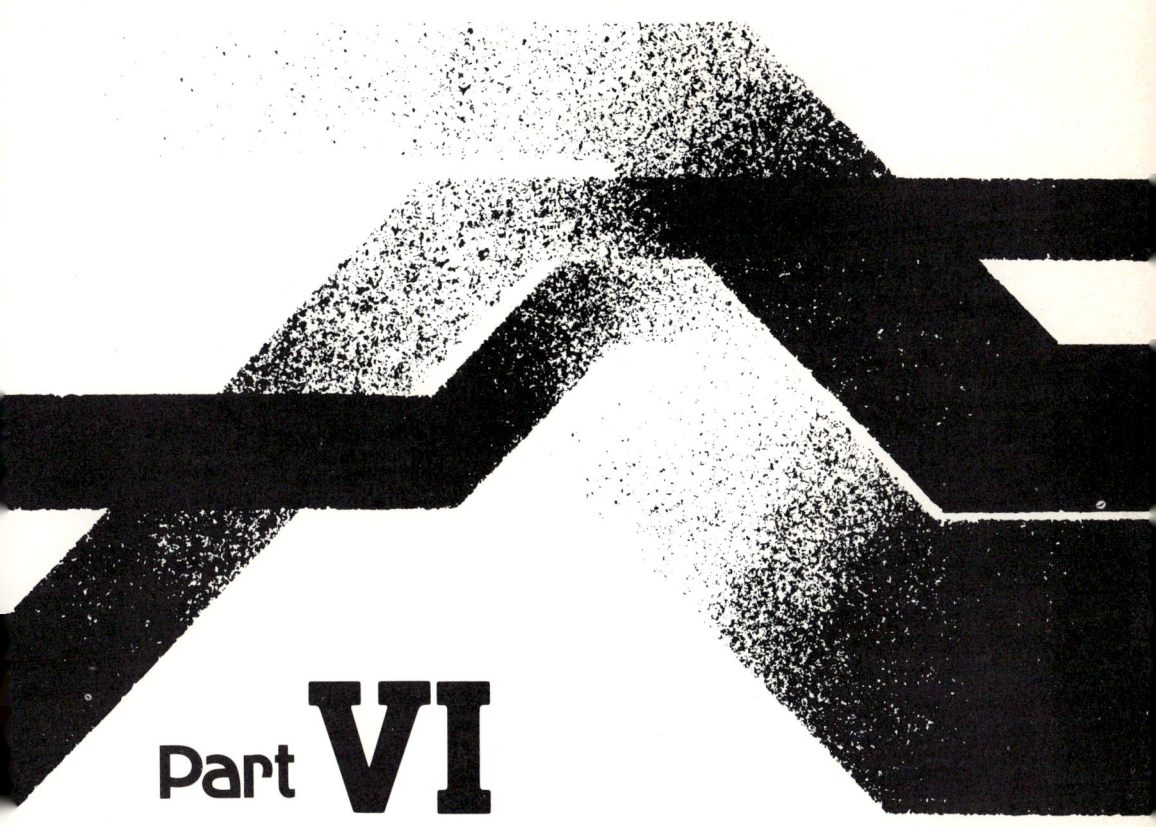

Part VI

Policy

Chapter 24. Monetary Policy
25. Fiscal Policy
26. Incomes and Other Supply-Oriented Policies

Chapter 24
Monetary Policy

In Part VI we refine our treatment of macroeconomic policy. In Chapters 24 and 25 we bring together the analysis of the response to monetary and fiscal policies developed previously, provide some discussion of the institutional features of the policy process, and consider the econometric evidence on the size and time path of the response of output and prices to monetary and fiscal policies. In Chapter 26 we introduce a third type of macroeconomic policy, incomes policy, which has its principal effect on the aggregate supply side of the economy. This differentiates it from monetary and fiscal policies which affect the economy primarily by influencing aggregate demand.

THE INSTITUTIONS OF MONETARY POLICY

Monetary policy is carried out by the Federal Reserve System (FRS). In this section we will consider the structure of the FRS and its relation to the legislative and the executive branches of government.[1]

The Structure of the FRS

The *Federal Reserve System* consists of 12 regional Federal Reserve Banks and a centralized Board of Governors. Each Federal Reserve Bank (FRB) has a board of directors selected in part by its member commercial banks and in part by the Board of Governors. The *Board of Governors* is the central decision-making unit and consists of 7 governors appointed by the President with the advice and consent of the Senate for overlapping, nonrenewable 14-year terms. Only one governor is permitted from each Federal Reserve district. The President designates the chairperson (and vice-chairperson) for 4-year terms which are not concurrent with the President's term.

---

[1] For a discussion of the institutions of monetary policy, see Lester Chandler and Stephen Goldfeld, *The Economics of Money and Banking* (New York: Harper and Row Pubs., Inc., 1977), Part 3; and *The Federal Reserve System: Purposes and Functions* (Washington: The Board of Governors of the Federal Reserve System, 1974).

The Federal Reserve Board is charged with the supervision of the regional Federal Reserve Banks and must approve the appointment of the president of each bank by its board of directors. The Board also must approve changes in the discount rate which are initiated by the regional banks and can set the required reserve ratios for member banks within limits dictated by congressional legislation.

All 7 of the governors serve on the committee responsible for the conduct of open market operations, the most important policy instrument under the Fed's control. The 12-member *Federal Open Market Committee* (FOMC) also includes the president of the New York Federal Reserve Bank and 4 of the other FRB presidents on a rotating basis. The president of the New York FRB is a permanent member of the FOMC because of the unique role of the New York FRB in the execution of monetary policy. However, all 12 FRB presidents generally attend and participate in discussions at FOMC meetings.

The FOMC meets about once a month to review the state of the economy and to decide how open market operations should be conducted to contribute to macroeconomic objectives. At each meeting the members vote on the nature of the policy and communicate their decision to the manager of the Open Market Account at the New York FRB in the form of a "directive." The manager then carries out purchases and/or sales from the system's portfolio of securities over the month (in between meetings) in accordance with the directive; however, it is normal for the manager to consult regularly with a representative of the FOMC during the intervening month.

The regional FRB's are "owned" by their member commercial banks. All national banks (banks with charters from the federal government) are required to be members of the FRS, but membership is optional for state-chartered banks. Each member bank is required to subscribe to the stock of its FRB equal to 6 percent of its own capital.[2] The FRB pays an annual dividend to its member banks limited to 6 percent of their subscription. The earnings of the FRS, primarily from its portfolio of government securities, in excess of its dividends and other costs of running the Federal Reserve System are paid to the Treasury.

The member banks elect six of the nine members of the board of directors of their respective FRB's. Three of these must be representatives of the banking community and the other three are designated "public" representatives and are selected with consideration to the interests of commerce, industry, agriculture, labor, services, and consumers. The remaining three members, including the chairperson, are selected by the Board of Governors. The board of directors' role is largely ceremonial, although they are responsible for appointing the president, subject to approval by the Federal Reserve Board.

○ The Relation of the FRS to the Legislative and Executive Branches of Government

The FRS is responsible to Congress in the sense that it must report regularly to Congress and that Congress can alter the institutional structure via amending the existing legislation. But the FRS is independent of the congressional appropriations

---

[2] The bank's capital is the amount that the owners of the bank have invested in the bank.

process because it pays all its costs out of its own earnings and until recently was exempt from audit by the government accounting office (GAO). The FRS is formally independent of the executive branch of government, although the President can exert influence by filling vacancies and appointing the chairperson, who is generally able to exert a powerful influence on the course of policy.

This degree of independence has been a continuing source of controversy. It has been defended as permitting the FRS to take a longer run perspective, immune from the short-run incentives associated with the electoral process that influence Congress and the executive branch. The long, overlapping terms provide for continuity, and the independence allows the Fed to exercise discipline on both the executive branch and Congress, who may be more willing to trade off future inflation for current gains against unemployment because the current declines in unemployment will get them reelected. However, such independence is difficult to reconcile with a commitment to the democratic process and, in addition, makes the coordination of monetary policy and other macroeconomic policies difficult. Recently, Congress has sought to improve the coordination of the Federal Reserve and executive branch. Under the provisions of the Full Employment and Balanced Growth Act of 1978, the Federal Reserve must report semiannually to Congress concerning its short-term policy goals and must comment on the compatibility of its policies with those proposed by the administration (as set forth in the most recent *Economic Report of the President*).

As we noted above, not all commercial banks are members of the FRS. Membership is optional (although required for banks with national charters) and the decision to join or remain a member of the FRS requires banks to balance the costs and benefits of membership. The costs include the opportunity cost of holding Federal Reserve stock at a return below that which banks could otherwise earn on the funds, the costs of more burdensome reserve requirements than those imposed by state banking authorities, and the costs of stricter reporting requirements and supervision of banking practices by the FRS as compared to state authorities. The benefits include access to the discount window and a variety of services that the FRS provides its members, although increasingly these services (such as check clearing services) are also available on at least a limited basis to nonmember banks. The proportion of member to total commercial banks and the proportion of assets in member banks to total assets of the commercial banking system have been declining and this has been a source of concern to the FRS.

The functions of the FRS fall into four broad categories: supervision of member banks, services to member banks (and to some extent to other financial institutions), services to the Treasury, and monetary policy. Services to the Treasury include acting as an agent for issuing and retiring Treasury securities, acting as an agent for receiving payments to and making payments by the Treasury, and providing general financial advice to the Treasury. Next, we will concentrate on the Fed's monetary policy functions.

THE INSTRUMENTS OF MONETARY POLICY

Policy instruments are variables under the direct and exclusive control of policy authorities. Monetary policy instruments are generally classified as either general or selective controls. *General controls* have their primary effect on either the net monetary base or the size of the money multiplier; these include open market operations, changes in reserve requirements, and changes in the discount rate. *Selective controls* have their primary influence on the allocation of credit among alternative uses. Examples of selective controls include margin (or down payment) requirements for loans to acquire securities and interest rate ceilings on rates paid by banks on savings accounts or charged by banks on loans. We will confine our attention to general controls in this chapter.

Open Market Operations

Open market operations involve the purchase or sale of government securities from the Fed's portfolio of securities. Open market operations are completely at the Fed's initiative, are flexible in both timing and magnitude, and can be carried out quietly, without the announcement effects that are associated with the more visible changes in discount rates and reserve requirement ratios.

Reserve Requirements

The Board of Governors can vary reserve requirements within a range set by legislation. The required reserve ratio varies with the size of total deposits at a member bank. The required ratio currently varies from 7½ percent on the first $2 million of demand deposits to 16½ percent on all deposits over $400 million. Separate reserve requirements are imposed on saving and time deposits (3 to 6 percent, depending on the maturity).

Even small changes in these ratios (such as ¼ or ½ percentage point) have large effects on the banking system, but the large impact of small changes means that changes in reserve requirements are not as flexible an instrument as open market operations. Also, changes in these ratios (or more precisely, increases) are unpopular with banks because by increasing the volume of idle funds, they directly reduce bank profits. Given the existing difficulty in attracting and retaining members, the Board of Governors is reluctant to use changes in these ratios as part of its policy.

The Discount Rate and Administration of the Discount Window

Member banks can borrow from their FRB either by the sale of eligible paper to their FRB (called *discounting*) or by securing a collateralized loan (called an *advance*). In the first case the bank sells a short-term bond issued by a business firm (i.e., a bank loan to a business firm) to its FRB at a discount; i.e., the bank receives less than the face value of the bond (loan). This discount imposes a cost on the borrowing bank. This was the way in which borrowing initially took place during the early years of the FRS, but most borrowing now consists of advances, secured by government securities owned by the bank. The rate on such borrowing is called the *discount rate* (r_d).

Borrowing is a privilege, not a right. This means that the Fed is not obligated to lend to its members as much or as often as the members request. In fact, it rarely refuses to lend to its members who are facing reserve needs. But after making the loan, the Fed will study the bank's situation and may ask the bank to reduce or retire its loan and refrain from further use of the discount window for some period if it determines that the bank is borrowing too often, too much, or for improper reasons.

The discount window is intended for three purposes: to help banks adjust to unforeseen needs for reserves (e.g., unexpected deposit losses or loan demand), to meet unusually large seasonal reserve needs, and to meet emergency situations. Banks have a variety of ways of meeting unforeseen reserve needs including the sale of securities, borrowing from other banks, or borrowing from households and businesses (by varying rates on liabilities such as large denomination time deposits called *certificates of deposit* or CD's), in addition to borrowing from the Fed. The Fed allows banks to borrow to permit them time to make more permanent adjustments to unexpected developments. However, it expressly forbids them from borrowing on a continuing basis to take advantage of the differential between the discount rate and the rate on bank earning assets.

The Federal Reserve is the "lender of last resort" when banks are in difficulty or when financial difficulties are widespread throughout the economy. In 1970, for example, Penn Central defaulted on its short-term bonds (called *commercial paper*). This made wealth owners reluctant to purchase commercial paper from other firms, and firms who had commercial paper outstanding and had to refinance this debt as it matured had to fall back on lines of credit that are usually established at banks for such contingencies. But the resulting increase in loan demand was more than the banks could accommodate. The Fed advised its members that loans were available from their FRB's to permit them to meet their lines of credit and as a result member bank borrowing soared. This borrowing however prevented a more serious financial collapse.

The Fed can influence the volume of borrowing by varying its discount rate. With a given discount rate, borrowing will increase as market rates increase because increases in market rates increase the cost of other ways of meeting temporary reserve needs. The Fed therefore generally varies its discount rate to keep it in line with open market rates. Variation in the discount rate can also be a dramatic vehicle for conveying a change in Fed policy; e.g., when the Fed changes the rate to initiate a change in interest rates rather than to follow changes in other interest rates. Such changes in the discount rate are said to have *announcement effects*. These, however, are more likely to be a nuisance than an aid to carrying out monetary policy since the announcement effect is far less predictable than the effect of the higher rate on borrowing or the effect of open market operations *(OMO)* on bank reserves and interest rates.

THE CHANNELS OF MONETARY POLICY

In the remainder of the chapter we will identify monetary policy with open market operations. In this section we consider the way in which open market operations affect aggregate demand and hence output and prices. We have discussed the way in which monetary policy affects the economy throughout the text. Here we summarize this discussion and relate it to the specification of the channels of monetary policy in large-scale income-expenditure econometric models. Then we develop the monetarist critique of the specification of the channels in econometric models and discuss the case for direct estimation of reduced forms as opposed to structural models.

○ The Channels of Monetary Policy in Income-Expenditure Models

The *income-expenditure approach* models the response of aggregate demand to monetary policy actions in terms of a two-stage process: the response of interest rates to monetary policy and the response of aggregate demand to changes in interest rates.[3] Our basic model is an example of this approach: the direct impact of an open market operation (I_r/L_r) can be separated into the impact of the *OMO* on the interest rate ($1/L_r$) and the effect of the change of the interest rate on aggregate demand (I_r).

In Parts III and V we further refined our treatment of the channels of monetary policy. We introduced the dual price view of investment (Tobin's q) as an alternative to the simple interest rate channel (Chapters 14, 20, and 22) and discussed the relevance of interest rates and/or relative price effects for decisions about consumer durables and residential construction (appendix to Chapter 14) as well as for decisions about fixed business investment. We introduced the *interest-induced wealth effect* (Chapter 13) and discussed its role in transmitting monetary policy to consumption expenditures. And we also discussed the role of liquidity constraints (Chapter 12) and credit rationing (appendix to Chapter 14) as channels through which monetary policy affects consumption and residential construction. Finally, in Chapter 20 we introduced multiple financial assets and the term structure equation linking the short-term rates on which monetary policy initially falls (given the preference of the Fed for carrying out most *OMO* in the short end of the market) to the long-term rates that influence consumption and investment decisions.

This description of the channels of monetary policy is generally consistent with the specification of the channels in large-scale econometric models, particularly the *FMP* model in which great care was exercised to model the way in which macroeconomic policy operates.[4] Long-term rates affect consumer durables and business fixed investment via a cost of capital variable and the long-term rate also affects state and local government construction expenditures. Residential construction responds to a q-type variable, the price of existing houses relative to the cost of producing new units, and is also influenced by credit rationing. And consumption depends on the net wealth of households which, in turn, depends on the interest rate.

○ The Monetarist Critique

The large-scale econometric models, such as the *FMP* model, suggest reasonably large multiplier responses to monetary policy, multipliers in the same general range

---

[3] For an example of the income-expenditure approach, see Warren L. Smith, "A Neo-Keynesian Approach to Monetary Policy," *Controlling Monetary Aggregates* (Boston: Federal Reserve Bank of Boston, 1969), pp. 105–126.

[4] The channels of monetary policy in the *FMP* model are discussed in Frank deLeeuw and Edward Gramlich, "The Channels of Monetary Policy," *Journal of Finance*, Vol. XXIV (May, 1969), pp. 265–290. For a discussion of the channels of monetary policy in a variety of econometric models, see G. R. Fisher and D. K. Sheppard, "Interrelationships Between Real and Monetary Variables: Some Evidence from Recent U.S. Empirical Studies," in Harry Johnson and A. R. Nobay (eds.), *Issues in Monetary Economics* (London: Oxford University Press, Ltd., 1974), 179–259.

as are associated with monetarist reduced forms, although the structural models indicate much longer lags than the reduced-form equations. Nevertheless, monetarists have been critical of the treatment of the channels of monetary policy in income-expenditure models. In this section we will discuss the nature of the monetarist critique.

Reduced Forms vs. Structural Models. Differences between the empirical strategies of monetarists and income-expenditure theorists tend to accentuate the perceived differences between their views of income determination. Income-expenditure theorists tend to build structural models and to derive policy multipliers via simulation experiments (e.g., as in the simulation analysis we did with the multiplier-accelerator model in Chapter 15). Monetarists tend to estimate reduced forms directly and to specify particularly simple reduced forms which include only two or three exogenous variables (generally some monetary aggregate, government expenditures, and taxes).

The preference for reduced forms can be explained by skepticism both about the state of knowledge concerning the structure of the economy and about our ability to operationally specify channels we perceive as being important so that they can be included in structural models. These considerations suggest that a reduced-form approach may be more successful in capturing the full impact of monetary change on expenditures than a structural approach. For example, Michael Keran notes:

> The major disadvantage in structural models is that the model builder may have omitted an important channel of transmission and, consequently, incorrectly estimated the magnitude of the monetary or fiscal influences. Indeed, even if a model builder has a good idea of the transmission channels, it may be technically impossible to estimate them because the channels have not or cannot be quantified.[5]

The channel that monetarists generally view as difficult to quantify is the response to changes in interest rates, and the channel some monetarists argue is incorrectly excluded from income-expenditure models is the direct impact of monetary change on aggregate demand. We consider each of these propositions below.

The Interpretation of the Interest Rate/Relative Price Channel. Monetarists generally agree that monetary policy operates primarily via interest rate and relative price effects. Nevertheless, they contend that it is extremely difficult, perhaps impossible, to model these effects in structural models. Milton Friedman and David Meiselman, for example, present an elegant description of the way in which monetary change affects aggregate demand via the impact on interest rates, but then argue that "while it is always possible to describe the effect of changes in the stock of money as operating through interest rates, it may not be very useful or illuminating to do so."[6] The reason it may not be very useful is partly because monetary change works through a very wide range of interest rates, some of which are implicit and unobservable, and partly because "the end result of a monetary change may not be a change in interest rates at all; it may be a change in either the general level of prices or output."[7]

---

[5] Michael W. Keran, "Monetary and Fiscal Influences on Economic Activity—The Historical Evidence," *Review* of the Federal Reserve Bank of St. Louis, Vol. 51 (November, 1969), p. 6.
[6] Milton Friedman and David Meiselman, "The Relative Stability of Monetary Velocity and the Investment Multiplier in the United States, 1897–1958," Commission on Money and Credit, *Stabilization Policies* (Englewood Cliffs, N.J.: Prentice-Hall, Inc., 1964), p. 217.
[7] *Ibid.*, p. 221.

It is easier, therefore, to describe the impact of a change in the money supply as acting directly on income.

In particular, monetarists expand the range of assets and accordingly the range of interest rates relevant to the transmission mechanism. In addition to including plant and equipment and residential construction, Milton Friedman and Anna Schwartz include ". . . also a host of other assets, even going so far as to include consumer durable goods, consumer inventories of clothing and the like and, maybe also, such human capital as skills acquired through training, and the like."[8] Friedman and Meiselman similarly urge inclusion in balance sheet adjustments of ". . . clothing in their closets and on their backs, food on their shelves. . . ."[9] Therefore, despite the fact that the monetary mechanism operates through interest rates and relative prices, monetarists maintain that it may not be possible to capture the full impact of monetary change on expenditures by incorporating a few interest rate or relative price terms in expenditure equations of a structural model. The empirical work of the monetarists has, therefore, relied primarily on reduced-form equations which simply attempt to measure the impact of monetary change on expenditures without investigating the channels through which it is transmitted.

Direct Impacts of Monetary Change on Aggregate Demand. Some monetarists have also suggested that income-expenditure models are misspecified because they ignore the *direct impact* of monetary change on expenditures.[10] We define *direct effects* as those effects of monetary change which are independent of prior changes in interest rates and/or relative prices.

Meiselman, for example, criticizes the assumption in traditional *IS-LM* analysis that the *IS* and *LM* curves move independently. He suggests that increases in the money supply lead directly to increases in aggregate demand (without any intervening change in interest rates) so that both *IS* and *LM* curves should shift in response to monetary change.[11] Schwartz makes a similar criticism of large scale income-expenditure models: the failure of these models to allow for a direct effect of money on expenditures suggests that they must underestimate the effect of monetary change on expenditures.[12]

But why include money in expenditure functions? Both authors suggest that a natural response to an excess supply of money is to increase demands for commodities as well as for financial assets. This follows, according to Schwartz, from an extended portfolio approach in which portfolios include consumer durables as well as money and bonds. Friedman also suggests that a distinguishing feature of monetarism is

---

[8] Milton Friedman and Anna Schwartz, "Money and Business Cycles," *Review of Economics and Statistics*, Vol. 45 (February, 1963), p. 61.

[9] Friedman and Meiselman, *op. cit.*, p. 218.

[10] Actually some of the same monetarists who provide eclectic treatments of the channels of monetary policy in one place, elsewhere attack such general treatments for failing to allow for direct effects on money on expenditures. For example, see the eclectic treatments by Friedman and Meiselman and Friedman and Schwartz cited above and the discussion of direct effects of money on expenditures by Meiselman, Schwartz, and Friedman we cite below.

[11] David Meiselman, "Discussion," *Controlling Monetary Aggregates* (Boston: Federal Reserve Bank of Boston, 1969), pp. 15–20.

[12] Anna Schwartz, "Comments on Modigliani and Ando," in Jerome Stein (ed.), *Monetarism* (New York: Elsevier North-Holland Inc., 1976), pp. 43–49.

the view that an excess supply of money is directly associated with increased spending on goods.

> For monetary theory, the key question is the process of adjustment to a discrepancy between nominal quantity of money demanded and the nominal quantity supplied.... The key insight of the quantity theory approach is that such a discrepancy will be manifested primarily in attempted spending, thence in the rate of change in nominal income.[13]

But an excess supply of money will generate increased demand for consumer durables only if it is also associated with an excess demand for consumer durables. And this takes us back to the specification of the demand for consumer durables. The demand for consumer durables may depend on income, interest rates, and wealth; but neither Meiselman, Schwartz, nor Friedman provides a rationale for including money in addition to these variables. If there is an open market purchase, for example, there will of course be an excess supply of money and an excess demand for bonds; but there will be excess demands for other assets (e.g., consumer durables) only to the extent that interest rates, income, or wealth (arguments in the respective asset demand functions) changes. We therefore conclude that monetarists have failed to provide theoretical support for the view that there is a direct effect of money on expenditures.

We will postpone our discussion of the income-expenditure counterattack on monetarist reduced forms until the next chapter because the key issue turns out to be the size of the fiscal policy multipliers rather than the monetary policy multipliers. We will find in the next section that structural model and reduced-form evidence agree that monetary policy has sizable multipliers.

EMPIRICAL EVIDENCE ON MONETARY POLICY MULTIPLIERS

In this section we discuss the empirical evidence on the size and time pattern of response of income to monetary policy. First, we discuss the evidence based on several large-scale econometric models, then the evidence from simple reduced forms.

Evidence from Econometric Models

In Table 24.1 we present some results of simulations of the response of real *GNP* to changes in nonborrowed reserves for three large-scale econometric models: the Data Resources (*DRI*) model, the Wharton III model, and the *FMP* model. The year and quarter in parenthesis next to the name of the model identifies the point at which the simulation began. The response to disturbances depends on *initial conditions* in these models; in particular, the lower the unemployment rate, the greater the response of prices and the smaller the response of output to expansionary policy. The models produce long-run results which conform to our classical model: approximate neutrality. In the long run, therefore, interest rates and output are independent

---

[13] Milton Friedman, "A Theoretical Framework for Monetary Analysis," *Journal of Political Economy*, Vol. 78 (March–April, 1970), p. 225.

of the level of high-powered money. In the short run, on the other hand, monetary change yields temporary effects on output and interest rates.

The short-run effects can be quite large and persist over several years. The output effect peaks in the 8th quarter in the *DRI* model and in the 12th quarter in the Wharton III model. As we noted in Chapter 15, these models generally respond with damped oscillations to disturbances. So, they may cycle after reaching their peak responses before converging to zero in the long run. The one-year multipliers vary from 4.5 to 7.0 and the two-year multipliers vary from 7.2 to 10.0.

Model	Quarter		
	1	4	8
DRI (1963 I)[14]	0	7.0	9.0
Wharton III (1962 I)[14]	1.4	4.5	7.2
FMP (1963 I)[15]	0.7	5.4	10.0

TABLE 24.1

The Response of Output to Changes in Nonborrowed Reserves: Evidence from Large-Scale Structural Models

○ Evidence from Monetarist Reduced Forms

The St. Louis Federal Reserve Bank did the pioneering work in estimation of simple reduced-form equations. The equation estimated by Leonall C. Andersen and Jerry L. Jordan related changes in nominal income to changes in nominal money supply and changes in nominal high employment government expenditures.[16] Taxes had essentially no effect and were therefore excluded from their preferred regression. Changes in money supply and government expenditures in the current and three lagged periods were included as independent variables. The exact specification was

$$\Delta X\$ = \sum_{i=0}^{3} a_i \Delta M_{t-i} + \sum_{i=0}^{3} b_i \Delta G\$_{t-i}. \tag{24.1}$$

Their results for the money multipliers are reported in Table 24.2. The first quarter impact is $1.5 billion for a $1 billion increase in the money supply and the multiplier builds to 5.8 by the fourth quarter and stabilizes there. These results are difficult to compare to those reported for the structural models because the latter

---

[14] From Table 4, pp. 68–69, in Carl Christ, "Judging the Performance of Econometric Models of the U.S. Economy," *International Economic Review*, Vol. 16 (February, 1975).

[15] From Table IV.3, p. 226, in G. R. Fisher and D. K. Sheppard, "Interrelationships Between Real and Monetary Variables: Some Evidence from Recent U.S. Empirical Studies," in Harry Johnson and A. R. Nobay (eds.), *Issues in Monetary Economics* (London: Oxford University Press, Ltd., 1974).

[16] Leonall C. Andersen and Jerry L. Jordan, "Monetary and Fiscal Actions: A Test of Their Relative Importance in Economic Stabilization," *Review* of the Federal Reserve Bank of St. Louis, Vol. 50 (November, 1968), pp. 11–24.

Quarter	1	4	8
Multiplier	1.5	5.8	5.8

TABLE 24.2
The Andersen-Jordan Results: The Cumulative Multipliers for the Response of Nominal Income to a Change in the Money Supply

were for real output and based on a change in nonborrowed reserves rather than money supply. Carl Christ also reports multipliers for nominal *GNP*: they are about the same as reported in Table 24.1 during the first year covered by the A-J equation. A change in nonborrowed reserves results in a multiple expansion of the money supply so that the results for a change in nonborrowed reserves should be a multiple of those for a change in the money supply. Frank deLeeuw and John Kalchbrenner estimated a reduced form like the A-J equation but using nonborrowed reserves instead of the money supply; the results are reported in Table 24.3.[17] The multiplier is smaller over the first year but larger at the end of two years. The 11.6 multiplier compares with the two-year nominal *GNP* multipliers of 11.0 and 6.8 in the *DRI* and Wharton III models, respectively. Thus, the structural and reduced-form evidence is not as far apart as might have been expected given the monetarist critique of the channels of monetary policy in econometric models.

Quarter	4	8
Multiplier	2.4	11.6

TABLE 24.3
The deLeeuw-Kalchbrenner Reduced-Form Results Using Nonborrowed Reserves

PROBLEMS IN THE EXECUTION OF MONETARY POLICY

The goals of monetary policy include maintaining full employment and price level stability. The principal instrument of monetary policy is open market operations. In the previous section we presented evidence confirming the potency of monetary policy actions. If there were no *conflicting objectives*, no *lags* in the response of goal variables to changes in policy instruments, and *complete information* about the values of both model parameters and exogenous variables, monetary policy (indeed, all macroeconomic policy) would be a simple exercise of solving for the unique value of the policy instrument for which the goal variables are at their desired levels. For example, in terms of our Keynesian *IS-LM* model, the execution of monetary policy would involve finding the value of the exogenous money supply for which the intersection of the *IS* and *LM* curves occurs at full employment. This case is depicted in Figure 24.1. If the Fed is assumed to know all model parameters (and therefore the slopes of the *IS* and *LM* curves) and all exogenous variables ($\bar{Z}$, $\bar{G}$, $\bar{T}$, and $\bar{L}$),

---

[17] Frank deLeeuw and John Kalchbrenner, "Monetary and Fiscal Policy: A Test of Their Relative Importance in Economic Stabilization—Comment," *Review* of the Federal Reserve Bank of St. Louis, Vol. 51 (April, 1969), pp. 6–11.

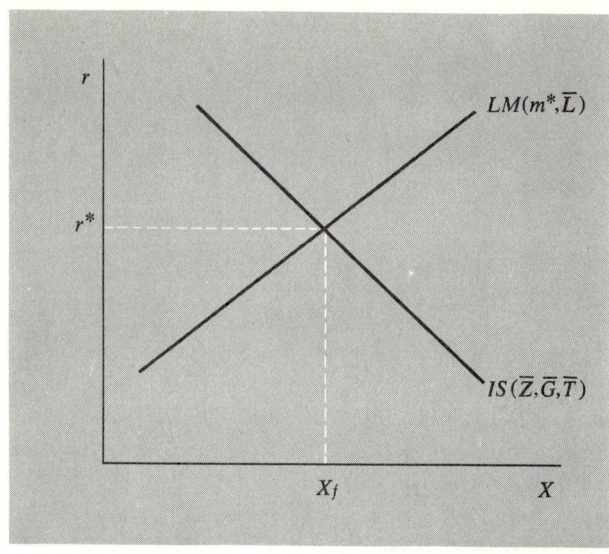

FIGURE 24.1
Monetary Policy in the Basic Keynesian Model:
One Target, No Lags, and Complete Information

it can simply set the money supply at the value which results in the *LM* curve intersecting the *IS* curve at X_f, the desired value of its single goal variable.[18] Adding an endogenous money supply only adds another link: now we find the value of high-powered money consistent with achieving full employment.

But monetary policy is obviously not as simple as the above analysis suggests. After all, the economy is only infrequently at full employment with price level stability. The conduct of macroeconomic policy is greatly complicated by the existence of conflicting objectives, lags in the response of goal variables to policy instruments, and uncertainty about the value of model parameters and exogenous variables. In the next three sections and in the two appendices at the end of the chapter we consider the implications of these complications for both the way in which monetary policy is carried out and for the precision with which we can expect policy authorities to meet their macroeconomic objectives.

---

[18] Alternatively, simply solve for the value of m which yields X_f (given $\bar{G}$, $\bar{Z}$, $\bar{T}$, and $\bar{L}$) from the reduced-form equation for income.

$$X_f = \frac{1}{D}(\bar{Z} + \bar{G}) - \frac{C_y}{D}\bar{T} - \frac{I_r/L_r}{D}\bar{L} + \frac{I_r/L_r}{D}m^*$$

To solve this, X becomes a predetermined variable (equal to X_f) and m becomes the unknown. We solve for the unique value of the money supply, m^*, consistent with X_f. One problem that arises even under these simple assumptions is insufficient instruments to achieve multiple goals. The number of independent instruments must be equal to or greater than the number of goal variables to permit policy to achieve target values of all the goal variables simultaneously. We discuss this problem further in Chapter 28.

○ Conflicting Objectives and Macroeconomic Policy

We have emphasized that the two principal objectives of macroeconomic policy are full employment and price level stability. There are additional goals such as the balance of payments equilibrium. We will postpone discussion of the latter objective until Chapter 27 and concentrate in this section on the full employment-price stability objectives.

We have discussed a variety of models that involve short-run and sometimes long-run trade-offs between unemployment and inflation in Chapter 18. The consensus view is that there is a short-run but no long-run trade-off between unemployment and inflation. In the long run, therefore, there will be no conflict between objectives *if* we set our target unemployment rate at the unique level consistent with price level stability (the nonaccelerating inflation rate of unemployment, u^*). If the policymakers set their unemployment target below u^*, on the other hand, they will induce accelerating inflation; in this case their two objectives become totally irreconcilable. Most econometric evidence suggests, for example, that the 5-year policy goals set by Congress in the Full Employment and Balanced Growth Act of 1978 (generally referred to as the Humphrey-Hawkins Act)—a 3 percent rate of unemployment for persons aged 20 years or over (which corresponds to an overall rate of about 4 percent) and a rate of inflation of 3 percent or less—are not consistent with each other.

But what if the economy is at u^* and there is also a positive rate of inflation? Assuming a natural rate-type model, the policy authorities can maintain the economy at u^* if they *accommodate* the inflation; i.e., set the rate of monetary growth equal to the inflation rate in our simple models. If the policy authorities insist on eradicating the inflation, they must push the unemployment rate above u^* for some period. The problem is *how much* above u^* and for *how long*? The appropriate policy in this case depends on the relative distaste for inflation compared to that for unemployment, the time rate of discount which determines how much weight to attach to price stability later relative to unemployment now, and the structure of the economy which determines "how much" and "how long." There is, unfortunately, no simple, indisputable answer to this policy dilemma. That is why economists can continue to disagree about policy even when their basic models are quite similar and why the conduct of policy often appears indecisive and without clear-cut direction.

If unemployment is initially above u^* and there is inflation, the policy is pretty much the same as if we begin at u^*. Do we want expansionary policy (to reduce unemployment) or restrictive policy (to reduce inflation)? Again, the answer is not obvious and our structural model alone will not permit us to answer this question.

Below we will leave this problem behind us by confining our attention to the Keynesian fixed price model in which there is a single goal variable, output. This will permit us to focus on the implications of lags and uncertainty for the implementation of policy. In appendices at the end of this chapter, we present a more formal treatment of the implications of both lags and uncertainty.

○ The Implications of Lags

Policy actions generally affect the economy gradually; i.e., the effects build up over time. In addition, policy does not respond immediately to offset disturbances;

instead, there is usually a delay between the need for policy and the policy action. In this section we discuss the sources of these lags, consider the empirical evidence on the length of the lags, and develop the implications of lags for the conduct of policy.

Inside and Outside Lags. There are two types of lags relevant to the policy process: inside and outside lags. The *inside lag* refers to the lag between the need for policy and the policy action. This is generally viewed as a *discrete lag*; e.g., it generally takes about six months after the need for a change in policy to implement the change. The inside lag in turn can be decomposed into recognition and decision lags. The *recognition lag* is the period from the need for action until this need is recognized by the policy authority. The *decision lag* is the period from recognition of the problem to the implementation of a policy action. The recognition lag should be the same for monetary and fiscal policy (the same information is available to both decision making units) but the decision lag is probably much shorter for monetary policy. Monetary policy changes can be implemented without legislative approval; the legislative process moves quite slowly and introduces a fairly long decision lag for fiscal policy.

The *outside lag* refers to the lag between policy action and the effect on goal variables. This lag does not take the form of a discrete lag or delay but rather of a gradual buildup in the effect in income over a number of periods. The outside lag is considered to be much longer for monetary than fiscal policy. Monetary policy generally impinges initially on short-term interest rates; there is a lag between the effect on short-term rates and the response of the long-term rates and equity prices that influence aggregate demand. As long-term rates and asset prices respond, orders for durable goods gradually change, and the change in orders yields a gradual response of production.

Empirical Evidence on Lags in Response to Monetary Policy. The evidence on lags related to monetary policy almost exclusively relates to the outside lag and this evidence is quite mixed.[19] The limited evidence on the inside lag suggests that it is quite modest, from three to six months.[20] There are four basic sources of evidence on the outside lag: lead-lag analysis, survey evidence, structural econometric models, and reduced-form equations. Friedman, for example, computes the lead of the peaks/troughs in the rate of growth of the money supply relative to the peaks/troughs in general business activity and concludes that the outside lag associated with monetary policy is about one to one and one-half years and that, in addition, the lag is highly variable from cycle to cycle.[21] This evidence on the length and variability of the lag is the basis for Friedman's skepticism about the potential for successful discretionary policy and his advocacy of fixed rules (e.g., constant growth rate in the money

---

[19] For surveys of evidence on lags in monetary policy, see Michael Hamburger, "The Lag in the Effect of Monetary Policy: A Survey of Recent Literature," *Monthly Review*, Federal Reserve Bank of New York (December, 1971), pp. 289–298; and Thomas Mayer, *Monetary Policy in the United States* (New York: Random House, 1968), Chapter 6.

[20] See Karl Brunner and Allan Meltzer, *The Federal Reserve's Attachment to the Free Reserve Concept* (Washington: U.S. House Committee on Banking and Currency, Subcommittee on Domestic Finance, 88th Congress, Second Session, 1964), p. 42.

[21] Milton Friedman, "The Lag in the Effect of Monetary Policy," *Journal of Political Economy*, Vol. 69 (October, 1961) pp. 447–466.

supply). The reduced-form results, on the other hand, generally suggest relatively short lags; for example, the Andersen-Jordan "St. Louis" equation indicates that the full response to monetary change occurs within a year.[22] Thomas Mayer's survey evidence, discussed in Chapter 15, suggests a total lag for construction expenditures of seven quarters.[23] Finally, structural econometric models suggest still longer lags, although there is a reasonable variance in the results from these models. The *DRI* model, for example, suggests a very short lag: three quarters of the peak response of real *GNP* occurs by the fourth quarter after the policy action and the cumulative peak response is achieved after only two years. In the Wharton III model, on the other hand, only about half the peak response occurs by the fourth quarter and the peak response does not occur until the fourth year.[24]

The *mean lag* (the time required for half the peak response) appears to be in the range of two to four quarters and the cumulative peak response appears to occur after at least four quarters, possibly quite a bit longer than that. We now consider the implications of such lags for the conduct of monetary policy.

Lags and the Effectiveness of Monetary Policy. The longer the lags, the greater the difficulty of carrying out stabilizing discretionary policy and the greater the potential that policy will turn out to be destabilizing. In particular, the longer the lag between a policy action and its impact, the greater the necessity of forecasting future values of exogenous variables to ensure that the policy will in fact turn out to be stabilizing rather than destabilizing.[25]

It may, however, be possible to compensate for the lagged response of aggregate demand to policy changes by increasing the size of policy actions. The lags involved are in part *delays* (e.g., the recognition and decision lags) and in part *distributed lags* (e.g., the outside lag). To the extent that the lags are distributed lags, a fraction of the total effect may occur in the first period. As long as there is some effect, the policymakers can compensate for the small initial effect by increasing the overall size of the policy action. In this case, however, the policy authority will have to offset the initial large policy actions in subsequent periods to maintain the goal variables at their desired levels. If the Fed acts aggressively to maintain output at its desired value each period, it may encounter the problem of *instrument instability*.[26] To maintain output on target, the Fed may have to increase then decrease its policy instruments in larger and larger amounts over time. Stabilizing its goal variables may require extraordinary instability in its instruments, an instability that may be inconsistent

---

[22] Leonall C. Andersen and Jerry L. Jordan, "Monetary and Fiscal Actions: A Test of Their Relative Importance in Economic Stabilization," *Review* of the Federal Reserve Bank of St. Louis, Vol. 50 (November, 1968), pp. 11–24.

[23] Thomas Mayer, "The Inflexibility of Monetary Policy," *Review of Economic Statistics*, Vol. 40 (November, 1958), pp. 358–374, and "Plant and Equipment Lead Times," *Journal of Business*, Vol. 33 (April, 1960), pp. 127–132.

[24] Carl Christ, "Judging the Performance of Econometric Models of the U.S. Economy," *International Economic Review*, Vol. 16 (February, 1975), pp. 68–69.

[25] The classic treatment of the way in which discretionary policy can turn out to be destabilizing is Milton Friedman, "The Effects of a Full Employment Policy on Economic Stability: A Formal Analysis," *Essays in Positive Economics* (Chicago: University of Chicago Press, 1953), pp. 117–132.

[26] The concept of instrument instability as well as the specific analytical treatment of it we employ below is from Robert Holbrook, "Optimal Economic Policy and the Problem of Instrument Instability," *American Economic Review*, Vol. LXII (March, 1972), pp. 57–65.

with the smooth functioning of the financial markets through which policy operates and, indeed, may be impossible to carry out because of constraints on the size of policy operations. The size of open market sales is, after all, limited by the size of the Fed's portfolio. In Appendix A at the end of this chapter we will illustrate the problem of instrument instability using numerical solutions of a simple model.

The Implications of Uncertainty

Even if discretionary policy can be implemented without a long inside lag and even if its effects occur with a relatively short outside lag, active manipulation of policy instruments may still be destabilizing if policymakers do not have complete knowledge of the structure of the economy and therefore of the effects of their policies. It is useful to distinguish two types of uncertainty that confront the policy authorities: (1) uncertainty about the values of the autonomous components of the endogenous variables (e.g., $\bar{Z}$ and $\bar{L}$ in our IS-LM models) and about the values of any exogenous variables (e.g., $\bar{I}$ in our simple Keynesian cross model of Chapter 6); and (2) uncertainty about the model that interrelates the economy's endogenous variables and, for a given model, about the values of the model parameters and hence policy multipliers. We have noted the alternative theories of consumption, investment, demand for money, and the Phillips curve in previous chapters. Even among those who agree on the model that explains a particular variable, there is disagreement concerning the precise values of model parameters (e.g., C_y, I_r, L_r, and L_x in our basic model of Chapter 10).

We will discuss the implications of the first type of uncertainty in Appendix B to this chapter. It does not require a major qualification of our analysis, although the existence of random shocks (via $\bar{Z}$, $\bar{L}$) does explain in part why policy fails to achieve its objectives. But it is uncertainty about model parameters and multipliers (generally referred to as *multiplier uncertainty*) that is most damaging to the ability to implement stabilizing discretionary policy. The more limited the knowledge of the structure of the economy, the greater the likelihood that attempts to vary policy instruments to achieve target levels of goal variables may have unanticipated and unfavorable results. In this case, policy authorities can reduce the risk of overshooting their targets by acting cautiously and varying their instruments less aggressively than they would if they had complete knowledge of model multipliers.[27]

RULES VS. DISCRETION

The problems of lags and multiplier uncertainty suggest that stabilizing discretionary policy may be difficult to implement. An alternative is to abandon active policy and rely instead on fixed rules. For example, Friedman has suggested that monetary policy be directed at achieving a constant rate of growth in the money supply. The preferred rate is the one consistent with price level stability, but the major benefits derive from maintaining a constant rate of growth as opposed to the particular rate

---

[27] The optimal use of policy in the case of multiplier uncertainty is developed in William Brainard, "Uncertainty and the Effectiveness of Policy," *American Economic Review, Papers and Proceedings*, Vol. 57 (May, 1967), pp. 411–425.

chosen.[28] The constant rate of money growth rule is an example of a rule *without feedback*; i.e., there is no response of monetary growth to deviations in output or prices from their desired paths. It is also possible to design rules which allow for such a response and we will give an example of a rule *with feedback* in the next chapter. Here we confine ourselves to a comparison of discretionary policy and rules without feedback.

Monetarists have generally been proponents of rules and nonmonetarists of activist policy. Indeed, Modigliani views this issue as the central one differentiating monetarists and nonmonetarists. Nonmonetarists, according to Modigliani, accept the practical message of Keynes's *General Theory* that

> . . . a private enterprise economy using intangible money *needs* to be stabilized, *can* be stabilized, and therefore *should* be stabilized by appropriate monetary and fiscal policies.[29]

○ The Case Against Activist Policy

The case against active policy rests on two propositions. The first proposition is that the private sector of the economy is inherently stable. This is a major tenet of monetarism and suggests the absence of a need for stabilization policy. Indeed, monetarists generally contend that the instability observed in the economy results mainly from government rather than private sector decisions. The inherent stability of the private sector results in part from the absence of large and persistent exogenous shocks (e.g., the absence of sharp autonomous changes in desired investment, consumption, or portfolio composition) and in part from the fact that the shocks that do occur have relatively small and only temporary effects on output and employment as a consequence of the economy's built-in stability. The built-in stability, in turn, results from the response of tax revenues to changes in income (discussed initially in Chapter 6 and in more detail in the next chapter), the response of interest rates to changes in income (discussed initially in Chapter 10), and the response of wages and prices to labor and commodity market disequilibrium (initially discussed in Chapter 9 and then in Chapters 17 and 18). We will discuss built-in stability more thoroughly in the next chapter. We simply note here that the degree of built-in stability depends on various parameters in the model; e.g., the negative feedback via the income-induced changes in the interest rate depends on the $(L_x/L_r)I_r$ term in our basic model multiplier of Chapter 10, and the negative feedback via wages and prices depends on the degree of price flexibility as reflected in the parameters in the Phillips curve developed in Chapter 18.

The second proposition in the case against policy activism is that even if the economy were subject to cumulative movements in output, employment, and inflation relative to target levels, discretionary policy might only compound the instability rather than dampen it. The danger that policy will turn out to be destabilizing follows

---

[28] See Milton Friedman, *A Program for Monetary Stability* (New York: Fordham University Press, 1953); and "The Role of Monetary Policy," *American Economic Review*, Vol. 58 (March, 1968), pp. 1–17.

[29] Franco Modigliani, "The Monetarist Controversy or, Should We Forsake Stabilization Policy," *American Economic Review*, Vol. 67 (March, 1977), pp. 1–19.

from the long inside lag, the long and variable outside lag, and the general uncertainty about the effect of policy on the economy. Thus, Friedman suggests that the most important objective of monetary management should be to "prevent money itself from being a major source of economic disturbance," and this leads to the prescription of a fixed rule.[30]

◯ The Case For Activist Policy[31]

The case for activist policy involves a rejection of the two propositions developed above; the economy needs to be and can be stabilized by appropriate use of stabilization policy. The first proposition in support of activist policy, then, is that the economy is subject to substantial and persistent disturbances arising in the private sector.

Nonmonetarists generally agree that the built-in stability properties of the economy substantially dampen the displacement arising from private sector disturbances. But there are both positive and negative feedback responses to disturbances, and nonmonetarists generally expect positive feedback to dominate initially so that output and employment decline for a period by a multiple of the downward demand disturbance, even though the income-induced decline in interest rates dampens the overall decline. This contrasts with the view associated with classical economists that negative feedback immediately dominates and quickly offsets any demand disturbances.[32] And given the gradual response of wages and prices to downward disturbances, nonmonetarists contend that an extended period of depressed levels of output and employment will result.[33] This residue of output and employment movements in response to disturbances provides the incentive to pursue active policy to offset the decline in income not quickly eliminated by negative feedback.

In addition, nonmonetarists contend that policy can be implemented with sufficiently short inside lags and with sufficient precision given our understanding of the structure of the economy. Nevertheless, there is wider recognition today compared to the mid-1960s among proponents of active policy of the limitations of active policy and the difficulty in "fine tuning" the economy by responding to even small departures of output and employment from target levels. Active policy however continues to have wide support in situations where a sizable displacement has occurred, such as in the 1974–1975 recession. On the other hand, many proponents of rules, such as

---

[30] Milton Friedman, "The Role of Monetary Policy," *American Economic Review*, Vol. 58 (March, 1968), p. 12.

[31] The case for activism is developed in Arthur Okun, "Fiscal-Monetary Activism: Some Analytical Issues," *Brookings Papers on Economic Activity* (1972:1), pp. 123–163; Franco Modigliani, "The Monetarist Controversy or, Should We Forsake Stabilization Policy", *American Economic Review*, Vol. 67 (March, 1977); and Robert J. Gordon, "What Can Stabilization Policy Achieve?" *American Economic Review, Papers and Proceedings*, Vol. 68 (May, 1978), pp. 335–341.

[32] For an excellent discussion of the interaction of positive and negative feedback responses to disturbances in the context of an interpretation of Keynes's critique of classical macroeconomics, see Axel Leijonhufvud, "Effective Demand Failures," *Swedish Economics Journal*, Vol. 75 (March, 1973), pp. 27–48.

[33] Tobin's discussion of the continuing relevance of Keynes's *General Theory* in James Tobin, "How Dead is Keynes?" *Economic Inquiry*, Vol. 15 (October, 1977), pp. 459–468, emphasizes the two points we have just developed: the element of exogeneity in private spending decisions and the slow response of wages and prices to downward demand disturbances.

Friedman, also allow for the use of discretionary policy to offset "major disturbances."[34] Therefore, the gulf between proponents of rules and activism is not nearly so great as it might at first appear.

○ The New Attack on Activism

The combination of the natural rate version of the Phillips curve (introduced in Chapter 18) and the rational expectations approach to expectation formation (discussed in Appendix B to Chapter 18) provides the basis for a new attack on active policy. According to the natural rate model, variations in employment arise from unanticipated inflation.[35] This contrasts with the Keynesian view that movements in output and employment result from the effects of changes in aggregate demand on markets in which wages and prices fail to adjust rapidly enough to maintain continuous market clearing. We contrasted these two views in Chapter 17. Adopting the natural rate view, policy can only affect employment and output if it can induce unanticipated inflation. But if policymakers act *systematically* to offset changes in employment, economic agents will be able to predict movements in policy instruments and policy will therefore not be able to affect employment and output.[36] As in the case of the traditional arguments against active policy, the natural rate-rational expectations view holds that policy is unnecessary as well as ineffective. Given that movements in output and employment arise from unanticipated inflation, departures from the natural rate can be expected to be short-lived. This view also leads, therefore, to the recommendation of fixed rules. We have discussed the limitations of the view that output and employment respond exclusively to unanticipated inflation in Chapter 17 and of the application of rational expectations to the analysis of a short-run response to policy actions in Appendix B to Chapter 18. It should be noted, however, that the view presented in this section is of quite recent vintage, and support for and against the natural rate-rational expectations approach is only now beginning to flow in. A thorough evaluation of this approach is therefore not possible at this time.

---

[34] Milton Friedman, "The Role of Monetary Policy," *American Economic Review*, Vol. 58 (March, 1968), p. 14.
[35] This also follows from the view introduced in Chapter 11 that changes in output reflect the response of aggregate supply to unanticipated changes in the price level.
[36] For an excellent development of this approach, see Thomas Sargent and Neil Wallace, "Rational Expectations and the Theory of Economic Policy," *Journal of Monetary Economics*, Vol. 2 (April, 1976), pp. 169–183.

APPENDIX

A The Problem of Instrument Instability

We can illustrate the problems of stabilizing income when income responds to policy changes with lags by the following simple model.[1] We will specify the reduced form for income as

$$\Delta X_t = \Delta Z_t + w_0 \Delta P_t + w_1 \Delta P_{t-1} \qquad (24A.1)$$

where ΔX is the change in income, ΔZ is the change in the single exogenous nonpolicy disturbance, ΔP is the change in the policy instrument, and w_0 and w_1, the weights on current and once-lagged ΔP, sum to one. If $w_0 < .5$, varying ΔP_t to maintain income unchanged ($\Delta X_t = 0$) in the face of a once-and-for-all decline in the nonpolicy disturbance term will require positive, then negative values of ΔP_t of progressively larger size.

In Tables 24A.1a and 24A.1b we provide an illustration using both a set of parameters that permit the policy authorities to maintain their goal variable on target without instrument instability ($w_0 = .55$ and $w_1 = .45$) and a set for which instrument instability arises ($w_0 = .45$ and $w_1 = .55$). Each case begins with a $10 billion exogenous decline in aggregate demand ($\Delta Z = -\$10$ billion). In the unstable case, the policy increase in period 1 required to offset the $10 billion exogenous decline in that period is a $22.22 billion increase in P; to find the ΔP required, simply solve for the ΔP for which $\Delta X_t = 0 = -10 + .45\Delta P_t$. ($\Delta P_{t-1}$ is zero initially.) This is not the end of the story, however, because income in period 2 will be affected by the change in policy instrument in the previous period; i.e., in period 2, ΔP_{t-1} will equal $22.22 billion. If the policy instrument remains unchanged in period 2, income would increase by $22.22 \times .55 = \$12.22$ billion. To keep income unchanged, the policy instrument will have to decline by $27.16 billion in period 2; i.e., we find the ΔP_t for which $\Delta X = 0 = .45\Delta P_t + .55(22.22)$. In subsequent periods ΔP will continue to cycle with each change, becoming larger and larger in absolute value. Stabilizing income period by period requires extreme instability in policy instruments.

(a) The Case of Instrument Instability: $w_0 = .45$, $w_1 = .55$				
Period	ΔZ_t	ΔP_t	ΔP_{t-1}	ΔX_t^*
1	−10	22.22	0	−10
2	0	−27.16	22.22	12.22
3	0	33.20	−27.16	−14.94

(b) The Stable Case: $w_0 = .55$, $w_1 = .45$				
Period	ΔZ_t	ΔP_t	ΔP_{t-1}	ΔX_t^*
1	−10	18.18	0	−10
2	0	−14.88	18.18	8.18
3	0	12.17	−14.88	−6.94

TABLE 24A.1
Monetary Policy and Instrument Instability

---

[1] This is the model employed by Robert Holbrook in "Optimal Economic Policy and the Problem of Instrument Instability," *American Economic Review*, Vol. LXII (March, 1972), pp. 57–65.

In Table 24A.1b we work out the results for the case where the ΔP's cycle becomes progressively smaller in absolute value.[2]

If instrument instability is a problem, the policy authority can stabilize income without having to undertake progressively larger and larger policy changes if it is content to move output back to its desired level *gradually*. For example, if the policy authorities increase P by $10 billion in period 1 and keep it at this level in subsequent periods, income will decline by $5.50 billion in period 1 [i.e., $\Delta X_1 = -10 + .45(10)$], but by period 2 income will be back at its desired value [$\Delta X_2 = .55(10) = +5.50$]. This strategy is illustrated in Table 24A.2.

Period	ΔZ_t	ΔP_t	ΔP_{t-1}	ΔX_t
1	−10	+10	—	−5.50
2	0	0	+10	+5.50
3	0	0	0	0

TABLE 24A.2
Gradualism and Instrument Instability

The case for gradual response is reinforced when we realize that policymakers are uncertain about the parameters (e.g., w_0 and w_1) in the economy as well as about the current values of the exogenous variables (the ΔZ's in this model). This reinforces their reluctance to act aggressively. Indeed, it is quite important to distinguish the problems of the *length* and *variability* of lags. Long lags may be offset by a *more vigorous* policy response subject to the problem of instrument instability. Variable lags mean that policymakers are uncertain about the effect of their policies and generally require a *more cautious* response of policy to disturbances.[3]

APPENDIX

The Implications of Uncertainty and Incomplete Information

In the models used in the previous chapter we assumed that the policymaker knew the values of all model parameters and exogenous variables so that it could, in principle, respond immediately to offset changes in exogenous variables. In fact, we simply do not know the current values of many of the variables in the economy. We get information on some variables more frequently than on others. For example, data on *GNP* and its components are available only quarterly (the value of production over each quarter) and are reported initially about a month after the quarter is over but generally revised over the next couple of months. The

---

[2] In the right-hand column of the table, ΔX_t^* is the change in income that would occur in period t if policy did not change (i.e., if $\Delta P_t = 0$).

[3] Milton Friedman in "The Effects of a Full Employment Policy on Economic Stability: A Formal Analysis," *Essays in Positive Economics* (Chicago: University of Chicago Press, 1953), pp. 117–132, is therefore concerned more with the variability than the length of lags and derives the result that the greater the uncertainty, the more cautious the optimal response of policy to disturbances. For an analysis which considers the problems associated with both length and variability of lags, see Stanley Fischer and J. Phillip Cooper, "Stabilization Policy and Lags," *Journal of Political Economy*, Vol. 81 (July–August, 1973), pp. 847–877.

unemployment rate is available monthly, money supply with a two-week lag, and quotes on interest rates are available almost continuously during operating hours in financial markets. This structure of information availability plays an important role in both the design of monetary policy and in limiting the ability of the Fed to achieve its macroeconomic objectives.

Incomplete Information and Uncertainty

The lack of information about current values of exogenous variables introduces uncertainty into the environment in which policy is conducted. The uncertainty associated with the lack of information about exogenous variables is compounded by our inability to predict endogenous variables precisely even if we knew current values of all exogenous variables. Consider our consumption function:

$$C = \bar{C} + C_y Y. \tag{24B.1a}$$

Even if we knew Y, we could not precisely predict consumption. This reflects the fact that both C_y and $\bar{C}$ are *random* variables. In the following analysis we will allow explicitly only for uncertainty about the autonomous component of our endogenous variables. We will write out consumption function as

$$C = \tilde{C} + C_y Y + U_C \tag{24B.1b}$$

where $\tilde{C}$ is the expected value of the autonomous component of consumption. The expected value of consumption is

$$\hat{C} = \tilde{C} + C_y Y \tag{24B.2a}$$

and the actual value is

$$C = \hat{C} + U_C \tag{24B.2b}$$

where U_C is a random variable (a variable whose value is governed by the laws of chance) with a zero mean. This means the best estimate of consumption is $\hat{C}$, given that the best guess is that U_C will turn out to be zero.

To introduce uncertainty into the *IS-LM* model, we include additive random components in the *IS* and *LM* equations (U_X and U_M, respectively):

$$X = C_y(X - \bar{T}) + I_r r + \tilde{Z} + \tilde{G} + U_X \tag{24B.3}$$

$$m = L_r r + L_x X + \tilde{L} + U_M. \tag{24B.4}$$

$\tilde{Z}$, $\tilde{T}$, $\tilde{G}$, and $\tilde{L}$ are expected values of $\bar{Z}$, $\bar{T}$, $\bar{G}$, and $\bar{L}$, respectively, and the U_X and U_M terms incorporate random components of both the exogenous variables and the structural equations. We can also add the money supply equation derived in Chapter 23:

$$m = \frac{1+c}{c+d}[nmb - F(r, r_d)]. \tag{24B.5}$$

In this case the policy instrument is the stock of high-powered money (*nmb*, the nonborrowed monetary base). To simplify, we do not include a random disturbance term in this equation.

Monetary Policy Under Uncertainty

To carry out monetary policy, the Fed must make some forecast about exogenous variables and the autonomous component of the structural equations. Given that the random components of the IS and LM curves have zero means, the Fed's best guess is that $U_X = U_M = 0$; i.e., it assumes that the prevailing values of $\bar{Z}$, $\bar{G}$, $\bar{T}$, and $\bar{L}$ will be equal to their expected values, $\tilde{Z}$, $\tilde{G}$, $\tilde{T}$, and $\tilde{L}$. Given the assumed values for the exogenous variables (and autonomous components of the endogenous variables), the Fed can solve the model for the value of high-powered money (nmb in this case) consistent with the desired value of income (X_f). This is referred to as a *certainty equivalence model*: the optimal policy of the Fed is to behave *as if* the expected values were the actual values of the exogenous variables and autonomous components of the structural equations.[1] The value of the instrument in this case will be the same as if the Fed knew with certainty that the current values of the exogenous variables and autonomous components were $\tilde{G}$, $\tilde{T}$, $\tilde{Z}$, and $\tilde{L}$.

We depict the solution graphically in Figure 24B.1. The position of the solid IS and LM curves reflects the expected values of $\bar{Z}$, $\bar{G}$, $\bar{T}$, and $\bar{L}$. The optimal setting of the policy instrument is the one that makes the expected value of income equal to its desired level, X_f. This is the most likely (expected) outcome. But $\bar{Z}$ in general will not turn out equal to $\tilde{Z}$; similarly with $\bar{G}$, $\bar{T}$, and $\bar{L}$. The dashed IS and LM curves are drawn for the *actual* levels of the exogenous variables and autonomous components of the structural equations and the optimal setting for the policy instrument (which, in turn, was based on expected values of $\bar{Z}$, $\bar{G}$, $\bar{T}$, and $\bar{L}$). These are the curves that determine the actual as opposed to the expected values of

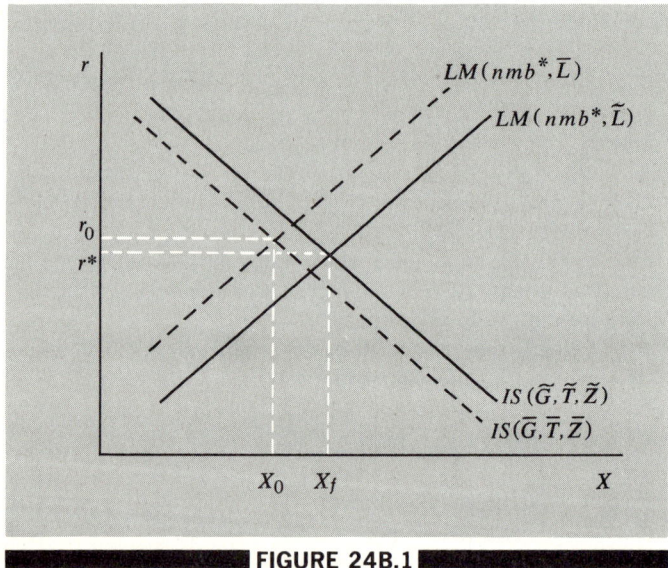

FIGURE 24B.1
Monetary Policy Under Uncertainty

---

[1] This is optimal provided that the values of the model parameters (C_y, I_r, F_r, L_x, L_r, F_{r_d}) are known with certainty. The only uncertainty is associated with the additive disturbance terms in the structural equations. If there is uncertainty about model parameters, the optimal policy response is more complicated. This case is developed in William Brainard, "Uncertainty and the Effectiveness of Policy," *American Economic Review, Papers and Proceedings*, Vol. 57 (May, 1967), pp. 411–425. Brainard shows that in this case the optimal response is more cautious than in the certainty equivalence case.

output and the interest rate. In Figure 24B.1 we have arbitrarily (randomly!) assumed that U_X turns out to be negative (e.g., $\bar{Z}$ turns out to be less than $\hat{Z}$) and U_M turns out to be positive (e.g., $\bar{L}$ turns out to be greater than $\hat{L}$). In the case pictured, X falls short of X_f. The monetary authorities cannot be faulted for missing their target. They operated without information on the true values of $\bar{Z}$, $\bar{L}$, $\bar{G}$, and $\bar{T}$ and perhaps did the best they could have under the circumstances. Or did they?

Intermediate Targets

In fact, the Fed *may* be able to improve upon the strategy of setting its instrument based on expected values of $\bar{G}$, $\bar{T}$, $\bar{Z}$, and $\bar{L}$. The alternative strategy employs an *intermediate target*; i.e., a target intermediate between the policy instrument (*nmb*) and the goal variable (X). An intermediate target is a variable which can be controlled by the Fed within narrow limits and about which the Fed has current information (or, at least, more frequent information than about the goal variable).[2] The two potential intermediate targets in our model are the interest rate and the money supply.

We assume the Fed can control either the interest rate or the money supply over the period between receipt of new information about the exogenous and endogenous variables. Therefore, we can treat either of these intermediate targets *as if* it were the instrument. Indeed, if the Fed follows an intermediate target strategy, the intermediate target is independent of the exogenous variables (i.e., an exogenous variable itself) whereas *the policy instrument responds to disturbances* (i.e., becomes an endogenous variable)! Before we explore the way in which endogenous movements in the policy instrument (*nmb*) *may* stabilize the economy, we introduce the three *LM* curves that are associated with the three strategies we will compare.

Three *LM* Curves

In Figure 24B.2 we depict three different *LM* curves: $LM(nmb^*)$ is the *LM* curve when the Fed sets its instrument and holds to it until it gets additional information about its goal variable. $LM(m^*)$ and $LM(r^*)$ are the *LM* curves when the Fed follows an intermediate target strategy—varying its policy instrument to maintain either r or m at fixed levels until more information is obtained about its goal variables.

If the Fed maintains $r = r^*$, the *LM* curve is horizontal; r^* will be the only interest rate consistent with financial market equilibrium. In Chapter 23 we found that the *LM* curve with an interest elastic money supply [corresponding to $LM(nmb^*)$] is flatter than an *LM* curve with an exogenous money supply [corresponding to our $LM(m^*)$].

To simplify the analysis, we begin by considering cases in which there are random disturbances in *either IS* or *LM* curves, but not in both. First, we consider the case of random real disturbances only and then we discuss the case of random financial disturbances only.

---

[2] The formal model underlying our analysis below is based on William Poole, "Optimal Choice of Monetary Policy Instrument in a Simple Stochastic Macro Model," *Quarterly Journal of Economics*, Vol. LXXXIV (May, 1970), pp. 197–216. See also Karl Brunner and Allan Meltzer, "The Nature of the Policy Problem," in K. Brunner (ed.), *Targets and Indicators of Monetary Policy* (San Francisco: Chandler Publishing Company, 1969), pp. 1–26; and Robert Holbrook and Harold Shapiro, "The Choice of Optimal Intermediate Economic Targets," *American Economic Review, Papers and Proceedings*, Vol. LX (May, 1970), pp. 40–46.

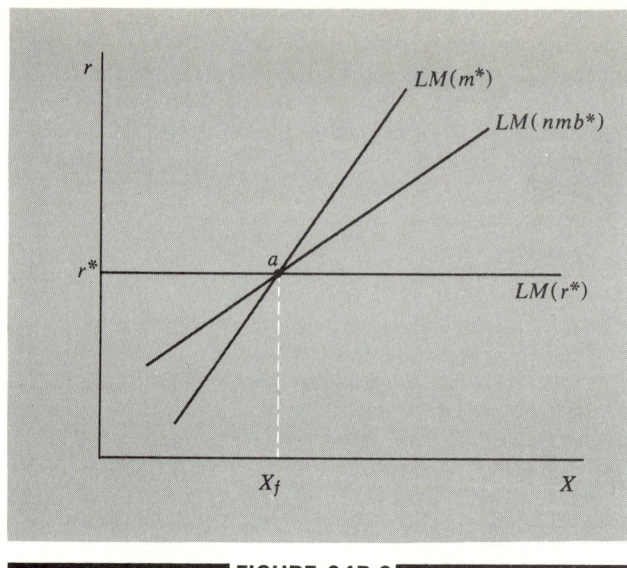

FIGURE 24B.2
The *LM* Curve Under Instrument and
Intermediate Target Strategies

Real Sector Random Disturbances Only

In this case the Fed can perfectly control the position of the *LM* curve under any of the three strategies, but there is a random component in the *IS* curve. Assume that there is a random decline in autonomous private demand; i.e., $\bar{Z}$ turns out to be less than $\hat{Z}$ (or, equivalently, U_X turns out to be negative). If the Fed had complete information, we would be back to the certainty case and it would not matter which of the three strategies the Fed pursued; indeed, the three strategies cannot be separated because setting its instrument at its optimal (certainty equivalence) value, nmb^*, results in the money supply and interest rates at m^* and r^*, respectively, and output at X_f. Therefore, the three *LM* curves intersect the *IS* curve at the same point (point *a* in Figure 24B.2) if all exogenous variables take on their expected values (or if the Fed knows the true values of all exogenous variables).

But the motivation for the intermediate target strategy is the structure of information availability discussed above. The Fed does not immediately know the magnitude of disturbances or the current level of income. Under the intermediate target strategy, it selects the value of the intermediate target which makes the expected value of income equal to its desired value (m^* or r^*) and *uses its policy instrument to offset the effect of random disturbances on its intermediate target.* It can do so because it receives frequent information about its intermediate target and exercises effective control over it by manipulating its policy instrument.

The consequences of following the three alternative strategies (associated with the three alternative *LM* curves) are depicted in Figure 24B.3. If the Fed follows a money supply policy, output declines from X_f to X_m. If the Fed follows an interest rate policy, output declines to X_r. And if the Fed follows an instrument (as opposed to intermediate target) policy, income declines to X_i. The best strategy, therefore, is the money supply policy and the worst is the interest rate strategy.

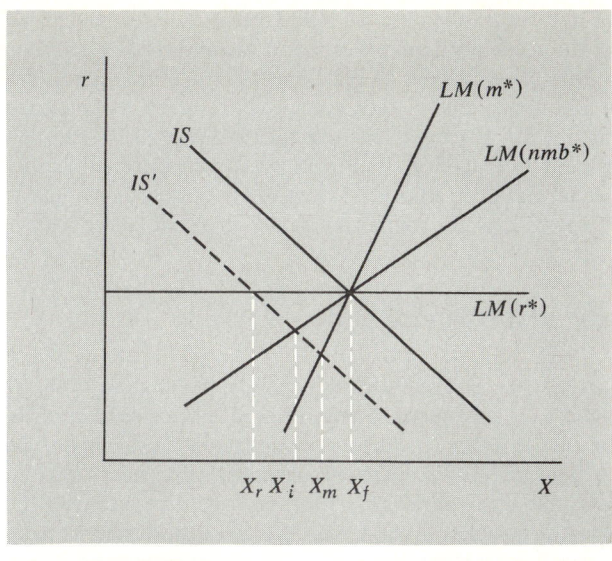

FIGURE 24B.3
Intermediate Targets and Real Sector Disturbances

To understand why the intermediate target strategy leads to different results than the instrument strategy, consider how the Fed responds to policy disturbances in the intermediate target cases. Indeed, this is the essential point, as noted above. Under an instrument strategy, the Fed does *not* respond to disturbances until it receives information about the disturbance or about the effect of the disturbance on income. When the Fed follows an intermediate target strategy, on the other hand, it responds immediately and automatically to disturbances as it acts to offset the influence of the disturbances on its intermediate target. Thus, the essential feature of the intermediate target strategy is the *induced* or *automatic* response of the policy instrument to disturbances. If these changes are stabilizing, the Fed will increase the precision with which it can meet its objectives by using an intermediate target. This is equivalent to enhancing the *built-in stability* of the system. For example, under the money supply strategy, movements of nmb to keep m equal to m^* are the *built-in* automatic components of policy. Movements in nmb to alter m^* are the *discretionary* components of policy.

We can trace through the way the Fed responds under r and m strategies. The initial decline in aggregate demand induces a decline in the interest rate which, in turn, induces a decline in the money supply (due to an increase in desired free reserves). Under the money supply strategy, the monetary authorities are induced to move the instrument in the appropriate direction; i.e., they increase high-powered money (nmb) to offset the impact of the reduction in aggregate demand on the money supply. Under the interest rate strategy, on the other hand, the monetary authorities are induced to operate in the wrong direction. As the interest rate declines, they *reduce* the level of high-powered money; this stabilizes the interest rate but further *destabilizes* the level of output. This analysis provides a rationale for the preference of controlling the money supply to controlling the instrument itself during the intervals between the receipt of information about exogenous and goal variables.

Note, however, that the appropriate strategy depends on where you are relative to where you want to be and on the strategy being pursued by the fiscal authority. If the economy is well below the target level of output, we may prefer a larger multiplier for the response of output to real sector disturbances because this will increase the leverage that the fiscal authority has over output. If the monetary authorities follow an interest rate strategy, the multiplier for fiscal policy will be larger than it would be under the other strategies and the relative superiority of the three strategies is, in fact, completely reversed. By stabilizing interest rates, the monetary authorities can offset both the negative feedback effects and the direct portfolio impact of bond-financed fiscal policy, assuring a greater increase in output than would be achieved with either of the other strategies. However, when it comes time for curtain calls, fiscal policy should not be a prima donna and should share the praise with monetary policy!

Monetary Sector Disturbances Only

Now we assume that the Fed knows with certainty the position of the *IS* curve but can only imperfectly control the *LM* curve because of random monetary disturbances. In Figure 24B.4 we depict the case of a random increase in the autonomous component of the demand for money; i.e., $\bar{L}$, the actual value of this autonomous component turns out to be greater than $\hat{L}$, its expected value (or, equivalently, U_M turns out to be positive). If the Fed follows an interest rate policy, it completely offsets the financial disturbance so that output remains unchanged.[3] If the Fed follows a money supply rule, on the other hand, output declines from X_f to X_m. And if the Fed chooses to pursue an instrument strategy, output declines to X_i. In this case the best strategy is an interest rate policy and the worst is a money supply strategy.

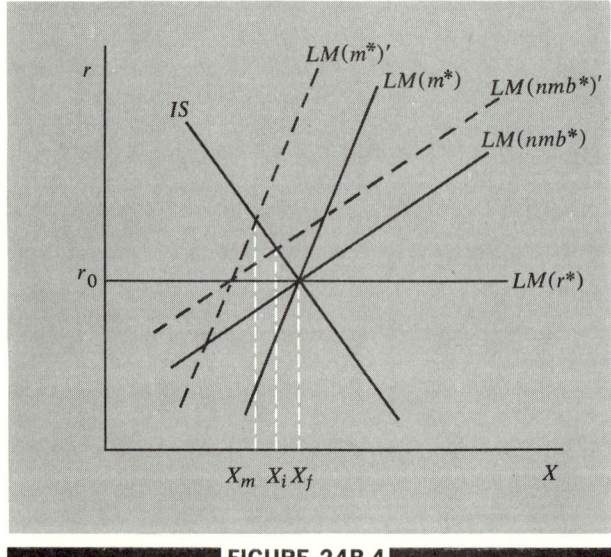

FIGURE 24B.4
Intermediate Targets and Financial Disturbances

The intermediate target strategies again induce responses of the policy instrument which in one case is stabilizing (the *r* policy) and in the other case is destabilizing (the *m* policy). The autonomous increase in the demand for money puts upward pressure on the interest

---

[3] Note that the $LM(nmb^*)$ and $LM(m^*)$ curves shift by equal amounts in the horizontal direction in this case ($\Delta X/\Delta \bar{L} = -1/L_x$ in each case) while the $LM(r^*)$ curve remains unchanged.

rate and hence tends to reduce output. Under an interest rate policy, the Fed responds by carrying out expansionary *OMO* until r is returned to its initial level. This will induce an increase in the money supply just equal to the autonomous increase in the demand for money. This is the one case where an intermediate target strategy permits a complete rather than partial offset to a random disturbance. The money supply strategy, on the other hand, induces the Fed to move its policy instrument in the wrong direction. The increase in the interest rate induced by the disturbance results in an increase in the money supply (via a decline in the demand for free reserves); in moving to offset the disturbance to the intermediate target (m), the Fed carries out restrictive *OMO* which further depresses output. Thus, the Fed stabilizes the money supply at the expense of destabilizing output in this case.

The General Case: Random Shocks from Both Sectors

In the general case when there are random shocks from both the real and financial sectors, the choice between the interest rate and the money supply will depend on the relative size of random shocks experienced in the two sectors and on the model parameters (which determine the multipliers that transform random shocks into changes in the goal variables). Evidence is rather scarce but the general view is that over periods of six months to a year, real shocks are more serious than financial shocks. This is the rationale for the Fed's use of monetary aggregate targets. Over very short periods (e.g., days, weeks), on the other hand, there may be large financial shocks which over months or quarters wash out. In this case, the Fed could set interest rates over short periods (e.g., months) and vary interest rates between months to achieve its long-run monetary growth targets. This is in fact what the Fed attempts to do.[4]

Limitations of the Intermediate Target Strategy

The intermediate target strategy may reduce the departures from target values of goal variables, but it will not in general fully offset disturbances. The problem is that if automatic movements of the instruments are required under the intermediate target strategy, the current value of the intermediate target variable will, in general, no longer be optimal.[5] Consider the case of the model with real disturbances only. If the Fed observes upward pressure on the money stock, it knows that there has been an upward disturbance on aggregate demand. The size of the discrepancy between the target value and the observed value of the money supply provides information on the size of the disturbance. The Fed must carry out open market sales more aggressively than required to simply get back to the initial target value of the money supply. Note also that an intermediate target strategy is only designed to enhance the economy's built-in stability. The Fed may be able to improve its control over goal variables by altering its setting for its intermediate target in response to new information about the exogenous variables and/or its goal variables; i.e., by carrying out discretionary policy.

---

[4] For more detailed discussions of the formulation and implementation of monetary policy, see William Poole, "The Making of Monetary Policy: Description and Analysis," *Economic Inquiry*, Vol. 13 (June, 1975), pp. 253–265; and Raymond Lombra and Raymond Torto, "The Strategy of Monetary Policy," Federal Reserve Bank of Richmond *Economic Review* (Sept.–Oct., 1975), pp. 3–14.

[5] For a discussion of the limitations of the intermediate target strategy, see John Kareken, "Discussion" in *Controlling Monetary Aggregates II: The Implementation* (Boston: Federal Reserve Bank of Boston, 1972); and Benjamin Friedman, "The Inefficiency of Short-Run Monetary Targets for Monetary Policy," *Brookings Papers On Economic Activity* (1977:2), pp. 293–335.

Part VI · Policy

● REVIEW QUESTIONS

1. In what sense is the Federal Reserve System "independent" of the executive and congressional branches of government? What control, if any, do these branches have over the Fed?

2. What are the pros and cons of the degree of independence the Fed has?

3. Can member banks borrow from the Fed at their own discretion? If not, what are the limitations on member banks borrowing?

4. What are the advantages of open market operations relative to other instruments under the Fed's control?

5. Describe the sequence of responses to an open market operation from its initial effect in financial markets to its ultimate effect on aggregate demand and income. What are the key parameters in the model that determine the overall effect on income?

6. What is the monetarist critique of the modeling of the channels of monetary policy in income-expenditure models?

7. What is the monetarist alternative to income-expenditure structural models and how does this overcome the problems of the former?

8. Is there substantial consensus or disagreement about the size of monetary policy multipliers?

9. Distinguish between the inside and the outside lags associated with monetary policy.

10. What is the problem of instrument instability?

11. Discuss the case against the discretionary use of policy instruments.

*12. Define an intermediate target and discuss the rationale for using one.

● PROBLEMS

* 1. Work out the time path of the policy instrument and output in response to a $5 billion increase in the disturbance term (Z) in the model given by equation (24A.1) for the two sets of values of the parameters given in the table below. Calculate the values of the change in the policy instrument and output for three periods.

	w_0	w_1
I	.40	.60
II	.60	.40

* 2. Demonstrate how a gradual policy response can avoid the problem of instrument instability using the parameter values given in the table above.

* 3. Assume there are stochastic disturbances in the real sector only. Compare the degree of built-in stability associated with an instrument and the two intermediate target

---

* The information necessary for solving these problems or questions can be found in the appendices.

strategies (money supply and interest rate targets) by solving for the reduced form for income and finding the multiplier on the disturbance term (U_X) in each case.

* EXERCISE

Each month the *Federal Reserve Bulletin* reports the record of policy actions of the Federal Reserve Open Market Committee. Look at a recent *Federal Reserve Bulletin* and discuss the nature of the policy directive. Explain the rationale for carrying out policy in the manner described.

---

* The information necessary for solving this exercise can be found in the appendices.

Chapter 25
Fiscal Policy

In this chapter we develop the institutions of fiscal policy, refine our modeling of the response of income to fiscal actions, and appraise the empirical evidence on the magnitude and time pattern of response of income to fiscal policy. We begin with a survey of fiscal institutions, including a discussion of the budget and the budget process. Next, we consider the appropriate measure of the economic stimulus associated with the budget and the role of fiscal institutions in enhancing the economy's built-in stability. We contrast the nature of built-in stability in Keynesian cross and Keynesian *IS-LM* models and then compare both of these models with the classical *IS-LM* model. We conclude the section with a discussion of a plan to improve fiscal built-in stability. In the next section we summarize the response of income to fiscal actions, bringing together the analysis presented in numerous preceding chapters and then discuss the empirical evidence on the response to fiscal policy. We conclude with a discussion of the monetarist critique of fiscal activism and an income-expenditure counterattack on monetarist empirical methodology.

FISCAL INSTITUTIONS

To appreciate the difficulty in the effective use of discretionary changes in fiscal instruments, it is useful to understand the interaction of executive and legislative branches of government in the fiscal decision-making process. We begin by discussing the government budget and then consider the process whereby both budget and tax proposals are implemented.

The Budget

There are a number of ways of organizing and reporting the government's budget. The budget concept we focus on is the national income accounts budget which presents the budget categories in a way that isolates the expenditure and tax revenue categories that are employed in the national income accounts' definitions of *GNP*, personal, and disposable income discussed in Chapter 2. Table 25.1 presents the *NIA* treatment of the government budget; the data are for 1977. The expenditures are separated into purchases of goods and services and transfer payments.

	1977 Actual
Receipts	
Personal Tax and Nontax Receipts	165.5
Corporate Profits Tax Accruals	57.4
Indirect Business Tax and Nontax Accruals	24.6
Contributions for Social Insurance	116.5
Total Receipts	364.0
Expenditures	
Purchases of Goods and Services	140.7
Defense	(92.0)
Nondefense	(48.7)
Transfer Payments	169.7
Domestic ("to persons")	(166.5)
Foreign	(3.2)
Grants-in-Aid to State and Local Governments	66.0
Net Interest Paid	29.3
Subsidies Less Current Surplus of Government Enterprises	6.1
Total Expenditures	411.8
Deficit (−)	−47.8

Source: From Table 18, p. 485, *The Budget of the United States Government: Fiscal Year 1979* (Washington: U.S. Government Printing Office, 1978).

TABLE 25.1

Federal Receipts and Expenditures in the National Income Accounts (in billions of dollars)

The deficit shown in the *NIA* budget does not fully indicate the borrowing requirements for the federal government. Net lending by the federal government is excluded from the *NIA* budget because net lending is an asset exchange rather than an expenditure for currently produced goods and services. But net lending (loan disbursements in excess of loan repayments) also must be financed. Table 25.2 reports the implications of the budget for borrowing requirements. The total need for financing was $53.7 billion in fiscal year 1977; $45 billion represented the basic expenditure deficit[1] and

---

[1] The expenditure deficit totals in Tables 25.1 and 25.2 differ slightly, reflecting slight differences in the measurement of expenditures and revenue flows in the *NIA* approach used in Table 25.1 and the unified budget approach underlying Table 25.2.

	1977 Actual
Budget Financing	
Budget Surplus or Deficit (−)	−45,040
Deficit (−), Off-Budget Federal Entities	−8,693
Total Deficit (−)	−53,733
Total Means of Financing Other than Borrowing from the Public	217
Total Requirements for Borrowing from the Public	−53,516
Change in Debt Held by the Public	53,516
Nonbank Investors	39,935
Commercial Banks	5,279
Federal Reserve System	8,302
Outstanding Debt, End of Year	
Gross Federal Debt:	
Debt Issued by Treasury	698,840
Debt Issued by Other Agencies	10,298
Total Gross Federal Debt	709,138
Held by:	
Government Agencies	157,295
The Public	551,843
Federal Reserve System	105,004
Others	446,839

Source: From Table 9, p. 435, *The Budget of the United States Government: Fiscal Year 1979* (Washington: U.S. Government Printing Office, 1978).

TABLE 25.2

Budget Financing and Outstanding Debt
(in millions of dollars)

$8.7 billion was due to deficits of "off-budget federal entities," federally owned and controlled agencies which, by law, are simply excluded from the budget. Most of the outlays for off-budget entities consist of net loans.

The federal government finances virtually all the deficit by borrowing from the public (via sale of government bonds). It does, however, hold some cash balances and deposits at both Federal Reserve Banks and commercial banks and can finance a minor portion of its deficit by drawing down such assets. During 1977 it used sources other than borrowing from the public to finance $217 million of its $53.7 billion deficit. Therefore, it sold $53.5 billion of additional bonds (in addition to "rolling over" maturing debt during the period). Table 25.2 indicates that most of the increase in debt was purchased by the nonbank public. The $8.3 billion of additional debt purchased by the Fed does not represent direct purchases from the government. Rather, it reflects Fed purchases of "old" debt associated with its conduct of open market operations over the year.

○ The Budget Process[2]

The executive branch prepares and submits its proposed budget to Congress in January for the fiscal year beginning the following October 1; e.g., in January, 1978, the President submitted his budget for the fiscal year October 1, 1978, to September 30, 1979 (the 1979 fiscal year). The budget process can be broken down into three phases: the preparation by the executive, consideration and possible revision by Congress, and execution of the budget by the executive.

Preparation of the Budget. The process of preparing the budget extends over a 20-month period beginning with an initial round of budget requests by various departments and ending with submission to Congress each January. The responsibility for coordinating the presentation of budget requests within the framework of some overall expenditure limit falls on the Office of Management and the Budget (OMB). Two themes interact throughout the preparation of the budget: program development and stabilization policy. During the first round departments submit requests. At the same time, the Council of Economic Advisors and the Treasury appraise revenue prospects and develop a fiscal policy in light of the economic outlook. On the basis of the fiscal considerations and revenue prospects, the OMB sets expenditure ceilings for the various departments and solicits a second round of budget requests. After a final overall review, the budget is submitted to Congress.

Congressional Budget Process. Congressional consideration of the budget was long hampered by lack of coordination between the program and fiscal considerations that were weaved together during the executive preparation stage. A 1974 reform, however, dramatically improved the congressional budget process. The budget is now considered by budget committees in each house and a concurrent resolution by these budget committees sets the overall limit on expenditures, its breakdown among various components, and determines the required level of revenue. The first concurrent resolution must be agreed upon by May 15 and provides the congressional vehicle for imposing an overall stabilization strategy. Both houses then act on various appropriation bills within the context of this resolution and then must agree on a second concurrent resolution by October 1 reaffirming or revising their first resolution. Congressional action on the budget is aided by the Joint Economic Committee which holds extensive hearings on the President's economic program and the Congressional Budget Office (CBO) which provides staff assistance to committees considering the budget. As we noted in the previous chapter, the Full Employment and Balanced Growth Act of 1978 specified precise, long-term targets for unemployment and inflation. The Act requires the administration to report each year on the relation of its current policies to these long-term goals.

---

[2] For an excellent discussion of the budget process, see David J. Ott and Attiat F. Ott, *Federal Budget Policy*, revised edition (Washington: The Brookings Institution, 1969); and Richard A. Musgrave and Peggy B. Musgrave, *Public Finance in Theory and Practice* (2d ed.; New York: McGraw-Hill Book Co., 1975).

Execution of the Budget. The President must sign or veto the budget bill within ten days. From this point, the execution of it is under the supervision of the OMB which oversees the allocation of the total among the various departments.

Tax Legislation

The tax side of fiscal decisions differs in one fundamental respect from the expenditure side. New legislation is not required each year. Tax rates, unless revised, remain in effect and generate a continuous flow of revenue. On the other hand, when the executive and/or Congress initiates tax bills to alter the structure of taxes or the revenue inflow from the tax system, there is a long process from recognition of the need for the legislation to enactment. Proposals to alter taxes may be initiated either by the executive or Congress. Unlike budget proposals which are acted upon concurrently by both houses, the Constitution requires that tax legislation originate in the House. Therefore, tax legislation is considered sequentially, first in the House and then in the Senate.

Proposals for Reform of Fiscal Decision Making

The process of fiscal decision making is generally regarded as being too slow and inflexible to permit effective discretionary stabilization policy. Some tax changes have taken over a year from the point at which the President requested the action to its passage; the important tax surcharge of 1968, for example, took 14 months and this was still faster than the 18 months required for passage of the Revenue Act of 1965. On the other hand, there are examples of quite speedy congressional action; e.g., the three-month period required for passage of the 1975 tax cut and the one-month action on cutting excise taxes in 1965. Still, on the whole, the slowness of the legislative process reduces the usefulness of discretionary fiscal policy.

There have been a number of suggestions to speed up the process. Both Presidents Kennedy and Johnson proposed presidential authority to initiate temporary tax changes within limits predetermined by Congress, but Congress has steadfastly opposed any infringement on its ultimate authority over tax and expenditure programs.

Another approach is to enhance the built-in stability associated with income-induced variations in expenditures and revenues under the existing tax schedule and transfer programs. We will postpone further discussion of this until we review and refine our analysis of fiscal built-in stabilizers.

THE ECONOMIC STIMULUS OF THE BUDGET AND MEASURING DISCRETIONARY POLICY CHANGES

In this section we identify the appropriate measure of the economic stimulus associated with the government's budget and consider the problem of identifying the direction and magnitude of changes in the budget associated with discretionary fiscal policy.[3]

---

[3] For an excellent discussion of the issues introduced in this and the following sections, see Alan S. Blinder and Robert M. Solow, "Analytical Foundations of Fiscal Policy," in Alan S. Blinder and Robert M. Solow, *et al.*, *The Economics of Public Finance* (Washington: The Brookings Institution, 1974), pp. 3–115.

○ Measuring the Stimulus Associated with the Budget

The stimulus associated with the budget is often identified with the magnitude of the deficit or surplus; e.g., the larger the surplus, the greater the restrictive impact of the budget. The identification of the expansionary thrust of the budget with the size of the budget surplus, however, contradicts our analysis of the balanced-budget multiplier. According to this analysis (see Chapter 6), government expenditures have a greater direct impact on aggregate demand (dollar-for-dollar) than an equal increase in tax revenue (C_y dollars decline in aggregate demand for each dollar increase in tax revenue).

The deficiency of the budget surplus as a measure of the expansionary influence of the budget is that it weights government expenditures and tax revenues equally. To accurately measure the stimulus associated with the budget, we must appropriately weight the various components. For the simple case of exogenous tax revenues, the *weighted surplus* is defined as

$$S_w = C_y \overline{T} - \overline{G} \tag{25.1}$$

where the weights on $\overline{T}$ and $\overline{G}$ are the numerators of the multipliers for T and G, respectively, in the reduced-form equation for income.

○ The Weighted Full Employment Surplus

The weighted surplus is an accurate measure of the stimulus associated with the budget. Budgets with smaller weighted surpluses are unambiguously more expansionary than budgets with larger surpluses. Furthermore, if G and T are exogenous, movements in the weighted surplus provide an unambiguous measure of changes in the posture of fiscal policy; e.g., decreases in S_w signal a move toward more expansionary policy.

However, if G and/or T are endogenous, movements in the weighted surplus will reflect the joint influence of changes in the level of income and changes in policy instruments. We will assume that G is exogenous and that net tax revenues are proportional to income ($T = tX$) so that the weighted surplus can be expressed as

$$S_w = C_y tX - \overline{G}. \tag{25.2}$$

Note that with fixed values for fiscal instruments ($\overline{G}, t$), the weighted surplus will automatically decline if income declines; this is, of course, simply a reflection of the built-in stability associated with endogenous tax revenues that we discussed initially in Chapter 6. Built-in stability is indeed useful, but we also discovered in Chapter 6 that fiscal built-in stability may only dampen the effect on income associated with disturbances; therefore, discretionary fiscal policy (changes in fiscal instruments) may be able to offset at least a portion of the remaining variation in income associated with exogenous disturbances. To evaluate the adequacy of discretionary fiscal policy, it is necessary to separate out movements in the weighted surplus due to changes in fiscal instruments from movements due to changes in income.

The change in the weighted full employment surplus (S_{wf})

$$S_{wf} = C_y tX_f - \overline{G} \tag{25.2'}$$

is often suggested as a measure of discretionary fiscal action. By measuring net tax revenues at a constant level of resource utilization, it permits us to isolate the net effect of changes in fiscal instruments on the weighted surplus. However, the weighted full employment surplus may yield misleading signals concerning the impact of fiscal changes when the policy changes are initiated at a level of income other than full employment. A better measure of fiscal actions is the *weighted initial surplus* (S_{wi})

$$S_{wi} = C_y t X_i - \overline{G} \tag{25.3}$$

where X_i is the prevailing or initial level of income. The analytical superiority of the weighted initial surplus will be further clarified in a problem at the end of this chapter.

Although the weighted surplus is superior analytically to the actual surplus as a measure of the expansionary thrust of the budget and the change in the weighted initial surplus is analytically superior to the change in the weighted full employment surplus as an indicator of the impact of changes in fiscal instruments, it is still possible that the qualitative information provided by S and S_w and by ΔS_{wi} and ΔS_{wf} will be the same; i.e., while S_w and ΔS_{wi} are analytically superior, we might not have been misled in practice by observing S and ΔS_{wf}. Arthur Okun and Nancy Teeters compare ΔS_f and ΔS_{wf}. They conclude that "the full employment surplus consistently tells the same story whether it is unweighted or weighted. . . ." Because of the insignificance of the weighting and possible disagreements concerning the value of the weights, they suggest "it is surely more practical to agree not to weight."[4] Indeed, the unweighted index remains the most widely cited measure of fiscal stimulus. They warn, however, that for major changes in the composition or size of the budget, the weighting scheme should be taken into account.

William Oakland compares ΔS_{wf} and ΔS_{wi}. He finds a close agreement in terms of direction of fiscal policy. On the other hand, the quantitative values of the two measures often differ, sometimes by a magnitude of two or more. Given the analytical superiority of ΔS_{wi} and the often large quantitative differences between ΔS_{wf} and ΔS_{wi}, Oakland suggests that ΔS_{wi} should be employed as the index of fiscal performance.[5]

BUILT-IN STABILITY

In our discussion of fiscal institutions, we noted that the legislative process does not move with the rapidity that seems essential for effective stabilization policy. While there are occasions in which fiscal policy changes were implemented within about one quarter following their recommendation by the President, there are many other cases in which more than a year was required to complete legislative action. The immobility of discretionary fiscal policy puts the burden on built-in stability (as well as on monetary policy) and we turn in this section to a theoretical refinement of

---

[4] Arthur M. Okun and Nancy H. Teeters, "The Full Employment Surplus Revisited," *Brookings Papers on Economic Activity* (1970), pp. 77–110. The quotes are found on p. 87.
[5] William H. Oakland, "Budgetary Measures of Fiscal Performance," *Southern Economics Journal*, Vol. 35 (April, 1969), pp. 347–358.

our analysis of built-in stability and empirical evaluation of the degree to which built-in stabilizers have cushioned the economy's response to disturbances.

We begin by discussing the evidence on the importance of *fiscal stabilizers*. Next, we consider the nature of built-in stability in a broader context by comparing the built-in stability in three models we have employed in previous chapters: the Keynesian cross, the Keynesian *IS-LM*, and the classical *IS-LM* models. This analysis suggests a way of improving built-in fiscal stability which we explore in the final part of this section.

○ Empirical Evidence on the Effectiveness of Built-In Fiscal Stabilizers

There is widespread agreement that built-in fiscal stabilizers have substantially dampened the amplitude of cyclical movements in income. Wilfred Lewis, in a careful study of fiscal policy in four early postwar cycles, concluded that "the built-in fiscal stabilizers have made a substantial contribution to the stability of the postwar economy."[6] Peter Eilbott estimates that fiscal stabilizers offset between 36 and 52 percent of the income declines during the three recessions between 1948 and 1960 and from 25 to 42 percent of the rise in income during the three expansions over this period.[7] The ranges reflect different values of parameters in his model. In a comparative study of fiscal policy in seven countries, Bent Hansen concluded that 32 percent of the business cycle was eliminated by the automatic fiscal stabilizers in the U.S. during the 1955–1965 period.[8]

○ The Nature of Built-In Stability in Three Models

The models that we have developed in previous chapters included three types of built-in stability: built-in stability due to income-induced changes in tax revenue (as in the Keynesian cross model in Chapter 6), due to income-induced changes in the interest rate (as in the Keynesian *IS-LM* model in Chapter 10), and due to price-induced declines in interest rates and increases in wealth (as in the classical model in Chapter 9). Any change in the structure of the economy which reduces positive feedback or increases negative feedback enhances built-in stability.

Endogenous Tax Revenues. Endogenous tax revenues (i.e., $T = tX$) reduce the positive feedback associated with the Keynesian consumption income multiplier and thereby reduce all model multipliers and improve the economy's built-in stability. Any disturbance which reduces aggregate demand and income also reduces tax revenues, so that disposable income falls by less than *GNP*, thereby cushioning the effect of the disturbance on consumption. Note that this aspect of built-in fiscal stability only dampens but cannot reverse or fully offset the effect of a disturbance on income. A simple example from the Keynesian cross model will illustrate this. If $C_y = .7$ and tax revenues are exogenous, the Keynesian cross multiplier for the response of income to an autonomous change in aggregate demand is

---

[6] Wilfred Lewis, Jr., *Federal Fiscal Policy in the Postwar Recessions* (Washington: The Brookings Institution, 1962), p. 15.

[7] Peter Eilbott, "The Effectiveness of Automatic Stabilizers," *American Economic Review*, Vol. LVI (June, 1966), pp. 450–465.

[8] Bent Hansen, *Fiscal Policy in Seven Countries, 1955–65* (Paris: Organization for Economic Cooperation and Development, 1969).

$$\frac{\Delta X}{\Delta Z} = \frac{1}{1-C_y} = 3.3. \tag{25.4a}$$

If we add endogenous tax revenues, the multiplier becomes

$$\frac{\Delta X}{\Delta Z} = \frac{1}{1-(1-t)C_y} = 2.0 \tag{25.4b}$$

where $t = .3$. A measure of the degree of built-in stability is the ratio of the two multipliers [equation (25.4b) divided by equation (25.4a)] called the *index of built-in stabilization* (σ).

$$\sigma = \frac{1-C_y}{1-(1-t)C_y} = .6 \tag{25.5}$$

The index indicates the percentage reduction in the income multiplier due to the existence of built-in fiscal stabilizers. The built-in stability in the economy does not derive exclusively from the fiscal stabilizers. In the next two sections we consider other components of the economy's overall built-in stability.

Negative Feedback in the Keynesian IS-LM Model. Assuming tax revenues are also endogenous in the Keynesian *IS-LM* model, built-in stability is greater in this model for real sector disturbances if the monetary authorities maintain a constant money supply (or constant supply of high-powered money). The added built-in stability reflects the *negative feedback* associated with income-induced changes in the interest rate. If autonomous private demand declines, for example, both tax revenues and the interest rate decline. The decline in the interest rate stimulates investment (and consumption if there is an interest-induced wealth effect), thereby cushioning the decline in income associated with the decline in autonomous aggregate demand. Once again, however, the built-in stability will only *partially* offset the disturbance.

The index of built-in stability for the economy with both endogenous tax revenues and income-induced variation in the interest rate relative to the Keynesian cross with exogenous tax revenues is

$$\sigma = \frac{1-C_y}{1-(1-t)C_y + \frac{L_x}{L_r}I_r} = .33$$

assuming $C_y = .7$, $t = .3$, $L_x = .2$, $L_r = -20$, and $I_r = -40$.

Price Flexibility and Built-In Stability in the Classical Model. The built-in stability in the classical model, on the other hand, provides for a *complete* rather than a partial offset to disturbances. If there is an autonomous decline in aggregate demand, prices fall. As prices fall, the real money supply and the real value of household net worth increase and this induces an increase in investment and consumption. As long as aggregate demand is below full employment, prices are falling and aggregate demand is rising. This process continues until the price decline has fully offset the effect of the disturbance on aggregate demand.

Proportional vs. Cumulative Controls

The distinction between built-in stability in the Keynesian cross and Keynesian *IS-LM* models, on the one hand, and the built-in stability in the classical model, on the other hand, is that the former is partial and the latter is complete. Both the endogenous tax revenues and income-induced changes in the interest rate are forms of *proportional controls*: in response to a decline in aggregate demand and income, proportional controls yield a *once-and-for-all* dampening effect proportional to the decline in income. Proportional controls only permit partial offsets. The price flexibility in the classical model, on the other hand, is an example of a *cumulative control*: in response to a decline in aggregate demand, cumulative controls yield *continuing* changes in some variable which are proportional to the *gap* between aggregate demand and the initial level of output. Thus, prices continue to decline at a rate proportional to the gap between aggregate demand and full employment output. Cumulative controls are therefore capable of fully offsetting disturbances.[9]

Improving Built-In Stability

Given the obstacles to effective discretionary fiscal policy, there have been a number of proposals to abandon discretionary policy altogether and to rely exclusively on an improved system of built-in stability. In this section we will consider the proposal by Milton Friedman, although there have been other similar proposals.[10] The proposal has three key elements.

1. Set government expenditures at a level that reflects the community's desire for public services. Do not vary G in response to cyclical developments.

2. Set tax rates to yield revenue equal to government expenditures when the economy is operating at full employment; i.e., set t so that

$$\bar{G} = tX_f. \tag{25.6a}$$

3. Finance all deficits by issuing money:

$$\Delta m \equiv \bar{G} - tX. \tag{25.6b}$$

The key feature of this proposal is the introduction of an automatic cumulative control via the link between income-induced changes in the deficit and increases in the money supply. The fixed price *IS-LM* model with the Friedman proposal now exhibits the same automatic tendency to return to full employment as in the flexible

---

[9] The distinction between these two types of controls is developed by A. W. Phillips, "Stabilization Policy in a Closed Economy," *Economic Journal*, Vol. 64 (June, 1954), pp. 290–323.

[10] Milton Friedman, "A Monetary and Fiscal Framework for Economic Stability," *American Economic Review*, Vol. 38 (June, 1948), pp. 245–264. See also Committee for Economic Development, *Taxes and the Budget: A Program for Prosperity in a Free Economy* (New York: CED, 1947).

price version. In both cases, the real money supply increases as long as output is below the full employment level; this stimulates aggregate demand until output again equals the full employment level. In the flexible price model, the increase in real money balances occurs at an unchanged nominal money supply as the price level declines in response to excess supply in the output market; in the fixed price model under the Friedman proposal, the increase in real money balances occurs at an unchanged price level as the nominal money supply increases in response to the deficit induced by the decline in income.

The Fiscal Drag and the Fiscal Dividend

In a growing economy tax revenues increase if the economy is maintained at full employment. The tendency of a balanced budget at full employment to be automatically transformed into a full employment surplus if government expenditures fail to grow at the same rate as tax revenues gives rise to what is referred to as *fiscal drag*. The budget automatically turns restrictive and becomes a drag on the economy. A more optimistic way of viewing the same phenomenon is that economic growth yields a *fiscal dividend*, the added revenue at unchanged tax rates. This fiscal dividend permits either growing government expenditures at unchanged tax rates or the same level of government expenditures at progressively lower tax rates or some combination of these. However, if neither of these options is exploited, the dividend becomes a drag!

THE RESPONSE OF INCOME TO DISCRETIONARY FISCAL ACTIONS

We have considered the response of income to fiscal actions throughout the text. In this section we summarize our treatment of the response to fiscal actions and relate it to the structure of large-scale income-expenditure models.

Summarizing the Response to Fiscal Actions

In this section we will sketch the main features of the response to fiscal actions we developed in earlier chapters.

The Direct Fiscal Impact. Changes in fiscal instruments have a direct impact on aggregate demand. G is a component of aggregate demand; therefore, changes in G initially alter aggregate demand dollar-for-dollar. Tax changes have their initial impact on disposable income and hence on consumption; a dollar decline in tax revenues initially increases aggregate demand by C_y dollars where C_y is the propensity to consume out of income.

The Simple Keynesian Income-Consumption Multiplier. In Chapter 6 we developed the role of the simple consumption multiplier. As income responds to fiscal actions, disposable income and hence consumption also increase. This positive feedback *multiplies* the response of income to fiscal actions. Taking $C_y = .7$, its long-run value according to empirical evidence is (see Chapter 12)

$$\frac{\Delta X}{\Delta G} = \frac{1}{1 - C_y} = 3.3. \tag{25.7a}$$

There are two important modifications of the simple consumption multiplier:

1. Endogenous tax revenues reduce all multipliers by reducing the positive feedback. As income increases, disposable income increases by less then *GNP*, dampening the response of consumption to fiscal actions. Assuming $t = .3$,

$$\frac{\Delta X}{\Delta G} = \frac{1}{1 - (1 - t)C_y} = 2.0. \tag{25.7b}$$

2. The life cycle hypothesis suggests that the short-run (e.g., one-year) multiplier will be still smaller. The first year value of C_y is estimated at about .4 (see Chapter 13). Therefore, assuming $w_0 C_y = .4$ and $t = .3$,

$$\frac{\Delta X}{\Delta G} = \frac{1}{1 - (1 - t)w_0 C_y} = 1.4. \tag{25.7c}$$

Negative Feedback. The negative feedback associated with income-induced changes in the interest rate further reduces the multiplier. We initially introduced this feedback response in Chapter 10. As income increases in response to expansionary fiscal action, the demand for money increases relative to the fixed money supply. As wealth owners attempt to sell bonds to acquire more money balances, the interest rate rises and this in turn restricts investment.

Taking $L_x = .2$, $L_r = -20$, and $I_r = -40$,

$$\frac{\Delta X}{\Delta G} = \frac{1}{1 - (1 - t)C_y + \frac{L_x}{L_r}I_r} = 1.1. \tag{25.8a}$$

There were a number of refinements of the income-induced rise in the interest rate introduced in subsequent chapters:

1. The interest-induced wealth effect (introduced in Chapter 13) makes consumption responsive to the income-induced rise in the interest rate and further reduces the multiplier. To capture this effect, we replaced I_r with $I_r + C_a g_r$.

2. Lagged response of investment to interest rate changes (introduced in Chapter 15), on the other hand, reduces the extent of negative feedback in the short run. We captured this by writing $I_r = \beta k_r$ where β is the speed of adjustment coefficient in the stock adjustment model of investment.

3. The term structure equation (introduced in Chapters 20 and 22) reduces the short-run response of long-term rates to income-induced increases in short-term rates. We captured this by replacing I_r with αI_r where α is the coefficient on the current short-term rate in the term structure equation.

The three refinements modify the multiplier as follows:

$$\frac{\Delta X}{\Delta G} = \frac{1}{1 - \underbrace{(1-t)w_0 C_y}_{\text{life cycle}} + \underbrace{(L_x/L_r)}_{\text{term structure}}(\underbrace{\alpha\beta k_r}_{\substack{\text{lagged} \\ \text{response} \\ \text{of investment}}} + \underbrace{C_a g_r}_{\substack{\text{interest-induced} \\ \text{wealth effect}}})} \tag{25.8b}$$

Setting $\alpha = .4$ (the sum of the weights in the first year in the term structure equation in Chapter 20) and setting $\beta = .25$ (assuming 25 percent of the increase in the capital stock occurs over the first year), and ignoring the $C_a g_r$ term, the one-year multiplier is 1.3.

The Accelerator. The accelerator (introduced in Chapters 14 and 15) has a profound influence on the short-run dynamics of income in response to fiscal actions; it increases the short-run response but may contribute to an oscillatory response of income to fiscal actions. Adding the accelerator term to the one-year Keynesian cross multiplier (with endogenous taxes and life cycle consumption function), for example, increases the multiplier from 1.4 to

$$\frac{\Delta X}{\Delta G} = \frac{1}{1 - (1-t)w_0 C_y - I_x} = 1.9 \tag{25.9}$$

when $I_x = .2$.

Bond Financing and Crowding-Out. The bond financing of changes in government expenditures and taxes has no effect in our two-asset framework as long as $L_a = 0$. If $L_a > 0$, on the other hand, bond financing has a cumulative restrictive effect, although the short-run multiplier remains unambiguously positive. The multiplier in this case (ignoring other refinements to the Keynesian *IS-LM* model discussed above) is

$$\frac{\Delta X}{\Delta G} = \frac{1}{1 - C_y + \dfrac{L_x + L_a(1 - C_y)}{L_r} I_r} \tag{25.10}$$

where the $L_a(1 - C_y)$ term in the denominator reflects the additional element of negative feedback in this case.

The long-run response to bond-financed fiscal policy depends on the interaction of the portfolio impacts and the direct wealth impacts; the latter have cumulative positive impacts on aggregate demand as long as income is rising in response to the fiscal action. The net effect of the interaction of the wealth and portfolio impacts is ambiguous; however, we noted in Chapter 22 that the model will be unstable if the portfolio impact dominates. In addition, the portfolio impact itself is ambiguous in a multi-asset framework (see the appendices to Chapters 20 and 22).

Price Flexibility. Price flexibility via the Phillips curve (see Chapter 18) insures that *long-run fiscal multipliers are all zero.* The economy eventually settles down at the noninflationary or nonaccelerating inflation rate of unemployment. The Phillips curve also makes *initial conditions* crucial in predicting the response of output to fiscal actions; the short-run response of output to fiscal actions is greater, the greater the initial slack in the economy.

Modeling Fiscal Action in Large-Scale Income-Expenditure Models

The *MPS* model indicates that the negative feedback responses (via the income-induced rise in interest rates and the Phillips curve) work more slowly than the expansive direct impact and positive feedback responses (via the consumption multiplier and accelerator). Therefore, output continues to expand for several quarters before the combined effect of the accelerator and negative feedback cause a turnaround in output. The peak cumulative multiplier is about 2.0 after 5 quarters and by 8 quarters the cumulative multiplier is close to zero, due more to the accelerator than to the role of negative feedback or the Phillips curve. Thereafter, income oscillates around zero before settling down. On the other hand, the *MPS* model assumes $L_a = 0$ and therefore does not allow for a restrictive cumulative impact associated with bond financing.[11]

EVIDENCE ON THE RESPONSE TO FISCAL ACTIONS

Below, we will report the evidence on the size and time pattern of the response to fiscal actions from both monetarist reduced forms and income-expenditure structural models.

The Monetarist Reduced-Form Results

The most widely cited monetarist reduced form was estimated by Leonall Andersen and Jerry Jordan.[12] We discussed their results for money multipliers in the previous chapter. Their cumulative multipliers for the response of nominal *GNP* to a sustained increase in nominal government expenditures is reported in Table 25.3. The multiplier builds up to almost unity by the second quarter, then declines to almost zero by the fourth quarter. Thus, the A-J reduced form indicates rapid nominal crowding-out in response to increases in government expenditures. Tax changes had virtually no effect and were excluded from their preferred equation.

---

[11] For a discussion of fiscal policy in the *MPS* model, see Franco Modigliani and Albert Ando, "Impacts of Fiscal Actions on Aggregate Income and the Monetarist Controversy: Theory and Evidence," in Jerome Stein (ed.), *Monetarism* (New York: Elsevier North-Holland Inc., 1976). The results reported for the fiscal multipliers in this paragraph differ somewhat from those reported in Table 25.4. This may reflect a combination of different initial conditions and different versions of the *MPS* model used to derive the multipliers in the two sources.

[12] Leonall Andersen and Jerry L. Jordan, "Monetary and Fiscal Actions: A Test of Their Relative Importance in Economic Stabilization," Federal Reserve Bank of St. Louis *Review* (November, 1968), pp. 11–24.

Period	Cumulative Multiplier
1	.40
2	.94
3	.91
4	.17

Source: Leonall Andersen and Jerry L. Jordan, "Monetary and Fiscal Actions: A Test of Their Relative Importance in Economic Stabilization," Federal Reserve Bank of St. Louis *Review* (November, 1968), p. 17.

TABLE 25.3

The Andersen-Jordan Equation: The Response of Nominal *GNP* to a Sustained Increase in Nominal Government Expenditures

○ Results from Income-Expenditure Structural Models

Fiscal multipliers derived via policy simulations of large-scale structural models are reported in Table 25.4. In contrast to the A-J equation, these models can be used to derive multipliers for changes in real or nominal *GNP* in response to changes in real or nominal government expenditures or changes in tax rates. In Table 25.4 we report multipliers for the response of real *GNP* to a sustained increase in real government expenditures. The multipliers generally build up over the first year and in some cases continue to increase over the second and third years. The peak multiplier is in the 1.5–2.5 range and the multipliers fall off to zero after as few as four years in the *MPS* model; Q^* in Table 25.4 indicates the period (in quarters) during which the multiplier goes to zero. Q^* is shown as a range rather than a specific quarter because the paper which reported the results only reported multipliers in every fourth quarter after the eighth quarter. The multipliers for changes in nominal *GNP* are larger since both output and prices initially increase in response to fiscal stimulus in these models. In addition, the effect on prices is generally a permanent one in these models; indeed, the increase in the price level is a key element in the mechanism whereby real private expenditures are ultimately crowded out by real government expenditures.

Model (initial Q)	1	4	8	12	Q^*
MPS	1.2	2.2	2.2	0.7	13–16
Wharton III (1965 I)	1.3	2.0	2.4	2.6	29–32
DRI (1962 I)	1.4	1.6	0.9	0.6	17–20
Michigan (1962 I)	1.4	1.7	1.4	1.0	37–40

Source: Gary Fromm and Lawrence R. Klein, "A Comparison of Eleven Econometric Models of the United States," *American Economic Review, Papers and Proceedings*, Vol. LXIII (May, 1973), p. 391.

TABLE 25.4

Cumulative Fiscal Policy Multipliers for Several Large-Scale Econometric Models: The Response of Real *GNP* to a Sustained Increase in Real Government Expenditures

All these models are nonlinear and therefore have multipliers which vary with initial conditions. We therefore noted the initial quarter of the simulation for the three models for which the initial quarter was reported. The multipliers tend to be larger over periods with considerable slack and smaller when the economy begins around full employment.

THE MONETARIST CRITIQUE AND INCOME-EXPENDITURE COUNTERATTACK

The monetarist critique of the treatment of fiscal policy in large-scale econometric models is motivated in part by dissatisfaction with the structure of those models, but it also reflects the skepticism about the usefulness of the structural model approach for the empirical estimation of policy multipliers and the resulting preference for the reduced-form approach. The income-expenditure theorists have responded to the monetarist critique both with a defense of their own models and with an attack on the adequacy of the reduced-form technique preferred by monetarists.

The Monetarist Critique

We noted above that monetarist reduced forms suggest smaller fiscal policy multipliers than income-expenditure structural models. The monetarist critique of income-expenditure (IE) modeling of fiscal policy attempts to explain why. There are two major criticisms: incorrect estimates of key parameter values and failure to model the cumulative impact of bond financing.

Judgments About Empirical Parameters. Monetarists generally hold that L_r is very small and the interest-responsiveness of aggregate demand (I_r in our simplest model) is quite large (in absolute values). The LM curve is viewed as positively sloped but very steep and the IS curve as both quite flat and subject to small shifts in response to fiscal actions because of a large (absolute) value of I_r. A high value of I_r combined with a low value of L_r produces a "minor" effect of fiscal action on aggregate demand.[13] The effects of the high I_r/low L_r and low I_r/high L_r sets of parameter values on the response of income to equal-sized autonomous shifts in aggregate demand are depicted in Figures 25.1a and 25.1b. This difference is often caricatured as the difference between the monetarist view that $L_r = 0$ and the IE view that $L_r = -\infty$ and/or $I_r = 0$. Neither of these attributions appears to apply to any of the major proponents of either monetarism or IE models. Nevertheless, as we learned in Chapter 10, L_r and I_r have asymmetric effects on fiscal and monetary policy multipliers; differences in judgment about these parameters are indeed an important element in the disagreement about the magnitude of fiscal multipliers. We noted in the previous chapter that monetarists view structural attempts to capture the interest rate-aggregate demand relation with considerable skepticism. In the case of fiscal policy, this means that such models are likely to understate the extent of negative feedback associated with income-induced increases in the interest rate.

---

[13] See, for example, Milton Friedman, "Comment on the Critics" in Robert J. Gordon (ed.), *Milton Friedman's Monetary Framework: A Debate With His Critics* (Chicago: University of Chicago Press, 1974), particularly pages 140–141.

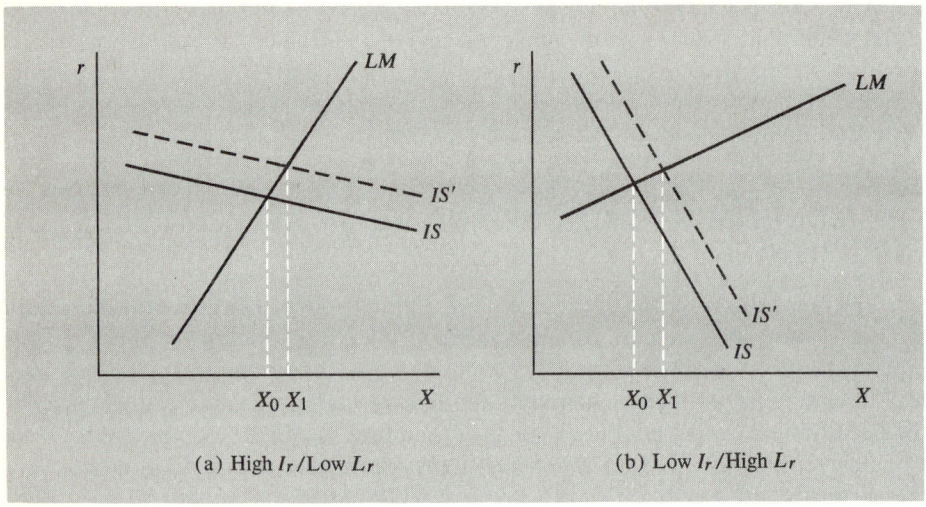

FIGURE 25.1
Monetarist and *IE* Views of Fiscal Policy: The Flow Effect

Impact vs. Cumulative Effects and Flows vs. Stocks. The second element in the monetarist critique is that whatever effect emerges initially from the *flow disturbance* (the once-and-for-all change in the level of government expenditures, ΔG) will be ultimately swamped by the effect of the associated changes in stocks. We know from the government financing constraint that a once-and-for-all change in G will result in continuing changes in money and/or bonds to finance the resulting deficit. If the deficit is financed by money issue, the continuing shifts in the *LM* curve may quickly swamp the effect of the once-and-for-all shift in the *IS* curve. If the deficit is financed by the sale of bonds, the increase in government bonds may crowd out private debt, raise interest rates, and quickly offset the positive flow multiplier.

○ The Income-Expenditure Counterattack

The *IE* counterattack points to the general consensus concerning the values of L_r and I_r in econometric models, the evidence in support of the pure transactions approach to the demand for money ($L_a = 0$), the logical implications of a negative cumulative impact of bond financing, and evidence suggesting that the simple monetarist reduced forms may themselves yield unreliable estimates of fiscal policy multipliers.

Parameter Estimates and Model Multipliers. Current econometric models estimate relatively low interest elasticities for the demand for money and higher and more pervasive interest response on aggregate demand than earlier generations of such models. Indeed, monetarists could well argue that many of these models already yield monetarist conclusions since the fiscal multipliers go to zero within a three- to five-year period. Nevertheless, these models do generally yield two-year multipliers for real *GNP* of about 2.0.

L_a and Fiscal Policy. First of all, we found in Chapter 22 that even if $L_a > 0$, the short-run effect of fiscal policy must be positive once the model is modified to include the relation between investment and private debt. Secondly, the theory underlying the transactions demand rejects the existence of a diversification demand for money and empirical evidence seems quite consistent with such transactions models. Finally, even if $L_a > 0$, the long-run response to bond-financed fiscal policy would not conform to the monetarist view. If bond financing has a restrictive impact, then we found in Chapter 22 that the negative cumulative multiplier becomes progressively larger and the model is unstable.[14]

The Unreliability of Reduced Forms. Recently there has been a growing body of literature on the unreliability of estimates of policy multipliers in simple reduced-form equations. There are three basic problems with the reduced-form approach, at least as implemented in the Andersen-Jordan equation: lack of attention to the problem of specifying the policy instruments, biases associated with the endogeneity of policy actions, and biases associated with the omission of nonpolicy exogenous variables.

1. *Specification of Policy Instruments.* The specification of policy instruments might seem like a simple task; in fact, it requires considerable care.

Fiscal Instruments. The simple reduced forms use high employment levels of G and T or high employment levels of the surplus. The latter is clearly inappropriate and the usual measures of high employment tax revenues also seem to be clearly inadequate. The change in the tax variable should be zero if there are no changes in tax rates, exemptions, etc.; the change in high employment tax revenues generally does not meet this restriction, suggesting a failure to isolate discretionary and automatic changes in tax revenues. A better measure is the *initial stimulus* measure; the discretionary change in tax revenues in this case is computed by multiplying the change in tax rates times the lagged tax base ($\Delta t \cdot X_{-1}$).

Monetary Policy Instruments. The specification of the monetary policy instrument is even more subject to controversy. If the Fed sets policy in terms of a reserve aggregate (such as nonborrowed reserves), changes in government expenditures will induce increases in both income *and money supply.* If the reduced form is estimated using the money supply as the policy instrument, the multiplier for an increase in government expenditures will be biased downward; the multiplier for a ΔG at unchanged money supply is equivalent to the sum of the fiscal multiplier for a ΔG and the monetary policy multiplier for open market sales required to maintain the money supply constant as interest rates rise in response to the fiscal action. Frank deLeeuw and John Kalchbrenner, for example, report much higher fiscal multipliers when nonborrowed reserves are employed as the monetary policy instrument.[15]

---

[14] Furthermore, in a multi-asset framework, $L_a > 0$ does not rule out a positive effect of bond financing on income due to the interaction of wealth and substitution effects. And if $L_a = 0$ in the multi-asset model, bond financing is unambiguously expansionary!

[15] Frank deLeeuw and John Kalchbrenner, "Monetary and Fiscal Actions: A Test of Their Relative Importance in Economic Stabilization—A Comment," Federal Reserve Bank of St. Louis *Review* (April, 1969), pp. 6–11.

2. *Endogenous Policy and Downward Bias on Reduced-Form Policy Multipliers.* We have been treating policy instruments as exogenous rather than endogenous variables. Policymakers, however, may respond systematically to changes in income; indeed, if policy is truly random, it is certain to destabilize rather than to stabilize income.[16] Assume that there is a single policy instrument and that it is manipulated so perfectly that all exogenous disturbances are immediately offset and income always remains unchanged. If we estimated the relation

$$\Delta X = \alpha_0 + \alpha_1 \Delta P, \tag{25.11}$$

the coefficient on ΔP would be *zero*! ΔP would generally be a large number (plus or minus) and ΔX would always be zero. In this case the small value of the policy multiplier reflects the effectiveness of the policy not the magnitude of the change in income associated with policy changes.[17]

3. *The Role of Omitted Exogenous Variables.* The simple reduced forms ignore all nonpolicy exogenous variables; they thus fail "to hold all other things constant" and this may bias the reduced-form multipliers if fiscal policy is systematically related to some of these omitted variables. For example, assume there is one nonpolicy variable (Z) and that the policy authority tries to move the instrument to offset movements in the disturbance; although the offset is not perfect, P and Z tend to move inversely. If we estimate X as a function of both Z and P, we will isolate the role of the policy instrument. However, if we omit Z, we will tend to get a downward biased estimate of the multiplier on P because the coefficient of P will tend to pick up the influence of movement in both P and the omitted (and correlated) exogenous variable Z. Thus, the role of omitted exogenous variables may simply be another example of the problem of estimating reduced forms when policy is endogenous.

Franco Modigliani and Albert Ando report an ingenious simulation experiment which confirms the bias associated with omitted exogenous variables in simple reduced forms.[18] Assume that we know the precise equations corresponding to our economy. We could then compare the simple reduced-form multipliers with our model multipliers which in turn are the "true" multipliers. Of course, we do not know the "true" equations but we can do the following experiment. Treat the equations of some econometric model (such as the *MPS* model) as if they were the "true" equations. The predicted values of the endogenous variables are now the "actual" data in our hypothetical economy and the policy multipliers derived from policy simulations are the "true" policy multipliers. We can now use "actual" values of income (the predicted value

---

[16] For a simple proof, see Milton Friedman, "The Effects of a Full Employment Policy on Economic Stabilization: A Formal Analysis," in Milton Friedman, *Essays In Positive Economics* (Chicago: The University of Chicago Press, 1953), pp. 117–132.

[17] For an excellent analysis of the implications of endogenous policy for empirical estimates of reduced-form parameters, see Stephen M. Goldfeld and Alan S. Blinder, "Some Implications of Endogenous Stabilization Policy," *Brookings Papers on Economic Activity* (1972:3), pp. 585–640.

[18] Franco Modigliani and Albert Ando, "Impacts of Fiscal Actions on Aggregate Income and the Monetarist Controversy: Theory and Evidence," in Jerome Stein (ed.), *Monetarism* (New York: Elsevier North-Holland Inc., 1976).

of income from the equations of the model) along with values of fiscal and monetary policy instruments to estimate a simple reduced form. Modigliani and Ando report that the fiscal multipliers estimated in this way are all biased substantially downward in the reduced forms. To determine whether correlation between omitted exogenous variables and fiscal instruments may be responsible for this result, they treat all untrended exogenous variables as constant at their sample means and all trended exogenous variables as constant trends. This removes any possible correlation with policy instruments. A new set of "actual" data is generated by solving for predicted values of all endogenous variables and a new reduced form is estimated. The fiscal multipliers now turn out to be quite close to the "true" values. The test demonstrates that omitted variables may bias reduced-form results. Of course, it does not definitively provide support for the multipliers of the structural models.

The specification of policy instruments and omitted exogenous variables may not be as serious a problem in large-scale econometric models. These models include government expenditures and a variety of tax rate parameters and permit a range of choices about the monetary policy instrument. They also include a wide range of nonpolicy exogenous variables. The endogeneity of policy, in principle, introduces biases into both structural models and reduced forms. There is some evidence, however, that the bias is much more serious for reduced forms.[19]

● REVIEW QUESTIONS

1. Discuss the institutional features of fiscal decision-making that account for the long inside lag of fiscal policy.

2. "The government deficit is an accurate measure of the stimulus associated with the prevailing budget." Comment.

3. Define the weighted surplus and discuss the choice of weights. How does the weighted surplus overcome the deficiency of the actual surplus as a measure of the stimulus associated with the budget?

4. Compare the nature of the built-in stability in

   (a) the Keynesian cross model with endogenous tax revenues,

   (b) the fixed price *IS-LM* model,

   (c) the flexible price *IS-LM* model, and

   (d) the fixed price *IS-LM* model under the Friedman proposal to set $G = tX_f$ and finance all deficits by increasing the money supply.

5. Discuss the sources of positive and negative feedback in response to an increase in government expenditures.

---

[19] Goldfeld and Blinder, *loc. cit.*

6. Many large-scale econometric models exhibit cumulative fiscal multipliers which decline to zero over a three- to five-year period. Discuss some of the features of these models that account for this result.

7. What are the central points in the monetarist critique of the treatment of fiscal policy in income-expenditure models?

8. Contrast the empirical evidence on fiscal policy multipliers based on reduced forms and structural models.

9. Discuss the basis for the income-expenditure critique of monetarist reduced forms.

● PROBLEMS

1. Compare the movement in the weighted full employment surplus (S_{wf}) and the weighted initial surplus (S_{wi}) in response to

   (a) a change in government expenditures (G)

   (b) a change in tax rates (t)

   (c) changes in G and t in the same direction

   (d) changes in G and t in opposite directions

   Construct the following diagram to make the comparisons. Measure income along the horizontal axis; include a vertical line at X_f to designate the full employment level of income. Measure the weighted surplus (S_w) along the vertical axis. Draw a line corresponding to the equation for the weighted surplus

   $$S_w = C_y tX - \bar{G}$$

   on the diagram. Identify the levels of S_{wf} and S_{wi} along this line. Then find the direction of changes in S_{wf} and S_{wi} in response to each of the changes in (a) through (d) above. Identify the cases where S_{wf} provides the correct signal and the cases where it may yield an incorrect signal about the direction of the policy-induced change in the stimulus associated with the budget.

2. Discuss the following quotes. Use an explicit model (or models) to support your answer.

   (a) "Built-in stabilizers can dampen but never reverse the impact of an exogenous disturbance."

   (b) "If the government sets its expenditures to equal the tax revenues that would be forthcoming at full employment, the economy will tend to return to full employment following any exogenous disturbance."

3. Set up a one-period fixed price *IS-LM* model under the Friedman proposal to set $G = tX_f$ and finance deficits by increasing the money supply. Derive the following multipliers for the response to an autonomous change in private aggregate demand:

(a) the one-period multiplier using a beginning-of-period specification of asset markets, (b) the one-period multiplier using an end-of-period specification, and (c) the equilibrium multiplier that reflects the long-run response to the disturbance.

● EXERCISE

Update Tables 25.1 and 25.2 using the latest available copy of *The Budget of the United States Government.*

Chapter 26

Incomes and Other Supply-Oriented Policies

In this chapter we turn our attention to policies that combat inflation and unemployment, other than the demand management policies discussed in the two previous chapters. Most of the policies discussed however are intended for use with rather than instead of or independent of demand management policies. In the first section we motivate the interest in alternatives or complements to demand management by considering the costs associated with combating inflation through demand management policies alone and then outline the variety of supply as opposed to demand policies that we will consider in this chapter. In the following three sections we discuss voluntary wage-price guideposts, mandatory wage-price controls, and indexation. In the final section we briefly consider a number of other supply-oriented policies.

THE MOTIVATION FOR SUPPLY POLICIES

The motivation for incomes policies in particular and aggregate supply-oriented policies in general is the limitations of demand management policies in combating the dual problems of inflation and unemployment. We noted in Chapter 11 that changes in aggregate demand tend, at least in the short run, to have symmetric effects on output and prices; or, in the context of our Phillips curve models in Chapter 18, stimulative demand management may induce increases in employment and output (at least in the short run) at the expense of (or perhaps in response to) increases in the rate of inflation. There has therefore been an interest in designing policies which affect prices and output asymmetrically; for example, policies which *shift* in the aggregate supply curve or the Phillips curve have the desirable property of affecting prices and output in this asymmetric fashion. We will group such policies under the heading of *aggregate supply policies*. Most of our discussion will be on policies to influence the wage and price setting behavior of firms and unions by exhortation, threat of specific actions, or legislation; the latter set of policies are generally referred to as *incomes policies*, reflecting the European usage of such policies as an attempt to reconcile conflicting income claims so as to avoid what we referred to as incomes inflation in Chapter 11. But aggregate supply policies also include policies to lower the amount of frictional unemployment; policies to increase the downward flexibility of wages and prices by increasing competition, in part by removing government regulations which contribute to inflexibility; and specific government actions to lower the price level. We also consider the role of indexation, the tying of nominal or dollar contracts to the price index to guarantee against unintended changes in real values of income or wealth due to inflation, as a means of reducing both the pain and distortions due to (unanticipated) inflation and of facilitating the transition to stable prices.

○ The Cost of Reducing Inflation in Terms of Permanent or Temporary Increases in Unemployment

To appreciate more fully the interest in alternatives or complements to demand management, consider the cost of reducing or eliminating inflation using such policies alone. Recall that inflation cannot be sustained without monetary accommodation. Traditional demand management, monetary restraint, remains a virtually unchallenged route to eliminating inflation. The problem however is the cost of such an antiinflation program in terms of the increased unemployment it induces (in the short run only under the expectations-augmented vertical long-run Phillips curve and in the short and long run under the traditional specification). These costs are sufficiently high that policymakers are reluctant to use the demand-oriented policies to reduce inflation; instead, monetary policy is directed at accommodating the inflation so that the level of output and employment are not automatically reduced via a decline in the real money supply.

In Figures 26.1a and 26.1b we depict the cost of using demand management policies to eliminate inflation, first in the case of a traditional Phillips curve and then for an expectations-augmented vertical Phillips curve. Demand management policy induces a *movement along* the traditional Phillips curve (*PC*) in Figure 26.1a. Initially the economy is at point *a* where inflation is $\dot{P}_0$. To reduce inflation to zero, demand management policies must move the economy from point *a* to point *b*; the cost of the elimination of inflation is the permanent increase in the unemployment rate from u_0 to u^* (the noninflationary rate of unemployment discussed in Chapter 18). We could then use Okun's Law to compute the loss in output *per year* of maintaining the economy at u^* rather than u_0.

The more relevant case, given the more widely held view that the long-run Phillips curve is vertical (or near vertical), is depicted in Figure 26.1b. Demand management policy initially induces a movement along the short-run Phillips curve (*PC,SR*); e.g., from point *a* to point *b*. The increase in unemployment, however, is only temporary in this case; as unemployment increases, wage gains and hence inflation are moderated and inflationary expectations are accordingly diminished. This in turn induces a downward shift of the short-run Phillips curve so that demand management policy ultimately results in a *movement along* the long-run Phillips curve (*PC,LR*); e.g., from point *a* to point *c*. Although the increased unemployment is only temporary, the cumulative loss of output may be very great, so that, as in the first case, policymakers are reluctant to impose such measures.

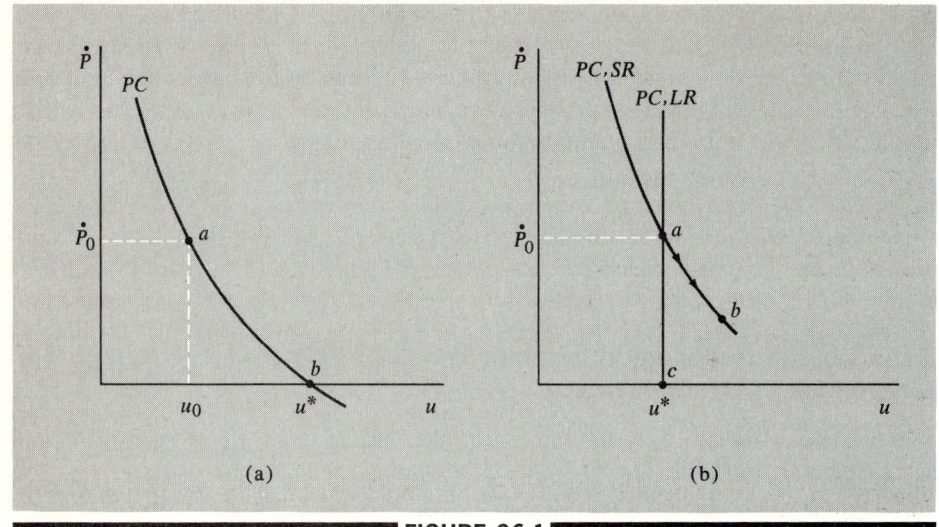

FIGURE 26.1
The Cost of Demand Management Policies

Figure 26.2 depicts the cycling-down of inflation via demand management policies based on the expectations-augmented inflation version of the Phillips curve. The initial impact of such policies is to induce slack in the economy; i.e., to raise u above u^*. As long as $u > u^*$, the inflation rate will be declining; the speed with which economic slack reduces inflation depends on the size of α and is, according to most estimates, quite small. In addition there is a powerful element of inertia, reflected in the expectations term, which depends on past rates of inflation (as in the adaptive expectations model discussed in Chapter 18). The decline in actual inflation rates gradually reduces expected rates, and this in turn feeds back (via the third link) to further reduce the actual rate. The inertia resulting from a small value of α and gradual response of $\dot{P}^e$ to $\dot{P}$ does not mean that demand management cannot cure inflation; it only means that the combination of the size of the rise in unemployment and the duration of the increase in unemployment will be such as to impose extremely high costs in the form of cumulative output loss.

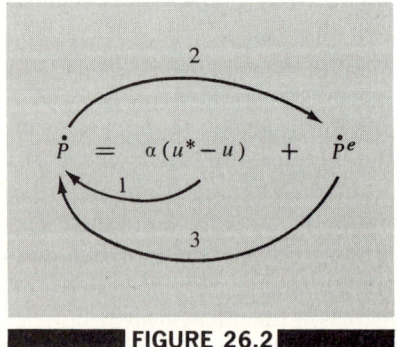

FIGURE 26.2
Cycling-Down the Rate of Inflation via Demand Management Policies

George Perry has recently provided evidence on the cost of demand management policies based on an estimated Phillips curve and a mark-up model of price determination.[1] Perry estimates that any unemployment rate in excess of 5.5 percent, if maintained long enough, will eliminate inflation; thus, 5.5 percent is his estimate of the nonaccelerating inflation rate of unemployment (*NAIRU*) we introduced in Chapter 18.[2] But an extra one percentage-point increase in the unemployment rate would lower the inflation rate by only 0.3 percentage points after one year and 0.7 percentage points after three years. Perry notes that an additional one percentage point of unemployment translates into a loss of one million jobs and a loss of $60 billion in output each year that unemployment remains one percentage point above *NAIRU*. At this rate, it would take about two decades to move from a 6 percent inflation rate to price stability.

While there is widespread agreement that there is an element of inertia in wage-price movements, Perry's estimate of the resulting cost of eradicating inflation seems implausibly high to many. His results may only reflect the dynamics of inflation and unemployment associated with the specific policies pursued during the estimation period. William Poole and William Fellner, for example, suggest that the speed with which inflation expectations can be reduced depends on the degree to which the government makes clear its commitment to eradicate inflation.[3] The Perry equation is based on a model of adaptive expectations in which inflation expectations gradually respond to past inflation rates and are independent of any additional information economic agents may possess such as announced monetary growth targets. Under rational expectations (discussed in the appendix to Chapter 18), economic agents form expectations based on all available information; their response to antiinflation policies will be influenced, in this case, by their perception of current and future policies. Nevertheless, there remains a consensus that the inertia is a serious problem even if the costs it implies for antiinflation policies are substantially smaller than those estimated by Perry.

⃝ The Motivation for and Types of Supply Policies

One motivation for supply policies is to reduce the costs (in terms of cumulative output loss) associated with this cycling-down of inflation rates. Increasing competitiveness in commodity and labor markets, for example, should increase α, making the inflation rate respond more vigorously to economic slack. By reducing the lag with which reductions in actual inflation rates are reflected in current wage demands, indexation is intended to speed up the second link in the cycling-down process, reducing the overall costs of the demand management approach. And price-wage guidelines and controls may permit the government to influence inflation-expectations independently of the unemployment rate. As actual inflation declines, the rate of monetary

---

[1] George Perry, "Slowing the Wage-Price Spiral: A Macroeconomic View," *Brooking Papers on Economic Activity* (1978:2), pp. 259–291. Similar results are presented in Arthur Okun, "Efficient Disinflationary Policies," *American Economic Review, Papers and Proceedings*, Vol. 68 (May, 1978), pp. 348–352.

[2] Perry estimates several alternative versions of a Phillips curve. Not all are vertical in the long run; the interpretation of the 5.5 percent unemployment rate as *NAIRU* holds only for the case of the vertical long-run Phillips curve.

[3] Comments by William Poole and William Fellner on the Perry paper cited above are in *The Brookings Papers on Economic Activity* (1978:2), pp. 259–291.

growth must also decelerate to remain consistent with the decline in inflation.

There is an alternative motivation for wage-price guidelines and controls that more accurately reflects the U.S. experience with both the wage-price guideposts in 1962–1966 and the freezes and phases of 1971–1974. In each case there was considerable slack in the economy, and policymakers were contemplating pursuing stimulative demand policies but feared an acceleration in inflation prior to overall demand pressing on the economy's productive capacity. The role of incomes policies in such a situation is to permit a freer use of stimulative demand management policies by reducing their cost in terms of accelerated inflation. Thus, wage-price guidelines and controls may be used to reinforce either restrictive or stimulative demand policies.

A third use of supply policies is to shift the long-run Phillips curve so that the unemployment rate corresponding to any given inflation rate is reduced. This involves reducing the u^* term in the Phillips curve by reducing the amount of frictional unemployment. Policies which improve the flow of information concerning unemployment and vacancies and increase the mobility of workers (among occupations and regions), policies which increase the incentive to search actively when unemployed, and policies which increase the incentive to remain employed for longer durations all tend to reduce the unemployment rate consistent with any given level of inflation. Another set of policies which can be used independently of demand management policies are those which result in a once-and-for-all shift in the aggregate supply curve. Many government programs such as minimum wage laws, agricultural price supports, and indirect as opposed to direct taxes directly raise the price level; i.e., involve upward shifts of the aggregate supply curve. Finding alternative methods of achieving the objectives of such policies may therefore permit once-and-for all reductions in the price levels.

WAGE-PRICE GUIDEPOSTS

The wage-price guideposts were introduced in 1962. There was at the time considerable slack and reasonably stable prices. The motivation for introducing the guideposts was to avoid a repetition of the experience from 1955 to 1958 when prices began to rise well before the economy reached what was regarded as full employment. The guideposts were introduced to complement stimulative demand management policies which were under consideration at the time and which were finally activated in the tax cut of 1964. It was hoped that guideposts would permit these stimulative policies to reduce the slack in the economy without an acceleration in inflation. In this section we will discuss the analytical basis of the guideposts, the development of the guidepost concept, and effectiveness of the guideposts.[4]

The Arithmetic of Wages, Prices, and Productivity

The introduction of guideposts in 1962 was an attempt to educate labor and business about the simple arithmetic of wages, prices, and productivity. The guideposts

---

[4] For an excellent survey of the theory of an experience with the guideposts, see John Sheahan, *The Wage-Price Guideposts* (Washington: The Brookings Institution, 1967).

were often referred to as "advisory" or "educational aids." The initial statement of guideposts, in the 1962 *Economic Report of the President*, emphasized the requirements of a noninflationary wage settlement.

> The general guide for noninflationary wage behavior is that the rate of increase in wage rates . . . in each industry be equal to the overall trend rate of productivity increase.[5]

This rule follows from the relationship between the real wage and the marginal product of labor (F_N) under perfect competition; i.e., $\frac{W}{P} = F_N$ and, taking logs and first differences,

$$\dot{P} = \dot{W} - \rho \tag{26.1}$$

where $\dot{P}$, $\dot{W}$, and ρ are proportional rates of change in prices, nominal wages, and productivity, respectively. The guidepost rule is to set

$$\dot{W} = \rho^* \tag{26.2}$$

where ρ^* is the economy's overall trend rate of growth in productivity. If prices are constant to begin with, this rule will result in real wages increasing at the same rate as productivity (as would occur under perfect competition).

The guide for the noninflationary price behavior was that prices should on average remain constant; with wages increasing at ρ^*, the trend rate of increase in productivity, unit labor costs would remain constant and prices should also remain constant. In particular, the rule was that prices should respond to the trend in unit labor costs in each industry, i.e.,

$$\dot{P}_i^* = \dot{W}^* - \rho_i^* \tag{26.3}$$

where $\dot{P}_i^*$ is the inflation rate in the ith industry, ρ_i^* is the trend rate of growth in productivity in that industry, and $\dot{W}^*$ is the rate of wage inflation associated with the guidepost rule. This implies that prices should remain stable in industries where the productivity trend is equal to the economy's overall trend, and prices should fall where productivity growth is above average and rise where it is below average.

◯ The Analytical Basis for the Guideposts

The guideposts were designed to avoid what Robert Solow has called "the problem of premature inflation," the tendency of wages and prices to begin to rise unacceptably rapidly prior to the economy reaching full employment.[6] While the existence of such premature inflation is consistent with the traditional specification of the Phillips curve, the guideposts were not in fact designed to cope with the response of prices or wages

---

[5] *The Economic Report of the President* (Washington: U.S. Government Printing Office, 1962), p. 189.

[6] For a cautious defense of the guideposts, see Robert Solow, "The Case Against the Case Against Guideposts," in George Shultz and Robert Aliber (eds.), *Guidelines, Informal Controls, and the Market Place* (Chicago: University of Chicago Press, 1966), pp. 41–54.

to excess demands—either to sectoral excess demand or to overall excess demand. The underlying model is rather one of cost-push pressure on prices and wages and the response of cost-push pressures to overall demand conditions in the economy. The important institutional feature of the economy, according to advocates of the guideposts, is that, in many sectors, prices are administered by large firms and wages set by bargaining with unions. In these sectors, prices and wages are not the outcome of impersonal supply and demand forces; rather, there is an important element of discretion in price and wage setting.[7] This leaves an element of autonomy in the wage-price decisions of firms and unions, and the resulting range of indeterminacy for wage and price movements suggests a possible role for government influence via incomes policies.

To generate the acceleration in inflation as the economy approaches (but remains below) full employment, there must also be a link between the cost-push pressures and the overall state of demand. This is provided by the presumed effect of the demand on market power of firms and/or on the ability of firms to exploit existing market power, inducing an increase in markups of prices over wages; and the effect of increases in the demand on the market power of unions or on the ability of unions to exploit their existing monopoly power and achieve higher wage gains. In the background, the Fed is assumed to be validating the resulting inflation so as to avoid the increase in unemployment that would otherwise result (at least in the short run) from such cost-push pressure on prices and wages.[8]

The purpose of the guideposts was to induce large firms and unions to behave as if they were perfect competitors. Wage gains would accordingly be limited to productivity gains, at least in the absence of inflation. And firms, by maintaining unchanged markups over variable costs (primarily unit labor costs), would then maintain overall price stability, assuming stability in nonwage variable costs.

○ The Limitations of the Guideposts

The guideposts were not designed to restrain inflation associated with excess demand and, therefore, presumably would not have been effective in reducing inflation associated with either sectoral or overall excess demand. Thus, the usefulness of the guideposts is linked to the cost-push nature of the inflation process. In addition, as long as inflation is affected by the state of aggregate demand, continued inflation requires monetary accommodation. Therefore, monetary restraint remains an effective means of controlling inflation. Any attempt by sectors with market power to increase prices will reduce real purchasing power and result in offsetting price declines elsewhere, provided that prices are flexible elsewhere and that the monetary authority is not accommodating the price increases. If prices do not fall elsewhere (because of downward price rigidity or sluggishness), cost-push pressures on prices will induce unemployment without accommodation and continuing inflation with accommodation. The Fed may opt for the latter, given its concern with the maintenance of full employment.

---

[7] This view is expressed in *Economic Report of the President*, 1962, p. 185.

[8] For a discussion of the logic of guideposts which emphasizes cost-push and demand elements, see Gardner Ackley, "The Contribution of Guidelines," in George Shultz and Robert Aliber (eds.), *Guidelines, Informal Controls, and the Market Place* (Chicago: University of Chicago Press, 1966), pp. 67–78.

○ The Breakdown of the Guideposts

The guideposts appeared to work effectively in the manufacturing sector where unit labor costs remained quite stable through the middle of 1966. The major departure within manufacturing was the failure of prices to fall in industries experiencing above-average productivity growth. The guidepost concept broke down, however, in response to price increases that continued in other sectors and that accelerated in the second half of 1965 and 1966. The equity concept of guideposts (i.e., real wage gains equal to the productivity trend) would require that the wage increases be allowed to recoup both the increases in productivity and the rise in the cost of living. This, however, would have undermined the stability of prices in manufacturing. Unit labor costs would rise, put upward pressure on prices, and set off a wage-price spiral, assuming the Fed was willing to accommodate the accelerated inflation, or an increase in unemployment otherwise.

There was no simple solution and the CEA sought to encourage a compromise; workers should accept wage increases which, although in excess of productivity gains, did not fully incorporate the increases in the *CPI*.[9] But the CEA abandoned any precise numerical guide for wage behavior in its 1967 report. The increased spending for social programs and the Vietnam War were now pushing the economy toward an excess demand situation far different from the environment in which wage-price guideposts were initially proposed. It is generally agreed that wage-price guideposts, to the extent that they were effective at all, affected wage-price behavior over the 1962–1966 period and thereafter were not a factor.

○ The Enforcement of the Guideposts

The wage-price guideposts in the 1962–1966 period were a voluntary program, enforced only by means of exhortation and admonition from the government. At the other extreme are the mandatory wage-price controls employed at times during 1971–1974; these imposed specific quantitative limits on wage and price changes carried the full force of law. In between, there is a range of measures that government can employ to support its guideposts, short of making them legally binding. The government can increase its pressure on firms and unions by setting up special agencies to review wage and price decisions. These reviews could be conducted prior to important wage-price decisions by requiring prenotification of such changes, or they could be conducted after such changes with the option of "rolling back" excessive wage and price increases. In addition, the government could threaten specific actions detrimental to firms and/or industries which failed to cooperate. The threat of tariff reductions, relaxed import quotas, increased antitrust scrutiny, and accelerated release of commodities from government stockpiles might be effective in some industries. The threat of withdrawal of government contracts could be effective in dealing with specific firms.

More recently there have been a number of suggestions for providing economic

---

[9] *The Economic Report of the President*, 1967, pp. 128–129.

incentives to comply with the wage-price guidelines suggested by the government. These plans are generally referred to as *tax-based incomes policies* (*TIP*) because they use the tax system to penalize noncompliance or reward compliance with the guidelines.[10] The *Wallich-Weintraub plan*,[11] for example, would impose a penalty tax on employers who grant excessive wage increases. Those who comply would pay the normal tax rate on corporate profits. Those who granted wage increases in excess of the guideline figure would pay higher tax rates; and the greater the noncompliance, the greater the increase in the tax rate. An alternative plan advanced by Okun[12] would reward employees for compliance with the guidelines by granting a tax reduction to workers if their firm's average increase in pay conformed to the target in the guidelines.[13]

○ Did the Guideposts Work?

Wage change remained moderate during the period from 1962 through 1965. But the effectiveness of the guideposts must be judged by whether or not wage gains were smaller than they would have been in the absence of the guideposts. Empirical studies of the effects of guideposts generally begin, therefore, by developing a model to determine what wage gains would have been in the absence of guideposts. Perry, for example, estimates a Phillips curve equation for wage change using quarterly data over the period of 1947–1960.[14] The basic form of the equation is

$$\% \Delta W_t = \alpha \left(\frac{1}{u_t}\right) + \beta \% \Delta P_{t-1} + \gamma \tag{26.4}$$

where $\% \Delta W_t$ is the percentage change in the nominal wage rate (straight-time hourly earnings) over the previous year, u_t is the unemployment rate, and $\% \Delta P_{t-1}$ is the percentage change in the consumer price index over the previous year, lagged one quarter.[15] Using data over the 1947–1960 period, Perry estimates the values of the structural parameters (α, β, and γ). Perry then uses this equation to determine the values for wage change in the 1962–1966 period that would have been expected on the basis of the actual values of unemployment and price change over the period

---

[10] For a discussion and analysis of the various proposals, see Laurence Seidman, "Tax Based Incomes Policies," *Brookings Papers on Economic Activity* (1978:2), pp. 301–348.

[11] Henry Wallich and Sidney Weintraub, "A Tax-Based Incomes Policy," *Journal of Economic Issues*, Vol. 5 (June, 1971), pp. 1–19.

[12] Arthur Okun, "The Great Stagflation Swamp," *Challenge*, Vol. 20 (Nov.–Dec., 1977), pp. 6–13.

[13] In October, 1978, the Carter Administration proposed a variant of the Okun plan in the form of *real wage insurance*. The Administration announced a specific numerical target for wage increases of 7 percent (and a somewhat less specific target for price increases). Under the real wage insurance plan, workers whose firms complied with the guidelines would be eligible for a tax rebate if inflation exceeded 7 percent; and the rebate would equal the excess of the actual inflation rate over 7 percent times their wage base. Congress has not yet considered the porposal. The guidelines are also backed by the threat of loss of government contracts by firms that fail to abide by the guidelines.

[14] George Perry, "Wages and the Guideposts," *American Economic Review*, Vol. 57 (Sept., 1967), pp. 897–904.

[15] Perry's equation also included the average profit rate and the change in the rate; we have excluded these terms to simplify the exposition.

and the estimated values of the α and β parameters that reflected the structure of the mechanism determining wages in the 1947–1960 period.

Perry found that the simulated values of wage change were systematically higher than the wage gains actually observed in the 1962–1966 period. Beginning in mid-1962, the prediction errors (actual wage change minus predicted wage change based on the Phillips curve equation) are negative for 15 consecutive quarters; this suggests that the guideposts restrained wage change relative to what would have occurred in their absence. The pattern of errors also appears plausible. At first, the overprediction is small, but it builds up gradually to substantial levels by 1964 and 1965. In a subsequent paper, Perry extends the analysis through 1967 and finds that the prediction errors become insignificant after 1966, consistent with the view that the guideposts effectively expired in 1966.[16]

Perry's results suggest a direct impact of guideposts on wages of 0.8 percentage points per year during the 1962–1965 period, with the effect reaching 1.5 percentage points in 1965. The overall or total effect on wages is still larger because of the indirect effect of lower wage change on price change (as via a markup model of price determination) and then the feedback of lower price change on wage change via the Phillips curve. The total effect of the guideposts over the period 1962–1965, taking into account this feedback via prices and Perry's Phillips curve equation, was to reduce wage and price inflation by over 1 percent a year.[17]

We have described in some detail the basic methodology that has been employed to evaluate the success of the guideposts, because the same approach has been applied to study the effects of controls in the 1971–1974 period. The essential feature of the method is to determine whether or not there has been a *shift* in the Phillips curve during the periods of the guideposts and of the controls and to measure the quantitative effect of the guideposts and controls by the size of the overprediction of wage change based on an equation estimated over a period prior to the policy in question. There are important limitations to this approach. First, it can at best yield results consistent with the hypothesis that guideposts or controls restrained wages; but it remains possible that changes in other factors not explicitly taken into account in the Phillips curve may have been at least partially responsible for the results. Secondly, attributing the overprediction to guideposts (or controls) is more plausible if the Phillips curve equation is stable over the period prior to guideposts or controls. If the equation is in general subject to unexplained shifts, the attribution of the particular shift during the period of guideposts or controls to those policies carries less weight. The Phillips curve was not, in fact, a particularly stable relation before (or after) the guidepost period. Perry's results, therefore, unfortunately like so many empirical findings in economics, strengthen the convictions of those already convinced and do not definitively resolve the question of whether or not guideposts did in fact restrain inflation.

---

[16] George Perry, "Wages and the Guideposts: Reply," *American Economic Review*, Vol. 59 (Sept., 1969), pp. 365–370.

[17] For a review of several empirical studies of the success of the guideposts, see John Sheahan, *The Wage-Price Guideposts* (Washington: The Brookings Institution, 1967).

MANDATORY WAGE AND PRICE CONTROLS

During the period of 1971 to 1974, mandatory wage and price controls were imposed in the U.S. in an effort to combat the inertia in price and wage movements.[18] The inflation during 1970 and 1971 (5.4 and 5.1 percent, respectively, in terms of the implicit *GNP* price deflation) reflected the inflationary expectations that had built up during the inflation generated by excess demand in the late 1960s. The Nixon Administration at first was content to rely on a gradual reduction in inflation in response to the economic slack associated with the 1969–1970 recession. We noted at the beginning of the chapter that such a gradual approach may be very long and painful in terms of cumulative output loss. As inflation persisted in 1970 and 1971 with apparently only slight response to the prevailing slack, the Administration became increasingly impatient with gradualism. And business and labor alike were calling for direct action to break the wage-price spiral.[19] The wage-price controls imposed in August, 1971, reflected the Administration's desire to pursue more stimulative demand management policies to reduce the economic slack while simultaneously attacking the inertia in inflation via incomes policy. The precise timing of the controls was also influenced by a deterioration in the U.S. balance of payments and the resulting heavy pressure on the dollar in the foreign exchange market.

The controls were initiated on August 15, 1971, with the imposition of a 90-day freeze on all wages, salaries, prices, and rents. The coverage of the controls was thus comprehensive with only raw agricultural commodities exempt. Unlike the guideposts of 1962–1966, the freeze and subsequent controls were enforceable in the courts although every effort was made to facilitate voluntary compliance by mobilizing public opinion about the importance of the program. Given the delays involved in legal proceedings and the ambiguities that might arise while the cases were unsettled, the threat of legal action was considered more valuable than the actual initiation of legal action. In fact, only eight legal actions were initiated by the government during the freeze and these were intended more to symbolize the government's determination to enforce the program than to resolve serious departures from the standards.[20]

The freeze had two primary objectives. First, it was a means of buying time while a more refined strategy for dealing with inflation was being developed. Secondly, it provided a dramatic signal of the determination of the Administration to combat inflation. This was particularly valuable in support of the international position of the dollar. Both by symbolizing the willingness to take necessary actions to curb inflation and by surpressing wage and price increases for 90 days, the freeze represented a shock treatment on inflation expectations.

---

[18] For general discussions of the experience with controls, see Arnold Weber, *In Pursuit of Price Stability*: *The Wage-Price Freeze of 1971* (Washington: The Brookings Institution, 1973); Robert F. Lanzellotti, Mary T. Hamilton, and R. Blaine Roberts, *Phase II Review*: *The Price Commission Experience* (Washington: The Brookings Institution, 1975); and Marvin H. Kosters, "Controls and Inflation: An Overview," in Joel Popkin (ed.), *Analysis of Inflation*: *1965–1974*, National Bureau of Economic Research (Cambridge, Mass.: Ballinger Publishing Company, 1977), pp. 121–189.

[19] See, for example, the discussion in Arnold Weber, *In Pursuit of Price Stability*: *The Wage-Price Freeze of 1971* (Washington: The Brookings Institution, 1973), Chapter 1.

[20] *Ibid.*, p. 96.

Following the 90-day freeze, Phase II was initiated with a goal of reducing the inflation rate to 2.5 percent. Under Phase II standards, wage increases were limited to 5.5 percent per year for new contracts. Assuming trend productivity growth of 3.0 percent a year, this would be consistent with the price objectives. The price policy was administered by use of an allowable cost rule whereby firms could pass through allowable costs on a dollar-for-dollar basis (where allowable labor cost increases were restricted to those within the 5.5 percent wage standard); this was backed up by a limitation on firms' profit margins (gross profits as a percent of sales), based on the highest two of the previous three fiscal years. The largest firms and unions were required to obtain advanced approval for wage and price increases; medium-sized units were required to submit reports after wage and price adjustments had been made. But all faced the same standards. As was the case with the freeze, problems mounted near the end of Phase II, and according to a study by three members of the Price Commission "there were indications that general cooperation with the control program was deteriorating" near the end of 1972.[21]

Phase III, introduced on January 11, 1973, was initially viewed as a transition toward decontrol. Its standards were somewhat relaxed compared to those under previous phases; it abandoned the necessity of prior approval and relaxed the rules relating to cost justification of price increases. It permitted, for example, price increases as necessary for efficient allocation of resources and to maintain adequate supply. The standards were both vague and self-administered. During the period in which Phase III was operative, dramatic price increases occurred among agricultural commodities and in the price of crude petroleum. The spread of these could not have been avoided under the stricter Phase II, but the resulting explosion in prices under Phase III led to an indictment of that program and eventually led to a second freeze, from June 13 to August 12, 1973, followed by the fourth and final phase of controls. Phase IV was a return to the somewhat stricter standards of Phase II but also a vehicle for dismantling controls, and by April 30, 1974, controls had been completely terminated.

In the following two sections we first consider the analytical foundation of mandatory wage and price controls and then review the evidence on the effectiveness of controls.

○ The Logic of Mandatory Controls

Mandatory wage and price controls take the form of either freezes on prices and wages (although often with some prices exempted from controls) or statutory ceilings on price and wage increases. The 90-day freeze imposed on August 15, 1971, was of the former kind; and Phases II, III, and IV were variants of the second. In analyzing the rationale for such controls, it is important to distinguish the costs and benefits of the controls in both the control and postcontrol periods. Such controls are invariably imposed temporarily and the critical issue is the degree to which the experience of reduced inflation during the control period is carried over to the postcontrol period.

---

[21] Robert F. Lanzellotti, Mary T. Hamilton, and R. Blaine Roberts, *Phase II Review: The Price Commission Experience* (Washington: The Brookings Institution, 1975), p. 198.

The Effects of Controls During the Period They Are Imposed

1. Price controls may directly suppress the inflation rate during the control period. The ability of controls to limit inflation depends on the initial economic environment (in particular, the degree of excess demand) as well as on the comprehensiveness of the controls and the strictness of their enforcement. The evidence suggests that the fairly strict controls, through Phase II at least, did have a moderating effect on inflation; but it should not be taken for granted that such controls are effective even within the control period.[22] Even if controls do successfully suppress inflation during the control period, this enforced moderation in inflation is the means to an end rather than the ultimate benefit to be derived from controls. Controls are generally advocated as a means of transforming the economic environment in such a manner that inflation will remain below its precontrol rate even after controls are eliminated. But before we discuss the transition to decontrol, we consider the other effects during the control period.

2. Controls impose explicit costs associated with administering and enforcing the system. These costs are imposed both on the government which must set up the administrative machinery and enforcement network and on private firms which may be required to prenotify the government of price decisions, report price decisions at regular intervals, and maintain a special staff to guarantee compliance. Lanzellotti, Hamilton, and Roberts estimate the sum of direct federal expenditures and costs incurred by firms to comply with Phase II regulations at $0.8 billion per year.[23]

3. Price controls may generate a misallocation of resources and thereby reduce the overall level of production. Controls may distort the allocation of resources both by inducing efforts to circumvent the controls and by impairing the ability of relative prices to signal appropriate movements in inputs and outputs in response to changing demand and supply conditions. Lanzellotti, Hamilton, and Roberts estimate the cost of the real resources diverted to circumvent controls as $0.5 billion per year under Phase II.[24] The costs associated with the immobilization of the relative price mechanism are likely to become progressively larger over time and to become especially severe as overall demand increases.

4. Controls interfere with the freedom of firms to set prices and workers and firms to bargain over wages. The political cost associated with this loss of individual freedom must be weighed in deciding whether or not to impose controls, and if imposed, how long their duration ought to be. Because such costs are intangible, there is a tendency to either ignore them or give them infinite weight, depending on one's predelections. While business and labor generally seem to be willing to tolerate short periods of interference in wage and price decisions in the hope of breaking the inertia of inflation, the political costs seem to become increasingly large and ultimately may limit the period for which controls are politically viable.

5. Controls may indirectly affect real aggregate demand and hence employment and output. Controls may affect aggregate demand through their effect on the price

---

[22] We discuss the evidence on the effectiveness of controls in the next section.
[23] Lanzellotti, Hamilton, and Roberts, *op. cit.*, pp. 190–192.
[24] *Ibid.*, pp. 192–193.

level and therefore on real money balances (the position of the LM curve in the r-X plane) and real net wealth and net exports (the position of the IS curve). Additional effects on aggregate demand may derive from the effect of controls on inflation expectations. According to the 1972 CEA report, the control program was "intended to stimulate spending and employment by reducing inflation-anxiety of consumers and businesses."[25] However, the 1974 report warned that "controls are sometimes thought to hold down spending. . . . If controls make people confident that inflation will moderate, they are less inclined to spend their money."[26] The two opposing effects reflect different aspects of inflation: in the former case, the controls increase spending by reducing uncertainty (about the rate of inflation during the control period); in the latter case, controls reduce spending by reducing the incentive to accelerate purchases to take advantage of lower prices today relative to tomorrow. The 1974 CEA report also warned that controls may introduce an element of uncertainty that affects long-term planning, hence investment; i.e., although controls may reduce the uncertainty associated with inflation over the control period, they may increase the uncertainty about longer term wage and price movements since these depend on the duration of and response to the relaxation of controls.

Although the effects of controls via their effects on uncertainty and inflation expectations are difficult to estimate, the effect via the estimated reduction in the inflation rate can more easily be translated into an estimate of the expansionary effect on output. Lanzellotti, Hamilton, and Roberts, for example, assume that controls left nominal aggregate demand unchanged and therefore simply redistributed the given nominal GNP between output and price changes. Their estimated 1.3 to 2.0 percentage-point reduction in the inflation rate during Phase II translates into a $15–$22 billion increase in real GNP.[27]

Another source of stimulus to output associated with controls derives from the increased latitude controls allow fiscal policy by providing "protection against the fact and expectation of inflation."[28] Indeed, in a study of Phase II by three members of the Price Commission, the reduction in inflation expectations is cited as "the secondary objective of Phase II" and the contribution to recovery by allowing a more stimulative fiscal policy as the primary objective.[29] Thus, controls may result in an expansion of output both by inducing a larger output response from unchanged policy settings (e.g., from a given level of M) and by inducing policy authorities to undertake more expansionary policy.

The Effects of Controls in the Postcontrol Period. The critical issue in evaluating the usefulness of controls is not their initial impact (i.e., their impact during the control period), but the duration of their effect as controls are relaxed and removed. As we noted above, controls are intended to provide relief from inflation rather than simply the temporary suppression of inflation. There are two key forces operative

---

[25] *The Economic Report of the President,* 1972, p. 24.
[26] *The Economic Report of the President,* 1974, p. 101.
[27] See Lanzellotti, Hamilton, and Roberts, *op. cit.,* Chapter VIII, pp. 103–106 for their conclusions about the effect on inflation; and Chapter XI, pp. 186–188 for their conclusions about the effects on output.
[28] *Ibid.,* p. 7.
[29] *Ibid.,* pp. 7–8.

in the transition from the control to the postcontrol period: the effects on inflation via the moderation in inflationary expectations during the control period and via the spurt in wages and prices immediately following the relaxation of controls in response to pressures that either existed at the time controls were imposed or that built up during the control period. We will consider each of these influences on inflation in this section.

1. Controls may reduce inflationary expectations in the postcontrol period. Controls are a direct attack on the inertia element in wage-price movements. Instead of cycling-down by operating directly on actual inflation rates via unemployment, controls attempt to influence inflation expectations directly by imposing a period of enforced moderation in wage and price movements. This view was emphasized in the 1972 CEA report:

> ... the control system can generate the expectation of reasonable stability that is essential to the achievement of reasonable price stability. And as that happens it will be possible to eliminate the controls.[30]

And Arnold Weber, Director of the Cost of Living Council which administered the freeze, noted that "... one of the primary objectives of the overall program was to dissipate inflationary expectations. ..."[31]

In terms of Figure 26.1, controls operate directly on the actual rate of inflation ($\dot{P}$), then on expected inflation ($\dot{P}^e$); the latter effect being successful, controls can be relaxed with lower $\dot{P}$ and $\dot{P}^e$ at the initial unemployment rate. Thus, controls permit a deceleration in inflation that works independently of changes in the unemployment rate. Of course, aggregate stabilization policies must be adjusted to be consistent with the reduced rate of inflation; in particular, the rate of monetary growth should decelerate along with the rate of inflation.

The key to modeling the effect of controls is therefore the specification of inflation expectations in the postcontrol period. Postcontrol inflation expectations can be expected to be influenced by four factors: (a) the actual inflation experience under controls, (b) the memory of the precontrol experience, (c) the perceived effect of any change in aggregate demand during the control period, and (d) the possibility of a catch-up effect in the period following elimination of controls.[32] The longer the duration of controls, the stronger the effect of the first and the smaller the effect of the second factor. Demand management policies inconsistent with the objective of lowering inflation, such as those implemented in 1972, will impair the effect of the control experience on inflation expectations via the third factor. The role of the fourth factor is considered in the next section.

2. There may be a *catch-up effect* following the relaxation of controls. Poole refers to the problem of how to emerge from the control regime so as to preserve

---

[30] *The Economic Report of the President*, 1972, p. 27.

[31] Arnold A. Weber, *In Pursuit of Price Stability: The Wage-Price Freeze of 1971* (Washington: The Brookings Institution, 1973), p. 39.

[32] A formal model of the formation of inflation expectations in the postcontrol period is developed in S. K. Gupta, L. H. Meyer, F. Q. Raines, and T. J. Tarn, "Optimal Coordination of Aggregate Stabilization Policy and Price Controls: Some Simulation Results," *Annals of Economic and Social Measurement*, Vol. 4 (Spring, 1975), pp. 253–270.

its beneficial influence on actual inflation rates as the "exit problem."[33] In the previous section we noted one element of the exit problem—the formation of inflation expectations in the postcontrol period. To the extent that inflation expectations are influenced by the control-restrained inflation experience, exit becomes possible. However, there is generally an attempt by wage earners and business firms to "catch-up" after controls are removed; i.e., to raise wages and prices to compensate for the inability to do so during the control period. The purpose and effect of these catch-up increases in prices and wages are not necessarily to restore prices to the level that would have prevailed in the absence of controls; that would imply a "law of conservation of price increases" according to which the prices rise following the relaxation of controls in proportion to the duration of controls and the deviation of the price level from what it would have been in the absence of controls. This ignores the self-perpetuating nature of wage-price increases that controls are designed to break. To the extent that controls hold wages and other costs down during the period in which they are operative, prices need not rise during or after controls. And to the extent that controls hold down price increases, wages need not rise by as much during or after controls.[34]

Nevertheless, the catch-up phenomenon is quite evident when controls are relaxed (as following the wage-price freeze in 1971 and the transition from Phase II to III in mid-1973) or removed (as during and after Phase IV). It is not, however, a mechanical response to return the price level to what it would have been in the absence of controls. Instead, it reflects attempts by workers and firms to reestablish traditional relationships among wages in different sectors and occupations and between wages and prices and prices and costs, relationships that were disturbed because controls prevented these adjustments from occurring in response to imbalances in these relationships that existed at the time controls were imposed or that developed during the control period because of the exemption of certain goods or sectors.

We have discussed previously the significance of relative wages or traditional wage differentials as an element influencing wage negotiations. When controls are imposed, it is inevitable that some workers have recently concluded negotiations while others are prevented from negotiating "comparable" wage gains during controls. The resulting wage differentials provide the basis for wage settlements delayed during the control period. Similarly, firms which had incurred cost increases prior to controls but had been prevented from raising prices during controls or those subject to cost increases due to price increases of uncontrolled commodities during the control period will move to restore more normal price-cost relations in the postcontrol period. For example, steel prices had been increased shortly before the freeze was imposed and the freeze did not allow users of steel to raise their prices to reflect the increased cost of new materials. And during the freeze and Phase II, firms which used as inputs uncontrolled raw agricultural products similarly found their profit margins squeezed.

The net effect of such developments is an inevitable bulge in wage-price movements when controls are relaxed or removed. If these are simply once-and-for-all adjustments

---

[33] W. Poole, "Wage and Price Controls: Where Do We Go from Here?" *Brookings Papers on Economic Activity* (1973:1).

[34] Poole, in the paper cited in footnote 33, suggested the possibility of what Paul Samuelson then labeled, "the law of conservation of price increases." Samuelson's comments are cited in the discussion of Poole's paper in *Brookings Papers on Economic Activity* (1973:1), pp. 300–302.

in relative wages or in prices relative to costs, they may not seriously interfere with the exit from control. But they are likely to have a dramatic psychological effect, discrediting the success of controls, and may escalate inflation expectations; in this case the catch-up may thoroughly offset any benefit controls may otherwise have had on inflation.[35]

Assessing the Effectiveness of Controls in 1971–1974

There have been a large number of studies of the effectiveness of the controls, particularly about the effects of Phase II.[36] The methodology employed in these studies is the same as was used by Perry to appraise the effectiveness of the wage-price guideposts: the comparison of actual wage and price changes with hypothetical simulated values derived from structural equations for wages and prices estimated using data prior to the control period.

The evidence is somewhat mixed and does not permit a definitive assessment of the success of the controls program. The weight of the evidence suggests, at best, a temporary effect which wore off as controls were relaxed in 1973 and then removed in 1974. Robert J. Gordon, for example, concludes that controls reduced the inflation rate by about two percentage points during Phases I (the freeze) and II.[37] Robert F. Lanzellotti, Mary T. Hamilton, and R. Blaine Roberts reach a similar conclusion.[38] There appears, on the other hand, to have been a much smaller restraining effect on wages during this period, suggesting that wages rose relative to prices and squeezed profit margins. Thus, Gordon warned against interpreting the restraint on prices as evidence of the "success" of controls. Any sustainable effect of controls requires restraining wages as well as prices. Any effect on prices at the expense of squeezed profit margins only sets the stage for a subsequent catch-up effect of prices relative to wages.[39] In a later study that considered the behavior of prices relative to wages through the year following the elimination of controls, Gordon concludes that the restraint on prices during Phases I and II (and indeed during much of Phase III) was completely offset during the following two years so that by the end of 1975 there was no evidence of a significant effect of controls on prices.[40]

---

[35] For an attempt to model the interaction of expectation-restraining and catch-up effects, see L. H. Meyer, F. Q. Raines, and M. J. O'Brien, "The Value of Coordinated Price Controls in a World of Virulent Inflation," paper presented at the Western Economics Association Meetings, June, 1976.

[36] A summary of a number of these studies can be found in John Kraft, "The Effectiveness of the Economic Stabilization Program: A Summary of the Evidence," in Paul H. Earl (ed.), *Analysis of Inflation* (Lexington, Mass.: Lexington Books, 1975), pp. 197–209. Other relevant studies are included in Joel Popkin (ed.), *Analysis of Inflation: 1965–1974*, National Bureau of Economic Research (Cambridge, Mass.: Ballinger Publishing Company, 1977). In addition, two papers by Gordon deserve mention: Robert J. Gordon, "The Response of Wages and Prices to the First Two Years of Controls," *Brookings Papers on Economic Activity* (1973:3), pp. 765–778, and "The Impact of Aggregate Demand on Prices," *Brookings Papers on Economic Activity* (1975:3), pp. 613–662.

[37] Robert J. Gordon, "The Response of Wages and Prices to the First Two Years of Controls," *Brookings Papers on Economic Activity* (1973:3), pp. 765–778.

[38] Robert F. Lanzellotti, Mary T. Hamilton, and R. Blaine Roberts, *Phase II Review: The Price Commission Experience* (Washington: The Brookings Institution, 1975), Chapter VIII.

[39] *Ibid.*

[40] Robert J. Gordon, "The Impact of Aggregate Demand on Prices," *Brookings Papers on Economic Activity* (1975:3), pp. 613–662.

INDEXATION

Indexation is the tying of nominal or dollar denominated contracts to the price level. Its purpose is to avoid the unintended changes in real incomes associated with unanticipated inflation. Workers would in effect bargain over real rather than nominal wages if their wage contracts were fully indexed; i.e., any price increase over the life of the contract would automatically raise their nominal wage. Thus, the rate of increase in nominal wages would equal

$$\dot{W} = \dot{W}^* + \dot{P} \tag{26.5}$$

where $\dot{W}^*$ equals the proportional rate of change in the nominal wage rate agreed to in the contract, assuming $\dot{P} = 0$ and $\dot{P}=$ the proportional rate of increase in the *CPI* over the life of the contract. $\dot{W}^*$ would be related to ρ, the rate of increase in productivity, but might be above or below ρ, depending on a variety of factors such as the existence of excess supply or demand for that particular type of labor. Similarly, social security and pensions could be fully indexed. And bonds could be issued carrying full indexation; the dollar repayment at maturity would be tied to the price index as would the coupon payments each period. Advocates of indexation generally recommend that governments index their wages, social insurance benefits, taxes, and long-term bonds and encourage but not require indexation in the private sector.[41]

The Case For Indexation

There are three basic arguments in support of indexation.[42] (1) Indexation promotes equity by preventing many arbitrary redistributions of income associated with unanticipated inflation; (2) indexation reduces the government's incentive to inflate; and (3) indexation, when combined with restrictive demand management policies, facilitates the transition to lower inflation or to price stability.

Indexation will not, in and of itself, lower the inflation rate. But it may aid in reducing inflation in two ways:

1. *Indexation reduces the government's incentive to inflate.* The government's incentive to inflate derives from the increased tax revenue and the reduced real cost of servicing the government's outstanding debt that results from increases in inflation. Under a progressive tax structure, inflation-induced increases in nominal incomes will push taxpayers into higher tax brackets so that their tax payments increase more than in proportion to the increase in their nominal incomes, thereby raising real tax revenue. Inflation also reduces the real value of exemptions and deductions which are fixed in nominal terms and gives rise to inflation-induced capital gains on which taxes must be paid. Government bonds pay coupons fixed in nominal terms. The coupons reflect inflation expectations at the time the bonds were issued. Any

---

[41] Some government wages, social security, and government retirement benefits to federal employees are already indexed.

[42] The case for indexation is presented in Milton Friedman, *Monetary Correction* (London: The Institute of Economic Affairs, 1974).

increase in inflation beyond the amount already reflected in the coupons reduces the real cost of debt service to the government.

Indexation of the tax structure and government bonds would eliminate the government's incentive to inflate. To index the tax structure, the tax brackets would be multiplied by the ratio of the price index in the given year to the price index in the year the tax tables were legislated; the same ratio would be used to adjust all deductions and exemptions. To index government bonds, the same ratio would be applied both to coupon payments and to the principal amount of the bonds.

2. *Indexation would reduce the cost in terms of cumulative output loss of a transition to a lower inflation rate.* The high cost of lowering inflation is due in part to the powerful element of inertia in wage and price movements. In terms of Figure 26.2, indexation should speed the response of the inflation expectations term to past inflation and therefore should speed the decline in the actual inflation rate. Under indexation, contracts do not lock in wage increases that both reflect past inflation and build in future inflation over several years. Instead, contracts are adjusted at least each year in light of recent inflation experience. This should substantially reduce the inertia in the wage-price movements we discussed earlier in the chapter.

The Case Against Indexation

There are four basic arguments against indexation: (1) Indexation reduces the cost of inflation and therefore will reduce the political will to reduce or eliminate inflation. (2) Indexation may signal an admission of defeat and a confession of failure and therefore increases expectations of inflation. (3) Although indexation would speed the transition to lower inflation rates if appropriate demand management policies were followed, it would also speed the response to inflationary disturbances. Note, however, that while indexation speeds the inflationary effect of, for example, an excessive monetary growth rate, the transition to higher inflation would occur more evenly and with less distortions under indexation. (4) While indexation may reduce the distortions and output loss associated with demand disturbances (e.g., changes in $\dot{M}$), it may aggravate the adjustment to supply side disturbances (e.g., temporary or permanent changes in the productivity trend). For example, assume wage contracts are negotiated for three-year periods. An indexed contract fixes the real wage for three years but allows the nominal wage to vary. The nonindexed contract fixes the nominal wage but permits the real wage to vary. Which structure is preferable depends on whether an adjustment in the real wage is part of the equilibrating response to the disturbance. Real wage adjustment is not necessary as part of a transition to lower inflation rates via demand management policies; indeed, any changes in the real wage would involve distortions and might increase the cost of the overall adjustment. On the other hand, consider the response to a downward shift in the productivity trend. The equilibrium response would be a decline in the real wage rate. This is, however, impossible over the life of indexed contracts. A decline in the productivity trend increases unit labor costs; any increase in prices, however, will also increase wages under indexed contracts, slowing the transition to a lower real wage.[43]

---

[43] For a thorough analysis of the implications of indexation for the response to demand and supply stocks, see Joanna Gray, "Wage Indexation: A Macroeconomic Approach," *Journal of Monetary Economics*, Vol. 2 (April, 1976), pp. 221–236.

The conclusion is that indexation would be, at best, a mixed blessing. The best solution is, even according to the most vigorous advocates of indexation, an unindexed economy with noninflationary monetary policy. Nevertheless, given an initial environment of substantial built-in inflation, indexation may reduce the cost of the transition to lower inflation rates enough to encourage policymakers to impose restrictive demand management policies that they might otherwise be reluctant to apply.

OTHER SUPPLY-ORIENTED POLICIES

In this section we will briefly discuss a number of other supply-oriented policies. These policies differ in an important respect from guideposts and mandatory controls. The latter are generally designed to cope with specific cyclical phenomena and therefore to be turned on and off in response to current economic developments. The policies we discuss below have a longer run dimension. They can generally be justified on efficiency grounds, represent a permanent change in the structure of labor or commodity markets, and are not intended to be turned on and off in response to short-term economic developments.

Policies to Improve the Efficiency of Labor Markets

We noted in Chapter 16 that the level of unemployment at "full employment" (which is at least a component of if not equal to the u^* variable in the Phillips curve) was determined in large measure by the amount of normal frictional unemployment. This frictional unemployment reflects the flows into unemployment associated with quits, layoffs, new entries and reentries, and the duration of the search process. Policies which reduce frictional unemployment shift the long-run Phillips curve, lowering the rate of unemployment at any given inflation rate.

Human Resources Programs. The motivation for *human resources programs* (traditionally referred to as "manpower programs") is to speed the match-up of unemployed persons to available jobs and to improve the quality of the match-ups so as to reduce frictional unemployment. The latter dimension of human resources programs is quite important, although it generally receives less recognition than the former. But increasing the speed of match-ups may encourage an increase in quits as well as a greater willingness to leave and reenter the labor force, increasing unemployment associated with these groups. Improving the quality of match-ups should increase the duration of employments among these groups, hopefully resulting in a net decline in their frictional unemployment.

Charles Holt and a number of colleagues have made several specific recommendations for human resources programs to reduce unemployment.[44] These policies aim to shift the Phillips curve by improving both the quality of matches and the efficiency of job search and by overcoming occupational and geographic mismatches of job vacancies and available workers. Special attention is focused on reducing high unemployment among young workers. The program features a substantial enlargement

---

[44] Charles C. Holt, C. Duncan MacRae, Stuart O. Schweitzer, and Ralph E. Smith, *The Unemployment-Inflation Dilemma: A Manpower Solution* (Washington: The Urban Institute, 1971); and "Manpower Proposals for Phase III," *Brookings Papers on Economic Activity* (1971:3), pp. 703–734.

of the employment service run by the federal government, closer cooperation between the employment service and schools, improved transition from school to work through work-study programs, occupational training to equip workers for jobs in areas where there are vacancies, and advisory and financial assistance for workers moving to new jobs to increase geographic mobility. The total cost of the program is $14 billion annually; part of this cost would be shared by business and part would be offset by higher tax revenues. Holt, *et al.,* estimate that the program can reduce the unemployment rate by about 2 percent, at a given rate of inflation.[45]

Unemployment Compensation. Unemployment compensation is another government program that may contribute directly to the amount of normal frictional unemployment. By reducing the cost of remaining unemployed, unemployment insurance encourages an increase in the duration of unemployment. Martin Feldstein notes that the combined effect of the level of benefits of unemployment compensation and their nontaxable status is to reduce greatly and sometimes completely eliminate any cost associated with remaining unemployed for another month or two.[46] The increased duration of search reflects both less intense search and more selective behavior. In addition, some who would otherwise drop out of the labor force continue to "search" in order to qualify for benefits. Stephen Marston, in a thorough empirical analysis of the effect of unemployment insurance, concludes that unemployment insurance increases the average duration of unemployment among insured job seekers by 16–31 percent compared to uninsured job seekers and that this in turn results in a "perceptible, but small" increase in unemployment of 0.2 to 0.3 percent of the labor force.[47]

○ Improving Price Flexibility

The high cost of reducing inflation via demand management policies reflects, in part, the small response of wages and hence prices to increases in the unemployment rate and the even smaller direct response of prices to declines in aggregate demand. In terms of Figures 26.1, the cost of reducing inflation can be increased by policies which increase α, the responsiveness of the inflation rate to the level of aggregate demand. Recall from our discussion of the nonlinearity of the Phillips curve in Chapter 18 that this parameter may be larger at low levels of unemployment than at high levels of unemployment: this is consistent with the asymmetry of wage and price responses to excess supply and demand and the downward relative inflexibility of wages and prices in the face of excess supply. The degree of price flexibility is often viewed as a function of the degree of market power which in turn is related to market concentration. Government policies could be directed at increasing the degree

---

[45] For an alternative estimate of the effects of the Holt, *et al.,* program, see Robert Hall, "Prospects for Shifting the Phillips Curve through Manpower Policy," *Brookings Papers on Economic Activity* (1971:3), pp. 659–70. Hall concludes that the Holt, *et al.,* program would reduce the unemployment rate by only 0.4 percentage points.

[46] Martin Feldstein, "Policies to Lower the Permanent Rate of Unemployment," in *Reducing Unemployment to 2 Percent.* Hearing before the Joint Economic Committee, 92nd Congress, 2nd session (Washington: U.S. Government Printing Office, 1972), pp. 24–28.

[47] Stephen T. Marston, "The Impact of Unemployment Insurance on Job Search," *Brookings Papers on Economic Activity* (1975:1), pp. 13–48.

Chapter 26 • Incomes and Other Supply-Oriented Policies

of competition, for example, by more aggressive antitrust policies, decontrol of regulated sectors such as trucking, and a reduction in protection from foreign competition by a decline in tariffs. However, few view such policies as having much potential, although the case for them may be stronger on the grounds of increased efficiency.

Policies to Reduce the Price Level

Many government decisions affect the price level directly as opposed to through their effect on aggregate demand; for example, the employer share of social insurance taxes, indirect taxes such as sales and excise taxes, and the costs imposed by social regulation of environment, health, and safety all tend to be shifted forward to higher prices for goods produced by business. In addition, agricultural price supports and minimum wages may directly raise prices and wages. In a recent study, Robert Crandall has considered the potential for reducing the price level by finding alternative approaches to meeting the objectives of these programs.[48] For example, direct taxes could be substituted for indirect taxes and direct subsidies or transfers for minimum wage and price supports. Just as these policies contribute to an upward shift in the aggregate supply curve, such substitutions would shift the aggregate supply curve downward, both lowering the price level and expanding aggregate demand.

But would these policies also reduce the inflation rate? If expected inflation is an important element in the inflation process and if inflation expectations are affected by recent actual inflation rates (as in the adaptive expectations model), then such policies may be effective in reducing the inflationary momentum. They would, first of all, result in lower inflation rates during the transition to a lower price level; this reduced inflation may restrain wage demands and hence further reduce inflation.[49] Demand management policies would also have to be adjusted to remain consistent with the lower rate of inflation. A more pessimistic scenario would relate inflation expectations to rates of monetary growth; this suggests the absence of any long-run effect of a once-and-for-all change in the price level on the inflation rate.

REVIEW QUESTIONS

1. Inflation can be eliminated by traditional demand management policies. Why bother with incomes or other aggregate supply policies?

2. Discuss the cycling-down of inflation via demand management policies.

3. What was the logic of the guide for noninflationary wage behavior in the wage-price guideposts?

4. Explain the way in which temporary mandatory controls may permit a permanent reduction in inflation.

---

[48] Robert Crandall, "Federal Government Initiatives to Reduce the Price Level," *Brookings Papers on Economic Activity* (1978:2), pp. 401–440.

[49] A model consistent with this result appears in Arthur Okun, "Efficient Disinflationary Policies," *American Economic Review, Papers and Proceedings,* Vol. 68 (May, 1978), pp. 348–352. Several of the comments on Crandall's paper cited above are skeptical about the effect on inflation of such policies.

5. The evidence suggests that inflation was not permanently lowered by the 1971–1974 episode of controls. Explain why controls may fail to be effective in moderating inflation.

6. Discuss the way in which controls may be used to complement stimulative demand management policies.

7. Discuss the case for and against indexation.

8. Discuss the determinants of the amount of unemployment at full employment. How can policy be used to affect this rate?

PROBLEMS

1. "There is a cumulative output loss associated with eradicating inflation in the case of a nonvertical Phillips curve. For a vertical Phillips curve there is only a temporary output loss." Comment.

2. "The fact that inflation remained moderate during the 1962–1966 period is evidence in support of the effectiveness of the guideposts program." Comment.

3. "Indexation speeds the effects of inflationary shocks and does not, in itself, reduce prevailing inflation. Therefore, it is worse than useless as an antiinflation device. It cannot help and can only make matters worse." Comment.

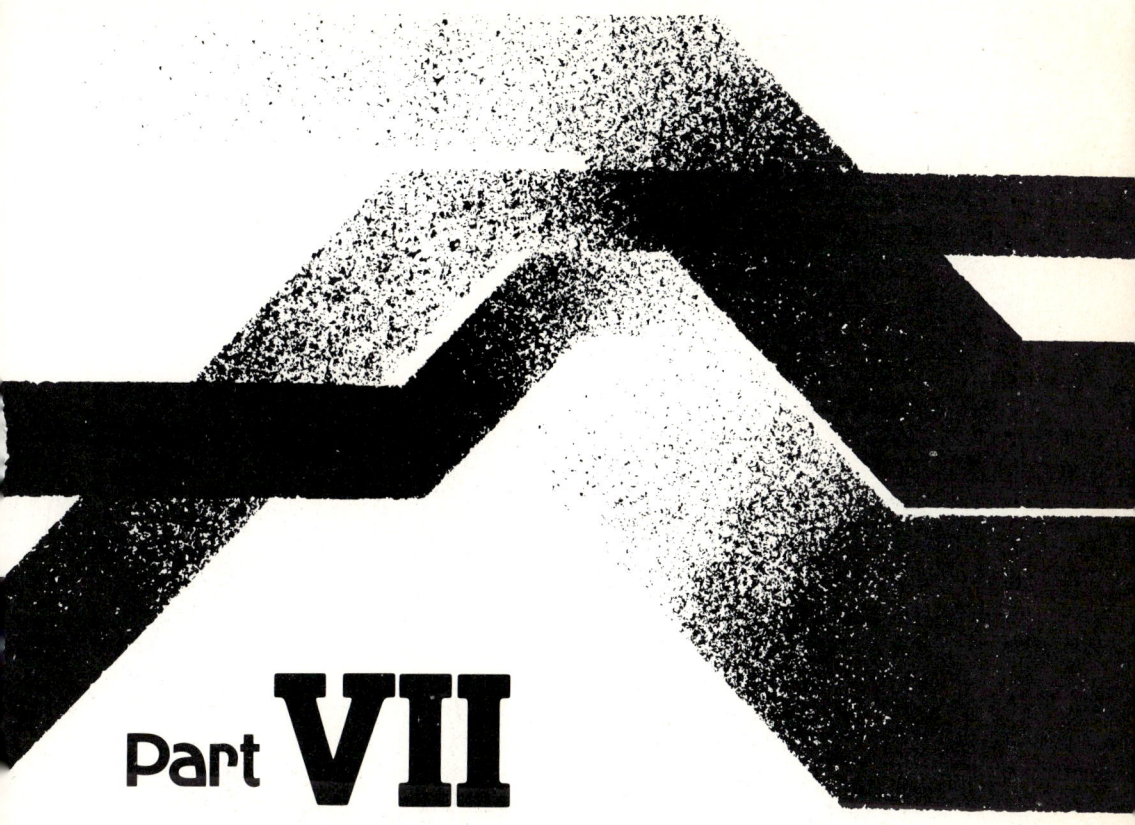

Part VII

Extension to an Open Economy

Chapter 27. Trade and International Capital Flows in Macroeconomic Analysis
28. Macroeconomic Policy in an Open Economy

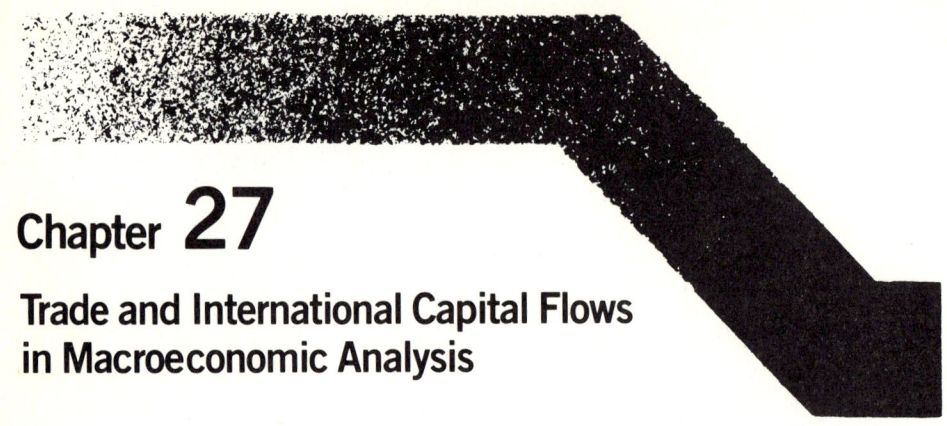

Chapter 27

Trade and International Capital Flows in Macroeconomic Analysis

Up to this point we have analyzed the determination of macroeconomic variables and the use of macroeconomic policy under the assumption of a closed economy; i.e., one in which there is neither trade in goods nor exchange of assets with residents of other countries. In this and the following chapter we introduce trade and international capital flows into our basic model and explore the implications for income, price, and interest rate determination and for the nature and limitations of policy in this environment. The fact that the open economy analysis is saved for the last is not a commentary on the relative importance of this topic; rather, it reflects a judgment about the usefulness of developing the models with the most restrictive assumptions first and then progressing by relaxing those assumptions.

This chapter develops the basic building blocks of the macroeconomics of an open economy. We begin by developing the accounting conventions for recording international transactions. Next, we discuss the role of relative prices in the open economy model and then the operation of the foreign exchange market which links the currencies of different nations. In the fourth section we modify the *IS* and *LM* curves to take into account international transactions and introduce a third equilibrium relationship corresponding to the balance of payments. In the final section we outline the various methods of dealing with payments imbalances and discuss alternative international arrangements to coordinate the response to such imbalances.

THE BALANCE OF PAYMENTS

The *balance of payments* (*BP*) is a summary of all economic transactions between the residents of one country and the rest of the world over a given period of time. The items recorded in the balance of payments are all *flows;* i.e., denominated in dollars per unit of time. A simplified presentation of the balance of payments appears in Table 27.1. The table includes three major categories of transactions: the current account, the capital account, and the balancing items. Each type of transaction within

Current Account

1. Exports and Imports of Goods and Services

    a. Merchandise

    b. Services

    c. Investment Income

$$1a + 1b + 1c = \text{Balance on Goods and Services}$$

2. Unilateral Transfers

    a. Private

    b. Government

$$1 + 2a + 2b = \text{Balance on Current Account}$$

Capital Account

3. Long-Term Capital Flows

4. Short-Term Private Capital Flows

$$1 + 2 + 3 + 4 = \text{Balance of Official Reserve Transactions}$$

_____ ("the line")

Balancing Items

5. Short-Term Official Capital Flows

6. Gold and Other International Reserve Movements

TABLE 27.1
The Balance of Payments

these accounts is registered as a credit (+) or a debit (−) and a net balance (surplus or deficit) can be computed for each type of transaction and each group of transactions. An item is entered as a credit when it increases the supply of foreign currency to residents of the country and as a debit when it increases the residents' demand for foreign currency. Note however that the double entry method of bookkeeping implies that each transaction must involve precisely offsetting debit and credit entries. For example, one cannot simply record an import of merchandise as a debit under current account transactions without recording how residents paid for those imports. The payment could have come from the sale, for example, of exports (a credit under current account transactions), or a sale of financial assets to the foreign residents (a capital inflow entered as a credit under the capital account); or by the government making available foreign exchange reserves to importers (entered as a credit in balancing items). This implies that the overall balance of payments must always balance; i.e., the sum of lines 1 through 6 must always be zero![1] The concept of surpluses or deficits in the balance of payments can therefore only apply to specific subgroups of entries; e.g., to each of the major accounts or to sums of accounts which exclude at least one.

The *current account* is divided into two major subgroups: (1) transactions involving currently produced goods and services between residents and the rest of the world and (2) unilateral transfers. The first category, generally referred to as *imports and exports of goods and services*, includes (a) transactions in currently produced goods (merchandise imports and exports), (b) transactions involving current services, and (c) investment income. Domestic purchases of foreign produced goods are called *imports* and are entered as debits (−) under merchandise (item 1a); e.g., the purchase of foreign autos is entered as a negative entry on line 1a. Foreign purchases of domestically produced goods are called *exports* and are entered as credits (+) on line 1a; e.g., the sale of agricultural commodities to foreign residents results in a positive entry on line 1a. *Current services* involve charges for professional and business services, shipping goods, transporting passengers, and all expenditures of tourists. For example, the shipment of U.S. goods on a foreign ship results in a debit entry on line 1b while the transport of foreign passengers on U.S. planes gives rise to a credit entry on the same line. The final line in the current account is for transactions involving the use of domestic technology and capital abroad and foreign technology and capital in the U.S.; i.e., for current services associated with capital. For example, dividends and interest paid by foreign firms to U.S. residents are entered as credits on line 1c while royalties for use of foreign technology in the U.S. are entered as debits. The balance on transactions involving merchandise trade is called the (merchandise) *trade balance* while the sum of lines 1a, 1b, and 1c is referred to as the *balance on goods and services* and is the item in the balance of payments that enters into the national income accounts discussed in Chapter 2.

The second subcategory in the current account is unilateral transfers between U.S. residents and foreigners and includes both private transfers (gifts or contributions) and government transfers (e.g., foreign aid). The sum of lines 1 and 2 is the *balance on current account*.

The *capital account* includes transactions involving the purchase/sale of assets between U.S. residents and the rest of the world. Subcategories include *long-term capital flows*, defined as those involving assets whose original maturity exceeds one year, and *private short-term capital flows*, defined as transactions among private parties

---

[1] Differences in the reporting of international transactions, however, may result in a discrepancy between the sum of total payments and the sum of total receipts. To insure that the balance of payments nevertheless "balances," an additional entry called *errors and omissions* is included in the balance of payments statistics. This item is not included in our simplified representation of the balance of payments in Table 27.1.

in the U.S. and abroad in assets whose original maturities are one year or less. Long-term capital flows involve both purchases of tangible physical assets (*direct investment*) and transactions in paper claims (*portfolio* or *financial investment*). A purchase of a foreign asset (referred to as a *capital outflow* although the physical asset or its ownership is in fact imported) gives rise to a demand for foreign currency and hence is entered as a debit.

The final category is referred to as *balancing* or *settlement items*. The distinction between the items "above" and "below" the line in Table 27.1 (i.e., between the first two categories and the third) is that the former arise out of normal business operations as well as from political considerations which are independent of the state of the overall balance of payments while the latter arise from the necessity (at least, under fixed exchange rates) to accommodate any imbalance between debits and credits for items above the line.[2] Thus, the distinction involves the underlying "motives" for the transactions. It is not surprising, therefore, that the precise point at which to draw "the line" has been a source of continuing controversy; as a consequence, several alternative measures of the overall surplus have generally been reported.[3] In Table 27.1 we show the most widely used measure of overall balance, the *official reserves transactions balance*. The balancing items in this definition include short-term official capital flows (e.g., those between official monetary authorities of the respective countries) and changes in official holdings of gold and other international reserve assets. If there is a net surplus of autonomous (above the line) items, the monetary authority will either acquire these additional units of foreign currency or use these inflows of foreign currency to acquire foreign government securities or gold or other currencies that are preferred as international reserves. Most countries hold their international reserves in dollars or dollar-denominated government securities. The process and necessity of acquiring such reserves will become clearer when we discuss the market for foreign exchange below.

THE EXCHANGE RATE, RELATIVE PRICES, ABSOLUTE PRICES, AND REAL INCOME

The currencies of the various nations are traded against each other on the foreign exchange market. The price of foreign exchange, called the *foreign exchange rate*, is usually quoted as the domestic currency price of a unit of foreign currency; for example, the German mark would be quoted as 0.50 dollars per mark in the U.S.[4]

---

[2] To maintain fixed exchange rates, governments must abort any excess supply or demand for foreign exchange that arises at the prevailing exchange rates. The balancing items are intended in this case to measure the extent of the prevailing excess supply or demand for foreign exchange. Under freely floating exchange rates, balancing items would be zero. Under a managed float, the balancing items provide a measure of the degree of government intervention in exchange markets. We will further discuss alternative arrangements concerning government intervention in the foreign exchange market later in this chapter.

[3] For a more thorough discussion of the balance of payments and a clear discussion of alternative measures of overall balance, see Robert Stern, *The Balance of Payments: Theory and Economic Policy* (Chicago: Aldine Pub. Co., 1973), Chapter 1; and Richard N. Cooper, "The Balance of Payments in Review," *Journal of Political Economics*, Vol. 74 (August, 1966), pp. 379–395.

[4] An exception is the British pound ("sterling") which is traditionally quoted in terms of the number of units of foreign currency per pound in the United Kingdom.

Note that, according to this convention, a *decline* in the value of the domestic currency (a decrease in the purchasing power of a dollar with respect to foreign goods) is equivalent to a *rise* in the foreign exchange rate; thus, an increase in the price of a mark from 0.50 to 0.60 dollars reduces the purchasing power of a dollar in terms of German goods. Of course, a decline in the value of the dollar against the mark is precisely equivalent to an increase in the value of the mark against the dollar.[5] The *exchange rate* is the rate of exchange between the *currencies* of two countries; in this section we consider whether it also provides a measure of the rate of exchange between the *goods* produced by the two countries. We will denote the dollar price of goods produced in the U.S. as $P(\$)$ and the foreign currency price of goods produced abroad as $P(£)$; £ is the symbol for the British pound or "sterling." We will use $P(£)$ as a proxy for the foreign currency price of all foreign goods. The exchange rate, e, is quoted as the number of dollars per pound ($/£).

○ The Keynesian Approach

Up to this point we have maintained a one-good framework so that relative prices of goods did not enter into the analysis. In the open economy case relative prices become central to the analysis. The assumption that usually underlies the simple extension of the Keynesian closed economy model to the open economy case is that prices of domestically produced goods are fixed in terms of the domestic currency; this is the natural counterpart of the "fixed price" assumption in the one-good closed economy model. The critical relative price, in this case, is the price of domestically produced goods relative to the price of foreign-produced goods (or, equivalently, the price of exports relative to the price of imports), denominated in a common currency; e.g., the ratio of the prices of export to import goods for the U.S. denominated in dollars is $P(\$)/eP(£)$. Where the prices of goods are fixed in terms of their respective currencies, changes in the exchange rate are the only source of changes in the relative price of imports and exports and relative prices vary systematically with changes in the exchange rate. To simplify, we assume $P(\$) = P(£) = 1$ in the fixed-price model so that these prices fall out of the explicit analysis and the influence of relative prices on import and export demands is captured by including the exchange rate as an argument in the demand functions for imports and exports.[6]

○ The Law of One Price and Purchasing Power Parity

This treatment of relative prices, however, violates the *law of one price*, according to which the price of any good should be the same in all locations, except for transport costs and government intervention (e.g., customs duties). This implies, in the absence of transport costs and governmental intervention, that $P_i(\$) = eP_i(£)$ for the ith commodity; i.e., the price of a given commodity denominated in a common currency

---

[5] When exchange rates are set by supply and demand on the exchange market, an increase in the exchange rate is called a *depreciation* of the dollar and a decrease in the exchange rate an *appreciation* of the dollar. When exchange rates are set at predetermined levels through government intervention, an increase in the exchange rate is called a *devaluation* and a decrease, an *upward revaluation*.

[6] An important paper in the development of the Keynesian approach to the open economy is Svend Laursen and Lloyd A. Metzler, "Flexible Exchange Rates and the Theory of Employment," *Review of Economics and Statistics*, Vol. 32 (November, 1950), pp. 281–299.

should be the same in all locations. This equality should be enforced by *commodity arbitrage*, the ability to profit by buying a good cheaply in one location and selling it at a higher price elsewhere. There are, however, several qualifications involved in moving from the level of individual commodities to price indices for domestic and foreign production and for imports and exports. First, not all goods are traded. Whether or not a particular good is traded depends on relative prices, although some goods such as houses and services will not be involved in international trade for any reasonable set of relative prices. The law of one price does not apply directly to nontraded goods. Therefore, although the law of one price may imply an equalization of the price of all traded goods in terms of a common currency, it does not imply that the price indices for domestic- and foreign-produced goods will be equalized since these indices are weighted averages of the price of traded and nontraded goods. Secondly, even if all goods were traded goods, the price indices for domestically produced goods would still differ across countries because these indices are weighted averages and the weights will differ across countries to reflect differences in relative quantities produced of each good. Thirdly, the law of one price does not restrict the relative price of imports and exports if countries specialize in the production of their export good(s). Note that the assumption of complete specialization provides a rationale for the Keynesian treatment of relative prices discussed above. It follows that the law of one price is more plausible for homogeneous goods traded on organized international auction markets, such as agricultural commodities and raw materials, but is less applicable to differentiated manufactured goods traded in monopolistically competitive and oligopolistic markets where prices tend to be based on markup over standard costs and where product differentiation provides scope for relative price movements.[7]

Assuming that countries do not specialize in the production of their export goods, ignoring the differences in weights in the price indices, and assuming that all goods are traded and that the goods produced in one country are perfect substitutes for goods produced elsewhere, the law of one price brings us in effect back to a one-commodity perspective. With $P(\$) = eP(£)$, the relative price of commodities (denominated in a common currency) produced in the two countries is $P(\$)/eP(£) = 1$ and is independent of the exchange rate. This case is the basis of the absolute version of the *purchasing power parity* (*PPP*) doctrine according to which the (equilibrium) exchange rate equals the ratio of the price levels in the two countries; i.e., $e = P(\$)/P(£)$.[8]

○ Nontraded Goods and Relative Prices

If we assume the law of one price holds for all traded goods but allow for the existence of nontraded goods, changes in exchange rates will not alter the relative price of imports and exports (traded goods) but may alter the relative price of traded

---

[7] For a discussion of the law of one price and some evidence on its consistency with observed prices of commodities in different countries, see Peter Isard, "How Far Can We Push the Law of One Price?" *American Economic Review*, Vol. 67 (December, 1977), pp. 942–948.

[8] For a thorough survey of the theory and applications of the *PPP* doctrine, see Lawrence H. Officer, "The Purchasing-Power-Parity Theory of Exchange Rates: A Review Article," International Monetary Fund, *Staff Papers*, Vol. 23 (March, 1976), pp. 1–60.

Part VII · Extension to an Open Economy

and nontraded goods and thereby affect the demands for imports and exports. For example, a devaluation that raised the price of traded to nontraded goods would induce a switching of expenditures from traded goods (imports) to domestically produced nontraded goods, thus reducing imports. Even in this case, imports and exports may be functions of the exchange rate.

○ Evidence on the Relation Between Exchange Rates and the Relative Price of Imports and Exports

There is, however, a substantial volume of evidence that the changes in exchange rates do in fact affect the relative price of imports and exports, at least in the short run.[9] This is consistent with the treatment in the Keynesian-type model, but inconsistent with the law of one price and purchasing power parity, although these may still be meaningful for very long-run analyses. This suggests that the Keynesian model provides a meaningful framework for short-run macroeconomic analysis. We will therefore assume that the key relative price in our model is the relative price of exports compared to imports and that this relative price can be identified with the exchange rate in the Keynesian version of our open economy model.

○ Absolute Prices and Real Income

Under Keynesian assumptions, we have to distinguish between the price index for domestic *output*, $P(\$)$, and the price index ($P$) that relates to the *expenditures* of home-country residents. The latter is a weighted average of prices of domestic- and foreign-produced goods where the weights reflect the relative importance of the two goods in total expenditures; i.e.,

$$P = \alpha P(\$) + (1 - \alpha) \, eP(\pounds) \qquad (27.1)$$

where α is the proportion of total expenditures allocated to domestic goods. $P(\$)$ corresponds to the implicit price deflator for *GNP* (a price index for goods produced in the U.S.) and P corresponds to the *CPI* (a price index associated with goods consumed by U.S. residents). Note that an increase in the dollar price of foreign output (either because of an increase in the exchange rate or because of an increase in the price denominated in foreign currency) increases the price index, P. With the real value of output produced in the U.S. unchanged, an increase in the consumer price index nevertheless reduces the real income concept relevant as a constraint on total expenditures by U.S. consumers. We can capture this by writing consumption expenditures as a function of both *GNP* and *e*. Thus, changes in exchange rates may induce both *substitution* and *real income* effects.

○ THE FOREIGN EXCHANGE MARKET

In Figure 27.1 we depict the two basic systems for determining exchange rates. The volume of foreign currency, assumed to be British pounds (£), is measured along the horizontal axis. The foreign exchange rate (*e*), the price of foreign exchange

---

[9] See, for example, Rudiger Dornbusch and Paul Krugman, "Flexible Exchange Rates in the Short-Run," *Brookings Papers on Economic Activity* (1976:3), pp. 537–575; and Peter Isard, "How Far Can We Push the Law of One Price?" *American Economic Review*, Vol. 67 (December, 1977), pp. 942–948.

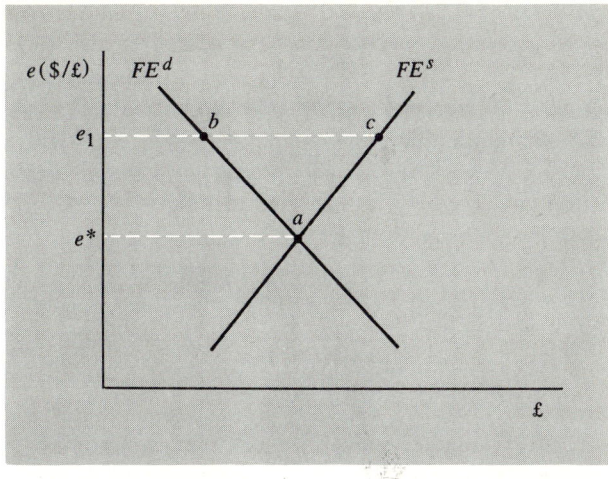

FIGURE 27.1
The Supply and Demand for Foreign Exchange

denominated as dollars per pound, is measured along the vertical axis. Under *flexible exchange rates*, exchange rates are determined by the supply of and demand for foreign exchange; the prevailing exchange rate in this case is the rate that clears the foreign exchange market, at e^* in Figure 27.1. Under *fixed exchange rates*, the monetary authorities of the various countries intervene in the foreign exchange market to maintain a predetermined pattern of exchange rates. If this exchange rate turns out to be above the equilibrium, as in the case of e_1 in Figure 27.1, the monetary authorities must prevent the excess supply at e_1 (equal to the horizontal distance bc) from putting downward pressure on the exchange rate. For example, the U.S. Fed may absorb the excess supply of sterling by purchasing the excess pounds; alternatively, the Bank of England may offset the excess demand for dollars by running down its reserve of dollars through purchases of pounds in the foreign exchange market.

○ Deriving the Shapes of the Supply and Demand Curves for Foreign Exchange

The supply and demand curves in Figure 27.1 reflect the response of international transactions to the level of the exchange rate. We assume for the moment that capital flows are independent of the exchange rate; they will therefore affect the position of the supply and demand curves but not their shape. The shapes of the supply and demand curves then reflect the response of imports and exports to the level of the exchange rate.

Exports give rise to a supply of foreign exchange (in payment for purchases of U.S. goods by foreigners) while imports give rise to a demand for foreign exchange (to pay for U.S. purchases of foreign goods). The real demand for both exports and imports is a function of the exchange rate, a measure of the relative price of these goods denominated in a common currency under the Keynesian assumptions being maintained in our analysis.

$$IM = IM(e) = \overline{IM} + IM_e e \tag{27.2}$$

$$EX = EX(e) = \overline{EX} + EX_e e \tag{27.3}$$

where $\overline{IM}$ and $\overline{EX}$ are the autonomous components of imports and exports, respectively, and IM_e and EX_e describe the response of imports and exports to a change in the exchange rate.

As we noted above, changes in exchange rates give rise to both substitution and real income effects. An increase in the exchange rate reduces the relative price of domestic output compared to foreign goods, inducing a substitution in favor of exports and away from imports. Domestic residents substitute domestic goods for foreign-produced goods, reducing imports; foreign residents substitute goods produced in the U.S. for goods produced in their own country, increasing U.S. exports. An increase in the exchange rate also reduces the real income of U.S. residents and increases the real incomes of foreign residents. The real income effect reduces the demand for imports and increases the demand for exports. The income effect thus reinforces the substitution effect. The effect of an increase in the exchange rate is therefore to reduce imports and increase exports. Hence, $IM_e < 0$ and $EX_e > 0$.

The supply of and demand for foreign exchange (FE^s and FE^d, respectively) reflect the *value* of the import and export demands; i.e., total desired *expenditures* on imports and exports, denominated in a common currency. In our example we denominate the value of imports and exports in the foreign currency. The foreign currency value of exports is $[P(\$)/e]EX$; this is the value of foreign exchange supplied to U.S. residents as a result of the sale of U.S. goods and services abroad. The foreign currency value of imports is $P(\pounds)IM$; this is the value of foreign exchange that U.S. residents demand in order to purchase goods produced abroad. Continuing with the assumption that $P(\$) = P(\pounds) = 1$, we write the supply and demand for foreign exchange as

$$FE^s = \frac{1}{e} EX(e) \tag{27.4}$$

$$FE^d = IM(e). \tag{27.5}$$

The demand for foreign exchange is unambiguously inversely related to the exchange rate; i.e., the FE^d curve is unambiguously negatively sloped. An increase in the exchange rate increases the dollar price of foreign-produced goods relative to domestic-produced goods, decreasing the real demand for imports. The foreign currency price of imports is unchanged, so the value of foreign exchange demanded to purchase imports (FE^d) unambiguously decreases. The slope of the supply curve, on the other hand, is ambiguous. An increase in the exchange rate reduces the foreign currency price of U.S. exports relative to foreign-produced goods and increases the *real demand* for exports; but the *value* of foreign exchange required to transact the higher demand for exports, $\left(\frac{1}{e}\right) EX$, may increase or decrease because the foreign currency price per unit of exports ($1/e$) declines while the units of exports (EX) increase. The effect of a change in the exchange rate on the supply of foreign exchange therefore depends on the *elasticity of demand* for U.S. exports (the percentage increase in the demand for exports in response to a given percentage change in the exchange rate). If demand is elastic, an increase in the exchange rate (a decline in the price per unit denominated in the foreign currency) induces a proportionately larger increase in the number of U.S. goods demanded for export so that the total expenditure on exports (the supply of foreign exchange) increases.

○ Disequilibrium and the Stability of the Foreign Exchange Market

Under flexible exchange rates, supply and demand determine the level of the exchange rate; e.g., in Figure 27.1 equilibrium occurs at an exchange rate of e^* where the FE^s and FE^d curves intersect. This is the only rate compatible with market clearing. At any rate above e^* there is an excess supply of foreign exchange, and at any rate below e^* there is an excess demand. When there is disequilibrium in the foreign exchange market, the exchange rate rises in proportion to the excess demand gap—the usual response of a price to market disequilibrium that we have assumed throughout. This disequilibrium adjustment can be formalized by

$$\dot{e} = \gamma(FE^d - FE^s) \tag{27.6}$$

where $\dot{e}$ is the proportional time rate of change in the exchange rate and γ is a positive constant. If the exchange rate were at $e_1 > e^*$, the excess supply equal to the distance bc in Figure 27.1 would put downward pressure on e until e^* was attained where supply and demand are equal. This suggests that the exchange market will always be stable when the demand curve is downward sloping and the supply curve is upward sloping.

If the supply curve is negatively sloped, on the other hand, the stability of the market depends on the relative slopes of the supply and demand curves. If the supply curve is steeper than the demand curve, as in Figure 27.2a, exchange rates above the equilibrium are still associated with excess supply and hence downward pressure on the exchange rate. Thus, the system remains stable. However, if the supply curve is flatter than the demand curve, exchange rates above equilibrium are associated with excess demand and hence *upward* pressure on the exchange rate. The exchange rate moves away from equilibrium in an explosive, unbounded fashion (beginning, of course, from a position of disequilibrium such as at e_1) and the foreign exchange market is unstable.

○ The Role of Demand Elasticities for Imports and Exports: The Marshall-Lerner Condition

The stability of the foreign exchange market thus depends on the relative responses of the supply and demand for foreign exchange to the exchange rate and these in turn depend on the relative responses of the supply and demand for imports and

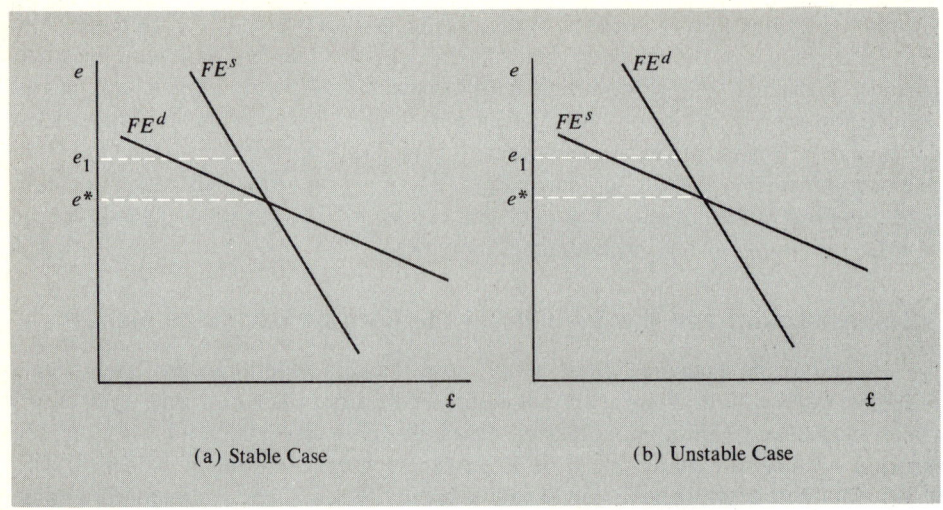

FIGURE 27.2
A Negatively Sloped Supply Curve and the
Stability of the Foreign Exchange Market

exports to exchange rates. The precise condition, called the *Marshall-Lerner condition* (which you can attempt to derive as a problem at the end of the chapter), is that the system is stable if the sum of the absolute values of the import and export demand elasticities exceeds unity.

Early empirical evidence on these elasticities suggested that the foreign exchange market might indeed be unstable. This "elasticity pessimism" gave way to "elasticity optimism" as improved econometric techniques resulted in higher estimates of these elasticities. It is now widely accepted that, at least in the long run, the Marshall-Lerner condition is fulfilled.[10] However, imports and exports respond gradually to a change in relative prices so that the short-run elasticity is much smaller than the long-run elasticity. As a result of lower short-run elasticities, the initial effects of the exchange rate depreciation may be to aggravate rather than improve the initial payments imbalance. The resulting time pattern of response of the trade surplus to a change in the exchange rate is sometimes referred to as the *J-curve phenomenon*, on account of the *J* pattern in Figure 27.3 where the trade balance is plotted against time. The trade balance is initially negative at point *A*. In response to the exchange rate depreciation, the trade deficit at first worsens (increasing from point *A* to point *B*) over the period from t_0 to t_1. Thereafter, it begins to improve, and in the long run, the trade deficit does indeed improve; at point *C* in Figure 27.3 the deficit is completely eliminated. Rudiger Dornbusch and Paul Krugman found, for example, that the elasticity of U.S. exports with respect to the relative price of imports and

---

[10] For a thorough empirical investigation of import and export elasticities, see Hendrick Houthakker and Stephen Magee, "Income and Price Elasticities in World Trade," *Review of Economics and Statistics*, Vol. 51 (May, 1969), pp. 111–125.

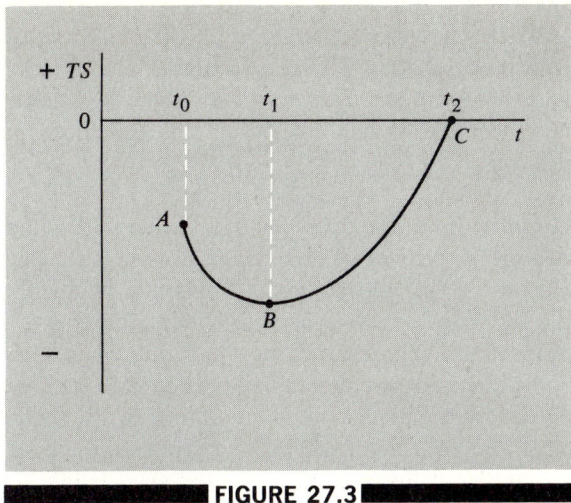

FIGURE 27.3

The Response of the Trade Surplus (*TS*) to a Change in the Exchange Rate: The *J* Curve

exports is only .33 for the first four quarters, less than 20 percent of the long-run elasticity.[11]

Capital Flows and Speculation

Up to this point we have focused on the supply and demand for foreign exchange associated with imports and exports of goods and services and viewed private capital flows as being determined independently of the exchange rate. Capital flows in this case affect the position of the supply and demand curves but not the stability of the market. For example, a net capital outflow would increase the demand for foreign exchange relative to the supply and require an increase in the exchange rate to induce a balancing excess of exports over imports. Capital movements may, however, be induced by a change in the exchange rate, based on the expectation that the exchange rate will continue moving in the same direction or will subsequently move in the *opposite* direction (toward its initial level). Such speculative capital flows may improve or damage the stability of the foreign exchange market.

Stabilizing Speculation. Assume, for example, that there is a temporary disturbance (e.g., an autonomous decrease in imports) which depresses the exchange rate. In the absence of speculative capital flows, the exchange rate decline will influence consumption and production decisions. But these adjustments may take a long time, and given the existence of adjustment costs, such changes in consumption and pro-

---

[11] Empirical evidence on the time path of adjustment can be found in Rudiger Dornbusch and Paul Krugman, "Flexible Exchange Rates in the Short-Run," *Brookings Papers on Economic Activity* (1976:3), pp. 537–575.

duction patterns may be undesirable. If speculators correctly foresee the temporary nature of the disturbance, they will recognize an opportunity to profit by purchasing foreign exchange now and reselling it later at a higher price. This will increase the demand for foreign exchange now relative to later, thereby stabilizing the exchange rate. The temporary decrease in imports has in this case been partially offset by speculative capital flows.

Destabilizing Speculation. If, on the other hand, a transitory decline in the exchange rate induces speculators to sell foreign exchange now in anticipation of buying it back later at a still lower price, speculation will increase fluctuations in the foreign exchange rate and may transform an otherwise stable market into an unstable one.

Speculative capital flows will generally be stabilizing when speculators correctly identify temporary disturbances and destabilizing when they incorrectly view temporary shifts in supply and/or demand curves as continuing further in the same direction. Note that speculators who are correct will make a profit. In the case discussed above, the speculators buy low and sell high. If, however, speculators are incorrect, they will suffer losses. This provides good reason for believing that speculators who are systematically incorrect will go out of business so that correct speculation will dominate. But there is no presumption that incorrect speculators are not continuously replaced by other incorrect speculators or that, even though speculation is on the average correct, there are not occasional episodes of destabilizing speculation. Note however that to result in market instability, incorrect speculators would have to dominate the market.

The issues of stability and speculation are also important under a "fixed" exchange rate system where occasional exchange rate adjustments are permitted to correct major, prolonged disequilibria. This corresponds to the adjustable peg system that prevailed from the end of World War II to 1973. Devaluation will correct a deficit position if the foreign exchange market is stable. When a serious, persistent disequilibrium puts an exchange rate under pressure, speculators have a *one-way option*: if there is a persistent deficit, they know that exchange rates can only remain constant or rise. There is no risk of a fall. Therefore, speculators sell foreign exchange and by worsening the excess supply may force a devaluation that otherwise might have been avoided. On the other hand, they may force a movement toward the equilibrium exchange rate that might have been postponed by the intervention in the foreign exchange market of the monetary authorities. In the latter case, perhaps the more typical case, such speculative capital flows cannot be meaningfully characterized as destabilizing.

INTEGRATING TRADE AND INTERNATIONAL CAPITAL FLOWS INTO THE *IS-LM* MODEL

In this section we revise the closed economy specification of the *IS-LM* model to incorporate trade and international capital flows. We begin with the modifications required in the commodity and money market equilibrium conditions (the *IS* and

LM curves, respectively) and then develop the role of the foreign exchange market in the analysis.

○ The Output Market

In the open economy case we must distinguish *expenditures* of domestic residents (sometimes called *absorption*, A) and domestic *production* (X). Part of domestic output is sold abroad (exports); thus, exports are a component of the demand for domestic output but not part of the expenditures by domestic residents. In turn, part of domestic expenditures are for goods produced abroad (imports); imports are part of domestic expenditures but not a component of the demand for domestic output. To simplify our model, we will assume that consumption expenditures are allocated between domestic- and foreign-produced goods but that all investment and government expenditures are for domestic output. We will refer to consumer expenditures on domestic output as C^h and consumer expenditures on foreign output as total imports (IM); it follows that total consumer expenditures (C) is the sum of consumption expenditures on domestic output and imports. Recall from our discussion earlier that domestic and foreign goods are being treated as distinct goods; therefore, we can compare them only in *value* terms, not in terms of physical units. To further simplify, we will assume initially that the prices of domestic and foreign goods are fixed in terms of their own currencies and that $P(\$) = P(£) = 1$; in this case the price of foreign output in terms of domestic output is given by the exchange rate. We can write total consumption expenditures in this case as

$$C = C^h + eIM \tag{27.7}$$

and total expenditures or absorption as

$$A = \underbrace{C^h + eIM}_{C} + I + G. \tag{27.8}$$

Total domestic production (or real *GNP*) is given by

$$X = C^h + I + G + EX. \tag{27.9}$$

Note that real *GNP* can be written alternatively as $C + I + G +$ net exports:

$$X = \underbrace{C^h + eIM}_{C} + I + G + \underbrace{EX - eIM}_{\text{net exports}} \tag{27.9'}$$

Not all consumption, investment, and government expenditures result in a demand for domestic output; part of these are for foreign-produced goods (imports). Therefore, we subtract imports from $C + I + G$ to get domestic demand for domestic output.

Part VII · Extension to an Open Economy

The total demand for domestic output is in turn increased by the demand for domestic output by foreign residents (exports). Hence we add on exports. The specification of our *IS* curve follows from the definition of real *GNP* given by equation (27.9).[12] The demand for domestic output of consumption goods by domestic residents is given by

$$C^h = C^h(Y,e) = \bar{C}^h + C_y^h Y + C_e^h e \qquad (27.10)$$

where $\bar{C}^h$ is the autonomous component of C^h. The demands for imports and exports are given by equations (27.2 and 27.3) above.

The demand for domestic output of consumption goods by domestic residents (C^h), like the demands for imports and exports, depends on the exchange rate, the unique determinant of the relative price of domestic and foreign goods, assuming fixed prices of these goods in terms of their respective currencies. Changes in the exchange rate have income and substitution effects. These reinforce each other in the case of exports but offset each other in the case of domestic demand for domestic output of consumption goods. An increase in the exchange rate reduces the relative price of U.S. to foreign-produced goods to U.S. residents and reduces the real income of U.S. residents. The substitution effect increases the domestic demand for domestic output of consumption goods (switches consumption expenditures from foreign to domestic output) while the income effect reduces expenditures on both domestic and foreign goods; the net effect on the domestic demand for domestic output of consumption goods and hence the sign of C_e^h are ambiguous. We will assume that the substitution effect dominates so that $C_e^h > 0$; however, the result that an increase in the exchange rate increases the demand for domestic output only requires that $C_e^h + EX_e > 0$.

C^h also depends on domestic (disposable) income; we assume $1 > C_y^h > 0$ and $C_y^h < C_y$, where C_y is the closed economy value of the marginal propensity to consume domestic output by domestic residents. This means that an increase in income results in a smaller increase in the demand for domestic output in an open economy because part of the increased expenditures is diverted to the purchase of foreign-produced goods. Exports also depend on foreign income, but foreign income is assumed to be exogenous in our analysis.

In the case of fixed exchange rates (assume $e = 1$ here for simplicity) our model will again involve only two unknowns, r and X. The *IS* curve in the open economy case is

---

[12] The traditional approach for respecifying the *IS* curve in the open economy case is to simply add on a net exports term to the closed economy specification of the *IS* curve. In this specification imports are included in consumption (and perhaps other components of domestic expenditure) and then subtracted off. We prefer to employ the definition of real *GNP* given by equation (27.9) in which imports do not appear at all. Egon Sohmen, in a series of articles, has drawn attention to the widespread misspecification of the *IS* and *BP* curves in the flexible exchange rate case. Our specification avoids the kind of error about which Sohmen warns. See, for example, Egon Sohmen, "Exchange Rates, Terms of Trade, and Employment: Pitfalls in Macroeconomic Models of Open Economies," *Kyklos*, Vol. 27 (1974), pp. 521–536.

$$\left.\frac{\Delta r}{\Delta X}\right|_{IS} = \frac{1 - C_y^h}{I_r}.^{13} \quad (27.11)$$

Given that $C_y^h < C_y$, the slope of the open economy IS curve (IS_o in Figure 27.4) is steeper than the slope of the closed economy IS curve (IS_c). To clarify why IS_o is steeper than IS_c, consider the decline in the interest rate required to restore output market equilibrium in response to an increase in domestic output in the closed and open economy cases. The increase in income results in a smaller increase in demand for domestic output in the open economy case because part of demand is diverted to foreign-produced goods (imports); therefore, the increase in output (ΔX equal to the distance ab in Figure 27.4) results in a greater excess supply in the commodity market (at point b) and hence requires a larger decline in the interest rate to restore commodity market equilibrium in the open economy case (from point b to point o) compared to the closed economy case (from point b to point c).

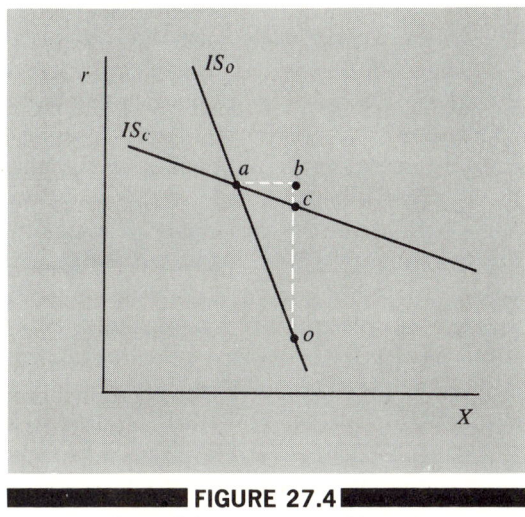

FIGURE 27.4
The IS Curves in the Closed
and Open Economy Cases

○ The Money Market

In the open economy case, balance of payments surpluses or deficits may affect the domestic money supply. To clarify this interaction, we must refine the definition

---

[13] Given that $C_y = C_y^h + IM_y$ (with $e = 1$), this can also be written in the more traditional form as

$$\left.\frac{\Delta r}{\Delta X}\right|_{IS} = \frac{1 - C_y + IM_y}{I_r}.$$

Given that $IM_y > 0$, the slope of the IS curve in the open economy case is clearly steeper than in the closed economy case where $IM_y = 0$.

of the nonborrowed monetary base introduced in Chapter 23. In that chapter we identified the Fed's portfolio of government securities (B_g^F) as the only source of the nonborrowed monetary base. The nonborrowed monetary base also includes official gold holdings (G) and foreign exchange holdings (FE^*) as (positive) sources of the base and foreign official holdings of domestic currency (f) as a negative source.

$$NMB = B_g^F + G + FE^* - f \tag{27.12}$$

Any increase in gold associated with settlement of payments imbalances (as under the gold standard from 1880 to World War I or under the gold exchange standard which prevailed from 1946 to 1971 when the U.S. abandoned convertibility of dollars into gold) or increases in official foreign exchange holdings associated with official intervention in the foreign exchange market automatically increase the nonborrowed monetary base and hence the money supply unless offset by domestic open market operations. Any increase in official holdings of a nation's currency by foreign central banks will decrease the foreign country's nonborrowed monetary base.

An example will clarify the effect of payments imbalances on domestic money supplies. Assume the U.S. has a deficit vis-a-vis West Germany and Germany acquires the excess supply of dollars to defend the exchange rate. We will see below that under the system that emerged from the Bretton Woods Agreement in 1944, intervention to support the exchange rate was generally conducted at the initiative of countries other than the U.S. by buying or selling dollars for their own currencies. The purchase of dollars with German marks increases the supply of marks outstanding; i.e., the FE^* component of the German NMB has increased. Without offsetting domestic operations, the German surplus has induced a domestic monetary expansion. The counterpart of the increase in official dollar holdings by the German central bank is the increase in foreign official dollar holdings on the Fed's balance sheet; i.e., an increase in f is a decrease in the U.S. nonborrowed monetary base (reflecting the fact that foreign official dollar balances are held as deposits with the Federal Reserve System, not with private commercial banks). However, West Germany will generally prefer to hold interest-earning dollar-denominated assets and will therefore exchange its dollars for U.S. government securities, either by purchasing them in the open market or through negotiations directly with the U.S. Treasury (but not from the Fed's own portfolio). The net result of such a purchase of U.S. securities will be to neutralize the effect of the German BP surplus on the U.S. money supply.[14]

On balance, then, the payments imbalance between the U.S. and Germany results in an expansion in the German money supply without any change in the U.S. money supply. The tendency of the U.S. money supply to be unaffected by the U.S. balance of payments reflects the special role of the dollar as a *reserve currency*, or a currency that is used as international reserves. We will explore below the special role of the reserve center, the country whose currency is used as international reserves. Consider, on the other hand, the effect of surplus/deficit positions between two countries whose

---

[14] Note that the FE^* term in the definition of the net source base includes both official holdings of foreign exchange and of foreign government securities.

currencies are not used as reserves. If France is a net deficit country and Germany a net surplus country, France will run down its dollar reserves, reducing its domestic monetary base and money supply while Germany acquires dollars and hence expands both its monetary base and money supply. In general, therefore, the domestic money supplies of both surplus and deficit countries are affected by payments imbalances.

The domestic monetary repercussions of international payments imbalances can be offset or *sterilized* in the short run by use of domestic open market operations. For example, if the German central bank responded to the increase in the FE^* component of its base by an equivalent-sized reduction in the B_g^F component via open market sales, the nonmonetary base would be unchanged; i.e., $\Delta B_g^F = -\Delta FE^*$ so that $\Delta NMB = 0$. Monetary authorities can and often do sterilize the effects of payments imbalances, but their ability to do so indefinitely is constrained by the size of their portfolio of government securities (limiting the magnitude of offsetting open market sales in the face of BP surpluses) and by the size of eligible security holdings available for them to purchase (limiting the offsetting open market purchases in the face of persistent deficits). This generally leaves considerable scope for sterilization operations and raises questions about the short-run efficacy of automatic changes in domestic money supplies induced by payments imbalances as an equilibrating mechanism. Empirical evidence suggests that some degree of sterilization is possible and indeed has been undertaken in the short run, although there is a wide range of experience. For example, Japan has been able to sterilize its surpluses while the German money supply has been dramatically influenced by its BP position.[15]

In the case of nonsterilized payments imbalances, the balance of payments becomes, in effect, a *shift parameter* in the LM curve, at least for nonreserve center countries. The effect of BP imbalances is *cumulative*; as long as a BP surplus persists, $\Delta FE^* > 0$ and the LM curve shifts outward. We will explore the implications of the monetary repercussions of payments imbalances, emphasized in the monetary approach to the balance of payments, in the next chapter.

○ The Balance of Payments and the Foreign Exchange Market

The balance of payments reflects the state of excess demand for foreign exchange; i.e., the BP surplus or deficit indicates the magnitude of intervention required to sustain the prevailing rate structure. The U.S. *balance of payments surplus, BP*, is defined as net exports minus net capital outflows, F, all denominated in dollars. Assuming $P(\$) = P(£) = 1$, we can write the BP surplus as

$$BP \equiv EX - eIM - F \qquad (27.13)$$

Net Capital Outflows and Interest Rates. We have already discussed the determinants of import and export demands. Net capital outflows depend on domestic and foreign interest rates (r and r_f, respectively). We will treat the foreign interest rate as exogenous. The modeling of net capital outflows presents the same difficulties we encountered

---

[15] For a discussion of the evidence on sterilization, see Marina v. N. Whitman, "Global Monetarism and the Monetary Approach to the Balance of Payments," in *Brookings Papers on Economic Activity* (1975:3), pp. 491–536.

in our development of the theory of net investment in Chapter 14. The basic decision relating to portfolio demands is a *stock* decision; i.e., how much wealth to hold at any time in domestic and foreign assets. This decision depends on both foreign and domestic interest rates. An increase in domestic rates will lead to a capital inflow as portfolio owners shift from foreign assets toward U.S. assets. Once the adjustment is completed, however, the capital inflow will end. In the long run, therefore, there is no relation between the level of the domestic interest rate and capital *flows*. We can formalize this in terms of the stock adjustment model we initially introduced for net investment in Chapter 4 and further considered in Chapter 14. The net demand for foreign assets (FA^d), or the difference between the U.S. demand for foreign assets and the foreign demand for U.S. assets, is a function of domestic and foreign interest rates:

$$FA^d = D(r, \bar{r}_f). \tag{27.14}$$

The higher the domestic interest rate relative to the foreign rate, the smaller the net demand for foreign assets by U.S. residents; hence, $D_r < 0$ and $D_{r_f} > 0$. Net capital outflows ($F = \Delta FA$) occur when the net demand for foreign assets exceeds current holdings.

$$F = \beta(FA^d - \overline{FA}) \tag{27.15}$$

where $\overline{FA}$ is initial (beginning-of-period) holdings of net foreign assets and β is a positive constant, the speed of adjustment of actual to desired holdings. Hence, we can write F as

$$F = F(r, \bar{r}_f, \overline{FA}) \tag{27.15'}$$

and since r_f and $\overline{FA}$ are fixed for short-run analysis, this reduces for our purposes to the conventional equation

$$F = F(r) = \overline{F} + F_r r \tag{27.15''}$$

where $F_r < 0$. But this equation must be used with caution because it is only meaningful for short-run analysis.

The BP Equation the BP Curve. The *BP* equation describes the combinations of the values of the interest rate and the output for which the *BP* surplus will be unchanged. We can set $BP = 0$ and find the combinations of r and X that will yield balance of payments equilibrium. To simplify, we consider the case of fixed exchange rates where $e = 1$:

$$0 = \overline{EX} - (\overline{IM} - IM_y Y) - (\overline{F} + F_r r).$$

Solving for the slope of the *BP* curve in the r, X plane in Figure 27.5, we obtain

$$\left.\frac{\Delta r}{\Delta X}\right|_{BP} = -\frac{IM_y}{F_r} > 0. \tag{27.16}$$

The positive slope indicates that an increase in income which worsens the trade balance can be offset by a rise in the interest rate and associated capital inflow. All points above and to the left of the *BP* line are points of surplus; e.g., at an unchanged interest rate, a decline in income reduces imports and results in a surplus (as at point *a*). All points to the right and below the *BP* line are correspondingly points of deficit; e.g., beginning from a point on the *BP* curve, a decline in the interest rate at an unchanged level of income induces a capital outflow and results in a deficit (as at point *b*).

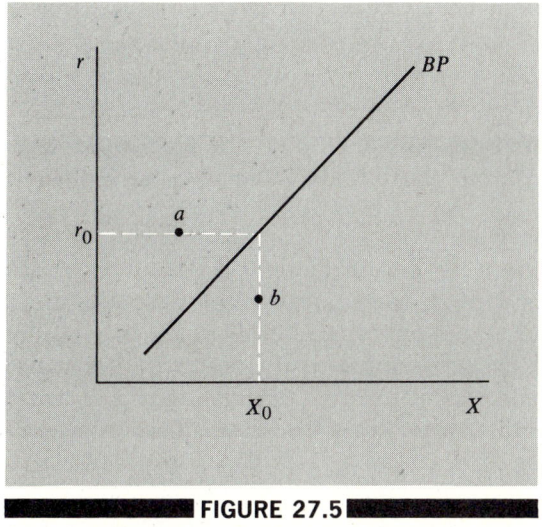

FIGURE 27.5
The Balance of Payments Curve

The BP Curve and Capital Mobility. The slope of the *BP* curve depends on the degree of *capital mobility*. If capital is perfectly immobile, then $F_r = 0$ and the *BP* line is vertical (the *BP* position is independent of the interest rate). On the other hand, if capital is perfectly mobile, $F_r = -\infty$ and the domestic interest rate cannot diverge from the world interest rate. If the domestic interest rate rises above the world rate, for example, capital continues to flow into the U.S. until the U.S. rate is driven back to the world rate. In this case the *BP* curve becomes horizontal at the prevailing world interest rate; i.e., $r = \bar{r}_f$ is the equation for the *BP* curve. Given that this is most likely to apply in the long run, there may still be scope for an upward-sloping curve in the short run. If we assume imperfect capital mobility, $-\infty < F_r < 0$, and the *BP* curve slopes upward. In this case increases in the domestic interest rate induce capital inflows, but not to the degree necessary to drive the interest rate back to its initial level. The three alternative versions of the *BP* curve, depending on the degree of capital mobility, are depicted in Figure 27.6. BP_0 assumes capital immobility; BP_∞, perfect capital mobility; and *BP*, imperfect capital mobility.

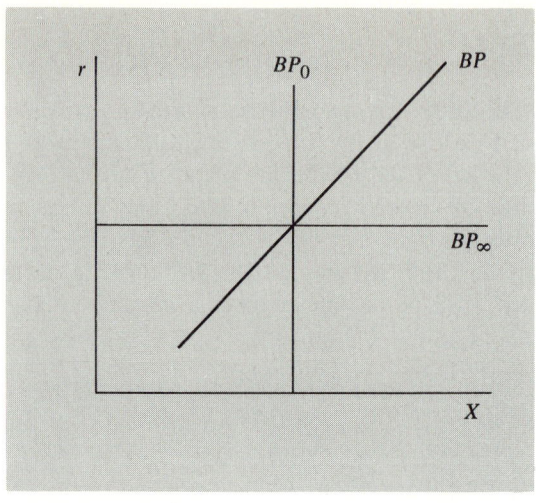

FIGURE 27.6
The *BP* Curve Under Alternative Assumptions
About Capital Mobility

In capital is imperfectly mobile, we must determine the relative positions of the positively sloped *BP* and *LM* curves. The two possible cases are depicted in Figures 27.7a and 27.7b. There remains disagreement in the literature about their relative slopes since there is no a priori reason why one or the other case should prevail.[16] The most widely held view is that the *BP* curve is steeper, but we will attempt to make clear as we go along when this assumption makes a difference in our conclusions.

The BP Curve Under Fixed and Flexible Exchange Rates. Under fixed exchange rates, the *BP* curve is not an equilibrium curve in the same sense as the *IS* and *LM* curves. This follows from the fact that under fixed exchange rates the exchange market need not be in equilibrium. The intersection of the *IS* and *LM* curves determines the equilibrium interest rate and output. These are substituted into the *BP* equation to determine whether a surplus or deficit exists. If the intersection of the *IS* and *LM* curves occurs below the *BP* curve, for example, the equilibrium interest rate and output results in a *BP* deficit. But the *BP* curve does not affect the simultaneous solution for the interest rate and output and is included only to permit us to determine the balance of payments implications of the *IS-LM* solution for *r* and *X*. Note, however, that *in the absence of sterilization* the *LM* curve will shift back as long as the deficit persists and this will ultimately restore *BP* equilibrium, although perhaps at the expense of price level objectives if prices are flexible or at the expense of domestic output

---

[16] Dwayne Wrightsman, for example, suggests that the *BP* curve is likely to be normally steeper than the *LM* curve as in our Figure 27.7a. See Dwayne Wrightsman, "*IS, LM*, and External Equilibrium: A Graphical Analysis," *American Economic Review*, Vol. 60 (March, 1970), pp. 203–208. Robert Stern, on the other hand, carries out his analysis using a *BP* curve flatter than the *LM* curve as in our Figure 27.7b. See Robert M. Stern, *The Balance of Payments: Theory and Economic Policy* (Chicago: Aldine Pub. Co., 1973), Chapter 10. Both authors note, however, that there is no a priori restriction on the relative slopes of the *LM* and *BP* curves.

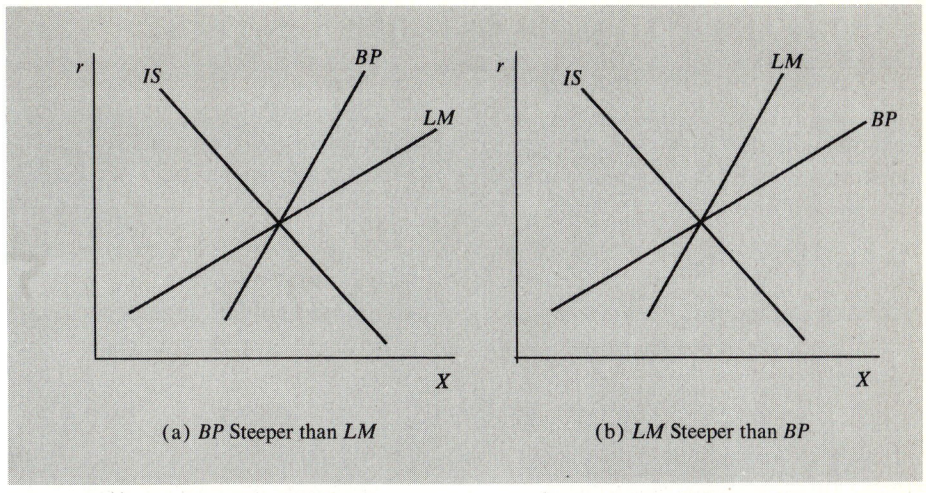

FIGURE 27.7
The Relation among the *IS*, *LM*, and *BP* Curves
with Imperfect Capital Mobility

and employment objectives if prices are sluggish in the downward direction. Over time, in the absence of sterilization, the *BP* deficit associated with the *IS-LM* curve solution will reduce the money supply, shifting the *LM* curve backward until all three curves intersect at the same point.

A change in exchange rates will shift both the *IS* and *BP* curves. An increase in the exchange rate encourages exports and induces a substitution of domestic demand from foreign to domestic output at given levels of income and the interest rate. Therefore, it is equivalent to an autonomous increase in aggregate demand and shifts the *IS* curve up and to the right. And an increase in the exchange rate moves the *BP* toward a surplus beginning at any point along the original *BP* curve (assuming the Marshall-Lerner condition is fulfilled); thus, the original curve must now be above the new curve, implying a downward shift in the *BP* curve.[17] As an exercise at the end of the chapter, you are asked to work out the explicit expressions for shifts in the *IS* and *BP* curves.

Under flexible exchange rates, the *BP* curve becomes a part of the simultaneous system that determines income, interest rate, and now, of course, the exchange rate. We have the usual graphical headache of three unknowns. We will stick to the *IS-LM-BP* framework showing only two of the unknowns on the axes. Each curve will be drawn for a given value of the exchange rate. Full equilibrium will require that all three curves intersect at the same point. If the *IS* and *LM* curves intersect off the *BP* curve, the exchange rate will rise or fall in response to the prevailing deficit or surplus, moving the curves until equilibrium is achieved.

---

[17] The *LM* curve could also be affected by the rise in the price level of goods purchased from abroad. However, to simplify the graphical analysis, we will ignore this effect which is likely to be quite small compared to the effects on the *IS* and *BP* curves. The latter effects will be further clarified in the next chapter.

METHODS AND SYSTEMS OF BALANCE OF PAYMENTS ADJUSTMENT

In this section we will discuss alternative methods of financing and correcting disequilibria in the balance of payments and then discuss the basic types of international monetary systems that provide a framework for coordinating the response of countries to payments imbalances.

Methods of Financing Payments Imbalances

Let us assume that a country finds itself with a payments deficit associated with a below-equilibrium exchange rate. There are a variety of methods of coping with this imbalance.

Financing the Deficit via Drawing Down International Reserves. One possibility is to finance or accommodate the deficit at the prevailing disequilibrium exchange rate; i.e., not to take measures to correct it but instead to prevent the imbalance from altering the exchange rate. Deficit countries can finance the resulting foreign exchange disequilibrium by drawing down reserves of foreign exchange; alternatively, surplus countries can offset the corresponding excess supply of the deficit countries' currency by purchasing the deficit countries' foreign exchange with the surplus countries' own currency, adding to their reserve holdings of foreign exchange. In general, countries hold their international reserves in gold and dollars, assets which have generally been acceptable in settlement of payments imbalances. Deficit countries run down their dollar reserves as they acquire their own currency in the financing operations while surplus countries acquire dollars in exchange for their own currencies.

But financing is not a permanent solution. It prevents the disequilibrium from upsetting the pattern of exchange rates but does not correct imbalances (except insofar as the financing operations are allowed to affect domestic money supplies). And financing cannot go on indefinitely. Deficit countries will ultimately run out of reserves (except if the reserves are liabilities on themselves) and surplus countries will become increasingly reluctant to accumulate reserves.

Financing the Deficit via Short-Term Capital Flows. An alternative short-run response is to raise domestic short-term interest rates relative to those abroad to induce a net capital inflow and thereby attain balance in overall international transactions. We include this as a means of financing rather than eliminating the deficit because the capital inflow associated with a once-and-for-all increase in the interest rate is only temporary. Like the financing of a *BP* deficit by drawing down official reserves, once-and-for-all increases in interest rates are effective for coping with *temporary* imbalances and for buying time to initiate and derive the benefit from policies to correct more persistent imbalances.

Methods of Correcting Payments Imbalances

The first three "corrective" policies are intended to eliminate imbalances while maintaining fixed exchange rates. Therefore, they are generally employed in combination with financing operations; the latter are used to defend the rate structure until the corrective measures become effective.

Domestic Price Adjustment. A deficit country can improve its payments position by using domestic policy (or allowing automatic forces associated with the effect of nonsterilized *BP* imbalances on the domestic money supply) to reduce the prices of domestically produced goods. A decline in the price of domestically produced goods makes domestic output more attractive to foreign residents and foreign goods less attractive to domestic residents, thereby both expanding the exports and reducing the imports of the deficit country. Similarly, surplus countries can allow their domestic prices to rise, discouraging exports and encouraging imports.[18]

Real Income Adjustment. Prices may be relatively sluggish in the downward direction so that the burden of adjustment in deficit countries to either (nonsterilized) declines in the money stock or explicit restrictive policy may fall on real income, at least in the short run. Declines in income reduce imports and hence also move the country toward balance in its international payments, although obviously at the expense of domestic objectives of high output and employment. If surplus countries face slack in their own economies, they can use stimulative policies to expand output, thereby encouraging imports and improving both the international payments and domestic employment situation. However, surplus countries will be reluctant to carry out stimulative policies beyond the point where inflation is accelerated and hence may leave the burden of income adjustment on deficit countries.

Direct Controls. A final method of preserving exchange rates in the face of a payments imbalance is to impose direct controls on current and/or capital account transactions so as to improve the overall payments situation. For example, deficit countries could (1) impose tariffs (taxes on imports which raise their price relative to domestically produced goods); (2) provide subsidies to export industries, improving their competitive position relative to foreign-produced goods; (3) impose quotas (limits to the number of goods that can be imported) or embargoes (prohibiting imports) on imports; (4) use exchange controls to limit foreign exchange to importers; or (5) use capital controls to preclude or limit capital flows.

Direct controls act to reduce the volume of world trade and to distort patterns of production, consumption, and trade. The use of controls, particularly those affecting current account transactions, is discouraged except as an emergency measure to allow time for the effects of other methods of adjustment. The General Agreement on Tariffs and Trade (GATT), for example, prohibits unilateral changes in tariffs and permits temporary quotas only under extreme conditions.

If the imbalance is persistent so that temporary financing is insufficient, if direct controls are avoided except as emergency measures, if both deficit and surplus countries

---

[18] Price adjustments shift the demand for exports and imports and hence the supply and demand curves for foreign exchange. To model this case, we must allow for variable levels of $P(\$)$ and $P(£)$ in our model. The demand for imports and exports depends on the relative price of exports to imports, $P(\$)/eP(£)$. The equation for the balance of payments in this case becomes $BP = P(\$)EX - eP(£)IM - F$. Note however that the same problem arises with respect to price changes as we noted for exchange rate changes. A decline in the domestic price level unambiguously reduces the demand for foreign exchange, equal to the decline in the real demand for imports times the unchanged foreign currency price of a unit of imports. The effect on the supply of foreign exchange, on the other hand, is ambiguous because of the offsetting effects of the decrease of the foreign currency price of exports and the increase in the real demand for exports. A decline in the domestic price level will reduce the excess demand gap in the foreign exchange market as long as the demand declines by more than the supply declines.

are reluctant to use domestic stabilization policies to correct international payments imbalances at the expense of domestic employment and price objectives, then a solution may still be achieved by altering exchange rates.

Allowing the Exchange Rate to Rise to Clear the Market. Allowing the exchange rate to rise (either by enforcing a new, higher exchange rate through government intervention or allowing the excess demand to drive up the exchange rate in a market free of government intervention) has the same effect as declining domestic prices in deficit countries and rising prices in surplus countries and is therefore a natural substitute for price flexibility. An increase in the exchange rate reduces the price of exports to foreign residents and increases the price of imports to domestic residents, thus encouraging exports and discouraging imports in the deficit country. Similarly, imports are encouraged and exports discouraged in the surplus country.

Systems of Coordinating the Responses to Payments Imbalances

In this section we discuss a number of international monetary systems, some hypothetical and some with historical counterparts. We use the term *international monetary system* to describe the set of institutions and conventions that govern the intervention (or nonintervention) of governments in exchange markets, the methods appropriate to correcting payments imbalances, and the nature and control of the reserve assets in which surpluses and deficits can be settled.

There are two polar cases of exchange rate regimes: fixed and flexible. However, during the postwar period, exchange rates have been neither perfectly rigid nor completely free. They have been managed via government intervention. From 1947–1971 this management took the form of a structure of exchange rates which was normally fixed but allowed under certain circumstances to change; this system is referred to as the *adjustable peg*. Subsequently, exchange rates were permitted to float, but governments continued to intervene in exchange markets to affect the rate structure; this is referred to as a *dirty* or *managed float* (presumably depending on whether you like the intervention or not!).

The adjustment procedures were discussed above. Under flexible exchange rates, no other method of correcting imbalances may be required. Under the managed float, on the other hand, surpluses and deficits have continued to be quite persistent so that other methods were often adopted or at least advocated along with exchange rate movement. Under fixed rates, surpluses and deficits must be financed temporarily while either automatic forces associated with the monetary repercussions of payments imbalances or alternative discretionary techniques of adjustment are initiated. A central problem for any fixed rate system is to encourage effective corrective action and allocate the burden of the adjustment among surplus and deficit countries.

Under freely floating exchange rates, no official international reserves need be held. There are no imbalances to be settled and no intervention in exchange markets. In other exchange rate regimes, agreements must determine acceptable means for settlement of payments imbalances and provide for the adequate growth of the reserve assets to accommodate the growth in international transactions.

Below we discuss four alternative systems that combine an exchange rate regime, a settlement procedure, and an adjustment process: the gold standard, freely floating exchange rates, the adjustable peg, and a managed float.

The Gold Standard. The gold standard is an example of a pure fixed rate regime. Under its simplest form, the *gold-specie standard,* the money supply of each country consists entirely of gold coins and each government commits itself to convert gold into coins at a nominal cost and to settle international payments imbalances by movements of gold. This is a simple procedure for ensuring fixed exchange rates since it essentially reduces to a single currency for all countries; after all, the different names, shapes, and imprints on a nation's gold coins are quite irrelevant to the exchange value of gold which depends on the weight of the gold alone.

However, there is no historical counterpart to this strict gold-specie standard. Generally gold was not the only form of money circulating domestically. During the period of the gold standard, from 1880 to World War I, there were always other currencies circulating with gold, such as silver or bank deposits. In this case the gold standard required governments to maintain convertibility between gold and other currencies at fixed prices. The net result would be the same as under the gold-specie standard provided that international movements of gold were permitted to affect national money supplies.

The gold standard thus prescribes fixed exchange rates, settlement of imbalances by gold flows, and involves adjustment to imbalances via changes in domestic money stocks automatically induced by international payments imbalances.

The model of the adjustment of payments imbalances under the gold standard usually presumes price and wage flexibility. Movements of gold induce changes in the money supply which in turn alter relative prices in surplus and deficit countries, encouraging exports and discouraging imports in deficit countries and discouraging exports and encouraging imports in surplus countries. These adjustments occur against the background of continuous full employment in both surplus and deficit countries. In practice, central banks generally attempted to avoid gold outflows by responding to deficits with an increase in domestic interest rates so as to induce offsetting capital inflows to current account deficits. In addition, they were reluctant to permit the gold flows that did emerge to influence domestic money supplies since price flexibility was never sufficient to avoid declines in domestic output and employment in response to monetary restraint.

The gold standard involves a single international reserve asset in which settlement is acceptable but leaves the growth of this reserve asset to be determined by gold discoveries and the state of technology for mining gold and by the price of gold relative to other goods.

Freely Floating or Flexible Exchange Rates. Like the gold-specie standard, there is no historical counterpart to the system of freely floating exchange rates. Since 1973, exchange rates have been flexible in the sense that governments are not committed to defending a predetermined structure but governments continue to intervene to at least smooth exchange rate movements. Under a freely floating exchange rate, governments do not intervene in exchange markets so that the balance of payments as defined on the basis of the autonomous items in Table 27.1 must be in continuous balance. The system is particularly simple: exchange rates are flexible, adjustment of disequilibrium occurs via exchange rate movements which continuously clear the foreign exchange market, and there are no imbalances to settle or reserve assets to hold.

The case for freely floating exchange rates is that it provides for equilibrium in the foreign exchange market without compromising domestic output and price objectives and provides for efficient world resource allocation by permitting unrestricted voluntary trade on free markets.[19] The case against freely floating exchange rates is based on fears that the foreign exchange market may be inherently unstable (failure of the Marshall-Lerner condition) or at least may be susceptible to destabilizing speculation. Even if the market is stable, there may be sizable short-run fluctuations in exchange rates; the resulting increase in exchange risk may reduce the volume of world trade.[20]

The Adjustable Peg. In 1944 international agreements were reached at the Bretton Woods conference to coordinate the response to payments imbalances so as to avoid the problems associated with both the fixity of exchange rates under the gold standard and the competitive manipulation of exchange rates employed during the 1930s to improve domestic employment at the expense of other countries. To accomplish this, a pattern of exchange rates was agreed upon. Under normal circumstances, participants were committed to defend this pattern. Surpluses and deficits were to be financed by flows of gold and foreign exchange acceptable as international reserves. Other corrective measures were to be initiated in response to persistent imbalances, although direct controls, particularly with respect to current account transactions, were discouraged. However, in cases of "fundamental disequilibrium," changes in the exchange rate pattern could be effected, subject to international agreement. In this way, it was hoped that the system would be freed from the necessity to compromise domestic stabilization objectives when large and persistent imbalances developed. The International Monetary Fund (*IMF*) was established to monitor the system.

Several problems emerged with the adjustable peg system: the absence of explicit criteria for "fundamental disequilibrium," the reluctance of countries facing imbalances to initiate adjustments which compromised domestic stabilization goals, the emergence of speculative capital flows when governments were reluctant to take corrective actions in the face of persistent imbalances, lack of agreement about the sharing of the burden of adjustment between surplus and deficit countries and between reserve center and other countries, the absence of a provision for the controlled growth of international reserves, and the instability inherent in the use of both foreign exchange and gold as reserves. Ultimately, these problems forced the breakdown of the adjustable peg system.

The exchange rate regime was a managed one, a compromise between the fixity of the gold standard and the complete flexibility of freely floating exchange rates.

---

[19] For a fuller discussion of the case for flexible exchange rates, see Milton Friedman, "The Case for Flexible Exchange Rates," in *Essays in Positive Economics* (Chicago: University of Chicago Press, 1953), and Egon Sohmen, *Flexible Exchange Rates: Theory and Controversy* (rev. ed.; Chicago: University of Chicago Press, 1969).

[20] It is possible to avoid some exchange risks by operating in the forward exchange market where foreign exchange can be bought or sold for future delivery. An importer with a commitment to purchase foreign goods in 60 days, for example, can purchase foreign exchange for delivery in 60 days and hence completely determine the dollar costs of the future transaction. Similarly, an exporter can sell the foreign exchange it will receive in the future on the forward market. In this way importers and exporters can avoid exchange risk. There are, however, costs of carrying out these operations (although forward exchange may sell at a discount or a premium against the spot rate) and they do not allow holders of long-term assets to avoid exchange risks.

Without well-defined standards for exchange rate changes, it operated more as a fixed rate system with only a few exchange rate changes between 1949, when rates were realigned in light of early experience, until 1967, when the system was in the process of breaking down. Nor were the adjustment procedures well-defined. With direct controls (tariffs, quotas, etc.) discouraged and exchange rate changes avoided except in extreme cases, the logic of the fixed rate system required price and income adjustments. These were not always initiated promptly, in part because of the reluctance of countries to compromise domestic stabilization objectives and in part because of the absence of agreement over the sharing of the burden of adjustment between surplus and deficit countries and between the reserve center (the country whose currency is used by others as international reserves) and other countries.

Deficit countries, as we noted above, face more immediate pressures to initiate adjustment: they must avoid running out of international reserves. Although surplus countries are not without incentives to seek corrective measures, their pressure is more remote and less binding. They suffer an opportunity cost in acquiring reserves rather than goods and ultimately face the constraint on the volume of open market sales required to sterilize the monetary repercussions of their surplus. As a result of the differences in the immediacy of the pressures to adjust, the burden fell primarily on deficit countries, and in the absence of direct controls or exchange rate changes, required compromise of their internal objectives to achieve balance in their international payments. To the extent that they took corrective actions, adjustment by deficit countries imparted a deflationary bias to the world economy.

The defense of the exchange rate structure was based on a two-tier structure. The U.S. agreed to maintain the convertibility of the dollar into gold while other nations committed themselves to stabilize their exchange rates relative to the dollar. This removed the U.S. from the immediate responsibility for intervention in exchange markets in defense of the rate structure, but it was also widely viewed as removing from the U.S. the opportunity to change exchange rates relative to all others. The U.S. could "in principle" alter its exchange rate relative to all others by changing the price at which it was willing to convert dollars into gold. It was widely believed that, "in practice," any such move by the U.S. would be "automatically" offset by parallel action of other nations as they continued to maintain unchanged exchange rates of their currencies *in terms of dollars*. In addition, action by the U.S. to raise the price of gold relative to the dollar would penalize those nations that agreed to hold their international reserves in dollars rather than gold and it was feared that such actions might be inconsistent with the continued role of the dollar as a reserve currency as long as the U.S. maintained convertibility of dollars into gold.[21]

As international capital flows expanded in the postwar period, manipulation of these capital flows through the effect of monetary policy on interest rates offered the possibility to achieve internal balance. We will discuss the policy-mix models in more detail in the next chapter. The effect of a once-and-for-all change in interest rates on capital flows is transitory so that this simply provided another means of short-run financing. In addition, the inflexibility of fiscal policy often left monetary

---

[21] For a discussion of both the technical issues and the prevailing views about the ability of the U.S. to unilaterally alter its exchange rate, see John Williamson, *The Failure of World Monetary Reform, 1971–74* (Lincoln Way, Great Britain: Thomas Nelson and Sons, Ltd., 1977).

policy with the impossible task of achieving both internal and external balance simultaneously. Indeed, when deficits persisted, capital flows often became destabilizing rather than stabilizing as speculators moved their funds to gain from anticipated changes in exchange rates. If a deficit persisted and a devaluation became a possibility, massive capital outflows from the deficit country could dramatically worsen the deficit based on the fundamental forces and force a devaluation that might otherwise have been avoided. Speculators faced minimal risk in such a situation, given that exchange rates could only remain constant or rise.

The reserve assets in the Bretton Woods system included gold and foreign exchange acceptable to surplus countries in settlement of imbalances. This dual system of reserve assets was referred to as the *gold exchange standard*. In practice the dollar emerged as the dominant foreign exchange reserve although a few countries held reserves in British pounds or French francs. Thus, the U.S. emerged as a reserve center country—one whose currency served as international reserves to others. With the supply of gold fairly stable, growth of international reserves depended on U.S. deficits. The inherent instability of this system was pointed out forcefully by Robert Triffin.[22] The gold exchange standard could meet the growing demand for international reserves only if the reserve center ran deficits. However, continued deficits by the reserve center would ultimately call into question its ability to maintain convertibility of its currency into gold. After running surpluses in the early years following the Bretton Woods accord, the U.S. began to run deficits after 1950. The supply of international reserves expanded accordingly, imparting an inflationary bias to the world economy (in contrast to the deflationary bias associated with pressure on deficit countries to seek adjustment). In large measure the pattern of surpluses and deficits reflected incompatible domestic policies in the surplus and deficit countries. We will see more clearly in the next chapter that fixed rate systems require coordination of domestic policies.

The U.S. responded to these deficits with benign neglect, viewing them as the passive response to the surpluses desired by nonreserve center countries in order to permit the latter to increase their supplies of international reserves to accommodate the growing volume of international transactions. This view was reinforced by the failure of surplus countries to initiate measures in order to avoid accumulating dollars. Surplus countries could initiate stimulative policies, raising income and/or prices. They could even raise their exchange rates. Finally, they could demand settlement in gold, a possibility intended to insure that even the reserve center will exhibit appropriate discipline with respect to its payments position.

For the most part, however, surplus countries avoided adjustment and accepted dollars. Dollars seemed safe and were more convenient than gold for settling imbalances; in addition, reserves could be held in interest-bearing dollar-denominated assets. And when the growth of dollars began to alarm nonreserve center countries, the U.S. asked for time to take corrective steps and successfully avoided conversion of dollars to gold. Nonreserve center countries increasingly felt locked into dollars in that widespread attempts to convert dollars to gold would be met by abandonment of the U.S. commitment to maintain such convertibility. Ultimately, the continued

---

[22] Robert Triffin, *Gold and the Dollar Crisis* (New Haven: Yale University Press, 1960).

deficits forced the U.S. to abandon the convertibility of dollars into gold in 1971, and surplus countries, unwilling to continue accumulating dollars, finally let their currencies float against the dollar. The adjustable peg system thus gave way to a managed float.

The Managed Float. Countries still accumulate and run down international reserves as they intervene on the exchange market. The rates nevertheless move day to day with supply and demand forces. Such intervention is rationalized as a means of smoothing out exchange rate fluctuations, thereby preventing transitory shocks from inducing changes in consumption and production patterns which will be costly to reverse and reducing exchange risk; in addition, intervention is rationalized as a means of offsetting destabilizing capital flows. However, there is simply no reliable procedure for isolating transitory from more permanent disturbances so that intervention may prevent or at least slow down the correction of fundamental imbalances. In addition, once the principle of intervention is accepted, the temptation exists to use the intervention to the advantage of domestic objectives; e.g., to drive exchange rates above their equilibrium level to encourage domestic employment.

● REVIEW QUESTIONS

1. If the balance of payments must always balance, what is the meaning of a balance of payments deficit?
2. What is the interpretation of the deficit on official reserve transactions?
3. Discuss the rationale for the Keynesian assumption that changes in the relative price of imports and exports are systematically related to changes in the exchange rates.
4. Define the law of one price and discuss its relation to the purchasing power parity doctrine.
5. What are the limitations of the law of one price?
6. What is the relation between the price index for domestic production, the price index for foreign production, and the price index relevant to expenditures by domestic residents?
7. Discuss the effects of a change in the exchange rate on real imports and exports.
8. Explain the sign of the slopes of the supply and demand curves for foreign exchange.
9. How can the balance of payments deficit influence the money supply?
10. What is the difficulty in specifying the equation for net capital flow?
11. Derive the slope of the balance of payments curve and discuss the relation of its slope to assumptions about capital mobility.
12. What is the difference in the role of the balance of payments curve in the fixed exchange rate and the flexible exchange rate cases?

Part VII • Extension to an Open Economy

13. Outline the various ways of coping with payments imbalances.

14. Discuss the advantages and disadvantages of flexible exchange rates.

● PROBLEMS

1. Assuming that capital flows are independent of exchange rates and that prices of domestic and foreign output are fixed in their respective currencies, the stability condition for the foreign exchange market requires that an increase in the exchange rate results in an excess supply in the foreign exchange market. Explain the logic of this condition and demonstrate that it leads to the condition that the sum of the absolute values of the elasticities of demand for imports and exports with respect to the exchange rate exceed unity (the Marshall-Lerner condition).

2. Work out the explicit expressions for the shifts in the *IS* and *BP* curves with respect to a change in the exchange rate.

3. Below are three alternative specifications of the *BP* curve. Explain the assumptions that underlie each case and explain the nature of the disequilibrium corresponding to points *a* and *b* in each diagram.

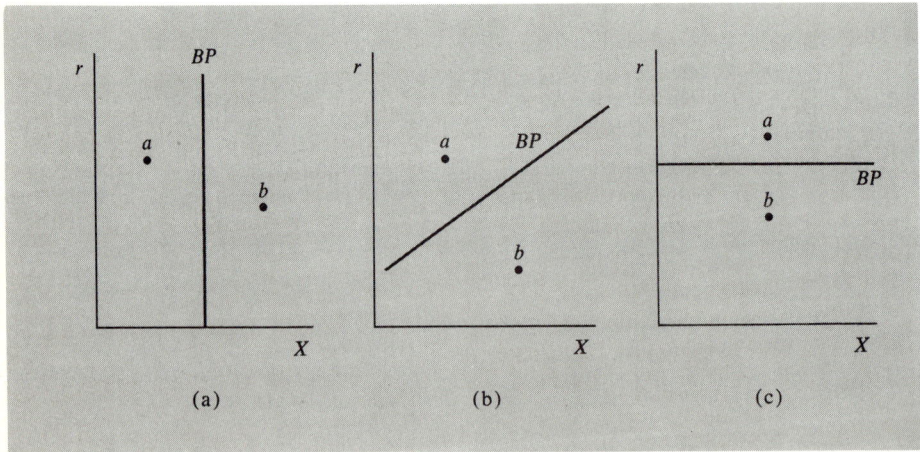

Chapter 28

Macroeconomic Policy in an Open Economy

The previous chapter developed the analytical structure we employ in this chapter—the extension of the *IS-LM* framework to the open economy. In this chapter we will use the framework to investigate the determination of prices, output, and interest rates in open economies and the way policies can be employed to simultaneously achieve balance in international payments (external balance) and domestic objectives with respect to employment and price level stability (internal balance). Our task is greatly complicated in the open economy case by the necessity of considering these problems under both fixed and flexible exchange rate regimes and under alternative assumptions about capital mobility and the sterilization of the monetary repercussions of payments imbalances as well as under the alternative assumptions of wage-price rigidity (Keynesian version) and complete wage-price flexibility (classical version).

The chapter is divided into four major sections corresponding to the various combinations of assumptions about exchange rates and prices: (1) fixed exchange rates and fixed prices, (2) fixed exchange rates and flexible prices, (3) flexible exchange rates and fixed prices, and (4) flexible exchange rates and flexible prices. Sterilization is only an issue under managed exchange rate regimes; we therefore consider the implications of sterilization only in the first two sections.

THE KEYNESIAN OPEN ECONOMY MODEL UNDER FIXED EXCHANGE RATES

Assuming fixed exchange rates, sterilization, and zero or imperfect capital mobility, the extension of the Keynesian model to an open economy involves only the simple revision of the *IS* curve discussed in the previous chapter and does not alter any qualitative conclusions reached on the basis of the closed economy model. However, imbalances cannot be financed indefinitely, so we also must explore the way in which policies can be used to attain internal and external balance simultaneously.

Part VII • Extension to an Open Economy

Finally, relaxing the assumption that monetary repercussions of payments imbalances are sterilized provides an automatic tendency toward external equilibrium.

○ Sterilization and Capital Immobility

When we assume sterilization and the absence of perfect capital mobility, the process of income and interest rate determination remains essentially unchanged in this model (at least as long as the lack of external balance does not require corrective measures). In this case the *IS* and *LM* curves alone determine the equilibrium values of income and the interest rate, and the position of the *BP* curve relative to the intersection of the *IS* and *LM* curves simply identifies the state of the balance of payments associated with the *IS-LM* equilibrium. While this model is of only limited interest given the impossibility of maintaining indefinitely both payments imbalances and sterilization of their monetary repercussions, it provides a simple point of departure for our analysis. Note, however, that the special position of the reserve center country makes its money supply independent of its *BP* so that in effect the monetary repercussions of its payments imbalances are automatically sterilized. On the other hand, its imbalances have effects on the money supplies of nonreserve countries unless they take specific action to sterilize this effect.

This model differs in only two ways from the closed economy model: the basic model multiplier is smaller so that internal disturbances generate smaller displacements from the initial position and the economy is subject to disturbances from external as well as internal sources. The smaller multiplier results from the fact that internal disturbances affect domestic imports so that part of any increase in aggregate demand falls on foreign rather than domestic goods; this implies, of course, that domestic disturbances affecting domestic imports are exogenous changes in the exports of some other country.

These modifications were reflected in the previous chapter in the revision of the *IS* curve in the open economy case to include exports and exclude imports from the demand for domestic output. Exports become the source of external stocks. The diversion of a portion of increases in aggregate demand to imports reduces the positive feedback associated with the consumption function. The multiplier result can be derived mathematically or diagrammatically for the simpler Keynesian cross case and the more complete *IS-LM* model.

The simplest framework to illustrate this is the Keynesian cross model. Assume both the interest rate and the exchange rate are fixed so that the *IS* curve reduces to one equation in one unknown:

$$X = \bar{C}^h + C_y^h Y + \bar{I} + \bar{G} + \overline{EX}. \tag{28.1}$$

We can solve for the basic multiplier, the response to some internal disturbance (such as an autonomous change in investment).

$$\frac{\Delta X}{\Delta I} = \frac{1}{1 - C_y^h} \tag{28.2a}$$

This compares to the closed economy case derived in Chapter 6 [and to which equation (28.2a) reduces if $C_y^h = C_y$]

$$\frac{\Delta X}{\Delta I} = \frac{1}{1 - C_y}. \tag{28.2b}$$

The open economy multiplier is clearly smaller, reflecting the additional leakage out of the income stream into imports in this case.[1] Therefore, domestic disturbances have smaller effects on income in the open economy case, at least under fixed exchange rates. In the problems at the end of the chapter you are asked to work out the relative responses of income to real and monetary disturbances in closed and open economy cases using *IS-LM* diagrams.[2]

○ The Policy Dilemma Under Sterilization and Capital Immobility

Given that payments imbalances cannot persist indefinitely, we must also consider how policy can be used to achieve external balance and whether such measures require compromise of domestic objectives. Internal balance in this model is simply a full employment level of output and is identified on the *IS-LM* diagrams by the vertical line $X = X_f$. We use the simplest case of capital immobility initially and then consider the implications of relaxing this assumption. Under capital immobility, payments equilibrium or external balance is the current account balance; i.e.,

$$EX(e) - eIM(Y,e) = 0 \tag{28.3}$$

where we continue to assume $P(\$) = P(£) = 1$. Given e, this is a vertical line at the unique level of output consistent with the current account balance.

If the *BP* and $X = X_f$ lines do not coincide, the use of domestic stabilization policies to affect the level of output cannot simultaneously achieve internal and external balance. We depict such a situation in Figure 28.1 where the intersection of *LM* and *IS* at point *a* yields both a balance of payments deficit and a below full employment level of production. Monetary and fiscal policies are alternative means of attaining *either* internal or external balance in this case, but stimulative policies which move the system to internal balance (at point *b* or point *c* depending on whether monetary or fiscal policy is used) do so at the expense of aggravating external balance; and, similarly, restrictive policies which move the system to external balance (at point *d* or point *e*) do so at the expense of increasing the departure from internal balance. Thus, this model suggests a policy dilemma; it is impossible to achieve internal and external balance simultaneously, and improving economic performance with respect to the one worsens it with respect to the other.

○ Exchange Rate Variation and Internal and External Balance

However, if we relax either the assumption of capital immobility or that of fixed exchange rates, we can achieve simultaneous internal and external balance. The basic

---

[1] Given that $C_y = C_y^h + IM_y$ (assuming $P(\$) = P(£) = e = 1$), we could also write (28.2a) as $\Delta X/\Delta I = 1/(1 - C_y + IM_y)$.

[2] One simplifying assumption we make throughout is to ignore foreign repercussions of domestic changes in income. When domestic income changes, we allow for the effect on domestic imports. Domestic imports are of course exports of some other country. Therefore, their income and their imports are also affected. But foreign imports are in part domestic exports. To capture this type of interaction, we would need to include the rest of the world sector to our model.

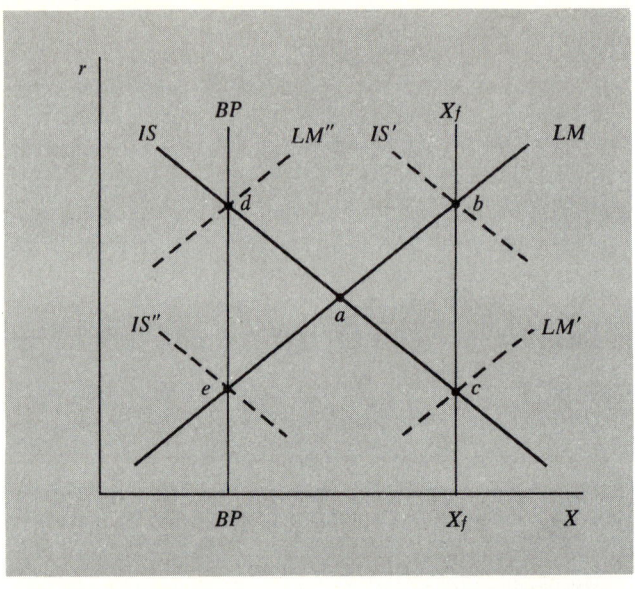

FIGURE 28.1

The Incompatibility of Internal and External Balance with Fixed Exchange Rates, Sterilization, and Capital Immobility

principle involved is that there must be at least as many independent instruments as objectives in order that all objectives can be met simultaneously. Instruments are independent when they have differential effects on the objectives. In the case above, monetary and fiscal policies were *not* independent instruments. Both affected internal balance via their influence on aggregate demand and output, and both affected external balance via their effects on aggregate demand and imports. In effect, these were two objectives and a single instrument.

Under the adjustable peg, exchange rate changes were available as a last resort. This provides the second independent instrument and permits simultaneous internal and external balance. An increase in the exchange rate (devaluation) by increasing net exports shifts both the *BP* and *IS* curves rightward (assuming the Marshall-Lerner condition is fulfilled). While devaluation results in movements in the direction of internal and external balance in this case, the simultaneous use of domestic stabilization policy (monetary and/or fiscal policies) will also generally be needed to achieve internal and external balance simultaneously.

○ Capital Mobility and the Policy-Mix Approach to Internal and External Balance[3]

As we noted in the previous chapter, such exchange rate changes were used only as a last resort under the adjustable peg system and were not available at all

---

[3] This section is based on Robert Mundell, "The Appropriate Use of Monetary and Fiscal Policy for Internal and External Stability," *IMF Staff Papers*, Vol. 9 (March, 1962), pp. 70–79. However, we use the traditional *IS-LM* framework and assume the money supply is the policy instrume controlled by the Fed, whereas Mundell treats the interest rate as the Fed's policy instrument.

under a pure fixed rate regime. A second solution, which is particularly attractive if the payments imbalance is viewed as temporary, is to finance the imbalance with short-term capital flows instead of out of official reserves. This, of course, requires that capital flows be interest sensitive. In Figure 28.2 we depict an initial payments imbalance, again a deficit, at a below full employment level of income; however, in contrast with the previous case, the *BP* curve is now upward sloping, allowing for imperfect capital mobility.

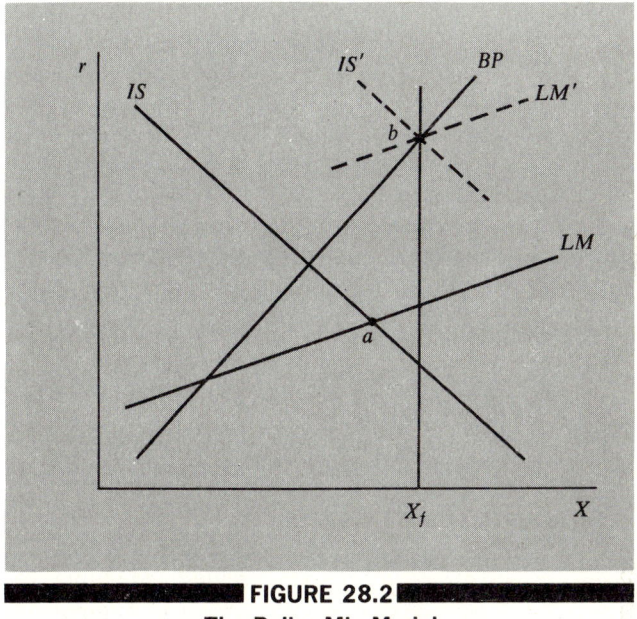

FIGURE 28.2
The Policy-Mix Model

The objective of simultaneous internal and external balance in the diagram requires the use of monetary and fiscal policies to move the intersection of the *IS* and *LM* curves from point *a* to point *b* where the *BP* curve and the $X = X_f$ line intersect. A combination of expansionary fiscal policy and restrictive monetary policy permits simultaneous internal and external balance at point *b*.[4]

There are, however, a number of important limitations to the policy-mix model. In the first place, it promises only a temporary rather than a permanent solution to

---

[4] We could view each instrument (monetary and fiscal policy) as being *assigned* to a particular objective (internal or external balance); for example, expansionary fiscal policy might be assigned to restore internal balance while restrictive monetary policy is assigned to ensure external balance. In a comparative static analysis, this assignment clearly does not matter (in that both assignments must ultimately lead to point *b* where internal and external balance are simultaneously achieved). There are, however, circumstances where the assignment of policy instrument to objective does matter. In particular, when each policy authority single-mindedly pursues a single objective without knowledge of the policy being pursued by the other, the assignment of instruments to objectives will determine whether or not the system converges over time to simultaneous internal and external balance. Thus, the assignment problem is really a question of dynamics under a special set of assumptions about the lack of coordination by policymakers. For a careful analysis of the assignment problem in the context of the pursuit of simultaneous internal and external balance, see Robert Mundell, *ibid*.

simultaneous internal and external balance. It is another means of *temporary financing* rather than correction of a payments imbalance; it permits policy authorities to finance an imbalance with short-term private capital flows, thereby economizing on official reserves. But a once-and-for-all increase in the interest rate induces capital flows only as long as it takes for portfolio balance to be restored at the new set of international interest rates. Therefore, the effect will gradually wear off and further monetary restriction will be required to maintain the capital flows. Secondly, the mix of monetary and fiscal policies is not irrelevant to domestic objectives since it affects the composition of domestic production—the mix between the production of capital and consumption goods. At point *b* in Figure 28.2, for example, the combination of restrictive monetary and expansionary fiscal policy drives up the domestic interest rate and may result in a smaller proportion of investment in total production than may be considered desirable. This, of course, implies that there are really three objectives (the composition of output at full employment being the third) and only two instruments. Finally, the mix models presume that there are two policy instruments available. If fiscal policy is too inflexible to permit effective use or the financial market in government securities is insufficiently developed to permit active monetary policy, the system reverts to one instrument and two objectives and the dilemma of conflicting objectives reemerges.

○ The Monetary Approach to the Balance of Payments: The Implication of the Absence of Sterilization[5]

In the absence of sterilization the monetary repercussions of payments imbalances will automatically move the system toward external balance. However, this may be at the expense of internal balance, at least in the short run, when price and wage inflexibility results in output rather than price level adjustments to policy restraint. Therefore, fiscal policy may still be required to achieve simultaneous internal and external balance.

In Figures 28.3a and 28.3b we illustrate the implications of the monetary repercussions of payments imbalances, first with capital immobility, then with imperfect capital mobility. At point *a* in both diagrams there is a *BP* deficit and output below full employment. If no explicit policies are undertaken, the deficit will induce backward shifts in the *LM* curve until income declines enough to restore payments equilibrium at point *b* in Figure 28.3a. If capital is immobile, policymakers intent on pursuing internal balance cannot permanently enforce an output level higher than X_0. For example, if fiscal policy is applied to move the system from point *a* to point *c* in Figure 28.3a where internal balance prevails, the larger deficit at point *c* will induce backward shifts in the *LM* curve until the system comes to rest at point *d*. Note that in this case the *BP* line becomes a true equilibrium condition: full equilibrium requires external balance. Thus, equilibrium requires the intersection of the *IS, LM,* and *BP* curves at the same point. In contrast, the X_f line simply identifies an objective in the fixed price model.

---

[5] For a discussion of the nature and origins of the monetary approach to the balance of payments, see Jacob A. Frenkel and Harry G. Johnson, "The Monetary Approach to the Balance of Payments: Essential Concepts and Historical Origins," in Jacob A. Frenkel and Harry G. Johnson, (eds.), *The Monetary Approach to the Balance of Payments* (London: George Allen & Unwin Ltd., 1976), pp. 21–45.

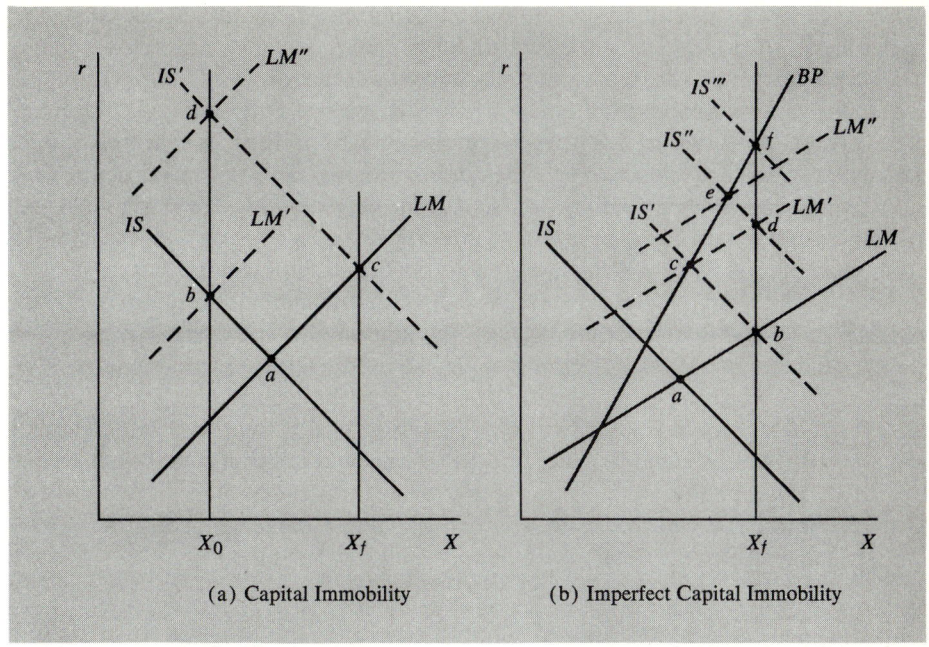

FIGURE 28.3
The Monetary Approach to the Balance of Payments

Allowing for imperfect capital mobility reintroduces the policy-mix approach to simultaneous equilibrium. In the present context that means the use of fiscal policy to supplement the automatic monetary response to payments imbalances. If the fiscal authority pursues internal balance without regard to external balance, the system will converge to simultaneous internal and external balance. For example, expansionary fiscal policy first moves the system to internal balance at point b. The resulting BP deficit, however, induces a backward shift in the LM curve until external balance is restored at point c. Fiscal policy is applied again to restore internal balance and the system ultimately converges to point f where both internal and external balance are achieved.[6]

○ Perfect Capital Mobility: The Nature and Limitations of Domestic Policy

Perfect capital mobility does not fundamentally alter the conclusions. The BP curve in this case is horizontal, reflecting the implication of $F_r = -\infty$: the domestic rate must equal the world interest rate. Otherwise, capital flows continue until the two rates are equated. If the intersection of the IS and LM curves occurs above or below the BP curve, capital flows are induced which automatically drive the BP to equilibrium. At the same time, the monetary repercussions of those imbalances induce

---

[6] This is an example of the convergence to equilibrium under a particular assignment of policies to objectives. Here monetary change automatically responds to external imbalances and fiscal policy is assigned to maintain internal balance.

shifts in the *LM* curve. The only full equilibrium occurs at the intersection of all three curves, such as at point *a* in Figure 28.4.

At point *a* internal balance prevails but output is below full employment. As in the previous case, monetary policy cannot be used to attain internal balance. A shift of the *LM* curve to *LM'*, for example, puts downward pressure on interest rates but this in turn induces a capital outflow driving the interest rate back to its initial level. The resulting deficit in the *BP* then pushes the *LM* curve backward until the original position is restored at point *a*. Thus, perfect capital mobility plus nonsterilization imply that monetary policy becomes totally ineffective.

Fiscal policy can, however, be used to achieve internal balance without interfering with the maintenance of external balance. An expansionary fiscal policy puts upward pressure on the interest rate (at point *d* for example). This induces a capital inflow and a surplus which in turn induces an increase in the money supply (shifting *LM* to *LM''*). The net result is another policy-mix: fiscal policy combined with automatic monetary adjustment achieves simultaneous internal and external equilibrium at point *c*. Indeed fiscal policy becomes more powerful in this case because it automatically induces monetary accommodation and because capital flows maintain the interest rate unchanged (hence, no income-induced rise in interest rates).

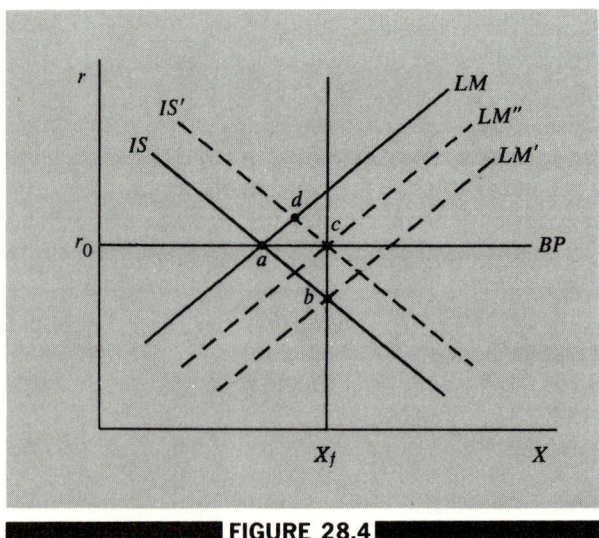

FIGURE 28.4
The Implications of Perfect Capital Mobility
Under Fixed Exchange Rates

○ THE CLASSICAL OPEN ECONOMY MODEL UNDER FIXED EXCHANGE RATES

In the classical model wage-price flexibility maintains full employment so that it might appear that internal balance is automatically achieved. However, internal balance must now be associated with price level or inflation objectives. With internal balance redefined in this way, conflict with external balance reemerges. For example, if the country faces a surplus, it can use domestic policies to raise its price level

The Classical Model with Capital Immobility and Sterilization

The specification of IS and BP curves in the flexible price-fixed exchange rate case are given by

$$\bar{X} = C^h[\bar{Y}, P(\$)/eP(£)] + I(r) + \bar{G} + EX[P(\$)/eP(£)] \tag{28.4}$$

$$EX[P(\$)/eP(£)] - \frac{eP(£)}{P(\$)} IM[\bar{Y}, P(\$)/eP(£)] - F(r) = 0. \tag{28.5}$$

In the flexible price case the position of the BP and IS curves in the r-X diagram depends on the price levels in both the U.S. and abroad. Internal balance requires that the IS and LM curves intersect along the vertical $X = X_f$ line. In Figure 28.5 this occurs at BP surplus (point a). BP equilibrium at the prevailing price level and exchange rates requires a level of real income in excess of the (maximum) full employment level that prevails. Assuming sterilization, this payments imbalance will persist and result in accumulation in official reserves. However, domestic policies can be used to attain internal balance at the expense of only temporary inflation. For example, an increase in the money supply will induce a rise in the domestic price level, P($), and increases in the price level shift all three curves. The BP curve shifts leftward as the increase in the relative price of domestic- compared to foreign-produced goods discourages exports and encourages imports. This price-induced decline in net exports shifts the IS curve downward and the increase in the price level shifts the LM curve backward. To achieve internal balance, the domestic price level must rise enough

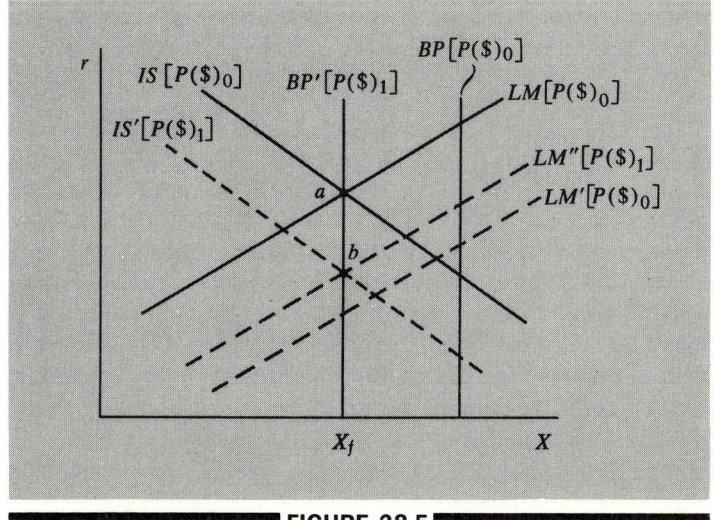

FIGURE 28.5
Internal and External Balance via Monetary Policy

to force the BP curve leftward until it coincides with the X-X_f line. In Figure 28.5, for example, the internal and external balance are attained at point b.

The results in this case can be further clarified using the r-P diagram we discussed in Chapters 7, 8, and 10. The LM curve is upward sloping as usual. Assuming capital immobility, the BP curve is vertical; i.e., there is a unique P($) consistent with external balance. The IS curve is now negatively sloped because both P($) and r affect aggregate demand. A decline in P($), for example, induces an increase in net exports; to maintain $X^d = X_f$, r must rise. Hence, the negative slope. In the case depicted in Figure 28.6 the intersection of IS and LM results in a price level below that at which BP equilibrium is possible; therefore, there is a surplus at point a. BP equilibrium can be restored by the use of monetary and/or fiscal policies. For example, expansionary monetary policy which moves the LM curve downward to LM' will achieve external balance at point b.

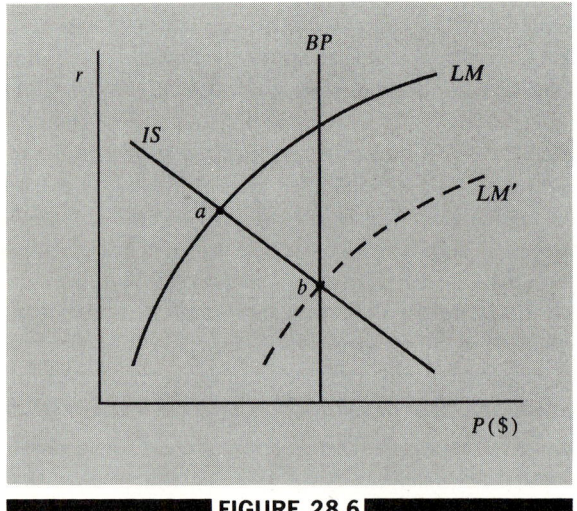

FIGURE 28.6
Internal and External Balance via Monetary Policy: The r-P Diagram

○ Incompatible Domestic Policies and External Balance

Assume external balance initially prevails in all countries and that they have adopted identical monetary policies so that they have identical rates of inflation. If the countries begin to pursue independent monetary policies and hence face differential inflation rates, external imbalances will emerge and become progressively larger over time. For example, countries inflating relative to others will find their BP's progressively moving to larger and larger deficit positions.

There are two solutions to the growing payments imbalances: coordinating domestic policies or letting exchange rates float. This is precisely the problem that ultimately resulted in the breakdown of the adjustable peg system. During the late 1960s and early 1970s the U.S. policy was more expansionary than many other industrial countries, particularly West Germany, and as a result the U.S. ran continuous deficits while Germany ran surpluses. With neither surplus nor deficit countries prepared to bring their domestic policies in line with the other, the only solution was to allow exchange rates to vary.[7]

○ Capital Mobility in the Classical Model

Interest-sensitive capital flows permit a monetary fiscal policy-mix to restore external balance without the necessity of price level changes. This case is depicted in Figure 28.7. At point a in Figure 28.7 there is internal balance (full employment and stable prices) but external imbalance (a BP deficit). A combination of expansionary fiscal and restrictive monetary policy raises the interest rate but maintains aggregate demand unchanged. At point b external balance has been restored without upsetting internal balance. However, as noted above, the interest-induced capital flows that were used to obtain internal balance should be viewed as short-run financing rather than a long-run solution for payments imbalances.

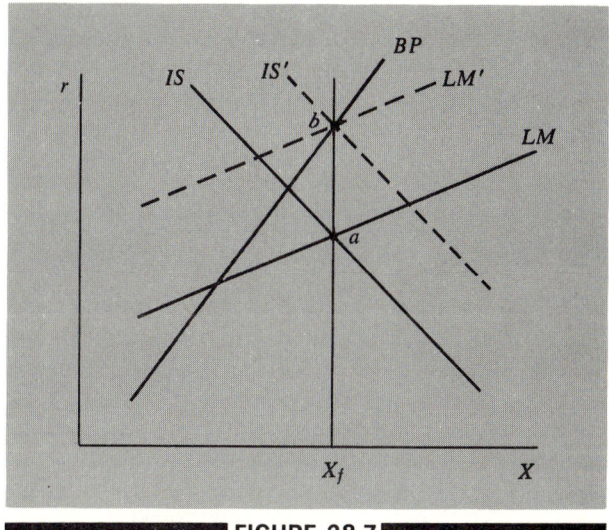

FIGURE 28.7
The Policy-Mix Solution to Internal and External Balance

○ The Classical Model Without Sterilization

If we allow for the monetary repercussions of payments imbalances, we get automatic forces moving the system to external balance. This, however, will generally be at the expense of internal balance if the latter is defined in terms of price level or inflation objectives. This can be illustrated most easily in the r-P framework. We can recycle Figure 28.6 for this purpose. At point a there is internal balance (the IS and LM curves having been drawn on the assumption that $X = X_f$) but there is

---

[7] This was precipitated also by the abandonment of the U.S. commitment to convert official dollar holdings into gold. The prospect of acquiring dollars under these circumstances was even less attractive than when convertibility was insured, and surplus countries ultimately let their currencies float.

a *BP* surplus. The surplus induces increases in the money supply and the *LM* curve moves downward until internal balance is restored at point *b*. In the long run, therefore, price stability and external balance are compatible provided that other countries maintain stable prices; in the short run, temporary inflation is required to attain external balance (at a higher relative price for domestically produced goods). The only difference from the sterilization case is that the adjustment to external balance occurs automatically. Fixed exchanged rates and nonsterilization therefore yield the same automatic tendency to external balance as flexible exchange rates.

On the other hand, the use of exchange rate changes in response to an external imbalance might still be justified as a much simpler way of rearranging relative prices of domestic and foreign goods than price level changes in each country. In contrast, many proponents of the monetary approach argue that allowing for the automatic tendency toward external balance inherent in the system permits smooth correction of payments imbalances while deriving the benefits of a pure fixed exchange rate system. These benefits are essentially those that accrue to the use of a single monetary unit within each country: a reduction in risks associated with trade and therefore an expansion in the volume of trade. It should be noted, however, that uncertainty may simply be transferred from exchange rate movements to price level and output movements when exchange rates are fixed and the monetary repercussions of external balances are not sterilized.

THE KEYNESIAN OPEN ECONOMY MODEL UNDER FLEXIBLE EXCHANGE RATES

Flexible exchange rates simplify the maintenance of internal and external balance in two respects. First, they provide an automatic mechanism that tends to push the economy toward external balance, at least if the foreign exchange market is stable. Secondly, by limiting both leakages from domestic disturbances and the influence of external disturbances, flexible exchange rates permit an independent domestic stabilization policy: freed from concern about external balance, domestic policy can now be focused exclusively on domestic objectives.

The model with flexible exchange rates is more complicated to analyze, however, because we now have a third unknown (e, as well as r and X) and a third equilibrium condition (the market for foreign exchange). Balance in international payments (i.e., equilibrium in the foreign exchange market) is now a fundamental part of the simultaneous system in contrast to its role in the Keynesian model, at least under sterilization. We can, however, derive some of the important implications by initially using the simpler Keynesian cross framework and assuming capital immobility. This removes one unknown (r) and one equilibrium condition (the *LM* curve), and it transforms the equilibrium condition in the foreign exchange market to current account balance.

The Response to Internal and External Disturbances Under Flexible Exchange Rates

Our model now consists of two equilibrium conditions (the commodity and foreign exchange markets) and two unknowns (output and the exchange rate). Each equilibrium condition indicates the combinations of e and X compatible with market equilibrium, given the prevailing values of the exogenous variables.

The equilibrium conditions in the commodity and foreign exchange markets are

$$X = C^h(Y,e) + \bar{I} + \bar{G} + EX(e) \\ = \bar{C}^h + C_y^h Y + C_e^h e + \bar{I} + \bar{G} + \overline{EX} + EX_e e \quad (28.6)$$

$$0 = EX(e) - eIM(Y,e) \\ = \overline{EX} + EX_e e - e\overline{IM} - eIM_y Y - eIM_e e. \quad (28.7)$$

To derive the response to an internal disturbance under flexible exchange rates, we solve for the $\Delta X/\Delta I$ multiplier:

$$\frac{\Delta X}{\Delta I} = \frac{1}{1 - C_y^h - eIM_y(Q)} \quad (28.8)$$

where

$$Q = \frac{C_e^h + EX_e}{EX_e - eIM_e - IM}. \quad (28.9)$$

Assuming the Marshall-Lerner condition is fulfilled, the denominator of equation (28.9) is positive; therefore, Q is positive but may be greater or less than one. We can compare the multiplier under flexible exchange rates with the multiplier when exchange rates are fixed,

$$\frac{\Delta X}{\Delta I} = \frac{1}{1 - C_y^h} \quad (28.8')$$

Comparing equations (28.8) and (28.8'), it is clear that internal disturbances have a larger effect under flexible exchange rates. This reflects the role of flexible exchange rates in countering the leakage of aggregate demand from domestic to imported goods under fixed exchange rates. Under flexible exchange rates, as imports increase in response to the increase in income, the exchange rate rises; this in turn reduces imports and increases exports, increasing the demand for domestic output by domestic residents and increasing the demand for domestic output by foreign residents. The net effect therefore is a larger multiplier under flexible exchange rates.

This result can be shown graphically as well. The XX and FF curves in Figure 28.8 depict the combination of e and X consistent with equilibrium in the commodity and foreign exchange markets, respectively, for given values of exogenous variables. Both curves are positively sloped. An increase in X at unchanged e results in excess supply in the commodity market; an increase in e increases aggregate demand. Hence, the XX curve is upward sloping. An increase in X induces an increase in imports and hence a deficit in the balance of payments; an increase in e reduces imports and increases exports and this can restore equilibrium. Hence, the FF curve is also upward sloping. In the problem section at the end of the chapter you are asked to

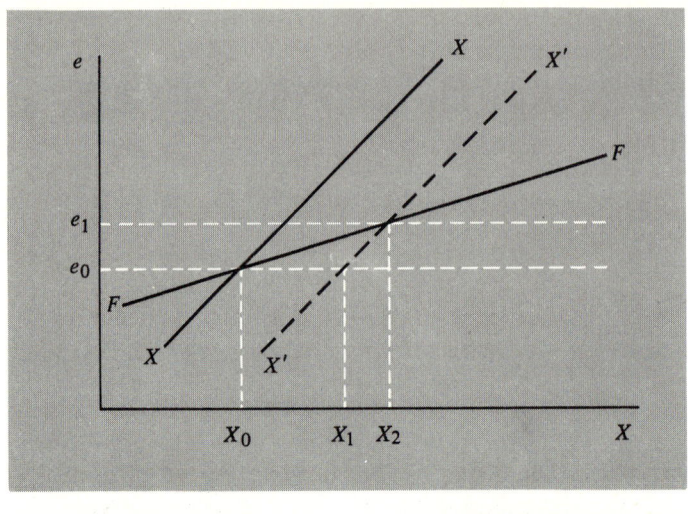

FIGURE 28.8
The Response to an Internal Disturbance Under Fixed and Flexible Exchange Rates

find the slopes explicitly and to demonstrate that stability requires that the XX curve be steeper than the FF curve, as depicted in Figure 28.8.

An autonomous increase in domestic demand for domestic goods shifts the XX curve outward. If exchange rates are fixed, output increases from X_0 to X_1. If exchange rates are flexible, the exchange rate rises and increases the response of income from X_1 to X_2.

○ Allowing for Capital Mobility, Interest-Responsive Investment, and the Money Market

The model developed above was useful in developing the essential feature of flexible exchange rates in models of income determination: flexible exchange rates reinforce the response to internal disturbances and counter the effects of external disturbances.

To develop a more complete model, we reintroduce interest-elastic investment. The IS curve is now

$$X = C^h(Y,e) + I(r) + \bar{G} + EX(e). \tag{28.10}$$

The foreign exchange market equilibrium condition now includes capital outflows.

$$0 = EX(e) - eIM(Y,e) - F(r) \tag{28.11}$$

The IS-LM-BP diagram is depicted in Figure 28.9. Equilibrium requires that all three markets be in equilibrium; hence, the three curves must intersect at a common point. There are three unknowns: e, r, and X. To permit the use of our r-X diagram,

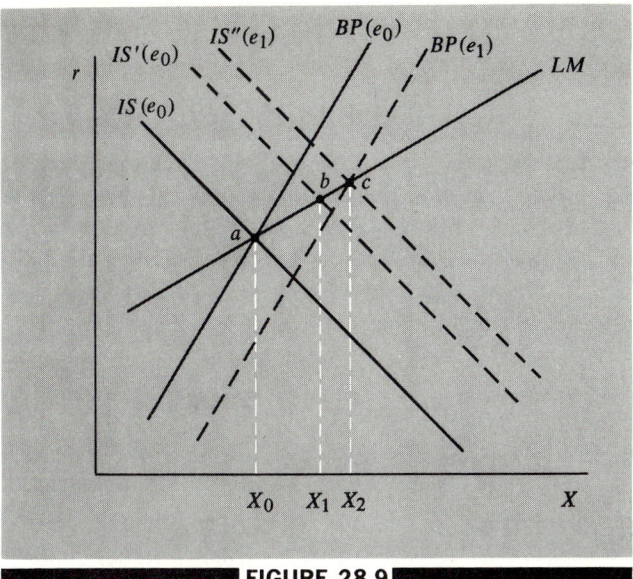

FIGURE 28.9
Flexible Exchange Rates in the *IS-LM* Model

each of the curves must be drawn for a fixed value of the exchange rate, initially the equilibrium value given the initial values of exogenous variables.

An internal disturbance shifts the *IS* curves alone initially. Under fixed exchange rates, the new equilibrium would be at point *b* where the deficit in the balance of payments was accommodated by the monetary authority. Under flexible exchange rates, the *IS* and *BP* curves shift as the balance of payments deficit induces a rise in the exchange rate. The *IS* curve shifts further to the right as depreciation increases aggregate demand, and the *BP* curve shifts rightward. As depicted in Figure 28.9 the net effect is to reinforce the increase in aggregate demand and income. Note however that if the *BP* curve were flatter than the *LM* curve, the shift in the *IS* curve would move the balance of payments toward a surplus, inducing a fall in the exchange rate; in this case flexible exchange rates dampen the increase in income associated with an internal disturbance.

◯ Monetary and Fiscal Policies Under Flexible Exchange Rates

External balance takes care of itself under flexible exchange rates. Domestic policy may therefore be directed toward the attainment of internal balance. Monetary policy increases income and puts upward pressure on the exchange rate; the increase in the exchange rate reinforces the effect of the monetary expansion, increasing the potency of monetary policy. The effectiveness of fiscal policy as a tool for attaining internal balance, however, depends on the degree of capital mobility. If capital is relatively immobile so that the *BP* curve is steeper than the *LM* curve, an increase in government expenditure increases income and induces a depreciation of the exchange rate; in this case, the movement in the exchange rate also reinforces the effect of fiscal policy. If capital is relatively mobile, on the other hand, an increase in government expenditure will increase income but also induce a decline in the exchange rate;

and the decline in the exchange rate will, in turn, tend to dampen the overall response of income to the fiscal operation.

○ Perfect Capital Mobility and the Effectiveness of Monetary and Fiscal Policies

Under perfect capital mobility, fiscal policy becomes completely useless. In addition, monetary policy works through completely different channels compared to the closed economy and fixed exchange rate cases. Assume that the initial equilibrium at point *a* in Figure 28.10 yields an income below the level at full employment. Expansionary fiscal policy will be useless because the increase in aggregate demand associated with the direct impact of the policy will be fully offset by the effect of the exchange rate decline required to maintain equilibrium in the foreign exchange market. The *IS* curve is initially increased to *IS'* in response to an increase in government expenditures, but the upward pressure on interest rates induces a capital inflow and the resulting appreciation of the dollar shifts the *IS* curve backward until the original equilibrium is restored.

An increase in the money supply to *LM'*, on the other hand, puts downward pressure on the interest rate, inducing a capital outflow and depreciation of the dollar. The depreciation shifts the *IS* curve rightward until at point *c* equilibrium is reestablished at a higher level of income and at the original interest rate. Thus, monetary policy does not expand income by increasing interest-sensitive components of aggregate demand. The interest rate is fixed at the world level and monetary policy works by inducing changes in the exchange rate and hence net exports.

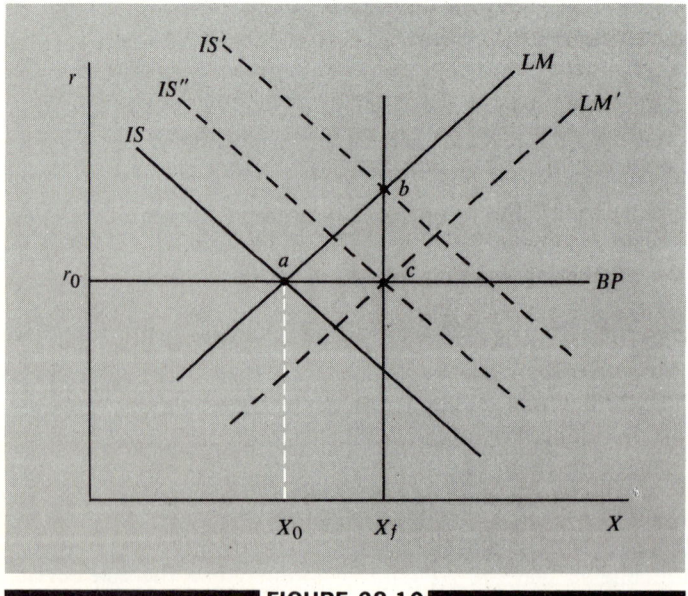

FIGURE 28.10
Monetary and Fiscal Policies: Flexible Exchange Rates and Perfect Capital Mobility

THE CLASSICAL OPEN ECONOMY MODEL UNDER FLEXIBLE EXCHANGE RATES

We found that under fixed exchange rates with sterilization, differential inflation rates would progressively increase payments imbalances and ultimately force abandonment of the fixed exchange rates; without sterilization, on the other hand, inflation rates automatically tend to converge. One way or the other, by conscious policy or automatic forces, fixed exchange rates therefore require coordinated monetary policies and inflation rates. Under flexible exchange rates, differential rates of inflation can persist as exchange rates vary to maintain external balance.

Consider the impact of differential rates of monetary growth. If country A runs a higher rate of monetary growth than country B, A's inflation rate will exceed B's by the differential in the rates of monetary growth (assuming for simplicity that real output is fixed at its full employment level in the two countries). For the moment, assume capital immobility. At a given exchange rate the relative price of A's goods to B's goods will increase for both A's and B's residents, increasing A's imports and B's exports and reducing A's exports and B's imports. This will move A's balance progressively toward a deficit and B's balance toward a surplus. If exchange rates are free to vary, the resulting excess demand for B's currency and the excess supply of A's currency will result in a depreciation in A's currency relative to B's (an increase in A's exchange rate relative to B's). To maintain balance in the foreign exchange market, the exchange rate must change so as to maintain an unchanged relative price for A's output relative to B's output. For $P(\$)/eP(£)$ to remain unchanged, for example,

$$\dot{e}/e = \dot{P}(\$)/P(\$) - \dot{P}(£)/P(£); \qquad (28.12)$$

i.e., the proportional rate of increase in the exchange rate must equal the differential in inflation rates.

Note that this relation also follows from the *absolute* version of the *PPP* doctrine discussed in Chapter 27. But we need not assume that $P(\$) = eP(£)$ to derive it. It requires only that $P(\$)$ be proportional to $eP(£)$. Equation (28.12) reflects the *relative* version of the purchasing power parity doctrine: the dollar price of commodities in the U.S. is *proportional* to the dollar price of commodities abroad so that the rates of change in dollar prices in the U.S. and abroad are equal.

The *PPP* doctrine, even in its relative form, is not fully consistent with empirical evidence. The *PPP* doctrine should apply to the response of exchange rates to differential inflation rates induced by differential rates of monetary growth, *holding constant all real influences on trade and inflation*. Thus, a once-and-for-all increase in the money stock should cause an equal percentage increase in a country's exchange rate *relative to what it would have been* in the absence of the monetary change. If over the period under consideration the country had enlarged its exports by force of its technological innovations (as in the case of Japan during the 1960s) or had reduced its imports due to the discovery of natural resources, the correspondence of exchange rates and relative inflation rates may fail to be observed. This is in part the failure of price indices to deal adequately with technological change and new products. This in no way, however, reduces the usefulness of the relative version of the *PPP* doctrine for the analysis of monetary disturbances.

Relaxing the assumption of capital immobility does not alter the basic conclusion of this analysis. With alternative rates of monetary growth and inflation, nominal rates will differ across countries to reflect differing inflation premiums. The nominal (and real) rates expected on securities denominated in the two currencies will be equalized in terms of a common currency. The nominal return in terms of the domestic currency on foreign securities depends on the nominal foreign interest rate and changes in the exchange rate. If country A's rate of monetary growth and hence inflation rate are 5 percent above country B's, A's exchange rate will depreciate 5 percent per year relative to B's, while A's nominal interest rate will be 5 percent above B's, reflecting differential inflation premiums. Therefore, A's residents can earn the same return (denominated in A's currency) by investing in A's or B's securities: if a resident of A can earn 10 percent on A's securities, it will also be able to earn 5 percent on B's securities (in terms of B's currency) and also obtain a 5 percent capital gain via the appreciation in B's currency relative to A's. Therefore, differential rates of monetary growth yield differential inflation rates and compensating movement in the exchange rates which maintain an unchanged relation between both the price of goods produced in A and B and the rates of return on securities denominated in A's and B's currencies. Of course, it is not *ex post* rates of return that are equated, only *ex ante* or expected returns.

There is considerable controversy about the implications of alternative exchange rate regimes for the level of world inflation. Under fixed rates, small countries find themselves unable to avoid inflation being imposed on them via the effects of rising prices of imported goods and the monetary repercussions of balance of payments surpluses. Thus, the European view attributed the worldwide inflation in the early 1970s to the inflation in the U.S. and the associated U.S. payments deficits which "forced" surpluses on European economies, making it difficult for them to avoid increases in monetary growth.

An alternative viewpoint is that fixed exchange rates impose discipline on countries to avoid inflation because inflation will induce deficits and threaten the countries' stock of official reserves. With this discipline removed under flexible exchange rates, more rather than less inflation may result from the existence of independent monetary policies.[8]

---

[8] For an interesting collection of papers on the contribution of alternative exchange rate regimes to the inflation process, see Lawrence B. Krause and Walter S. Salant (eds.), *Worldwide Inflation: Theory and Recent Experience* (Washington: The Brookings Institution, 1977).

Chapter 28 • Macroeconomic Policy in an Open Economy

APPENDIX

A Monetarist Model of the Balance of Payments and World Inflation

The result derived above that domestic monetary expansion will be offset by the monetary repercussions of the ensuing imbalances in international payments under fixed exchange rates and no sterilization can also be derived using a monetarist model of the balance of payments.[1] As was typical of the early monetarist analysis of closed economy models, the open economy approach focuses exclusively on the supply and demand for money. The demand for money is given by the basic equation we have used previously:

$$\frac{M}{P} = L(r,X). \qquad (28A.1)$$

The supply of money is also conventional—a multiplier (assumed constant for simplicity but it could be interest-elastic without affecting the results) times high-powered money, which we will treat as the monetary base.

$$M^s = kB \qquad (28A.2)$$

The base in turn is viewed as the sum of a domestic component (D) and international reserves (R).

$$B = D + R \qquad (28A.3)$$

Equilibrium of course prevails when the supply and demand for money are equal.

$$M^s = M^d \qquad (28A.4)$$

Substituting equation (28A.3) into equation (28A.2) and equations (28A.1) and (28A.2) into equation (28A.4) yields

$$R + D = (1/k)PL(r,X). \qquad (28A.4')$$

Now for the key assumptions: Output (X) is fixed at full employment. The price level and interest rate are fixed by the "small country" assumption;[2] i.e., the domestic interest rate must equal the world interest rate (perfect capital mobility and small country assumption) and the price level is pegged to world prices (the law of one price and the small country assumption).

Note that if we accept these assumptions, $X = \bar{X}$, $r = \bar{r}$, $P = \bar{P}$, and the entire right-hand side of equation (28A.4') is fixed. Therefore, the left-hand side must also be fixed; this implies that the domestic monetary authority cannot control its own stock of high-powered

---

[1] The monetary approach to the balance of payments is developed in Harry Johnson, "The Monetary Approach to the Balance of Payments," in Jacob A. Frankel and Harry G. Johnson (eds.), *The Monetary Approach to the Balance of Payments* (London: George Allen & Unwin Ltd., 1976), pp. 21–45.

[2] A small country cannot affect world prices or interest rates; it is a "price taker," like a firm operating in a perfectly competitive market.

money. Any change in the domestic component will be completely offset by a change in its international reserves; i.e., $\Delta R = -\Delta D$. Thus, the conclusion: *the balance of payments is a purely monetary phenomenon.* Note also that if world prices are increasing at a 10 percent rate, the stock of money must also increase at that rate—either by increases in D, R, or some combination. There is no way, at least for a small country, to follow an independent monetary policy and avoid coordinating rates of monetary growth under fixed exchange rates.

It should be clear that we can derive essentially the same conclusions from the framework developed above. However, the broader framework does not assume the convergence of inflation as a consequence of commodity arbitrage but rather as part of the adjustment to domestic monetary expansion. That approach therefore is not subject to the criticisms that apply to the extension of the law of one price to price indices. Note also that both models make some restrictive assumptions which reduce their relevance to short- or even medium-run analysis; e.g., output is fixed and there is no sterilization.

Global Monetarism[3]

The previous analysis does not, however, provide a model of the determination of the world price level to which all countries are tied. The monetarist model of world price level (and world inflation) parallels their approach to inflation in a closed economy: inflation is a monetary phenomenon. The monetarist model of world inflation, sometimes referred to as *global monetarism*, views the world as a closed economy and the world price level (P^w) as being determined by the supply and demand for the world money supply (M^w). The *world money supply* is simply the sum of national money supplies denominated in a common currency. For example, using a two-country model of the world,

$$M^w = M(\$) + eM(\pounds) \tag{28A.5}$$

where $M(\$)$ is the U.S. money supply, $M(\pounds)$ is the rest of the world's money supply, and e is the exchange rate (\$ per £).

The demand for real money balances depends on real world income, y^w, taken as exogenous. Thus, equilibrium in the world money market requires that the supply and demand for world money balances be equal:

$$M^w = P^w k^w y^w. \tag{28A.6}$$

Given the assumption that k^w is fixed and y^w is exogenous, M^w determines P^w.

● REVIEW QUESTIONS

1. Why can't payments imbalances be continued indefinitely?
2. What is meant by internal and external balance?

---

[3] For a thorough discussion of global monetarism, see Marina v. N. Whitman, "Global Monetarism and the Monetary Approach to the Balance of Payments," *Brookings Papers on Economic Activity* (1975:3), pp. 491–536.

3. What is the policy dilemma under fixed exchange rates and capital immobility?
4. How is the policy dilemma resolved when capital is imperfectly mobile?
5. What are the limitations of the policy-mix model?
6. Explain why there is a deficit at point *a* in both Figures 28.3a and 28.3b.
7. What are the implications of payments imbalances when we rule out sterilization?
8. What is the difference in the role of the *BP* curve under sterilization and nonsterilization?
9. Is internal balance assured in the classical model?
10. Explain the need for coordinated domestic policies under fixed exchange rates.
11. Explain the relative size of multipliers for the response of income to an autonomous change in investment under fixed and flexible exchange rates, assuming capital immobility and a Keynesian cross framework.
12. Explain the implications of perfect capital mobility under flexible exchange rates for the effectiveness of monetary and fiscal policies.
13. What is the difference between the absolute and relative versions of the purchasing power parity doctrine?

● PROBLEMS

1. Using the Keynesian cross diagram, compare the response of income to an autonomous change in the demand for domestic output in the closed economy case with the response under fixed exchange rates in the open economy case. Explain the assumptions required to permit the comparison.
2. Assuming capital immobility, use *IS-LM* curve analysis to make the comparison called for in question 1.
3. Make the same comparison for an increase in the money supply using *IS-LM* curve analysis.
4. Derive the shifts in the *BP* and *IS* curves corresponding to Figure 28.1 (capital immobility) in response to a change in the exchange rate.
5. Explain why a change in the exchange rate must generally be supplemented by monetary and/or fiscal policy to permit simultaneous attainment of internal and external balance.
6. Derive the multiplier given by equation (28.8).
7. Derive the slopes of the *FF* and *XX* curves depicted in Figure 28.8.
8. Explain why stability requires that the *XX* curve be steeper than the *FF* curve.
9. Compare the response of output to an increase in government expenditures under fixed exchange rates when the *BP* is steeper than the *LM* curve and when the *LM* curve is steeper than the *BP* curve.

INDEX

A

absolute income hypothesis, 212–213, 219; defined, 212–213
absorption, defined, 545
acceleration hypothesis, 357–358
accelerator, 283–292, 498; crowding-out and, 289–290; disequilibrium and, 253; interest rate snapback and, 290–292
accelerator model, 260–262; flexible, 261; permanent, 261–262
accounts: automatic transfer, 388; national income, 24–33; negotiable order of withdrawal, 388
activist policy: case against, 472–473; case for, 473–474
actual investment, defined, 102
adaptive expectations model, 362–363; fooling and, 354–355; of job search, 309
additional worker hypothesis, 303
adjustable peg, 558–561; defined, 556
adjustment costs: cyclical variation in hours and, 301–302; defined, 258; external, 258; internal, 258; nonhomogenous workers and, 324; theory of investment and, 257–260
adjustment function, kinked wage, 342
administered rate, defined, 386
advance, defined, 459
aggregate demand: applications to other components of, 269–273; autonomous change in private, 140, 179; deficiency of, 320; direct impacts of monetary change on, 463–464
aggregate demand curve, 198–200; defined, 198
aggregate supply curve, 192–198; derivation of, 193; differences in two specifications of, 197–198; money illusion and, 195–197; response of output to demand disturbances and, 200–202; rigid nominal wages and variable prices on, 193–195; supply of labor and, 193–195
aggregation among individual labor markets, 342–343
amortizing, defined, 76, 248
Andersen, Leonall C., 465, 499
Ando, Albert, 216, 221, 222, 504–505
announcement effects, defined, 460
anticipated inflation, fully, 355
appreciation, defined, 536 n.5
arbitrage, commodity, 536
asset demand: for money, 375–385; specification of, 406–407
asset management, 442
asset market equilibrium in period models, defined, 94 n
auction model, continuous, 307–308, 328–329; and search models, limitations of, 330–331
automatic transfer accounts, defined, 388
autonomous vs. induced changes in endogenous variables, 16–17
average propensity to consume, defined, 213
aversion, risk, and preferred habitat theory, 401

B

balanced-budget fiscal policy, 139–140, 177, 243–244; defined, 117, 136
balanced-budget multiplier, 116–117
balance of payments, 532–535; defined, 532; foreign exchange market and, 549–553; monetary approach to, 568–569; world inflation and, monetarist model of, 581–582
balance of payments adjustment, methods and systems of, 554–561
balance sheet constraint, defined, 71; household, 70–72; in continuous models, 93–94
balance sheet identity, defined, 70; demand for bonds and, 392–394
balance sheets, 38–47; of commercial banks, 439–441; of Federal Reserve System, 439–441; of nonbank public, 439–441; of three sectors, simplified, 64–65; sectoral, 39–41
balancing (settlement) items, defined, 535
bank portfolio behavior, commercial, 442–443
barter economy, defined, 369
benchmark unemployment rate, defined, 317
Board of Governors, 456
bond, 42–45; corporate, 39; defined, 43, 388; demand for, 82; demand for, and balance sheet identity, 392–394; financing constraints and, supply of, 394–397; government, 39; government, sale of, 156–157; government financing constraint and supply of government, 79–80; household demand for, 70; supply of, 78
bond financing: crowding-out and, 498
Brainard, William C., 255, 392
Bretton Woods: conference, 558, system, 560
Brinner, Roger, 361
Brumberg, Richard, 216
Brunner, Karl, 385
budget constraint: government, 431–434; household, 67–68
built-in stabilizer, 279
business cycles, 54–56; defined, 54; properties of, 285–287
business investment, fixed, 27–28
business taxes, indirect, 31
business transfers, 31

585

C

capital: Cobb Douglas production function and, 264; demand for, 250–253, 263–265; demand for, uncertainty and, 252–253; household portfolio behavior and, 397; marginal efficiency of, 252
capital account, 534
capital consumption adjustment (*CCAdj*), defined, 30
capital consumption allowances (*CCA*), 31–32
capital flows: financing deficit via short-term, 554; international trade, 544–553; long-term, 534; private short-term, 534–535; speculation and, 543–544
capital gains, defined, 240
capital immobility: classical model with, 571–572; policy dilemma under, 565; sterilization and, 564–565
capital mobility, 576–577; balance of payments and, 551–552; in classical model, 573; perfect, 569–570, 578
capital stock, long-run profit-maximizing level of, 250
catch-up effect, defined, 522
certainty equivalence model, defined, 478
certificates of deposit, defined, 460
Christ, Carl, 466
civilian labor force, defined, 51
classical adjustment mechanism, 240–241, 338–339, 415, 417; conditions under which it breaks down, 150–154
classical assumptions, 84–89; Keynesian and, 84–89; on price and wage flexibility, 85–86
classical demand curve for labor. See notional demand curve
classical excess demand inflation, defined, 202
classical model, 126–130; adjustment mechanism in, 147–150; built-in stability in, 494–495; capital mobility in, 573; equilibrium real interest rate in, 158; important propositions based on, 158–166; Keynesian model and, versions of, 96–97; price flexibility in, 494–495
classical open economy model: under fixed exchange rates, 570–574; under flexible exchange rates, 579–580
Cobb Douglas production function, 263; demand for capital and, 264
commerical banks, 439–443; balance sheets of, 439–441; portfolio behavior, 442–443
commercial paper, defined, 460
commodity arbitrage, defined, 537
common stock (equity), 45
congressional budget process, 489
consol (perpetuity), defined, 44
consumer durable expenditures, 272–273
consumer price index (*CPI*), 207; defined, 36
consumption: as a function of current and lagged values of income, 231–236; autonomous component of, 16; defined, 66, 224; income and, 210–212; induced component of, 16; measured, 228; permanent, 228; savings over the life cycle, time patterns of and, 219–220; transitory, 228
consumption (saving) function, 66, 71 n.4; income-constrained, 211–212; notional, 210–211; short-run, instability of, 214
consumption multiplier model, simple, 100–113
contractions, defined, 54
contracts, explicit and implicit, 323–324
controls: direct, 555–556; effects of during the period they are imposed, 520–521; effects of in postcontrol period, 521–524; general, 459; in 1971–1974, assessing effectiveness of, 524; mandatory, logic of, 519–524; mandatory wage and price, 518–524; proportional vs. cumulative, 495; selective, 459
corporate bonds, defined, 39
corporate profits, defined, 30
corporate profit tax liability, defined, 31
correspondence principle, defined, 113
cost-push inflation, defined, 202
coupon, defined, 43
CPI. See consumer price index
Crandall, Robert, 529
critical interest rate, defined, 377
critical rate of inflation, 317
crowding-out, 163–166, 181–183; accelerator and, 289–290; bond financing and, 498; bond market and, 427–429; wealth effect in, 421–422
currency, defined, 39; holdings and money supply process, 446–447; reserve, 548
current account: balance on, 534; defined, 534

D

debt claim (or loan or bond), 42–45; defined, 42
debt-financed fiscal policy, 243, defined, 136
deflator, implicit *GNP* price, 36–37
deLeeuw, Frank, 466, 503
demand: asset, specification of, 406–407; effective, 88; elasticity of, 541; private, increase in autonomous component of, 157; private aggregate, autonomous change in, 140, 179; supply curves for foreign exchange and, 539–541; supply disturbances, response of price level to and, 202–207; supply model and, 14–15; value of import and export, 540
demand curve: aggregate, 198–200; effective, 75; income-constrained, 299–301; notional, 75, 296–299
demand deficiency, problem of, 326–327; unemployment defined, 52
demand deposits, defined, 39, 388
demand-pull inflation, defined, 202
depreciation, allowance, defined, 262 n
depreciation, defined, 27, 536 n.5
devaluation, defined, 536 n.5
dichotomy, defined, 158; neutrality, and quantity theory of money, 241; neutrality and, existence of, 158
diminishing returns, law of, 73

direct controls, 555–556
dirty (managed) float, defined, 556
discounting, defined, 459
discount rate, 459–460; defined, 442
discouraged worker hypothesis, 303–304
discrete analysis, 7. *See also* period analysis
disposable income, defined, 66; total, 222
disposable personal income (DI): defined, 32; personal and, 32–33
distributed lags, defined, 470
dividend: defined, 31; fiscal, 496
dividend price ratio, defined, 384
domestic price adjustment, 555
Dornbusch, Rudiger, 542
Duesenberry, James, 225–226
dynamic analysis, defined, 109
dynamic model, 233; *IS-LM*, 284; properties of, 285–287

E

Eckstein, Otto, 361
econometric models, evidence from, 464–465
economic growth, 4; sources of, 332–334
effective demand, 88; for commodities, income-constrained or, 211
effective demand curve, defined, 75
Eilbott, Peter, 493
Eisner, Robert, 261
elasticity, defined, 10; demand, for imports and exports, 541–543; of demand, defined, 541; of demand for money, real income, 412–413; of substitution, constant, 263
employed, defined, 51
employment: hours and, response of to changes in demand for labor, 301–302; output and, cyclical movements in, 334–335; output and, cyclical variation in, 327–331; unemployment and, defining, 50–51; unemployment and, measurement of, 50–52
Employment Act of 1946, 3
Enzler, Jared, 206
equilibrium: asset market, in period models, 94 n; defined, 13; disequilibrium and, 105–106; impact multipliers and, 233–235; in the four markets, 80–82; labor market, 355; labor market and unemployment, 310–314; pure wealth approach with end-of-period and beginning-of-period, 423–425; simultaneous, 90
equilibrium condition, 13–14, 89; two versions of, 101–102, 114
equilibrium multiplier, defined, 109
equity (common stock), 45; defined, 39; market value of, 45
escalator clause, 36; defined, 325 n
excess reserves, defined, 441
exchange costs, 69; explicit, 69; implicit, 69
exchange rate, 535–538
expectations model: adaptive, 362–365; adaptive, and fooling, 354–355; rational, 362–365

exports: defined, 29, 534; import demands and, value of, 540; imports and, demand elasticities for, 541–543; imports and, exchange rates and relative price of, 538
external adjustment costs, defined, 258

F

Fed. *See* Federal Reserve System
Federal Open Market Committee, 457
Federal Reserve Banks (FRB), 456
Federal Reserve System (Fed), 80, 143, 143 n.10, 395, 439–452; balance sheets of, 439–441; behavior of, 443; Board of Governors, 456; Federal Open Market Committee, 457; relation to legislative and executive branches of government, 457–458; structure of, 456–457
feedback effect: negative, 174; positive, 174
Feldstein, Martin, 528
Fellner, William, 511
final good: defined, 26; vs. intermediate goods, 26–27
financial asset: defined, 39
financing constraint: government, 394–396; investment, and supply of private bonds, 396–397; supply of bonds and, 394–397
fiscal drag, defined, 496
fiscal institutions, 486–490
fiscal instruments, 503; cumulative vs. impact effects of changes in, 395–396; supply of government bonds and, 395
fiscal policy, 156–157, 175–177; balanced-budget, 117, 136, 139–140, 177, 243–244; bond-financed change in government expenditures, 137–139; bond-financed change in net taxes, 139; debt-financed, 136, 243; direct wealth effects and, 243; effectiveness of, 185–188; in three-asset model, 435; long-run effect of, 431–434; monetary policies and, effectiveness of, 241–245, 578; monetary policies under flexible exchange rates and, 577–578; monetary policy multipliers and, term structure equation and, 429–431; money-financed, shifts in *IS* and *LM* curves, 142–143; with endogenous tax revenues, long-run response to, 432–434
fixed exchange rates, 539
flexible accelerator model, defined, 261
flexible exchange rates, 539
floating exchange rates, freely or flexible, 557–558
foreign exchange market, 538–544; balance of payments and, 549–553; disequilibrium and stability of, 541
foreign exchange rate, defined, 535
free reserves, 447
frictional (search) unemployment: defined, 51, 311; wage illusion and, 313–314
Friedman, Benjamin, 364
Friedman, Milton, 227–229, 261, 307, 385, 410, 415, 462–464, 469, 471, 473–474, 495–496
Frisch, Ragnar, 287

full employment: defined, 52–53; labor services, growth of, 332–333; level of employment, defined, 313; meaning of, 52–54, 314–317; price stability and, incompatibility of, 349–351; surplus, weighted, 491–492
Full Employment and Balanced Growth Act of 1978, 458, 468, 489

G

General Agreement on Tariffs and Trade (GATT), 555
general controls, 459
global monetarism, defined, 582
GNP. See gross national product
goal variable, defined, 16
gold exchange standard, defined, 560
Goldfeld, Stephen, 385–387
gold-specie standard, defined, 557
gold standard, 557
Gordon, Robert J., 524
government expenditures, 79; bond-financed change in, 137–139, 175–176; change in financed by change in tax receipts, 177; increase in by sale of government bonds, 156–157
government financing constraint, 135, 394–396; supply of government bonds and, 79–80
gross national product (GNP), 25–33; as measure of macroeconomic activity, 25; defined, 7; gap, defined, 57; gap and Okun's Law, 57; nominal, 33; price deflator, implicit, 36–37; real, 33
gross private domestic investment, 28
growth: cycles and, 56–59; cyclical experience vs., long-run, 59; full employment labor services, 332–333; of money supply, increase in rate of, 161–163; rate, secular, 59; rate of labor productivity, 333–334; recessions, defined, 59; sources of economic, 332–334; trend rate of, 56
guideposts, 512–517

H

Hamilton, Mary T., 521, 524
Hansen, Bent, 493
Hicks, J. R., 287, 370, 375, 383
high-powered money or monetary base, defined, 441
Holt, Charles, 527–528
household, 66–72; balance sheet constraint, 70–72; budget constraint, 67–68; budget identity, defined, 67; businesses, and government behavior of, 65–80; capital portfolio behavior and, 397; demand for bonds, 70; demand function for commodities, notional, 211; sector, 63; wealth, 72
human resources programs (manpower), 527–528
Humphrey-Hawkins Act. See Full Employment and Balanced Growth Act of 1978

I

IMF. See International Monetary Fund

implicit (imputed) cost, defined, 248
implicit exchange costs, defined, 69
implicit GNP price deflator, 36–37
imports: defined, 534; export demand and, value of, 540; exports and, demand elasticities for, 541–543; exports and, exchange rates and relative price of, 538
income: consumption and, 210–212; consumption as a function of current and lagged values of, 231–236; disposable, 66; disposable labor, 222; disposable personal, 32; exogenous, 411; expected, as function of current and past levels of actual income, 222; expected, proportional to current income, 222; measured, 228; national, 29–31; other charges against, 31; permanent, 227; permanent, operational definition of, 228–229; personal, 32; personal and disposable personal, 32–33; proprietors', 30; real, 535–538; real, absolute prices and, 538; rental, 30; response of to discretionary fiscal actions, 496–499; total disposable, 222; transitory, 228; wealth and, relation between propensities to consume out of, 218–219
income-constrained consumption function, 211–212
income-constrained demand curve, 299–301
income effect, 382; defined, 68; real, 538
income hypothesis: absolute, 212–213, 219; relative, 225–227
income side of NIA, 29–33
incomes inflation, 204–205
incomes policies: defined, 508; tax-based, 516
indexation, 525–527
indirect business taxes, 31
indirect wealth effects: defined, 237; direct and, 237–240
induced investment, 275–283; implications of with stable model, 281–283; pulling-in and, 282; stability of Keynesian model with, 278–281
inflation, 4; accelerating, 317; as monetary phenomenon, 160; classical excess demand, 202; constant rate of, 317; continuing, 159; cost of reducing, 509–511; cost-push, 202; critical rate of, 317; demand, 202–203; demand-pull, 202; demand shift, 207; diminishing returns, 202; eradicating of, 357; expected, coefficient on rate of, 354; fully anticipated, 355; incomes, 204–205; price level and, 59–60; profit-push (markup), 204–205; quantity theory of money and, 159–161; self-liquidating nature of, 349; supply, 203–207; temporary, 159; unanticipated, absence of, 353; unanticipated, and unemployment, short-run trade-off between, 356–357; wage-push, 204–205; with simultaneous recession, 203; world, and balance of payments, monetarist model of, 581–582
inflationary bias, 341, 347
inflation expectations: empirical evidence on role of, 358; influence of, 353–354; Phillips curve, natural rate view and, 351–358
instrument instability, 470, 475–476
interest-induced wealth effect, 237–240, 461; effectiveness of monetary and fiscal policies and, 244–245; empirical evidence on importance of, 245

Index

interest rate: as real phenomenon, 160; critical, 377; equilibrium real, in classical model, 158; expected, 376; income-induced rise in, 181; lagged adjustment of investment to change in, 292–294; links, breakdown of in adjustment mechanism, 151–153; net capital outflows and, 549–550; of return (i) and present value (PV) rules, comparison of, 266–268; of return rules, multiple values of, 267–268; parameters of monetary and fiscal policy, 185–188; "q" as argument in investment function vs., 255–256; real and monetary influences on, 179–180; relative price channel, 462–463; response of to monetary change, 161–163, 180–181, 283; snapback and accelerator, 290–292; term structure of, 397–403; trap and term structure theory, 401–402; unique equilibrium real, 155
intermediate good: defined, 26; final vs., 26–27
intermediate targets, 479; strategy, limitations of, 483
internal adjustment costs, defined, 258
internal funds: defined, 262 n; profits and, 262–263
internal rate of return rule, 254; present value rules and, 254–256
international capital flows and trade, 544–553
International Monetary Fund (*IMF*), 558
international monetary system, 556
intertemporal substitution effect, defined, 153
intertemporal utility function, 217
inventory valuation adjustment (*IVA*), defined, 30
investment: actual, 102; alternative models of, 256–263; defined, 247; direct, 535; fixed business, 27–28; gross domestic, 247; gross private domestic, 28; income-induced, 118; interest-responsive, 576–577; inventory, 27–28, 272; lagged adjustment of to change in interest rate, 292–294; net, 75; perfectly reversible, 251; portfolio (financial), 535; production function, and demand for capital, 262–265; stock adjustment model of, 257; theory of, and adjustment costs, 257–260; theory of net, 254–256; unintended, 102
investment financing constraint: defined, 78; supply of private bonds and, 396–397
IS curve, 89, 122–123; classical, 127–128; classical, slope of when there is a wealth effect, 131; Keynesian, 124–125; *LM* curves and, shifts in, 142–143; *LM* steeper than, 280–281; shifts in, 137–140; steeper than *LM*, 280. *See also* IS-LM model
IS-LM model: dynamic, 284; integrating Phillips curve into, 347–349; integrating trade and international capital flows into, 544–553; negative feedback in Keynesian, 494; stability analysis of, 276–281

J

J-curve phenomenon, defined, 542
job search, adaptive model of, 309
Jordan, Jerry L., 465, 499
Jorgenson, Dale, 268; model of optimal capital accumulation, 268–269

K

Kalchbrenner, John, 466, 503
Kane, Edward, 399
Keran, Michael, 462
Keynes, J. M., 89, 148 n, 151, 252, 324–325, 376, 378, 402, 409–410, 415, 417–418, 425 n.14, 472
Keynesian approach, 536
Keynesian counterrevolution, 415
Keynesian cross model, 100
Keynesian model, 122–126; deriving reduced forms for, 173–174; disequilibrium assumptions for, 172; important properties of, 179–185; income determination in, numerical example of, 189–190; simple, stability of, 277–278; with induced investment, stability of, 278–281
kinked wage adjustment function, 342
Koyck lag distribution, 232–233
Krugman, Paul, 542

L

labor: demand for, 73–75, 81, 296–302; demand for, response of employment and hours to changes in, 301–302; marginal physical product of, 73; notional demand curve for, 296–299; supply of, 68, 81, 302–310; supply of, aggregate supply curve and, 193–195; supply of, money illusion and, 307–310
labor force participation, 302–304; rate, defined, 302; wage illustion and, 309–310
labor market, 81; aggregation among individual, 342–343; classical and Keynesian treatment of, 84–89; disequilibrium in, unemployment and, 319–327; equilibrium and fully anticipated inflation, 355; equilibrium in, and unemployment, 310–314; nonlinear wage adjustment in, 341–342; policies to improve efficiency of, 527–528; role of dispersion of unemployment among individual, 342–343; unemployment rate as proxy for excess demand in, 343–345
lags, 468–471
Laidler, David, 385
Lanzellotti, Robert F., 521, 524
law of diminishing returns, defined, 73
least squares method, defined, 20
Lewis, Wilfred, 493
life cycle hypothesis, 216–223; defined, 216–217; deriving a testable specification of, 221–222; problems with operational specification of, 235–236; two-period example of, 217–218
lifetime resources, defined, 217
Lipsey, Robert, 339, 344
liquidity, defined, 221, 400
liquidity constraints, 220–221
liquidity preference, defined, 425 n.14
liquidity premiums, 399–400
liquidity trap, 151, 180 n, 418–420; defined, 378
LM curve, 89, 122–123 n; classical, 128–130; extended, 449–450; income determination and, 410–413; *IS* and, shifts in, 142–143; *IS* steeper

than, 280; Keynesian, 125–126; shifts in, 140–142; steeper than *IS*, 280–281. *See also* IS-LM model
loanable funds approach, 425 n.14; defined, 148 n
long-term capital flows, defined, 534

M

macroeconomics: defined, 3; microeconomics, vs., 3; problems in, 3–5
Malkiel, Burton, 399
managed float, 556, 561
mandatory wage and price controls, 518–524
marginal cost, defined, 74
marginal efficiency of capital, defined, 252
marginal physical product of labor, defined, 73
marginal propensity to consume, defined, 212
marginal revenue, defined, 74
marginal revenue product curve, defined, 249
marginal unit of capital, defined, 255
Marshall-Lerner condition, 541–543; defined, 542
Marston, Stephen, 528
Mayer, Thomas, 470
mean-variance model, defined, 381
medium of exchange, 369
Meiselman, David, 462–464
Meltzer, Alan, 385
microeconomics: defined, 3; macroeconomics vs., 3
Mincer, Jacob, 303–304
Modigliani, Franco, 216, 221–222, 236, 245, 371, 403, 430, 472, 504–505
monetarist, 163
monetarist approach, 413–415
monetarist critique, 461–464, 502–505
monetarist model of balance of payments and world inflation, 581–582
monetary and fiscal policies: effectiveness of, 241–245, 578; multipliers, term structure equation and, 429–431; under flexible exchange rates, 577–578
monetary approach to balance of payments, 568–569
monetary policy, 155–156, 177–178; channels of, 460–464; decisions, defined, 395; defined, 136; direct wealth effects and, 242; effectiveness of, 185–188; empirical evidence on lags in response to, 469–470; income-expenditure models, channels of, 461; institutions of, 456–458; instruments, 458–460, 503; lags and effectiveness of, 470–471; multipliers, empirical evidence on, 464–466; open market operations, 140–142; powerless, 183–185; problems in execution of, 466–471; under uncertainty, 478–479
money: asset demand for, 375–385; bond financing and, relative effect of, 433; bonds and, financial market impact of changes in supply of, 407; central issue in demand for, 370–371; defined, 368 n, 388–389; functions of, 369–370; functions of, and theory of demand for money, 368–371; high-powered, or monetary base, 441; implications of extreme values of interest responsiveness of demand for, 409–420; integer constraint in transactions model of demand for, 389–390; interest-responsive demand for, 415–417; inventory theoretic models of demand for, 371; portfolio demand for, 383–384; quantity theory of, 159–161, 168, 241; real income elasticity of demand for, 412–413; speculative demand for, 376–379; theory of demand for, 368–371; transactions demand for, 371–375
money, demand for, 68–70, 413–415; autonomous change in, 142, 156, 178–179; by noncash managers, 389–390; portfolio approach to asset holdings and, 383–385; pure transactions and pure wealth models of, 423–425
money illusion: absence of, 161 n, 353; aggregate supply curve and, 195–197; concept of, 354; cyclical variation in employment and output and, 327–331; defined, 195, 307; labor supply and, 307–310; permanent, 327–328
money market, 81–82, 547–549, 576–577
money supply: change in, 155–156; endogenous, 449–452; exogenous nominal, 410; increase in growth rate of, 161–163; interest-responsive, 450–452; nominal, 80; once-and-for-all increase in, 161; world, defined, 582
money supply process, 439–443; currency holdings and, 446–447; models of, 443–449
multiperiod loan, defined, 43
multiple expansion of deposits, simple model of, 444–446
multiplier, 106–108; balanced-budget, 116–117; basic model, 174; defined, 17, 105, 174; downward bias on reduced-form policy, 504; empirical evidence on monetary policy, 464–466; equilibrium, 109; for classical model, mathematical derivation of, 167–169; impact and equilibrium, 233–235; interpreting, 174–175; model, 281–282, 502; monetary and fiscal policy, term structure equation and, 429–431; simple Keynesian income-consumption, 496–497; unambiguous $\Delta X/\Delta G$, and saving, 422–423
multiplier model, 15; defined, 15; simple consumption, 100–113

N

national income (*NI*), 30–31; defined, 29
national income accounts (*NIA*), 24–33; defined, 24; income side of, 29–33; product side of, 28–29
national wealth, defined, 38
natural rate of unemployment, 317; defined, 353
negative feedback effect, defined, 174
negotiable order of withdrawal accounts, defined, 388
net capital outflows and interest rates, 549–550
net interest, defined, 30
net investment: defined, 75; theory of, 254–256
net national product (*NNP*), defined, 27
net wealth, 66
neutrality: defined, 158, 163 n.21; dichotomy, and quantity theory of money, 241; dichotomy and, existence of, 158

NIA. See national income accounts
normal good, defined, 68
NNP. See net national product

O

Oakland, William, 492
Office of Management and Budget (OMB), 489
official reserves transactions balance, defined, 535
Okun, Arthur, 57, 236, 335, 492, 516
Okun's Law, 4, 334–335; defined, 57, 335; *GNP* gap and, 57
OMB. *See* Office of Management and Budget
OPEC. *See* Organization of Petroleum Exporting Countries
open market operations, 140–142, 177–178, 407, 459; defined, 80; effect of, 433–434
open market purchase, defined, 136, 140
opportunity cost, defined, 76–77
Organization of Petroleum Exporting Countries (OPEC), 202, 206

P

paper claims, varieties of, 42–45
par, 43
payments imbalances: methods of correcting, 554–556; methods of financing, 554; systems of coordinating responses to, 556–561
period analysis: continuous and, 6–7; defined, 7
period models: asset market equilibrium in, 94 n; continuous and, flows and stocks in, 92; *EOP* specification of, 94; Walras' Law and, 94–96
permanent accelerator model, 261–262
permanent consumption, 228
permanent income: defined, 227; operational definition of, 228–229
permanent income theory, 227–229; basic assumptions of, 227–228
perpetual inventory approach, 237
perpetuity (consol), defined, 44, 239
Perry, George, 316, 511, 516–517
personal income (*PI*): defined, 32; disposable, 32; disposable personal and, 32–33
Phelps, Edmund S., 363
Phillips, A. W., 337, 339
Phillips curve: breakdown in 1970s of traditional, 351; eclectic specifications of, 359–362; inflation expectations and, natural rate view, 351–358; integration into *IS-LM* framework, 347–349; macroeconomic implications of traditional, 347–351; specification of natural rate, 353–355; traditional specification of, 339–351; two-stage, 361–362; vertical, 355
Pierce, James, 206
Pigou, A. C., 152, 153 n.7
policy instruments, 135–136; defined, 15, 135, 458; monetary, 503; nonpolicy disturbances and, 134–137; specification of, 503
policy variable, defined, 15

Poole, William, 511, 522
portfolio: composition of, 148 n; diversifying, 69; investment component of, 68; transactions component of, 68
portfolio approach: operational specification of, 384–385; to asset holdings and demand for money, 383–385
portfolio behavior: capital and household, 397; commercial bank, 442–443
portfolio composition, 71–72
portfolio (financial) investment, defined, 535
positive feedback effect, defined, 174
positive time preference, 42
potential output, 56–59; cyclical behavior of actual relative to, 57–59; defined, 56
present value, 42
price deflator, implicit *GNP*, 36–37
price expectations: destabilizing of, 153; static, 153
price flexibility, 499; improvement of, 528–529; in classical model, 494–495; wage flexibility and, classical assumptions on, 85–86
price index, 33–38; constructing, 34–35; consumer, 36; defined, 33; hedonic, 37; particular, 35–37; problems in construction of, 37–38; weighted, 34; wholesale, 36
price-induced wealth effect, 237, 240–241; defined, 238
price level: equilibrium, 159; expectations, 353; inflation and, 59–60; not pure monetary phenomenon, 160; policies to reduce, 529; response of to demand and supply disturbances, 202–207
prices: absolute, 535–538; absolute, and real income, 538; effective, 258; exogenous, 411; flexibility of, 147; inflexible, 151; law of one, 536–537; market, 27; money, of goods and services, 33; relative, 535–538; relative, and nontraded goods, 537–538; relative, of imports and exports, 538; variable, on aggregate supply curve, 193–195; wage controls and, mandatory, 518–524; wages, and productivity, arithmetic of, 512–513; wages and, rigid, Keynesian assumptions on, 87–89
price taker, defined, 581 n.2
probability distribution, defined, 19
production function, 72–73; Cobb Douglas, 263; Cobb Douglas, and demand for capital, 264; constant elasticity of substitution, and demand for capital, 264; defined, 72; demand for capital, and investment, 262–265; investment and, 264–265
productivity: growth rate of labor, 333–334; labor hoarding and cyclical variation in, 302; wages, and prices, arithmetic of, 512–513
product side of *NIA*, 28–29
profits, 45; actual, 262; corporate, 30; internal funds and, 262–273; undistributed, 31
profit tax liability, corporate, 31
propensity to consume: average, 213; marginal, 212; out of income and wealth, relation between, 218–219
proprietors' income, defined, 30
prospective yield, defined, 252
purchasing power parity, 536–537; defined, 537

pure expectations hypothesis, defined, 398
pure transactions approach, defined, 385
pure wealth approach: defined, 385; with beginning-of-period equilibrium, 423–424; with end-of-period equilibrium, 424–425

Q

quantity: *ex ante*, 13; *ex post*, 13; price adjustments or, in disequilibrium, 321–324
quantity theory, crude, 410–415
quantity theory of money, 168; defined, 160; inflation and, 159–161; neutrality, dichotomy, and, 241
quid pro quo, defined, 26

R

random variable, defined, 19
rates of return, real vs. nominal, 45–47
rational expectations model, 362–365; limitations of, 365
real asset: defined, 39; financial asset vs., 39
real feedback response, defined, 181
real *GNP*, defined, 33
real income, 535–538; absolute prices and, 538
real income adjustment, 555
real income effects, 538
real income elasticity of demand for money, 412–413
real interest rate: equilibrium, in classical model, 158; unique equilibrium, 155
real money balances, demand for, 82
real sector random disturbances, 480–482
real sectors, financial sectors and, random shocks from, 483
real variables, 158
real wage rate: defined, 68; nominal or real wage adjustments to above equilibrium, 325; nonequilibrium, 319
recession: amplitude of, 55; defined, 54; growth, 59; inventory, 272; with simultaneous inflation, 203
recognition lag, defined, 469
recontracting, 322
recurring flow, defined, 66
reduced forms, 189–190; defined, 17, 105; explicit solution to models and, 104–105; for Keynesian model, deriving, 173–174; monetarist evidence from, 465–466; structural equations and, 17; structural models vs., 462; unreliability of, 503–505
relative income hypothesis, 225–227
required reserves, defined, 441
reservation wage rate, defined, 308
reserve currency, defined, 548
reserve requirements, 459
reserves: excess, 441; excess, and borrowing, adding, 447–449; free, 447; international, financing deficit via drawing down, 554; required, 441; surplus, 444
retained earnings, defined, 31, 262 n

risk averse, defined, 323
risk aversion: and preferred habitat theory, 401; uncertainty, and asset demand for money, 379–382
risk averter, defined, 381
risk lovers, 381 n.18
risk neutral, defined, 323
risk premium, 252
Roberts, R. Blaine, 521, 524
rules vs. discretion, 471–474

S

Samuelson, Paul, 113, 284, 287, 339, 344, 347
saving (consumption) function, 71 n.4
savings deposits, defined, 388
Schultze, C. L., 207
Schwartz, Anna, 385, 463–464
search model, 308–310, 330; continuous auction models and, limitations of, 330–331
sectoral balance sheets, 39–41
sectoral net wealth, 38–39; defined, 39
secular growth rate, 59
selective controls, 459
settlement (balancing) items, 535
simultaneous equilibrium, 90
Solow, Robert, 339, 344, 347, 513
speculation: capital flows and, 543–544; destabilizing, 544; stabilizing, 543–544
speculative demand for money, 376–379
spillover effect, defined, 211–212
stability, built-in, 117, 492–496; improving, 495–496; in classical model, 494–495; incompatibility of with price, full employment, 349–351; nature of in three models, 493–495
stability analysis of *IS-LM* model, 276–281
static analysis, defined, 109
static price expectations, defined, 153
Steindel, Charles, 236
stochastic specification, 18–20
stock variables, defined, 96
store of value, 370
structural equations: and reduced forms, 17; defined, 17
structural parameters, defined, 17
structural unemployment, 51–52; defined, 51
subsidies, 31
substitutability: *ex ante*, 262–265; *ex post*, 265
substitution effects, 38, 382, 538; defined, 68, 250; intertemporal, 153
superneutrality, defined, 163 n.21
supply: endogenous money, 449–452; exogenous, nominal money, 410; in the four markets, 80–82; labor, and money illusion, 307–310; nominal money, 80; world money, 582
supply, money. *See* money supply
supply and demand curves for foreign exchange, 539–541
supply and demand disturbances, response of price level to, 202–207
supply and demand model, 14–15

supply-oriented policies, 527–529
supply policies: aggregate, 508; motivation for, 508–512; motivation for and types of, 511–512
surplus: balance of payments, 549; current, of government enterprises, 31; weighted, 491; weighted full employment, 491–492; weighted initial, 492
Sutch, Richard, 403, 430

T

target variable, defined, 16
tax-based incomes policies, defined, 516
taxes: exogenous, long-run response with, 431–432; indirect business, 31; net, bond-financed change in, 139; transfers or bond-financed changes in, 176
tax legislation, 490
tax rates, 117
tax revenues, 79, 117; endogenous, 493–494; endogenous, long-run response to fiscal policy with, 432–434
technological change, defined, 56
Teeters, Nancy, 492
temporary inflation, defined, 159
term structure approach, operational specification of, 402–403
term structure equation and fiscal and monetary policy multipliers, 429–431
term structure of interest rates, 397–403; defined, 398
three-asset model, 406–407; fiscal policy in, 435; implications of, 435–436
three-period lag distribution, 233
time deposits: defined, 388; savings and, 39–40
time horizon, 85, 180
time series for consumption and income, 20
Tobin, James, 255, 376, 392, 418
trade and international capital flows, 544–553
trade balance, defined, 534
transactions approach: defined, 370–371; pure, 385
transactions demand for money, 371–375; formal model of, 373–375
transactions model of demand for money, integer constraint in, 389–390
transfer payment, defined, 26
transfers: business, 31; taxes or, bond-financed changes in, 176
transitory consumption, defined, 228
transitory income, defined, 228
Treasury, 80, 143, 143 n.10, 457–458, 489
Triffin, Robert, 560

U

uncertainty: demand for capital and, 250–253; implications of, 471; incomplete information and, implications of, 476–483; monetary policy under, 478–479; multiplier, 471; risk aversion, and asset demand for money, 379–382

undistributed profits, defined, 31
unemployed, defined, 51
unemployment, 4; below natural rate, maintenance of, 357–358; cost of reducing inflation in terms of, 509–511; defined, 313; defining employment and, 50–51; demand deficiency, 52; equilibrium in labor market and, 310–314; frictional, 51, 311; frictional (search), wage illusion and, 313–314; labor market disequilibrium and, 319–327; measurement of employment and, 50–52; natural rate of, 317, 353; nonaccelerating inflation rate of, 317; noninflationary rate of, 315, 345, 359; role of dispersion of, among individual labor markets, 342–343; short-run trade-off between unanticipated inflation and, 356–357; structural, 51–52; types of, 51–52; vacancies and, 311–313
unemployment compensation, 528
unintended investment, defined, 102
utility approach, defined, 370
utility function, intertemporal, 217

V

vacancies: defined, 312; unemployment and, 311–313
valuation of product, 27–28
variable prices on aggregate supply curve, 193–195
variance, defined, 19
velocity, 413–415; defined, 413

W

wage adjustments: efficacy of, 324–327; in each labor market, nonlinear, 341–342; nominal or real, to above equilibrium real wage rate, 325
wage and price controls, mandatory, 518–524
wage and price flexibility, classical assumptions on, 85–86
wage illusion: defined, 309; employment acceptance decision and, 310; frictional (search) unemployment and, 313–314; labor force participation and, 309–310
wage-price adjustment, speed of, and persistence of disequilibrium, 322–324
wage-price guideposts, 512–517
wage rate: above equilibrium real, 325; nonequilibrium real, 319; real, 68; reservation, 308
wages: prices, and productivity, arithmetic of, 512–513; relative, concern about, 324; rigid nominal, on aggregate supply curve, 193–195
Wallich-Weintraub plan, defined, 516
Walras' Law: and period models, 94–96; defined, 95
wealth: beginning-of-period value of, 221; defined, 236–237; household, 72; income and, relation between propensities to consume out of, 218–219; in the money demand function, 420–425; national, 38; net, 66; perpetual inventory definition of, 72; sectoral net, 38–39

wealth effect, 236–245; direct, 241–244; direct, and fiscal policy, 243; direct, and monetary policy, 242; direct and indirect, 237–240; in crowding-out, 421–422; in money demand function, 421–422; price-induced, 237–238, 240–241; slope of classical *IS* curve with, 131

Weber, Arnold, 522

weighted full employment surplus, 491–492

weighted initial surplus, defined, 492

weighted price indices, defined, 34

weighted surplus, defined, 491

wholesale price index (*WPI*), defined, 36

WPI. See wholesale price index

Y

yield: holding period, 44; prospective, 252